Documents in Communist Affairs

Documents in Communist Affairs

1979

Edited by
Bogdan Szajkowski

University College Cardiff Press

335.4309
D65
1/7927
ayn 1981

First published 1979 in Great Britain by
University College Cardiff Press, P.O. Box 78,
Cardiff, CF1 1XL, Wales, in association with
Christopher Davies (Publishers) Ltd.,
52 Mansel Street, Swansea, Wales.

ISBN 901426 97 0

Printed by Salesbury Press Ltd., Llandybïe, Dyfed.

Moim

Rodzicom

Editorial Board

Acknowledgements

The Editor gratefully acknowledges the following who have very kindly supplied him with the material included in this volume: the Embassies of: the Socialist Federal Republic of Yugoslavia, the Socialist Republic of Romania, the Socialist Republic of Vietnam, the Mongolian People's Republic, the United States of America, the People's Republic of Bulgaria, Democratic Kampuchea and the Permanent Mission of Ethiopia to the United Nations.

In addition thanks are due to the following: The Information Section of the Council for Mutual Economic Assistance; Mr. Gerard Streiff of the Section Politique Exterieure of the French Communist Party; Appeal for Polish Workers International Committee — London Office; the Information Section of the Belgian Communist Party; Mr. Adolfo Lopez of the Spanish Communist Party; Directorate-General Information of the Commission of the European Communities; Keston College; Foreign Relation Section of the University of Tirana Scientific Library.

I am particularly grateful to Mr. Renee Laffeter and *Le Monde* for their kind co-operation.

A very substantial number of documents in this volume have been translated and appear here for the first time in English translation. For expert translations I am very grateful to Dr. Geoff West of the Department of Languages and Linguistics of the University of Essex, Mrs. Rowena Gaskell, Mr. Dewi Llud Williams, Mr. Gianni Delgado-Morgan, Mr. Sabah Kubba, Dr. Alfred White of the Department of German UCC and Mr. Geoff Swain of the Department of History UCC.

The Editor also wishes to acknowledge Mrs Ivy Walker, Mrs Shirley Bolton and Miss Julie Cornish of the University College, Cardiff Printing Unit for their help and continuous assistance in the publication of this volume.

Lastly, my very special thanks go to Mr. Michael Breaks for expertly compiling the index.

Contents

9

Asia

International Meetings

Latin America

Soviet Union and Eastern Europe

Western Europe

Introduction

The enthusiastic reception which greeted the first volume of Documents in Communist Affairs and the firm establishment of University College Cardiff Press has enabled me to present this second volume of documentary material on contemporary communism. This edition contains material from original sources which became available during the 1978 calendar year. Most of the documents included have never before been published and for those that have appeared previously elsewhere, sources are given in brackets in the titles. Several of the documents included appear here for the first time in translation.

The material has been divided into sections as follows: Africa, Asia, The Arab World, International Meetings, Western Europe and the Soviet Union and Eastern Europe, thus enabling the reader to find the material more easily.

Readers of the previous volume of Documents in Communist Affairs will see that there is an obvious continuity between the first and present edition. All the major issues in the communist world which were documented in the first volume recur in varying stages of development in this edition.

In the first section, on Africa, a substantial amount of material which is included, relates to the continuing hostilities in the Horn of Africa, with particular emphasis being placed on its international dimensions. Thus the material presents the Cuban, Soviet and Chinese views on their respective roles in Africa and in world affairs in general. The African section also includes illuminating views on the ongoing Ethiopian revolution and its ideological and strategic significance to the developments both in Africa and for the world communist movement.

Part of the section on Asia is devoted to the internal developments in post-Maoist China and includes, among others, the constitution of the People's Republic of China, Hua Kuo-feng's report to the Fifth National People's Congress and a highly significant editorial from the *People's Daily* on the theory of genius and the theory of practice, which officially heralded the start of the de-Maoisation process. Considerable space is also given to the documents relating to the consolidation of the new directions in China's foreign policy — here illustrated by the Treaty of Peace and Friendship between China and Japan; the communiqué on the establishment of diplomatic relations with the United States and the trade agreement between China and the EEC.

A great deal of material in the Asian section relates to the internal developments in what, until 7 January 1979, was called Democratic Kampuchea (now People's Republic of Kampuchea) and the deteriorating relations between Democratic Kampuchea and Vietnam, the background to which can be found in the previous volume. The escalation of this conflict to open hostilities between the two socialist countries and the creation of the Cambodian National United Front for National Salvation (the anti Pol Pot liberation movement) and its programme are fully documented here. This, together with the rapidly worsening relations between Vietnam and China and the intensification of the Sino-Soviet dispute not only undermine the stability and security of South East Asia, but also negate one of the cornerstones of Marxist-Leninist ideology — proletarian internationalism. This unique collection of documentary material on the contesting Asian communist countries not only reflects the fragility of the situation in that part of the world, but also indicates the serious situation in which the international communist movement finds itself and the severe repercussions which might follow.

The Latin-American section includes only one document — on Cuba and the Movement of Non Aligned Countries. This might seem surprising in view of the numerous pronouncements which have emerged from the various communist parties in Latin America. However this publication does not set out to catalogue indiscriminately the vast material appearing on communism each year. The Editor felt that the statement by Carlos Rafael Rodriguez was by far the most significant document from a communist source to come from Latin America during 1978.

Similarly, in the section on the Arab world, the Manifesto of the Communist and Workers' Parties of the Arab Countries was felt to be of prime importance.

In the section of the Soviet Union and Eastern Europe the Reader will find some of the more important material relating to the Eleventh Congress of the League of the Communists of Yugoslavia. The precarious situation in the Balkans and its importance in the approaching post-Tito era is reflected in the number of relevant documentary material that originated from Yugoslavia, Bulgaria, Albania, and Romania. The section also includes the exchange of letters between China and Albania which culminated in the breaking off the close relations between the two countries, the ending of China's aid to Albania and the creation of a new pro-Albanian division in the international communist movement.

This second volume of Documents also includes some of the more important dissident material from Eastern Europe and the Soviet Union, much of it smuggled out from the respective countries. The amount of documentary material which continues to emerge from dissident sources and which is an important record of contemporary history is considerable. Understandably, therefore, only a very minute portion could be printed in this volume.

The election of Pope John Paul II could not have passed unrecorded in a publication of this nature and three documents on his election are therefore included.

The section on Western Europe continues the discussion on Euro-communism which has been well documented in the previous edition. This year's exchanges have been much more salient and the PCI-CPSU Communique suggests a possible rapprochement between the Euro-communists and the Soviet and Eastern European parties. The same section also includes documentary material on some of the most important develop-ments among two of the Western European parties: the historic first legal congress of the Spanish Communist Party and the French parliamentary elections. The importance of the forthcoming elections to the European Parliament and the communist attitudes to the European Economic Community are illustrated in some of the material both in this section and the one on the Soviet Union and Eastern Europe.

This volume would not have been possible without the support and continuous encouragement I received from Dr. C.W.L. Bevan, C.B.E., the Principal of University College, Cardiff, to whom I am greatly indebted.

I should like to thank the international editorial board and in particular Dr. Vladimir Kusin and Mr. Michael Waller and the Board's Chairman, Professor Richard M. Griffiths. Thanks are also due to the Secretary of University College Cardiff Press, Mr. D.P.M. Michael, C.B.E., and Mr. Bryan Turnbull, Assistant Registrar of University College, Cardiff and Mrs. Val Dobie for their kind help and advice.

I am also grateful to Mr. Michael Kaser of St. Antony's College, Oxford, for kindly writing the comment on China's aid to Albania.

Dinas Powis
4 January 1979.   Bogdan Szajkowski

Africa

Tass Statement

(Complete Text). Pravda, 19 January, 1978.

Reports have been recently disseminated in the foreign press, as well as statements by officials, above all those of Somalia, and in places far beyond that country, which present in a deliberately distorted manner the origin and current development of the armed conflict between Somalia and Ethiopia. It is alleged, in particular, that Soviet military personnel, as well as "thousands" of citizens of other socialist countries, are taking part in combat operations on the Ethiopian side. Rumours are also circulated, alleging that with their help an invasion of Ethiopian troops into Somali territory is being prepared, and that for this purpose the USSR Defence Minister has secretly arrived in Ethiopia. Provocative fabrications have also been put in circulation regarding an imaginary participation of Soviet ships and aircraft in the military operations taking place in Ethiopia.

Tass is authorised to state that all these inventions are absolutely groundless and their purpose is obvious: by distorting the actual state of affairs to cover up the designs being nurtured by some quarters in the West for their own interference in the Somali-Ethiopian conflict.

The truth is that the Soviet Union, for its part, did everything possible to prevent an armed conflict between Somalia and Ethiopia from breaking out. However, when the Somali leaders, contrary to common sense and the efforts of the true friends of the Somali people, began military operations against Ethiopia and when Somali troops invaded her territory, the Soviet Union, as always in such cases, sided with the victim of aggression. At the request of the government of Ethiopia it is giving her appropriate material and technical assistance in repulsing the aggression. In doing so, the Soviet Union proceeds from its fundamental foreign policy principles, regardless of the fact that this might be followed and was actually followed by the known unfriendly steps of the Somali leadership against the Soviet Union itself.

It is precisely those who are now trying to cast aspersions on the Soviet Union and the other socialist countries who actually encouraged the Somali leadership at the time to start the aggression, promising to aid Somalia with weapons. They did so publicly and, as later became known, during informal contacts with the Somali leadership. Now that the expansionist plans of the Somali leaders are failing, their sponsors abroad are trying to come to their rescue both by continuing arms supplies to Somalia through third countries and by public assurances of possible open military aid. At the same time they are trying to intimidate Ethiopia and those countries which support her just struggle against external aggression.

And all this is being done at the time when, on the one hand, regular Somali forces still remain on part of Ethiopian territory captured by them and when, on the other hand, the Ethiopian leadership has stated officially that its only objective is to free its lands and that it has no intention of sending its forces to Somalian territory.

As to the Soviet Union, just as before, it comes out for a peaceful settlement of the Somali-Ethiopian conflict through negotiations based on reciprocal respect by the sides for the sovereignty, territorial integrity, inviolability of borders and non-interference in each other's internal affairs. Of course, the necessary prerequisite for such a settlement must be the unconditional and speedy withdrawal of Somali troops from Ethiopian territory. There are plenty of examples of what happens when military operations are ended without the immediate withdrawal of the invader troops from the foreign lands captured by them. Suffice it to look at the still explosive situation in the Middle East.

Those who stubbornly refuse to learn a proper lesson from this bitter experience must carry full responsibility for the possible consequences of encouraging the aggressor, which may further complicate the Somali-Ethiopian conflict and lead to a new sharpening of the situation throughout the world.

Warning in Good Time
Commentary of "People's Daily".
(Complete Text). Hsinhua News Agency 11 January, 1978.

Somali President Mohamed Siad Barre recently warned once again that "if the situation in the Horn of Africa has turned for the worse, those who had created tense situation in Africa should take the responsibility". This is a timely warning. The Soviet Union is hatching new military actions in the Horn of Africa, said the Western press in their recent reports. Judging from the actions taken by the Soviet Union in Africa recently, these reports are certainly not fabrications.

An incident which attracted close attention throughout the world is that the Soviet Union suddenly dispatched 225 transport aircraft, or about 15% of its air transport capacity, to carry military supplies to the Horn of Africa, and other parts of Africa, between late November and early December last year. During the three-week period these aircraft took off from air bases in the Soviet territory to fly to Africa over nearly 10 countries' airspace, without asking for permission. Radar stations in many Soviet neighbouring countries simultaneously detected this extraordinary large-scale airlift. A number of these countries ordered their air forces to be on all-round alert. Meanwhile, the Soviet Union launched a satellite to coordinate the air transport.

According to Western analysts, the massive Soviet airlift was not only for the transport of munitions but was also a large exercise designed to test the Soviet Air Force's capability to move Soviet troops or mercenaries to Africa for new military interventions. During the same period, large numbers of freighters carrying military hardware sailed from Soviet ports to the Horn of Africa.

Meanwhile, CGS of the Soviet Army and Navy N.V. Ogarkov and First Vice-Minister of Defence S.L. Sokolov visited the coastal areas of the Mediterranean and the Red Sea to engage in bustling activities with ulterior motives.

This is an ill omen which shows that the Soviet social-imperialism will never take its defeat lying down after being driven out of Somalia and excluded from the negotiations on the Middle East question. Moscow is in a hurry to create tension in the Horn of Africa — when the Arab countries are turning their eyes elsewhere — trying to threaten them from the flanks so as to reverse its unfavourable position and strengthen its hand in its intensified rivalry with the United States in this area.

The Arab and African people have already heightened their vigilance against this Soviet scheme. Exposing to the world the danger of Soviet intervention on 8th January, Sudanese President Jaafir Mohamed al-Nemery pointed out that the Soviet Union is playing the imperialistic tactics of utilizing Africans to fight Africans so as to realize its despicable aim. To smash the superpower scheme of dividing and sabotaging the Afro-Arab anti-imperialist and anti-hegemonist front, many Arab and African leaders have appealed for strengthening of unity. In face of the African and Arab States which are fighting in unity, all interventionist schemes of Soviet social-imperialism are doomed to failure.

Mengistu Haile Mariam. Address to the Nation.

(Complete text). Granma 19 February, 1978.

* The address of the Chairman of the Provisional Military Administrative Council and of the Council of Ministers of Socialist Ethiopia was delivered over radio and television on 30 January, 1978.

For centuries the broad masses of Ethiopia have fought a bitter, protracted struggle against the colonialists, arrogant invaders and racist powers to defend themselves against those same antipeople and antipeace forces. It is easy for anyone who has observed the long history of struggle of the Ethiopian people, and the glorious victories won by them over the centuries, to discern the fact that struggle and victory are characteristics of the Ethiopian people. This long history of struggle of the Ethiopian masses furnishes firm and dependable foundations for the present Democratic Revolution.

And yet, while the masses of Ethiopia have a long history of bitter and victorious class struggle behind them, they have also come through a long history of exploitation, oppression, devastating poverty and indescribable suffering.

During the defunct feudo fascistic oppressive system, the death of which was brought about by the masses, the overwhelming majority of the Ethiopian people was subjected to a life of slavery and sharecropping, in which the Ethiopian's labour was exploited and he was divested of all human dignity and humiliated in every way possible. It must be remembered that 90% of the people were dependent on agriculture to earn their squalid subsistence, and, of these, 70% were sharecroppers. These share-croppers were forced to pay 75% of what they produced in kind to the nobility and absentee landlords, who enjoyed a life of luxury in the various urban centres.

In addition to giving the greater part of their production to the landlords, sharecroppers were also under the obligation to transport, store and deliver all that was owing to the landlord. The broad masses, therefore, who were always out front, ready to sacrifice themselves in defence of the territorial integrity, freedom and honour of the motherland, lived as dispossessed outlaws in their own country. Not only was their property subject to economic exploitation, they were also denied any form of political rights.

Members of the ruling class under the feudo-fascistic system had recourse to the myth of divine celestial power which they put before and tried to impose on the masses; they tried to make out that this mysterious power could only be wielded by the royal family. In doing so, they resorted to despotism and even ended up by deceiving themselves into believing that the ruling class was a sui generis species of Homo sapiens. The ruling class not only denied the masses freedom of speech, expression and association and the right to organize themselves to have a share in political power; it also forced the masses to worship it, much as one would worship an idol. Like many other countries, Ethiopia is a country inhabited by many nationalities professing different religious creeds.

The discredited former régime's system of divide and rule has been abolished, its place being taken by a system which guarantees religious freedom and equality for all nationalities. We are determined to protect those rights to the full and to guarantee their being applied in practice. Our programme of the Ethiopian National Democratic Revolution, which is our guide, clearly explains that by abolishing exploitation; oppression; nepotism; bribery; and tribal, religious and sex discrimination, we aim to establish a society in which justice, equality and peace prevail. These are prerequisites for the transition to collective progress and at the same time reflect the hopes and aspirations of the oppressed Ethiopian masses.

I have tried to explain briefly that our Ethiopia has over the centuries been subjected to repeated tests of foreign invading forces, that internally the masses have been subjected to indescribably inhuman treatment on the part of the feudal ruling clique, that the broad Ethiopian masses have never succumbed either to any chance foreign aggression or to the slavery with which they had been burdened internally; they have rather waged a long, bitter struggle and continue to do so.

On recalling the long, bitter struggle of the broad masses, we would like to mention the sacrifices made by Ethiopian fighters, peasants, workers, the men-in-uniform, intellectuals and students. We recall with pride and admiration the just and fruitful struggles that these progressive, patriotic sons and daughters of our country have waged in various places over the ages. Through their decisive struggle for the economic, political and cultural demands of the masses, those revolutionaries have made important contributions to the growth of the ongoing revolution, to its achievements, which will continue to be carried forward.

The Ethiopian Revolution, which was spontaneous, has reached its present stage. The popular victories won in the short time since the beginning of the Revolution have, on several occasions, been made public in detailed form. It has been manifestly shown during the past three years that the victories gained by our people's Revolution were received with jubilation and given constant support by Africans and by all progressive peoples of the world. This goes to show that our struggle is contrary to the exploitation, oppression and aggression perpetrated against the broad masses of the world and that it is contrary to discrimination on the grounds of religion and sex; that it is an integral part of the revolutionary struggle of the oppressed peoples of the world.

We would like to take this opportunity to express our revolutionary gratitude to the peace-loving socialist countries and other progressive forces that have given us their unreserved and true support to make up our forces bent on achieving the objectives of our programme of the National Democratic Revolution: to uphold the territorial unity and integrity of Ethiopia, to further our Revolution and to enable the Ethiopian people to reach a higher stage of development. The broad Ethiopian masses and the Revolution will always remember this debt of gratitude which has been recorded forever in the pages of history.

On the other hand, there are reactionary forces which, from the start of the Revolution, have been conspiring to undermine our independence, to dismember our country and to subvert our Revolution.

As our Revolution has gained in clarity and depth, so these reactionary forces are now planning to expand the scope of the illegal war they have unleashed against us on several fronts, under the coordination of international imperialism.

They are making ready to line up together in combat formation against us.

For several years now the Arab régimes in neighbouring regions, determined to make their long-cherished dream of expansion come true and desirous of having the Red Sea under their control and for their exclusive use, have been coordinating, organizing and arming reactionaries at home who have been scared by the Ethiopian Revolution and others afflicted by narrow feelings based on nationality.

Since these reactionary forces with expansionist intentions particularly believe in the separatist banditry that began to operate in the Eritrea region in northeast Ethiopia 16 years ago, and whose rebirth could well be their only opportunity of holding back the Ethiopian Revolution, they have, aside from supplying arms, money and occasionally personnel on a much greater scale than before, spared no effort to undermine the attempts we have been making to solve the problem in the region in a peaceful way. And we continue to do so. .

In addition to the conspiracy which imperialist and reactionary forces in these parts have been plotting and are still plotting in the north of Ethiopia, they are also extremely serious in fixing their sinister sights on the east of Ethiopia and are working hand in glove with the reactionary ruling classes of Mogadishu.

What is the cause of the unscrupulous and, as the whole world knows, illegal war of aggression that Somalia is perpetrating at present in the east and south of Ethiopia?

Who thought up the arrogant jingoist dream of Greater Somalia in the first place?

The entire world knows that, after the colonialists divided the whole of Africa up among themselves, the end of World War II witnessed the growth of a new movement in history. When this inexorable pressure forced colonialism to gradually leave Africa, imperialism, which was determined to prolong its life, hurriedly devised a way of having itself reappear under the cloak of neocolonialism. The arrogant expansionist concept of Greater Somalia is one of the neocolonialist stratagems contrived by imperialism. Colonialism left not only Somalia but also many other developing countries with a similarly venomous heritage.

True to the expansionist dream it inherited from the colonialists, Somalia, on gaining independence, became obsessed by the annexation of considerable portions of Ethiopia and Kenya, plus the whole of Djibouti. This ambition does not only appear in the Constitution of Somalia and inlaid on its national emblem;[1] it has also been openly repeated over and

[1] In Somalia's view the five-pointed national star symbolizes the five branches of the nation characterized by a single language, predominantly nomadic way of life and century old dedication to the Islamic faith. When in July 1960 the former British Somaliland and Italian Somaliland united to form the independent Republic of Somalia left outside the

over again on various occasions by its leaders. To make this dream come true, the leaders of Somalia have been making elaborate preparations for 17 years now to hurl their forces upon us.

So as to win support for realizing this ambition, they perversely identified the people of Somalia as an Arab people.

What is more, without having the slightest conviction about socialist philosophy, the leaders of Somalia have been trading with the name of socialism so as to amass arms. They praised the Soviet Union as their great friend while publicly lashing out at the Western countries. But now, the Soviet Union and other really socialist countries not only refuse to serve as an instrument for the expansionist ambitions of the sick leaders of Somalia; they have also, as a question of principle, made no bones about their opposition to such adventurism given Somalia's antipeople and antipeace aims. This is why the leaders of Somalia, with their characteristic lies and brazen opportunism, and, having taken an 180 degree turn, are now lavish in their praise for the countries they had previously vulgarly denounced, slandering those they had admired only shortly before.

Right after we declared that socialism was our guiding principle, we sought the ways and means whereby the oppressed peoples of Ethiopia and Somalia might cooperate in the best way possible in the interests of peace, progress and good neighbourliness in our area instead of furthering the unscientific contradictions aided and abetted by imperialism in the horn of Africa. To this end, we even went as far as to propose to the leaders of Somalia, who have become drunk on the dream of expansionism, a confederation that would initially comprise the two countries.

These positive objectives and popular measures taken by Ethiopia in all goodwill were fully appreciated by the Soviet Union, other socialist countries and all peace-loving peoples, all of whom made considerable efforts towards this end being realized. The reply of the rulers of Somalia to all these appeals for good neighbourliness and peace was, however, that of going ahead with feverish preparations, in alliance with imperialism, to unleash a war of aggression on Ethiopia.

As a result, within a short time, the Ethiopian Revolution thus exposed the empty pretensions of Somalia as regards being progressive.

Immediately after the rise of our Revolution, just after the historic law nationalizing the land, the regular forces of Ethiopia had to take on many

ultimate goal of Somali statehood were three remaining branches of the nation. The first was the Somali community in the French territory of Djibouti; the second the Ogaden and other Somali clans in Harar Province of Ethiopia; and the third the Somali tribesmen living in Northern Kenya. The Somali constitution approved by a popular referendum on 20 June, 1961 stated "The Somali people is one and indivisible" (Article 1) and "the Somali Republic will promote by all legal and peaceful means, the union of all Somali territories" (Article 6, paragraph 4). Although the 1961 constitution was suspended as a result of the 1969 military coup the Revolutionary Charter published at that time proclaimed as one of the objects of the revolution the "fight for the unity of the Somali nation". (Ed) duties and simultaneously had to put up resistance to the traitorous bandits of Eritrea and protect the at that time unarmed oppressed peasants against the reactionary former landlords in the 14 administrative regions of the country. Blinded by the disease of expansionism, the ruling classes of Somalia at that moment tried to take the east and south of Ethiopia, deploying an infantry force of over 40,000 regular troops who carried out large-scale acts of sabotage and unbridled destruction. It is thanks to the valiant and firm stand of our heroic forces on the eastern and southern fronts that some of the infiltrators were annihilated while the rest fled in total disarray.

Having for the second time equipped their forces with better and more balanced military training and instruction, as well as with arms such as light artillery and mortars, they started the war which was but a prelude to the later war of invasion. They followed this up by taking railroads and bridges to pieces and destroying them and, therefore, not only prevented agricultural produce and other basic daily supplies from reaching the people of Djibouti but also threw the Ethiopian economy into crisis, some 60% of foreign trade in particular.

They also destroyed settlement projects, partially financed through international aid, set up to rehabilitate Ethiopian victims of the drought area and nomads whose subsistence depended entirely on the whims of nature. Human losses ran into the thousands, while damage to property amounted to hundreds of millions' worth. They cruelly massacred defenceless children, women and old people; they set fire to and plundered towns where many people lived and destroyed crops.

Moreover, they demolished lines of communication and agricultural and industrial enterprises.

Although the two-phase guerrilla type invasion unleashed by the sick ruling classes of Somalia over the last two years has caused a great loss in lives of innocent Ethiopian citizens and occasioned considerable damage to property and government institutions, not to mention the realization of their objective to capture the western and central regions of Ethiopia, they too were caused to suffer great losses and demoralization. Consequently, the ruling classes of Somalia unleashed their third open war of aggression on July 23, 1977, and, mobilizing all their war machinery (deploying tanks, artillery and aviation), invaded our territory, penetrating 700 kilometers into the eastern part and 300 kilometers into the southern part of the country. Not content with this, they are still extending their invasion.

Revolutionary Ethiopia (a victim of illegal, barefaced aggression) at that point publicly raised the matter before the Organization of African Unity and before the whole world. We also took foreign reporters to the war front and showed them and explained to them whose territory it was and which the places were where fighting was taking place between the forces of the illegal Somalian aggressors and the Ethiopians defending it. We showed visiting reporters the many varied modern arms and equipment utilized by Somalia against defenceless children, old people and women; the tanks and artillery captured from the enemy; the fighter planes shot down by our defence forces; and members of the regular forces of Somalia captured by our forces. On doing so, we furnished them with a correct panorama and the true state of affairs.

During this period, the arrogant ruling classes of Somalia — who through their very acts have corroborated their expansionist ambition and illegal invasion by defiling the tombs of valiant Ethiopians who gave their lives in defence of their frontiers and their freedom on driving out the colonialists who had repeatedly tried to invade the country — have shown reporters towns of ours invaded by them: namely, Gode, Kebridehar, Degehabour and Jijiga.

On taking note of the fact that the Somalian invasion forces had stepped up their action, the Committee of Good Offices of the Organization of African Unity met in Libreville, Gabon, in August 1977, and attempted to find a peaceful solution to the problem with the participation of representatives of the Governments of Somalia and Ethiopia. True to its responsibilities as a nation and to the trust and respect it has for that organization, Ethiopia participated fully in the meeting, whereas the representatives of Somalia arrogantly left the gathering, thus publicly demonstrating their supreme lack of respect and scorn for the whole of Africa and for peace.

Later, in violation of the resolution passed by the Committee within the framework of the basic principles of the OAU Charter, which deplores the conflict and urges that each country respect the territorial integrity and not interfere in the internal affairs of the other, Somalia instead extended the area under invasion.

Somalia has violated the Charter of principles of the United Nations, which, among other things, urges all member states, in the sphere of international relations, to abstain from the use of threats or force against the political liberty of a country and to abstain from violating the territorial integrity and sovereignty of another state. On pointing out this very fact, Ethiopia explained in detail to the 32nd Session of the General Assembly of the United Nations the nature of the act of aggression that Somalia continues to perpetrate against this country.

When I gave a press conference for the international mass media on September 18, 1977, on making a general outline of the Somalian war of aggression, I indicated that it was only a question of time before the unjustifiable euphoria and premature jubilation of the mentally unbalanced, shortsighted Somalian rulers and their mercenary illegal aggression rapidly turned into laments, distress and moans of desperation. Now that the broad Ethiopian masses have risen up in unison behind the motto "Revolutionary Ethiopia or Death," they have been fortified with the bravery inherited from their forebearers and subsequently armed with revolutionary fervour and decision to carry onto the offensive a just, unceasing war to protect our territorial integrity and our Revolution. As a result, the cries of the rulers of Somalia the invader and of its accomplices have begun to echo in all corners of the earth.

The leaders of Somalia and their accomplices know well that the Ethiopian people are fighting for a just cause, that is, for justice, equality, peace and protection of the age-old unity and territorial integrity of the country, and that we will neither turn back nor rest without achieving these noble and just aims. Instead of withdrawing the troops they sent to Ethiopia in the hope of fulfilling their illegal, illusory and arrogant expansionist mission, the Somalian leaders have resorted to what they consider to be a new tactic and political strategy; a sick strategy that, by disorientating and confusing the peoples of the world, prepares them for worse mistakes and horrors that are far more serious. When on the attack, they vociferate as if they were the victims or try to make out that Ethiopia is going to invade them, a policy for which its inventors could only be absolved if they were to go to their grave. What is exceedingly surprising and saddening is the antipeople and antipeace propaganda war of certain governments bent on making this an international conflict in the horn of Africa, thus bringing about even greater destruction, and this when they are very familiar with the Somalian leaders' malevolent mission of invasion and destruction and are deliberately concealing the naked truth from the peaceloving masses whom they supposedly represent. These people echo the foxy howls of the arrogant leaders of Somalia to the effect that "Ethiopia is going to invade Somalia." What these antipeople and antipeace forces take to be tactical and secret is clear to us. As the old Ethiopian saying goes, "He who wishes to take a scoopful of grain out of the can approaches with a handful"; these are clear indications that the illegal war of invasion that is being waged in Ethiopian territory will henceforth be perpetrated not only by Somalia but by other forces as well. Those same governments will bear the responsibility for the sad consequences their actions may have in the future.

Time and history will bear witness to this.

What should be particularly borne in mind is that during the last 25 years the United States of America has been the main supplier of arms to Ethiopia.

It must be remembered that, with a view to preserving independence and safeguarding its frontiers, two years ago Ethiopia signed an agreement with the United States for the purchase of arms for defence[2] with money

[2] On 17 March, 1975 the US State Department announced that the United States had agreed to supply Ethiopia with military equipment worth $7.000,000 (Ethiopia's request was for $30.000,000). Under separate agreement signed in Washington on 25 April, 1975, the Ethiopian Ministry of Agriculture was to be provided with $15.000,000 while the total US economic aid to Ethiopia for the 1975 financial year was $31.000,000. (Ed).

collected from the poor Ethiopian masses. While we were awaiting delivery after payment had been made, the United States suspended arms supplies to Ethiopia,[3] just a few months before Somalia was to unleash its war of aggression on the country. Consequently, on carrying out such an act, the U.S. Government not only indirectly encouraged Somalia to aggress against Ethiopia but also did not condemn the arrogant aggression, even after it was unleashed.

In this sense, there are certain instructive parallels in history. For example, the Ethiopian people will never forget the arms embargo of the Western European countries and the United States when fascist Italy committed a similar act of aggression against Ethiopia in 1935. I would like to emphasize here the damage the United States did to Ethiopia on that opportunity.

In August 1935, the U.S. import and export banks declared their intention of not granting credit to Ethiopia for buying arms and munitions. In October that same year, the Government of the United States levelled an embargo on arms to Ethiopia. It is evident that these measures deprived Ethiopia of its vital capacity for defence, while at the same time it aided the invader, fascist Italy, giving the Italians strength added to their advantage. Six weeks after Mussolini's invading forces entered Addis Ababa, on May 5, 1936, the United States lifted the embargo on the export of arms to Ethiopia. This policy of the U.S. Government to back the arrogant, barefaced, open aggression not only left Ethiopia defenceless but also created a situation whereby fascist Italy, which was not lacking in arms, could purchase them in the United States, if necessary, once having occupied the

[3] William Schaufele, US Assistant Secretary of State for African Affairs, stated in reply to questions before the US Senate Foreign Relations Subcommittee on African Affairs on 8 August, 1976 that the Ethiopian Government was unstable, prone to violations of human rights, incapable of managing the country's deteriorating economy, beset by "insurgencies and incipient insurgencies", and using US — supplied arms against the Eritrean secessionist movements. He also warned that the degree of US cooperation which since 1952 amounted to $350.000,000 in economic aid and $275.000,000 in military assistance would "depend largely on the course finally taken by the new revolutionary régime". On 24 February, 1977 the US Secretary of State Cyrus Vance reported to the Senate Foreign Appropriations Committee that the Administration had decided to reduce military and economic aid to Argentina, Uruguay and Ethiopia in the fiscal year beginning on 1 October, 1977, because of human rights violations in those countries. The State Department published on 12 March, 1977 reports on human rights in 82 countries. On 23 April, 1977, the Ethiopian authorities closed all US services in the country except the US Embassy and the US Agency for International Development. The services effected by the closure were the Military Assistance and Advisory Group, its Naval Medical Research Unit, the Kagnew communications centre near Asmara, the US Cultural Centre in Addis Ababa, the US Consulate General in Asmara and six small libraries in various other towns.
On 27 April, 1977 the Government of the United States announced that it had suspended its arms supplies to Ethiopia and that no deliveries had been made of F-5E fighter-bombers, M-60 tanks and ammunition. (Ed).

country. History will not forget that, spurred on by the backing he received, Mussolini even went so far as to express his gratitude in a jubilant speech he gave in a public square in Rome on June 20, 1936.

As we now witness the recent meeting of representatives of the Governments of the United States, Great Britain, France, Italy and the Federal Republic of Germany, with the aim of coordinating their backing for and plotting with Somalia the invader an act which is contrary to peace and the basic interests of the peoples, it would seem that history repeats itself and that these same forces are trying to enact anew the perfidy and injustice which they perpetrated against the Ethiopian people in 1935.

Although certain Western governments betrayed Ethiopia by conniving with Mussolini during the invasion by fascist Italy, the Ethiopian people will always appreciate the fact that the broad masses of Western Europe and the United States exposed and condemned the plotting their governments were up to and also fought resolutely for the freedom and independence of Ethiopia; and they did everything they could to bring about a change in their rulers' policy. Today we also trust that the broad masses of Western Europe and the United States, who are lovers of peace and goodwill, will find it difficult to look with indifference upon the conspiracies and multiple acts of injustice that their governments have been committing and continue to commit against Ethiopia. That is why we urge them to awaken their conscience and make themselves heard, that they may give a just verdict and, in so doing, thwart the conspiracy.

Vociferating with obvious pleasure and satisfaction, the Western news agencies have been thinking up headlines declaring that the invading forces of the reactionary ruling classes of Mogadishu have captured towns of revolutionary Ethiopia, such as Jijiga, Neghelle, Harar and Diredawa, and that in the north the antipeople bandits have captured Asmara and Massawa. These sources, that all this time have been affirming that Ethiopia is annihilated and dead, have now, in the same breath, started to go on about how Ethiopia is armed to more than capacity and is preparing to invade or about to invade Somalia. We are firmly convinced that the peoples of the world will observe, analyse and come to a correct verdict as to up to what extent a mind that has been stopped up and riddled with lies, intrigue and outrage and a conscience bemused by love of riches can manage to delude someone.

Why do the imperialists and their lackeys, who know full well that the protests uttered by Somalia are false and that the victim is revolutionary Ethiopia, stand on the side of the rulers of Somalia and so disorient the peoples of the world? Is it because they are concerned about the broad masses of Somalia? Or is it because, as they profess in word, they are truly concerned about peace and the well-being of humankind? If this was the case, why did they not make every attempt to prevent the dishonest Siad Barre from unleashing his criminal invasion instead of encouraging him and helping to egg him on to adventurism, lies and arrogance? Knowing full well that the immediate withdrawal of the forces of invasion of Somalia from Ethiopian territory was at that moment the only decisive solution for reaching peace, why did they not advise him to withdraw his forces?

The tactics and objective of these ruling antipeople and antipeace forces, as they are employed and perceived at present in the horn of Africa, are not new, but old, and they have been employed and will continue to be employed against many oppressed peoples and developing countries. It is the old, dilapidated, shamefaced policy and conspiracy of dividing, exploiting and weakening, known otherwise as neocolonialism or indirect government. Having failed in their sinister designs on the oppressed peoples of the Far East, the Middle East and Latin America, not content with the cruelty to which they have subjected these sister peoples who are fighting against diseases, hunger, ignorance and abject poverty, they now turn to Africa.

At present Africa has formed a common front and is rapidly advancing by means of its historic continental organization. In today's age, Africa is making great advances in the economic, political and cultural fields and is solving for itself problems related to these and other spheres.

Although there are in Africa certain sick opportunist forces, victories are being gained through fighting together against the old and new forms of colonialism. In southern Africa, freedom fighters are making the racists and fascists give in.

As a result of the victories scored by Africa and the historic struggle for freedom, a well-defined line is being drawn in Africa between those in favour of freedom, progress and unity and those against.

Africa is a continent with vast reserves of yet unexploited resources that could benefit other countries.

Africa has a young and progressive labour force that can be fully trusted to carry through revolutionary change and the progress of the continent.

Together with its struggle against imperialism, this progressive, emerging force is forging an alliance with the oppressed peoples the world over, with the oppressed peoples of the Middle East, the Far East and Latin America and with other progressive, peace-loving forces.

Africa's emerging and progressive forces are undergoing an unparalleled transformation that is the fairest in the whole world.

This is why the antipeople and antipeace forces are putting into effect every imaginable scheme and manoeuvre to stave off this historic tide and to subvert this growing force.

We believe that the peoples of the world, the world's emerging forces and all peaceloving and progressive peoples would be making a monumental mistake if they looked on the flame that has been lit in the Horn of Africa with indifference.

The oppressed masses, the emerging forces and the progressives of Africa and other places want and are making every possible effort to create bonds of friendship with the broad masses of America and Western Europe, based not on the old-type diplomacy or lord-servant relationship but rather on equality and fraternity, which do not stand for exploitation, oppression, racism and overt aggression.

However, how can anyone enjoy a drink of pure water when those who contaminate it are still at large?

The imperialists bedeck their cities with skyscrapers and fragrant flowers while at the same time testing their weapons by using them without the slightest qualms against the oppressed peoples of the world. Can anyone imagine a more heinous crime being perpetrated by man against man?

The conspiracy against the entity and the Revolution of Ethiopia has a neocolonial nature and is conducted by imperialism.

Siad Barre, who is both the cause and instrument of the conspiracy, is spouting absurd propaganda when he claims that he's seeking peace and that Ethiopia is about to invade Somalia. The ruling classes of Somalia have been engaging in all kinds of dealings with the reactionary Arab ruling classes, trying to obtain weapons and financial and troop support with the aim of extending their jihad[4] war to face up to the economic upheaval and widespread concern caused by the reactionary invasion they have been carrying out for the last few months. In their effort to obtain weapons from the imperialist countries, thereby making the war an international affair, Siad Barre's emissaries have also spread the rumour around the Western European capitals and Washington that Ethiopia will invade Somalia, and they have also tried to sow confusion among African leaders and peoples, but to no avail.

The real truth is far removed from the propaganda spread by the reactionary ruling classes of Somalia and their allies. The atrocities perpetrated against Ethiopia by the Italian fascists constituted the worst crime committed against our country in all its history, and the crime that is being perpetrated now by the Mussolini of Mogadishu unquestionably ranks second to it.

It is quite obvious that President Carter's recent meetings and consultations with Middle East and Western European leaders are aimed at making use of the propaganda about Somalia on the verge of being invaded and finding the way through which the Horn of Africa — chiefly Ethiopia and the Red Sea — is to fall under the control of anti-Ethiopia forces.

When he said that he was certain that Somalia would look for peace President Carter was trying to present Somalia, the invader, as a lover of peace and Ethiopia, the invaded, as the aggressor.

---

[4] In Arabic holy war, literally 'great effort'. Muslims are obliged to fight non-Muslims until the latter accept either the religion of Islam, or the status of protected subject. In principle, any war by a Muslim country against a non-Muslim one may qualify as Jihad, but Muslim tradition requires Jihad to be proclaimed officially. (Ed).

After his meeting with President Carter, the Shah of Iran said that he would not remain indifferent should Ethiopia violate Somalia's border. It is evident that he was paving the way for an excuse to ship arms to Somalia openly instead of doing it in secret, the way he has been doing. The ruling classes of Iran and Saudi Arabia have informed Carter of their decision to support Somalia in its flagrant invasion of Ethiopia, and have agreed on the following proposals with the aim of supplying arms to Somalia's war arsenal and thus enable that country to extend the invasion:

1. Iran, Saudi Arabia, Kuwait and West Germany would provide Somalia with the money it needs to purchase the weapons for the invasion;

2. Egypt would supply Somalia with as many weapons as it possibly could from the armament received from the Soviet Union to combat Israel and would ask the United States for weapons to replace those sent to Somalia;

3. The U.S. bases located in Saudi Arabia, Iran and West Germany would furnish whatever amount of arms Somalis requested using Iran as the transfer point;

4. All further supplies of arms by Western Europe and the United States would be guaranteed;

5. Iran would participate directly by sending troops to fight alongside the Somalian soldiers in case Somalia were too weak to achieve its goals of expansion after the weapons were delivered.

6. The Iranian army would launch its war of intervention from Oman, with air support from Saudi Arabia; and

7. An anti-Ethiopia military pact would be signed immediately that would include the governments of the Persian Gulf and of the Gulf states.

The other anti-Ethiopia front consists of the conspiracy against our Revolution and our entity put into effect by such petrodollar régimes as those of Kuwait, the Union of Arab Emirates and other reactionary ruling classes that would provide Somalia with arms, money and troops. The ruling classes of Abu Dhabi and Jordan recently declared a jihad by calling on the Islamic nations and others to lend support to Somalia. This bellicose and reactionary declaration urged the Arab world to "deploy its military forces alongside those of Arab Somalia."

The crimes that are being committed against black peoples by the decadent régimes of Saudi Arabia, Iran, Kuwait and the Gulf states are not limited to Ethiopia. Instead of siding with the African peoples who sympathize with them in their struggle against Israel, those Arab countries are doing everything within their power to bolster the economy of the arch-enemy of the African people — the racist, fascist régime of South Africa — by investing in its commercial and industrial development. They have also turned a deaf ear to Africa's demands that oil shipments to that racist and illegal régime be suspended, while at the same time sparing no effort to divide, bleed and weaken Africa and to eliminate the Palestinian people, who do not have a state of their own.

Broad masses of Ethiopia and friendly oppressed and progressive peoples of the world, in addition to the aforementioned forces that have lined up against a developing, nonaligned country that is trying to solve its domestic social and economic problems and establish a free society where justice, equality and opportunity for all will prevail, an extraordinary situation has come about as a result of the agreement arrived at following an urgent meeting held behind closed doors in Washington by NATO member countries — the USA, Great Britain, West Germany, Italy and France — with the aim of secretly arming Somalia.

These five great powers make up the majority of the standing members of the UN Security Council, which is considered a guarantor of world peace by all the peoples on earth.

According to the communiqué issued following the meeting, these powers proposed that Somalia negotiate with invaded Ethiopia, but they did not condemn Somalia for being the attacker. This is extremely deplorable.

This is the kind of world we still live in.

This was the position adopted by the standing members who play such an important role in the UN body that is entrusted with safeguarding peace.

Many years have passed since the hypocritical League of Nations, responsible for World War II and the death of millions of persons, was discredited and replaced.

We used to believe that the attitude of those governments and the general world situation had changed considerably, but we were very much mistaken. And we might ask as an aside: what can the world learn from this? In our opinion, few people know as well as do the people of Great Britain, Germany, France and Italy what the results, both constructive and destructive, of the wars they fought in were; those wars that have gone down in the history of the world and that were instigated by certain naive, arrogant groups. How is it possible that this lesson has been forgotten within a period equivalent to the age of a mature person?

We would like to ask a number of questions of those who have asked us to negotiate with Somalia and of Somalia itself, which has openly and arrogantly invaded our territory to satisfy its thirst for expansion and still continues to invade some of our territory, wantonly murdering our innocent people.

How did Washington and the people of the United States react when the Japanese attacked and bombed Pearl Harbour?

What did Churchill and those British officials who are still alive say in the House of Commons in the dark hours when Hitler's warplanes flew over British skies following the fall of France?

Is it perhaps that they look upon the Ethiopian people as making up a society devoid of feelings and incapable of fighting for its honour, its territorial integrity, its freedom, its unity, its rights and its Revolution?

Or is it that they think that the Ethiopians who, every second, every minute, are torn to pieces by the tanks, the artillery and the machine guns of the arrogant Somalian troops are but the skeletons of donkeys?

We leave the answers to these questions to the conscience of the peace- and freedom-loving peoples of the world.

One thing that we Ethiopians would like to remind the world of is that, apart from opposing the colonialists, expansionists, racists and fascists and defending ourselves against their attacks, never in our long history did we cross our neighbours' borders as invaders or violate the rights of others. Even today we have no territorial disputes with anybody or expansionist aims or intentions to take over territory belonging to our neighbours.

We are struggling to consolidate our unity, national integrity and national independence.

We are struggling to establish a completely free society devoid of exploitation, oppression, injustice and differences based on religion, tribe or sex; a society where peace, justice, equality and social progress prevail.

All we ask for is the proper respect for and materialization of the principles contained in the UN Charter and established more than 32 years ago where special mention is made of the nations' common determination to protect future generations from the scourge of war and not to make use of force unless such force is used for collective security and to maintain international peace and security.

We will continue our just and legitimate defensive struggle without any hesitation whatsoever with the purpose of cleaning up our territory and driving out the arrogant forces of Somalia, in keeping with Article 51 of the UN Charter, unless the illegal and arrogant ruling classes of Somalia un- conditionally and immediately — I repeat, **immediately** — withdraw their invasion troops.

Those member states of the UN and peoples that have committed them- selves to the defence of justice and peace have the international, moral and legal duty to side with us in our legitimate struggle.

People of Ethiopia:

What is expected of us in this decisive hour of trial?

To remain alert, organized and armed. That the progressive, patriotic and oppressed classes rise up in unison. That incessant efforts be made on the war front and in the productive and professional fields; and the determination to withstand any sacrifice for the sake of our just struggle and goal.

We have but one option: Revolutionary Ethiopia or death. A day of freedom is preferable to perpetual shame and disguised slavery.

We will not fall prey to panic, regardless of how many antipeople and antipeace forces are mobilized and united against us.
The struggle will continue!
We will win!

Berhanu Bayih*

The Ethiopian Revolution: A Hard Period.

(Complete Text). World Marxist Review, vol. 21 no. 4. April 1978.

* Member, Standing Committee, Provisional Military Administrative Council of Socialist Ethiopia.

Q. When we met the last time[1] you said that the PMAC had approved a Programme of the National Democratic Revolution. What new elements has it brought to the development of the revolutionary process in Ethiopia?

A. The Programme of the National Democratic Revolution lays down the guidelines for our revolutionary process. It establishes Ethiopia's entry upon the path of socialist orientation and sets as the goal of the national democratic stage the formation of a people's democratic republic led by the working-class party. This, the Programme says, will lay "a sound foundation for transition to socialism".

As you see, we accept the theory of the non-capitalist way of development. When we call our country "Socialist Ethiopia" we do not mean that we have already built up a socialist society. We merely want to show what we want, what our goal is. We are now at the stage of national democratic revolution. And we are aware that it will take much time before we can go over to socialist construction.

The key task today, according to the Programme, is to unite all the Marxist-Leninist organisations and groups which are active in Ethiopia. At first, we envisage their co-operation at every level, then formation of a united front on the basis of a common platform, and finally, complete organisational unity on the basis of ideological unity, which will mean the establishment of a Marxist-Leninist party, a proletarian party.

Marxist-Leninist party leadership, we believe, is a necessary condition for Ethiopia for full victory by a broad revolutionary front of all the anti-feudal and anti-imperialist forces, and it is our goal to form such a front. It may include mass organisations (trade unions, women's, youth and other organisations) and other progressive democratic parties, even if they are not Marxist-Leninist parties. Adoption of a joint action programme for

[1] See World Marxist Review, August 1976.

struggle against imperialism, feudalism and bureaucratic capitalism is to be the main criterion. These are the three reactionary class forces which determine the nature of the present Ethiopian society as a semi-feudal and semi-capitalist society, and that is what the Ethiopian revolution seeks to change. The establishment of a broad revolutionary front will make it possible to hold elections to a National Assembly, which is to proclaim a People's Democratic Republic.

Consequently, one of the chief aims of the Ethiopian revolution is to hand power over to the people. This requires the establishment of a revolutionary Marxist-Leninist party of the proletariat, to act as the leading force in a broad national democratic front.

There are now five revolutionary Marxist-Leninist organisations and groups in Ethiopia, namely, the All-Ethiopian Socialist Movement, the Marxist-Leninist Revolutionary Organisation, the Revolutionary Seded (Fire), the Labour League and the Revolutionary Struggle of the Oppressed Peoples of Ethiopia. In June 1977, they proclaimed the establishment of the United Front of Ethiopian Marxist-Leninist Organisations on the basis of their common Action Programme. But for the time being they have their independent organisations.

Mass democratic organisations began to take shape from the very start of the revolution. The most important of these is the All-Ethiopian Trade Union, which was founded in 1977. Trade unions are being organised at the enterprises, in the industries and on a national level. The new trade unions have earned the greatest hatred of the reactionaries. You may be aware that both the first and the second chairmen of the All-Ethiopian Trade Union were killed by counter-revolutionary terrorists.[2]

Peasant associations are another important form of mass democratic organisation. Grass-roots peasant associations elect delegates to associations formed on the level of districts and provinces. The All-Ethiopian Peasant Association, which was founded in September 1977, is now acquiring organisational form. Peasant associations, which now bring together over 7 million farmers, enjoy fairly broad rights. For all practical purposes, they exercise the functions of local self-administration. They have their own executive bodies, judicial bodies and security agencies. Self-defence detachments have been set up everywhere. Their members have been given some military training and provided with weapons.

Urban dwellers' associations are another form of mass organisation. The grass-roots associations — *kebele* — of which more than 1,000 have already been set up, join in higher-level associations and then form urban centres. The members of each centre elect their executive organs. The Congress of the Urban Centre nominates three persons from its midst, one of

[2] Tewodros Zekele was killed in February, and Temesgen Madezo in September 1977.

whom is appointed mayor by the government. These centres also set up judicial organs, security agencies and self-defence detachments.

Women's and young people's associations are also being set up, but for the time being only on the local and not yet on the national level. Let me add that those who head various types of associations at all levels are also targets of counter-revolutionary terrorist attacks. This provides fresh proof that the imperialists and reactionaries regard the establishment of mass organisations and their adoption of revolutionary ideas as a great threat to themselves.

Q. What are the main achievements and problems of the Ethiopian revolution in the socio-economic sphere?

A. First of all, there is the agrarian reform, which is perhaps the most radical in Africa. Under a decree issued by the PMAC in March 1975, all the land in the rural localities has been nationalised and proclaimed to be the Ethiopian people's collective property. This is a tremendous achievement for a country 90% of whose population is peasant. The same PMAC decree simultaneously abolished land rent in every form, debt payments, and so on. Land can now now longer be either sold, divided or mortgaged.

Each peasant family has the free use of a plot of land not more than 10 hectares in area. The big farms are not to be broken up but will be and are being converted into state farms. The establishment of co-operatives of peasant associations is being encouraged, including both service co-operatives and producer co-operatives. Peasants are already working simultaneously on their own plots and in the collective fields. They also help to cultivate the fields of families who have lost their bread-winner, where the bread-winner is at the front, or where the head of the family is old. The state farms will help to boost agricultural production, while setting an example for the peasants and showing them how to use modern methods in agriculture. In addition, the state farms supply peasants with fertilisers and render various types of services, especially those involving farming machinery.

Of course, the agrarian reform ran a different course in the various parts of the country. The point is that in the past there was a substantial difference between the system of landownership in the north and the south of Ethiopia. In the north, only 7% of the land belonged to the feudal lords, the rest being officially in communal ownership. Nominally, every peasant had the right to a plot of land, but there was a land shortage because of the very high density of the population in that part of the country.

In the south, feudal and church landownership was the prevalent form. The bulk of the peasants had no land and were tenants who had no rights and who could be driven off their plots at any time. Overall, 60% of the farm land in Ethiopia belonged to less than 1,000 families. The feudal lords took up to 75% of the peasants' crop.

Nationalisation, as I have said, was proclaimed everywhere. In the north, it was naturally easier to put it through right away. Incidentally, apart from expropriating the land which belonged to the feudals, the reform also destroyed many feudal customs and institutions which were not directly connected with landownership, like the so-called *gulte*, the right to collect taxes which the emperor gave the feudal lord for services rendered. Other feudal levies were also abolished. The peasants at once realised that their existence, their living standard was improving. Peasant associations and co-operatives, and co-operative shops in the towns are also being successfully established.

In the south, the reform caused much sharper upheavals. There, the feudal lords, who were in possession of virtually all the land, put up armed resistance. However, they were defeated, killed, driven out or disarmed, and strong peasant associations have now been set up in the area. A campaign, known as *Zemecha* — Development through Co-operation — had a great part to play. In the course of it, 60,000 students, teachers and soldiers went to the rural localities to support and teach the peasants. Let us note that within a year of the proclamation of the agrarian reform, farm output increased by 30%.

In the towns, the land and all the extra houses (in the towns, one family can now own no more than one house) have been proclaimed government property. This reform dispossessed the same feudal lords and aristocrats who had owned tracts of land and many houses in the towns. Rent was reduced by between 15 and 50%. In addition, taxes, which have now been unified and are collected by urban dwellers' centres, are being used to meet the needs of local development.

In Ethiopia, banks, insurance companies and the major industrial enterprises have been nationalised. Thus, the commanding heights of the economy are in the hands of the state. However, provision has also been made for some participation by local private capital in the country's development. This is in accord with the present stage, the stage of national democratic revolution. A ceiling has been established for private investment.

Mixed enterprises are also to be set up and developed. This implies co-operation between the government and foreign capital in developing industry. But if one takes the capitalist countries, only some of the old firms have by now joined the government in setting up mixed enterprises. Others have preferred to stop production.

The task now is to develop to the utmost mixed enterprises set up jointly with socialist countries. Ethiopia has engaged in co-ordinating economic plans with them, and has been receiving assistance from them. We believe that planning is the basis of success in economic activity. We now have a Central Planning Commission, but like other agencies it has a shortage of trained personnel. We seek to overcome these difficulties, making use of experts from socialist countries and sending our students to study there.

We also have other numerous difficulties arising from the war, the need to beat back the aggression, or from overt sabotage by counter-revolutionaries. One should bear in mind, after all, that two "political parties" — the Democratic Union[3] and the People's Revolutionary Party[4] — and seven so-called liberation — actually separatist — fronts[5] are now fighting the Ethiopian revolution with support from external reactionaries.

Q. What are the main problems the Ethiopian revolution has to face in its ideological-organisational work?

A. This is an exceptionally important sphere of activity. The revolution cannot advance without a revolutionary workers' party. But Lenin said that there can be no revolutionary party without a revolutionary ideology.

Such a party could not emerge under the monarchy because of the persecution of progressive forces and the weakness of our working class. That is why when the revolution began we invited all the Ethiopians who had studied in other countries and had adopted Marxist-Leninist ideas to return home. We asked them whether they were willing to co-operate with the PMAC on the basis of its programme. They agreed. A Provisional Office for Mass Organisational Affairs was set up.[6] When it began to operate, it turned out that these men were members of various groups, the five groups mentioned above, and that they have different views on a number of substantial matters. That is why we began to encourage them to co-operate and establish ideological unity. The PMAC believes that it would be a mistake to issue a formal decree merging these groups and proclaiming the establishment of a proletarian party "from the top". They must attain ideological and then organisational unity by themselves, and in the process win over to their side the industrial workers, the vanguard of the proletariat.

We have entrusted the Provisional Office with the preparations for setting up a Marxist-Leninist party and with carrying on agitation and propaganda work among the masses. It has been given all the necessary

[3] An anti-Marxist front formed in 1975 by liberals who had been exiled in Haile Selassie's time. They have since been joined by civil servants and soldiers fleeing the excesses of the new régime. The movement is strongest in Gondar, Tigre and Gojjam provinces where it has also attracted local leaders. (Ed).

[4] Formed by militant trade unionists and students against the Haile Selassie's régime. It describes itself as Marxist-Leninist and wants to end military rule. The Ethiopian People's Revolutionary Party (EPRP) operates powerful urban guerilla groups that have assassinated senior government officials and supporters.(Ed).

[5] The Tigre People's Liberation Front (TPLF) Oromo National Liberation Front (ONLF) Afar Liberation Front (ALF) Western Somali Liberation Front (WSLF) Eritrean Liberation Front (ELF) Eritrean People's Liberation Front (EPLF) Eritrean Liberation Front (EPLF) Eritrean Liberation Front — Popular Liberation Forces (ELF—PLF). (Ed).

[6] The creation of the Office was announced in the Programme of National Democratic Revolution on 21 April, 1976. (Ed).

facilities, means of transport, etc. It set up its branches everywhere, including districts and villages. An Ideological School has been established in Addis Ababa. We have displayed full trust in these people, supplied them with weapons and provided protection from the EPRP killers. We have recommended them to the people.

However, after a little while one of these groups, namely, the All-Ethiopian Socialist Movement, or MEISON for short, decided that it was the strongest and aspired to subordinate the other groups. In the summer of 1977, the PMAC decided to reorganise the Provisional Office. The idea behind its decision was to give all the groups within it equal rights both in the work of the Office itself and - and this is highly important — in guiding the Ideological School.

When this had been done, some MEISON leaders were disappointed. Soon there came the Somali aggression against Ethiopia. In addition, the separatist movement in Eritrea was intensified, and the country's unity was threatened on every side. These were combined with the activities of internal counter-revolutionaries. And just when the battle of Dire Dawa (Ogaden region) was being fought, some of the MEISON leaders went into hiding.

It later turned out that it was the right-wing opportunist elements who had taken flight. They issued a statement listing all the dangers threatening the country and declared that the situation was hopeless. They claimed that the PMAC was doing nothing to save the country and the revolution. However, they miscalculated in expecting that the peasants would support them. Actually, the peasants arrested many of them. When the peasants handed them over to the revolutionary authorities, they said: "These are traitors, they themselves told us that the revolution should be defended to the end, and here is what they have done." The flight of some of the MEISON leaders spelt their political suicide. They were not supported by the people, and the group's left wing condemned them.

But the revolution was hit. Let me say briefly that among those who fled were men like Haile Fida, Chairman of the Office, two ministers, the Minister of Education and the Minister of Housing and Urban Development, who was also responsible for the urban dwellers' centres, and his brother, a permanent secretary of the Ministry of Culture. This left vacant posts in the Mass Organisation Office and several other establishments, and these are not easy to fill. But the unity of the five Marxist-Leninist groups is now stronger and more solid, for the fugitive leaders had only paid lip-service to unity, while secretly working against it.

Q. How does the PMAC intend to start solving the nationalities question on Ethiopia?

A. Our Programme of National Democratic Revolution envisages a solution of the nationalities problem through a recognition of the right of each nationality in Ethiopia to self-determination in the form of regional autonomy. Ethiopia has many tribes and nationalities. We believe that recognition of each nationality's right to self-determination and regional autonomy is the correct way to solve the nationalities question in line with socialist principles and Ethiopia's objective conditions. We seek to translate it into practice, notably, in Eritrea, for which we have worked out a special nine-point programme.[7]

The PMAC has already proclaimed the equality of all the nationalities in the sphere of religion, language, culture, and so on. It is our intention to give all the nationalities of Ethiopia an opportunity to use their national language, to develop their economy and national culture, to enjoy all rights and to be free from any exploitation. We regard the nationalities question as an organic part of the overall question of class struggle.

Concerning the choice of form in which the self-determination of the country's nationalities is to be realised, namely, regional autonomy, that is Ethiopia's sovereign business. After all, this is not a liberation of colonies but free development of nationalities within revolutionary Ethiopia.

Q. What, in your opinion, has the Ethiopian revolution done for the world-wide anti-imperialist struggle?

A. The Ethiopian revolution can have a very important international role to play. Its successes can largely promote the anti-imperialist struggle, and not only in Africa. They will also be a contribution to the socialist transformation of the world.

Our region is of tremendous strategic importance. If the Ethiopian revolution advances successfully, it will mean that our country will continue to play a big positive role within it, and also in Africa as a whole. Imperialism is aware of this, and that is why it has been using its agents within and outside the country to undermine the development of our revolution.

Socialist Ethiopia's foreign policy is based on principles like peace, equality of all states, non-interference in their domestic affairs, non-alignment, and so on. These principles are clearly set out in the Programme of National Democratic Revolution.

Some ask us whether there is a contradiction between such a policy and our orientation on stronger friendship with the socialist countries. But we

[7] The PMAC's Nine Point Programme announced on 16 May, 1976, provided for:
"full participation by the people of the Eritrean administrative region in the country's political, economic and social movements with the rest of the Ethiopian people"; "immediate autonomy to the people of the . . . region in collaboration with the progressive forces"; "any necessary assistance for the return of all Ethiopians who have fled to neighbouring and other countries" and for their rehabilitation; the release of political prisoners, or a reduction of their sentences, "as soon as peace prevails"; the lifting of the state of emergency (which had been extended to cover the whole of Eritrea in February 1975) "when peace prevails and . . . the major points mentioned above are in the process of implementation"; and the establishment of a "special commission" for the region to "work on the implementation" of the points concerning refugees, rehabilitation and political prisoners.

The proposals were rejected on 17 May by the ELF—PLF. (Ed).

are sure that there is no contradiction here. After all, non-alignment means pursuit of an independent foreign policy. Our relations with other countries are our own business, they are a matter of our independent policy. Ethiopia is fighting against imperialism and internal reaction, and this is a struggle that cannot be carried on single-handed. Close relations with the socialist countries are needed also for successful socialist construction.

Fidel Castro. Speech Marking the Hundredth Anniversary of General Antonio Maceos' Baragua Protest.

(Excerpts). Granma, 26 March, 1978.

. . . Distance practically doesn't exist for revolutionaries in the world today.

I was saying that a detailed report was published yesterday.[1] We might point out that it has been a tradition in our revolutionary process to report on the facts and tell the truth. Every citizen who read those reports yesterday knew there wasn't a single lie there. This has always been our practice from the time of our struggle in the Sierra Maestra and all during these 20 years: the truth, confidence in the people and information for the people. The Revolution works with the masses, merges with the masses and the truth. That's why nobody had any doubts that what Granma said yesterday was the truth and nothing but the truth.

Some imperialist news agencies have said that the Cuban people officially found out about our internationalist aid to Ethiopia yesterday. Well, if they want to say "officially," yes, we admit it; but unofficially — in the way we know about things and the way we do things and know how to do them among ourselves — everybody knew about it a long time ago.

It was the same with our internationalist aid for Angola. The people know about it because we don't do things any other way than with the people. Of course, there are situations in which certain things can't be published officially, because if you must undertake a complicated and dangerous operation you must do so in a discreet manner; there is no need to go around telling everybody about it. But, who if not the workers and peasants of our reserve forces and the soldiers and officers of our regular forces fulfilled this mission? All the combat units knew about it and so did all the reserve units. And, as was the case with Angola, there weren't 1,000 or 10,000 but hundreds of thousands of our compatriots who were willing to fulfill this internationalist mission.

[1] See "Summary of the Military Operations that led to the Great Victory of the Ethiopian Revolution in Ogaden", Granma, 14 March, 1978. (Ed).

We never do anything behind the backs of the people. Very often the masses are told about many things that are not published on the front pages of the newspapers through the Party and the mass organizations . . .

Our Revolution isn't seeking glory or prestige; it simply fulfills its internationalist postulates and principles! Of course, we couldn't discuss our internationalist aid to Ethiopia publicly until the Ethiopians did. As long as they felt that keeping quiet was the right thing, we did likewise. When the Ethiopians discussed the matter publicly, we, our Party, were then in a position to do the same. It wasn't going to be a secret known to millions of people forever. Now it's a national and international secret. . .

First of all, we would like to say that we deeply regret the conflict between Somalia and Ethiopia; we did all we could to avoid it. Roughly a year ago, around this time — perhaps it was later than March 20, I don't remember exactly — we organized a meeting in Aden between the leaders of Ethiopia, Yemen and Somalia and ourselves in an effort to solve the problems between Somalia and Ethiopia, precisely to avoid a war; to avoid a development which would constitute a betrayal of the international revolutionary movement; to prevent the leadership of Somalia, with its territorial ambitions and aggressive attitude, from going over to imperialism. We weren't able to prevent it.

In Somalia there were two forces: forces of the right and forces of the left. For many years they talked to the masses about socialism and progress, but there was a powerful reactionary group in the government, right-wingers who advocated an alliance with imperialism, Arab reaction, Saudi Arabia, Iran, etc. They gradually caused the left-wingers to lose ground in the country, upholding, as reactionaries always do everywhere, the banner of chauvinism. Since they lack a social, political and revolutionary doctrine, reactionaries resort to playing upon people's basest instincts, and they especially resort to chauvinism. . .

Chauvinism, however, isn't the only thing which explains the timing of the attack. Ethiopia was ruled by a feudal régime for many years, and that régime was done away with by the Ethiopian Revolution. Ethiopia is a country in which peasants make up 85 or 90% of the population. Before the Revolution and practically up to 1973, even slavery existed in Ethiopia. Those who weren't serfs or peasants tied to the land and oppressed by the landowners might well have been slaves.

Thus, the Ethiopian Revolution meant an extraordinary change for the people of Ethiopia; many millions of exploited peasants were liberated, and the bondage of the exploited masses ended. They didn't have a very large working class, but it was also liberated by the Revolution. Women, who were especially oppressed and subjected to terrible injustices, were liberated by the Ethiopian Revolution.

The Ethiopian Revolution not only did away with feudalism; it also decided to advance toward socialism. One of the most important events to take place in Africa during the last few years was precisely the Ethiopian Revolution. . .

In February 1977 the most important, radical and revolutionary elements, headed by Comrade Mengistu Haile Mariam,[2] took over the leadership of the Ethiopian Revolution and announced their intention to build socialism, and it was then that the ties between Ethiopia and imperialism were broken. It was at that precise moment that, the right-wing faction of the Government of Somalia felt the time to invade Ethiopia had come, because they knew that invading Ethiopia meant cooperating with imperialism in the destruction of a great revolution and that imperialism would be delighted. Furthermore, they knew that the NATO powers would also be delighted if Somalia helped eliminate the Ethiopian Revolution. . .

But at the Aden meeting the leaders of Somalia solemnly pledged, solemnly committed themselves not to invade Ethiopia ever, not to attack Ethiopia militarily. In fact, they already had everything planned, and the attack began in July.

Ethiopia is a big country, it has a large population, it has soldiers and very good soldiers at that. That's why, in answer to their request, we initially decided to send them a few dozen instructors and advisers — the figure might have come to a few hundred — to train units and teach them how to handle modern weapons of a type they weren't familiar with. Since the Emperor was an ally of the United States, the Ethiopians had U.S. weapons; then they started to receive supplies from the socialist countries which they didn't know how to handle.

We felt that helping them to train their army would be a provisional measure, because when the Ethiopian army has been trained and well armed you can be sure that nobody — nobody — will bother them. You can be sure of that!

Why did it become necessary for us to send fighters? Because of the scope and magnitude of Somalia's aggression. Somalia had been preparing itself for a number of years. It had even been upholding the banners of socialism; it claimed to be a progressive country, an ally of the progressive world — I'm talking about the Somalian Government — and all along it had been building up an army. Somalia had hundreds of tanks, hundreds of artillery pieces, planes, many motorized infantry brigades, and nearly all those weapons and units were used during the invasion of Ethiopia.

At that time, Ethiopia had to struggle all over the country against groups of counterrevolutionary bandits aided from abroad and directed by feudal elements, and against the secessionist movements in the north,[3]

---

[2] 3 February. (Ed).

[3] Refers to the three guerilla groups fighting for the independence of Eritrea; The Eritrean Liberation Front, The Eritrean People's Liberation Front and the Eritrean Liberation Front — Popular Liberation Forces. (Ed).

that are still getting help today from countries in the region. Ethiopia was faced with a very difficult situation, with no time to spare. If the Ethiopians had had a little more time, they would have learned how to handle all those tanks, artillery pieces and other modern weapons. We along with other socialist countries, would have contributed to training personnel. But the critical situation created by the invasion in late November led the Ethiopian Government to make an urgent request that we send tank, artillery and aviation specialists to help the army, to help the country, and we did so.

As Granma explained, our specialists started arriving in Ethiopia in mid-December and early January. We sent tank, artillery and aviation specialists, since the Ethiopians didn't have the time to learn how to handle that weaponry in view of the situation. They really didn't need infantry; there were plenty of infantrymen. If some Cuban medium-sized units such as battalions were sent to the east, it was to ensure cooperation with the tank and artillery contingents operated by Cuban personnel, since you must bear in mind the language problem and the fact that there are times when a tank unit must have cooperation with the infantry assured.

But actually our main support for Ethiopia involved sending specialists. The Ethiopians already have artillery and tank units, and I'm sure that soon they'll have excellent cadres to handle that equipment. They have more than enough soldiers, and training an infantryman is easier than training a tank or artillery specialist. We might add that the Ethiopian infantry is made up of very brave and courageous soldiers who have tremendous fighting potential.

Our cooperation became indispensable, the specialists were sent, and, as was reported in Granma, Cuban motorized infantry units participated in the final stage of operations alongside the Ethiopian infantry.

We might point out — as was published yesterday — that in seven weeks practically all the occupied territory in Ogaden was liberated, an area of more than 320,000 square kilometers. The invaders had overrun 320,000 square kilometers, an area three times the size of Cuba! From January 22 to March 14, practically the entire area was liberated; only a few towns were left and their capture was just a matter of time, since the Ethiopian forces didn't have enough vehicles and in many of those places they had to go on foot. So, for all practical purposes, the war on the eastern front has ended.

Cooperation between Ethiopians and Cubans was magnificent. There were artillery units made up of Cuban specialists and Ethiopian personnel. In a few days they started to understand one another by using signs and numbers, and the artillery group was operating smoothly. In spite of the language differences, they got along very well and there was a great deal of comradeship, confidence and brotherhood, and problems were solved smoothly.

I repeat that we don't want to seem as if we are boasting, as if we were indulging in exaggerated praise for our fighters, but we do think that it's only fair to say that the Cuban internationalist fighters stood out for their extraordinary effectiveness and magnificent combat ability. It is really admirable to see how many sons of our people were capable of going to that distant land and of fighting there as if fighting in their own country. That is proletarian internationalism! Brave and efficient revolutionary soldiers soon struck up a wonderful friendship and close ties with the admirable Ethiopian revolutionary fighters; they were welcomed in an extraordinarily affectionate manner by the Ethiopian people, and I know their leaders are very grateful to our people for this help.

The war against the invaders is practically over. Ethiopia has publicly stated it will not cross Somalia's border. This seems to us completely just and correct, because the war was fought not to invade another country, much less to seize land which belongs to others. It was an absolutely just, defensive war to protect territory invaded by foreign aggressors until such a time as those aggressors could be thrown out. Of course this means that the attacks on Ethiopia from Somalia will cease, because we can't imagine that any country would be willing to tolerate attacks launched from the borders of another country indefinitely without responding appropriately. But we know the Ethiopian Government was absolutely sincere in its assurance that its troops would not cross the Somalian border. Actually, from the military point of view there is no need to do so, since the attacking forces have been completely defeated, and we fully support the position of the Ethiopian Government.

What will happen in Somalia? There's no telling. But it is clear that the right-wing faction, which imposed its aggressive and adventurist line on the Government of Somalia, has suffered a great defeat. Naturally, even amidst defeat the imperialists are trying to encourage this group and are man-oeuvring. However, there are also progressive and left-wing forces in Somalia, and we shall see what happens in the coming weeks. Of course, this is a matter that only concerns the people of Somalia, not any of us or any other country.

The imperialists have assumed a very hypocritical position during the conflict, because they knew that Somalia was invading Ethiopia right from the start, in July. The United States and the NATO countries knew about it and remained silent; they didn't say a word and they were delighted. They provided weapons for the aggressors — weapons from the United States and from NATO member states — by way of Saudi Arabia, Iran and other countries, and as the Somalians advanced they didn't say a word. When Somalia had occupied nearly all of Ogaden, the imperialists were optimistic; but when the Ethiopians began receiving internationalist aid, when they started to get weapons from the socialist camp and internationalist Cuban fighters began to arrive, the imperialists raised a real hue and cry. Then they insisted that there had to be a meeting of the OAU, the UN, etc., etc., and they talked about the need for a cease-fire. When, though, did they start talking about a cease-fire? When the aggressors started to lose the war.

As long as Somalia's forces advanced, the imperialists didn't say a word. When things started to change after the Ethiopians' first successful battles, when they realized that the situation could change quickly, then they raised the hue and cry and unleashed a propaganda drive all over the world, talking about the Cuban internationalist fighters — the Cuban troops as they call them — in Ethiopia. When the tables began to turn, they started to talk about a cease-fire, something which they hadn't done for all those months when the reactionary aggressors advanced. Of course, the Ethiopian Government quite correctly said that there could be no cease-fire, as long as part of its territory was occupied. That's also our revolutionary philosophy: there can be no cease-fire as long as there is occupied territory.

The first counterattacks and the offensive followed, and the enemy troops were roundly defeated. They had to pull out in great haste, leaving behind tanks, cannon, artillery, all kinds of weapons, to escape being surrounded and captured because they had been defeated, completely defeated. We must point out that there was nothing voluntary about the withdrawal of Somalia's troops. If they had stayed four more days, just four more days, virtually all their troops in Ogaden would have been surrounded. Due to the way the revolutionary forces advanced and captured the main communication centres, if the enemy hadn't undertaken a speedy withdrawal, the remains of Somalia's army would have been surrounded in Ogaden. Thus, the aggressors have been forced to leave. They can't fool anybody at all by saying that the Somalian Government made the gesture of withdrawing its troops, because had the Somalians not done so they would have lost what little they had left. That's the situation: they left as a result of the military operations in which they were defeated.

That's the truth; there's no need to lie. We feel that the war between Somalia and Ethiopia has ended for the time being since the territory has been liberated. I don't think the Somalians will be stupid enough to fall into the temptation of attacking Ethiopia again on their own; but just as reactionary countries, NATO states and imperialism encouraged them once they might do so again. . .

What does the presence of the Soviet Union's 'foreign legion' in Africa mean?
Commentary by Hsinhua Correspondent.
(Complete Text). Hsinhua News Agency, 2 April, 1978.

Nineteen days have elapsed since Somalia completed its troop withdrawal from Ogaden on 14th March. Yet there is still no sign that the

Cuban troops, whom the world public call the "foreign legion" of the Soviet Union, would withdraw from the Horn of Africa. Instead, word comes that Cuba is sending reinforcements to the Horn of Africa and south-eastern Africa.

People now raise the question: Since the original pretext for the military intervention no longer exists, why is it that the mercenary troops in the pay of the Soviet Union should hang on first in Angola and then in the Horn of Africa? And to what part of the African continent will the Kremlin direct this scourge next?

The lesson one has learnt from this is: Once the mercenary troops of the Soviet Union stepped on the soil of an African region or country, they would not quit easily. This is because their military actions in Africa are not merely acts of military intervention against one region or one country; they are closely related to the ambitions of social-imperialism for world domination and to its increasingly intense rivalry with the other superpower. This "foreign legion" formed by Cuban troops is but a tool of the Kremlin for world hegemony.

Nikita Khrushchev introduced missiles into Cuba in 1962. This action showed that as early as the 1960s, when the Soviet Union was beginning to degenerate into social-imperialism and to contend for supremacy with US imperialism, the masters of the Kremlin already singled out Cuba as their base for confrontation and rivalry with the United States. In the past 10 years or more when the Soviet Union has completely degenerated into social-imperialism, it has not only turned Cuba into a military springboard in the Caribbean but also placed the Cuban armed forces under its control. The 20-odd Cuba-based Soviet Tu-95B long-range reconnaissance bombers are making regular flights near the USA proper. Cienfuegos of Cuba has been turned into a base for the Soviet special task fleet to make constant presence in the Caribbean. A strategic highway best suited for military aircraft in wartime is being built in Cuba. The Soviet Union has poured more than 3,000 million US dollars' worth of military hardware into the western hemisphere after the US armed forces.

The Cuban troops have made their presence as the Soviet Union's "foreign legion" in some regions of the world at a time when the rivalry between the two superpowers for hegemony in Europe and its flanks has become ever more acute. They were transported from far-off Caribbean to Angola. Equipped with Soviet arms and led by Soviet generals, the Cuban forces in Angola started their expeditions in the African continent. Then came the armed invasion of Zaire engineered by the Soviet Union and Cuba. Then follows their armed intervention in the Horn of Africa.

In an article carried in the French paper *Le Monde* on 10th February discussing the strategic significance of the presence of the Soviet "foreign legion" in Africa, defence expert Jacques Isnard says; "Under the umbrella of nuclear deterrent which is aimed at 'freezing' the situation in certain regions of the world, notably in Europe, the Soviet Union has perfected a military capacity of long-distance intervention which relies on the existence of a new 'foreign legion' in its service; Cuban units and technicians of central Europe.'' According to the intent of the Kremlin, a Cuban expeditionary corps of professional soldiers ''can be put in the first line of the scene where the Soviets would not like very much to occupy themselves''.

It is very obvious that by supplying Cubans with money and weapons for them to fight in Africa, the Soviet Union aims to establish its own spheres of influence in Africa, encircle Europe from the flanks, and pose a threat to the lifeline, namely the sea route for petroleum transport, of the Western countries. The using of Cuban troops by the Soviet Union to carry out armed intervention in Africa also indicated that social-imperialism has developed into a stage when it would not scruple to launch a limited conventional war to realize its strategic ambition for world supremacy.

After the Soviet mercenaries staged an armed intervention in Angola, the US Weekly *Clarion* pointed out that Cuba had become a Trojan Horse installed by the Soviet Union in the Third World. Cuba's status as a weak nation being subjected to prolonged colonial oppression, its leader's ''revolutionary'' cloak and even the complexion of its black troops which makes it difficult to differentiate them from the Africans, all these are factors in the Kremlin choice of Cuba as its cat's paw to cover up its armed expansion in Africa.

Western information agencies estimated that Cuban troops in Africa have now exceeded 40,000, or nearly one-third of the strength of the Cuban regular force. To equip this ''foreign legion'', the Soviet Union has sent armaments worth over 1,000 million US dollars to Africa. For sending these Cubans to Africa the Soviet Union organized a massive long-range air and marine transport unprecedented since world war two. Judging by the fact that the Kremlin has set such a big chip in this gambling and that Soviet mercenaries have been fighting in Africa for the past three years, it is clear that the Soviet Union, after long deliberation, has taken an ambitious strategic action in Africa, an action which it will never give up lightly.

In the Caribbean crisis in October 1962 after the United States spotted the missiles which Khrushchev had furtively sent to Cuba, US President John F. Kennedy, in a grim trial of force with the Soviet Union, ordered a naval blockade of Cuba. Reeling back from his acts of adventurism in the subsequent confrontation, Khrushchev turned to capitulationism and pulled the Soviet missiles and bombers out of Cuba and even agreed to the humiliating demand for inspection by US ships on the way home.

Now, 16 years later, the Soviet Union and Cuba were emboldened to commit flagrant military intervention in Africa. As the British MP Winston S. Churchill put it, ''this new crisis finds the West in acute disarray, lacking the will to challenge the brazen Soviet aggression at any point. The United

States sits paralysed as reinforcements leave Cuba by sea and by air, beneath their very nose.''

Nor has the United States reacted in any way to the fact that Soviet aircraft and warships and even nuclear-powered submarines stay at Cuban bases and that Soviet pilots took the place of the Cuban ones sent to Africa and fly patrol missions just off the US limits.

The change that took place in the last 16 years points to the decline of an imperialist power of the old order and the meteoric rise of a social-imperialist upstart. Today, the Soviet Union has become the most dangerous source of another world war.

However, historical development is inexorable. The United States, for many years the world gendarme, had once engineered the invasion of Cuba by mercenaries it formed of Cuban exiles, but the whole venture ended in abject fiasco, and it has been on the decline. Who would care to assert that Soviet social-imperialism, now throwing it weight around all over the world, will not drift into the same rut of US imperialism.

Cuban-Ethiopian Joint Communique.

(Complete text). Granma, 7 May, 1978.

At the invitation of Comrade Fidel Castro Ruz, First Secretary of the Central Committee of the Communist Party of Cuba and President of the Council of State, Comrade Mengistu Haile Mariam, Chairman of the Provisional Military Administrative Council of Socialist Ethiopia, made an official, friendly visit to the Republic of Cuba, April 21-27, 1978.

During his visit, Chairman Mengistu Haile Mariam was accompanied by a high-level delegation that included: Lieutenant Colonel Tesfaye Gebre Kidan, member of the Standing Committee of the PMAC, in charge of Defence; Major Endale Tessema, member of the Standing Committee of the PMAC, in charge of Social Affairs; Second Lieutenant Tamirat Ferede, member of the Standing Committee of the PMAC, in charge of Information; Second Lieutenant Mengistu Gemetghu, member of the Standing Committee of the PMAC and Special Assistant to the Chairman; Captain Melaku Tefera, member of the PMAC Congress and its delegate in Gondar Province; Lieutenant Tessema Belai, member of the PMAC Congress and its delegate in Kaffa Province; Second Lieutenant Bahefu Alemu, member of the PMAC and its delegate in Gojjam Province; Aymro Wondmagenehu, Ethiopian Ambassador to Cuba; Doctor Tefera Wonde, Minister of Public Health; Colonel Doctor Feleke Gedle Giorgis, Minister of Foreign Affairs; Tesfaye Mekonnen, General Secretary of the Office of Political and Mass Organizations Affairs; Getachew Kibret, Political Advisor in the Chairman's Office; Addis Antenen, Vice-Commissioner of the Central Planning Commission.

Upon arrival in Havana, the Chairman of the PMAC Comrade Mengistu Mariam was warmly welcomed by Comrade Fidel Castro, who congratulated him and, through him, the entire Ethiopian people, on major achievements in defending the revolutionary gains and the sovereignty of their country from external aggression and the intrigues of international reaction and expressed his wishes for more brilliant successes in the future for revolutionary Ethiopia.

During its stay in Cuba, the Ethiopian delegation witnessed the great demonstrations of love and solidarity offered by the Cuban people along the visitor's extensive tour of Havana, Cienfuegos, Santiago de Cuba and the Special Municipality of Isle of Pines, as well as in the historical mass rally held in Revolution Square where the distinguished visitor gave a vibrant address which reaffirmed the revolutionary and anti-imperialist road of the Ethiopian process, as well as the indestructible bonds of friendship that link the two countries in their common struggle for socialism.

The Government of Cuba awarded the Playa Girón National Order to Comrade Mengistu Haile Mariam in recognition of his great contribution to the cause of the freedom of his people and the further strengthening of the bonds of friendship and cooperation between Cuba and Ethiopia.

Comrades Mengistu Haile Mariam and Fidel Castro held fraternal meetings in which problems common to both countries were analyzed. They also discussed the cooperation between Cuba and Ethiopia, the exchange of information on the advances made by both countries in the tasks concerning the building of the new society, as well as topical international issues.

Cuba was also represented by: Ramiro Valdés, Guillermo Garcia, Blas Roca, Carlos Rafael Rodríguez Osvaldo Dorticós, Armando Hart, Sergio del Valle, Pedro Miret and Arnaldo Milián, members of the Political Bureau of the Communist Party of Cuba; Antonio Pérez Herrero and Raúl Valdés Vivó, members of the Central Committee Secretariat of the Communist Party of Cuba; Division Generals Senén Casas, Abelardo Colomé and Arnaldo Ochoa, Lionel Soto, head of the Central Department of Foreign Affairs of the Central Committee, also members of the Central Committee; and José Pérez Novoa, Cuban Ambassador to Ethiopia.

Comrade Lt. Col. Mengistu Haile Mariam apprised Comrade Fidel Castro of the achievements and progress of the Ethiopian Revolution. The Ethiopian Leader described the struggle waged by the Ethiopian people against the intrigues of imperialism, internal and external reaction, and the heroic defence by the Ethiopian people of the revolutionary gains and the territorial integrity of their country. In this connection, Comrade Mengistu Haile Mariam expressed profound appreciation to the people of Cuba, the Communist Party and the Government of Cuba and to Comrade Fidel Castro for the resolute support and internationalist assistance rendered to the Ethiopian Revolution in this struggle.

He emphasized that Ethiopia intends to firmly pursue the anti-imperialist and anti-colonialist course in its foreign policy and seeks to develop and strengthen the relations of friendship and cooperation with all countries and peoples.

The Ethiopian Leader expressed the high regard in which the Ethiopian Revolution holds the continued economic, social and cultural success of the Cuban Revolution and its consistent, principled and internationalist foreign policy being carried out under the correct guidance of the Communist Party of Cuba, its First Secretary Commander-in-Chief Comrade Fidel Castro Ruz. He paid special tribute to Fidel Castro and his Comrades-in-arms, whose revolutionary zeal, heroism, uncompromising stand and successive victories against imperialism during the last two decades have made Cuba an inspiring example for a whole generation of progressive mankind.

The Cuban side expressed its admiration for the heroic battles waged by the Ethiopian people in defence of its Revolution and hailed the historic victory over the aggression in the Eastern and Southern Regions of Ethiopia. The progress and consolidation of the revolution in Ethiopia constitutes a further positive development in Africa's contemporary history and a significant contribution to the struggle against imperialism, colonialism, reaction and racism.

The Cuban side highly values the major achievements of the Ethiopian people in such a short period during which it completely liquidated one of the most backward régimes of our times, thus paving the way to freedom for millions of human beings who have been subjected for centuries to the yoke of exploitation by feudal lords and the bourgeoisie.

On analyzing the international situation, both sides noted with satisfaction the positive changes which have taken place in the world correlation of forces in favour of socialism, national independence, social progress and world peace. This change in favour of these trends has been a direct result of the increased strength and political influence of the community of socialist countries, specially of the Soviet Union, the great victories achieved by the people's national liberation movements, the struggles of the working class and other progressive forces for social progress and peace.

Ethiopia and Cuba express their support for the necessary policy of détente present in the international relations as a result of those changes, and condemn with the utmost firmness the actions of the reactionary groups of capitalist régimes opposed to détente.

Both sides spoke in favour of the earliest possible conclusion of a treaty on the complete and general prohibition of nuclear weapon tests and a convention banning chemical weapons. Emphasis was made on the urgency of prohibiting the development and production of new types of weapons systems of mass destruction. The sides expressed themselves in favour of the conclusion of a comprehensive agreement on this matter.

The Republic of Cuba and Ethiopia pronounced themselves in favour of making the principle of the non-use of force an inmutable law of international life and will seek to achieve the early conclusion of a world treaty on the non-use of force in international relations.

On analyzing the situation in the Horn of Africa, both sides condemned the sinister activities of imperialism and its reactionary allies in the region aimed at promoting wars among the African peoples so as to keep the countries of that region under their control and at the service of their exploiter interests. In their pursuit of further aggressive designs, they coordinate their forces against the Ethiopian Revolution, they encourage secessionism, territorial claims on alleged ethnic and religious grounds in an attempt to achieve their expansionist ambitions and thereby revise the existing borders.

They emphasized that the Red Sea is an international waterway of paramount interest to the international community and to the coastal states, in particular to Ethiopia. They, therefore, strongly condemned the joint NATO powers naval exercises that are being held in the Red Sea for provocative, intimidating and destabilizing purposes. The two sides vigorously rejected such imperialist designs to make the Red Sea serve the policies of imperialism and reactionary Arab régimes and supported the efforts to make the Red Sea a zone of peace, free from imperialist interference.

Both sides denounced the current campaign launched by the Somalian ruling clique, as well as by the United States and other imperialist powers and their collaborators in the region, aimed at slandering Ethiopia and its people, by accusing them of false aggressive plans against Somalia whose armed forces had treacherously attacked the Ethiopia territory.

Cuba reaffirmed its belief that in order to achieve durable peace in the Horn of Africa it is an indispensable condition for Somalia to renounce formally and unconditionally its expansionist designs and territorial claims on Ethiopia, Kenya and Djibouti, and abandon all acts directed against the sovereignty and territorial integrity of those countries. Both sides reiterated their adherence to the principle of inviolability of state borders, as it has been recognized by the OAU and the United Nations Charters and decisions.

Cuba and Ethiopia view with concern the situation in the Middle West and strongly condemn the recent Israeli aggression against Lebanon. Only with the withdrawal of Israel from the Arab territories occupied since 1967, respect for the legitimate rights of the Palestinian Arab people to have their own independent State, and the recognition of the PLO as their legitimate representative, will it be possible to obtain a just and lasting peace which guarantees the independent existence of all the countries in the region.

Both sides reiterate their solidarity with the patriotic and progressive forces united in the Rejection Front against imperialism's manoeuvres and Arab reaction's capitulating policy.

They expressed their solidarity with the People's Democratic Republic of Yemen which courageously confronts the aggressive actions of imperialism and reaction.

Ethiopia and Cuba support the just struggle of the people of Western Sahara to exercise their right to self-determination.

On analyzing the situation in Southern Africa, both sides reaffirmed their support for the struggle of the peoples of Zimbabwe and Namibia to achieve their independence from the racist Rhodesian and South African régimes. They condemned the Anglo-American manoeuvres aimed at dissolving Zimbabwe's patriotic armed forces in order to promote the neo-colonialist designs that seek to replace the white minority régime by a puppet government made up of servile instruments for imperialist domination. Both sides reaffirmed their continuing support for the Patriotic Front of Zimbabwe.

Concerning Namibia, both sides reaffirmed their support for its independence and reaffirmed their unwavering support for SWAPO as the sole and legitimate representative of the Namibian people. They condemned all attempts to dismember any part of the Namibian territory and to establish a puppet régime to guarantee the exploiter interests of imperialism.

They also expressed their solidarity with the genuine freedom fighters of South Africa, who are struggling to liquidate the fascist régime of racial oppression as represented by the hateful apartheid system.

Cuba and Ethiopia condemned the aggressions launched against the Front Line State of Angola, Mozambique, Tanzania, Zambia and Botswana, because of their support for the liberation movements in Southern Africa.

Both sides expressed their support for the Angolan revolution under the leadership of the MPLA-Workers Party, headed by Comrade Agostinho Neto, and denounced the continued actions by imperialism, reaction and South African fascists, that aim at crippling the development of the Revolution in that sister country. The triumph of the Angolan people against the South African invasion and the defeat of all the counterrevolutionary groups that tried to set up a neocolonial régime, improved the conditions for the struggle for freedom of the African peoples.

On analyzing the situation in the Indian Ocean, both sides denounced the imperialist manoeuvres and the existence of military bases like that of Diego Garcia which threaten the sovereignty and legitimate interests of the peoples of the area.

They expressed their support for the just demand of the Comoro Government for the restoration of the Mayotte Island.

Both sides hail the successes of the heroic Vietnamese people under the leadership of its Marxist-Leninist Party founded by President Ho Chi Minh, and express their solidarity with the Socialist Republic of Vietnam in its efforts to repair the devastating destructions wrought on their country in the war of aggression by United States imperialism, and to peacefully build a socialist society.

At the same time, both sides express their support for the struggle of the Korean people for a peaceful and independent reunification without foreign interference.

With respect to the situation in Latin America and the Caribbean, both sides hail the struggles of these peoples against U.S. imperialism and ultra-reactionary régimes like those in Chile, Paraguay, Uruguay and other countries. Both sides reaffirm their full support for the just cause for independence of the Puerto Rican people. They express their solidarity with the Panamanian people, who struggle for the full exercise of national sovereignty, and with the Nicaraguan people, whose struggle began by the great Latin American patriot Augusto César Sandino.

U.S. imperialism is trying new methods in which it combines the demagogic defence of supposedly suppressed "human rights" while it desperately tries to stop and crush the peoples struggle for national and social liberation and oppresses many millions of its own workers as well as Blacks and those of Latin American or other origins.

The United States Government, which has installed aggressive military bases all over the world and maintains hundreds of thousands of soldiers in foreign countries, pretends to be the champion of non-intervention. Among these bases is Guantánamo Base, in Cuba, imposed as a colonial enclave contrary to International Law and against the will of the Cuban people. That base dates back to the turn of the century, that is, the same period when other predatory actions such as the occupation of the Canal Zone in Panama, the subjection of the Puerto Rican nation, and the establishment of a neocolonial régime in Cuba took place.

Cuba and Ethiopia reaffirm their adherence to the Non-Aligned Movement and express their firm resolve to work within its framework, for the preservation of its principles of struggling against imperialism, colonialism, neocolonialism, racial discrimination, apartheid and Zionism. Both sides demand the establishing of a new international economic order that should encourage the struggle against underdevelopment and promote the social progress of all peoples.

The Ethiopian side expressed its support for the VI Summit Conference of the Non-Aligned Movement which will take place in Havana in 1979, as well as the readiness of the Ethiopian youth to participate with deep enthusiasm in the XI World Festival of Youth and Students for peace and international solidarity.

The Cuban side expressed its support for the holding in Ethiopia of the Conference of Solidarity with the African and Arab peoples in their struggle against imperialism, colonialism, reaction and racism.

The two sides emphasized the urgency to reinforce the unity between the countries of the so-called Third World and its natural allies, the socialist countries, because the consolidation of that common front is the best guar-antee for world peace and a decisive factor for the successful development of the struggle for a better future of the peoples that face imperialist aggressions.

Both sides recognize the significant contribution that the Soviet Union and other countries of the socialist community have made and still make to the cause of the national liberation of peoples.

On behalf of the Provisional Military Administrative Council and of the Council of Ministers of Socialist Ethiopia, Comrade Mengistu Haile Mariam extended invitations to Comrade Fidel Castro and Raúl Castro to make friendly visits to Socialist Ethiopia.

The invitations were accepted and the exact dates for the visits will be set through mutual consultation.

Mengistu Haile Mariam. Speech at mass rally in Havana.*

(Excerpts), Granma, 7 May, 1978.

* The rally was held in Havana's Revolution Square on 26 April, 1978.

. . . Popular discontent, caused by the exploitation and oppression suffered by the Ethiopian masses over centuries, led to the growth of a student move-ment with the watchword "Land to the tiller." The result of student agita-tion among the masses was that Marxism-Leninism was adopted as the correct strategy of struggle.

This struggle involved the whole country and turned into the tumult-uous Revolution of February 1974. Workers, peasants, soldiers, students, democratic elements and other strata of the oppressed classes rose up in revolution to rock the very foundations of the fascist feudal régime of Haile Selassie.

They intensified the struggle, and, by means of a coordinated movement of the masses and the armed forces, the monarch who had ruled the country for over 50 years was deposed in Sepember 1974, and the monarchy that had lasted centuries was abolished once and for all.

Due to the fact that the great masses had been deprived of their political rights under the old régime, there wasn't even one politically organized group that could take power. Consequently, the armed forces took on the responsibility of state leadership, and, for the first time in the long history of the Ethiopian masses, state power had been taken from the hands of the monarchs and the aristocracy.

The overthrow of Haile Selassie, a fact of unparalleled importance in the history of struggle of the Ethiopian people, has helped bring about bright prospects for organizing the great masses. Thus guiding the action of the Ethiopian masses by means of a programme, The Programme of the National Democratic Revolution,[1] tremendous victories for the people have been won against imperialism, feudalism and bureaucratic capitalism over these last four years.

Among these victories, I would like to mention briefly the following:

— The land problem, that was a burning issue in the long struggle of the peasantry, has been solved by nationalizing all rural land.

— The basic means of production and distribution such as the banks and insurance companies that were instruments of exploitation in the hands of the imperialists and the local comprador bourgeoisie have been nationalized to the benefit of the broad masses.

— Urban land and additional houses, which were complementary means of exploitation of urban dwellers, have also been nationalized.

— The schools are now controlled by the masses.

— A new labour law has been passed.

— To strengthen and safeguard the coordinated struggle of the masses and to achieve their legitimate emancipation by the only way, through socialism, the Programme of the National Democratic Revolution was drawn up and is being carried out.

— To further the political awareness of the masses and enable them to organize themselves to play the role of bulwark of the Revolution, we have set up a provisional office for the organizational affairs of the masses and the Marxist-Leninist Political School.

— The broad masses will achieve final victory over their enemies only when they are politically aware, organized and armed. The conditions are being created for workers, peasants and progressive forces to participate in the revolutionary process.

— Equality for all nationalities and religions has been recognized, and the means for enforcing this are already being worked out.

— The government has created favourable conditions and is taking all measures it deems necessary to help the progressive forces set up their vanguard: the Party of Labour.

Comrades, all these victories have not been won without sacrifice. As you revolutionaries know full well through your own struggle, wherever there is a revolution there will also be counterrevolution. Similarly, victories are always accompanied by difficulties. That is the dialectical truth. The internal and external alignment of forces with regard to the Ethiopian Revolution has taken different forms at different times and can be divided into two categories. These two categories are: revolutionaries and counter-revolutionaries.

[1] The Programme of National Democratic Revolution issued on 21 April, 1976. Listed as the government's main objectives (i) the total eradication of feudalism, bureaucratic capitalism and imperialism and the laying of a firm foundation for transition to socialism; and (ii) the establishment of a People's Democratic Republic.

Internally, the revolutionary forces are made up of workers, peasants, soldiers, left-wing elements of the petty bourgeoisie, progressive and patriotic elements. The external forces are represented by the socialist countries and the democratic forces.

The counterrevolutionary forces include, internally, the aristocrats, feudal elements, the right-wing petty bourgeoisie and, externally, international imperialism, reactionary ruling cliques and imperialism's lackeys.

The so-called EPRP (Ethiopian People's Revolutionary Party), the self-styled EDU (Ethiopian Democratic Union), the secessionist groups, the ruling reactionary cliques in Somalia and some of the Arab states all have the same objectives, the same ends; they are the supports of international imperialism, especially U.S. imperialism, and they carry out its instructions and do all they can against the great masses of the Ethiopian people.

As the great masses of the Ethiopian people matured even further in struggle, so the antipeople forces had to resort to new plans. Gnawing away at the Revolution from the inside by means of political and economic sabotage, the antirevolutionary forces resorted to assassination.

Many true revolutionaries, labour leaders, peasant leaders, leaders of mass organizations, soldiers and patriots were assassinated in full daylight by paid criminals. All this was carried out so as to pave the way for counter-revolution. But the great masses stood firm with ironclad determination.

On several occasions they tried to carry out a coup d'etat. However, the masses didn't take even one step backwards. In fact, their revolutionary fervour, courage and decision to safeguard the Revolution by means of vigilance were strengthened even further.

Recognizing how vain its attempts were in this respect, imperialism began to coordinate the efforts of its fifth column with those of the secessionist groups in the north, and finally they collaborated in the overt invasion unleashed by the Somalian reactionary ruling class in the east and south of the territory of revolutionary Ethiopia. . .

The Ethiopian masses will always remember the fraternal internationalist aid they were given by Cuba, the Soviet Union, the Democratic Republic of Yemen, the German Democratic Republic and other countries.

The struggle of the oppressed peoples of the world, which has been increasingly organized since the Great October Revolution of 1917, has manifestly triumphed in revolutionary Ethiopia.

Comrades, we will never forget the support given by the people of revolutionary Cuba, on the basis of Leninist principles, to the Revolution of the great masses of Ethiopia when our Revolution was facing grave danger, threatened as it was by the invasion of the reactionary army of Somalia, coordinated by imperialism. My comrade, the great revolutionary leader Fidel Castro, the people, the Party and the Government of revolutionary Cuba went to great lengths to try to prevent the Somalian reactionary ruling classes from beginning hostilities. But since madness has taken hold of the rulers of Somalia, a madness that must surely destroy them, the peace efforts of Comrade Fidel Castro were fruitless.

Thus, upon realizing the danger this represented to the very existence of revolutionary Ethiopia, the people of revolutionary Cuba backed all the measures taken by the great Ethiopian masses who, to save their Revolution, grouped together under the watchwords, "Revolutionary motherland or death," and "All for the front." In addition to that support, the people of revolutionary Cuba were also beside the great Ethiopian masses and took part in the decisive battle for victory.

You, the sons and daughters of revolutionary Cuba, known well among the oppressed peoples of the world for your Leninist and internationalist positions, have travelled thousands of kilometers to close ranks with the great masses of revolutionary Ethiopia, have endured their want, have shared their suffering, have lived their life and indeed de facto have died their death.

This internationalist aid has contributed immensely to the success of the struggle of the Ethiopian masses to drive the reactionary army of Somalia out of our revolutionary country in a short time. And as a result of this, the fraternal links uniting the peoples of revolutionary Cuba and revolutionary Ethiopia have been sealed with blood. I want to repeat once and again these words: have been sealed with blood; have been sealed with blood.

The best way of expressing the fraternal links that exist between the people of our two revolutionary countries is in the historic words of Comrade Fidel Castro on the occasion of the centennial of the Baraguá Protest when he said: "There's a special flower, a wreath, a tribute being paid to this centennial of our glorious General Antonio Maceo, and that is the successful fulfilment of Cuba's internationalist mission in Ethiopia. It is as if the descendants of General Antonio were paying him a great tribute . . . . We feel so close, so near to and such brothers of the Ethiopian revolutionaries, it's as if they were here with us, as if they were with Maceo. . . ."

Comrades, although we have emerged victorious from the aggression unleashed on us in the east and in the south of Ethiopia, the struggle our Revolution is waging against the antipeople forces has still not ended. Revolutionary Ethiopia still has a long hard struggle ahead. Since the forces of reaction have never resigned themselves to the thrust of the oppressed peoples, they will continue to fight against us.

That is why imperialism, the reactionary Arab classes and the fifth columnists are conspiring together to frustrate our Revolution, backing the traitors in the Administrative Region of Eritrea who are at present scheming to sell their homeland for petrodollars.

All the NATO countries that have been defeated in the east of Ethiopia now turn their sights to the north. They are out to get in the north what they failed miserably to achieve in the east.

The Eritrean secessionists, who pretended to be progressives in the period of the now defunct monarchical domination, have shown themselves to be mere opportunists. Since the beginning of the popular insurrection of February 1974, which guided the masses along the path of the National Democratic Revolution to attain many victories, they have shown their true face. It has been clear that these secessionist groups are antipeople, reactionary and conspiratorial. The revolutionary process has unmasked these forces, and it is becoming increasingly clear that, contrary to what they say, they have always been against the people and not with the people; that they are reactionary and not progressive; that they are antipeople rather than for the people.

It is by now an undeniable fact that these groups in the Administrative Region of Eritrea are agents of imperialism and Arab reaction and that they are trying to turn Eritrea into a base and fortress of these reactionary forces with the aim of strangling the people's Revolution.

They are carrying out wild counterrevolutionary attempts to prevent the masses of the region of Eritrea from enjoying the fruits of the Revolution.

The position of the Ethiopian masses is clear. The masses of the region of Eritrea, together with their brothers and sisters, will eliminate these secessionist groups. And they will turn the region of Eritrea into a revolutionary fortress.

Nevertheless, I should say that the gravity of the situation should not be underestimated. The secessionists are not alone, numerous reactionary forces are backing them. The great masses of revolutionary Ethiopia also know that, in their struggle against the present danger, they have internationalist support.

And yet revolutionary Ethiopia has tried over and over again to solve the problem of the Administrative Region of Eritrea by peaceful means. Ethiopia, of course, will continue along the same path.

The Nine-Point Political Declaration of the Provisional Military Administrative Council is one of the measures taken to this end.

Nonetheless, the secessionist groups have not accepted these repeated calls for peace. What they have done is to intensify their antipeople conspiracy.

As a result, the great masses of Ethiopia are determined to intensify their just revolutionary struggle to destroy this antipeople conspiracy. And we are certain that the masses of Cuba will be together with us in our efforts for peace and in the revolutionary class struggle.

Comrades, we live in an era in which socialism is winning decisive victories over imperialism. This is an era in which the frontiers of imperialism are shrinking, while those of socialism are expanding, with the destruction of reactionary and exploitative systems.

Despite this, imperialism cannot be underestimated as an enemy. The internal feuds and rivalries that once prevailed in the imperialist system are now being tempered. At the same time, since the great victories of social-sim are more and more all the time, imperialism has cause for concern. Brooding over the humiliation it has suffered over the victories gained first by the oppressed masses in Cuba, then in Vietnam, recently in Angola and now in Ethiopia, imperialism should realize what is inevitably in store for it.

It is because it realizes this that it has had to tone down its internal feuds and mobilize all its forces to wage the final battle.

And this is clearly reflected in the imperialist attempts to surround Ethiopia from all directions and envelop its Revolution in a violent storm. The Ethiopian masses, however, have withstood all these attempts with firm determination.

Since international imperialism is increasingly mobilizing its forces, the oppressed masses of the world must constantly ensure the consolidation of unity in struggle.

There can be no doubting that the unity of the oppressed peoples of the entire world in their struggle for national independence, democracy and socialism will guarantee final victory.

Revolutionary Ethiopia is fully aware of the important role it plays in this struggle of the oppressed peoples of the world for national independence, democracy and socialism, and, as such, is committed to giving its unlimited revolutionary support to these struggles. . .

Statement of the Government of the USSR on Africa

(Complete Text). Tass, 22 June, 1978.

The growth of tension in the African continent, resulting from the aggressive actions of a group of leading NATO countries headed by the USA, arouses the legitimate anxiety of the peaceable States. The armed conflict in the Horn of Africa, the unceasing military provocations against Angola, the intervention of Zaire, the formation of so-called "pan-African" and in fact anti-African armed forces under the command of NATO officers, the coup staged by mercenaries on the Comoros — this is a far from complete list of just the recent imperialist actions. It is evidence that an offensive is being conducted against the national liberation forces in Africa. The colonialists would like once again to impose their dictates upon the African peoples, though this is obviously hopeless.

In the current situation, the Soviet Government deems it necessary to express its views on the topical problems of the situation in and around Africa.

1. Tremendous changes have taken place in Africa over the last quarter of a century. Colonial empires have collapsed; and the question of abolishing the last seats of colonialism and racialism on African soil has been raised on the practical plane. Great political and socio-economic changes are taking place in the liberated countries of Africa; an unswerving process of consolidation is going on among the young States. A number of African countries have embarked on the road of progressive social development, making their choice in favour of a socialist orientation. The role and significance of the African countries in the world arena is growing. They are making an ever greater contribution to the struggle for detente, for strengthening peace, and asserting the principles of equal rights in political and economic relations between States.

The Soviet Union is profoundly sympathetic towards these changes. The USSR and the other countries of the socialist community have vigorously supported and continue to support the just struggle of the African peoples. It was after all on the initiative of the socialist countries that the UN General Assembly in 1960 adopted the Declaration on granting independence to colonial countries and peoples. The development of relations between our State and the African countries is determined by the objective convergence of interests in connection with the fundamental problems of our time. In its relations with the States of Africa, the Soviet Union invariably adheres to the principles of solidarity with the peoples' struggle for independence and freedom, national and social progress, genuine equality, respect for sovereignty and territorial integrity, non-interference in internal affairs and mutually-advantageous co-operation. This principled foundation of our relations is of lasting significance.

2. But the forces of imperialism, racialism and reaction do not want to accept the positive changes in Africa. They want to continue exploiting the African peoples and the continent's natural wealth. They continue to think in colonialist categories of "zones of influence", and to this day they refuse to regard Africans as equal partners.

In the past, too, the imperialists and their accomplices often launched military ventures in Africa, provoked inter-State conflicts, and encouraged separatist actions in order to weaken the corresponding African countries. They have on their conscience many State coups and anti-Government plots, notorious "secret operations", and the extermination of such glorious sons of free Africa as Patrice Lumumba, Marien Ngouabi, Eduardo Mondlane, Amilcar Cabral, and others.

At present imperialist interference in the affairs of Africa has assumed a particularly cynical and dangerous character. A particularly apt example of this is the operation in Shaba Province, Zaire, carried out in order to preserve the control of Western monopolies over Zaire's copper, cobalt, uranium, diamonds and other natural resources, and ensure the military-strategic and selfish interests of the West. The example of Zaire shows that the imperialist powers are resorting to direct military action against Africans using their own armed forces, thus reviving the worst times of colonial plunder. They obviously want to assume once more the role of the gendarme of Africa, to rule the destinies of its peoples, although nobody has ever elected them into this office.

The adoption by the leading Western powers of a course of collective and aggressive military-political action is a new and dangerous moment in Africa. The guiding role in implementing this action belongs to the United States which is making extensive use of the NATO apparatus for its aims. There is an attempt to extend the sphere of action by this aggressive bloc to Africa.

This is precisely what was discussed at the latest session of the NATO Council in Washington and at the conference of the five leading NATO states in Paris. For the West, the internal events in Zaire were only a pretext for NATO to formalize its long-standing plans to create a "mechanism for rapid reaction" to changes in the African continent that are not to the taste of the Western imperialist powers. The danger posed by such actions to the African peoples, and not only to them, is obvious. Also disturbing are the activities of some NATO countries to knock together pro-imperialist military-political groupings in West Africa and the Red Sea area with the obvious intention of attaching these groupings to the NATO bloc.

The dispatch to Zaire of the so-called "pan-African force" on the initiative of the above-mentioned countries serves the aim of expanding imperialist interference in Africa's affairs. The attempt to "Africanize" NATO operations in Zaire by using military units from some African countries cannot delude anyone. The "pan-African force" acts under the control and in the interests of definite NATO powers, and any attempts to legalize it in any way may have dangerous consequences for all African countries.

Another aim of the intervention in Zaire is to exert direct pressure on the patriotic forces of Zimbabwe and Namibia, and on the so-called "frontline" States of Africa, and to impose a neo-colonialist solution of the Rhodesian and Namibian questions. The recent talk in Britain about the possibility of launching similar operations to protect the West's interests in Rhodesia is very indicative in this respect.

Thus a new phase in the development of the policy of the Powers — for which the colonialist and racialist order is like balm for the soul — is now evident. This policy is directed towards stemming by all possible means the anti-imperialist struggle in Africa and not only towards preserving, but also towards strengthening the positions of these Powers there, and directing the development of African States into the framework of the neo-colonialist "partnership" which is suitable for these Powers. It is this that is actually concealed behind the hypocritical talk of some highly-placed people in the West about their desire to see Africa free of foreign domination and respect the strivings of its peoples.

3. The vicious anti-Soviet campaign which has been unleashed in the leading NATO countries is an integral part of the afore-mentioned efforts. It is obviously designed to sow mistrust in the Soviet Union and other socialist countries, isolate Africa from its natural allies, and leave the African countries matched singly against the combined forces of neo-colonialism and imperialist reaction. Refuge is being taken in slander of the most shameless kind against the Soviet Union, Cuba and other countries of the socialist community.

In an attempt to justify the NATO intervention in Zaire, which the Soviet Union resolutely condemns, a persistent effort is being made to spread the myth about the involvement of the USSR, Cuba and a number of African countries in the events of Zaire, although the obvious mendacity of this version has already been exposed repeatedly both in Soviet official statements and in the statements made by Governments of other countries.

Just as groundless are the contentions that the aid given by the USSR and Cuba to some African countries, primarily to Angola and Ethiopia, and to the national-liberation movements in southern Africa creates a threat to peace and stability in the continent and undermines the process of relaxation of international tension. The legitimacy of such aid derives from the charter of the United Nations organization, from the decisions of this organization and from other authoritative international forums.

One cannot fail to see the principled difference between the assistance given by socialist countries to the States and peoples of Africa and the armed interference in the internal affairs of Africa as put into practice by Western countries in their own narrow, selfish interests. The assistance given by socialist countries serves the just cause of the liberation of the peoples from racialist-colonialist slavery and the cause of protecting the sovereignty and territorial integrity of States from outside encroachments. The Soviet people are rightly proud of their assistance to the furtherance of these lofty aims.

Detente by no means implies the artificial restriction of objective processes of historical development. It is not a charter of immunity for anti-popular, corrupt and venal régimes, nor for any special rights and priviliges inherited from the colonial past or obtained by means of unequal deals and agreements. And it does not bestow any right at all, to suppress the just struggle of the peoples for their national liberation and social progress or to interfere in their internal affairs. It is the right of the peoples that the imperialist circles want to abrogate. While hypocritically pronouncing about the "indivisibility of detente" and the need to extend it to all areas of the globe, the NATO countries, above all the United States, are acting by their deeds in Africa in a directly opposite direction.

Detente would only gain if the remaining seats of racialism and colonialism in the world are swiftly liquidated. These seats of racialism and colonialism are the unfortunate heritage of colonial domination which is hated by the peoples, an obstacle to the progress of the African peoples and a source of international tension.

4. The racialist régime in Pretoria, which itself presents a threat to international peace, is an accomplice of the Western Powers. It is actively building up its military might with the assistance of NATO and strives to gain access to nuclear weapons.

The changes in Africa are not to the liking of the Peking leaders either, who, in accordance with their chauvinistic, hegemonistic and selfish considerations would like to see the continent an arena of serious international complications and conflicts. The Peking leadership, along with NATO and the Republic of South Africa, is an active co-participant in building up tension in Africa. It has joined forces with imperialism, with the elements of aggression and reaction, neo-colonialism and racialism and thereby ranked itself with opponents not only of socialist countries, but also the entire national-liberation movement, the unity of African peoples, and the struggle of African countries for their independence and freedom, against imperialist domination. This was the situation during the events in Angola and in the Horn of Africa. Peking's perfidy also manifested itself fully in connection with the NATO intervention in Zaire.

5. The desire of the former colonialists to return to Africa with arms in hand under the false pretext of protecting it from he soviet and Cuban "threat" arouses concern among all peoples, but particularly all African peoples. They rightly view this as a real danger, heralding the restoration of colonial rule, the creation of punitive forces of imperialism against forces of social progress, and the institution in the continent of neo-colonialist relations based on exploitation and plunder in an attempt to undermine progressive régimes. And all this is directed against the political and economic independence of African States, with the aim of undermining this independence.

The African peoples see the actions of the Western imperialist circles as an attempt to weaken at all costs and, if possible, to destroy the unity of African countries and thus split them, in face of the pressure that is being brought to bear on them. Under threat is the very existence of the Organisation of African Unity, which is an important instrument in the struggle for the common interests of African States. It is not by chance that many African leaders are strongly condemning the imperialist military intervention in Zaire and the attempts to create in the continent groupings directly or indirectly associated with NATO.

The efforts being made to solve African problems behind the backs of Africans is rightly being taken as an insult to Africa, as a refusal to take into consideration its increased role in the international arena. It can be confidently asserted that the peoples of Africa will not allow the colonialists to delude them. As for these colonialists, while hypocritically speculating on the slogan of "African solidarity", they are in actual fact vigorously recruiting henchmen and promoters of their policy from among the puppet and anti-popular régimes. To these intrigues independent Africa opposes true African solidarity, the united will of the freedom loving peoples and their resolve to uphold the independence of their countries and their free internal development.

6. The Soviet Union's policy towards Africa is clear and consistent. In the developing countries, as everywhere, it is on the side of the forces upholding the cause of national independence, social progress and democracy. It treats them as its comrades in struggle. In this the Soviet Union seeks no advantages for itself, it is not after concessions, nor does it press for political domination, or solicit military bases. The USSR is entirely on the side of the African peoples struggling against the further retention, in any form, of the vestiges of colonialism and racialism in Africa, against neo-colonialism.

It is natural, therefore, that the Soviet Union has consistently supported and continues to support the liquidation of the racialist régime in Rhodesia and the handing over of full power to the Zimbabwe people in the person of the Patriotic Front, the immediate and full withdrawal of the Republic of South Africa from Namibia and the handing over of power to SWAPO, the genuine representative of the people of its country, and the abolition of the system of apartheid in the Republic of South Africa.

Proceeding from respect for the right of every people to choose its course of development independently, the Soviet Union resolutely condemns the military and political interference of imperialism in the internal affairs of independent African States and the infringement of their sovereignty and territorial integrity. The military interventionist actions of imperialist Powers in various parts of the African continent are a challenge to the whole of independent Africa, to the aims of the Organisation of African Unity and the principles of its Charter, a challenge to the United Nations Organization. Such actions as the creation by the NATO bloc of some "pan-African force", are nothing but the setting of Africans against Africans, a means of suppressing liberation movements in Africa by using the hands of Africans themselves.

The Soviet Union consistently supports the speediest swiftest possible liquidation of the seats of tension in the African continent, and the settlement of existing differences between individual African States. It is against attempts to set African States at loggerheads and against the whipping up of fratricidal conflicts and wars. All responsibility for the possible consequences of whipping up tension in the Africa continent rests with the aggressive circles of the West. The provocative actions of these circles and their accomplices are condemned by the world public and by the Soviet people. The independent African States and the progressive and peace-loving forces of the whole world must display vigilance and rebuff these actions.

The interests of peace and development in Africa demand an immediate end to imperialist interference in the affairs of African countries, the respect for their right to an independent and free existence and to the maintenance of equal relations with all States in accordance with the principles and aims of the United Nations Charter. For its part, the Soviet Union, just as in the past will continue to do everything in its power to enable developments in Africa to proceed precisely in this direction, and it is prepared to unite its efforts with all who are guided by the same lofty aims.

Solidarity has had a special significance for the African and Arab struggles in our times.

Speech by Fidel Castro Ruz, at the opening ceremony of The International Conference of Solidarity with the struggle of the African and Arab Peoples against Imperialism and Reaction, Addis Ababa, 14 September, 1978.

(Complete Text).

Dear Comrade Mengistu Haile Mariam;
Distinguished delegates and guests:
    The privilege of attending the celebrations of the fourth anniversary of the Ethiopian Revolution has given me the chance to be with the leader of the Ethiopian Revolution, Comrade Mengistu Haile Mariam, at the opening ceremony of this conference.
    The problems of Africa and the Middle East stand at the centre of today's international situation, and your decisions will not only influence the question of international détente, on which concern throughout the world is focused. But in addition they will determine the destiny of the African peoples and of the Arab people of Palestine, and hence the course of the struggle of the countries which are fighting in Asia, Africa and Latin America to achieve, consolidate and develop their national independence; and thus, with full equality and rights, to join the tide of progress carrying humanity towards higher economic and social goals.
    This conference is being held at a time when Africa is the chief concern of the most aggressive imperialist forces, who would wish to hold back the uncontainable advance of the African peoples.
    In the days following the defeat of Nazi fascism in World War II, the crisis of the colonial system led to the legal independence of dozens of African countries. The Arab countries of the north, and a significant group

of countries of Black Africa including Guinea, Senegal and Ghana, achieved this legal independence without the need to resort to a final armed confrontation with their former colonial oppressors.

But the imperialists used their former ties òf economic dominance and their political influence in order to transform that formal beginning of independence into a sad reality of neocolonial systems. Sometimes by assassinating great figures like Patrice Lumumba, sometimes by means of reactionary coups, at other times by means of political penetration and economic corruption — the imperialists gradually substituted colonial vassalage with the more subtle, but no less sinister system of socio-economic neocolonialism. Just a few isolated régimes were left fighting heroically to maintain their independence.

However, in the seventies we have seen the resurgence of the struggle for national independence. To an appreciable degree this has been influenced by the fact that neocolonial imperialism does not have anything better to offer the peoples it tries to dominate. But the heroic and resolute struggle of the African peoples has also a decisive influence. Foremost are those whose struggles brought about the crisis and defeat of Portuguese colonialism, such as Angola, Mozambique, Guinea Bissau and Cape Verde, as well as the valiant and resolute determination of the peoples of Zimbabwe, Namibia and South Africa to rid themselves of the shameful and brutal domination of colonialism, the bloodthirsty and oppressive white minorities and apartheid.

In Angola the imperialists tried to use the abominable South African racist régime and their puppet governments in countries bordering Angòla to crush the MPLA Government led by Agostinho Neto and bring about a new reverse, like that of the fifties, which would restrict the independence of Angola, Mozambique and Guinea Bissau and would once again isolate Tanzania, Zambia, the Republic of Guinea and other democratic and progressive governments.

The victory in Angola prevented this historic reverse from taking place, and the heroic and victorious action of the Ethiopian people in introducing a profound and authentic revolution to the northeast of Africa, to a strategically situated country with an ancient culture and more than 30 million inhabitants, made a decisive contribution to the struggle of the black and Arab countries of Africa. These victories have converted the African continent, as we said, into an area that is decisive for the confrontation of imperialism by the peoples both here and in Latin America and Asia, who wage the final battle for real independence and for the profound, just and humane social changes that history demands.

The African peoples' solidarity with one another, solidarity between the African peoples and the Arab countries of Africa and the Middle East, the solidarity of all the underdeveloped and developing peoples with their brothers in this part of the world; as well as the solidarity of the progressive forces of the whole world, the socialist countries, and the working class and progressive forces in the developed capitalist countries with the cause of Africa and the Arab countries, are an indispensable part of this historic battle. Solidarity has had a special significance for the African and Arab struggles in our times.

The imperialists and their reactionary agents attack the presence of Cuba in Africa, when it is no more than an expression of this necessary and courageous solidarity which you yourselves defend and practice. We could answer them by repeating the words of various African heads of state, who have said that there is not a single Cuban in Africa who has not been asked to come by an independent state exercising its sovereignty and in order to defend a just cause.

We have come here to say to you, the representatives of the progressive and revolutionary organizations of the peoples of Africa, the Middle East and other parts of the world, that we are with you in your decision in favour of solidarity which has inspired this enthusiastic gathering.

To those who accuse us of promoting armed confrontation by the African peoples against their oppressors, we say that Cuba is not opposed to any peaceful solution to the struggle for independence of the African peoples, essentially in Zimbabwe and Namibia, so long as the solution is a fair one and is accepted by the peoples' legitimate representatives — the Patriotic Front and SWAPO — and by the African states that have supported them. But at the same time we say that the main responsibility for the failure to achieve a peaceful solution lies in the fact that while the Anglo-American leaders talk about peace, they seek to achieve it maintaining intact the repressive and reactionary structures created by Smith and Vorster to impose their hateful white minority and apartheid régimes.

While this situation continues, and those fighting in Zambabwe and Namibia go on risking their lives in this arduous struggle, the Patriotic Front and SWAPO can count on the same resolute cooperation they have received from revolutionary Cuba until now.

The imperialists persist in supporting the Zionist reactionaries and their illegal occupation of Arab territories, in particular, of Palestinian territories.

The Camp David talks are a desperate attempt to maintain the diplomacy of conceding the Arab and Palestinian peoples their rights in partial instalments, and to prevent the presence of the Arab countries and their allies at the Geneva negotiations, which they hope to cancel.

In Latin America there is no future for the régimes that have taken the road of fascism

The difficulties are many, but in Africa and in all parts of the world the struggle of the peoples advances. In Latin America there is no future for the régimes that have taken the road of fascism — a road that has been renovated by the CIA and the transnational corporations. Panama has won recognition of its right to the Canal. A glorious chapter of Nicaraguan history is being written by the Sandinista Front, and the country's entire people have joined the uprising against the tyrant Somoza. In its Special Committee on Decolonization, the UN has acknowledged that Puerto Rico is a Yankee colony.

We could add (leaving the text for a moment) that this great victory won by our people, won by Latin America in particular, which opposes the annexation of Puerto Rico and opposes the devouring of the Latin-American community by U.S. imperialism — that this victory was achieved with the aid of countries which firmly supported the just position and as a result of two great events: the victory of the Ethiopian Revolution and the victory of the Afghanistan Revolution.

We must say here at this solidarity conference that one of the most inspiring examples of internationalist spirit and political honour given us by Comrade Mengistu and the Ethiopian Revolution was his decision to vote for the just position on the Puerto Rican question at the Special Committee on Decolonization.

In the same way we must salute the courageous stand taken by the Government of Afghanistan, which also supported the resolution.

And so the revolutionary family grows year by year, and the correlation of forces changes in favour of the independence of the people, in favour of our struggles.

As we speak here today, we recall speaking in Algeria in 1973. At that time Guinea Bissau, Angola and Mozambique were still fighting. Just a few years have passed, and today these countries are in the vanguard of the world's progressive movement, and they are not with us here as liberation movements but as independent, sovereign and revolutionary states.

And who would have dreamt just four years ago that feudal Ethiopia, an ally of imperialism, would today be one of the most resolute bastions of the progressive movement and liberation movement in the world?

In the same way, I am sure that before long Namibia and Zimbabwe will also be represented at this conference as independent and sovereign states. And that, by perhaps a somewhat more distant date, the brutal, repugnant and hateful colonialism, fascism and racism will have disappeared from South Africa.

Near here Afghanistan has overthrown feudalism and advances like a second Ethiopia, while the people of Iran fight valiantly for their freedom.

Now not even the imperialists — the imperialists who talk so much about human rights and support the Shah of Iran, one of the most repressive régimes in the world — now not even the imperialists are sure that this régime will survive.

The most important thing in this struggle is to maintain the unity of the forces that are fighting and of the countries that are supporting them.

Historically the most important weapon the imperialists have used against the people of Africa and every part of the world has been division. Division between countries, division between races, division between revolutionary forces. If there is anything we would wish to emphasize in this brief speech, it is that unity must be the constant watchword of all those who oppose the system of domination that imperialism is trying to preserve.

Precisely here lies the vile significance of the role of the Chinese leadership. If those who fight for democracy and national independence of the peoples have righteously condemned the Chinese leaders for supporting the murderers of the Chilean people, for their aggression against heroic Vietnam, for encouraging fratricidal war in Indochina, and for their attacks on Angola and Ethiopia, then the Chinese leaders merit such denunciation even more for their devious and obscene divisionist policy.

We visited Ethiopia for the first time 18 months ago. We came to meet the leaders of this Revolution in which we had seen from afar an example of the most profound social changes in the African continent. Because it must not be forgotten that there was slavery in Ethiopia until the Revolution. In the Addis Ababa exposition we have seen the iron and steel fetters used to chain tens of thousands of this country's citizens. But we also came with the purpose of trying to find just political solutions that would prevent divisions and war between the peoples of the Horn of Africa, and the shedding of blood in internal struggles. We did not succeed because of a great charlatan — who I will not mention by name, nor is there need to — who posed under the banner of socialism but believed that Ethiopia was militarily so weak that he would be able to carve it up, realize his expansionist dreams in opposition to the decision of the African countries, and at the same time be of service to the imperialists he had already sold out to.

Eighteen months later we have come back to Ethiopia, now victorious thanks to the heroism of its warrior sons and to the support of international solidarity, as Comrade Mengistu put it two days ago. What's more, it is a now powerful Ethiopia. The massive parade on Tuesday has given proof of the enormous tide of people who keep pace with the revolutionary change. And yesterday's military parade has shown us the degree of organization and discipline achieved by the combative and courageous sister people of Ethiopia.

Let us remind those who are ignorant of some things in this world, that one of the most combative, courageous and heroic soldiers in the world is the Ethiopia soldier.

We reaffirm today our close and indestructible alliance with the Ethiopian Revolution, and our certainty that the Ethiopian leaders will be able to find revolutionary, just and Marxist-Leninist solutions to their problems, and that they will be able to preserve not only the territorial integrity of Ethiopia, but also the union of all in a great revolutionary Ethiopia.

Comrades, permit me to salute you, the representatives of the best forces from all continents, and on behalf of my people to thank you for the solidarity you have always shown us. Also let me convey to you the Cuban Revolution's message of struggle and encouragement, and urge that your duty be fulfilled.

Revolutionary internationalis, is one of the laws of our struggle. We cannot triumph in isolation. Large-scale assistance, or the simplest support of popular rebellions strengthens us all, since they are the expression of a new humanity, which fights for a more just society.

We join with you in condemning the racist and aggressive régimes of South Africa, Zimbabwe and Israel, and the bloody régime of the Shah of Iran. With you, we support the Polisario Front, the Patriotic Front of Zimbabwe, SWAPO and the South African organizations. And like you, we also condemn the imperialist powers who use NATO as their advance guard to intervene militarily in Africa and give political support to the anti-popular and reactionary régimes of Africa and the Middle East.

We are infinitely more powerful than the imperialists and their agents, because we are the standard-bearers of social progress and justice. History is on our side; our scientific and just ideas are invincible.

Long live solidarity between the peoples!

Declaration of the International Conference of Solidarity with the struggle of the African and Arab peoples against Imperialism and Reaction.
Addis Ababa, 14 September, 1978.
(Complete Text).

1. We, the representatives of the governments, parties, national, inter-national and regional organizations and national liberation movements that are participating in the International Conference of Addis Ababa, from September 14-17, 1978, express our solidarity with the struggle of the Africa and Arab nations against imperialism, colonialism, neocolonialism, Zionism and racism; and for their freedom, independence and social, economic and cultural progress.

2. The speeches by the president of the Provisional Military Administrative Council and of the Council of Ministers of Ethiopia, Lieutenant Colonel Mengistu Haile Mariam, and by the first secretary of the Communist Party and president of the Council of State and Council of Ministers of Cuba, Fidel Castro, at the opening ceremony; as well as a great number of messages from various heads of state have been a source of inspiration for all the participants.

3. The participants in this Conference note with enthusiasms the resolute struggle of the African and Arab peoples against the forces of war, aggression, expansionism and colonialism, and for their national rights, vital interests, and national and economic independence.

4. Their struggle is a significant factor in the global cause of all progressive forces to establish a just and lasting peace, national independence and international cooperation based on equality.

5. Alarmed by the heroic and indomitable struggle of the oppressed masses of Africa, the Middle East, Asia and Latin America, the imperialists resort to new tactics to impose a new form of oppression, trying to maintain their hegemony over the economic potential of the newly independent countries by introducing the neocolonialist master. As a result, some new nations obtained independence in name only, not real independence. With a view to safeguarding their economic relations of exploitation and their strategic interests, the imperialist powers, mainly the U.S. imperialists, have in some cases managed to hand over power to puppet régimes, adopt measures to corrupt and subordinate existing régimes, and employ various techniques to bring down progressive régimes.

6. The African and Arab peoples, as well as other peoples in arms, have intensified their struggle against both internal and external enemies.

7. The unity of action between the forces of socialism and the national liberation movements which emerged in the struggle against colonialism, and for freedom and independence, has now become a factor of fundamental importance for world progress and development. The struggle for peace and disarmament has always been one of the basic aims of progressive forces and of the socialist countries, because the struggle for real independence and economic development is closely related to the struggle for peace and disarmament. The correct road is one of cooperation on the basis of equality, especially with the socialist countries. The consolidation of a strong anti-imperialist front is imperative. It should include the socialist countries, the national liberation movements, the progressive sectors of the developing countries, and the working class and democratic forces of the capitalist world.

8. The Conference of Addis Ababa notes that the imperialists, supported by local reactionaries, are trying to hold back the movements of the Arab and African nations to achieve development following the path of national independence, social progress and international solidarity. Imperialism is using every possible means to try and obstruct the elimination of the racist régimes of southern Africa, and the creation of a just and lasting peace in the Middle East.

9. This conclusion is supported by the following facts: the NATO interference in Zaire; the growing number of imperialist and reactionary intrigues in the Red Sea area, in the Horn and in other parts of Africa; the attempt to create the so-called Pan-African forces under the control of the

NATO governments; the efforts being made to establish a military pact in the South Atlantic; the use of mercenaries; the attempts to crush the valiant struggle of the Palestinian people for their national rights, to impose treaties on the Middle East that would harm the interests and legitimate aspirations of the Arab nations, and to create tensions in Lebanon and in the south of the Arab Peninsula, especially directed against the People's Democratic Republic of Yemen.

10. The Conference has studied the behaviour of the Chinese leaders and notes with indignation and shock their collaboration with reactionary imperialist and fascist régimes such as Chile, the South African Government and Israel.

11. Those participating in the Conference also denounce the complicity of the Chinese leaders in the aggression against Angola and Ethiopia, and their chauvinist and expansionist policy towards socialist Vietnam. The anti-Soviet position of the Chinese leaders does not serve the cause of the national liberation movement.

12. In expression of our unshakable determination to eliminate the racist strongholds in southern Africa, we resolutely declare our support for the liquidation of the Rhodesian racist régime, the transfer of absolute power to the people of Zimbabwe, the complete withdrawal of South Africa from Namibia, and the elimination of the system of apartheid and of Bantustans from the racist Republic of South Africa.

13. We condemn the declaration of martial law by the fascist Smith régime and the resulting arrest of hundreds of members of the Patriotic Front, and promise our firm support to the Patriotic Front of Zimbabwe, the South West Africa Peoples' Organization (SWAPO) in Namibia and the African National Congress (ANC) of South Africa — the sole authentic representatives of their peoples.

14. The Conference also condemns the Western imperialist powers who, with the collaboration of their racist agents, are coordinating efforts to impose neocolonial solutions on the peoples fighting in Zimbabwe and Namibia.

15. The Conference salutes the firm position of the Front Line States — Angola, Botswana, Zambia, Mozambique and Tanzania — in the cause of unlimited support for the national liberation struggle of the peoples of southern Africa.

16. The Conference declares its support for the independence and self-determination of the heroic people of Western Sahara, fighting under the leadership of the POLISARIO Front.

17. Socialist Ethiopia's victory over the forces of feudalism, imperialism, and internal and external reaction is convincing proof of the indestructible and inexhaustible power of nations that have chosen the road of freedom and progress. We, the participants in this international conference, declare our fraternal and militant solidarity with the people of

Ethiopia, and we wish the citizens of this ancient Africa country unshakable unity, peace and prosperity.

18. We, the participants in this Conference, send fraternal greetings of solidarity to the Palestinian Arabs who firmly and valiantly oppose the incessant machinations of imperialism, Zionism and Arab reaction, and struggle courageously for the inalienable national right of the Palestinians for a return to their homeland, self-determination and the establishment of their independent state. The Conference promises to give its determined support to the Palestine Liberation Organization (PLO), sole legitimate representative of the Palestinian Arabs. It condemns the policy of searching for partial solutions to the Arab-Israeli conflict, and declares its support for the full liberation of all occupied Arab territories.

19. The participants in this Conference wish to emphasize the great contribution that the Non-Aligned Movement has made to the struggle of nations fighting against imperialism and against the last strongholds of colonialism and racism. We declare our full confidence in the success of the Non-Aligned summit meeting due to be held next year in Havana, the capital of Cuba.

20. The International Conference of Addis Ababa declares its profound appreciation and admiration for the Soviet Union, Cuba and other socialist countries, as well as for the progressive forces of the world, for their internationalist aid and unselfish support of the African and Arab nations in their just struggle. Cuba's practical and effective solidarity has become a very significant factor for the liberation of Africa and the consolidation of its independence.

21. The Conference firmly declares that the triumph of the peoples the world over against the forces of imperialism and reaction is inevitable.

22. There will be freedom and democracy, peace and progress for the African and Arab nations and the entire world.

Mozambique — Angola Joint Communique, Maputo, 20 September, 1978.

(Excerpts)

At the invitation of the President of Frelimo and President of the People's Republic of Mozambique, Samora Moises Machel, the President of the MPLA Party of Labour and President of the People's Republic of Angola Agostinho Neto, accompanied by his wife, paid a friendly official visit at party and state level to the People's Republic of Mozambique from 16th to 20th September 1978. . .

Both sides hailed the results of the recent talks in Luanda between the delegations of the two parties and states which resulted in the signing of an agreement of economic, scientific and technical co-operation and of a commercial agreement.

They also hailed the creation of a joint commission and the results of its first session. The two delegations expressed a firm wish to put into effect the agreements signed by taking the necessary action for the development of economic relations, particularly in the field of commercial exchanges. . . Bilateral talks were also held on industry, foreign trade, fisheries, transport and communications, vocational training, agriculture, information, education, culture and sports. During the visit the two Heads of State signed a treaty of friendship, co-operation and mutual aid. . .

The Presidents of the People's Republic of Mozambique and the People's Republic of Angola expressed their firm conviction that the development of bilateral co-operation between the two states reflected the aspirations of the two peoples. It was an important factor in strengthening the struggle for economic independence, building socialism in the two countries, and strengthening African unity and socialism in the world at large.

The delegations analyzed in depth the international situation, having previously stressed the identity of principle underlying their foreign policies, based on specific situations and the objective interests of the two peoples and revolutions. Both sides attached the greatest importance to strengthening unity between members of the international revolutionary movement. . .

The two delegations stressed the continuous strengthening of unity with all socialist countries. They acknowledged the advance of the progressive forces in their struggle against all forms of exploitation and oppression, and reaffirmed the importance of the non-aligned movement in keeping peace for the economic and social development of peoples and denounced imperialist divisionist manoeuvres aimed at isolating the movement from its natural allies. . . and reaffirmed that their decision to build socialist societies, based on Marxist-Leninist principles and proletarian internationalism, was in harmony with the true ideals of the movement. In this connection, they hailed the decision to hold in Havana the sixth summit of the movement of non-aligned countries.

Both sides reaffirmed their determination to fight and destroy the international economic order established by imperialism so as to build a new, progressive economic order free from exploitation and based on the rights of peoples to possess and use their natural resources.

In their analysis of the present situation in Asia, the two parties hailed the victory of the people of Afghanistan. They appealed to the peoples of Vietnam and Cambodia, under their parties' leadership, to find a peaceful solution to their conflict; a solution based on the principles and traditions of friendship, solidarity and militant internationalism forged in the common struggle against imperialism. The two countries expressed their solidarity with efforts now being made by the Democratic People's

Republic of Korea for the peaceful and independent reunification of the country within the framework of democratic principles and without foreign interference and demanded the withdrawal of all foreign troops from South Korea. They also strongly condemned Zionism and all imperialist manoeuvres against the Arab peoples, especially in the Middle East, and reaffirmed their support for the struggle of the Palestinian people led by the PLO.

As far as East Timor was concerned, the two parties supported the Democratic Republic of East Timor, led by Fretilin, in its just struggle against the colonial expansionism of the Indonesian régime and in defence of the right of the Timorese people to self-determination and independence.

In their analysis of the situation in Latin America, the two countries hailed the victories achieved against imperialism in this area of the world. At the same time, they expressed their repugnance for the régime oppressing the Chilean people, condemned the occupation of Puerto Rico by US imperialism, and reaffirmed their solidarity with the Latin American peoples who continued to resist and fight dictatorial régimes and imperialist manoeuvres.

The two delegations also hailed the republic of Cuba for its militant and exemplary actions in the anti-imperialist struggle and its internationalist support for other peoples, in particular in the African continent.

In their analysis of the present situation in Africa, both sides denounced imperialist manoeuvres in the form of direct military intervention against African peoples, namely in the invasion of the Comoro islands, in the militarization and occupation of the Indian Ocean, and in attempts to create divisions in the ranks of the liberation movements, between independent states and within the OAU.

The two parties expressed support for the Saharan Democratic Republic led by the Polisario Front in its just struggle against colonial expansionism and in defence of the Saharan people's right to self-determination and national independence.

In particular the two delegations analyzed the present situation in southern Africa, having pointed out that the balance of power had altered decisively in favour of the peoples struggling for their liberation in this part of our continent. . . against oppression and exploitation — and especially the defeat of the invading racist army of the Pretoria régime by the heroic Angolan people led by the MPLA. The situation was still that of daily direct confrontation with some of the most aggressive and criminal forces in the imperialist system.

Both sides strongly condemned the constant attacks, invasions and massacres of which the people of the countries frontally opposing the last bastions of racism, colonialism and apartheid in southern Africa were victims. They both hailed the victories achieved by the Zimbabwean people led by the Patriotic Front, and reaffirmed their total support for the armed struggle as the only way for the achievement of national independence. They strongly condemned the manoeuvres of imperialists who by constant manipulation intended to destroy the Patriotic Front, divide the frontline states, create conditions which would justify direct imperialist intervention in the region and set up a neocolonialist régime in Zimbabwe.

The People's Republic of Mozambique and the People's Republic of Angola expressed their total and unconditional support for SWAPO as the sole, genuine, representative of the Namibian people and condemned the colonial domination and dilatory and divisive manoeuvres by Vorster's racist régime. . . The People's Republic of Mozambique also strongly condemned the use of Namibian territory as a launching-pad for constant provocation, attacks and acts of subversion against the sovereignty and territorial integrity of the People's Republic of Angola by the racist authorities of the Pretoria régime. By the same token the People's Republic of Angola resolutely condemned the systematic and barbarous attacks launched by the racist and illegal régime of so-called Rhodesia against the People's Republic of Mozambique.

It was also stated that the setting-up of a military bloc in the South Atlantic, with the active participation of the Pretoria régime, and the attempt to stop the transformation of the Indian Ocean into a peace zone, constituted increasing threats to the security and sovereignty of African countries and to the international community in general.

The two sides firmly condemned the Pretoria régime and policy of Bantustanization and urged an end to the policy of apartheid and terror carried out by the racist authorities against the South African people. They denounced imperialist support for the racist régime, namely through the supply of arms, including nuclear arms, which was aimed at suppressing the working class, arming the racist régime for attacks against sovereign and neighbouring countries and perpetuating the existence of apartheid. Both sides expressed their solidarity with, and total support for, the African National Congress, ANC, which, in difficult conditions, was mobilizing and leading the South African people in their struggle against apartheid and towards national liberation.

President Agostinho Neto thanked President Samora Machel for the extremely fraternal cordial and militant hospitality which he and his entourage had received from the people, Party and Government of the PRM during the visit. At the conclusion of the talks, the President of the MPLA party of Labour and President of the People's Republic of Angola, invited the President of Frelimo and of the PRM to pay an official visit at party and state level; an invitation which President Samora Machel was pleased to accept on behalf of the people, Frelimo and the Mozambican state. The date of the visit would be fixed later.

The Arab World

Manifesto of the Communist and Workers' Parties of the Arab Countries

For the creation of an effective progressive patriotic front of the Arab world to fight against imperialism, Zionism and reaction, to thwart the capitulatory plans, to liberate the territories occupied by Israel, to ensure the legitimate rights of the Arab people of Palestine, to consolidate independence, for democracy and social progress.

(Complete Text.).

It is being increasingly confirmed today that our epoch is the epoch of transition from capitalism to socialism. The balance of world forces is continually changing in favour of peace, liberation, democracy and socialism.

This is demonstrated by the strengthening of the power of the Soviet Union and the countries of the socialist camp, in economic, political and military fields, and in the strengthening of the relationship between them, in the continuous need for struggle in order to consolidate the pillars of peaceful co-existence between states with different social systems, and in the intensification of the struggle to stabilize the detente and enlarge its circle to include military detente and comprehensive disarmament.

It is also shown by the strengthening of the role of the international patriotic liberation movements, for the sake of the common struggle against imperialism; and it is reflected in the attitude taken by some countries against capitalism, and in the enhancement of their relations with the socialist countries; it is apparent in the increase of their positive role in the revolutionary process. The role of the developing countries, namely the liberated ones, is increasing in the formulation of international policy, of the United Nations, the Non-Alignment Movement, and in the Organisation of African Unity. It is also shown in the expansion and socio-economic transformation in some of the countries of the patriotic liberation movement, after the termination of the colonial régimes.

It is illustrated by the increasing crisis of the international capitalist régimes where the advanced capitalist countries witness a continual crisis in the political, economic, and ideological fields; it is reflected in the contradictions emerging between the imperialist countries and their monopolies, and in the increasing struggle of the labour movement and the expansion of the roles and influence of the Communist parties.

The international imperialist and capitalist régimes which lost historical initiative in defining trends of international development, still possess the capacity to obstruct the progress of nations and to disrupt the international situation. Therefore, international imperialism is becoming more evil, and its conspiratory role is increasingly expanding against the forces of peace, freedom and socialism in the world. In order to achieve its goals it has employed modern and sophisticated techniques. Having succeeded in its attempts at direct interference in the internal affairs of other nations, it has now proceeded to rely on the activities of the local reactionary régimes which it uses as a weapon not only in the suppression of the progressive movements in the various regions of the world but also as a basis for reactionary conspiracies. This type of involvement occurred especially in the wake of the new American administration; which has once more returned to the policy of the cold war and dislodgement of the international situation, to the intensification of the arms race and the production and development of modern arms, for example, the Neutron bomb, as well as continuous efforts in the strengthening of military pacts, especially NATO. It is also trying to establish new types of military bases and pacts, for instance the early alarm bases in the Sinai and the Arabian Gulf Security Pact and Red Sea Security Pact.

Economic involvement, particularly in the energy area, is playing a prominent role in stabilizing and regaining imperialist bases, for the international agency which is controlled by American petroleum monopolies is exerting a great influence on undermining the results achieved by petroleum nationalisation. This policy is clearly reflected in the efforts that have been made by the American petroleum monopolies to obstruct the marketing of nationalised petroleum as well as to impede the development of the associated petroleum industry. American imperialism and international petroleum monopolies are becoming more active in order to increase their influence in the Middle-East and also in causing a rift within OPEC, thereby guaranteeing continuous and permanent access to petroleum at prices appropriate to their interests. They attempt to achieve cooperation with the reactionary petroleum exporting countries in the Middle East.

Imperialism, especially in recent years, has stepped up its activity in the ideological sphere, particularly by fermenting nationalist sentiments, setting people and various forces against each other, inciting religious and communal discord, spreading anti-communism and anti-Sovietism, resorting to subversion of and attempting to split the national-liberation movement. Undoubtedly, Carter's proclaimed "human rights" slogan is only a ploy for spreading the campaign against socialism and to hamper the process of detente. By dividing the world into the "poor and the rich", "North and South", imperialism and Maoism pursue the aim of slandering the socialist system and eroding its relations with the national liberation movement.

Contingents of the Communist movement highly assess the role of the CPSU — the glorious party of Lenin, the outstanding achievements of the

Great October Socialist Revolution. The new Constitution of the USSR reflects the enormous and inspiring successes achieved by the peoples of the Soviet Union in building mature socialism and in deepening socialist democracy, in advancing towards communism and in the struggle for a stable universal peace.

A larger role for the International Communist Movement
    World developments confirm the decisive role played by the world Communist movement and its successes in the struggle for peace, freedom, democracy and socialism. Today the role of the Communist parties in the world is increasing and the movement's influence is expanding in making every effort to strengthen the unity of the Communist movement on the principles of Marxism-Leninism and proletarian internationalism. This unity is a crucial factor in fulfilling the movement's objectives. It is essential to safeguard the purity of its theory, to wage a struggle against any attempts at its distortion, to rebuff all attacks on the experience of building real socialism, from wherever may come.
    The present Chinese leadership is following the former Maoist policy, proceeding, both at the state and party level, from the policy of hostility towards the Soviet Union and the world Communist movement, intensifying international tension, supporting imperialism's attempts to return to the cold-war policy, encouraging imperialist military blocs and subversion of the national liberation movements on various continents. This was demonstrated by the Chinese attitudes to the developments in the Sudan, to the fascist coup d'etat in Chile, and to the events which took place in Angola, Ethiopia and so on. The Chinese leadership also encouraged Sadat's initiative along with the activities of the reactionary rulers of the Middle East. The Chinese leadership rejected all the principled and sincere efforts of the Soviet Union, including its recent initiative to normalise relations between the two countries on the principles of peaceful coexistence and good-neighbourliness.
    The Communist and Workers' parties of the Arab countries reaffirm their condemnation of this anti-Marxist policy that runs counter to the peoples' aspirations to freedom, independence, progress, peace and socialism, serving only the interests of imperialism and its puppets in various countries. They appeal to the Chinese leadership to renounce this course, which is inflicting enormous harm on the interests of the Chinese people themselves and the interests of their further development and to respond to the Soviet initiative to normalise relations between the two states.
    Recently, Socialist Vietnam has been subjected to dangerous provocation on her borders with Kampuchea, which was aimed at distracting Vietnam from dealing with the consequences of the liberation war and at preventing her from consolidating her unity and progress on the road to socialism. It also aimed at preventing Vietnam from exercising her positive

influence as a major revolutionary power in South East Asia as well as on the rest of the world. But Vietnam has dealt with that conflict by showing her readiness to seek a peaceful solution through negotiation and not through the application of power. Vietnam's attitude has gained wide support from the national and progressive Arab circles.

The Arab national liberation movement has won substantial successes in the course of its struggle, as witnessed by the gaining of political independence, the establishment of progressive patriotic régimes in a number of Arab countries, by many political, economic and social gains that serve as the basis for moving forward along the road of economic justice and the gradual elimination of dependence on the world capitalist market. The Arab national liberation movement, which is a part of the international revolutionary patriotic movement, is playing a prominent military role as demonstrated by the strengthening of its militant role against imperialism and its basis and influence in the area; it is also demonstrated by its support of the nation's struggle for freedom and independence.

The Arab National Liberation Movement is Enriched by Deep Progressive Concepts

Throughout that long struggle so many Arab reactionary régimes fell as a result of their adherence to imperialism and Zionism; their attempts to strangle mass movement and their betrayal of the Arab Palestinian people's cause. During that struggle the representatives of the national and progressive circles have come to power and supported slogans of socio-economic progress and unity. Accordingly, the Arab national liberation movement has been enriched with deep progressive socio-economic and political, as well as intellectual concepts. However, all these concepts are related to the position of the social forces where the labouring class, along with the working masses and the revolutionary intelligensia, and many other elements from the petit-bourgeoisie in both town and city have begun to play a more active part in the current developmental process. Furthermore, during that period, the organic inter-relationship between the national and patriotic struggle has increased. It also became obvious that socio-economic development has become more inter-related with the struggle against imperialism and its reactionary monopolies on one side and more concerned with developing mutual relations with the socialist countries on the other. In fact, the change which has taken place in the position of class powers has been reflected in the increased role of the parties and revolutionary powers including our Labour and Communist parties of the Arab countries; it has also been reflected in its increasing intellectual influence, the widespread influence of scientific socialist thoughts and the adaptation of socialist thought by some of the circles of the Arab national liberation movements, strengthening the cooperation between Arab Labour and Communist parties along with the Communist parties of the Soviet Union, as well as the other parties of the socialist countries.

The Arab national liberation movement has achieved these goals through large-scale struggles that have taken place throughout the years. Those struggles, however, have been undertaken by the political, patriotic and progressive forces, whether communist, democratic, revolutionary or progressive, and have represented all trends. It has also relied on the support given by the working masses. All this has taken place for many reasons — the positive potentials of the international situation, the change that has taken place in favour of socialism, the good relationship existing among the various groups of the Arab national liberation movements and also the good relations between the progressive and patriotic régimes and the socialist countries along with the different progressive powers of the world.

The present stage of the Arab national liberation movement is essentially a stage of national democratic revolution, which is proceeding in new circumstances, where the objectives of national liberation and social progress converge and their solution becomes increasingly vital and complex in view of the aggravation of the class struggle.

An important feature of the present stage is the deep-rooted process of political and class differentiation in the Arab national liberation movement. Certain forces seek to block the movement's further development in solving general national problems, as well as in the social and economic spheres. This poses a threat to the Arab liberation movement, for ceasing the struggle is tantamount to retreat. There are forces, moreover, that are abandoning the Arab liberation movement and inasmuch as their interests coincide with those of neocolonialism, are adopting a hostile stance towards the movement. On the other hand, there are forces seeking to deepen the development of this movement, invigorate its national anti-imperialist aspects, and deepen its economic and social content while relying on the popular masses and their enhanced activity. That is the goal of the working class, peasantry and working people in general, the Communist and Workers' parties of the Arab countries, the revolutionary democratic circles and movements.

The process of differentiation varies depending on development levels and objectives facing the country concerned. It grows deeper with the sharpening of the class battles around the issue of the prospects of socio-economic development, and with the intensification of the struggle against imperialism and reaction.

The major achievements of the Arab national liberation movement in the political, economic and social spheres, the deepening of its patriotic and progressive content and the expansion of its ties with the world revolutionary movement, have led to the activisation and military expansion of the forces of imperialism, Zionism and reaction. These forces resort to ever more varied and brutal methods and rely increasingly on the reactionary and ultra-right forces in the region of planning and carrying out this offensive, which is aimed at restoring full American control and domination over the Arab world, a major economic and oil-producing centre, with great strategic significance. American imperial assault in the area is part of a comprehensive imperial strategy which is embodied in a variety of imperial activities in different parts of the world and manifested in certain prominent characteristics such as American imperialist attempts (after ten years of imperialist Zionist aggression on the Arab countries) to impose submissive settlements in order to control the whole area.

Within the present international situation of the balance of power (which is limiting direct imperialist influence in the area to achieve its goals and ensure its continuity) American imperialism is seeking to create a new situation through which it can guarantee its continuous control over the area. In order to achieve the goal American imperialism is relying more and more heavily on the rulers of Israel and local reactionary rulers of the Arab countries. It is also making great efforts to establish and expand its military bases and also to revitalise past military pacts such as the Central Treaty Organization whilst, at the same time, creating new ones with different forms and also establishing new types of military installations such as early warning alarm bases.

US imperialism is out to overthrow the progressive national régimes or to bring them under its influence. To this end it uses the stick and carrot method and various forms of subversive actions in these countries, seeking, in particular, to split the unity of the national contingents, to effect economic penetration, to harness the economies of these countries to the chariot of the imperialist monopolies, and to conduct subversive activity in the sphere of culture, information and education.

Imperialism and its allies in the Arab region are out to deal blows at Arab-Soviet friendship and cooperation in the political, economic, cultural and military spheres so that the Arab liberation movement would find itself facing the plots of imperialism, Zionism and reaction without the support of its true and powerful ally, to isolate it from the world revolutionary movement. Imperialism is expanding its campaign against the ideological front and trying to create centres of instability and confrontation among the Arab countries and to encourage Arab progressive forces to fight with each other at both regional and national levels. It also aims to disseminate sectarian and/or religious fanaticism.

Sadat's visit to Israel and his capitulatory course, which represents an open challenge to the national and patriotic sentiments of the Arab peoples, was the culmination of the retreat in the political, economic and social spheres that has been in evidence in Egypt over the recent period. The main purpose of Sadat's visit, along with a series of activities related to it, has been to stifle the military and political power of Egypt and to divert the

Arab countries from the path of struggle against imperialism and occupation into bases of alliance with the forces of imperialism. The aim is to undermine the efficiency of the Arab African liberation movement. Nonetheless, the main result of Sadat's new activities is to weaken the chances of bringing about a just peace in the area and also to contribute towards the increased arrogance of Israeli rulers, encouraging them to continue their expansionist ambitions. However, Israel's negative attitude is demonstrated by its constant declarations not to withdraw from the West,Bank and the Gaza Strip, expanding its policy of establishing more settlements in the pan-occupied territories including Sinai, total and absolute rejection of the just rights of the Arab people of Palestine and by the evil aggression in South Lebanon and its ultimate occupation.

At the same time as the Egyptian régime stands invalid and submissive in front of the increasing aggression of Israel, which is enjoying the continuous support of American imperialism, Egypt is directing its efforts towards confronting and eliminating the progressive and patriotic movements and régimes whether in the Arab area or in the African countries and it is also creating conflicts and problems in these areas.

Settlement of the Middle East crisis is the key link in the struggle waged by the Arab national liberation movement against imperialism, Zionism and reaction, for economic and social progress.

As before, this struggle is developing between two basic tendencies, between national liberation and the reactionary, pro-imperialist, capitulatory trends.

The national liberation trend places the emphasis on an overall settlement of the Middle East problem on the basis of full liberation of the occupied territories, ensuring the legitimate rights of the Arab people of Palestine, including the right to return to their home and to set up an independent state on the West Bank of the Jordan and in the Gaza Strip. This trend holds that a just and stable Middle East peace can only be reached on such a basis, through persistent struggle against imperialism and by strengthening the alliance with the USSR and other forces of progress and liberation throughout the world while using various means, opportunities and methods of struggle. But the reactionary imperialist trend is based on the principle of non-adherence to the goal of the liberation of all the occupied Arab territories and in the prevention of the Arab Peoples of Palestine from deciding their destiny; it is also based on the refusal to recognize the PLO as the sole representative of the Palestinians, the pursuit of partial and individual settlement concerning Palestinian issues and finally on the dissemination of a submissive spirit. It is a fact, that the USA is not satisfied with arming Israel and granting her all sorts of assistance, but it is also trying to force the Arab countries to follow Sadat's example and to accept the submissive settlements by various coercive means, whether military or economic.

The latest events in Lebanon have represented one of the most dangerous conspiratory circles and a solid base for confrontation against imperialism. Nevertheless the danger of Israel's aggression against Lebanon has contributed to the strengthening of the unity of the Lebanese patriotic movement based on progressive principles, and to its increasing reliance on mass support. It has also strengthened the cohesion of the Lebanese patriotic movement with the Palestinian resistance movement, ultimately raising the level of the patriotic struggle against reactionary Zionist imperialist conspiracy.

During the drafting and signing of the Sinai agreement an armed struggle broke out in Lebanon, launched by the forces of international reaction in fulfilment of the plans of imperialism, reaction and Zionism.

In the conditions resulting from Sadat's visit to Israel and the failure of his capitulatory line, as well as the continuing US-Zionist plot, the struggle broke out anew in Lebanon, and the extensive Israeli aggression in the south of Lebanon rendered it even more dangerous. Israeli aggression against Lebanon, was not only an attempt to occupy part of Lebanese territory but also aimed at undermining the Palestinian resistance movement, eliminating Palestinian existence, crushing the Lebanese patriotic movement and exposing Syrian integrity to danger thereby obliging her to retreat from the policy of opposing Sadat's capitulatory settlement. It was also intended to weaken the rejectionist front by giving a hand to the Zionist and isolationists' attempts. That aggression was also aimed at the elimination of the Arab national identity from Lebanon, coercing it to succumb to the reactionary, fascist, sectarian powers. It was further aimed at the creation of a sectarian entity on part of Lebanon's territory.

Solution of the key national task at this stage requires the overcoming of contradictions and narrow interests and the establishment of relations of close cooperation between Syria, the Palestine resistance movement and the national movement in Lebanon, with the aim of banishing the Israeli occupationists from southern Lebanon, of thwarting the Zionists' plans and of solving the Lebanese crisis on the basis of ensuring the country's independence and Arab character, as well as safeguarding the forces of the Palestine revolution.

The Palestine resistance movement occupies an important place in the ranks of the Arab national liberation movement as a key contingent in the struggle being waged in the region against imperialism, Zionism and reaction and in obstructing the implementation of subversive plans. It is also a key element in flying the banner of struggle for a right and just cause, that is, the Arab Palestinian cause. Because of that the PLO and the resistance movement is subjected to military attacks from Israel and the isolationist elements in Lebanon. It is subjected to continuous acts of oppression and aggression and attempts to control it and to limit its independence. These moves are all intended to take a stranglehold on the revolutionary inclination of the Palestinian resistance movement in order to divide it and create an alternative.

But all these attacks and coercive measures will be defeated in the face of heroism and consciousness of the patriotic forces and the Palestinian masses; they will be overcome in the face of the continuous cohesion of the Palestinian movement with the forces of the Arab liberation movements. They will also be defeated with the help and international support of the forces of peace, of progress and socialism, namely from the Soviet Union.

Within this framework of struggle, the Palestinian masses inside the occupied territories are waging a continuous battle against the occupation and Sadat's submissive settlement policy, and against all the plans aimed at abrogating the rights of the Arab masses of Palestine and undermining the role of the PLO as its sole legal representative.

The sequence of events in the Middle East throughout the past three decades have proved that no genuine peace can be achieved in the area without recognition of the patriotic rights of more than 3 million Palestinians.

The Gulf area and the Arab peninsula have become the focus of increasing interest by the imperialists, namely the Americans, in their plans directed against the Arab nations and their liberation movements. This has come about because this area is the largest source of production and export of oil petroleum of which its territories have an immense reserve. It is also an important sea route for marketing the oil, while in addition the area enjoys an important strategic position which has an impact on the economy of international capitalism.

The economic importance of the area is increasing and coincides with the emergence of an energy crisis and inflationary phenomena which are used to lessen the monetary crisis in the capitalist countries; it also comes at a time when there are continuous efforts being made to control the patriotic régimes and encourage the provision for heavy armament against patriotic Arab and African liberation movements.

The imperialist plans in the area are increasingly based on the establishment of many permanent and temporary military bases and the infiltration of thousands of military experts especially in the oilfields. The aim of this policy is to secure the total occupation of the area through the creation of armed bases for total destruction and means of communication. The aim is also to support the reactionary régime in the confiscation of common liberties such as in the cases of Bahrain and Kuwait and also to direct a blow at the Oman people. These imperialist plans are also intended to create political and military alliances such as the Gulf Security Programme and Red sea security with the aim of increasing Zionist and imperialist domination in the sea routes of the area.

In the western part of the Arab world the elements of unrest are increasing, yet the causes of these conflicts in that part of the world are simple, they can be solved through peaceful and political means by negotiation. These problems can be solved in such a way as to serve the interests of all those who live in that area. Obviously, the continuing instability in the western part of the Arab world works in favour of the imperialists. Thus the French imperialists have begun to threaten the area with interference and collaboration with American imperialism. Naturally this would endanger the progress and patriotic achievements of the nations in this area, namely Algeria, Morocco and Mauritania.

The Communist and Workers' parties of the Arab countries consider that a firm unity of interests and common aims unite the Arab and African peoples, who in varying forms are together countering the aggressive policy of imperialism and reaction.

The events of the Horn of Africa represent a dangerous plot against the African and Arab liberation movement, particularly against the revolutionary régimes in Ethiopia and Democratic Yemen. The Somali leadership has aided these plans and violated the decisions of the Organization of African Unity concerning recognition of the existing borders of the African States and settlement of border issues by peaceful means. The Somali government has also, to the advice given, invaded the territory of Ethiopia. Naturally in so doing it has exposed Somali's national independence and the Somali people's achievements to grave danger.

The highest interests of the Arab national liberation movement require that these plans must be frustrated and that an end must be put to imperialist and reactionary interference. The Ethiopian revolution must be protected, and the Eritrean problem solved by peaceful means on the basis of self-determination of the people, in accordance with the common military interests against reaction and imperialism.

Experience has taught us that depending on reactionary movements and imperialism would endanger patriotic independence and crush progressive achievements. Therefore, the revolutionary leadership which is heavily reliant on a deep and comprehensive mass support, inspired by revolutionary thought and assisted by the Soviet Union and other socialist forces, along with other progressive forces in the world, should secure victory. The continuous support offered by Cuba to the struggle of the Ethiopian peoples and other African nations represents a good example of international military solidarity.

Some of the Arab reactionary régimes which are supported by imperialism have always co-operated and formulated common plans with Zionism and the rulers of Israel. But what is the most unendurable thing in that cooperation is that it has now become more open and obvious, that the rulers of Egypt have joined it having deserted the struggle against Israeli occupation.

A Continuous Role of Retrogression and Submission

The imperialist offensive would have been less effective and the true face of Arab reaction less pronounced had not a number of negative aspects that have emerged in the recent period, prejudiced the Arab national liberation movement. Those negative aspects are represented in a continuous inclination inside certain elements of the Arab patriotic liberation movements towards following a more lenient policy with local reactionary rulers and imperialism, and also in the estrangement of other patriotic elements from the patriotic camp in order to join the opposite side.

Within that framework the intruding bourgoisie has played an increasing role in accelerating the trends of retrogression and capitulation, and in the pursuit of economic liberalisation. That social strata is developing and becoming stronger in collaboration with the state sector, state system, commerce and tender sector. Naturally, in circumstances where mass supervision and vigilance are non-existent, the social strata (the intruding bourgeoisie) would become a more dangerous force.

This social strata would also develop attitudes contrary to the national liberation aspiration and against the patriotic interests of the people. This will be achieved over a period of time because it is not participating in the process of social activity. Therefore it will regard itself as nearer to the interests of reaction, Zionism and imperialism. Hence it is not strange to discover that this phenomenon has already begun to appear in one form or another in some of the progressive countries. This phenomenon necessitates complete vigilance and adherence to a policy of resistance by force. It has become very clear in recent years the extent to which that phenomenon is dangerous to the working masses and the frameworks within which they work, for instance political organizations, unions and democratic organizations, and in the restriction of the liberties of the people.

It is essential to consistently follow a line of relying on the support of the masses, to provide conditions for the manifestation of their creative energies and initiatives, and to ensure democratic freedoms, above all, the freedom to set up political and trade union organisations, freedom of expression and the press. Failing this, it will be impossible to defend and develop the progressive gains, counter the plots of imperialism, Zionism and reaction and safeguard national independence and sovereignty.

In Circumstances of Fulfilling Democratic Liberties and Guaranteeing Mass Participation

The masses of labourers, peasants and revolutionary intelligensia which form the comprehensive, social and patriotic militant foundations should participate actively in determining their country's destiny. All this depends to a great extent on the realisation of democratic liberties and mass participation in the progressive and patriotic battles.

It is obvious that the negligence of mass demands has been an important factor for the progressive régimes in weakening their countries, for as long as the social transformations are deep, equal and responsive to mass demands, then the mass of labourers, peasants and intelligensia will play an active role in the battle of construction and liberation. But these conditions would only be created when public institutions became free of destructive elements, when revolutionary institutions based on democratic principles were established and when, in the fight against bureaucracy complete reliance was placed on the popular supervision of the state institutions as well as on other services and production sectors.

In the face of the expanding onslaught of imperialism, Zionism and reaction, it is imperative to ensure the active participation of the broadest social strata in defending and developing progressive gains, safeguarding national sovereignty and in rebuffing the plotting of imperialism, Zionism and reaction.

The struggle against the economic offensive of internationally organised monopolies, against the policy of "economic liberalisation" propagandised by the reactionary circles in the Arab world, plays an important part in organising a rebuff to imperialist pressures. It is essential to display vigilance and not to permit subordination of economic and trade relations to the world capitalist market, to step up the struggle against the plunder of national wealth, above all of oil, and to make sure that the oil revenues are not used to alleviate the crisis of world capitalism, to subvert the Arab and African progressive patriotic régimes, and establish domination over other countries of the region.

In countering the imperialist onslaught vital importance is attached to the struggle in defence of the state sector, to its expansion and improved management, to averting the efforts of the hostile elements aimed at undermining it and to deepening the socio-economic changes in various fields.

In this connection the importance of strengthening economic and commercial cooperation with the states of the socialist community as a way of achieving economic independence and resolving the objectives of economic development, is becoming increasingly clear. It is possible to resist and curb this vicious imperialist assault. To achieve this goal the Arab patriotic liberation movement possesses all the military, economic and political potential. For the Arab masses have already undertaken courageous battles against imperialism and for liberation and social progress. Those battles have benefited the Arab masses and their political and progressive vanguards as well as their popular organisations, in becoming more experienced and victorious.

The Factors Leading to the Defeat of the Imperialist Conspiracy

There are certain factors which make the possibility of defeating imperialist conspiracy easy for the following reasons:

1. The existence of progressive and patriotic régimes antagonistic to imperialism, with power and ability to take the initiative of leadership from the forces of right and Arab reactionary elements.

2. The existence of political organisations and revolutionary movements, particularly working class parties, which are capable of mobilising the popular masses in times of fatal battles.

3. The solidarity of the Soviet Union, the socialist countries and the forces of progress in the world with the Arab patriotic liberation movement.

4. The emergence of an international situation at a time when the balance of power is becoming more in favour of socialist countries, while the crisis of international imperialism is increasing and becoming more detrimental.

The political, economic and popular potentials of the Arab patriotic liberation movement can confront the recent developments of the Arab situation and can also confront the vicious imperialist assault, if they are well organised; the widely popular official reactions against Sadat's initiative has proved the existence of such a possibility. The popular reawakening of these attitudes has begun to crystalize and has become more active against submissive attitudes, capitulation and imperialism. All this has been reflected in the demonstration of the masses and acts of mass denunciation of Sadat's initiative in various Arab countries and even in the West Bank and the Gaza strip. The masses of Palestine have thus proved their loyalty to the PLO and their rejection of occupation and submission. The progressive and patriotic forces of Egypt are playing a bold and prominent role against the Sadat treachery to the Arab cause.

The popular masses in the Arab countries hail the formation of a front of staunchness and resistance as a major gain in the struggle against the onslaught of imperialism and Zionism, for thwarting the capitulatory policy. The results of the Tripoli summit and the People's Congress represent an important step in that direction. These results were consolidated and developed at the summit meeting in Algiers. A statement adopted at this meeting emphasises the need to wage a resolute struggle against imperialism and Zionism, against the course followed by the Egyptian régime, to strengthen friendship and cooperation with the Soviet Union and all forces of progress and socialism across the world.

The Significant Steps on the Road to a Progressive and Patriotic Arab Front.

The Arab progressive and patriotic forces together with all forces of progress, freedom and socialism in the world have held the results at both the Tripoli and Algiers summit conferences and they saw in them a significant step towards the development of Arab solidarity and as a step directed against Sadat's submissive policy. These conferences represent important developments on the road to establishing Arab progressive and patriotic front. No doubt this front will be strengthened and become more powerful if Iraq participates in it. The political circumstances of the area and its geographical location has denoted the significance of such a front which should include Iraq, Syria and the PLO. What is required now above all is the intensification and consolidation of the results of Tripoli's and Algiers' summit conferences and the exertion of all possible efforts to establish a militant programme for confrontation which all the Arab patriotic régimes would support. It is also most important to guarantee the participation of the representatives of all the progressive and patriotic trends in the activities of the general trustee for the Arab Popular Conference by mobilising all potentials in every Arab gathering against Zionism and imperialism.

It is becoming more obvious throughout the struggle against imperialism and its allies and conspiracies, that the Arab masses are trying to achieve a wider Arab progressive front to lead its united fight against the common enemy. This is in order to curb all the attempts which aim at drowning the slogans of Arab militant solidarity. The Arab masses are also trying to create that front among the progressive and patriotic powers in their fight against imperialist assault. That front also aims at confronting the Arab reactionary régimes which are trying to follow calls for Arab solidary in order to distract the attention of the Arab masses from the struggle against imperialist activities, Zionism and reactionary régimes that are always conspiring against their just national cause. This popular desire of unity of action and struggle is connected with the legitimate desire for Arab unity which must be founded on the principles of continuous antagonism against imperialism and determination for consistent action on the road to social progress, through complete reliance on a wider base of the masses, through the realisation of democratic liberties by means of political organisations and professional unions and freedom of expression. That desire is also related to the wish for continuous cooperation with socialist countries and the revolutionary democratic forces of the world. Hence the intensification of the potentials of the Arab confrontationist countries (including the PLO) against Israel is imperative.

Consolidation of Independence and its Protection through Co-operation and Friendship with the Socialist Countries

Since the Arab states began to achieve independence and fight for its protection and consolidation, the experiment of modern history has demonstrated that such an aim would be impossible without the co-operation and friendship of the Soviet Union and other socialist countries on a frank and sincere basis.

The armies of Syria have fought alongside the advanced Soviet technical armies since 1956 but the Egyptian régime today is trying to deviate from that policy and has begun to seek a new source of arms. Unfortunately, this tendency is enjoying the moral and financial support of the

Arab reactionary régimes, such as Saudi Arabia. However, Sadat's inclination to disarm the Egyptian army is in line with the submissive policy he is following in all fields. But on the other hand it has become obvious through experience that imperialism is not the real source of armament to the Arab countries, including Egypt, as some of the Arab countries aim to liberate the occupied territories one day.

The slogan of "looking for new sources of arms" is a dangerous one, which aims at directing a harmful blow against the progress of Arab countries, especially against the aggressive countries in order gradually to subjugate them to reactionist and imperialist control.

In fact, improvement and increase of the fighting potentials of progressive Arab armies and the proper application of modern fighting techniques is beginning to play a prominent part in the present situation, as the accumulation of arms themselves is insufficient without the required technical knowledge of their use.

Life has Proved the Necessity of the Progressive and Patriotic Fronts
The progressive and patriotic fronts which are formed in certain Arab countries have proved to be necessary. They have embraced progressive and patriotic parties, including the communist parties. This has reflected an objective reality. The cooperation within the framework of these fronts has achieved success in political and socio-economic fields and has also played a prominent role in mobilising the masses in their fight against imperialism and its allies.

Life has confirmed the need for the patriotic and progressive fronts that have been set up in a number of Arab countries. They consist of national and progressive parties, including the Communists, which reflects objective reality. Cooperation in the framework of these fronts has ensured successes in the political, economic and social spheres. They had a role to play in mobilising the masses for the struggle against imperialism and its henchmen.

Vital Objectives of the Struggle.
The programme of struggle against imperialism, Zionism and reaction, to thwart the capitulatory course, for the liberation of the occupied Arab territories and to ensure the national rights of the Arab people of Palestine presupposes the implementation of the following objectives:

1. Formation of a broad progressive patriotic front on the scale of the entire Arab world, comprising all progressive patriotic forces and streams, built on the basis of a realistic concrete fighting programme and leading to the expansion and cohesion of the base of staunchness and resistance, with the aim of effecting the necessary changes in the situation of the Arab national liberation movement and at raising it to the level of the tasks of the present stage while simultaneously developing and strengthening Arab soli-

darity in the name of launching a joint struggle against the overall plans of imperialism.

2. Defence of the progressive patriotic régimes against attempts to overthrow or subvert them, enhancement of their role in the struggle against imperialism, Zionism and reaction.

3. Strengthening the front of staunchness and resistance, by eliminating all its weak points, enabling it to counter the increasingly serious attacks, to resolutely reject the capitulatory course of Sadat, while following a consistent line of struggle against imperialism, US imperialism first of all, Zionism and reaction, and rebuffing their various plans and manoeuvres in the region.

4. Creation of political, material and military prerequisites to ensure the staunchness of the Syrian front in face of the Zionist enemy, formation of close fighting relations between Syria, the Palestine resistance movement and the progressive patriotic movement in Lebanon.

5. Full political, material and military support to the forces of the Palestine revolution on the basis of safeguarding their independence in adopting political decisions expressing the independent national identity of the Arab people of Palestine, which will help to maintain and strengthen their present potential in the struggle for the right of the Arab people of Palestine to return to their home, for self-determination, setting up an independent national state and to full restoration of their legitimate national rights, in the struggle conducted under the leadership of the Palestine Liberation Organisation as the sole legitimate representative of that people.

6. Support for the struggle of the Lebanese national movement and all forces seeking to safeguard the unity and Arab character of Lebanon, against Israeli aggression and for the unconditional banishing of the occupationists from the southern regions of the country, against the isolationist Zionist plans that are designed to deprive Lebanon of its Arab identity and to turn it into a racist communal formation.

7. Support for the national democratic movement in Egypt in its struggle against Sadat's line, so that Egypt can once again take its natural position in the Arab front of struggle against imperialism and the Israeli occupation.

8. Intensified struggle to thwart the plans to set up new military blocs and to dismantle the military bases in the region of the Persian Gulf and the Arabian Peninsula which serve aggressive purposes, for the withdrawal of foreign troops and to maintain the independence of the states of this region, to ensure freedom of navigation in accordance with the rules of international law.

9. Ensurance of the broadest democratic freedoms for the masses, the popular movements and progressive forces to display their initiatives, renunciation of any manifestations or forms of restricting the activity of these forces, abrogation of the repressive anti-Communist laws still in force in a number of Arab countries.

10. Enhancement of the effectiveness of the national fronts and alliances, enrichment of the content of their activity, and increasing the role and activity of their participants, as well as the role of the mass popular organisations for the maximum and more effective mobilisation of forces and opportunities in the face of the intensified imperialist, Zionist and reactionary plots.

11. Deepening of the democratic socio-economic transformations, strengthening economic independence, satisfaction of the demands of the popular masses, consolidation of their role in resolving the fate of their country with the aim of ensuring a stable material foundation and mass base for the struggle against the alliance of imperialism, Zionism and reaction.

12. Steadfast strengthening of friendship and cooperation with the Soviet Union in all spheres in the interests of the struggle against imperialism, Zionism and the capitulators, in the interests of the development and progress of our peoples.

13. Promotion of relations of cooperation and solidarity with the revolutionary movements and régimes in Africa, support for their struggle against the plots of imperialism and reaction, for the just struggle being waged by the peoples of South Africa, Zimbabwe and Namibia and their revolutionary organisations against racial discrimination and for national liberation.

14. Invigoration of the struggle to consolidate the unity of the world Communist movement on the principles of Marxism-Leninism and proletarian internationalism.

15. Invigoration of the struggle against all anti-Communist and anti-Soviet trends and tendencies.

Jordanian Communist Party
Socialist Vanguard Party of Algeria
Sudanese Communist Party
Iraqi Communist Party
Lebanese Communist Party
Party of Progress and Socialism of Morocco
Egyptian Communist Party

Mid-April 1978

Asia

The Constitution of The People's Republic of China

(Adopted on March 5, 1978 by the Fifth National People's Congress of the People's Republic of China at its First Session)*
(Complete Text). Hsinhua News Agency, 10 March, 1978.

* This is the third Constitution of the People's Republic of China since its proclamation on 1 October, 1949. The first, comprising of 104 articles, was promulgated by the First Session of the First National People's Congress on 20 September 1954. The Second constitution comprising of 30 articles was adopted by the First Session of the Fourth National People's Congress on 17 January 1975.

The "Report on the Revision of the Constitution" that proceeded the adoption of the present constitution was delivered by Marshall Yeh Chien-ying on 1 March 1978. For the text of the Report see: Peking Review, No. 11, March 17, 1978, pp. 15-28. (Ed.).

Preamble

After more than a century of heroic struggle the Chinese people, led by the Communist Party of China headed by our great leader and teacher Chairman Mao Tsetung, finally overthrew the reactionary rule of imperialism, feudalism and bureaucrat-capitalism by means of people's revolutionary war, winning complete victory in the new-democratic revolution, and in 1949 founded the People's Republic of China.

The founding of the People's Republic of China marked the beginning of the historical period of socialism in our country. Since then, under the leadership of Chairman Mao and the Chinese Communist Party, the people of all our nationalities have carried out Chairman Mao's proletarian revolutionary line in the political, economic, cultural and military fields and in foreign affairs and have won great victories in socialist revolution and socialist construction through repeated struggles against enemies both at home and abroad and through the Great Proletarian Cultural Revolution. The dictatorship of the proletariat in our country has been consolidated and strengthened, and China has become a socialist country with the beginnings of prosperity.

Chairman Mao Tsetung was the founder of the People's Republic of China. All our victories in revolution and construction have been won under the guidance of Marxism-Leninism-Mao Tsetung Thought. The fundamental guarantee that the people of all our nationalities will struggle in unity and carry the proletarian revolution through to the end is always to hold high and staunchly to defend the great banner of Chairman Mao.

The triumphant conclusion of the first Great Proletarian Cultural Revolution has ushered in a new period of development in China's socialist revolution and socialist construction. In accordance with the basic line of the Chinese Communist Party for the entire historical period of socialism, the general task for the people of the whole country in this new period is: To persevere in continuing the revolution under the dictatorship of the proletariat, carry forward the three great revolutionary movements of class struggle, the struggle for production and scientific experiment, and make China a great and powerful socialist country with modern agriculture, industry, national defence and science and technology by the end of the century.

We must persevere in the struggle of the proletariat against the bourgeoisie and in the struggle for the socialist road against the capitalist road. We must oppose revisionism and prevent the restoration of capitalism. We must be prepared to deal with subversion and aggression against our country by social-imperialism and imperialism.

We should consolidate and expand the revolutionary united front which is led by the working class and based on the worker-peasant alliance, and which unites the large numbers of intellectuals and other working people; patriotic democratic parties, patriotic personages, our compatriots in Taiwan, Hongkong and Macao, and our countrymen residing abroad. We should enhance the great unity of all the nationalities in our country. We should correctly distinguish and handle the contradictions among the people and those between ourselves and the enemy. We should endeavour to create among the people of the whole country a political situation in which there are both centralism and democracy, both discipline and freedom, both unity of will and personal ease of mind and liveliness, so as to help bring all positive factors into play, overcome all difficulties, better consolidate the proletarian dictatorship and build up our country more rapidly.

Taiwan is China's sacred territory. We are determined to liberate Taiwan and accomplish the great cause of unifying our motherland.

In international affairs, we should establish and develop relations with other countries on the basis of the Five Principles of mutual respect for sovereignty and territorial integrity, mutual non-aggression, non-interference in each other's internal affairs, equality and mutual benefit, and peaceful coexistence. Our country will never seek hegemony, or strive to be a superpower. We should uphold proletarian internationalism. In accordance with the theory of the three worlds, we should strengthen our unity with the proletariat and the oppressed people and nations throughout the world, the socialist countries, and the third world countries, and we should unite with all countries subjected to aggression, subversion, interference, control and bullying by the social-imperialist and imperialist superpowers to form the broadest possible international united front against the hegemonism of the superpowers and against a new world war, and strive for the progress and emancipation of humanity.

Chapter One

General Principles

Article 1 The People's Republic of China is a socialist state of the dictatorship of the proletariat led by the working class and based on the alliance of workers and peasants.

Article 2 The Communist Party of China is the core of leadership of the whole Chinese people. The working class exercises leadership over the state through its vanguard, the Communist Party of China.

The guiding ideology of the People's Republic of China is Marxism-Leninism-Mao Tsetung Thought.

Article 3 All power in the People's Republic of China belongs to the people. The organs through which the people exercise state power are the National People's Congress and the local people's congresses at various levels.

The National People's Congress, the local people's congresses at various levels and all other organs of state practise democratic centralism.

Article 4 The People's Republic of China is a unitary multinational state.

All the nationalities are equal. There should be unity and fraternal love among the nationalities and they should help and learn from each other. Discrimination against, or oppression of, any nationality, and acts which undermine the unity of the nationalities are prohibited. Big-nationality chauvinism and local-nationality chauvinism must be opposed.

All the nationalities have the freedom to use and develop their own spoken and written languages, and to preserve or reform their own customs and ways.

Regional autonomy applies in an area where a minority nationality lives in a compact community. All the national autonomous areas are inalienable parts of the People's Republic of China.

Article 5 There are mainly two kinds of ownership of the means of production in the People's Republic of China at the present stage: socialist ownership by the whole people and socialist collective ownership by the working people.

The state allows non-agricultural individual labourers to engage in individual labour involving no exploitation of others, within the limits permitted by law and under unified arrangement and management by organizations at the basic level in cities and towns or in rural areas. At the same time, it guides these individual labourers step by step on to the road of socialist collectivization.

Article 6 The state sector of the economy, that is, the socialist sector owned by the whole people, is the leading force in the national economy.

Mineral resources, waters and those forests, undeveloped lands and other marine and land resources owned by the state are the property of the whole people.

The state may requisition by purchase, take over for use, or nationalize land under conditions prescribed by law.

Article 7 The rural people's commune sector of the economy is a socialist sector collectively owned by the masses of working people. At present, it generally takes the form of three-level ownership, that is, ownership by the commune, the production brigade and the production team, with the production team as the basic accounting unit. A production brigade may become the basic accounting unit when its conditions are ripe.

Provided that the absolute predominance of the collective economy of the people's commune is ensured, commune members may farm small plots of land for personal needs, engage in limited household sideline production, and in pastoral areas they may also keep a limited number of livestock for personal needs.

Article 8 Social public property shall be inviolable. The state ensures the consolidation and development of the socialist sector of the economy owned by the whole people and of the socialist sector collectively owned by the masses of working people.

The state prohibits any person from using any means whatsoever to disrupt the economic order of the society, undermine the economic plans of the state, encroach upon or squander state and collective property, or injure the public interest.

Article 9 The state protects the right of citizens to own lawfully earned income, savings, houses and other means of livelihood.

Article 10 The state applies the socialist principles: "He who does not work, neither shall he eat" and "from each according to his ability, to each according to his work."

Work is an honourable duty for every citizen able to work. The state promotes socialist labour emulation, and, putting proletarian politics in command, it applies the policy of combining moral encouragement with material reward, with the stress on the former, in order to heighten the citizens' socialist enthusiasm and creativeness in work.

Article 11 The state adheres to the general line of going all out, aiming high and achieving greater, faster, better and more economical results in building socialism, it undertakes the planned, proportionate and high-speed development of the national economy, and it continuously develops the productive forces, so as to consolidate the country's independence and security and improve the people's material and cultural life step by step.

In developing the national economy, the state adheres to the principle of building our country independently, with the initiative in our own hands and through self-reliance, hard struggle, diligence and thrift, it adheres to the principle of taking agriculture as the foundation and industry as the leading factor, and it adheres to the principle of bringing the initiative of both the central and local authorities into full play under the unified leadership of the central authorities.

The state protects the environment and natural resources and prevents and eliminates pollution and other hazards to the public.

Article 12 The state devotes major efforts to developing science, expands scientific research, promotes technical innovation and technical revolution and adopts advanced techniques wherever possible in all departments of the national economy. In scientific and technological work we must follow the practice of combining professional contingents with the masses, and combining learning from others with our own creative efforts.

Article 13 The state devotes major efforts to developing education in order to raise the cultural and scientific level of the whole nation. Education must serve proletarian politics and be combined with productive labour and must enable everyone who receives an education to develop morally, intellectually and physically and become a worker with both socialist consciousness and culture.

Article 14 The state upholds the leading position of Marxism-Leninism-Mao Tsetung Thought in all spheres of ideology and culture. All cultural undertakings must serve the workers, peasants and soldiers and serve socialism.

The state applies the policy of "Letting a hundred flowers blossom and a hundred schools of thought contend" so as to promote the development of the arts and sciences and bring about a flourishing socialist culture.

Article 15 All organs of state must constantly maintain close contact with the masses of the people, rely on them, heed their opinions, be concerned for their weal and woe, streamline administration, practise economy, raise efficiency and combat bureaucracy.

The leading personnel of state organs at all levels must conform to the requirements for successors in the proletarian revolutionary cause and their composition must conform to the principle of the three-in-one combination of the old, the middle-aged and the young.

Article 16 The personnel of organs of state must earnestly study Marxism-Leninism-Mao Tsetung Thought, wholeheartedly serve the people, endeavour to perfect their professional competence, take an active part in collective productive labour, accept supervision by the masses, be models in observing the Constitution and the law, correctly implement the policies of the state, seek the truth from facts, and must not have recourse to deception or exploit their position and power to seek personal gain.

Article 17 The state adheres to the principle of socialist democracy, and ensures to the people the right to participate in the management of state affairs and of all economic and cultural undertakings, and the right to supervise the organs of state and their personnel.

Article 18 The state safeguards the socialist system, suppresses all treasonable and counter-revolutionary activities, punishes all traitors and counter-revolutionaries, and punishes newborn bourgeois elements and other bad elements.

The state deprives of political rights, as prescribed by law, those land-lords, rich peasants and reactionary capitalists who have not yet been reformed, and at the same time it provides them with the opportunity to earn a living so that they may be reformed through labour and become law-abiding citizens supporting themselves by their own labour.

Article 19 The Chairman of the Central Committee of the Communist Party of China commands the armed forces of the People's Republic of China.

The Chinese People's Liberation Army is the workers' and peasants' own armed force led by the Communist Party of China; it is the pillar of the dictatorship of the proletariat. The state devotes major efforts of the revo-lutionization and modernization of the Chinese People's Liberation Army, strengthens the building of the militia and adopts a system under which our armed forces are a combination of the field armies, the regional forces and the militia.

The fundamental task of the armed forces of the People's Republic of China is: To safeguard the socialist revolution and socialist construction, to defend the sovereignty, territorial integrity and security of the state, and to guard against subversion and aggression by social-imperialism, imperial-ism and their lackeys.

Chapter Two

The Structure of The State

Section I

The National People's Congress

Article 20 The National People's Congress is the highest organ of state power.

Article 21 The National People's Congress is composed of deputies elected by the people's congresses of the provinces, autonomous regions, and municipalities directly under the Central Government, and by the People's Liberation Army. The deputies should be elected by secret ballot after democratic consultation.

The National People's Congress is elected for a term of five years. Under special circumstances, its term of office may be extended or the succeeding National People's Congress may be convened before its due date.

The National People's Congress holds one session each year. When nec-essary, the session may be advanced or postponed.

Article 22 The National People's Congress exercises the following functions and powers:

(1) to amend the Constitution;

(2) to make laws;

(3) to supervise the enforcement of the Constitution and the law;

(4) to decide on the choice of the Premier of the State Council upon the recommendation of the Central Committee of the Communist Party of China;

(5) to decide on the choice of other members of the State Council upon the recommendation of the Premier of the State Council;

(6) to elect the President of the Supreme People's Court and the Chief Procurator of the Supreme People's Procuratorate;

(7) to examine and approve the national economic plan, the state budget and the final state accounts;

(8) to confirm the following administrative divisions: provinces, autonomous regions, and municipalities directly under the Central Governments;

(9) to decide on questions of war and peace; and

(10) to exercise such other functions and powers as the National People's Congress deems necessary.

Article 23 The National People's Congress has the power to remove from office the members of the State Council, the President of the Supreme People's Court and the Chief Procurator of the Supreme People's Procuratorate.

Article 24 The Standing Committee of the National People's Congress is the permanent organ of the National People's Congress. It is responsible and accountable to the National People's Congress.

The Standing Committee of the National People's Congress is composed of the following members:

the Chairman;

the Vice-Chairmen;

he Secretary-General; and

other members.

The National People's Congress elects the Standing Committee of the National People's Congress and has the power to recall its members.

Article 25 The Standing Committee of the National People's Congress exercises the following functions and powers:

(1) to conduct the election of deputies to the National People's Congress;

(2) to convene the sessions of the National People's Congress;

(3) to interpret the Constitution and laws and to enact decrees;

(4) to supervise the work of the State Council, the Supreme People's Court and the Supreme People's Procuratorate;

(5) to change and annul inappropriate decisions adopted by the organs of state power of provinces, autonomous regions, and municipalities directly under the Central Government;

(6) to decide on the appointment and removal of individual members of the State Council upon the recommendation of the Premier of the State Council when the National People's Congress is not in session;

(7) to appoint and remove Vice-Presidents of the Supreme People's Court and Deputy Chief Procurators of the Supreme People's Procuratorate;

(8) to decide on the appointment and removal of plenipotentiary representatives abroad;

(9) to decide on the ratification and abrogation of treaties concluded with foreign states;

(10) to institute state titles of honour and decide on their conferment;

(11) to decide on the granting of pardons;

(12) to decide on the proclamation of a state of war in the event of armed attack on the country when the National People's Congress is not in session; and

(13) to exercise such other functions and powers as are vested in it by the National People's Congress.

Article 26 The Chairman of the Standing Committee of the National People's Congress presides over the work of the Standing Committee; receives foreign diplomatic envoys; and in accordance with the decisions of the National People's Congress or its Standing Committee promulgates laws and decrees, dispatches and recalls plenipotentiary representatives abroad, ratifies treaties concluded with foreign states and confers state titles of honour.

The Vice-Chairmen of the Standing Committee of the National People's Congress assist the Chairman in his work and may exercise part of the Chairman's functions and powers on his behalf.

Article 27 The National People's Congress and its Standing Committee may establish special committees as deemed necessary.

Article 28 Deputies to the National People's Congress have the right to address inquiries to the State Council, the Supreme People's Court, the Supreme People's Procuratorate, and the ministries and commissions of the State Council, which are all under obligation to answer.

Article 29 Deputies to the National People's Congress are subject to supervision by the units which elect them. These electoral units have the power to replace at anya time the deputies they elect, as prescribed by law.

Section II

The State Council

Article 30 The State Council is the Central People's Government and the executive organ of the highest organ of state power; it is the highest organ of state administration.

The State Council is responsible and accountable to the National People's Congress, or, when the National People's Congress is not in session, to its Standing Committee.

Article 31 The State Council is composed of the following members:

the Premier;

the Vice-Premiers;

the ministers; and

the ministers heading the commissions.

The Premier presides over the work of the State Council and the Vice-Premiers assist the Premier in his work.

Article 32 The State Council exercises the following functions and powers:

(1) to formulate administrative measures, issue decisions and orders and verify their execution, in accordance with the Constitution, laws and decrees;

(2) to submit proposals on laws and other matters to the National People's Congress or its Standing Committee;

(3) to exercise unified leadership over the work of the ministries and commissions and other organizations under it;

(4) to exercise unified leadership over the work of local organs of state administration at various levels throughout the country;

(5) to draw up and put into effect the national economic plan and the state budget;

(6) to protect the interests of the state, maintain public order and safeguard the rights of citizens;

(7) to confirm the following administrative divisions: autonomous prefectures, counties, autonomous counties, and cities;

(8) to appoint and remove administrative personnel according to the provisions of the law; and

(9) to exercise such other functions and powers as are vested in it by the National People's Congress or its Standing Committee.

Section III

The Local People's Congresses And the Local Revolutionary Committees at Various Levels

Article 33 The administrative division of the People's Republic of China is as follows:

(1) The country is divided into provinces, autonomous regions, and municipalities directly under the Central Government;

(2) Provinces and autonomous regions are divided into autonomous prefectures, counties, autonomous counties, and cities; and

(3) Counties and autonomous counties are divided into people's communes and towns.

Municipalities directly under the Central Government and other large cities are divided into districts and counties. Autonomous prefectures are divided into counties, autonomous counties, and cities.

Autonomous regions, autonomous prefectures and autonomous counties are all national autonomous areas.

Article 34 People's congresses and revolutionary committees are established in provinces, municipalities directly under the Central Government, counties, cities, municipal districts, people's communes and towns.

People's congresses and revolutionary committees of the people's communes are organizations of political power at the grass-roots level, and are also leading organs of collective economy.

Revolutionary committees at the provincial level may establish administrative offices as their agencies in prefectures.

Organs of self-government are established in autonomous regions, autonomous prefectures and autonomous counties.

Article 35 Local people's congresses at various levels are local organs of state power.

Deputies to the people's congresses of provinces, municipalities directly under the Central Government, counties, and cities divided into districts are elected by people's congresses at the next lower level by secret ballot after democratic consultation; deputies to the people's congresses of cities not divided into districts, and of municipal districts, people's communes and towns are directly elected by the voters by secret ballot after democratic consultation.

The people's congresses of provinces and municipalities directly under the Central Government are elected for a term of five years. The people's congresses of counties, cities and municipal districts are elected for a term of three years. The people's congresses of people's communes and towns are elected for a term of two years.

Local people's congresses at various levels hold at least one session each year, which is to be convened by revolutionary committees at the corresponding levels.

The units and electorates which elect the deputies to the local people's congresses at various levels have the power to supervise, remove and replace their deputies at any time according to the provisions of the law.

Article 36 Local people's congresses at various levels, in their respective administrative areas, ensure the observance and enforcement of the Constitution, laws and decrees; ensure the implementation of the state plan; make plans for local economic and cultural development and for public utilities; examine and approve local economic plans, budgets and final accounts; protect public property; maintain public order; safeguard the rights of citizens and the equal rights of minority nationalities; and promote the development of socialist revolution and socialist construction.

Local people's congresses may adopt and issue decisions within the limits of their authority as prescribed by law.

Local people's congresses elect, and have the power to recall, members of revolutionary committees at the corresponding levels. People's congresses at county level and above elect, and have the power to recall, the presidents of the people's courts and the chief procurators of the people's procuratorates at the corresponding levels.

Deputies to local people's congresses at various levels have the right to address inquiries to the revolutionary committees, people's courts, people's procuratorates and organs under the revolutionary committees at the corresponding levels, which are all under obligation to answer.

Article 37 Local revolutionary committees at various levels, that is, local people's governments, are the executive organs of local people's congresses at the corresponding levels and they are also local organs of state administration.

A local revolutionary committee is composed of a chairman, vice-chairmen and other members.

Local revolutionary committees carry out the decisions of people's congresses at the corresponding levels as well as the decisions and orders of the organs of state administration at higher levels, direct the administrative work of their respective areas, and issue decisions and orders within the limits of their authority as prescribed by law. Revolutionary committees at county level and above appoint or remove the personnel of organs of state according to the provisions of the law.

Local revolutionary committees are responsible and accountable to people's congresses at the corresponding levels and to the organs of state administration at the next higher level, and work under the unified leadership of the State Council.

Section IV
The Organs of Self-Government of National Autonomous Areas

Article 38 The organs of self-government of autonomous regions, autonomous prefectures and autonomous counties are people's congresses and revolutionary committees.

The election of the people's congresses and revolutionary committees of national autonomous areas, their terms of office, their functions and powers and also the establishment of their agencies should conform to the basic principles governing the organization of local organs of state as specified in Section III, Chapter Two, of the Constitution.

In autonomous areas where a number of nationalities live together, each nationality is entitled to appropriate representation in the organs of self-government.

Article 39 The organs of self-government of national autonomous areas exercise autonomy within the limits of their authority as prescribed by law, in addition to exercising the functions and powers of local organs of state as specified by the Constitution.

The organs of self-government of national autonomous areas may, in the light of the political, economic and cultural characteristics of the nationality or nationalities in a given area, make regulations on the exercise of autonomy and also specific regulations and submit them to the Standing Committee of the National People's Congress for approval.

In performing their functions, the organs of self-government of national autonomous areas employ the spoken and written language or languages commonly used by the nationality or nationalities in the locality.

Article 40 The higher organs of state shall fully safeguard the exercise of autonomy by the organs of self-government of national autonomous areas, take into full consideration the characteristics and needs of the various minority nationalities, make a major effort to train cadres of the minority nationalities, and actively support and assist all the minority nationalities in their social revolution and construction and thus advance their socialist economic and cultural development.

Section V
The People's Courts and the People's Procuratorates

Article 41 The Supreme People's Court, local people's courts at various levels and special people's courts exercise judicial authority. The people's courts are formed as prescribed by law.

In accordance with law, the people's courts apply the system whereby representatives of the masses participate as assessors in administering justice. With regard to major counter-revolutionary or criminal cases, the masses should be drawn in for discussion and suggestions.

All cases in the people's courts are heard in public except those involving special circumstances, as prescribed by law. The accused has the right to defence.

Article 42 The Supreme People's Court is the highest judicial organ.

The Supreme People's Court supervises the administration of justice by local people's courts at various levels and by special people's courts; people's courts at the higher levels supervise the administration of justice by people's courts at the lower levels.

The Supreme People's Court is responsible and accountable to the National People's Congress and its Standing Committee. Local people's courts at various levels are responsible and accountable to local people's congresses at the corresponding levels.

Article 43 The Supreme People's Procuratorate exercises procuratorial authority to ensure observance of the Constitution and the law by all the departments under the State Council, the local organs of state at various levels, the personnel of organs of state and the citizens. Local people's pro-curatorates and special people's procuratorates exercise procuratorial authority within the limits prescribed by law. The people's procuratorates are formed as prescribed by law.

The Supreme People's Procuratorate supervises the work of local people's procuratorates at various levels and of special people's procuratorates; people's procuratorates at the higher levels supervise the work of those at the lower levels.

The Supreme People's Procuratorate is responsible and accountable to the National People's Congress and its Standing Committee. Local people's procuratorates at various levels are responsible and accountable to people's congresses at the corresponding levels.

Chapter Three
The Fundamental Rights And Duties of Citizens

Article 44 All citizens who have reached the age of 18 have the right to vote and to stand for election, with the exception of persons deprived of these rights by law.

Article 45 Citizens enjoy freedom of speech, correspondence, the press, assembly, association. procession, demonstration and the freedom to strike, and have the right to "speak out freely, air their views fully, hold great debates and write big-character posters."

Article 46 Citizens enjoy freedom to believe in religion and freedom not to believe in religion and to propagate atheism.

Article 47 The citizens' freedom of person and their homes are inviolable.

No citizen may be arrested except by decision of a people's court or with the sanction of a people's procuratorate, and the arrest must be made by a public security organ.

Article 48 Citizens have the right to work. To ensure that citizens enjoy this right, the state provides employment in accordance with the principle of overall consideration, and, on the basis of increased production, the state gradually increases payment for labour, improves working conditions, strengthens labour protection and expands collective welfare.

Article 49 Working people have the right to rest. To ensure that working people enjoy this right, the state prescribes working hours and systems of vacations and gradually expands material facilities for the working people to rest and recuperate.

Article 50 Working people have the right to material assistance in old age, and in case of illness or disability. To ensure that working people enjoy this right, the state gradually expands social insurance, social assistance, public health services, co-operative medical services, and other services.

The state cares for and ensures the livelihood of disabled revolutionary armymen and the families of revolutionary martyrs.

Article 51 Citizens have the right to education. To ensure that citizens enjoy this right, the state gradually increases the number of schools of various types and of other cultural and educational institutions and popularizes education.

The state pays special attention to the healthy development of young people and children.

Article 52 Citizens have the freedom to engage in scientific research, literary and artistic creation and other cultural activities. The state encourages and assists the creative endeavours of citizens engaged in science, education, literature, art, journalism, publishing, public health, sports and other cultural work.

Article 53 Women enjoy equal rights with men in all spheres of political, economic, cultural, social and family life. Men and women enjoy equal pay for equal work.

Men and women shall marry of their own free will. The state protects marriage, the family, and the mother and child.

The state advocates and encourages family planning.

Article 54 The state protects the just rights and interests of overseas Chinese and their relatives.

Article 55 Citizens have the right to lodge complaints with organs of state at any level against any person working in an organ of state, enterprise or institution for transgression of law or neglect of duty. Citizens have the right to appeal to organs of state at any level against any infringement of their rights. No one shall suppress such complaints and appeals or retaliate against persons making them.

Article 56 Citizens must support the leadership of the Communist Party of China, support the socialist system, safeguard the unification of the motherland and the unity of all nationalities in our country and abide by the Constitution and the law.

Article 57 Citizens must take care of and protect public property, observe labour discipline, observe public order, respect social ethics and safeguard state secrets.

Article 58 It is the lofty duty of every citizen to defend the motherland and resist aggression.

It is the honourable obligation of citizens to perform military service and to join the militia according to the law.

Article 59 The People's Republic of China grants the right of residence to any foreign national persecuted for supporting a just cause, for taking part in revolutionary movements or for engaging in scientific work.

Chapter Four
The National Flag, the National Emblem and The Capital

Article 60 The national flag of the People's Republic of China has five stars on a field of red.

The national emblem of the People's Republic of China is: Tien An Men in the centre, illuminated by five stars and encircled by ears of grain and a cogwheel.

The capital of the People's Republic of China is Peking.

Hua Kuo-feng

Unite and Strive to Build a Modern, Powerful Socialist Country!

Report on the Work of the Government delivered at the First Session of the Fifth National People's Congress on February 26, 1978. (Excerpts). Hsinhua News Agency, 10 March, 1978.

The Struggle Over the Last Three Years and The General Task for the New Period

Since the Fourth National People's Congress our country has gone through a severe test in sharp and complex struggles between the two classes and between the two lines. Led by the Chinese Communist Party, the people of our country finally smashed the anti-Party "gang of four" of Wang Hung-wen, Chang Chun-chiao, Chiang Ching and Yao Wen-yuan after repeated and intense trials of strength. This tremendous victory marked the successful conclusion of China's first Great Proletarian Cultural Revolution and the beginning of a new period of development in its social-ist revolution and socialist construction.

The 11th National Congress of our Party held last year comprehen-sively summed up the Party's struggle against the "gang of four." It was truly a life-and-death struggle between the proletariat and the bourgeoisie, a decisive and historic battle. The crux of the struggle was whether to uphold Chairman Mao's proletarian revolutionary line or to follow the gang's counter-revolutionary revisionist line, whether to persevere in the dictator-ship of the proletariat or to institute a fascist dictatorship of the bourgeoisie, whether to make China a prosperous, modern and powerful socialist country or to reduce it to its former semi-colonial and semi-feudal status. It was around these focal questions that we waged one soul-stirring struggle after another against the gang. . .

Looking back at this period of our history, we can see that the destiny of our Party and country hinged on the struggle against the "gang of four". This counter-revolutionary clique of conspirators exploited the positions and power they had usurped to collect landlords, rich peasants, counter-revolutionaries and bad elements as well as a small band of careerists, rene-gades, newborn counter-revolutionary elements, gangsters and smash-and-grabbers to make havoc of the Party, army and country. They practised fascist dictatorship and ruthlessly persecuted revolutionary cadres and people. They sabotaged the national economy and disrupted socialist construction in every field. The consequences were extremely grave. As a result of their interference and sabotage between 1974 and 1976 the nation lost about 100 billion yuan in total value of industrial output, 28 million tons of steel, and 40 billion yuan in state revenues, and the whole economy was on the brink of collapse. In some regions and departments where bad characters were in power because of the gang's support, protection and connivance, production came to a standstill in factories, land was parcelled out to peasant households for individual farming, corruption, embezzlement and profiteering became widespread, class enemies went berserk, unreformed landlords, rich peasants, counter-revolutionaries and bad elements attempted to recover lost privileges and seek revenge, and in some cases there was even capitalist restoration. Had this situation been allowed to go on, our country would have changed colour and our people would have suffered grave disasters. The smashing of the "gang of four" averted a major split in the Party and a major retrogression in our country's history, and thus enabled our people to continue their advance along the socialist road charted by Chairman Mao. . .

Fellow Deputies! The overthrow of the "gang of four" is another great turning point in the history of our revolution. The general task facing our people in the new period of development in socialist revolution and socialist construction is firmly to carry out the line of the 11th Party Congress, steadfastly continue the revolution under the dictatorship of the proletariat, deepen the three great revolutionary movements of class struggle, the struggle for production and scientific experiment, and transform China into a great and powerful socialist country with modern agriculture, industry, national defence and science and technology by the end of the century.

Back in 1963, Chairman Mao incisively pointed out, **"In the 105 years from the 1840s to the middle of the 1940s, almost all the imperialist countries of the world, whether large, medium or small, committed aggression against our country and waged war against us. Except for the last war, namely, the War of Resistance Against Japan, which resulted in the surrender of Japanese imperialism owing to internal and external causes, all these wars ended in our defeat and the signing of treaties with humiliating terms. That was due to two factors, first, a corrupt social system and, second, a backward economy and technology. Now our social system has changed and a basic solution has occurred as far as the first factor is concerned. But the solution is still incomplete, because class struggle still exists. There is some change too in regard to the second factor, but it will require several more decades to bring about a complete change. If in the decades to come we don't completely change the situation in which our economy and technology lag far behind those of the imperialist** countries, it will be impossible for us to avoid being pushed around again." And he added, "In planning our work we should start from the possibility of being attacked and do our utmost to change the backward state of our economy and technology in not too long a period of time, otherwise we will make mistakes."

Chairman Mao here summed up the history of imperialist aggression against China and our people's struggle against it over the past century. He regarded the transformation of our economic and technological backwardness as a question of life and death for the nation, bringing into sharp relief the importance and urgency of socialist construction. In studying Chairman Mao's teachings afresh, we can all see more clearly than ever that the socialist modernization of our agriculture, industry, national defence and science and technology is not merely an important economic task, it is, above all, an urgent political task. . .

Speed Up Socialist Economic Construction

In order to make China a modern, powerful socialist country by the end of the century, we must work and fight hard in the political, economic, cultural, military and diplomatic spheres, but in the final analysis what is of decisive importance is the rapid development of our socialist economy. . .

By the end of this century, the output per unit of major agricultural products is expected to reach or surpass advanced world levels and the output of major industrial products to approach, equal or outstrip that of the most developed capitalist countries. In agricultural production, the highest possible degree of mechanization, electrification and irrigation will be achieved. There will be automation in the main industrial processes, a major increase in rapid transport and communications services and a considerable rise in labour productivity. We must apply the results of modern science and technology on a broad scale, make extensive use of new materials and sources of energy, and modernize our major products and the processes of production. Our economic and technical norms must approach, equal or surpass advanced world levels. As our social productive forces become highly developed, our socialist relations of production will be further improved and perfected, the dictatorship of the proletariat in our country consolidated, our national defence strengthened, and our people's material well-being and cultural life substantially enriched. By then, China will have a new look and stand unshakably in the East as a modern, powerful socialist country.

The ten years from 1976 to 1985 are crucial for accomplishing these gigantic tasks. In the summer of 1975, the State Council held a meeting to exchange views on a perspective long-term plan. On the basis of a mass of material furnished by investigation and study, it worked out a draft outline of a ten-year plan for the development of our economy. The outline was discussed and approved by the Political Bureau. The "gang of four" attacked the State Council meeting as "the source of the Right deviationist wind" and labelled the outline a "revisionist document." This was just plain slander and vilification. After the gang's downfall, the State Council revised and supplemented the outline in the light of China's fine political and economic situation and in accordance with the ardent desire of the whole nation to accelerate the four modernizations. The draft outline of the plan is now submitted to you for consideration.

According to the plan, in the space of ten years we are to lay a solid foundation for agriculture, achieve at least 85% mechanization in all major processes of farmwork, see to it that for each member of the rural population there is one *mu*[1] of farmland with guaranteed stable high yields irrespective of drought or waterlogging, and attain a relatively high level in agriculture, forestry, animal husbandry, sideline production and fisheries. The plan calls for the growth of light industry, which should turn out an abundance of first-rate, attractive and reasonably priced goods with a considerable increase in percapita consumption. Construction of an advanced heavy industry is envisaged, with the metallurgical, fuel, power and machine-building industries to be further developed through the adoption of new techniques, with iron and steel, coal, crude oil and electricity in the world's front ranks in terms of output, and with much more developed petrochemical, electronics and other new industries. We will build transport and communications and postal and telecommunications networks big enough to meet growing industrial and agricultural needs, with most of our locomotives electrified or dieselized and with road, inland water and air transport and ocean shipping very much expanded. With the completion of an independent and fairly comprehensive industrial complex and economic system for the whole country, we shall in the main have built up a regional economic system in each of the six major regions, that is, the southwest, the northwest, the central south, the east, the north and northeast China, and turned our interior into a powerful, strategic rear base.

According to the ten-year plan, by 1985, we are to produce 400 billion kilogrammes of grain and 60 million tons of steel. In each of the eight years from 1978 to 1985, the value of agricultural output is to increase by 4 to 5% and of industrial output by over 10%. The increase in our country's output of major industrial products in the eight years will far exceed that in the past 28 years. In these eight years, state revenues and investments budgeted for capital construction will both be equivalent to the total for the past 28 years. As fellow Deputies have reviewed the various economic targets in the ten-year plan, there is no need to list them now. The accomplishment of the ten-year plan will bring about tremendous economic and technological changes and provide the country with a much more solid material base, and, given

[1] One fifteenth of a hectare.(Ed.)

another period of hard work over three more five-year plans, the stage will be set for China to take its place in the front ranks of the world economy. . .

To turn the plan into reality, we must also adopt effective measures and strive to solve a number of problems bearing on our whole economy.

First. Mobilize the Whole Nation and Go in for Agriculture in a Big Way.

Agriculture is the foundation of the national economy. If agriculture does not develop faster, there will be no upswing in our industry and economy as a whole, and even if there is a temporary upswing, a decline will follow, and there will be really serious trouble in the event of major natural calamities. We must have a clear understanding of this. Predominantly agricultural provinces must make an effort to develop agriculture, and pre-dominantly industrial provinces must make still greater efforts. All trades and professions must do their best to support and serve agriculture.

In order to effect an upswing in agriculture, we rely mainly on learning conscientiously from Tachai, practising scientific farming and speeding up mechanization. In line with the principle of **"taking grain as the key link and ensuring an all-round development,"** the state is planning to take the following measures to develop agricultural production:

(1) While attaining a country-wide increase in grain production, focus on the two following tasks. One, run the 12 large commodity grain bases and all our state farms efficiently and enable them to achieve a twofold or threefold increase in marketable grain in a space of eight years. Two, help low-yield, grain-deficient areas to become self-sufficient and achieve a surplus within two or three years.

(2) While ensuring a rise in yields per unit, organize planned reclam-ation of wasteland by the state farms and people's communes so as to obtain a fair increase in cultivated acreage year by year, provided such reclamation does not affect water and soil conservation and the protection of forests, grasslands and aquatic product resources.

(3) In accordance with the principles of specialized planting and rational distribution, build a number of bases for the production of cotton, edible oil, sugar and other cash crops where conditions are suitable, and turn them into the state's main sources of supply for these products.

(4) Strive to develop forestry, animal husbandry, sideline production and fisheries, do a good job of developing the forest regions, plant trees around every house and every village, by roadsides and watersides, build livestock breeding areas, set up fresh-water and marine fishing grounds, and actively promote rural sideline occupations and commune- and brigade-run enterprises. In this way it will be possible considerably to expand the afforested areas and greatly increase the output of animal and aquatic products and increase the proportion of commune and brigade income derived from sideline occupations and enterprises.

(5) Mobilize the masses to forge ahead with farmland capital construction and stress soil improvement and water control. The state must take charge of large-scale water conservancy projects, continue to harness such big rivers as the Yellow River, the Yangtze, the Huai, the Haiho, the Liaoho and the Pearl River, carry out the key projects to relieve drought in northwest, north and southwest China properly, and undertake projects to divert water from the Yangtze to areas north of the Yellow River. In the localities work must be initiated to build medium-sized and small water conservancy works suiting local conditions and to improve low-yield fields on mountain slopes, alkaline land and red soil.

(6) From the top organs to the grass-roots units, set up and perfect a system of agro-scientific research and agro-technical popularization; implement the Eight-Point Charter for Agriculture in an all-round way, with stress on cultivating and popularizing fine strains of seed, improving farming methods, extensively exploring various sources of fertilizer, making a big effort to develop organic fertilizer and making proper use of chemical fertilizer.

(7) In order to hasten the mechanization of agriculture, strive to manufacture more, better and cheaper farm machinery, chemical fertilizer and insecticide that meet specific needs, to a good job of supplying complete sets of farm machinery and of their maintenance, repair and management, and step up the training of farm technicians.

(8) Make an extra effort to build up mountain areas and in particular give attention and assistance to construction in the old revolutionary base areas so as to accelerate their economic progress.

(9) Strengthen the leadership of the poorer production teams and help them to transform themselves economically and catch up with the richer teams as soon as possible.

In order to ensure the implementation of the above measures, the state has planned to make appropriate increases in the proportion of its financial expenditures allocated to investments in agricultural capital construction and to operating expenses and to make corresponding arrangements for materials and equipment.

To increase agricultural production, it is imperative to bring into full play the socialist initiative of our peasant masses. Otherwise, the measures for increasing production will come to naught and socialist agriculture will not grow smoothly. All communes and brigades must deepen education in the Party's basic line, persistently imbue the peasants with socialist ideas and keep on overcoming the spontaneous tendencies towards capitalism. It is necessary to adhere to the principle of running the people's communes democratically, diligently and frugally so as to ensure efficient management. Matters of importance should be decided through discussion at the general meetings of commune members or the conferences of their representatives, and not by a few people. To start farmland capital construction, improve farming methods, draw up plans for planting and work out ways to increase production, it is necessary to solicit opinions from the commune members and give full consideration to their practical experience in such matters. We must proceed from reality and adopt measures suiting local conditions. Coercion, commandism and arbitrary orders should be firmly opposed. Commune and brigade finances should be open to the supervision of the masses through the periodic publication of their accounts. Sponging and taking more than one's share, overdrawing and using funds for purposes other than those originally intended, and extravagance and waste on the part of cadres must be banned. . .

The state farms are agricultural units owned by the whole people. They must play an exemplary role in building a modern, large-scale socialist agriculture. We must sum up experience, fully tap our potentialities and run the existing state farms well so as to provide the state with more agricultural and animal products. Meanwhile, we must actively set up more state farms to give our state-owned agriculture a big fillip.

Second. Speed Up the Development of the Basic Industries and Give Full Scope to the Leading Role of Industry.

As the economy becomes modernized, the leading role of industry, and especially that of the basic industries, becomes more and more prominent. We must **take steel as the key link**, strengthen the basic industries and exert a special effort to step up the development of the power, fuel and raw and semi-finished materials industries and transport and communications. Only thus can we give strong support to agriculture, rapidly expand light industry and substantially strengthen the national defence industries.·

In developing the basic industries, we must endeavour to strengthen our work in geology and in the opening up of new mines so that geological surveying and the mining industry will meet the needs of high-speed economic construction.

In developing the basic industries, we must be good at tapping the potential of the existing enterprises and at renovating and transforming them as well as at integrating this task with the building of new enterprises. In the next eight years, and especially in the next three years, our existing enterprises must be the foundation for the growth of production. We must make full use of existing equipment, make sure that complete sets of equipment are available, introduce technical transformation in a planned way and carry out extensive co-ordination between specialized departments. This will gain us time and speed and will save on investment. Meanwhile, the state plans to build or complete 120 large-scale projects, including ten iron and steel complexes, nine non-ferrous metal complexes, eight coal mines, ten oil and gas fields, 30 power stations, six new trunk railways and five key harbours. The completion of these projects added to the existing industrial foundation will provide China with 14 fairly strong and fairly rationally located industrial bases. This will be decisive in changing the backward state of our basic industries.

In capital construction, we must keep to the principle of concentrating our forces and fighting a battle of annihilation to achieve economy in our investments, high quality in our work and short building cycles, and we must rapidly acquire the capacity to streamline production and get optimum results. With regard to the 120 large-scale projects in the state plan for the next eight years, the whole country, from the top levels to the grass roots, must cooperate closely and select competent leading cadres, fine technical personnel and skilled workers for the concerted battle to accomplish these projects successively with greater, faster, better and more economical results.

It is essential to adhere to the policy of the simultaneous development of large, medium-scale and small enterprises. While it is important to run the large modern enterprises well, every attention must also be given to the development of medium-scale and small enterprises. All provinces, municipalities and autonomous regions must utilize local resources, strive to make a success of medium-scale and small coalfields, small power stations, mines, cement and chemical fertilizer plants, strengthen and improve medium-scale and small iron and steel and non-ferrous metal enterprises, and try to produce more chemical raw materials. All medium-scale and small enterprises should come under the plans, get their raw materials from local sources and work hard to improve production and management techniques. Where they compete with the large enterprises for supplies of raw and semi-finished materials or for fuel or power, the matter must be given overall consideration and properly solved to ensure that the needs of the large enterprises are fully met.

The machine-building industry which has the vital task of equipping all branches of the economy should be organized in accordance with the principle of co-ordination between specialized departments. It should come under a unified plan, do a good job in the standardization, serialization and general utilization of its products, work hard to turn out high-grade machines and equipment and produce more and better sets of large modern precision machinery. The national defence industries should turn their production capacity to good account, diligently carry out research and the trial production and then the outturn of more and better modern conventional and strategic weapons. Serious efforts should be made to implement the policy of integrating military with non-military enterprises and peacetime production with preparedness against war, and fully tap the potential of the machine-building and national defence industries.

Along with the strengthening of the basic industries there should be a vigorous development of light industry. We should explore and open up more sources of raw materials, try to increase the supply of agricultural raw materials, substantially increase the ratio of such petrochemically produced raw materials as chemical fibres and plastics to all raw materials used in light industry, greatly expand the production of textiles, sugar and paper and other light industrial products, and see that the provinces and autonomous regions achieve self-sufficiency in ordinary light industrial products as early as possible. We should continue and expand the production of popular traditional articles, and efficiently arrange the production of articles of daily use, miscellaneous goods, handicraft wares and commodities specially needed by the minority nationalities.

In building our industry we should apply the principle of combining industry and agriculture and town and country. Where conditions permit, the workers and staff and their families should get organized for agricultural and sideline production, as in the Taching Oilfield. We should as far as possible avoid crowding the big cities with new construction units and should build more small and medium-sized towns and cities.

Third. To a Good Job in Commerce and Develop Foreign Trade.

Socialist commerce is a bridge that links industry with agriculture, urban areas with rural areas and production with consumption. It is essential to make a success of commerce, for it promotes the rapid growth of the economy, consolidates the worker-peasant alliance and serves to meet the people's daily needs. Those who work in shops and supply and marketing departments are part of the working class. They are inseparably linked with the general process of production, and since what they do is lofty revolutionary labour they should command the respect of all. The commercial departments should firmly implement the policy of **"develop the economy and ensure supplies,"** give strong support to industrial and agricultural production and wholeheartedly serve the people in meeting their daily needs. We should organize the exchange of industrial goods with agricultural products well, stimulate the interchange of urban and rural products, provide the markets with adequate supplies, appropriately expand commercial networks or centres, increase the variety of goods on the market, and improve the quality of service to customers. We should tighten price and market controls and deal resolute blows to speculation and profiteering.

There should be a big increase in foreign trade. In our export trade, attention should be given both to bulk exports and exports in small quantities. While expanding the export of agricultural and sideline products, we should raise the ratio of industrial and mineral products in our exports. We should build a number of bases for supplying industrial and mineral products and agricultural and sideline products for export. We should earnestly sum up our experience in foreign trade and, in accordance with the principle of equality and mutual benefit, handle our business transactions flexibly and successfully.

Fourth. Encourage Socialist Labour Emulation and Be Active in Technical Innovation and Technical Revolution.

The masses have a vast reservoir of enthusiasm for socialism. Socialist labour emulation is a good and important method of bringing the initiative and creativeness of the people into full play and of achieving greater, faster, better and more economical results in developing the economy. Each and every locality, trade, enterprise, establishment and rural commune and production brigade should fully mobilize the masses and bring about an upsurge in emulating, learning from, catching up with and overtaking the advanced units, and helping the less advanced units.

The main aim of the labour emulation is to increase production and practice economy, that is, to strive to step up production, improve quality, raise labour productivity, economize on materials, cut down costs and increase profits. At present, some enterprises seek to increase production to the neglect of quality of products and quantity of materials consumed, causing much waste. This does not square with the requirement of achieving greater, faster, better and more economical results. Failure to achieve high quality, economize on materials and provide the state with constantly increasing profits will make it impossible for the economy to achieve sustained and high-speed development. All enterprises are required to reach their previous peak production levels in terms of economic and technical norms before the year is out, and those that have already done so should strive to catch up with or surpass domestic and world advanced standards. In the course of labour emulation, attention should be paid to combining work with adequate rest so as to keep up the enthusiasm of the masses. Moreover, all departments and enterprises should break down the boundaries between trades and create more for the state by actively undertaking the multiple utilization of resources and so turning "waste" into wealth. We must resolutely combat the spend-thrift style, which pays no attention to quality and economic accounting, and the prodigal bourgeois style of indulgence in extravagance and waste. We must foster the fine tradition of waging hard struggles and building the country with diligence and thrift.

For our economy to develop at high speed, we must break free from conventions and use advanced techniques as much as possible. The broad masses have inexhaustible creative power and are fully capable of making a great leap forward in science and technology by relying on their own strength. Our workers, peasants and intellectuals should be creative and dauntless; they should dare to think, dare to speak out and dare to act and should unfold a widespread movement for technical innovation and technical revolution in urban and rural areas, coming up with new and better ways to do things and turning their talents to full account. All localities and departments must keep abreast of current developments in technology at home and abroad, work out plans and measures for employing and popularizing new techniques, strive to learn advanced science and technology, domestic and foreign, and must not get stuck in a groove and rest content with old practices. We must increase technical exchanges and fight against the rotten bourgeois style of refusing to share information. Commendations and proper awards should be given to those units that have achieved marked successes in adopting new techniques, developing new technologies and turning out new products as well as to those collectives and individuals who have made inventions.

Fifth. Strengthen Unified Planning and Give Full Play to the Initiative of Both the Central and the Local Authorities.

Planned economy is a basic feature of the socialist economy. We must resolutely put an end to the anarchy resulting from the interference and sabotage of the "gang of four" and bring all economic undertakings into the orbit of planned, proportionate development. In formulating plans, we must follow the mass line, and both the central departments and the localities should do more investigation and study, endeavour to strike an overall balance, make the plans bold as well as sound and allocate manpower, material and money where they are most needed so that the various branches of the economy, develop in co-ordination. A strict system of personal responsibility must be set up at all levels, from the departments under the State Council to the provinces, municipalities and autonomous regions right down to the grass-roots units, so that each leading cadre has his clear-cut responsibilities and nothing is neglected. Fulfilment of the state plan will thus be effectively ensured. We must check up regularly on how the localities, departments and grass-roots units are carrying out their plans. We shall commend those who fulfil their plans satisfactorily where the plan is not fulfilled because of their poor work and bureaucracy. In the case of serious failures necessary disciplinary action will be taken.

The law of value must be consciously applied under the guidance of the unified state plan. We must study in earnest the price parities between industrial and agricultural products and between raw and semi-finished materials, fuel and manufactured goods. To promote production, we must appropriately raise the purchase prices of agricultural products and, as costs are cut down, properly reduce the prices of manufactured goods, especially those produced to support agriculture. We must fully utilize finance, banking and credit in promoting and supervising economic undertakings so as to spur all enterprises to improve management, pay due attention to economic results and accumulate more capital for the state.

Given the strengthening of unified central leadership, it is necessary to develop the initiative of both the central and the local authorities. While the former must have absolute control on major issues, power should devolve on the latter with respect to minor ones. Power is to be centralized where necessary, while active support is to be given to the local authorities in undertaking what should be put in their charge. The principle of transferring the management of certain enterprises to the localities should be adhered to. However, instead of washing their hands of these enterprises, the central departments should enthusiastically assist the local authorities to run them well. Key enterprises and research and designing institutions that have a bearing on the economy as a whole should be put under dual leadership. The central departments in charge should assume the chief responsibility, but the provinces, municipalities and autonomous regions must shoulder some responsibility too. We must conscientiously sum up experience, gradually reform and perfect the management of enterprises and control over planning, materials and finance. Both the central departments and the localities must have the overall interest in mind and work for the strengthening of the unified leadership of the central authorities. While we must put out foot down on the tendency of the central departments to take too much upon themselves and hamper the local authorities' initiative, we must also oppose the tendency of regions or departments to attend only to their own individual interests to the neglect of the unified state plan.

Sixth. Uphold the Principle of "From Each According to His Ability, to Each According to His Work" and Steadily Improve the Livelihood of the People.

Throughout the historical period of socialism, we must uphold the principles of "He who does not work, neither shall he eat" and "from each according to his ability, to each according to his work." In applying them we must firmly put proletarian politics in command, strengthen ideological and political work and teach and encourage everybody to cultivate the communist attitude towards labour and to serve the people wholeheartedly. With regard to distribution, while we should avoid a wide wage spread, we must also oppose equalitarianism and apply the principle of more pay for more work and less pay for less work. The enthusiasm of the masses cannot be aroused if no distinction is made between those who do more work and those who do less, between those who do a good job and those who do a poor one, and between those who work and those who don't. All people's communes and production brigades must seriously apply the system of fixed production quotas and calculation of work-points on the basis of work done and must enforce the principle of equal pay for equal work irrespective of sex. The staff and workers of state enterprises should be paid primarily on a time-rate basis with piecework playing a secondary role, and with additional bonuses. There should be pecuniary allowances for jobs requiring higher labour intensity or performed under worse working conditions. In socialist labour emulation, moral encouragement and material reward must go hand in hand, with emphasis on the former. As regards the reform of the wage system, the relevant departments under the State Council should, together with the local authorities, make conscientious investigation and study, sum up experience, canvass the opinions of the masses and then submit a draft plan based on overalll consideration to the central authorities for approval before it is gradually implemented.

Chairman Mao said, "**We must lay emphasis on the development of production, but consideration must be given to both the development of production and the improvement of the people's livelihood.**" We must carry forward our fine tradition of diligence, thrift, plain living and hard work so as to accumulate more capital for increasing production and promoting construction. At the same time, as production rises, we must gradually improve the livelihood of the people, so that in normal harvest years 90% of the commune members can receive a bigger income every year, and staff members and workers can have their wages increased step by step, provided that the state plan is fulfilled. Great efforts must be made to increase the supply of non-staple foodstuffs for urban consumers. Large and medium-sized cities and those factories and mines which are in a position to do so should build production bases for non-staple foodstuffs and set up well-run mechanized or semi-mechanized pig and poultry farms. We must improve the living conditions of the urban and rural population by systematically supplying the countryside with materials needed for building houses and resolving the problem of providing living quarters for staff members and workers. Vigorous action should be taken to develop collective welfare and urban public utilities so as to facilitate production and provide amenities for the people. We must strive to ensure safety in production and the protection of labour. The elimination of pollution and the protection of the environment are a major issue involving the people's health, an issue to which we must attach great importance. We must draw up regulations to protect the environment and make sure that related problems are satisfactorily solved.

We are not yet acquainted with many of the problems that crop up in economic construction. In particular, in many respects modern production remains an unknown kingdom of necessity to us. In accordance with Chairman Mao's instructions, the leading cadres at all levels must use their brains and assiduously study Marxism-Leninism, economics, production management and science and technology so as to "**become expert in political and economic work on the basis of a higher level of Marxism-Leninism.**" We must study hard and work well, sum up experience, attain a better grasp of the laws governing socialist economic construction, master the art of guiding and organizing modern production, raise the level of economic management and do our economic work in an ever more meticulous, thoroughgoing, practical and scientific way, thus propelling the national economy forward at high speed.

Develop Socialist Science, Education and Culture

In the wake of the new upsurge in economic construction a new upsurge of construction in the cultural sphere will follow. We must raise the scientific and cultural level of the entire Chinese nation to a much higher level so that our working people will master modern techniques of production and scientific knowledge. At the same time, we must build a vast army of working-class intellectuals. Only thus can we successfully fulfil the grand target of building a modern, powerful socialist country.

In the last 28 years, guided by Chairman Mao's revolutionary line, we have achieved much in the spheres of science, education, literature and art, public health, physical culture, the press and publishing. The explosion of the A-bomb and the H-bomb, the launching and retrieval of man-made satellites — all these mark a new level of the development of our country's science and technology. Junior middle school education has become general in practically all cities and towns and primary school education in most villages. Institutions of higher learning and secondary technical schools have trained large numbers of students in professional skills. However, our scientific, educational and cultural work has suffered severely from interference and sabotage by Liu Shaochi and Lin Piao, and most of all by the "gang of four." The gap between our own and the advanced world scientific and technical level which had been narrowing has widened again in recent years. The quality of school education has fallen sharply. In all fields of endeavour there are not enough trained younger men and women ready to take over from older experts. A new liberation has come with the smashing of the "gang of four." The tremendous exuberance of the masses of workers, peasants, soldiers and intellectuals is becoming a mammoth force for storming the citadels of science, revitalizing education and creating a brilliant culture.

Modern science and technology, which are characterized mainly by the use of atomic energy and the development of electronic computers and space science, are experiencing a great revolution leading to the emergence of new industries and spurring the advance of technology by leaps and bounds. To catch up quickly with the dramatic changes in modern science and technology and rapidly transform our backwardness in these fields are important and indispensable steps for the speedy development of our economy and the strengthening of our national defence. This is a matter to which our whole Party, army and nation must give close attention. Scientific research should be comprehensively planned with due attention to both short- and long-range targets and in the light of the needs of our national construction and the trends of modern science and technology. All branches of science and technology should be developed in co-ordination, with special emphasis on focal ones so that there is enough concentration to make a breakthrough. Scientific and technical personnel should be widely mobilized and their efforts organized, with proper division of labour and close co-ordination, to speed up research into urgent scientific and technical problems in economic construction and national defence. They should produce results in advanced scientific and technical research so as to achieve high and steady yields and fine quality at low cost in agriculture, the all-round development of agriculture, forestry, animal husbandry, sideline production and fisheries, and the building of a modern, large-scale socialist agriculture. They should make contributions towards the technical transformation of the industrial departments, towards prospecting for and discovering more mineral resources and, in particular, towards rapidly transforming the weaker links in our economy, that is, fuel, electricity, raw and semi-finished materials industries, and transport and communications, so as to put our industries on an advanced technological basis as early as possible. The prediction of natural calamities and our ability to cope with them should be improved. We must strive to develop new scientific techniques, set up nuclear power stations, launch different kinds of satellites, and step up research into laser theory and its application, attach importance to the research on genetic engineering and above all to research on integrated circuits and electronic computers and their widespread application. We must strive to apply the latest techniques in scientific experiment and set up a number of centres for sophisticated experimentation. Full attention must be paid to theoretical research in the natural sciences, including such basic subjects as modern mathematics, high energy physics and molecular biology. Negligence in this respect will make it impossible for us to master and apply the results of advanced world science and technology and properly solve important problems in our construction, to say nothing of making major discoveries or inventions. . .

In the sphere of philosophy and the social sciences, we should make a study of the past as well as the present state of Chinese and world politics, economics, military affairs and ideology. . .

We must organize forces to map out a national development plan for philosophy and the social sciences and for research into philosophy, economics, politics, military sciences, law, history, education, literary theory, linguistics, ethnology and religion. Comrades working on the ideological and theoretical front must strive to contribute to spreading and developing Marxist philosophy and social sciences.

We must correctly carry out the policy of making education serve proletarian politics and combining it with productive labour, have a correct orientation, ensure the success of the revolution in education and accelerate the training of our students so that they develop in an all-round way, morally, intellectually and physically, and become workers with both socialist consciousness and culture. All professions and trades should attach due weight to education and fully support it. We should run well schools at all levels and of all types, and primarily the key universities and schools. In order to improve the quality of education, it is necessary to take effective measures to train teachers, to compile new textbooks speedily and to utilize modern aids fully. By 1985, in the main eight-year schooling should be made universal in the rural areas and ten-year schooling in the cities. We should fully tap the potential of existing institutions of higher learning, actively expand the student enrolment, rapidly set up new colleges and institutes and endeavour to run the vocational and technical schools and colleges well. We must break free from old rules and conventions and spot, train and foster talents in all fields. Spare-time education should be actively promoted to satisfy the demand for learning on the part of cadres, workers, peasants, soldiers and school graduates who have gone to the countryside. We should set up an appropriate examination system. Spare-time students who have attained college graduate level and have proved themselves qualified by passing an examination should be given the same treatment as college graduates in their employment. Our present college graduates should be enabled to put what they have learnt to good use and further effort should be made to train them and raise their level. In recent years, large numbers of students selected from among workers, peasants, soldiers, and school graduates who had been to the countryside were trained in colleges and universities. They are a new force in our contingent of intellectuals and should be given every care and assistance to grow and mature.

The vital task on the front of literature and art now is conscientiously to implement Chairman Mao's directive on readjusting the Party's policy in this sphere. Our work should be strengthened and the present shortage of all genres of literature and art caused by the sabotage of the "gang of four" should be rapidly overcome. The repertories of the performing arts should be enlarged to enrich the people's cultural life. Literature and art must keep to the orientation of serving the workers, peasants and soldiers. Workers in literature, drama, the film, music, the fine arts, choreography and *chuyi*[2] should be mobilized and encouraged to go to factories, rural areas and army units to experience life at its source and create more. We should give special attention to the film with its huge audience, because its impact is immense. We should redouble our efforts to produce more fine films. There should be variety in the subject matter of our literature and art. Modern revolutionary themes should be dominant, particularly those reflecting the three great revolutionary movements of the socialist period, but attention should also be given to historical and other themes. Revolutionary realism combined with revolutionary romanticism should be encouraged in artistic creation. We should give great emphasis to literary criticism. We should be active in organizing cultural centres, film projection teams and various forms of spare-time cultural activity for the masses. Local operas should be revived and the distinctive literature and art of our different nationalities developed. For half a century and more our great leader Chairman Mao led the Chinese people in great revolutionary struggles that brought epoch-making changes. Our writers and artists should have lofty aspirations and strive to produce fine works of art depicting the glorious deeds and achievements of Chairman Mao, Premier Chou, Chairman Chu Teh of the N.P.C. Standing Committee and other proletarian revolutionaries of the older

[2] Popular forms of ballad singing etc.(Tr.)

generation, and the militant course of the people's revolutionary struggle led by our Party.

In health work, we should continue the policy of putting the stress on the rural areas and run county and commune hospitals well. The rural co-operative medical service should be strengthened and expanded and the professional proficiency of barefoot doctors raised. At the same time, medical and health work in the cities and in factories and mines should also be done well. We should earnestly strengthen the leadership over rural and urban hospitals, consolidate the management system, and raise the quality of medical care and nursing. Attention should be given to the health work for women and children. Doctors and nurses should be well trained. Medical research should be intensified and medical institutions be provided with advanced technical equipment. The policy of emphasizing preventive medicine should be implemented and patriotic sanitation movements aimed at wiping out pests and diseases should be launched. The policy of combining Chinese traditional and Western medicine should be pursued so as to create a new integrated Chinese medicine and pharmacology. We should vigorously promote mass sports to improve the people's physique. We should rapidly develop the ranks of our athletes and strive to scale the world's peaks in sports.

Family planning is a very significant matter. Planned control of population growth is conducive to the planned development of the national economy and to the health of mother and child. It also benefits the people where production, work and study are concerned. We must continue to give it serious attention and strive to lower the annual rate of growth of China's population to less than 1% within three years.

We should make a success of our press and broadcasting work and accelerate the development of television so as to be able to utilize the mass media fully in our propaganda and education. We should improve our publishing work and lose no time in changing the present state of affairs in which books and periodicals are few, the process of printing is long-drawn-out and printing techniques leave much to be desired. Libraries of all types should be promoted so that a network serving the masses and scientific research can be established.

Giving full scope to the abilities of intellectuals is important for speeding up the development of our science, education and other cultural undertakings and building a modern, powerful socialist country. . .

"**Let a hundred flowers blossom, let a hundred schools of thought contend**" is the basic policy for making China's socialist science and culture flourish. Its essence is to adopt a policy of "opening wide" within the ranks of the people while adhering to the six political criteria so as constantly to expand the positions of Marxism in matters of ideology and to promote science and culture. Only by firmly carrying out Chairman Mao's policy of a hundred flowers and a hundred schools can people cultivate the ability to distinguish fragrant flowers from poisonous weeds through comparison and struggle, and thus promote what is correct and overcome what is wrong. Only thus can different styles and trends in art and different viewpoints and schools of thought advance through discussion and mutual stimulation, and only thus can we turn out fine and competent people, register first-rate scientific achievements and produce fine literature and art. Of late, our academic circles have started a spirited discussion on a number of theoretical questions that had been bedevilled by the "gang of four." This is an auspicious sign and should be supported and encouraged. Where there is controversy in academic discussions and literary criticism, we should avoid hasty conclusions. We should seek solutions not through such over-simple measures as administrative orders but through full discussion and practical experience.

   "We shouldn't demand perfection." This is a point of substance to bear in mind while implementing the policy of a hundred flowers and a hundred schools. To demand perfection, to require gold to be one hundred per cent pure and man to be flawless, is a manifestation of metaphysical thinking. The "gang of four" searched everywhere for false charges to level at people and stopped at nothing to throttle socialist science and culture. We must try hard to remove their pernicious influence, warmly support and care for new socialist things and foster their sturdy growth. As long as works of literature and art conform to the six political criteria and pass muster artistically, they should be allowed to appear. After publication or appearance they can be revised and improved in the light of comments and suggestions from the public.

   To accelerate the development of socialist science and culture we must stick to the policy of **"making the past serve the present"** and **"making things foreign serve China."** We must conscientiously study the advanced science and technology of all countries and turn them to our account. We must be critical in assimilating things from our ancient culture and from the culture of foreign countries, taking the essence and discarding the dross and weeding through the old to bring forth the new, in order to promote a socialist culture which is national in its traits and rich in the characteristics of the age.

   The "gang of four" vehemently opposed Chairman Mao's policies of letting a hundred flowers blossom and a hundred schools of thought contend and of making the past serve the present and things foreign serve China. It wildly pushed fascist cultural autocracy and a policy of prohibition. It put into cold storage all the highly rated films made before the Cultural Revolution and progressive films imported from abroad. It prohibited the performance of good historical plays and traditional operas. It banned large numbers of local operas, songs and dances of the nationalities, modern plays and excellent Chinese and foreign music. It stopped the publication of the finest literature, whether Chinese or foreign, disbanded the mass organizations devoted to scientific and cultural advancement and arbitrarily put books under lock and key. And so on and so forth. Cultural poverty and insipidity was the result of the gang's perversion and wrong-doing, and this aroused strong dissatisfaction among the people. We must deepen our criticism of the gang's cultural autocracy and policy of pro-hibitions and deal effectively with such problems as still require attention, in accordance with Chairman Mao's consistent teachings and the Party's policies.

The basic task on the ideological and cultural fronts is to promote what is proletarian and liquidate what is bourgeois. All reactionary theories, whether feudal, capitalist or revisionist, and all that is decadent in the cultural sphere, must be criticized and repudiated and must not be allowed to spread with impunity. Truth always exists by contrast with falsehood and grows in struggle with it, and so it is in the case of fragrant flowers and poisonous weeds. In struggling with things non-Marxist and anti-Marxist, we should not adopt a policy of prohibiting people from coming into contact with the false, the ugly and the hostile, for **"it is a dangerous policy"** and **"it will lead to mental deterioration, one-track minds, and unpreparedness to face the world and meet challenges."** Our purpose in providing the people with selections of needed negative material is to fortify and immunize them. To correctly implement the policies of letting a hundred flowers blossom and a hundred schools of thought contend and of making the past serve the present and things foreign serve China will definitely strengthen the leading role of Marxism-Leninism-Mao Tsetung Thought in the spheres of science and culture. It will certainly not lead to bourgeois liberalization as the reactionaries at home and abroad fondly hope. If anything, it will bring about a flourishing socialist science and culture. . .

Consolidate Our Political Power and Strengthen The Great Unity of the People of All Nationalities

To make China a great modern, powerful socialist country, we must further strengthen the state apparatus of the dictatorship of the proletariat, give full play to popular democracy, enhance the great unity of the people of all nationalities, develop the revolutionary united front and mobilize all positive factors.

The revolutionary committees at various levels are local government organs of the dictatorship of the proletariat. In the last few years these committees were paralysed in many places because of interference and sabotage by the "gang of four," and there were even cases where power was usurped by them and their followers. We must re-elect these committees at the various levels and do a good job in building up our political power in strict accordance with the five requirements for successors in the revolu-tionary cause and with the principle of combining the old, the middle-aged and the young laid down by Chairman Mao. Prior to this session of the National People's Congress, all the provinces, municipalities and autonomous regions had at one time or another convened people's congresses at which outstanding people from the ranks of workers, peasants, revolutionary armymen, revolutionary cadres, and intellectuals, outstanding people who had made genuine, publicly acknowledged contributions, and representatives from all circles were elected to new revolutionary committees. This has had the warm support of the masses. People's congresses will be held in the cities directly under provincial authorities, in the autonomous prefectures and in the counties and communes throughout the country during the year to elect new revolutionary committees. As the organ of state power at the prefectural level is an agency of the provincial authorities, no revolutionary committee will be established at this level. With the exception of those factories, mines or other enterprises where government administration is integrated with management, factories, production brigades, schools and colleges, shops, Party and government organizations and other enterprises and establishments will no longer set up revolutionary committees inasmuch as they do not form a level of government. In lieu of revolutionary committees, a system of division of responsibilities should be adopted with factory directors, production brigade leaders, school principals, college presidents, and managers taking charge under the leadership of Party committees. . .

Under the unified leadership of the Party, revolutionary committees at all levels must attach importance to the role played by the trade unions, the Poor and Lower-Middle Peasants' Associations, the Youth League, Women's Federations and other popular organizations, and through them maintain close ties with the masses and do a good job in every field.

The Chinese People's Liberation Army founded personally by Chairman Mao is the staunch pillar of the dictatorship of the proletariat. Over the past 50 years, this army has performed meritorious services, defeating internal and external enemies, defending our socialist motherland and taking part in the socialist revolution and socialist construction. It deserves to be hailed as a heroic people's army. During the Great Proletarian Cultural Revolution, it again made significant contributions in the "three support's and two military's"[3] and in crushing the three bourgeois headquarters of Liu Shao-chi, Lin Piao and the "gang of four." The People's Liberation Army should continue to implement Chairman Mao's important instructions, **"It is necessary to consolidate the army"** and **"Be ready to fight in a war."** It must grasp the key link of class struggle and run its affairs well, promote its glorious traditions, strengthen its political work and its political and military training, run the military academies well, step

[3] Support industry, support agriculture, and support the broad masses of the Left; and military control and political and military training. (Tr.)

up preparations against war and deepen the mass movements for learning from the model soldier Lei Feng, the "Hard-Boned Sixth Company" and the First Air Force Division. We must work hard to raise to a new height the military and political quality of our army, its preparations against war and the degree of its revolutionization and modernization. We must uphold the system under which our armed forces are a combination of the field armies, the regional forces and the militia; we should continue to build up the militia organizationally, politically and militarily and give full scope to its role in the socialist revolution, socialist construction and the defence of the motherland.

Let the whole nation learn from the Liberation Army and the Liberation Army learn from the whole nation. In order to cement the ties of unity between the army and the people and between the army and the government, not only must the revolutionary committees at all levels seriously attend to the work of supporting the army and giving preferential treatment to the families of the armymen but the People's Liberation Army units must do likewise in supporting the government and cherishing the people. Moreover, they must make proper arrangements for retired, demobilized and disabled armymen and armymen transferred to civilian jobs. In particular, they must be warm in their concern for the political well-being of revolutionary armymen who have made contributions in the long years of revolutionary war and take effective measures to solve any difficulties in their livelihood.

The people's public security organs, the procuratorial organs and people's courts are important instruments of the dictatorship of the proletariat. They must be further consolidated and built up. In accordance with Chairman Mao's teaching on correctly distinguishing and handling the two types of contradictions which are different in nature, we must firmly implement the principles and policies set down by the Central Committee concerning the struggle against the enemy and deal sure, accurate and relentless blows to the handful of class enemies, with the emphasis on accuracy. We must **enforce dictatorship over the reactionary classes and elements and all those who resist socialist transformation and oppose socialist construction**. We must also exercise dictatorship over new bourgeois elements, thieves, swindlers, murderers, arsonists, criminal gangs, smash-and-grabbers and other scoundrels who seriously disrupt public order.

Dictatorship over the enemy and democracy among the people are the two inseparable aspects of the dictatorship of the proletariat. Only when we deal resolute blows to the enemy can we ensure that the people will really become masters of their own affairs. Only when we give full play to democracy among the people can we deal effective blows to the enemy and truly protect the people. Only when we give full scope to democracy can we correctly practice centralism, work out policies and methods consistent with Chairman Mao's revolutionary line and promptly spot and correct shortcomings and mistakes in our work. Only thus can we closely unite the people and fully mobilize everyone's revolutionary initiative. Chairman Mao pointed out, **"Without broad democracy among the people, it is impossible for the dictatorship of the proletariat to be consolidated or for political power to be stable. If unity is to prevail throughout the Party and the nation, we must give full play to democracy and let people speak up."** We must follow Chairman Mao's teachings, listen modestly to the opinions of the masses and treat seriously the letters the people send in and the complaints they make when they call. We will never allow suppression of opinion, much less retaliation against those who make criticisms. Our Constitution lays down in clear terms the rights of the people. The organs of the state at various levels must take effective measures to ensure that the people enjoy and exercise these rights. Violation of these rights will be dealt with strictly and in serious cases will be punished according to law.

It is essential to strengthen the socialist legal system if we are to bring about great order across the land. Our laws protect the people's interests. Basing ourselves on the new Constitution which is to be discussed and adopted at this session, we should draw on our 28 years of experience with the dictatorship of the proletariat, give a ready ear to the opinions of the masses and gradually make and perfect our socialist laws. We should give wide publicity to the significance of cultivating a sense of respect for socialist laws. Cadres should be law-abiding, as should the masses and indeed everyone. We should rely on the masses in enforcing public order and dealing firmly with crimes of different kinds.

China is a unitary state with more than 50 nationalities. Chairman Mao consistently stressed cementing the ties of unity among all nationalities and called on the people of all nationalities to make concerted efforts to build out great socialist motherland. We must thoroughly unmask and criticize the "gang of four" for their counter-revolutionary crime of undermining Chairman Mao's nationality policy and strengthen the unity of all nationalities. We must conduct re-education in this policy, with the emphasis on opposing great-nationality chauvinism while at the same time directing our attention to overcoming and preventing local nationality chauvinism. All nationalities should respect, help and learn from one another. The policy of regional national autonomy must be conscientiously implemented and the right of the minority peoples to equality and autonomy must be guaranteed without fail. We must try very hard to train cadres from minority nationalities and promote the outstanding ones to leading positions. We must run the nationality institutes well and stress the use and development of the spoken and written languages of the minority nationalities. Comrades of the Han nationality who work in a minority nationality area must learn the area's language and respect its customs and ways. As to old and backward customs and habits, it is up to the people of the minority nationalities concerned to reform them step by step according to their own will. The handful of class enemies who try to sow discord among the nationalities and undermine national unity must be fully exposed and resolutely dealt with.

To give sincere and active help to the minority nationalities to develop their economy and culture is a major task in our nationality work, in building up our border regions and in consolidating our national defence. The minority nationalities should foster the revolutionary spirit of hard struggle and self-reliance, and the state should help them in a planned way with funds, materials and personnel to ensure "**the growth of agriculture, animal husbandry and industry from year to year, greater economic prosperity from year to year, and rising living standards of the people from year to year**" in the minority areas.

In accordance with the provisions in the Constitution, we shall continue to implement the policy of freedom of religious belief, which embraces freedom to believe in religion, freedom not to believe, and freedom to propagate atheism. We must expose and strike at the class enemies who carry on counter-revolutionary activities in religious garb.

An important component of Chairman Mao's proletarian revolutionary line is the development of the revolutionary united front which is led by the working class and based on the worker-peasant alliance, and which unites the large numbers of intellectuals and other labouring people, patriotic democratic parties, patriotic personages, our compatriots in and from Taiwan, Hongkong and Macao, and our countrymen residing abroad. The revolutionary united front was one of the magic weapons by which we defeated the enemy in the period of the new-democratic revolution. In the period of socialist revolution, this revolutionary united front continues to be consolidated and expanded and is playing an important role. We must make further efforts to ensure the full implementation of Chairman Mao's principles and policies concerning the united front, uniting with all the forces that can be united and mobilizing all positive factors to serve the socialist cause. . .

Overseas Chinese who have returned from abroad have played a positive role in building the motherland. As before, we must seriously try to carry out the state's policies and pay attention to the political progress, work and well-being of all returned overseas Chinese and the relatives of overseas Chinese and give them proper preferential treatment, so as to bring their enthusiasm for socialism into fuller play. Our countrymen residing abroad and foreign nationals of Chinese descent who return to the homeland to visit their relatives and friends should be provided with the necessary facilities. The concern and preferential treatment extended to the relatives of overseas Chinese will equally be extended to the relatives in China of foreign nationals of Chinese descent.

Taiwan is part of the sacred territory of China. The people in and from Taiwan are our kith and kin. The liberation of Taiwan and the unification of the motherland are the common aspirations of the whole Chinese people, our Taiwan compatriots included. We resolutely oppose anyone scheming to create what is called "two Chinas," "one China, one Taiwan," "one China, two governments" or an "independent Taiwan." We place our hopes on the people of Taiwan and resolutely support their patriotic struggle against imperialism and the Chiang clique. As for the military and administrative personnel of the Kuomintang in and from Taiwan, it has been our consistent policy that "all patriots belong to one big family," "whether they come over early or late." It is our hope that they will clearly see the general trend of events and take the road of patriotism and unification of the motherland. The Chinese People's Liberation Army must take all the preparations necessary for the liberation of Taiwan. We are determined to realize the behest of Chairman Mao and Premier Chou and, together with our Taiwan compatriots, accomplish the sacred task of liberating Taiwan and unifying the motherland.

The International Situation and China's Foreign Policy

The international situation has been developing in a direction favourable to the people of the world in the last three years. . .

The people of Kampuchea, Vietnam and Laos defeated the U.S. aggressors after long years of war and bloodshed. Egypt, the Sudan and Somalia categorically abrogated their treaties with the Soviet Union and expelled the Soviet specialists from their countries. Zaire heroically routed the mercenary troops engaged in the invasion masterminded by the Soviet Union. The people of Africa will no longer tolerate the superpowers' riding rough-shod over them, and have angrily shouted such slogans as "Hands off African affairs!" and "Russia, get out of Africa!" Faced with the superpowers' threats, the second world countries of Western Europe and other regions are making greater efforts towards unity against hegemonism. The unswerving struggles waged by the people of the world have struck crushing blows to the superpowers which, beset with difficulties at home and abroad and threatened by growing crises, find the going tougher than ever. The course of world events has further borne out the correctness of Chairman Mao's theory of the three worlds.

Unreconciled to their reverses, the two hegemonist powers are intensifying their contention for world domination and frantically pushing their policies of aggression and war. At the same time the factors for revolution are growing, so obviously are the factors for war. The danger of a world war is a growing menace to the people of the world. So long as social-imperialism and imperialism exist, war is inevitable. The contention between the two hegemonist powers reaches every corner of the globe, but the cockpit is Europe. They work overtime to preach "detente" and "disarmament," with no other purpose than to fool people and hide their arms expansion and war preparations. A latecomer among imperialist powers, the Soviet Union relies mainly on its military power to carry out expansion; yet it goes about flaunting banners of "socialism" and "support for revolution" to dupe people and sell its wares. It is the most dangerous source of a new world war. Since things differ from one country to another, the people of each country must determine their own fighting tasks in the light of its specific conditions. But so far as the overall world situation is concerned, there is a strategic task common to the people the world over, and that is to consolidate and expand the international united front against hegemonism, oppose the policies of aggression and war pursued by the superpowers, and in particular by Soviet social-imperialism, and strive to put off the outbreak of a new world war. At present, some people in the West follow a policy of appeasement towards the Soviet Union with the fond hope of saving themselves at the expense of others. This can only whet the ambitions of the aggressors and hasten the outbreak of war. Our attitude towards a new world war is: **"First, we are against it; second, we are not afraid of it."** We believe that the outbreak of war can be put off, but then the people of all countries must close ranks, sharpen their vigilance, prepare against all eventualities, oppose appeasement, resolutely struggle against the war machinations of the superpowers and foil their strategic dispositions. In this way, even if the superpowers gamble with war, the people of the world will not be caught in a vulnerable state of unpreparedness. We are revolutionary optimists. The future of the world is bright, though the struggle of the people of the world may be arduous and protracted and the road tortuous. Victory is sure to go to the people of the whole world.

The Chinese Government and people uphold proletarian internationalism and are determined to carry out Chairman Mao's revolutionary line in foreign affairs. Following Chairman Mao's theory of the three worlds, we should strengthen our unity with the proletariat, oppressed people and oppressed nations of the world, with the socialist countries and with the third world countries, unite with all countries subjected to aggression, subversion, interference, control and bullying by the superpowers and form the broadest united front against superpower hegemonism. We are ready to establish and develop relations with all countries on the basis of the Five Principles of mutual respect for sovereignty and territorial integrity, mutual non-aggression, non-interference in each other's internal affairs, equality and mutual benefit, and peaceful coexistence. We support all the oppressed people and nations in their revolutionary struggles.

We have always maintained that all countries, whether big or small, or equal and that the big should not bully the small, the strong not domineer over the weak, the rich not oppress the poor. We oppose the superpowers' interference in the internal affairs of other countries and their attempts to monopolize international affairs. No country should seek hegemony in any region or impose its will on others. Whether a country treats others on an equal footing or seeks hegemony is a major criterion by which to tell whether or not it follows the Five Principles of Peaceful Coexistence and whether it is a genuine or sham socialist country. A socialist country should set an example in treating others as equals. We firmly stand on the side of the people of the world and will never seek hegemony or strive to be a superpower, neither today nor in the future when we have become a modern, powerful socialist country. We shall always follow Chairman Mao's teaching that we should **get rid of great-nation chauvinism resolutely, thoroughly, wholly and completely**.

The people of the world support each other in their just struggles. we are only fulfilling our bounden internationalist duty when we render assistance to other countries. We will continue to apply the Eight Principles on providing aid to other countries as proclaimed by Premier Chou En-lai in 1964. We strictly respect the sovereignty of recipient countries and never attach any political strings, ask for any privileges or interfere in the internal affairs of these countries. In rendering assistance, we aim at helping the recipient countries to be self-reliant and not at making them dependent on the aid-giving country. As a developing country China can provide only a limited amount of aid. Nevertheless, we will try our best to do this job well.

Before liberation quite a few people left China to make a living abroad. They have contributed their share to the progress of the economy and culture of host countries and have forged bonds of deep friendship with the people there. The policy of our government has been consistent; it supports and encourages the overseas Chinese voluntarily to take the citizenship of the countries in which they have made a new home, but it opposes any attempt to compel them to change their citizenship. All those who have voluntarily acquired the citizenship of their country of domicile as well as those who are already citizens automatically forfeit their Chinese citizenship, but their ties of kinship with the Chinese people remain. As for those who decide to keep their Chinese citizenship, we expect them to abide by the law of the country in which they reside, respect the customs and ways of its people and live amicably with them. While it is the duty of the Chinese Government to protect their legitimate rights and interests, it is hoped that safeguards to this effect will be provided by the countries concerned. We would like to see Chinese nationals residing abroad serve as a bridge to foster the friendship between the Chinese people and the people of the countries concerned.

China is a socialist country. It belongs to the third world and has experience and tasks in common with the other third world countries. We resolutely support the developing countries and people of Asia, Africa, Latin America, Oceania and other regions in their struggles against imperialism, colonialism and hegemonism and in their struggles to win and preserve national independence, defend state sovereignty, develop the national economy, protect national resources and establish a new international economic order. We highly appraise the non-aligned movement, which plays a positive role in the struggles against imperialism, colonialism and hegemonism, and give it firm support.

We have consistently worked for greater unity with the other socialist countries and the development of relations of friendship, mutual assistance and co-operation with them on the basis of Marxism-Leninism and proletarian internationalism. We steadfastly support them in their efforts to integrate the universal truth of Marxism-Leninism with the concrete conditions in their own countries and to carry on their revolution and construction independently, and we steadfastly support them in their struggle to oppose foreign aggression and subversion and to safeguard their independence, sovereignty and territorial integrity. We hold that the socialist countries should likewise adhere strictly to the Five Principles of Peaceful Coexistence in their relations with one another. Should differences arise, they should seek a solution through friendly consultation. We pledge our firm support to the Korean people's just struggle for the independent and peaceful reunification of their fatherland.

The Chinese people maintain traditional ties of friendship with the people of Southeast Asian countries. In the last few years China has established diplomatic relations with Malaysia, the Philippines and Thailand, and there has been a new growth in friendly contacts and economic and cultural interchange. It is our desire to restore or establish diplomatic relations with all the other countries in this region. We support the countries of Southeast Asia in their efforts to strengthen regional economic co-operation and bring about the neutralization of Southeast Asia.

The good neighbourly relations we have with Burma, Bangladesh, Sri Lanka, Nepal, Pakistan, Afghanistan and Iran are steadily getting better and better. We support the proposals put forward by the countries concerned to make the Indian Ocean a peace zone, South Asia a nuclear-free zone and Nepal a zone of peace. The Chinese people have always cherished feelings of friendship for the Indian people. The people of both countries wish to see an increase in friendly contacts and an improvement in their relations. There are questions pending between China and India; nevertheless, relations can be further improved provided serious efforts are made on both sides.

The Middle East question has long remained unsettled and the trouble is due to superpower support for Israeli aggression and superpower contention for hegemony in the region. The situation in the Middle East is still in a state of flux. We stand four-square behind the people of the Arab countries and the Palestinian people in their just struggle to recover lost territories and regain national rights. We are against Israeli aggression and against the contention between the Soviet Union and the United States in this part of the world. The Middle East question cannot be solved unless Israel withdraws from the occupied Arab territories and the national rights of the Palestinian people are restored. We are convinced that ultimate victory will go to the people of the Arab countries and the Palestinian people provided they set store by the general interests of their fight against the common enemy, uphold unity and persevere in struggle. China maintains good relations with most of the Arab countries and hopes to establish and develop relations with the remaining ones.

In recent years, there has been great progress in the friendly and co-operative relations between China and the African countries. The people of Africa are waging a hard struggle to win the complete emancipation of the continent. We firmly support the people of Zimbabwe, Namibia and Azania in their just struggle against colonialism and racism and for national independence and liberation. In accordance with their strategic need to compete for global hegemony, the superpowers are stepping up their contention in Africa. We resolutely support the African countries in their struggle against aggression, subversion and intervention by the super-powers, and by Soviet social-imperialism in particular. Africa belongs to the people of Africa. The African people can settle their own problems by themselves so long as they strengthen unity and exclude outside inter-ference.

In recent years there has been a gradual extension of the relations between China and Latin American countries. We are ready to establish and develop relations with more Latin American countries and enhance mutual understanding and friendship. We support the Latin American countries in their struggle to safeguard their independence and sovereignty, to defend their maritime rights, to promote regional economic co-operation and to establish a Latin American nuclear-free zone. We also support the people of Panama in their unrelenting struggle to recover the Panama Canal.

There have been satisfactory developments in the relations between China and the second world countries, with a steady increase in friendly contacts and economic and cultural interchange. We are ready to develop our relations with them in diverse fields. We support them in their struggle against threats, interference, subversion and control by the superpowers, and particularly by Soviet social-imperialism. We support the West Euro-pean countries in their efforts to unite against hegemonism, and we hope to see a united and powerful Europe. We also hope to see closer contacts between the second and third world countries on the basis of the Five Principles of Peaceful Coexistence.

China and Japan are close neighbours separated only by a strip of water, and the friendship between their two peoples goes back to ancient times. Since the normalization of relations, contacts and exchanges have been growing in many fields and a long-term trade agreement was recently signed. It is in the fundamental interests of the people of China and Japan to conclude at an early date a treaty of peace and friendship based on the joint statement of the two governments. We firmly support the Japanese people in their just struggle to recover their four northern islands. The people of China and Japan should live in friendship for countless generations.

China and the United States differ in social system and ideology, and there are fundamental differences between them. Yet the two countries have quite a few points in common on some issues in the present international situation. The Sino-U.S. Shanghai Communique issued in 1972 has brought a new turn in the relations between the two countries. These relations will continue to improve provided the principles laid down in the Communique are seriously carried out. At present, the attitude of the U.S. Government towards the question of Taiwan is the obstacle to the normalization of Sino-U.S. relations. The Chinese people are determined to liberate Taiwan. When and how is entirely China's internal affair, an internal affair which brooks no foreign interference whatsoever. If the relations between the two countries are to be normalized, the United States must sever its so-called diplomatic relations with the Chiang clique, withdraw all its armed forces and military installations from Taiwan and the Taiwan Straits area and abrogate its so-called "mutual defence treaty" with the Chiang clique. This is the unswerving stand of the Chinese Government. The people of China and the United States have always been friendly to each other. We are willing to increase contacts between the people of our two countries and promote mutual understanding and friendship.

China and the Soviet Union were once friendly neighbours. The people of the two countries forged a profound friendship in their long revolutionary struggles. The Sino-Soviet debates on matters of principle were provoked by the Soviet leading clique through its betrayal of Marxism-Leninism. The fact that the relations between the two countries have sunk to such a low point today must be traced to the social-imperialist policy pursued by this clique. The debates on matters of principle must go on. At the same time, we have always held that such debates should not impede the maintenance of normal state relations on the basis of the Five Principles of Peaceful Coexistence. The Soviet leading clique has expressed its desire to improve Sino-Soviet state relations in words, but in actuality it stubbornly clings to its policy of hostility towards China. It has gone to the length of arrogantly demanding that we change Chairman Mao's revolutionary line. this is nothing but a pipe dream. If the Soviet leading clique really desires to improve the state relations between the two countries, it should prove its sincerity by deeds. First of all, in accordance with the understanding reached between the Premiers of the two countries in 1969, it should sign an agreement on maintaining the status quo on the borders, averting armed clashes and disengaging the armed forces of both sides in the disputed border areas, and then enter into negotiations on resolving the boundary question. It should also withdraw its armed forces from the People's Republic of Mongolia and the Sino-Soviet borders, so that the situation there will revert to what it was in the early 1960s. How Sino-Soviet relations will develop is entirely up to the Societ side.

Chairman Mao taught us: **"Dig tunnels deep, store grain everywhere, and never seek hegemony,"** and **"Be prepared against war, be prepared against natural disasters, and do everything for the people."** We must maintain a high level of vigilance and be prepared against a war of aggression launched by the superpowers. **We will not attack unless we are attacked; if we are attacked, we will certainly counterattack.** The heroic People's Liberation Army and the millions of militia, together with the people of the whole country, must go all out to strengthen preparedness against wars and be ready at all times to wipe out any enemy that dares to invade us.

Fellow Deputies!

Reviewing the past and looking forward into the future, we are fortified by our boundless confidence that we will win new and still greater victories in our socialist revolution and socialist construction.

The socialist modernization of our agriculture, industry, national defence and science and technology is a great and unprecedented undertaking and a profound revolution, too. There will be momentous changes in town and country, in the productive forces and the relations of production, in the economic base and the superstructure, and in the political, economic military, cultural and other spheres. In this great struggle, many new situations and new things will emerge and challenge our understanding, and many new contradictions and new problems will arise and challenge us to resolve them. Our thinking and our style and methods of work must be improved and raised to a new level. We must study hard and well, try to grasp new things as they come along, and tackle new problems as they crop up. In this way we shall be able to adapt ourselves to the new situation and tasks.

Our tasks are glorious as well as arduous. Our future is bright. We must free ourselves from superstitions, emancipate our minds, be dauntless and revolutionary in the task of **"transforming China in the spirit of the Foolish Old Man who removed the mountains,"** be firm and unyielding, and work hard to reach our great goal through indomitable struggle.

The great banner of Chairman Mao is the invincible banner of unity in struggle and of continued revolution for the people of all nationalities in our country. For over half a century, this glorious banner has guided us out of darkness to a world of light, taken us past innumerable hidden reefs and enabled us to overcome countless difficulties and win triumph after triumph. On our road of continuing the revolution under the dictatorship of the proletariat, the banner of Chairman Mao will guide us in continuing to vanquish all internal and external class enemies, surmount all kinds of difficulties and hardships, achieve miracles and make a greater contribution to humanity. . .

West European Unity Against "Hegemonism", Commentary of 'People's Daily'.

(Excerpts). Hsinhua News Agency, 21 February 1978.

Europe is now the focus of contention between the two superpowers, the Soviet Union and the United States, for domination of the world. As their rivalry intensifies and Soviet threat is growing in the area, public attention is drawn to the development in the situation of West European unity against hegemonism.

In spite of difficulties and obstacles standing in the way of unity, the West European countries have made continuous advances in their united efforts against the common threat. They are co-operating more effectively with each other in many spheres within the framework of the EEC, which has been enlarged from the original six to the present nine member States and is negotiating to admit new members. Militarily, they are working in concert to co-ordinate their steps. Their united efforts are manifesting themselves in many forms, in co-operation between nations or in the regional framework. The ties between the EEC and the Third World countries are getting closer and closer, politically and economically.

It should be pointed out that all such fruitful results of West European unity against hegemonism have been achieved under very difficult circumstances. In the past year, Western Europe was in the grip of slow economic recovery and slackened growth, compounded by serious unemployment and inflation. Disputes even arose among the nations because of their contradictions and discordant opinions over this or that issue. Despite all this, the West European countries forged ahead in their efforts to harmonize their attitudes against hegemonism. This proves to the hilt that to stand together against hegemonism is the common wish of all countries and people of Western Europe. This public sentiment is now the general trend.

A united, strong Europe serves exactly the interests of the countries and people of Europe. Historically, the major countries of Western Europe were themselves imperialist powers contending for control of Europe. Consequently, there was no question of West European unity against hegemonist Powers then. But things are different today. The Soviet Union and the United States have emerged as two superpowers overwhelming all other countries in the world. The formerly advanced capitalist countries have found themselves in a changed position, subject to bullying and threat by the two superpowers, Soviet social-imperialism in particular. It is precisely in these historical circumstances that the need arises for the West European countries to hand together to safeguard their independence and sovereignty and ensure their national survival.

There is at present a struggle for and against control between the West European countries and the United States, but the greatest danger to the Europeans comes from Soviet social-imperialist aggression and expansion.

In the past few years in particular, the Soviet Union constantly dispatched reinforcements to Europe, renewed arms and equipment, deployed latest-type missiles and staged large-scale military manoeuvres. It developed its military superiority in central Europe numerically and qualitatively, and reinforced its Atlantic and Mediterranean fleets, thus increasing Soviet military threat to the northern and southern flanks of Europe. It conducted unscrupulous aggression and expansion in Africa and the Middle East and set up strategic points there in an effort to encircle Western Europe from its flanks in a roundabout way. Recently it sent large quantities of weapons to Africa and directly dispatched military personnel and foreign mercenaries to interfere with the affairs in the Horn of Africa. This has aroused grave concern among the West European countries. In the face of the avaricious desire and menacing paws of the polar bear, the West European countries have no other choice but to unite to cope with the threat. Union means strength, while disunion means weakness.

A more united and powerful Europe is also in full conformity with the interests of the world people's struggle against hegemonism as a whole. To dominate the world, the Soviet Union must first of all conquer Europe because it is where finance, industrial output, agricultural production, science and technology of the contemporary world are comparatively concentrated and developed. Whoever occupies Europe can make use of its manpower, material and financial resources for a war for conquering the world. Hitler had begun carrying out his frenzied war plan by launching aggression on Europe. Therefore, to foil the superpower plot of aggression and war in Europe is of major significance. At present, the mounting struggle against hegemony waged by the countries and people of the world, the Third World in particular, is dealing a powerful blow to superpower hegemonism. The united struggle against hegemonism waged by the countries and people of Western Europe becomes an important component part of the world people's struggle against hegemonism. Stressing on "speaking with one voice", the West European communities have in recent years begun paying attention to improving their relations with the Third World countries on the basis of mutual respect for sovereignty and equality. They called for "dialogue" in place of confrontation with the Third World countries and backed the African and Arab countries' struggle against hegemonism in a number of issues. This attitude of the West European countries has won the approval of the Third World. They are playing an ever more important role in international affairs.

It should be noted that the path of unity against hegemonism of Western Europe is by no means smooth. The Soviet Union is never willing to see a powerful, united Western Europe which will be a grave obstacle to Soviet contention for hegemony in Europe. The more Western Europe is divided and weak, the more profitable it is to the Soviet Union. Up to now, the Soviet Union is still obstinately refusing to extend formal recognition to the

EEC, and repeatedly sows discord among its members in an attempt to obstruct its growth and expansion. Resorting to every possible means, tough and soft, it steps up military deployment to pose a threat to Western Europe while resorting to the "detente" fraud and spreading deceptive arguments of all sorts to divide the West European countries and dull their vigilance, so as to be able to defeat them one by one. All this is aimed at breaking West European unity so that it can one day extend to Western Europe the "community" it has set up in Eastern Europe, and dominate the whole of Europe.

Under the aggressive Soviet offensive, certain Western Europeans favour appeasement and concession to the Soviet Union to gain momentary ease. This appeasement mentality is particularly obvious on the other side of the Atlantic, which has an inevitable effect on Western Europe. This makes the West Europe situation more dangerous. In short, such mentality is a result of a fear for the Soviet Union. Do not irritate the Soviet Union, some people suggest, otherwise it will launch a third world war which will "destroy Europe". Therefore, they are not active in promoting West European unity against hegemonism, holding that only more economic benefits can "soften the Soviet Union". They believe that Europe could only be saved through the benevolent aspirations of "disarmament" and "detente". Of course, this is sheer illusion. Facts have proved that more economic benefits provided by the West have "strengthened" the Soviet Union and "weakened" the West itself. It is a policy of "bringing about its own destruction". All the fear about irritating the Soviet Union is completely groundless. To any aggressor, the more you are afraid of him, the more vicious he would become, no matter if you irritate him or not. It is especially dangerous to seek "benevolence" from the aggressor.

Trade Agreement between the European Economic Community and the People's Republic of China.

(Complete Text). Official Journal of the European Communities, No. L 123/3, 11 May 1978.

The Council of the European Communities
and
The Government of the People's Republic of China,

DESIRING to develop economic relations and trade between the European Economic Community and the People's Republic of China on the basis of equality and the mutual advantage of the two Contracting Parties and to give a new impetus to their relations,

have decided to conclude this Agreement the terms of which are as follows:

Article 1

The two Contracting Parties will endeavour, within the framework of their respective existing laws and regulations, to promote and intensify trade between them.

To this end they confirm their determination:

(a) to take all appropriate measures to create favourable conditions for trade between them;

(b) to do all they can to improve the structure of their trade in order to diversify it further; and

(c) to examine, each for its own part and in a spirit of goodwill, any suggestions made by the other Party, in particular in the Joint Committee, for the purpose of facilitating trade between them.

Article 2

In their trade relations the two Contracting Parties shall accord each other most-favoured-nation treatment in all matters regarding:

(a) customs duties and charges of all kinds applied to the import, export, re-export or transit of products, including the procedures for the collection of such duties or charges;

(b) regulations, procedures and formalities concerning customs clearance, transit, warehousing and transhipment of products imported or exported;

(c) taxes and other internal charges levied directly or indirectly on products or services imported or exported;

(d) administrative formalities for the issue of import or export licences.

2. Paragraph 1 of this Article shall not apply in the case of:

(a) advantages accorded by either Contracting Party to States which together with it are members of a customs union or free trade area;

(b) advantages accorded by either Contracting Party to neighbouring countries for the purpose of facilitating border trade;

(c) measures which either Contracting Party may take in order to meet its obligations under international commodity agreements.

Article 3

The two Contracting Parties will make every effort to foster the harmonious expansion of their reciprocal trade and to help, each by its own means, to attain a balance in such trade.

Should an obvious imbalance arise, the matter must be examined within the Joint Committee so that measures can be recommended in order to improve the situation.

Article 4

1. The People's Republic of China will give favourable consideration to imports from the European Economic Community. To this end the com-

petent Chinese authorities will ensure that Community exporters have the possibility of participating fully in opportunities for trade with China.

2. The European Economic Community will strive for an increasing liberalization of imports from the People's Republic of China. To this end it will endeavour progressively to introduce measures extending the list of products for which imports from China have been liberalized and to increase the amounts of quotas. The procedure for implementation will be examined within the framework of the Joint Committee.

Article 5

1. The two Contracting Parties shall exchange information on any problems that may arise with regard to their trade and shall open friendly consultations, the the intention of promoting trade, for the purpose of seeking mutually satisfactory solutions to those problems. Each of the two Contracting Parties will ensure that no action is taken before consultations are held.

2. In an exceptional case, however where the situation does not admit any delay, either Contracting Party may take measures, but must endeavour as far as possible to hold friendly consultations before doing so.

3. Each Contracting Party will ensure that, when taking the measures referred to in paragraph 2, the general objectives of this Agreement are not prejudiced.

Article 6

The two Contracting Parties undertake to promote visits by persons, groups and delegations from economic, trade and industrial circles, to facilitate industrial and technical exchanges and contacts connected with trade and to foster the organization of fairs and exhibitions by both sides and the relevant provision of services. As far as possible they must grant each other the facilities concerning the above activities.

Article 7

Trade in goods and the provision of services between the two Contracting Parties shall be effected at market-related prices and rates.

Article 8

The Contracting Parties agree that payments for transactions shall be made, in accordance with their respective existing laws and regulations, in currencies of the Member States of the Community, Renminbi or any convertible currency accepted by the two parties concerned in the transactions.

Article 9

1. An EEC-China Joint Committee for Trade shall be set up, comprising

representatives of the European Economic Community on the one hand and representatives of the People's Republic of China on the other.

2.   The tasks of the Joint Committee shall be as follows:
    — to monitor and examine the functioning of this Agreement,
    — to examine any questions that may arise in the implementation of this Agreement,
    — to examine problems that could hinder the development of trade between the Contracting Parties,
    — to examine means and new opportunities of developing trade between the Contracting Parties and other problems relating to their trade,
    and
    — to make recommendations that may help to attain the objectives of this Agreement.

3.   The Joint Committee shall meet once a year, in Brussels and Peking alternately. Extraordinary meetings may be convened by mutual agreement, at the request of either Contracting Party. The office of chairman of the Joint Committee shall be held by each of the two Contracting Parties in turn. Where both Parties consider it necessary, the Joint Committee may set up working parties to assist it in its work.

Article 10

As far as the European Economic Community is concerned, this Agreement shall apply to the territories in which the Treaty establishing the European Economic Community is applied, and under the conditions laid down in that Treaty.

Article 11

This Agreement shall enter into force on the first day of the month following the date on which the Contracting Parties have notified each other of the completion of the legal procedures necessary for this purpose. It is concluded for a period of five years. The Agreement shall be tacitly renewed from year to year provided that neither Contracting Party notifies the other Party in writing of its denunciation of the Agreement six months before the date of expiry.

However, the Agreement may be amended by mutual consent of the two Contracting Parties in order to take account of new situations.

In witness whereof, the undersigned, being duly authorized thereto, have signed this Agreement.

Done at Brussels on the third day of April in the year one thousand nine hundred and seventy-eight, in two copies in the Danish, Dutch, English, French, German, Italian and Chinese languages, each text being equally authentic.

Draft Treaty on Good-Neighbourhood and Co-operation between the USSR and Japan.

(Complete Text). Izvestia, 23 February, 1978.

The Union of Soviet Socialist Republics and Japan, seeking to promote the consolidation of peace and security in the Far East, in the Pacific basin and throughout the world.

Convinced that peaceful co-operation between both States on the basis of the aims and principles of the United Nations Charter accord with the aspirations of the Soviet and Japanese peoples, the broad interests of international peace.

Guided by the desire fully to overcome the elements of estrangement and distrust in their mutual relations, engendered in the past.

Prompted by solicitude for creating an atmosphere of good-neighbourhood and goodwill between both countries.

Reaffirming thei intention to continue talks on the conclusion of a peace treaty.

Desiring to express in contractual form their resolve to create a firm and long-term foundation for the development of all-round co-operation between them, above all, in the political sphere, and also in the sphere of the economy, science, technology and culture, have agreed as follows:

Article 1

The Union of Soviet Socialist Republics and Japan regard the maintenance of peace, extension and strengthening of relaxation of tension and strengthening of international security as one of the main aims of their policy.

They express a desire to exert efforts for the consolidation of universal peace on the Asian continent, in the Pacific basin and throughout the world.

Article 2

The Union of Soviet Socialist Republics and Japan shall settle their disputes exclusively by peaceful means and undertake in their mutual relations to refrain from the threat of force or its use.

The high contracting parties shall develop and strengthen relations of good-neighbourhood and mutually-advantageous co-operation on the basis of peaceful coexistence.

Article 3

The Union of Soviet Socialist Republics and Japan undertake not to allow the use of their territories for any actions which could prejudice the security of the other party.

Article 4

The high contracting parties undertake to refrain from any actions encouraging any third party to take aggressive actions against either of them.

Article 5

The Union of Soviet Socialist Republics and Japan shall maintain and widen regular contacts and consultations on important international issues concerning the interests of both States through meetings and exchanges of views between their leading statesmen and through diplomatic channels.

Should a situation arise, which, in the opinion of both sides is dangerous for maintaining peace, or if peace is violated, the sides shall immediately contact each other with the aim of exchanging views on the question of what can be done for improving the situation.

Article 6

The Union of Soviet Socialist Republics and Japan declare their determination to continue efforts for ending the arms race, of both nuclear and conventional weapons, and attaining general and complete disarmament under effective international control.

Article 7

Considering trade relations to be an important and necessary element of strengthening bilateral relations and attaching great significance to economic co-operation between the Union of Soviet Socialist Republics and Japan, the parties shall actively promote the growth of such relations, contribute to co-operation, between the appropriate organizations and enterprises of both countries and to concluding appropriate agreements and contracts, including long-term ones.

Article 8

Attaching great significance to scientific and technical co-operation between the Union of Soviet Socialist Republics and Japan, the parties will promote in every way possible an expansion of mutually beneficial and all-round co-operation in these fields on the basis of the treaties and agreements which exist or will be concluded between them.

Article 9

Being interested in the preservation and rational use of biological resources of the world ocean, the Union of Soviet Socialist Republics and Japan shall continue broadening co-operation in this field on the basis of the appropriate agreements and with due regard for the legislation of the parties.

Article 10

The high-contracting parties shall encourage the development of relations between Government institutions and public organizations in the field of science, arts, education, television, radio and sports, contributing to a mutual enrichment of achievements in these fields, to strengthening the feeling of respect and friendliness of the peoples of those countries for each other.

Article 11

The Union of Soviet Socialist Republics and Japan shall strive that the relations and co-operation between them in all the above listed fields and any other fields of mutual interest be built on a durable and long-term basis. With this aim in view, the parties shall establish, where it is deemed advisable, joint commissions or other joint bodies.

Article 12

The Union of Soviet Socialist Republics and Japan do not claim and do not recognize anyone's claims to any special rights or advantages in world affairs, including claims to domination in Asia and in the area of the Far East.

Article 13

This treaty shall not affect the bilateral and multilateral treaties and agreements concluded earlier by the Union of Soviet Socialist Republics and Japan, and is not directed against any third country.

Article 14

This treaty shall be subject to ratification and enter into force on the day of the exchange of instruments of ratification to be done in the city of . . . . . done at .... on .... In two copies, each in the Russian and Japanese languages, both texts being equally authentic.

Soviet Statement on the Resumption of Japanese-Chinese Treaty Negotiations.*

(Complete Text).

* The Statement was presented on 19 June, 1978 by Dmitry Polansky, the Soviet Ambassador to Japan, to Keisuke Arite, the Japanese Foreign Minister.

According to statements by Japanese officials, the government of Japan has decided to resume negotiations with the People's Republic of China on the conclusion of a treaty of peace and friendship.

How she should conduct her relations with China is certainly a matter for Japan herself and this is also true with regard to the treaty. However, it is natural that the Soviet Union cannot remain indifferent when actions are involved which directly affect its interests.

The Soviet side has repeatedly expressed its attitude to the substance of the projected Japanese-Chinese treaty, and this attitude is well known to the Japanese government. It has been pointed out in particular that the Peking leadership wants to sign with Japan a treaty such as would be directed against the Soviet Union. It has also been pointed out that in the event of a treaty being concluded with the provisions directed against the USSR, the Soviet side would be compelled to draw certain conclusions and introduce certain correctives in its policy towards Japan.

Events of the recent period show that the hostility of the Peking leadership towards the Soviet Union, which has been made a matter of national policy, is assuming even more extreme forms. China is intensifying the line of frustrating the process of détente, worsening the danger of war and setting certain states against others.

In such conditions, whether or not Japan wants this to happen, on signing a treaty with China she would objectively be tied to the Peking leadership's line in foreign policy which runs counter to the interests of ensuring peace and security in the Far East.

We should like to express the hope that the government of Japan will show due concern for the future of Soviet-Japanese relations and will take no steps that may raise obstacles to their development and throw away all the positive gains that have been achieved in our relations through persistent efforts on the part of both countries.

Treaty of Peace and Friendship Between the People's Republic of China and Japan.

(Complete Text). Hsinhua News Agency, 12 August, 1978.

The People's Republic of China and Japan,

Recalling with satisfaction that since the Government of the People's Republic of China and the Government of Japan issued a joint statement in Peking on 29th September 1972, the friendly relations between the two Governments and the peoples of the two countries have developed greatly on a new basis.

Confirming that the above-mentioned joint statement constitutes the basis of the relations of peace and friendship between the two countries and that the principles enunciated in the joint statement should be strictly observed.

Confirming that the principles of the Charter of the United Nations should be fully respected.

Hoping to contribute to peace and stability in Asia and in the world.

For the purpose of solidifying and developing the relations of peace and friendship between the two countries.

Have resolved to conclude a treaty of peace and friendship and for that purpose have appointed as their plenipotentiaries:

The People's Republic of China: Huang Hua, Minister of Foreign Affairs.

Japan: Sunao Sonoda, Minister for Foreign Affairs.

Who, having communicated to each other their full powers, found to be in good and due form, have agreed as follows:

Article 1

(1) The contracting parties shall develop durable relations of peace and friendship between the two countries on the basis of the principles of mutual respect for sovereignty and territorial integrity, mutual non-aggression, non-interference in each other's internal affairs, equality and mutual benefit and peaceful coexistence.

(2) In keeping with the foregoing principles and the principles of the United Nations Charter, the contracting parties affirm that in their mutual relations, all disputes shall be settled by peaceful means without resorting to the use or threat of force.

Article 2

The contracting parties declare that neither of them should seek hegemony in the Asia-Pacific region or in any other region and that each is opposed to efforts by any other country or group of countries to establish such hegemony.

Article 3

The contracting parties shall, in a good-neighbourly and friendly spirit and in conformity with the principles of equality and mutual benefit and non-interference in each other's internal affairs, endeavour to further develop economic and cultural relations between the two countries and to promote exchanges between the peoples of the two countries.

Article 4

The present treaty shall not affect the position of either contracting party regarding its relations with third countries.

Article 5

(1) The present treaty shall be ratified and shall enter into force on the date of the exchange of instruments of ratification which shall take place at Tokyo. The present treaty shall remain in force for 10 years and thereafter shall continue to be in force until terminated in accordance with the provisions of Paragraph 2 of this article.

(2) Either contracting party may, by giving one year's written notice to the other contracting party, terminate the present treaty at the end of the initial 10-year period or at any time thereafter.

In witness whereof the respective plenipotentiaries have signed the present treaty and have affixed thereto their seals.

Done in duplicate in the Chinese and Japanese languages, both texts being equally authentic, at Peking, this 12th day of August 1978.

The People of China and Japan Will Remain Friends for All Generations to Come, Editorial, People's Daily.

Editorial article published by People's Daily on 14 August, 1978.
(Complete Text).

Entrusted by Japan's Prime Minister Takeo Fukuda and the Japanese Government, Foreign Minister Sunao Sonoda came to Peking for talks on the conclusion of the Sino-Japanese Peace and Friendship Treaty. Through joint efforts of China and Japan, the two parties reached agreement and the signing ceremony was held in Peking on 12th August. Chairman Hua Kuo-feng and Vice-Premier Teng Hsiao-ping were present. Chinese Foreign Minister Huang Hua and Japanese Foreign Minister Sunao Sonoda signed the treaty for their respective countries. This is another great event in the history of relations between the two countries, following the normalization of diplomatic ties. The signing of the treaty conforms with the common aspirations of the Chinese and Japanese peoples for peaceful and friendly coexistence for all generations to come, and also in the fundamental interests of these two peoples and all other peoples in the Asia-Pacific region. There is no doubt that it will hold great practical significance and far-reaching historical importance for further strengthening and developing the relations of peace, friendship and co-operation between the two countries and for preserving peace and security in the Asia-Pacific region. The Chinese people greet it with enthusiasm.

To conclude a Sino-Japanese Peace and Friendship Treaty was an important stipulation of the Sino-Japanese Joint Statement. Former Japanese Prime Minister Kakuei Tanaka and former Japanese Foreign Minister Masayoshi Ohira visited China in September 1972 and signed the Sino-Japanese Joint Statement with the Chinese Government bringing about the normalization of relations between the two countries and writing a new page in the history of their relations. The Sino-Japanese Joint Statement is a historical document of far-reaching significance for the relations between the two countries; it is also the basis for developing friendly and good-neighbour relations between them. In accordance with the Joint Statement, the Chinese and Japanese governments in subsequent years signed agreements on trade, aviation, navigation and fisheries and this year signed a long-term trade agreement. Since the two governments started talks on the peace and friendship treaty in accordance with the Joint Statement, the people of Japan and friendly Japanese personages inside and outside the Government have made great efforts to promote its early conclusion. On their part, the Government and the people of China have always taken a positive attitude and done their best to promote its early conclusion. This common wish of the Chinese and Japanese peoples has now come true. All the fundamental principles laid down in the Sino-Japanese Joint Statement are reaffirmed in the treaty. The Sino-Japanese Peace and Friendship Treaty is a political summation of relations between the two countries up till now, and a new starting point for the development of friendly, good-neighbour relations between the two countries.

The Chinese Government has always maintained that relations with all countries should be established and developed on the basis of the five principles of peaceful coexistence. Despite the difference in social system, China and Japan can and should establish peaceful and friendly ties on the basis of the five principles — mutual respect for sovereignty and territorial integrity, mutual non-aggression, non-interference in each other's internal affairs, equality and mutual benefit, and peaceful coexistence. The treaty stipulates that China and Japan should establish "durable relations of peace and friendship" and that "in their mutual relations, all disputes shall be settled by peaceful means without resorting to the use or threat of force". The establishment and development of durable relations of peace and co-operation between the two countries, with a combined population of nearly 1,000 million, will be a powerful, positive factor for the maintenance of peace, security, stability and prosperity in the Asia-Pacific region.

At present, hegemonism is engaged in evil-doing all over the world, carrying on aggression, interference, expansion and subversion everywhere. This is the harsh reality, an objective fact of the current world situation. Wherever hegemonism extends its sinister hand, peace and security are menaced and tranquillity is disturbed. Therefore, opposition to hegemonism is a major task in the work of defending peace and an important item in the Sino-Japanese Peace and Friendship Treaty.

The government and the people of China, following the teaching of the great leader and teacher Chairman Mao on "never seeking hegemony", have repeatedly declared that China will never seek hegemony. China does not seek hegemony now and will definitely not seek it in the future even when its economy is more developed and the four modernizations are achieved. We are very happy to note that the principle of opposing hegemonism, which is in accord with the historical tide, is expressed in the Sino-Japanese Peace and Friendship Treaty. The treaty stipulates: "The contracting parties declare that neither of them should seek hegemony in the Asia-Pacific region or in any other region and that each is opposed to efforts by any other country or group of countries to establish such hege-mony." The commitment of China and Japan not to seek hegemony through explicitly writing an "anti-hegemony" clause into the Sino-Japanese Peace and Friendship Treaty is an innovation in international treaties. It conforms to the aspirations of the Chinese and Japanese peoples and all other peace-loving peoples of the world and is sure to have a far-reaching impact in international affairs.

Now, the people of China and Japan are happy at the signing of the Sino-Japanese Peace and Friendship Treaty. The people of Asian and Pacific countries are happy too. And so are all peace-loving countries and people throughout the world. Only Soviet social-imperialism is not happy. Ever since Sino-Japanese treaty negotiations began, the Soviet Union has taken an attitude of ludicrous hostility. Recently, it has put out repeated statements and speeches shamelessly attacking and slandering China's foreign policy, while using pressure of all sorts, threats and blackmail against Japan. The development of friendly relations between China and Japan and the signing of the treaty seem to become a thorn in the flesh for the Soviet Union. It flies into a rage at the very word "anti-hegemony", fully revealing its sordid features. But the historical tide of Sino-Japanese friendship is not to be stemmed by the Soviet Union. The signing of the Sino-Japanese Peace and Friendship Treaty proclaims the ignominious bankruptcy of the Soviet social-imperialist plot to interfere and sabotage.

China and Japan are neighbours, joined by a strip of water. Friendly contacts between the two peoples go far back into the past. Wars between China and Japan during half a century from the end of the 19th century caused the Chinese people major hardships. The Japanese people, too, suffered much. But in the two thousand years' history of contacts between the two countries, that was, after all, only a brief interval. The Chinese people's great leader Chairman Mao Tsetung and beloved Premier Chou En-lai held great hopes for Sino-Japanese friendship and make painstaking efforts for its development. The signing of the peace and friendship treaty marks a new stage in the friendly relations between the two countries and will open up broader prospects for furthering and promoting their friend-ship and co-operation. The Chinese nation and the Japanese nation are both great nations. The people of the two countries are both industrious and courageous. We hope and believe that on the way forward the people of China and Japan will be able to join hands still better and through repeated efforts overcome all interference and obstruction and remain friends for all generations to come.

Memorandum of the Government of the Democratic People's Republic of Korea, Pyongyang, 1 February, 1978

(Complete Text).

The reunification of Korea is unanimous desire and aspiration of the entire Korean people and the peaceloving people the world over.

Today, however, the domestic and foreign splittists have become more undisguised in their "two Koreas" plot to keep Korea split for ever, going against the demand of the times.

Considering that it is necessary for preventing the danger of permanent division of the country and the nation and bringing earlier the reunification to expose in all nakedness before the world the "two Koreas" plot of the domestic and foreign splittists, the Government of the Democratic People's Republic of Korea publishes this memorandum.

Creation of "two Koreas" is the basic principle of US policy towards Korea

Divide and rule — this is the habitual tactics of the imperialists. The United States applies this ruling method in Korea, as it does in every part of the world. Having occupied south Korea in 1945, the United States converted it into its colony and rigged up the south Korean puppet régime by abusing the name of the United Nations. The United States dreaming of world domination could not be content with the occupation of south Korea alone. It was for this reason that it started the Korean war in 1950. But, it sustained a shameful defeat in this war. Far from drawing a lesson from this, the US ruling circles instigated the south Korean authorities to cry for the "unification by prevailing over communism" while persistently intensifying the policies of aggression and war in Korea after the war.

The wild ambition for "unification by prevailing over communism" to dominate the whole of Korea by force of arms came a cropper.

In face of the ever growing might of the Democratic People's Republic of Korea and the mounting revolutionary struggle of the Asian people, the United States found itself further on the defensive. Thus, voices began to become louder in the United States calling for the "reshaping" of the US Asian policy and the perpetuation of the split of Korea. The "report on the study of the Asian policy", ("Conlon report") submitted to the US Senate Foreign Relations Committee in 1959 claimed that "there is no proper way for the unification of Korea . . . and the governments of two Koreas should continue to exist till the foreseeable future". Following this, the *Washington Post* said that ". . . there can be no unification of Korea. Divided Korea will be far better than a unified communist Korea". (Washington, October 31, 1959, "UPI"; Washington, December 22, 1960, "Tongyang").

In particular, following the announcement of the "Nixon doctrine" the US ruling circles entered the stage of openly pushing ahead with the "two Koreas" plot in real earnest early in the 1970's. In his article "US Asian policy" reflecting the "Nixon doctrine", Scalapino, the then US Asian policy maker, wrote that the United States should "recognize each of split Korea as an independent and sovereign state and make both of them observe the principles of peaceful co-existence and non-aggression against each other".

When the North-South Joint Statement was made public and north-south dialogue started in Korea in 1972 the United States used this as the best means of creating "two Koreas" and zealously encouraged the south Korean authorities to take the road of split, not reunification. The south Korean authorities immediately put into practice the "two Koreas" plot stepped up by the US behind the curtain of the dialogue.

On July 7, 1972, Pak Jung Hi stated at a "cabinet meeting" that "it took 300 years for Silla to unify the country" and that "the people should cool down excessive optimism, hasty enjoyment and excitement. . . and strive to build up national strength." And Li Hu Rak who was Co-chairman of the Seoul side to the North-South Co-ordination Commission, said at the very place where the North-South Joint Statement was made public that "north-south relations have now gone over from confrontation without dialogue to confrontation with dialogue," inciting antagonism and confrontation between the north and the south. The south Korean authorities turned down all the reasonable and realistic proposals advanced by our side in the north-south dialogue and finally went the length of making public the socalled "special statement" in June 1973, thus openly announcing to the world the "policy" of freezing and perpetuating the division of the country. The assertion of Pak Jung Hi in the "special statement" was that the north and south of Korea, being split as they are, should enter the United Nations separately. The south Korean authorities described this treacherous assertion as one "helpful" to "detente" and "international cooperation" but, it was actually aimed at splitting our nation into two for ever and keeping south Korea indefinitely as a colony of the imperialists.

The US and Japanese authorities did not bother to conceal the fact that this treacherous act of Pak Jung Hi was instigated by them. On July 20, 1973, former US Secretary of State Rogers, during his south Korean trip, said that he actively supported the simultaneous entry of the north and south of Korea into the United Nations and that the United States would "make every possible diplomatic effort" for it. And Misuno, the then Permanent Undersecretary of Foreign Affairs of Japan, stated: "Frankly speaking, Pak was persuaded by the Japanese Foreign Ministry to make public the June 23, statement. Fortunately, the south Korean government complied with it and the statement came into being." (Seoul, July 20, 1973, "Tongyang"; Japanese Journal *Gunji Hyoron*, No. 4, 1976). The "two Koreas" policy of the Nixon administration was taken over by the Ford administration. Former US Secretary of State Kissinger in an "interpellation" at an upper midwest meeting in Minneapolis on July 15, 1975, said his candid opinion was that the Korean question would not find an internal solution in the foreseeable future.

By perpetuating the division of Korea, the United States intended to keep south Korea as a colony and military base indefinitely and realise its domination of Asia and the world with south Korea as a stronghold. The "two Koreas" plot of the preceding US authorities is carried on by the present US authorities. At the present stage the splittists try to create an international climate for rigging up "two Koreas" through the "cross recognition" of the north and south of Korea and, furthermore, legalize the division of Korea through the United Nations. This is the strategy of the splittists to create "two Koreas".

"Cross recognition" argument for creating climate for permanent split

Today the domestic and foreign splittists claim that an "international climate" should be created for making "two Koreas." It was for this purpose that they conceived an argument about the "cross recognition" of the north and south of Korea. "Cross recognition" is meant to create "two Koreas" through the "alternate recognition" of the north and south of Korea by socialist and capitalist countries. This was an "invention" made by the Ford administration to perpetuate division.

A "high-ranking official" of the United States who accompanied Ford during his Far Eastern tour in November, 1974, said that the United States was ready to negotiate with north Korea if the socialist countries expressed "their readiness to recognize south Korea as a state and have negotiations with it" (Japanese Yomiuri Shimbun, November 22, 1974). Kissinger who had long hatched the plot for "cross recognition of the north and south of Korea," said in his speech at the 30th Session of the UN General Assembly on September 22, 1975 that if "north Korea and her allies" "improve relations" with south Korea, the United States "is ready to take similar action." In his "new Pacific doctrine" made public in Honolulu on December 7, 1975, Ford, talking about a "constructive arrangement" for the solution of the Korean question, revealed the intention of the United States to make countries surrounding Korea recognize the "existence" of the south Korean "régime" through "negotiations" and realise "cross recognition" in this course.

This "cross recognition" argument was more loudly vociferated by the Japanese authorities. Asked by an opposition party member as to "how he thought of the idea of simultaneous recognition of the north and south of Korea by four big powers. . .," Miyazawa, former Japanese Foreign Minister, said at the Foreign Affairs Committee of the House of Councillors on December 24, 1974 that "if an agreement is reached among the countries concerned, our country will also approve it" and that "it will result in giving up the reunification of Korea. . ., but it will be a step forward from the present state."

At that time "Asahi Shimbun" said that the statement of Miyazawa on "the method of cross recognition of the north and south of Korea, which was brought forward "with Ford's Far Eastern trip as an occasion," subsequently confirmed by Kissinger and strongly insisted on by south Korea, clearly expressed the stand of the Japanese government. In March 1977 Hatoyama, former Foreign Minister of the Fukuda government, following suit of his predecessors, stated that the concrete way of co-existence of the north and south is to make them recognize each other, "cross recognition of the north and south." (Jiji, March 11, 1977, Tokyo). The present south Korean authorities are frantically scheming to realise the "cross recognition" plot of the United States and Japan.

Saying that it is their "policy to establish relations with East European communist states which have differing systems and ideals", they blared that they "approve the cross recognition of north and south of Korea by the western side and communist bloc".

Those who obstinately opposed the national liberation struggle and national self-determination of the oppressed peoples, acting as a servant of the imperialists, have gone so far as to disguise themselves as a "friend" of the countries of the new-emerging forces in order to make their way into these countries. In an attempt to justify their argument, the advocates of "cross recognition" claim that an "international mediation" by big powers is a "reasonable way" to "guarantee" peace in Korea and settle the question of Korea's reunification.

This is an entirely illogical assertion.

The question of Korea's reunification is an internal affair of the Korean people, which allows no third party's intervention or interference. Tension persists in Korea and her reunification has not been achieved up to this day not because of the absence of "international mediation" but because of the interference of outside forces in the internal affairs of our country and their splitting manoeuvres. The Korean question must not be made a plaything of outside forces or used by anyone as a lever in the political bargaining. Talking about "international mediation" on the question of Korea's reunification is contrary to the will of our people to solve the question of reunification independently, the North-South Joint Statement whose keynote is the three principles — independence, peaceful reunification and great national unity and the UN resolution which welcomed and supported it.

After all, this is intended to justify the interference of outside forces in our country and their splitting policy. The advocates of the "cross recognition" even claim that the countries which have state relations only with the Democratic People's Republic of Korea should establish "diplomatic relations" with south Korea, alleging that as the south Korean authorities are in "Power", they should not be ignored.

As for the present "régime" of south Korea, it is not an independent government with which the independent states should have relations. The south Korean 'régime" is a tool for executing the colonial policy of the United States. This "régime" represents none of the Korean people.

Anyone who takes the stand of respecting the interests of the Korean people and desiring peace in Korea and her peaceful reunification should not discuss the question of recognizing the present "régime" of south Korea, but reject its splitting machinations, support and encourage the just struggle of the south Korean people for the democratization of society and national reunification and help establish a democratic government in south Korea.

"UN Membership" argument for justifying division

The splittists within and without including those of the United States regard the UN as a favourable theatre for freezing the division of Korea and creating "two Koreas". The splittists try to fabricate "two Koreas" through the UN. This is designed to justify the division of Korea by applying in divided Korea the general practice that today all countries admitted to the UN have their existence and position internationally recognized as independent states. This is why the splittists have persistently tried to realize "simultaneous entry into the UN" by the north and south of Korea and "separate admission of south Korea to the UN". The methods employed for perpetuating division through the UN were, without exception, aimed at keeping Korea divided indefinitely, not at realising the reunification of Korea. Their splitting manoeuvres, however, met fiasco each time.

Nevertheless, the splittists are now hatching all kinds of schemes to realize at any cost the "simultaneous entry into the UN" by the north and south of Korea or "separate admission of south Korea to the UN".

Pak Jung Hi, with the active backing of his masters, is going around, eagerly begging everyone not to obstinately oppose or obstruct south Korea's admission to the UN. South Korean "foreign minister" Pak Dong Jin said: "Our policy is to enter the UN at any rate whether it may be separate or simultaneous admission of the north and south." The splittists are describing the admission of south Korea to the UN as a "realistic method" for Korea's reunification.

This, however, is nothing but a sophistry to veil their splitting machination. Their real aim is to see the Democratic People's Republic of Korea compelled to enter the UN with the admission of south Korea to it. In regard to this a Japanese paper exposed that the admission of south Korea to the UN was intended to produce "an effect on the simultaneous entry of north and south Korea into the UN". It is ridiculous indeed that a "régime" which is not entitled to enter the UN, isolated and rejected within and without, makes much ado about the admission to the UN. The south Korean authorities charged the United Nations with "inability" and "weakness" when it took a favourable measure for Korea's reunification. But they clamour about the "advantage" of the admission to the UN when they want to use it for their splitting machination. Entirely unjustifiable is the plot of the splittists to create "two Koreas" through the UN. If south Korea is "admitted to the UN" or the north and south of Korea enter the UN being separated from each other, Korea, a single national state will be recognized internationally as two states and Korea's division be fixed permanently. As a result the eagerness of the Korean people for reunification will be realized, division will continue indefinitely, the situation will not be stabilized in Korea and the tension and the danger of war will constantly persist there.

The Government of the Democratic People's Republic of Korea has clarified many a time its consistent stand that our country should not enter the UN before its reunification and should be admitted to it after the reunification or at least as a single state under the name of the Confederal Republic of Koryo after the institution of confederation. The just stand of the Government of Democratic People's Republic of Korea fully reflects the unanimous desire of the entire Korean people to prevent the permanent division of the country and the nation and realize the reunification and enjoys the unequivocal support of the world peaceloving people.

"Equilibrium of strength theory" for backing division by force of arms

The imperialists who seek domination and subjugation have always resorted to the policy of "strength". The "equilibrium of strength theory" loudly advertised by the splittists in Korea is an offspring of their policy of aggression. In the "equilibrium of strength" the United States seeks to maintain its domination over south Korea and backs the permanent division of Korea with "strength".

Rumsfeld, former US Defence Secretary, in his "defence report of fiscal 1977" presented to Congress on January 27, 1976 said that "our greatest concern in Northeast Asia is the power balance on the Korean peninsula" and told a "joint press interview" on May 27 of the same year that the US would do its best to help south Korea maintain the power balance with north Korea in the military aspect.

"Testifying" at a subcommittee of the House Appropriations Committee on the "foreign aid bill for fiscal 1976" on November 15, 1975

Kissinger stated: "there is no other way of protecting the interests of the United States in south Korea but to strengthen the defence capacity of south Korea". (south Korean "Radio Munhwa", November 16, 1975)

It is none other than the Japanese and south Korean authorities that are dancing to the tune of the "equilibrium of strength theory" of the US. At a session of the House of Representatives on September 16, 1975, Miki, Ex-prime Minister of Japan, said: "for Japan . . . the immediate task is to maintain the present equilibrium between north and south Korea and prevent a sudden change. For this the continued presence of the US troops is needed". And Japanese Prime Minister Fukuda, at an "exclusive press interview" on December 3, 1976 said that "the reduction or withdrawal of the US troops" occupying south Korea might "result in shattering the balance and security on Korean peninsula" and "furthermore undermining the security of Japan and Asia." When working our the "Japan-US Joint Statement" in March 1977, he persisted that the word, "reduction" not "withdrawal," should be used in connection with the US troops pullout from south Korea (Jiji, March 22, 1977, ,Washington).

On January 26, 1976 Pak Jung Hi ranted: "there is no other bright idea but building up our own strength. Our immediate task is not unification." In March 1977 he told the Japanese ambassador to south Korea that "a hasty withdrawal of the US troops is not desirable" and begged Japan to strive to prevent it. (south Korean "Radio Chungang," January 26, 1976; south Korean "Radio Munhwa" March 17, 1977). The splittists within and without are now steadily reinforcing the armed forces in south Korea in accordance with the "equilibrium of strength theory".

The United States has already hurled 6,847,300,000 dollars into south Korea in military "aid". Now it schemes to further increase the military "aid" under the pretext of "compensatory measure" to offset the "withdrawal" of its ground forces. South Korean Radio Munhwa on July 20, 1977 reported the US defence study report disclosed that 8,000 million dollars worth of weapons would be turned over to south Korea in four to five years as a "compensatory measure" to offset the "phaseout of the US ground forces. On July 22, 1977, the "US Eighth Army Radio" reported the same news quoting a "Pentagon source." Now the United States is further increasing the naval and air forces in south Korea, shipping in large quantities of modern weapons of destruction and continues bringing ammunition from different military bases in Okinawa and Japan and the Pacific region.

Not without reason did Kraff of the Brookings Institute in the United States, disclosed the scheme to reinforce the armed forces under the cloak of the "withdrawal" of the US ground forces.

"Testifying" on the "withdrawal" of the US ground forces at the "US-Japan policy symposium" in Tokyo, Japan last year, he stated there was prevailing argument in the United States of late that the US troops occupying south Korea are rather being reinforced than being withdrawn.

On the instructions of the United States to promote "cooperation" within the framework of the "US-Japan-south Korea triangular military system," the Japanese ruling circles are seeking to hold a main position in the "Power balance" on the Korean peninsula. To this end, they are working to put fresh muscles into the "Japan-south Korea military cooperation system" through the "reinforcement" and "redeployment" of the Japanese Self-Defence Forces, while increasing support to the nursing of the south Korean key industries.

Under the slogan of "allout security," the south Korean authorities are actively speeding up the "modernization" of the south Korean puppet army and further strengthening the military fascist system, claiming that the "most urgent task is to build up strength." In an attempt to check the US troops pullout, they also committed a filthy international bribery and even mumbled that the situation is far more strained in Korea. All the facts indicate that the splittists' drive for the reinforcement of armed forces intended to perpetuate the division of Korea by "strength" will eventually lead to another war in Korea. The "two Koreas" plot of the advocates for the "equilibrium of strength theory" finds clear manifestation also in their call for "north south co-existence" and "non-aggression treaty."

On July 10, 1972 Tanaka, Ex-Prime Minister of Japan, at the "first cabinet meeting" characterized the then international situation as "an era of thaw" and said that Japan should pursue a "multilateral diplomacy suited to the thaw between the east and the west" and she "cannot but recognize that there exist two Koreas is our desirable diplomatic goal." On January 28, 1975, Ex-Prime Minister of Japan Miki also said that he "hoped for the peaceful co-existence of the north and the south of Korea" (Jiji January 28, 1975, Tokyo) Pak Jung Hi in "new year press conference" on January 18, 1974, said that "the north and south should conclude a non-aggression treaty. . . and co-exist peacefully" and in his "interview" with a reporter of the Japanese paper "Sankei Shimbun" on May 30, 1976, stated that "there is no other way but north-south peaceful co-existence for creating conditions for unification. (Hapdong, January 18, 1974, Seoul; south Korean "Kyonghyang Sinmun", June 1, 1976)

The Japanese and south Korean authorities claim that the "co-existence" of the north and the south and conclusion of a "non-aggression treaty" is a "realistic way" for "preserving peace" and the "prerequisite to reunification." But this is nothing but a sophism for justifying their policy of permanent split. The Japanese journal *Ushio* laid open long ago the real picture of the "two Koreas" plot of the splittists within and without when it said that it was originally a "drama in which the Pak Jung Hi régime is dancing in accordance with a US script with the United States as the stage director and Japan as the producer." None of the "theories" brought forward by the splittists within and without and the methods used by them can be justified and they are designed to perpetuate the division of Korea and create "two Koreas."

Korea must be reunified into one

The "two Koreas" plot of the splittists within and without is wholly contradictory to the will and purpose of our people and the world peace-loving people who unanimously desire the reunification of Korea. The Government of the Democratic People's Republic of Korea and the entire Korean people sternly denounce the "two Koreas" plot of the splittists to permanently split the country and the nation into two as an intolerable insult to the Korean people and wanton violation of the dignity and sovereignty of the nation.

There is no reason or ground for one Korea to remain divided into "two Koreas" permanently. The Korean people have been a homogeneous nation from old times and a resourceful people who have inherited one language and the same culture and custom in one Country and one soil through a long history spanning 5,000 years. It is unthinkable that Korea which remained one organism through a long history of thousands of years should be divided into "two Koreas" in our era, the era of independence when all the countries of the world, big and small, are advancing toward independence and sovereignty.

The Korean people categorically opposed from the beginning the division of the country and the nation and earnestly wish to be reunified into one, recovering the inherent appearance of our nation. The division which has continued for over 30 years spells immeasurable misfortunes and sufferings to the Korean people. The commonness of the homogeneous nation is gradually disappearing and millions of blood-relatives split into the north and south have been unable to meet with each other or hear about each other's fate though one new generation has grown up. The division of the country and the nation is indeed most heart-rending to anyone of the Korean people.

When the misfortunes and sufferings brought by the past history of division are so great, the splittists within and without are now engaged in manouevres to obstruct the reunification of Korea at any cost and split for ever into two the land of the fatherland linked by the same vein and our people who are of the same blood. Can there be more serious crime than this?

The "two Koreas" plot of the splittists within and without should never be tolerated. The US ruling circles should clearly see the unshaken will of the Korean people to end the division and achieve reunification and the reality today when the just struggle of the peaceloving people of Asia and the rest of the world against domination and subjugation and for independence and sovereignty is mounting high and give up the "two Koreas" policy, take measures to completely and immediately withdraw all the US troops and all the mass destruction weapons including nuclear weapons from south Korea in accordance with the U.N. resolution and their pledges, and should take their hands off Korea. The Japanese government should not play the role of a "detached force" in accordance with the script of "two Koreas." As a zealous follower of this policy of the United States contradictory to the interests of the peoples of Korea and Japan, it should no longer take an action obstructive to the reunification of Korea. If the south Korean authorities think they could prolong their remaining days by the "two Koreas" plot, intensifying their fascist repression of all patriotic elements struggling for democracy and peaceful reunification, that is a mistake.

Those who persist in the manoeuvres for permanent split, going against the people's will for reunification, are fated to meet the same end as the successive traitors who went to ruin, bringing the curses of the whole nation on their heads. The struggle for the reunification of Korea is the common cause of peace in Asia and the world.

Only when Korea is reunified and developed as one state, can the root cause of split and war be eradicated in this area and the peace in Asia and the world preserved and consolidated.

The world must advance more dynamically under all circumstances toward the reunification of Korea. When the world energetically heads for the reunification of Korea, the "two Koreas" plot of the splittists within and without will be thwarted and frustrated and the Korean people's just cause of peace and peaceful reunification further accelerated. Any country which really wants peace in Korea and her peaceful reunification must in any event be drawn into or respond to the "two Koreas" plot of the splittists within and without which can no more be tolerated either from the national point of view, humanitarian point of view or from the viewpoint of world peace. The Korean people are greatly inspired by and always grateful for the positive support and encouragement extended by the world peace-loving people to our just struggle to reunify the country, rejecting outside forces.

The Government of the Democratic People's Republic of Korea and the entire Korean people earnestly appeal to the governments and peoples of the socialist countries and the non-aligned countries and the governments and peoples of the peaceloving countries of the world to strongly oppose and reject the arguments on "cross recognition," "UN membership" and all other manifestations of the "two Koreas" plot of the splittists within and without aimed at permanently splitting one Korea into two and actively help the Koreans realize the country's reunification independently and peacefully by themselves.

The Korean people express the hopes that especially the American people who see at first hand the wrong Korean policy of the US ruling circles directly responsible for Korea's division and the Japanese people who feel nearer than any others the Korean people's sufferings caused by division will join more actively in the struggle against the "two Koreas" plot of the US and Japanese reactionaries and the splittists within and without.

No splittists can ever break the rock-firm will and unshakable purpose of the Korean people who always consider it their legitimate right and noblest and most sacred duty to take back the land and people lost to outside forces and establish the sovereignty of the nation.

The Korean people, with the positive support and encouragement of the peaceloving people the world over, will thwart and frustrate the "two Koreas" plot of the splittists within and without and certainly achieve the independent and peaceful reunification of the country, the greatest desire of the people.

Pyongyang, February 1, 1978.

Interview with Hafizullah Amin, Deputy Prime Minister and Minister for Foreign Affairs of the Democratic Republic of Afghanistan by Cuban Journalists.

(Complete Text). Granma, 4 June, 1978.

What are the main principles on which the new Afghan Government's foreign policy is based?

Those principles have already been explained in a political declaration issued by the president of the Revolutionary Council and prime minister, Nour Mohamed Taraki.

The document explains in detail the steps to be followed in observing a policy of non-alignment, a positive and active neutrality policy to establish good relations with neighbouring countries and to consolidate the broadening of friendly relations with our great neighbour to the north, the Soviet Union, with which we have had relations for 60 years.

We refer to this as our peaceful borders with the Soviet Union, and it constitutes a good, friendly example to the rest of the world that these relations are not only unbreakable but will continue to develop for the benefit of both countries.

With respect to Pakistan, I would like to say that we also want to maintain good relations with it. We hope that the only political problem that exists between Afghanistan and Pakistan — the national question of the

Balush and Pashthum people — will be settled on the basis of our historical background, and we hope that the solution will be reached via peaceful negotiations between the two governments.

We have very good relations with India which go deep into the roots of our history, and we wish to establish relations with Iran and China.

Taking into account the present world balance of forces, what is your opinion as to the role that the Movement of the Non-Aligned Countries should play?

We are very interested in the Movement, and hope that through the strong consolidation of the non-aligned countries it will be possible to combat the attack of colonialism in both its old and new forms, to prevent the attacks on peoples everywhere in the world and to protect them.

Would you be so kind as to tell us what were the main causes of the revolutionary uprising that took place recently in your country?

As you know, President Daud, who referred to his régime as the Republic of Afghanistan, promised the people many things but actually gave them nothing. He leaned toward the country's reactionary forces. He wouldn't lay a hand on the feudal lords and kept feudalism in power. The people were becoming poorer and poorer, they had no jobs, no food, no housing, no clothes. . . .

The people couldn't put up any longer with the oppression to which they were subjected by the old régime. The despotism, the tyranny, and the nepotism became intolerable and brought about the downfall of Daud's régime.

On April 27, when the developments that led to the present democratic and revolutionary process in Afghanistan occurred, you were in prison along with President Taraki and other leaders. Would you tell us about those developments?

I should explain something to you about our Party and how the uprising came about. Our Party held its first Congress on January 1, 1965, under the leadership of Nour Mohamed Taraki, who was elected general secretary on that occasion.

For 13 years the Party worked among the workers and peasants, among the intellectuals and other strata of the people, and especially over the last few years among the army in a very subtle, secret fashion. Thus, the Party had a strong base within the Army, as it had among the people.

When Daud's régime turned toward the reactionary circles it began to arrest our Party leaders. Comrade Taraki and several other Party leaders were arrested in the early hours of April 26. I was placed under house arrest at the very beginning, that is, on April 26.

When I learned that Comrade Taraki was in prison and since I had been previously given orders by the Party regarding the organizations and planning of the revolutionary movement, I was able to make contact with the Party members who were active inside the army and who kept in contact with me, because, as a member of the Central Committee, I was in charge of the work among the army.

I turned in the map and all the plans for the revolutionary uprising which was scheduled to begin at 9.00 a.m., April 27. I was arrested at 11.00 a.m., but the plan was put into effect because all our members in the army remained in contact in keeping with the plan I had given to them. Thus the revolution began on the morning of the 27th.

I should point out that the names of the members of the Central Committee and the news that they had been arrested were broadcast over the government radio station on the evening of April 26. Contrary to what the régime expected, this helped the revolutionaries' plans, because it gave added encouragement to our Party members in the army.

In addition, Daud's régime issued a warning to the army, because it was taken for granted that the members of the Party would not be happy about the measures taken by the government.

However, most of the officers in the army were members of our Party. For example, in the air force, which was distributed among military airports, the command was controlled by the Party, that is, a plane couldn't take off by orders of the government. And the tank regiments were also under the full control of our Party members.

Our men manned the tanks and planes at 9.00 a.m., and the struggle got under way according to the instructions given to the members of the Party by Hafizulla Amin, whom they knew was in charge of Party work among the military.

Thus, the revolution got started, and went on to develop everywhere according to the plan I had turned in.

The tanks reached the prison at 5.00 p.m. We were rescued and those who were Party members were taken aboard the tanks to Radio Afghanistan, which served as the revolutionary headquarters. There, the officers turned over their command to me, I conducted the revolution from 5.00 p.m. April 27 to 9.00 a.m. April 28.

Shortly after 5.00 p.m. on April 27, the Party leadership prepared a communiqué that was broadcast at 7.00 p.m. When it was heard all over the country, our officers arrested all the generals in the various regiments and put them in prison. With the exception of one province, where the general and the governor died, the members of our Party assumed the leadership of all the regiments without running into any resistance.

For all these reasons we call our movement the April 27 Revolution.

In your opinion, what are the principal dangers and obstacles — both internal and external — that Afghanistan must face on the way to the consolidation of the revolutionary process?

Within the country itself, I see no danger on the part of the people, because the masses have strongly supported the revolution. However, as you know, wherever there is a real revolution, a revolution that heralds a socialist revolution, there begins resistance on the part of the agents of imperialism and reaction.

Thus, it's quite likely that the imperialist circles and their lackeys will want to encourage the fanatic, religious leaders with the help of the feudal lords who feel they are in danger and, in that sense, there might be problems.

At any rate, since we have the support of the people and of friends all over the world, we are confident that we can crush any kind of resistance to our revolution.

What is the present state of Afghan-Cuban relations and what is their outlook?

Revolutionary Cuba is well loved by the people of Afghanistan. This is the feeling of our people and our Party. But this is nothing new because, especially since the time our Party was founded, our people have been told all about Cuba and its great leader, and the information has been welcomed throughout the country.

The members of our Party, as well as all those who practice a progressive policy, are in favour of the establishment of a permanent Cuban embassy in Afghanistan.

When I left Afghanistan, some of my comrades asked me to return with a Cuban ambassador.

We are sure that revolutionary Cuba will be willing to help us in any field, especially that of the economy.

I would like to express my satisfaction for the friendly, brotherly hospitality given me. All of the members of the delegation representing our country are very grateful for the hospitality given us by the people of Cuba.

This comes as no surprise to us, because we knew beforehand that these fraternal relations between our countries existed, but now we see them demonstrated in practice. I would like to express my happiness and to have you convey my feelings to the people of Cuba.

Treaty of Friendship and Co-operation Between the Socialist Republic of Romania and Democratic Kampuchea

(Complete Text).

Prompted by the common wish to strengthen and develop relations of brotherly friendship, militant solidarity, and co-operation between the Romanian Communist Party and the Communist Party of Kampuchea, between the governments and peoples of the two countries, on the basis of Marxism-Leninism and of the rules of observing independence, national sovereignty, territorial integrity, the right of each nation to decide upon its own destiny, nonaggression, noninterference in the domestic affairs of another state, equality, and mutual advantage.

Persuaded that the manifold development and strengthening of relations of friendship and co-operation between the two countries fully accord with the interests of the Romanian and of the Cambodian peoples, and serve the cause of social progress, of peace and international co-operation.

Eager to make their contribution to the strengthening and development of friendship and co-operation with the socialist countries, with the non-aligned, developing, and other countries, in a spirit of justice, peace, and independence, on the basis of full equality of rights.

Reasserting their resolution to strengthen their militant solidarity with the communist and international workers' movement on the basis of the principles of respecting independence and equality of rights, noninterference in others' internal affairs, and the right of each party independently to work out its domestic and foreign policies, its strategy and revolutionary tactics to accord with the specific historical, social, and national conditions under which it operates.

Reasserting their will to strengthen their resolute and constant support of all revolutionary movements in the world, of the movements of national liberation of the oppressed peoples and nations, of the struggle of the peoples for the defence and strengthening of their independence, sovereignty, and integrity, against imperialist, expansionist, colonialist, and neo-colonialist policies of racism and apartheid, of pressure or ultimatums, or of any other attempt to dominate other states and peoples.

Determined to make an active contribution to the defence of peace and international security, to examining and settling the major international issues confronting mankind, to achieving general and total disarmament and, above all, nuclear disarmament, to establishing a new economic and international political order, to bring about a better and more just world.

Reaffirming their full support of the goals and principles of the United Nations Charter, and their determination to contribute to adjusting the UN to the realities of the contemporary world, to the demands of international life.

The Socialist Republic of Romania and Democratic Kampuchea have decided to conclude the present Treaty of Friendship and Co-operation.

Article 1

The high contracting parties will base and develop their bilateral relations, as well as their relations with other states, on the following principles:

Point 1. The inalienable right of each nation to decide its own destiny, to choose and develop, in full freedom and independence, its political, economic, and social systems, in keeping with its national aspirations, without any outside interference, pressure, or constraint;

Point 2. The inviolable right of every state to existence, freedom, national independence, and sovereignty; the obligation of all states to refrain from any act or attempt to restrain or subordinate any other state's prerogative to exercise all these rights;

Point 3. The full equality of the rights of all states, irrespective of their size, level of development, or political, economic, or social system;

Point 4. The right of all states to participate in international co-operation freely and have access, on an equal footing, to the sources of raw materials and energy, to the achievements of modern science and technology;

Point 5. The sovereign, inalienable and imprescribable right of each state to use all its natural wealth and other resources to serve its own national interests, without any outside restriction;

Point 6. The right of all states to co-operate among themselves and to take part on a fully equal footing in the examination and settlement, through peaceful means and in the interest of all nations, of problems connected with international peace and security;

Point 7. The obligation of the states not to intervene, in any form or under any pretext, in the domestic and foreign affairs of any other state;

Point 8. The obligation of each state to respect the territorial integrity and frontiers of every other state, to refrain from making any attempt upon the national integrity of another state; the obligation of all states not to recognize territorial gains or other advantages obtained by force;

Point 9. The obligation of all states to refrain, in international relations, from using any military, political, economic, or other form of restraint, from threating the use of force, or actually using it, under any pretext, in any circumstances or any form, against any another state;

Point 10. The legitimate right of every state to defend itself lawfully against any armed attack;

Point 11. The obligation of all states to settle all their international differences exclusively by peaceful means, based on genuine respect for all principles included in the present article.

The high contracting parties consider that these fundamental principles should be strictly observed by all states and that any infringement of them can never be justified, under any circumstances.

Article 2

The high contracting parties will develop contacts between the representatives of the parties, governments, and parliaments of the two countries, to the fullest extent possible, in order to gain a better mutual knowledge and to make it possible to exchange experiences in various sectors of socialist construction; they will encourage co-operation between the trade union, youth, women's, and other mass organizations of their two countries.

Article 3
Commensurate with the possibilities provided by the economic potential and the natural resources of the two countries, the high contracting parties will develop trade and economic links, and will co-operate in the scientific and technological fields, on a fully equal footing, on the basis of mutual advantage and fraternal mutual aid.

Article 4
The high contracting parties will develop exchanges and co-operate in science, education, culture, the arts, and other fields of mutual interest, in order to improve mutual knowledge of the intellectual and cultural achievements of the two nations.

Article 5
The high contracting parties declare that they are opposed to any imperialistic, expansionist, colonialist, or neocolonialist policy, to the use of force, or issuing of ultimatums, or attempt to dominate other peoples, against any act that might threaten or prejudice the national unity or stability of any other state.

They will continue to support the rightful struggle of all nations for national liberation, to put an end to colonialism and neocolonialism, in the struggle for the defence and consolidation of independence and national sovereignty, for independent socioeconomic development, for the fulfilling of all nations' fundamental aspiration for peace and progress.

Article 6
The high contracting parties will co-operate in the field of international relations to abolish inequality, and to establish a new, just, and equitable economic and political order in the world, a better world where justice, democracy, equality, and peace among states will reign, to fulfil all nations' fundamental aspirations and interests.

Article 7
The high contracting parties will continue to campaign for the implementation of general and complete disarmament, and primarily of nuclear disarmament. They emphasize the need completely and totally to destroy nuclear weapons, and all other types of mass destruction weapons, as well as the need for the nuclear states to make a formal promise that they will not use such weapons against countries that do not possess them.

They will make efforts to bring about prompt adoption of measures capable of producing a halt to the arms race, a dismantling of all foreign military bases, and a withdrawal of all foreign troops from the territories of other states, and of creating nuclear-free zones and abolishing military blocs.

Article 8

In order to implement the provisions of the present treaty, the high contracting parties will engage in periodic consultations and exchanges of information, and will co-operate in international organizations and meetings.

Article 9

The high contracting parties declare that the provisions of the present treaty do not contravene the obligations falling upon either of them from other treaties to which they are party, or the standards of international law.

Article 10

The present treaty will come into force on the date it is signed and in accordance with the constitutional provisions of the two states.

Done at Pnom Penh, on 29 May 1978, in two copies, in Romanian and in Khmer languages, with both texts being equally valid.

Interview with Comrade Pol Pot
Secretary of the Central Committee of the Communist Party of Kampuchea, Prime Minister of the Government of Democratic Kampuchea with Delegation of Yugoslav Journalists.

(Complete Text). Ministry of Foreign Affairs, Phnom Penh, 17 March, 1978.

We are happy that the delegation of Yugoslav journalists has come and paid a visit to Democratic Kampuchea. This visit will strengthen the ties of friendship between our two countries and peoples. Like Kampuchea, Yugoslavia is a non-aligned country and has always resolutely defended its independence. Therefore, the friendship between our two countries lays on the same basis.

We have respect and affection for Comrade President Tito and the friendly peoples of Yugoslavia. Comrade President Tito and Yugoslav peoples have always extended to us support and aid. We have great sympathy for President Tito and the peoples of Yugoslavia. We would like to express to them our thanks.

I was in Yugoslavia. It was in 1950, in Zagreb, in a brigade of workers. So I feel great sympathy for President Tito and the Yugoslav peoples.

You are now in Kampuchea as friends.

Q. Respected Comrade Pol Pot, you are going, soon, to celebrate the third anniversary of the liberation of your country. Please tell us what are the outstanding achievements in national construction and rehabilitation during these past three years.

A. It is a pleasure for me to answer your question. During the past three years we have achieved a large number of good results. However, first of all, I would like to tell you that at the same time we still have a lot of work to do. The first outstanding result is that we have solved the agricultural problem, particularly with regard to growing rice. To have succeeded in increasing the rice yield means that we have enough rice to feed our people. In 1976 we planned to get a yield of three tons of paddy per hectare. We achieved 80 tp 90% of this objective. This enabled us to solve the problem of the people's livelihood and still have rice available for export. In 1977, we planned to produce three tons of paddy per hectar on land growing one crop a year and six tons of paddy per hectare on land growing two crops a year. We fulfilled nearly 100% of this plan. That is why our 1977 rice yield has increased over that of 1976. We could then improve the living conditions of our people and export more rice. Our slogan is: "When we have rice, we can have everything". This is because when the people have rice to satisfy their needs, we also have rice for export and then we can import all the necessary commodities.

Our successes in agriculture have resulted from the fact that we have developed the basis for it — irrigation systems. The existence of irrigation systems is an important factor which can secure a high yield for rice and other farm products. Along with the development of agriculture, there can also be development in other fields. Industry, handicrafts, social action and culture can develop and expand in accordance with our agricultural line.

Another outstanding success is the fact that we have eradicated malaria which was a scourge for more than 80% of our population. In the past our people were affected by malaria each year and had difficulty in carrying out their work. Now that we have solved more than 90% of the malaria eradication problem, our people's health is far better than before.

Another outstanding result is the basic elimination of illiteracy which was a social disease in the old society. It is true that in that society there were some universities, secondary and primary schools in large cities and towns, but the majority of our people in the countryside were illiterate. Now, we have fundamentally solved this problem. Our people can read and write. This is a foundation which enables the people to gradually enhance their culture. It is not just one section of our population but the entire people who can learn and study. We have adopted this foundation for the development and advancement of our education.

As for other results, they are less important, but I would like to tell you that we have established and developed a health system throughout the country. Each cooperative has its own medical centre and pharmaceutical centre where medicines are prepared according to national and traditional methods, which has helped to improve greatly the health of our people. The present situation is different from that in the old days. In the past there were doctors only in Phnom Penh and in the big cities. Now we have doctors stationed throughout the country in all cooperatives and even in the most remote areas. The level of these medical personnel is still only elementary, but continuing on this basis we will gradually improve our medical capability.

With regard to the cottage industry and small industrial workshops, there are no spectacular achievements, but we have set up workshops everywhere. Every cooperative has its own cottage industry and workshops; they are the bases for the development of our handicrafts and for the gradual industrial development of our country.

These are the outstanding results which were due to the efforts of our people under the leadership of our Communist Party of Kampuchea. The people have done all this by themselves; they have seen the results and have taken pleasure in them.

Q. During our short stay in your beautiful country, we have seen signs that your revolution is completely cut off from the past. So what sort of a model for a society are you now trying to build?

A. We don't have any model upon which to build a new society. The special National Congress held at the end of April 1975 clearly noted the determining role in the revolution, in the national liberation war played by workers and peasants, who form the overwhelming majority of the populace. They have been the ones who have endured the heaviest burden in the revolution, they must continue to enjoy the revolutionary rewards. This has also been stipulated in the preamble to our Constitution. We desire to build a prosperous and happy Cambodian society in which all enjoy equality, happiness and a society free from all class or individual forms of exploitation, in which everyone strives to increase production and to defend the country. It is on this basis that we are striving to build a new society. It is with this aim that we are striving to build the present new society. Therefore, the trend of our effort to build a new society is based on the aspiration of the people, especially our workers and peasants who represent the majority.

The people have realized that this way of building society is good, and they will continue to carry on the work. However, if they ever decide that this way is not good they will stop it. It is up to the people. Our experiences have proved that we are entirely dependent upon the people in waging the revolution and the national liberation war. If the people attempt a task, they will certainly succeed, but if the people do not want to do something, we cannot do anything in their place.

For this reason, I would like to point out to you that we do not have any preconceived model or pattern of any kind for a new society. This means that we are working with the aim of serving the people's aspirations, as specified in the preamble of our Constitution — the Constitution of our Democratic Kampuchea.

Q. As we have seen in the current phase of your revolution, you have mobilized all national forces to develop agriculture. Would you have any intention to develop industry also? And how would you establish the technical basis, that is to say, how are you going to train the necessary cadres essential for this purpose? As far as we know, you have no universities, colleges or technical schools at present.

A. We have both the desire and plan to build our industry quickly. By relying on our agriculture, we endeavour to develop industry. It is our view that in order to have an independent economy we must develop our agriculture, cottage industry and other sectors. Thus it is an orientation to which we are paying great detail. However, where can we obtain the necessary capital to build the industries? We must depend on agriculture to create capital. For example, we now have trade relations with our Yugoslav comrades. We export our farm products and import the industrial goods we need for our agricultural sector and our industry as well. At the same time, our principle is to train as many technical cadres as possible as quickly as possible.

Speaking of universities and higher and secondary education as it existed in the past, it seems that we have none. However, we are now developing our technical ranks at our bases. In the co-operatives there are several types of workshops where people are trained on the job. This sort of training is available in all factories in Phnom Penh and in the provinces as well. In this way, people work and are trained at the same time.

Before liberation, there were a number of graduates who had been educated in Phnom Penh, the provinces or abroad. But, as far as concret results are concerned, these graduates could not serve the industrial or cottage industry movements as well as the people of the present day. The technical cadres now emerging from our bases enable our people to produce more. Using this experience, we have trained technical cadres in our bases and have gradually increased their technical ability. They do practical work and gain practical experience; and if they make mistakes, they can correct them and thus improve their knowledge.

Before liberation, some of you had been several times in Kampuchea. At that time, there were very few national technicians; they were outnumbered by foreign technicians. That is why we are now striving essentially to train national technicians. As concrete results of our training programme let us take an example of a hydrological project on the Prek Twot river. Many years were spent on construction work without success. In 1976-77, however, we succeeded in building five dams. By doing practical work, we gain practical experience. We believe that if we wait any longer, we shall never be able to give timely support to the production movement and we shall never be able to solve the problems of the people's livelihood.

I could cite other examples. In fact, we are now capable of building our own rice husking machines, pumps with engines, rice-threshers, and other kinds of engines. We make some of this mechanical equipment completely by ourselves; we have adapted other imported machines for our own purposes. In the past, this was not possible; everything was imported from abroad.

In brief, we pay great attention to the problem of industrial development and to the training of our national technicians. We shall develop the level of their knowledge by our own means. We think that we can do so to a certain degree. In combining closely the studies with the concrete practice, they have progressively gained more experience. Then, they will go to friendly countries for training so that they could improve their scientific and technical knowledge. These are the principles on which we rely, but we will send our trainees only to friendly countries.

Q. We have seen that your cities have no population. Can you explain the aim of this operation? Why have you abolished the role of money, the salary system and the trade network? Is this a temporary trend in the social changes and revolutionary transformations in your society, or is it a model society that you are trying to create on a long term basis.

A. The first reason was an economic one, to ensure food supply for many million inhabitants in the cities. When we examined this problem, we saw that it was beyond our capability. It would be impossible for us to feed so many millions of towns-people. To take these people to the countryside and relocate them in cooperatives would be a good solution, as the cooperatives had ricefields and other means of production at their disposal. We have cooperatives which are willing to have the townspeople live and work with them. The cooperatives own oxen, buffaloes and all other means of production in common. Our strength is in the countryside; our weakness is in the cities. Therefore, we came to the conclusion that we had to ask the people to go and live in the countryside in order to solve the food problem. If we could solve the problem of food supplies, the people would gain confidence in us. Staying in the cities meant starvation. A hungry people would not believe in the revolution.

Such was the economic reason. However, in addition to the economic reason, there was also the problem of defending the country and maintaining national security. Before our liberation we had already learned of a plan to defeat us by the US imperialists and their lackeys. According to this plan, after our victory and our entry into Phnom Penh, they would create difficulties there in the political, military, economic and other fields in order to destroy our revolution. Consequently, we evacuated the city's population to the countryside, in the cooperatives, in order to solve the food problem and, at the same time, to defeat the advance of US imperialists' plans so that they could not attack us when we entered into Phnom Penh.

Thus, this action was not pre-planned. It was the realization that a food shortage was imminent and that there was a need to solve the problem of food for the people, as well as the realization that there was a plan by US lackeys to attack us, that prompted us to evacuate the cities.

Concerning the function of the money, the salary and trade systems, I would like to tell you the following: In 1970-71, we had already liberated 75 to 80% of our country. At that time, we had the political and military power, but not the economic power. The economy was in the hands of landlords and capitalists. These people received everything that was produced, because they had the money to do so. In the liberated areas, we fixed the price of paddy at 30 riels a tao (12 kilograms), the price at which the population must sell the paddy to the revolutionary administration. But, the landlords and tradesmen bought it at 100 to 200 riels a tao and then they sold it to the Lone Nol clique. As for us, we had nothing. The population faced many difficulties in food supply. It was the same for our army. These difficulties affected our national liberation war. After having examined this situation, we decided to establish cooperatives so that they could take in hand the economy, the agricultural production in the countryside, the management, distribution, supply system and the exchanges between cooperatives on one hand and, on the other hand, between cooperatives and the State. In this way we could control the agricultural production and solve the problem of livelihood for the people. The people were enthusiastic and sent their sons and daughters to join the Army to fight against the enemy.

As the cooperatives started providing support for each other, the role of money became increasingly less important. In 1974, it was reduced by 80%. Before liberation, only the State used money. It used it to buy various products in the areas not yet liberated for the needs of the liberated areas under its control. After these experiences, we asked for the people's opinion and we were told that money was not needed as everything was traded on a barter system within the cooperatives. Therefore, in the liberated zone at the time — which represented more than 90% of the territory and was inhabited by almost 6,000,000 people — we completely solved this problem. When the people left the cities they all received the support of the cooperatives. Therefore we have ceased to use money up to the present.

What will happen in this respect in the future? That would depend on our people. If the people judge it is necessary to go back and use money we shall do so. But, if the people consider it is not necessary to use money, they will then decide accordingly. Therefore, in the future this problem would depend on the concrete situation. That is what we have told you that we have no blueprint or pre-established model. That would depend on the development of the people's revolutionary movement and the progressively acquired experiences.

Concerning the salary system, this was a habit also acquired in the past. In the revolutionary movement, especially during the national liberation war, there was no salary either among the cadres or in the army. As for the inhabitants, they had no salary either. Before liberation, in the liberated areas, cadres, army population, that is nearly 6 million inhabitants, were already used to living without salary. Moreover, the truth is that in the past, the majority of the people received no wage at all; only functionaries did.

We have noticed that in the old days, the majority of our people had no salary. Only the functionaries had salary. Therefore, having been used to this, the people from the cities were absorbed into the cooperatives, the military and civil cadres, men and women fighters and workers have continued to live following the régime of supply in practice during the war. We consider that this practice has avoided a heavy burden on the people and allowed us to keep this money mainly for national defence and edification. What will be the situation in the future? That would depend on the concrete situation and the people.

Concerning the trade network, the State and cooperatives cooperate with each other to organise it. The State gathers cooperative products and distributes them throughout the country or exports them abroad. The State imports the products from abroad to distribute them throughout the country. This is the method we have used so far, on which we practised during the war.

The future also depends on the actual situation. That is to say, we do not take the present system as a permanent one. Neither is it a transitional one. We have been practising this method in accordance with the actual situation and will continue to do so. The determining factor is the people.

Q. As we see it, Democratic Kampuchea faces many problems and difficulties of all kinds with her neighbours. What is your opinion and how could you solve these problems and overcome the present difficulties?

A. Like all other newly liberated countries, Democratic Cambodia is experiencing difficulties. This is a normal situation. Historically speaking, to our knowledge, the difficulties being experienced by our Democratic Cambodia are not as serious as those of several other newly liberated countries. Of course, Democratic Cambodia certainly has difficulties.

The main difficulty arises from the fact that we have been adhering to the principle of independence, sovereignty and self-reliance and of deciding by ourselves our own destiny. This position runs counter to some countries, that is, the expansionists and the imperialists. But we assess that in upholding this principle of independence, sovereignty and self-reliance, our difficulties are less serious than those that we would face if the nation and the people of Kampuchea were subjugated or absorbed. Therefore, we prefer to stand by our principle of independence, sovereignty territorial integrity, and non-alignment and of deciding by ourselves our own destiny in overcoming all obstacles.

As for the question of how to solve these difficulties, it depends on both our side and the side of those opposing us. We have successively tried to solve this issue through negotiations. Immediately after liberation, in June 1975, myself and other comrade leaders, went to Hanoi. We decided to go and showed our goodwill in seeking to solve our long-standing problems. There were many problems, but one in particular, that of the border, to be discussed. We held that Cambodia wanted nothing more than to live in peace and we asked that the border, which in 1966-67 the Vietnamese side solemnly recognized and promised to respect, be the boundary between the two countries in an attempt to preserve, strengthen and expand the friendship between our nations and peoples. We did not claim our former territories. Neither did we claim our former islands. We did not claim even an inch of land. The Vietnamese did not deign to reply for they have fostered greater ambitions, that is to take possession of the whole Kampuchea under the form of an "Indochina Federation" by sending every year many hundreds of thousands or millions of Vietnamese to come and instal themselves in Kampuchea. In 30 years or more, the people of Kampuchea would become a national minority. That is very clear.

In May 1976, we invited the Vietnamese to come and negotiate in Phnom Penh. At first, they did not want to come. When they arrived, they said that they had come because we had insisted on inviting them. During the negotiations, Vietnam rejected the borders that it had recognized in 1966 and 1967. They said that in 1966 they had agreed with Kampuchea on this point because at that time they had been compelled to fight US imperialism. Consequently, it had been a deception. Furthermore, they proposed a new border demarcation which took away a vast part of our territorial waters. We saw this as sheer expansionism. No hint of friendship could be detected. They thought that they could put pressure on us because ours was a small country. We did not comply. The talks were therefore a failure.

At the same time, they continued to use military forces to attack us in the border region in an attempt to coerce us into capitulating. Again, we did not comply. How can we agree with them. It is unacceptable for us to become a slave of the Vietnamese after making allout efforts to fight the imperialists and their lackeys. It is unacceptable to our people and our army.

How then will we proceed to solve this issue? We are solving it in accordance with the actual situation. If they truly respect our sovereignty and independence, if they have true friendship, there is no difficulty in solving it. It can be solved immediately. However, if they persist in taking Kampuchea, we will have to adopt a position for the defence of our independence, sovereignty and territorial integrity. However, it is our opinion that these difficulties will be solved gradually. First, we will have to safeguard our independence, sovereignty and territorial integrity at all costs. In order to succeed in this endeavour, the entire people must be united, strive to maximize production and improve their living standard. Also, we must export more to secure more capital to finance national construction and defence.

At the same time, we hold that friends of the Democratic Kampuchea all over the world are standing on the side of our country and that the number of these friends is steadily growing.

We hold that many countries cherish independence and that some of them — Yugoslavia, to cite just one example — have a firm stand for independence. These independence-minded countries can see who is right and who is wrong, who wants peace and friendship and who is expansionist and aggressive. The independence, and justice-loving countries have seen this more and more clearly. The trend, as we feel it, is becoming more and more favourable to us. Therefore, those who have been committing expansionism and aggression against us should realize, also gradually, that they can no longer carry out aggression, expansionism and annexation against Kampuchea. Only then will we be able to solve the problem. Nevertheless, we have to continue to cope with the prevailing situation.

Q. Many articles have been written throughout the world with or without reason, to the effect that your country is very closed. Are you considering making it more open to the world? If so, what principle and direction will you follow?

A. Since our liberation, we have gained one friend after another. After liberation, there were many problems to be solved, such as rehabilitating the country and improving the people's livelihood. This is called putting one's house in order, re-establishing order inside the country. While we were carrying out these tasks, we were honoured by the successive visits of our friends. We hold that, in the future, a steadily increasing number of friends will call on us. There were some in 1975; more visited us in 1976; still more in 1977; and more will visit us in 1978. In the years to come, an increasing number of friends will visit us.

We are opening up to you, inviting you to visit us, to come to our country. We expect that more friends will be invited to come and see us, and that friendship will be further strengthened and expanded with all these friendly peoples and countries.

Regarding the personages and various organizations showing friendship with and justice to Kampuchea, we have invited and will invite more of them to visit our country, in our opinion, the trend is that more and more friends will come and visit us. Nevertheless, it is imperative for us to prepare our house and put it in order to the best of our ability in order to receive our friends.

As you can observe during your visit, the war brought much destruction to our country. Many who did not know Phnom Penh before and during the war, thought that Phnom Pehn had been spared. Immediately after liberation, Phnom Penh did not look the way it does now. It was extremely filthy and was encumbered with networks of barracks and rolls of barbed wire. Now, we have removed, dismantled and cleaned up all this.

Q. *The relations between Democratic Kampuchea and Socialist Yugoslavia appear in friendship and cooperation. What possibilities would you find to increase this cooperation and to extend the collaboration between our two friendly countries?*

A. Democratic Kampuchea and Yugoslavia are friendly countries and this friendship is based on the policy of non-alignment and independence. On this basis, we have ties of solid friendship to develop and strengthen our relations in all fields in the future. The relations in various fields have been developed and strengthened according to the possibilities of our two countries. As far as Kampuchea is concerned, we are striving to build up our country, increase our production and develop our trade exchanges with Yugoslavia. At present, our agricultural production cannot yet meet all our Yugoslav friends' demands. For example, in the case of rubber, we produce a fair quantity but the quality is not yet up to standard. We are striving to improve the quality of our production in order to increase our trade. Regarding other fields, we will continue to maintain our relations in order to cooperate with each other as much as possible. It is our opinion that the trend in this cooperation is excellent, because it is based not only on economic or commercial exchanges but also on good political and friendly relations.

Q. *When we return to our country, we will present to our readers and TV audience the successful outcome of our visit and the questions to which Democratic Kampuchea is devoting its attention primarily as well as the portraits of the leaders of this friendly non-aligned country. Therefore, let us ask you this last question: Comrade Pol Pot, who are you? What is the past of the Comrade Secretary of the Central Committee of the Communist Party of Kampuchea?*

A. I would like to say that I am glad to answer this question. But, first let me tell you that I myself as well as the other leading comrades are just a tiny part of the Kampuchean national movement and Kampuchean people's revolutionary movement. The history of my life is as follows: I am the son of a peasant. When I was young, I helped my parents in their work. Later on I stayed in a monastery, as was our custom, to receive an education. I lived there for six years, two years of which I spent as a monk. You are the first to know some of the details of my life.

When I was older, I attended a primary school of general education. I completed the course at this school but failed to go on to a secondary school, as I did not sit the entrance examination. At that time, in order to

attend a secondary school, you had to sit an examination. I therefore
returned home and helped my parents on the land. Later, I entered secondary school and finished the primary grade. I then switched to a secondary
electrotechnical school where I studied for only just over a year. I studied
many technical subjects, especially electricity.

After obtaining a scholarship, I went abroad to study. I went to France.
The first year there I made great efforts and became a fairly good student.
Later, I joined the progressive student movement. As I spent most of the
time on revolutionary activities, I did not attend many of the classes at
school. I attended the technical school less during the last two years. The
state then cut short my scholarship, and I was forced to return hom, where I
secretly joined the revolutionary movement of Phnom Penh.

Afterwards, I joined the maquis against French colonialism. After the
1954 Geneva Agreement was signed, I returned to the capital and resumed
my underground activities. In public, I worked as a lecturer in geography,
history and morals in a private school. My underground work was mainly
among students, intellectuals, workers and peasants.

In 1963, I could no longer stay in Phnom Penh. I again went into the
maquis. This is why my name was not well known. Even Lon Nol's secret
service, which kept following me and knew my name, had no idea of my
position. In Phnom Penh, I was the general responsible for our movement
in the capital. I was also in charge of liaison with the countryside.

I joined the maquis in 1963 and I came back to Phnom Penh on April
24, 1975.

In 1960, the Congress of the Party elected me as member of the Central
Committee and member of the Standing Committee of the Central Committee of the Party.

In 1961, I was Deputy-Secretary of the Standing Committee.

In 1962, our comrade Secretary of the Party was secretly assassinated by
the enemy. I assumed then the function of acting Secretary.

In 1963, the Second Congress of the Party elected me as Secretary. And
the following Congresses confirmed me successively in this position.

In the countryside, I stayed mainly in the most remote areas. I travelled
all over the country. I know fairly well my people, the geographical and
economic situation of my country. My base was in the region of the national
minorities, that is in the North-East region. I am very familiar with these
national minorities. They were very miserable. They wore only very small
loin cloths. They had no salt to eat. Now, one cannot distinguish them from
the other people. They wear the same dress and live like everyone. They
have enough rice, salt, medicines and other products. Their living
conditions have been considerably improved.

I would like to tell you about a particular fact. In 1950, when I was a
student abroad, I was in a brigade of workers in Zagreb for more than a
month during my vacation. I had contacts with Yugoslav people and I

attended the Yugoslav folkloric performances. So, from that time, I had ties of friendship with the Yugoslav people.

Statement of the Government of the Socialist Republic of Vietnam on Relations with Kampuchea, Hanoi, 5 February, 1978.

(Complete Text).

In its statement of 31st December 1977, the Government of the Socialist Republic of Vietnam proposed that Vietnam and Kampuchea meet as soon as possible at any level to settle the border question between the two countries in a spirit of fraternal friendship.[1] This proposal has won the approval and support of the governments and peoples of peace- and justice-loving countries as well as large sections of world public opinion. The Vietnamese and the Government of the SRV sincerely thank their brothers and friends the world over for this approval and support.

It is regrettable that the Government of Democratic Kampuchea has so far persisted in rejecting the proposal for negotiations of the SRV Government. On the other hand, the Kampuchean side keeps using its armed forces for attacks on many places in Vietnamese territory all along the border, particularly in Kien-Giang, An Giang, and Tay Ninh provinces, perpetrating new barbarous crimes against the Vietnamese people. It is striving to arouse hatred against Vietnam; it continues making cynical slanders alleging that the SRV has committed aggression against Kampuchea, interfered in Kampuchea's internal affairs, carried out subversive activities against Kampuchea, and tried to force Kampuchea into a Vietnam-dominated "Indochinese federation. . .". The Government of the SRV energetically rejects these slanderous allegations by the Government of Democratic Kampuchea. Obviously, Kampuchea is deliberately trying to increase tension on the Vietnam-Kampuchea border, to deteriorate the relations between Vietnam and Kampuchea and to render the settlement of problems concerning the relations between the two countries more and more difficult and complicated.

The SRV Government and the Vietnamese people once again reaffirm that it is their unswerving principled position to resolutely defend the independence, freedom, sovereignty and territorial integrity of Vietnam, and at the same time to constantly respect the independence, freedom, sovereignty and territorial integrity of Kampuchea as well as of other countries; and to uphold solidarity with the Kampuchean people, to make ceaseless efforts to

[1] For complete text see: B. Szajkowski (ed.) *Documents in Communist Affairs — 1977*, pp. 174-177.

rapidly settle problems concerning the relations between the two countries through negotiations.

Vietnam and Kampuchea are two neighbour countries, the two peoples have long been together in the struggle against their common enemy — the imperialist aggressors — to secure independence and freedom. Now they share the earnest aspiration to strengthen solidarity, long-term cooperation and mutual assistance in building their respective countries into prosperous ones, in keeping with the specific conditions of each country. The SRV Government is of the view that through negotiations in the spirit of anti-imperialist solidarity of the non-aligned movement and in the spirit of the non-aligned movement and in the spirit of the UN Charter, the Vietnam-Kampuchea border question will be correctly solved in the interests of each people and to the benefit of peace and security in South-East Asia and elsewhere in the world.

Desirous to reach an early settlement of problems concerning the relations between Vietnam and Kampuchea, the SRV Government makes the following proposals:

(1) An immediate end shall be put to all hostile military activities in the border region. The armed forces of each side shall be stationed within their respective territory 5 km from the border.

(2) The two sides shall meet at once in Hanoi or Phnom Penh or at a place on the border to discuss and conclude a treaty, in which they will undertake to respect each other's independence, sovereignty and territorial integrity, to refrain from aggression, from the use of force or the threat to use force in their relations with each other, from interference in each other's internal affairs, and from subversive activities against each other, to treat each other in an equal footing, and to live in peace and friendship in a good neighbourly relationship.

The two sides shall sign a treaty on the border question on the basis of respect for each other's territorial sovereignty within the existing border.

(3) The two sides shall reach agreement on an appropriate form of international guarantee and supervision.

To create favourable conditions for the negotiations between the two countries, it is necessary to put an end to any propaganda creating hatred between the two nations, to all divisive acts detrimental to the existing solidarity and friendship between the two peoples.

The SRV Government calls on the Government of Democratic Kampuchea to make a positive response to the above-mentioned fair and logical proposal in the immediate and long-term interests of the peoples of Kampuchea and Vietnam and to the benefit of their friendship.

The SRV Government calls on the governments and peoples of countries friendly to the Vietnamese and the Kampuchean peoples, on international organizations and on peace and justice-loving people throughout the world to support the proposal of the SRV Government and to make positive contributions to bring about early negotiations between Vietnam and Kampuchea, to the benefit of peace and security in South-East Asia and in the world.

Facts about the Vietnam-Kampuchea border question.

Ministry of Foreign Affairs of the Socialist Republic of Vietnam, Hanoi, 7 April, 1978.

(Complete Text).

In its 31st December, 1977 statement, the Government of Democratic Kampuchea presented the Vietnam-Kampuchea border question as follows:

(1) ". . . Right after the liberation of Kampuchea, the Vietnamese army attacked and occupied Kampuchea's Vai island and simultaneously carried out provocations and encroached on Kampuchean territory, to depths of from one metre to tens of kilometres."

(2) ". . . In June 1975. . . a delegation of the CPK were in Hanoi to settle the border question with Vietnam. . . In keeping with the decision made in 1966 by the government of Kampuchea and the South Vietnam, National Front for Liberation. But, on that occasion, the Vietnamese side ignored the good-willed proposals of the Kampuchean side; in fact, they paid no attention to the Kampuchean proposals."

(3) ". . . In May 1976, still wishing to settle the Kampuchea-Vietnam border question in a friendly way, the Government of Democratic Kampuchea invited the Vietnamese side to hold negotiations in Phnom Penh. The Vietnamese side came to Democratic Kampuchea with a hostile attitude, with no intention of solving the frontier question. . . On the contrary, the Vietnamese side tried to revise the existing Kampuchea-Vietnam border, the sea border in particular. . ."

But in his 6th January, 1978 statement, the spokesman of the Ministry of Information and Propaganda of Democratic Kampuchea said that "the clashes along the frontiers are only one of Vietnam's many pretexts to invade, threaten and put pressure on Kampuchea. . . to force it into an Indochinese federation."

Then, on 30th January, 1978, Phnom Penh radio reaffirmed that "the Kampuchean frontiers have been clearly delineated and established in international agreements; the Provisional Revolutionary Government of the Republic of South Vietnam and the Government of North Vietnam also gave their recognition to them in written documents in 1966. Therefore, there is no question of the border not being clearly delineated. . ."

So, within a short period, Democratic Kampuchea has on the one hand asserted the existence of border disputes between Kampuchea and Vietnam and clamoured about its "good will", but on the other also said that the border between the two countries had already been clearly defined and internationally recognized, including by Vietnam; at the same time it has slanderously accused Vietnam of using border clashes as a pretext to invade Democratic Kampuchea.

What are the facts about the Vietnam-Kampuchea border question? This document will shed light on this problem.

I The truth about the Vietnam-Kampuchea border question

Regarding the Vietnam-Kampuchea border question the Government of the Democratic Republic of Vietnam, the National Liberation Front for the Liberation of South Vietnam and the Provisional Revolutionary Government of the Republic of South Vietnam as well as the present Government of the Socialist Republic of Vietnam have always stood for a negotiated settlement, keeping with the principle of respect for each other's sovereignty and territorial integrity and in a spirit of equality, mutual respect, friendship and good neighbourhood.

On 9th March and 14th April, 1960, the Saigon puppet administration laid claim to seven islands along the Kampuchean coast, namely Hon Dua (Koh Takeav), Hon Nan Trong (Koh Thmey), Hon Nang Ngoai (Koh Ses), Hon Tai (Koh Antay), Hon Tre Nam (Koh Po), Hon Kien Vang (Koh Ankrang), and Hon Keo Ngua (Koh Ses).

On 20th June, 1964, the then Kampuchean Head of State, N. Sihanouk sent a letter to the President of the Presidium of the Central Committee of the NFLSV, Nguyen Huu Tho, expressing a desire to meet and exchange views with the President in connection with the border question, in which he stated: ". . . We give up all territorial claims in exchange for an unambiguous recognition of the existing borders and of our sovereignty over the coastal islands illegally claimed by the Saigon administration. . ." On 18th August, 1964, Head of State N. Sihanouk sent another letter to President Nguyen Huu Tho, reaffirming: ". . . For its part, Kampuchea only demands recognition of its existing land border as drawn on the maps commonly used up to 1954 and recognition of its sovereignty over the coastal islands illegally claimed by the Saigon régime without any justification whatever. . ."

The NFLSV agreed to the meeting requested by Head of State N. Sihanouk, and in October and December 1964, the two sides started negotiations in Peking. During these negotiations, the delegation of the NFLSV expressed its good will and desire to conclude an agreement between the two parties. However, the Kampuchean side claimed sovereignty over Vietnam's Hai Tac Nam and Tho Chu island (both of which lie south of the Brevie line). The Kampuchean side also put forward a map with nine corrections of the pre-1954 map and with the Vietnam-Kampuchea border redrawn in such a way as to encroach on Vietnamese territory. In addition, it linked the border question with other issues, such as privileges for Khmers residing in South Vietnam. That is why the 1964 negotiations failed to achieve any results.

In March 1965, in the resolution of the conference of the Indochinese peoples held in Phnom Penh, the delegations of the Vietnam Fatherland Front and the NFLSV once again reiterated ". . . respect for the sovereignty, independence, neutrality and territorial integrity of Kampuchea and undertook to continue to do so and to avoid any action inconsistent with these principles. . ."

In August 1966, at the request of Head of State N. Sihanouk, a delegation of the NFLSV headed by Mr Tran Buu Kiem, member of its Central Committee Presidium, went to Phnom Penh to continue negotiations on the border question. In the course of the negotiations, the Kampuchean side once more demanded an amendment of the land border as drawn on the 1:100,000 map published by the Geographical Service of French Indochina widely used before 1954.

As regards the sea border, the Kampuchean side rejected the Brevie Line and said "if administrative control of these islands is considered to be territorial sovereignty over them, South Vietnam will then have an advantage, because among the islands south of the Brevie Line is Phu Quoc island, which comes under the sovereignty of Kampuchea. . ." The Kampuchean side also linked the border question with many other issues, such as privileges for Khmers residing in South Vietnam, Kampuchean navigation rights on the Mekong River and the use of Saigon's sea port. It considered its proposals as an indivisible whole and demanded that the NFLSV accept it as such. These were absurd demands and because of them the negotiations had to be adjourned. At the last meeting, on 17th September, 1966, the Kampuchean side requested that "the negotiations be suspended for the time being. . ."

Such are the facts about the August 1966 negotiations. Nevertheless, the Government of Democratic Kampuchea said in its 31st December, 1977 statement[1] that in 1966 the NFLSV had officially recognised the sea borders of Kampuchea. The Government of the SRV categorically rejects this falsification by the Government of Democratic Kampuchea. The Kampuchean side did not accept the proposals of the NFLSV and put forward absurd demands, and as a result no agreement was reached during the negotiations.

On 9th May, 1967, the Royal Government of Kampuchea appealed to all countries to respect the territorial integrity of Kampuchea within its existing borders. In responding to this appeal, the Central Committee of the NFLSV

[1] For complete text see: B. Szajkowski (ed.).*op.cit.*, pp. 166-171.(Ed.).

took into consideration the request by Head of State N. Sihanouk in his letters of 20th June and 18th August, 1964, that "the existing Kampuchean land border as drawn on the maps commonly used up to 1954 be recognized. . ." and on 31st May, 1967, declared that it: "(1) Reaffirms its consistent stand to recognize and undertakes to respect Kampuchea's territorial integrity within its existing borders. (2) Recognizes and undertakes to respect the existing frontiers between South Vietnam and Kampuchea. . ."

On 8th June, 1967, the Government of the Democratic Republic of Vietnam also declared that it: "(1) Recognizes and undertakes to respect Kampuchea's territorial integrity within its existing borders. (2) Fully approves the 31st Mary, 1967, statement by the Central Committee of the NFLSV recognizing the existing frontiers between South Vietnam and Kampuchea."

In April 1970, together with the other participants in the summit conference of the Indochinese peoples, Prime Minister Pham Van Dong of the Democratic Republic of Vietnam and Nguyen Huu Tho, Chairman of the Presidium of the Central Committee of the NFLSV and President of the Advisory Council of the PRGRSV, once more declared:

"As regards the relations between the three countries, the parties are determined to abide by the five principles of peaceful coexistence: mutual respect for sovereignty and territorial integrity; non-aggression; mutual respect for the political régime of each country and non-interference in the internal affairs of others; equality and mutual benefit; peaceful coexistence. The parties respect the fundamental principles of the 1954 Geneva agreements on Indochina, recognize and pledge respect for the territorial integrity of Kampuchea within its existing borders, and respect the 1962 Geneva agreements on Laos. The parties affirm that all problems arising in the relations between the three countries can be solved through negotiations conducted in a spirit of mutual respect, mutual understanding and mutual assistance." (Joint Declaration of the Summit Conference of the Indochinese Peoples, 25th April, 1970).

From May 1975 up to the present:

The 31st December, 1977, statement of the Government of Democratic Kampuchea says, among other things: "Right after the liberation of Kampuchea, the Vietnamese army attacked and occupied Kampuchea's Vai island, and simultaneously carried out provocations and encroached on Kampuchean territory to depth of from 0.1 metre to tens of kilometres. . ."

The Government of the SRV categorically denies these slanderous allegations of the Government of Democratic Kampuchea. The fact is that as early as 1st May, 1975, the Kampuchean authorities ordered their armed forces to encroach on Vietnamese territory in a number of places in border areas from Ha Tien to Tay Ninh, causing great human and material losses to the local populations.

On 4th May, 1975, Kampuchean troops landed on Phu Quoc island and on 10th May, 1975, they launched attacks from the mainland and from Hon Troc (Vai island) on Vietnam's Tho Chu island and occupied it. Tho Chu island lies far south of the Brevie Line. The Kampuchean authorities launched repeated attacks on this island with their armed forces, destroyed villages, killed many people and abducted 515 inhabitants of the island. In spite of the protest made by the Vietnamese side, the Kampuchean troops maintained their occupation of Tho Chu island. For this reason on 25th May, 1975, Vietnamese local armed forces were compelled to use their legitimate right of self-defence to drive the intruders out of Tho Chu island and, on 6th June, 1975, pursued them as far as Hon Troc (Vai island).

The Kampuchean troops' encroachments upon Vietnamese territory were admitted on 2nd June, 1975, by Pol Pot, Secretary of the Central Committee of the Communist Party of Kampuchea, when he received Comrade Nguyen Van Linh, representative of the Vietnam Workers Party, but he argued that the Kampuchean troops' "Ignorance of local geography" had been the cause of these painful bloody clashes.''

For its part, the Vietnamese side ordered its armed forces to withdraw from Hon Troc (Vai island) after driving out the perpetrators of this land seizure. In a meeting on 10th August, 1975, between Comrade Nguyen Van Linh, representative of the Vietnam Workers Party, and Nuon Chea, Deputy Secretary of the Central Committee of the CPK the Vietnamese side made it clear that Vietnamese armed forces were no longer stationed on Hon Troc (Vai island). It also declared that it would return to the Kampuchean side nearly 600 Kampuchean troops captured during encroachments on Vietnamese territory. At this meeting, Deputy Secretary Nuon Chea said: "Regarding the Vai island question, on behalf of our party, we would like to express our deep thanks to you", and admitted that "unawareness of the border problems", had resulted in these incidents. As for the 515 inhabitants of Tho Chu island abducted by the Kampuchean army, nearly three years ago now, the Kampuchean side has not returned them to Vietnam, nor has it given any information about what has become of them.

In another paragraph of the 31st December, 1977, statement of the Government of Democratic Kampuchea, one can read: "In June 1975. . . , a delegation of the Communist Party of Kampuchea went to Hanoi to settle the border question with Vietnam . . . but, on that occasion, the Vietnamese side ignored the good-willed proposals of the Kampuchean side; in fact, they paid no attention to the Kampuchean proposals.''

This is a complete and brazen fabrication. The fact is that a delegation of the Communist Party of Kampuchea headed by Pol Pot, Secretary of the Central Committee of the Communist Party of Kampuchea, paid a friendship visit to Vietnam in June 1975. On 12th June, 1975, the head of the delegation of the Communist Party of Kampuchea made it clear that the purpose of the visit was to strengthen the solidarity between the two parties and the two peoples, and to express deep gratitude to the Vietnamese Workers Party, the Government of the Democratic Republic of Vietnam, and the Vietnamese people, for their continuous, multiform and very precious support to the Kampuchean people. During the talks, the Kampuchean side suggested the conclusion of treaty of friendship between the two countries encompassing economic exchanges trade, the movement of the two populations across the border for their livelihood, the question of national frontiers, and other matters, but did not request immediate negotiations during that visit on the settlement of the border question.

The Vietnamese delegation welcomed the idea of signing such a treaty of friendship, emphasized that both sides had to respect each other's independence and territory so that solidarity could be strengthened and fraternity be maintained between the two peoples, and agreed that the two sides would engage in negotiations on a border treaty also.

After this visit, the Vietnamese side had occasion to bring up the Kampuchean suggestion about the conclusion of a treaty of friendship and a border treaty, but the Kampuchean side kept silent and never referred to this question again.

On April 1976, the Central Committee of the Vietnamese party and that of the Kampuchean party agreed to hold a meeting between high-ranking representatives in June 1976 to discuss the settlement of the border problem, and prepare for the signing, at state level, of a border treaty.

To prepare for this high-ranking meeting, a preliminary meeting was held in Phnom Penh from 4th May to 18th May, 1976, at the request of the Vietnamese side. At this meeting, the Vietnamese side put forth logical and sensible proposals regarding the principles for solving the border question, on land and on the sea, between the two countries.

As regards the land border, the two sides agreed to use the 1:100,000 map printed by the French and widely used before 1954.

As regards the sea border, the Vietnamese side agreed to take the Brevie Line as the demarcation line with regard to sovereignty over the islands. As for the actual border on the sea, there has been no legal text delineating such a border agreed to by both parties yet. In US puppet times, the Saigon and the Lon Nol puppet administrations carried out sea patrols along a demarcation line different from the Brevie Line. Therefore, in the view of the Vietnamese side, the Brevie Line could not be taken as the actual border — on the sea. The Kampuchean side, however, insisted on taking the Brevie Line as the border on the sea. The meeting was still in progress when the Kampuchean side asked for a "temporary adjournment", allegedly to have time to "get instructions" from the members of the Standing Committee of the Kampuchean party who were not available in Phnom Penh at that time. The Vietnamese side proposed the resumption of the meeting on many occasions, but got no response from the Kampuchean side.

The following clarification concerning the Brevie Line should be made: On 31st January, 1939, after considering the proposals made by the governors of "Cambodia" and "Cochin-China",[2] the Indochinese Governor-General, J. Brevie, issued a circular demarcating the respective administration and police zones into whose jurisdiction the islands in the sea areas of "Cambodia" and "Cochin-China" fell. The circular stated:

> . . . I deem the existing state of affairs untenable; the inhabitants of these islands are compelled to make their various applications to the administration of Cochin-China, at the price of either a long sea-crossing or a long journey through Cambodian territory. Consequently, I have decided that all the islands situated north of a line drawn at right angles to the coast at the frontier between Cambodia and Cochin-China, and making an angle of 140 (degrees) with the meridian North, as on the map attached hereunto, will from now on be administered by Cambodia. All the islands situated south of this line, including the whole island of Phu Quoc, will continue to be administered by Cochin-China. It is understood that the demarcation line drawn in this manner will skirt the north of Phu Quoc island, passing 3 km from the extreme points of the northern coast of this island.

The above-mentioned circular also pointed out: "Of course, only the matters of administration and the police are considered here, the question of whose territory these islands are remains outstanding."

The territorial waters of French Indochina, "Cochin-China" and Cambodia included, were delineated according to he 1st March, 1888, Law of the French Republic, i.e. three nautical miles wide (5,556 km). This proves that the French authorities of the time had no intention of taking the Brevie Line as the border on the sea between "Cochin-China" and "Cambodia". Therefore the Brevie Line only demarcated the administrative and police zones of the islands; it is not interpretable in any way as the sea border between the two countries.

On 19th May, 1976, Ieng Sary, member of the Standing Committee of the Central Committee of the Communist Party of Kampuchea, Vice-Premier in charge of External Affairs, received the Vietnamese delegation to the preliminary meeting, saying, "On behalf of the Party, Government and people of Kampuchea, we thank the Vietnamese delegation for having come and worked in Kampuchea". Then he added: "Though the meeting has not reached a solution on any major problem, its discussions have been highly significant, and the meeting helps both sides understand each other better and clearly realize the necessity of solidarity between the two parties and two countries".

On 23rd May, 1976, Nuon Chea, Deputy Secretary of the Central Committee of the Communist Party of Kampuchea, addressed a letter to Comrade Pham Hung, member of the Political Bureau of the Central Committee of the Vietnamese Workers Party, which reads in part "Our two delegations' recent work was very successful in further consolidating and

[2] One of the five states of the former French Indochina. It became part of Vietnam in 1949. (Ed.)

strengthening our militant solidarity. . . Our two delegations understood each other, sympathized with each other and were extremely sincere with each other, as the comrades-in-arms and revolutionary brothers they are.''

The facts about the May 1976 preliminary meeting and the above-mentioned statements by the leaders of the Communist Party of Kampuchea and Government of Democratic Kampuchea belie the distortions in the 31st December, 1977, statement of the Government of Democratic Kampuchea that "the Vietnamese side came to Democratic Kampuchea with a hostile attitude, with no intention of solving the border question", that "the Vietnamese side tried to revise the Kampuchea-Vietnam border, the sea border in particular". These facts also completely refute the allegation made by Pol Pot, Secretary of the Party Central Committee and Prime Ministry of the Government of Democratic Kampuchea, when interviewed by Yugoslav journalists on 17th March, 1978, that Vietnam "proposed another border with a view to seizing a large sea area "from Kampuchea".

In its 31st December, 1977, statement, the Kampuchean side deliberately used vague wording in an attempt to deceive public opinion: "In June 1977, the Vietnamese on the one hand, continued their invasion of Kampuchea along the border, and on the other, they pretended that they were still in favour of negotiations with the Kampuchean side on the border question, in order to slacken Kampuchea's vigilance and to launch surprise attacks against it".

In fact, after the preliminary meeting in Phnom Penh in May 1976, the Vietnamese side went ahead with implementing the three measures agreed upon: (1) The two sides strive to educate with cadres combatants, and people of their respective countries in the border areas with a view to strengthening solidarity and friendship and avoiding conflicts; (2) all conflicts must be settled in a spirit of solidarity, friendship, and mutual respect; and (3) the liaison committees of the two sides must investigate any conflicts and meet to settle them.

Far from doing the same, the Kampuchean side launched continuous military attacks against Vietnam and encroached on Vietnam's territory. April 1977 marked an increase in the Kampuchean authorities' mobilization of a very large force, of many divisions with the strong support of artillery clusters based in Kampuchea, to carry out concerted attacks on almost all border areas, from Ha Tien in Kien Giang Province to Tay Ninh, to loot, to burn houses and to kill people in a most savage manner, causing very great losses to the local inhabitants, and committing extremely barbarous crimes of the type described in detail in the White Paper published in January 1978 by the Department of Press and Information of the Ministry of Foreign Affairs of the SRV. At the same time, the period January-May 1977 saw the Kampuchean side successively cut off all relations between the liaison committees of Kampuchean and Vietnamese border provinces.

In view of this very serious situation, on 7th June, 1977, the Central Committee of the Communist Party of Vietnam and the Government of the SRV sent a letter to the Central Committee of the Communist Party of Kampuchea and the Government of Democratic Kampuchea, in which they expressed "the sincere desire to rapidly settle the border question, to put an end to the bloody incidents detrimental to the militant solidarity and fraternal friendship between Vietnam and Kampuchea". They also proposed that "a high-level meeting between our two parties and governments be convened as soon as possible, in Phnom Penh or in Hanoi, at the convenience of the Kampuchean side".

In their reply dated 18th June, 1977, the Central Committee of the Communist Party of Kampuchea and the Government of Democratic Kampuchea held that a meeting was necessary, but they proposed to "wait until the situation returns to normal and some time without further border clashes elapses. . ." before any meeting be held. It should be pointed out that it was nevertheless the Kampuchean side, and no one else which increased its military attacks, encroached on Vietnamese territory, savagely massacred Vietnamese civilians and sabotaged the peaceful labour of the Vietnamese people in all the provinces along the border. In such conditions, with the Kampuchean side continuing its wild military operations, how could the border situation "return to normal . . . without further border clashes" so that the two sides might meet?

Besides its military attacks and encroachments upon Vietnamese territory the whole length of the border, the Kampuchean side circulated a map of Democratic Kampuchea, scale 1:2,000,000 (printed in the August 1977 issue of the pictorial magazine *Democratic Kampuchea Advances*) on which the national sea border of Kampuchea was drawn according to the Brevie Line. It should be pointed out that even the former Royal Government of Kampuchea never drew the national sea border according to the Brevie Line. In 1973 and 1974, the Royal Government of National Union of Kampuchea printed and published a map of the same scale (1:2,000,000) but never drew the national border wither on land or on the sea as it was drawn in the August 1977 map. This action of the Kampuchean side testified to its land greed and territorial ambitions.

Each time the Kampuchean side violated the territorial sovereignty of Vietnam, the Vietnamese side always informed it of the fact promptly and requested it to stop all violations without delay. But the Kampuchean side always denied the facts in an attempt to elude its responsibility. For instance, Kampuchean troops had perpetrated many crimes in a number of places along Vinh Te canal in An Giang Province; but Pol Pot, Secretary of the Central Committee of the Communist Party of Kampuchea, although admitting violations of Vietnamese territory, said they were caused by ignorance of the border, resulting in very painful and bloody clashes (May 1975). Another time, following incidents in March 1977, the Kampuchean

Ministry of Foreign Affairs stated that "Kampuchea has never encroached even one inch on the territory of Vietnam." About incidents taking place from 27th April to 2nd May, 1977, the Kampuchean side said that the clashes had occurred in Kampuchean territory and the Kampuchean troops "only did their duty in defending their territory".

So, the Kampuchean side has not only contradicted itself in words; its words do not match its deeds; and these contradictions all the more clearly reveal its wicked design of systematic grabbing of Vietnamese land in the border region.

Since 31st December, 1977, the Government of Democratic Kampuchea has, on the one hand, persisted in rejecting the proposal for negotiations made by the Government of the SRV. On the other, it has kept launching attacks with its armed forces on many areas in Vietnam's territory all along the border, committing new barbarous crimes against the Vietnamese people. It has endeavoured to fan up national hatred against Vietnam, continued to brazenly slander to the SRV saying it has invaded Kampuchea, interfered in its internal affairs, carried out subversion against it, and tried to pressure it into a Vietnam-controlled "Indochinese federation". The Government of the SRV categorically denies all these slanderous allegations of the Government of Democratic Kampuchea.

The above-mentioned facts have borne out that the Kampuchean side has deliberately aggravated the tense situation on the Vietnam-Kampuchea border, caused the relations between Vietnam and Kampuchea to deteriorate, and created more difficulties and complications in connection with finding a solution to the problems concerning the relations between the two countries.

II The correct way to settle the Vietnam-Kampuchea border question

The above-mentioned facts prove that the Kampuchean authorities have made a volte face, that they do not want a correct settlement of the Vietnam-Kampuchea border question, and that they deliberately initiated the border clashes to kindle national hatred against Vietnam and to divert attention from the domestic purging and repression against their people.

Regarding problems relating to the frontiers between neighbouring countries, the position of the Communist Party of Vietnam and the Government of the SRV is very clear: (1) Sovereignty and territorial integrity is a sacred question of each nation: (2) between neighbouring countries, there are often disputes whose origins are historical regarding questions of frontier and territory, questions which are sometimes very complicated and require careful study and examination; (3) the countries concerned should study these problems in a spirit of equality, mutual respect, friendship and good-neighbourliness, so as to find a negotiated solution to these problems.

With regard to the Vietnam-Kampuchea border question, in its 31st December, 1977, statement, the Government of the SRV affirmed:

"Vietnam is resolved to defend its independence, sovereignty and territorial integrity, and at the same time it always respects Kampuchea's independence, sovereignty and territorial integrity, and does all it can to preserve the militant solidarity and great friendship between Vietnam and Kampuchea. This is a principled stand, a just and unswerving stand of the SRV".

"Once again, the Government of the SRV proposes that the two sides meet as early as possible at whatever level, so as to together solve the border issue between the two countries in a spirit of fraternal friendship."

On 5th February, 1978, the Government of the SRV once again put forward the following reasonable and sensible three-point proposal aimed at solving all problems concerning the relations between Vietnam and Kampuchea through negotiations. (1) An immediate end shall be put to all hostile military activities in the border region; the armed forces of each side shall be stationed within the respective territory 5 km from the border. (2) The two sides shall meet at once in Hanoi or Phnom Penh, or at a place on the border, to discuss and conclude a treaty in which they will undertake to respect each other's independence, sovereignty and territorial integrity, to refrain from aggression, from the use of force or threats to use force in their relations with each other, from interference in each other's internal affairs, and from subversive activities against each other, to treat each other on an equal footing, and to live in peace and friendship as good neighbours. The two sides shall sign a border treaty on the basis of respect for each other's territorial sovereignty within the existing borders. (3) The two sides shall reach agreement on an appropriate form of international guarantee and supervision.

Regarding the Vietnam-Kampuchea border question, the Communist Party of Vietnam and the Government of the SRV have adopted a consistent stand, i.e. (a) the existing land frontiers, as drawn on the 1/100,000 map printed by the French and widely used before 1954, will be taken as land borders between the two countries; (b) the Brevie Line drawn in 1939 will be adopted for purposes of determining sovereignty over the islands; (c) regarding the sea border question, the two parties will negotiate a fair and reasonable settlement.

Regarding the land border, the two parties have agreed to use the 1:100,000 map printed by the French and widely used before 1954; the two parties have also agreed on the division of the islands; but they still hold different views regarding the border on the sea. Regarding this question a basis for the two parties to negotiate a settlement already exists:

On 12th May, 1977, the Government of the SRV issued a statement defining the territorial sea, the contiguous zone, the exclusive economic zone and the continental shelf of the SRV, Article 7 of this declaration states: "The Government of the SRV will settle through negotiations with the countries concerned all matters relating to the maritime zones and the continental shelf of each country, on the basis of mutual respect for independence and sovereignty in accordance with international law and practices."

On 15th January, 1978, the spokesman of the Ministry of Foreign Affairs of Democratic Kampuchea made a statement reaffirming the Kampuchean position on the territorial sea, the contiguous zone, the exclusive economic zone, and the continental shelf of Democratic Kampuchea. Point 6 of that statement reads: "Regarding countries involved in the problem of determining the above-mentioned maritime zones, the Government of Democratic Kampuchea will deal with each according to the actual situation."

The Government of the SRV maintains that, on the basis of these two statements, the two sides can negotiate and delineate a sea border between the two countries.

The Government of the SRV appeals to the Government of Democratic Kampuchea to respond positively to the proposals put forth in the two statements of 31st December, 1977, and 5th February, 1978, by the Government of the SRV, and come to the conference table to settle the border problem and other problems concerning the relations between the two countries.

The Government of the SRV is convinced that "by means of negotiations in the spirit of solidarity against imperialism of the non-aligned movement, and in keeping with the spirit of the Charter of the UN organization, the problems concerning the relations between Vietnam and Kampuchea will be correctly settled in the interests of the people of each country, and for the benefit of peace and security in South-East Asia and the world".

Hanoi, 7 April, 1978.

Annex

Department for Political Affairs
No - 867 -API

Letter of the Governor-General,
31 January, 1939

Subject: Islands in the Gulf of Siam

Hanoi, 31st January, 1939

From: The Governor-General of Indochina
Grand Officer of the Legion of Honour

To: The Governor of Cochin-China (1st Bureau)
Saigon

I have the honour to bring to your knowledge that of late, I have further examined the question of the islands in the Gulf of Siam, the possession of which is disputed by Cambodia and Cochin-China.

The position of this string of islands, scattered along the Cambodian coast and some of them located so close by this coast that the continuing alluvial deposits must join them to the Cambodian coast in a relatively near future, makes it necessary, from logical and geographical point of view, for these islets to be placed under the administration of the latter country.

I deem the existing state of affairs untenable; inhabitants of these islands are compelled to make their various applications to the administration of Cochin-China, at the price of either a long sea-crossing or a long journey through Cambodian Territory.

Consequently, I have decided that all the islands situated north of a line drawn at right angles to the coast, at the frontier between Cambodia and Cochin-China, and making an angle of 140 (degrees) with the meridian North, as on the map attached hereunto, will form now on be administered by Cambodia. The protectorate will, in particular, take charge of the police of these islands.

All the islands situated south of this line, including the whole island of Phu Quoc will continue to be administered by Cochin-China. It is understood that the demarcation line drawn in this manner will skirt the north of Phu Quoc island, passing 3 km from the extreme points of the northern coast of this island.

The administration and police powers with regard to these islands will therefore be clearly distributed to Cochin-China and Cambodia in order to avoid any dispute in the future. Of course, only the matters of administration and the police are considered here. The question of whose territory these islands are remains outstanding. You will be so kind to take action so that my decision will be immediately put into effect.

Please acknowledge receipt of this letter.

Signed: Brevie.

Facts on the "Indochinese Federation" question.

Ministry of Foreign Affairs of the Socialist Republic of Vietnam, Hanoi, 7 April, 1978.

(Complete Text).

Since December 31, 1977, the Kampuchean authorities have slander-ously accused the Socialist Republic of Vietnam of "having long had the strategic design of turning Democratic Kampuchea into a member of the Indochinese Federation and a "slave of Vietnam" (December 31, 1977 Statement by the Government of Democratic Kampuchea), of "standing for the establishment of an Indochinese Federation with only one party, one country, one people" (January 17, 1978 Speech by Pol Pot, Secretary of the Central Committee of the Communist Party of Kampuchea, Prime Mini-ster of the Government of Democratic Kampuchea), and of "desiring to seize the whole of Kampuchea through the formation of an Indochinese Federation" (Pol Pot, Secretary of the Central Committee of the Comm-unist Party, Prime Minister of the Government of Democratic Kampuchea in answer to Yugoslav journalists on March 17, 1978).

The Socialist Republic of Vietnam deems it necessary to state the following truth:

I. From 1930 to 1951:

The Indochinese Communist Party and the "Indochinese Federation":
In 1930, the Indochinese Communist Party came into being with the historic mission of leading all the Indochinese nations in the struggle for the "complete independence of Indochina and for lands to the peasants" (Con-stitution of the Indochinese Communist Party).

The Resolution on the policy of nationalities adopted by the Party in March 1935, stipulated: *After driving the French imperialists out of Indo-china, every nation has the right to self-determination; it may join the Indo-chinese Federation or set up a separate state; it is free to join or leave the Federation; it may follow whichever system it likes. The fraternal alliance must be based on the principles of revolutionary sincerity, freedom and equality.*

The June 1941 Resolution of the 8th Plenum of the Central Committee of the Party stressed: *"After driving out the French and the Japanese, we must correctly carry out the policy of national self-determination with regard to the Indochinese peoples. It is up to the peoples living in Indo-china either to organize themselves into a Federation of Democratic Repub-lics or to stand separately as national states".*

As is well known, by the end of the 19th century, Vietnam, Laos and Kampuchea, three neighbouring countries on the Indochinese peninsula, were one after another occupied by the French colonialists. On the one hand, the French colonialists crushed them as states, took away even their names, and merged them into what was called French Indochina, overseas territory of France; a colonial system was imposed on all three countries, with a unified apparatus in various fields, military, political, economic, financial. . . placed under the centralized direction of a French Governor General. On the other hand, carrying out their wicked "divide-and-rule" policy, the French colonialists cut Vietnam into Tonkin, Annam and Cochin-China with three different forms of Government, which with Laos and Kampuchea made up five regions of French Indochina. They also sowed division among the Vietnamese people, and between Vietnamese, Laos and Kampuchea, using one people to fight another, and undermining the solidarity among the people of the Indochinese countries so as to dominate them more easily.

In these circumstances, *the founding of the Indochinese Communist Party was a historical necessity, meeting the* pressing demands of the liberation struggle of all peoples who lived together in "French Indochina", whose destinies were bound together, and who had to concentrate all their forces to defeat the common enemy and foil the latter's wicked plan to use Indochinese to fight Indochinese. The Party's slogan of "making Indochina completely independent and advancing toward an Indochinese Federation" which was raised in this context and *based on exercising the national right of self-determination, conformed to the situation of the 1930's and 1940's* and aimed at uniting the peoples of Vietnam, Laos, and Kampuchea against the French colonialists and the Japanese fascists.

During the 21 years of its existence, the Indochinese Communist Party fulfilled its glorious historical mission. *With the last-mentioned slogan, the three Indochinese peoples, closely united, rose up as one to seize power in the Autumn of 1945* and otherthrow the Japanese fascists. Thereafter, they fought a long war of resistance against the French colonialist aggressors.

II. In February 1951: At the proposal of the Vietnamese Communists, the Indochinese Communist Party disbanded. Vietnam, Laos and Kampuchea each had its party government, army and national united front, completely independent of each other; at the same time, they were united in the struggle on the principle of free choice, equality, mutual assistance and respect for each other's sovereignty, the question of an Indochinese Federation was never raised again.

As early as 1941, at its eighth Central Committee meeting the Indochinese Communist Party, observing the new conditions internationally and in Indochina had already realized the need "to awaken the traditional national spirit among the people" and stood for solving the national liberation question within the context of each country and establishing in each country a separate National United Front against the French and Japanese. In implementation of this resolution, the League for the Independence of Vietnam (Vietminh) was founded in Vietnam, the Lao Patriotic Front (Itsala) in Laos, and the Khmer Patriotic Front (Itsarac) in Kampuchea.

In February 1951, at the second Congress of the Indochinese Communist Party, in the Political Program presented by comrade Truong Chinh, then Secretary General of the Party, it was pointed out that: "Since 1930, with Indochina colonised, the peoples of Vietnam, Kampuchea and Laos, under the leadership of the working class and its political party, have together fought the French colonialists. Today, with the development of the revolutionary movements in Vietnam, Kampuchea and Laos, the three nations have grown into three separate states. It is still the three nations' revolutionary task to fight imperialism, though there exist some differences".

Therefore, on the initiative of the Vietnamese communists and with the concurrence of the Lao and Kampuchea communists, the Congress adopted the resolution: "Because of the new conditions in Indochina and in the world, *Vietnam will establish a Vietnam Workers' Party with a political program and constitution suited to Vietnam's conditions. Laos and Cambodia will also found their respective revolutionary organizations suited to the conditions of their respective countries*".

As a result, there came into being the Vietnamese Workers' Party, the Cambodian People's Revolutionary Party (now the Communist Party of Kampuchea) and the Lao People's Revolutionary Party.

Along with the resolution to establish a separate party in each country the second Congress of the Indochinese Communist Party placed emphasis on solidarity and co-ordination by the peoples of Vietnam, Kampuchea and Laos in the struggle against the common enemy.

Following the correct line of the Congress, on March 11, 1951, there was convened a Conference of representatives of the Viet-Khmer-Lao Peoples' Alliance, including representatives of the three countries' respective National United Fronts namely the Lien-Viet of Vietnam, the Itsala Front of Laos and the Itsarac Front of Kampuchea; the Conference adopted a resolution "to form the Viet-Khmer-Lao Peoples' Alliance *based on the principle of free choice, equality and mutual assistance*" in order to "carry on the long struggle by all the people and in all fields to wipe out the French colonialists, to defeat the U.S. interventionists, and to totally liberate the three countries", "to oppose all divisive schemes of the enemy" "to promote mutual understanding and to strengthen the solidarity among the three nations" and "to wholeheartedly help each other in all fields. . ."

This closely co-ordinated struggle was the most important factor which led to the signing of the 1954 Geneva Agreements on Indochina, and the elimination of colonial rule over the Indochinese countries. It forced the French colonialists and U.S. interventionists to recognize and undertake to respect the independence, sovereignty, unity, and territorial integrity of the three countries.

With the other participants in the Geneva Conference on Indochina, *the Democratic Republic of Vietnam solemnly affirmed in the final statement of the conference that:* "In relations between Kampuchea, Laos and Vietnam, all participants in the Geneva Conference *pledge to respect their sovereignty, independence, unity and territorial integrity and to refrain from any interference in their internal affairs*".

After the 1951 Congress of the Indochinese Communist Party, and following the 1954 Geneva Conference in particular, the "Indochinese Federation" question passed forever into history; as did French Indochina. Like Laos and Kampuchea, Vietnam has never referred to the Indochinese Federation question again.

When the 1962 Geneva Agreement on Laos was signed, the Democratic Republic of Vietnam, together with other participants in the Conference, solemnly declared that:

" a) *They will not commit or participate in any way, in any act which might directly or indirectly impair the sovereignty, independence, neutrality, unity or territorial integrity of the Kingdom of Laos*;

b) They will not resort to the use or threat to use force or any other measure which might impair the peace of the Kingdom of Laos;

c) *They will refrain from all direct or indirect interference in the internal affairs of the Kingdom of Laos. . .*"

In response to the proposal by Head of State Norodom Sihanouk for a meeting of 14 countries which would seek to guarantee Kampuchea's independence and neutrality, Premier Pham Van Dong, in his August 28, 1962 note, unilaterally and solemnly declared that: "*The Government of the Democratic Republic of Vietnam has unswervingly respected the independence, neutrality, and territorial integrity of the Kingdom of Kampuchea*: It wishes to promote a durable and lasting friendship with the Kingdom of Kampuchea *on the basis of the five principles of peaceful co-existence and the ten Bandung principles*".

In March, 1965, the two zones of Vietnam, together with the other participants in the Conference of the Indochinese Peoples convened by Head of State N. Sihanouk in Phnom Penh, solemnly *declared to strictly respect "Kampuchea's sovereignty, independence, neutrality and territorial integrity, and to avoid any action that does not conform to these principles"* (Resolution on Kampuchea adopted by the Conference).

In response to the May 9, 1967 communiqué by the Government of the Kingdom of Kampuchea appealing to all countries to respect Kampuchea's territorial integrity within its existing borders, on May 31st, 1967, the Central Committee of the South Vietnam National Front for Liberation solemnly declared:

1) To reaffirm its unswerving stand, *i.e. to recognize and undertake to respect Kampuchea's territorial integrity within its existing borders.*

2) *To recognize and undertake to respect the existing borders between South Vietnam and Kampuchea. . ."*

Thereafter, on June 8, 1967, the Government of the Democratic Republic of Vietnam issued a statement which read in part: "Proceeding from its consistent policy towards the Kingdom of Kampuchea, i.e. to respect its independence, sovereignty neutrality and territorial integrity, the Government of the Democratic Republic of Vietnam solemnly declares:

1) *It will recognize and undertake to respect Kampuchea's territorial integrity within its existing borders.*

2) It fully agrees with the May 31, 1967 Statement of the Central Committee of the South Vietnam National Front for Liberation, recognizing the existing borders between South Vietnam and Kampuchea. *The Government of the Democratic Republic of Vietnam recognizes and undertakes to respect these borders".*

In the Vietnam-Kampuchea Joint Statement of January 8, 1968 on the occasion of the visit to Vietnam of Minister for Foreign Affairs N. Phurissara of the Kingdom of Kampuchea, "the Government of the Democratic Republic of Vietnam once more reaffirms its respect and full support for the Kingdom of Kampuchea's peace and neutrality policy, once again reaffirms *its recognition of and pledge to respect Kampuchea's territorial integrity within its existing borders".*

In the April 25, 1970 Joint Declaration of the Summit Conference of the Indochinese Peoples, together with the other participants, the Government of the Democratic Republic of Vietnam and the Provisional Revolutionary Government of the Republic of South Vietnam solemnly undertook that: "In *relations between the three countries, the parties are determined to apply the five principles of peaceful coexistence: respect for each other's sovereignty and territorial integrity; non-aggression; respect for each other's political system, non-interference in each other's internal affairs; equality and mutual benefit; and peaceful coexistence.* The parties reaffirm that all the problems in the relations between the three countries could be solved through negotiations in the spirit of mutual respect understanding, and assistance".

Also at this Conference, "on behalf of the people and the Government of the Democratic Republic of Vietnam", Prime Minister Pham Van Dong undertook once more *"to recognize and promise to respect Kampuchea's territorial integrity within its existing borders".*

In the June 7, 1970 Vietnam-Kampuchea Joint Communiqué issued during Head of State Norodom Sihanouk's visit to Vietnam "once again, the Government of the Democratic Republic of Vietnam solemnly declares that *it will strictly respect Kampuchea's independence, peace, neutrality, sovereignty and* political system within its existing borders".

In the February 8, 1971 Vietnam-Kampuchea Joint Statement on the occasion of Head of State N. Sihanouk's visit to Vietnam, *"the Democratic Republic of Vietnam reaffirms its recognition of and pledge of respect for the territorial integrity of Kampuchea within its existing borders"*, and together with the Kampuchea side, it undertook that: "In relations between the two countries, the two sides *are determined to apply for five principles of peaceful co-existence: respect for each other's sovereignty and territorial integrity: non-aggression; respect for each other's political system and non-interference in each other's internal affairs; equality and mutual benefit; peaceful co-existence.* . . The peoples of Vietnam and Kampuchea together with the fraternal people of Laos are determined to strengthen their solidarity, . . . to totally defeat the U.S. imperialist aggressors . . . , *in order to turn Indochina into a peaceful region of independent states, so that South Vietnam, Kampuchea and Laos may follow the path of independence, peace and neutrality, and the people of each Indochinese country may decide their internal affairs by themselves without foreign interference"*.

At a meeting in Vietnam in May 1971 to welcome the Lao people's delegation headed by President Souphanouvong, Prime Minister Pham Van Dong solemnly declared: *"The People and the Government of the Democratic Republic of Vietnam always desire an independent, peaceful, and genuinely neutral Kingdom of Laos at its western borders.* The also desire to unceasingly consolidate and develop the good neighbourly relationship and lasting cooperation with the Kingdom oy Laos *on the basis of the five principles of peaceful co-existence and in keeping with the Joint Declaration of the Summit Conference of the Indochinese Peoples"*. In their May 30, 1971 Joint Statement, Vietnam and Laos undertook "to resolutely press ahead with and intensify their struggle, together with the Kampuchean people, *in order to make Indochina a peaceful region of independent states"*.

During the visit to Vietnam in November 1971 of the delegation of the National United Front and the Royal Government of National Union of Kampuchea headed by Special Envoy Ieng Sary (now Deputy Prime Minister), Nguyen Duy Trinh, Deputy Prime Minister and Minister for Foreign Affairs, affirmed: *"It is the policy of the Government of the Democratic Republic of Vietnam to strictly respect the independence, peace, neutrality, sovereignty and territorial integrity of Kampuchea within its existing borders and to respect the national rights and the political system of Kampuchea"*. (Excerpt from his speech at the reception in honour of the Delegation on November 10, 1971). In the November 16, 1971 Joint Statement, the Vietnamese and the Kampuchean sides, once more reaffirmed their determination to endeavour, together with the fraternal Lao people, " *to make the Indochinese peninsula a truly peaceful region of independent states, to ensure that South Vietnam, Kampuchea and Laos may follow the path of independence, peace and neutrality."* "In relations between the two countries, *the two sides reiterate their determination to implement the five principles of peaceful co-existence: respect for each other's sovereignty and territorial integrity; non-aggression; respect for each other's political system and non-interference in each other's internal affairs; equality and mutual benefit; peaceful co-existence.*

On the occasion of Head of State N. Sihanouk's visit to Vietnam in May 1972, the Vietnamese and the Kampuchean sides once more solemnly undertook that: "No brute force, no insolent threat, no perfidious scheme of the U.S. imperialists can prevent the three Indochinese countries from pursuing their lofty aims of totally liberating Indochina and *making Indochina a free and peaceful peninsula of independent and sovereign states, so that South Vietnam, Kampuchea and Laos may follow the path of independence, peace and genuine neutrality*". (Excerpt from the Vietnam-Kampuchea Joint Statement of March 5, 1972).

In the October 28, 1972 Vietnam-Kampuchea Joint Communiqué regarding Head of State N. Sihanouk's visit to Vietnam, the Vietnamese and the Kampuchean sides "reaffirm that *the affairs of each Indochinese country must be solved by its own people. This is a sacred and inalienable right of each nation.* The two sides *strictly respect and resolutely support each side's position regarding the settlement of its internal affairs* in accordance with each country's characteristics and interests and with Indochina's general situation".

When the Paris Agreement on ending the war and restoring peace in Vietnam was signed in 1973, together with the other parties participating in this conference, the Government of the Democratic Republic of Vietnam and the Provisional Revolutionary Government of the Republic of South Vietnam solemnly pledged in Artle 20 of the Agreement:

" a) The parties participating in the Paris Conference on Vietnam *shall strictly respect the 2954 Geneva Agreements on Cambodia and the 1962 Geneva Agreements on Laos, which recognized the Cambodian and the Lao Peoples' fundamental national rights, i.e. the independence, sovereignty, unity, and territorial integrity of these countries. The parties shall respect the neutrality of Cambodia and Laos* . . .

c) *The internal affairs of Cambodia and Laos shall be settled by the people of each of these countries without foreign interference.*

d) The problems existing between the Indochinese countries shall be settled by the Indochinese parties *on the basis of respect for each other's independence, sovereignty, and territorial integrity, and non-interference in each other's internal affairs*".

Together with the other parties participating in the March 1973 International Conference on Vietnam, the Government of the Democratic Republic of Vietnam and the Provisional Revolutionary Government of the Republic of South Vietnam reaffirmed their commitment in article 8 of the Act of this Conference: "With a view to contributing to and guaranteeing peace in Indochina, the Parties to this Act acknowledge the commitment of the parties to the Agreement to *respect the independence, sovereignty, unity, territorial integrity, and neutrality of Cambodia and Laos* as stipulated in the Agreement''.

During the visit to the liberated zones of Laos in November 1973 by the Delegation of the Vietnamese Workers' Party and the Government of the Democratic Republic of Vietnam, comrade Le Duan, First Secretary of the Central Committee of the Party, solemnly declared: "The Vietnamese people always desire to have an independent, peaceful, and genuinely neutral Laos. . . along their western borders. . . The Government of the Democratic Republic of Vietnam is prepared to establish friendly relations and lasting co-operation with the National Coalition Government of Laos, in order to consolidate and develop the good neighbourly relations with the Kingdom of Laos *on the basis of respect for each other's sovereignty and territorial integrity, respect for each other's political system and non-interference in each other's internal affairs, refusal to allow any other country to use the territory of one country for interference in and aggression against the other, equality and mutual benefit*''. In their November 4, 1973 Joint Statement, the Vietnamese side and the Lao Patriotic Front reiterated that the purpose of their fight was *"to make Indochina a peaceful peninsula of genuinely independent and free states''*.

In March 1974, a delegation of the National United Front and the Royal Government of National Union of Kampuchea, headed by Vice-Premier Khieu Samphan, (now President of the State Presidium) paid a visit to Vietnam. In their April 1, 1974 Joint Statement, the Vietnamese and the Kampuchean sides affirmed: "The people of Vietnam and Kampuchea, together with the fraternal people of Laos, are determined to hold high the banner of solidarity and friendship of the Summit Conference of the Indochinese Peoples and to persistently endeavour to *make Indochina a peaceful peninsula of genuinely independent, sovereign and free states. . .''*

Vietnam has always strictly respected the fundamental national rights of Kampuchea and Laos and the independence of the fraternal Parties of the two countries. At the same time it has tried its best, together with the Lao and the Kampuchean sides, to actively contribute to the solidarity between the three countries. The militant solidarity and wholehearted mutual support and assistance were an objective necessity for the struggle of each Indochinese people against the common enemy, the U.S. imperialist aggressors and their lackeys. In the course of the struggle, the three Indochinese peoples have endeavoured to foster that solidarity, in the interests of the people of each country and for the sake of the common revolutionary cause of this region.

During the 1960's, coupled with "Special War" and "Local War" in South Vietnam, and the air and naval "war of destruction" against North Vietnam, the U.S. imperialists, on two occasions, launched a "special war" to oppose the independence, peace, and neutrality of the Kingdom of Laos. And, together with the Saigon puppets, they brought pressure to bear on the Kingdom of Kampuchea in order to force it to abandon its policy of independence, peace, and neutrality. In such conditions, the Third Congress of the Vietnamese Workers' Party held in August 1960 adopted a resolution *"to welcome and support Kampuchea's policy of peace and neutrality and to further develop the relations of friendship with the Kingdom of Kampuchea"*, *"to support the Lao People's struggle to carry out their policy of peace, genuine neutrality* and national concord, and to express the desire to establish relations of friendship with the Kingdom of Laos".

In implementation of this resolution *and at the request* of the peaceful and neutral Government of the Kingdom of Laos, the Vietnamese people stood shoulder to shoulder with the fraternal Lao people and wholeheartedly supported them in their fight against the U.S. aggressors. As a result, the 1962 Geneva Agreement on Laos was signed, "recognizing the sovereignty, independence, neutrality, unity and territorial integrity of the Kingdom of Laos. . ."

The Democratic Republic of Vietnam strongly supported the proposals made in the early 1960's by N. Sihanouk, Head of State of Kampuchea, to convene a conference of 14 countries to guarantee the independence and neutrality of the Kingdom of Kampuchea.

In March 1965, an Indochinese Peoples' Conference was held in Phnom Penh at the initiative of Head of State N. Sihanouk. In its resolution, the Conference reiterated "the need *to consolidate the sincere and firm solidarity of the Indochinese peoples on the basis of equality of interests, mutual understanding and mutual concession. . .*" Vietnam made every effort to contribute to the success of the Conference.

In Mid-1967, in order to help Kampuchea resist the pressure of the United States and the Saigon puppet administration, the two parts of Vietnam quickly responded to the appeal made by the Royal Government of Kampuchea, in its May 9, 1967 Communiqué calling on other countries to respect the territorial integrity of Kampuchea within its existing borders.

In 1970, the U.S. imperialists staged the March 18 coup with overthrew the Royal Government of Kampuchea, destroying its independence, peace and neutrality. The U.S. imperialists' aim was to turn Kampuchea into a U.S. military base and neo-colony and, at the same time, to encircle and weaken the war of resistance of the Vietnamese and the Lao peoples.

To cope with this great danger, a Summit Conference of the Indochinese Peoples was convened on March 24 and 25, 1970 in Canton, China, at the initiative of Head of State N. Sihanouk and with the agreement of the Vietnamese and Lao parties. The Conference made public a now famous joint declaration appealing to the three peoples to "strengthen their solidarity . . . and determination to defeat the U.S. imperialists and their agents, to preserve their sacred national rights and the basic principles of the 1954 and 1962 Geneva Agreements, so as to make Indochina a truly independent and peaceful region".

The Kampuchean communists themselves, who were then leading the war of resistance in their country, also heartily welcomed the great success of the Conference. On May 1, 1970 Messrs. Khieu Samphan, Hu Yun, and Hunim, in the capacity of representatives of the Kampuchean people's United Resistance Movement declared: "The content of the Joint Declaration of the Summit Conference of the Indochinese Peoples is most clear-sighted, correct and valuable. The three Indochinese peoples have to endeavour to carry it out at any cost". "We solemnly declare that we totally and resolutely support the Joint Declaration of the Summit Conference of the Indochinese peoples".

In May 1970, the U.S. imperialists sent tens of thousands of U.S. and Saigon puppet troops to invade Kampuchea, thus extending the war to the whole of Indochina. In implementation of the Joint Declaration of the Summit Conference of the Indochinese People and at the request of Kampuchea, the Vietnamese people and their armed forces fought in co-ordination with the Kampuchean people and their armed forces and dealt punishing blows at the U.D. imperialists and their agents, compelling the U.S. and the Saigon puppet troops to withdraw from Kampuchea.

The strengthened solidarity and the co-ordinated struggle of the three Indochinese peoples created a tremendous force that dramatically changed the balance of forces on all battle fields in Indochina in favour of the revolutionary and patriotic forces of Vietnam, Laos, and Kampuchea. The invincible strength of the three peoples, who closely united with each other, wholeheartedly supported and helped each other in their persistent struggle, and who received wide support from progressive people all over the world, finally defeated the U.S. aggressors and brought their puppet administrations to total collapse, winning a victory of great significance: the total liberation of all three countries in the same year of 1975.

Appreciating the militant solidarity of the peoples of Vietnam, Laos, and Kampuchea, comrade Kayson Phomvihan, Secretary General of the Central Committee of the People's Revolutionary Party of Laos, Premier of the People's Democratic Republic of Laos, pointed out that the Vietnamese Workers' Party "has made an extremely great contribution to the building of the militant unity and alliance between Vietnam, Laos and Kampuchea, which has objectively and practically become one of the most decisive factors for the success of the revolution in each country in the past as well as in the future" (Speech at the Fourth National Congress of the Vietnamese Workers' Party).

Regarding the relations between Vietnam and Laos, he said: "In the history of the world's revolution, there are many brilliant examples of proletarian internationalism, but nowhere and never before can we find such a lasting and comprehensive special militant unity and alliance. Over 30 years have elapsed, but it remains as pure as ever before. Such a solid unity and alliance *has greatly enhanced the spirit of independence and sovereignty and all subjective factors of each nation and, combining their strength, the two nations have fought together and won victory together, fulfilling their lofy historic mission towards their respective peoples and toward the world's revolutionary movement.* The Vietnam-Laos relationship has become a pure, faithful and exemplary, rarely found, ever consolidating and finely developing special relattionship'' (Speech welcoming the Fourth National Congress of the Vietnamese Workers' Party).

Regarding the Vietnam-Kampuchea solidarity, and Vietnam's correct policy towards Kampuchea, Ieng Sary, head of the Delegation of the National United Front and the Royal Government of National Union of Kampuchea (now Vice Premier of the Government of Democratic Kampuchea), said during his visit to Vietnam in November 1971. *"The solidarity between the peoples of Kampuchea and Vietnam has been very beneficial to our two peoples. . . The two peoples have always firmly upheld the principle of equality and mutual respect in keeping with the April dochinese Peoples"* (Speech at the reception of November 1971).

In March 1974, during his visit to Vietnam, Vice Premier Khieu Samphan (now Chairman of the State Presidium) said: "The militant solidarity and fraternal friendship between our two peoples *have been strengthened day after day since they rely on a correct basis: mutual assistance on an equal footing and respect for each other's sovereignty in keeping with the spirit of the Joint Declaration of the 1970 Summit Conference of the Indochinese Peoples"* (Speech at the meeting of March 30, 1974). Pol Pot, Secretary of the Central Committee of the Communist Party of Kampuchea, said when he spoke about Kampuchea's victory: *"'all these victories cannot be separated from the assistance of our brothers and comrades-in-arms, the Party and people of Vietnam. . . The relations between our two Parties, based on mutual respect and absolute non-interference in each other's internal affairs, constitute a factor that cannot be dissociated from our victory* (Letter of October 3, 1974 to the Central Committee of the Vietnamese Workers' Party). In the talks between the Delegation of the Communist Party of Kampuchea and the Delegation of the Vietnamese Workers' Party held in Hanoi in June 1975, Pol Pot, Secretary of the Central Committee of the Communist Party of Kampuchea, said: "Though our victory stems from subjective factors *we should not have had it but for the assistance of the Vietnam Workers' Party, the Vietnamese army,* and the world people, *especially the Vietnamese people"*.

At this new stage, the people of Vietnam, Laos and Kampuchea have gained total independence and sovereignty and are making every effort to build their respective countries, the policy of the Vietnamese Party and State towards the other two fraternal Parties and countries, Laos and

Kampuchea is consistent and unchanged; it has been clearly expounded in the Resolution of the Fourth Congress of the Vietnamese Workers' Party: *"To endeavour to preserve and develop the special relationship between the Vietnamese people and the people of Laos and Kampuchea,* strengthen the militant solidarity, mutual trust, long-term cooperation and mutual assistance in all fields between our country and the two fraternal countries in *accordance with the principle of complete equality, respect for each other's independence, sovereignty and territorial integrity, and respect for each other's legitimate interests,* so that the three countries, which have been associated with one another in the struggle for national liberation, will for ever be associated with one another in the building and defence of their respective countries, *in the interests of each country's independence and prosperity".*

In its relations with the People's Revolutionary Party of Laos and the Communist Party of Kampuchea, the Communist Party of Vietnam always remains faithful to the revolutionary principles of the two Declarations of the Conferences of Representatives of the Communist and Workers' Parties held in Moscow in 1957 and 1960 and consistently advocates: "All *Communist and Workers' Party are independent, equal and, at the same time, duty bound to support and assist one another"* (Report presented at the Third Plenum of the Central Committee of the Vietnamese Workers' Party in December 1960).

In keeping with this spirit, on July 18, 1977, the Socialist Republic of Vietnam and the People's Democratic Republic of Lao signed the Treaty of Friendship and Cooperation and the Treaty on the Delineation of National Borders between the two countries. These treaties are of "great historic significance"; they "mark a new all-side development of the special relationship between Vietnam and Laos for the sake of the defence of national independence and the building of socialism in each country and respond to the earnest aspirations and vital interests of each people". The signing of the Treaty on the Delineation of National Borders "has reaffirmed the two parties' determination to build the Vietnam-Laos border into one of lasting fraternal friendship between the two countries. This treaty is a splendid illustration of how to settle problems relating to national interests in a spirit of harmoniously combining genuine patriotism with pure proletarian internationalism; it is a brilliant example of the policy of friendship and good neighbourhood pursued by the Socialist Republic of Vietnam and the People's Democratic Republic of Laos" (Joint Declaration between Vietnam and Laos, July 19, 1977).

With regard to Democratic Kampuchea, the Socialist Republic of Vietnam has persistently advocated a correct settlement of the border clashes through consultations and agreement between the two sides. On June 7, 1977, the Central Committee of the Communist Party of Vietnam and the Government of the Socialist Republic of Vietnam sent a letter to the Central

Committee of the Communist Party of Kampuchea and the Government of Democratic Kampuchea, expressing their "sincere desire to rapidly settle the border question, to end the bloody clashes detrimental to the militant solidarity and fraternal friendship between Vietnam and Kampuchea", to build a border of lasting friendship between the two countries" and proposing "to hold as early as possible a high-level meeting between the leaders of the two Parties and the two Governments. . .". It is very regrettable that the Kampuchean side has refuted this proposal, that it has publicly started a border war between the two countries and at the same time, increased slanderous charges against the Socialist Republic of Vietnam.

Following its December 31, 1977 Statement on February 5, 1978 the Government of the Socialist Republic of Vietnam put forward a three-point proposal to the Kampuchean side, which included: an immediate and to all hostile military activities in the border region; signing by the two parties of documents undertaking to respect each other's independence, sovereignty and territorial integrity within the existing borders, to refrain from the use of force, particularly from interference in each other's internal affairs and from subversive activities against each other; and agreement between the two sides on an appropriate form of international guarantee and supervision.

The Kampuchean side has so far ignored and not responded to this fair and reasonable proposal of the Socialist Republic of Vietnam.

III. The Kampuchean authorities' allegation about the so-called "Vietnam-dominated Indochinese Federation with only one party, one state, and one people" is completely groundless.

The history of 100 years of foreign domination experienced by the Indochinese peoples has proved that the imperialists, whether they were the French colonialists, or the Japanese fascists or the U.S. imperialists, had all used Indochina as a theatre of war, applied their traditional "divide-and-rule" policy, used one country as a springboard for aggression against another, used one people to fight another with the aim of conquering all the three countries. The solidarity of the peoples of the three countries against the common enemy was an objective requirement of the revolutionary cause of each people, a factor of decisive importance to win victory in the national liberation struggle as well as in the long-term cause of national defence and construction carried out by each people. To be lasting, this solidarity must be based on equality and mutual respect, it must serve the national interests of each country, in accordance with the interests of the world people. The Indochinese Communists in the past, as well as the leaders of the three Parties and three countries later on, did all they could to build and foster the militant solidarity and fraternal friendship between the three nations, while scrupulously respecting the fundamental national rights of each people and the independence of each Party.

The unswerving policy followed by the Vietnamese Party and Government with regard to the two fraternal countries and Parties is to foster "militant solidarity and to promote long-term and friendly cooperation with them on the basis of respect for the fundamental national rights of each country. With regard to Kampuchea, now as in the past, in hard times as well as in days of victory, Vietnam's policy is consistent and its feelings are unchanged: solidarity with and wholehearted support to Kampuchea, respect for its independence, sovereignty, Unity, territorial integrity, political system, independent and sovereign line, and non-inference in its internal affairs.

With its correct line and actions as well as by its concerted fight against the common enemy, Vietnam has done its utmost to contribute to the lofty solidarity between the three nations and to fulfil its international duties towards the common cause of revolution.

All true revolutionaries, and patriots are duty-bound to defend and promote this lofty solidarity. Only the imperialists and world reactionaries are striving to undermine it.

Why then have the Kampuchean authorities distorted history and confused black and white, in an attempt to slander the Socialist Republic of Vietnam? "The Indochinese Federation" is a historical matter, and for the past twenty years and more, it has no longer been referred to. If the "Indochinese Federation" question really stands on the way of the friendly relations between the two countries, why should they not agree to sign with the Socialist Republic of Vietnam a treaty in which they undertake to respect each other's independence, sovereignty, and territorial integrity, to refrain from aggression, from the use of force or the threat to use force in the relations with each other, from subversive activities against each other, to treat each other on an equal footing, and to live in peace and friendship in a good neighbourly relationship", and "a treaty on the border question on the basis of respect for each other's territorial integrity within the existing borders" as proposed by the Vietnamese side on February 5, 1978? The fact that they raise this historical matter again, just as they have done with the historical question of territory between the two countries, is but a stratagem to arouse national hatred and enmity. The policy of fanning national hatred and enmity between Kampuchea and Vietnam and sabotaging the friendship between the two peoples is part of their policy of creating border conflicts with neighbouring countries, applying a closed-door foreign policy, enhancing narrow nationalism and rejecting international and regional cooperation (such as the cooperation concerning the Mekong River). The Kampuchean authorities' foreign policy is aimed at serving their intensified repression of the people at home and their purging of revolutionaries and patriots opposed to their erroneous line; it is also aimed at consolidating their power and diverting public opinion at home, which has become indignant at their criminal policies.

Undermining the traditional solidarity between the three nations, the Kampuchean authorities are not only betraying their people's close comraides-in-arms but also cutting across their people's sacred feelings and national interests. Although the imperialists have been forced to withdraw from Indochina, they have not given up their vicious intention to sabotage the independence and peace of the three Indochinese countries. By undermining the militant solidarity between the three peoples, the Kampuchean authorities are committing a crime which is encouraged by the imperialists and world reactionaries and for which they must be held fully responsible to their own people and to history.

The Government of the Socialist Republic of Vietnam affirms the following:

1) "The Indochinese Federation" is a question which has passed forever into history. Ever since 1954, after Vietnam, Laos and Kampuchea restored their national sovereignty and territorial integrity and won international recognition, it has no longer been mentioned by the Laotians, the Kampucheans or the Vietnamese. Holding high the banner of national independence and socialism, the Government of the Socialist Republic of Vietnam once again affirms that there is no such question as the Indochinese Federation.

2) The Government of the Socialist Republic of Vietnam unswervingly honours its commitments in the Geneva Agreements on Indochina (1954) and the Geneva Agreement on Laos (1962), the Paris Agreement and the Act of the International Conference on Vietnam (1973) as well as other international documents it has signed concerning its relations with Laos and Kampuchea: strict respect for the independence, sovereignty, unity, territorial integrity, political system and the independent and sovereign line of the two fraternal countries — Laos and Kampuchea — respect for the independence of the People's Revolutionary Party of Laos and the Communist Party of Kampuchea, non-interference in the internal affairs of Laos and Kampuchea. It is prepared to sign with Kampuchea a treaty on mutual respect and a treaty concerning the border between the two countries, as has been proposed in its February 5, 1978 Statement.

3) The Government of the Socialist Republic of Vietnam will continue to make every effort to preserve and strengthen the militant solidarity and fraternal friendship between the Vietnamese and the Kampuchean peoples, and between the peoples of the three countries on the Indochinese peninsula.

The Vietnamese people are confident that in the end justice will prevail, and the solidarity and friendship between the Vietnamese and the Kampuchean peoples will prevail.

Hanoi, 7 April, 1978.

Note of the Ministry of Foreign Affairs of Democratic Kampuchea, Phnom Penh, 15 May, 1978.

(Complete Text).

Democratic Kampuchea is always endowed with a firm will to live in peace and to maintain close relations of friendship with all neighbouring countries on the basis of equality and mutual respect.

In order to create conditions favourable for solving rapidly the problems caused by the acts of violation and aggression perpetrated by the Socialist Republic of Vietnam against Democratic Kampuchea, the Government of Democratic Kampuchea addresses this note to the Government of the Socialist Republic of Vietnam in order that it takes the following urgent measures:

1) To stop carrying out any attack of aggression, invasion and annexation against the territory of Democratic Kampuchea; to stop any act of provocation and violation against the territory, territorial waters and airspace of Democratic Kampuchea; to stop machine-gunning, pounding, bombing and carrying out air-raids against the territory and territorial waters of Democratic Kampuchea;

2) To stop sending spying agents to gather intelligence in the territory, territorial waters and islands of Democratic Kampuchea; to stop carrying out any act of subversion and interference in the internal affairs of Democratic Kampuchea; to stop carrying out attempts of coups d'etat or other forms of activities aiming at overthrowing the Government of Democratic Kampuchea;

3) To definitively abandon the strategy aiming at putting Kampuchea under the domination of Vietnam in the "Indochina Federation" following the doctrine of "one party, one country and one people" in the "Indochina" belonging to Vietnam;

4) To respect the independence, sovereignty and territorial integrity of Democratic Kampuchea; to respect the rights of the Kampuchea's people to decide by themselves their own destiny.

If the Socialist Republic of Vietnam carries out concrete acts in conformity with this note in 4 points during a period of 7 months, from now up to the end of 1978, by stopping during this period all acts of violation or aggression against the independence, sovereignty, territorial integrity and security of Democratic Kampuchea, then an atmosphere of friendship and confidence would surely be created. In this atmosphere, the Kampuchea's side and the Vietnamese side will meet together in order to sincerely seek for a correct and definitive solution to the various problems.

The Government of Democratic Kampuchea considers and is convinced that this is the only way which would be in conformity with the interest of the Vietnamese people and the Kampuchea's people, which would create friendship between Vietnam and Kampuchea, between the peoples of Vietnam and Kampuchea, and would allow Vietnam and Kampuchea to live in good neighbourhood, peace, and in prosperity. And it is the only way which would be in conformity with the principles of non-alignment and the interest of the peoples the world over and contribute to the peace in this region.

But if the Socialist Republic of Vietnam obstinately persists in carrying out acts of provocation, violation, aggression and annexation against the territory of Democratic Kampuchea, then the so-called negotiations propagated by Vietnam would be nothing but just a continued piece of dupery and the face of aggression and annexation of the Socialist Republic of Vietnam against Democratic Kampuchea would be further spurned by the independence- and justice-loving peoples the world over.

Phnom Penh, May 15, 1978.

Note of the Ministry of Foreign Affairs of the Socialist Republic of Vietnam to the Foreign Ministry of Democratic Kampuchea.

(Complete Text.).

The Foreign Ministry of the Socialist Republic of Vietnam presents its compliments to the Foreign Ministry of Democratic Kampuchea and has the honour to clearly express Vietnam's views regarding the 15th May, 1978 Note of the Kampuchean Foreign Ministry as follows:

It is the principled stand of the Vietnamese people and the Government of the Socialist Republic of Vietnam to resolutely defend the independence, freedom, sovereignty, and territorial integrity of Vietnam, while at the same time respecting the independence, freedom, sovereignty and territorial integrity of Kampuchea and of other countries; to consistently unite with the Kampuchean people and to tirelessly endeavour to quickly settle problems in relations between the two countries through negotiations.

In its 5th February, 1978 statement, the Government of the Socialist Republic of Vietnam put forward a three-point proposal:

(1) An immediate end shall be put to all hostile military activities in the border regions; the armed forces of each side shall be stationed within their respective territory 5 km from the border.

(2) The two sides shall meet at once in Hanoi or Phnom Penh, or at a place on the border to discuss and conclude a treaty, in which they will undertake to respect each other's independence, sovereignty and territorial integrity, to refrain from aggression, from the use of force or the threat to use force in their relations with each other, from interference in each other's

internal affairs, and from subversive activities against each other, to treat each other on an equal footing, and to live in peace and friendship in a good-neighbourly relationship. The two sides shall sign a treaty on the border question on the basis of respect for each other's territorial sovereignty within the existing border.

(3) The two sides shall reach agreement on an appropriate form of international guarantee and supervision.

The *aforesaid* three-point proposal has been widely approved and supported by world public opinion, but the Government of Democratic Kampuchea has not yet officially expressed its attitude. On 10th April, 1978, the Deputy Prime Minister and Foreign Minister of the Socialist Republic of Vietnam addressed a Note to the Deputy Prime Minister in charge of Foreign Affairs of Democratic Kampuchea, reiterating the three-point proposal and requesting a positive response from the Government of Democratic Kampuchea.

It is most regrettable that the Kampuchean side refused to accept this Note.

As the Vietnamese side has pointed out on many occasions, in order to have a pretext for launching a border war against Vietnam, the Kampuchean side has not ceased to slanderously accuse Vietnam of carrying out aggression and subversion against Kampuchea and forcing it into an Indochinese federation. In its 15th May, 1978 Note, the Kampuchean side based itself on these slanderous allegations to demand that Vietnam meet four conditions during a seven-month period, from now to the end of 1978, before the two sides can meet. The Vietnamese people and the Government of the Socialist Republic of Vietnam resolutely reject these absurd demands because they are aimed only at deliberately prolonging the border war and undermining the settlement of problems in relations between the two countries through peaceful negotiation.

Wishing to end the armed conflict and bloodshed immediately, and to sit at the negotiating table at once to settle problems in relations between the two countries, the Government of the Socialist Republic of Vietnam now proposes that:

(1) The two sides shall issue a joint statement or each side shall make a separate statement to cease all hostile military activities in the border regions at the earliest date possible to be agreed upon by the two sides and to station their armed forces within their respective territories, 5 km from the border.

(2) On the same date, the diplomatic representatives of Vietnam and Kampuchea in Vientiane or in another mutually acceptable capital shall meet to discuss and quickly reach agreement on the date, place, and level of a meeting between representatives of the Vietnamese Government and the Kampuchean Government, to settle problems in relations between the two countries.

The Government of the Socialist Republic of Vietnam hopes that the Government of Democratic Kampuchea will give an early positive response to the aforesaid proposal, in the immediate and long-term interests of the Kampuchean and the Vietnamese peoples, for the benefit of peace and security in South-East Asia and the world.

The Foreign Ministry of the Socialist Republic of Vietnam takes this opportunity to renew to the Foreign Ministry of Democratic Kampuchea the assurances of its high consideration.

Hanoi, 7 June, 1978.

Declaration of the Kampuchean National United Front for National Salvation. 3rd December 1978.

(Complete Text.).

Dear and respected compatriots, Dear cadres and combatants, Dear compatriots abroad,

Throughout the long period when Cambodia was under the yoke of colonialism, imperialism and feudalism, many of our compatriots, cadres and combatants have developed our forefathers's glorious tradition, and, despite innumerable difficulties and sacrifices, they have relentlessly struggled with sublime heroism against Frensh and US imperialism with a view to restoring independence and freedom for the country, thus glorifying our magnificent land of Angkor. Particularly during our patriotic war against US imperialism, while relying on our own forces and at the same time enjoying the sympathy, support and assistance of socialist countries and peace and justice-loving people the world over, our people won the glorious victory of 17th April, 1975, totally liberating our country, opening for the Cambodian people a new era, the era of independence, freedom and socialism.

Following the restoration of our total independence, our people could have enjoyed peace, devoted might and main to national reconstruction, and established relations of solidarity and friendship with socialist countries and all peace loving countries, independence and freedom in South-East Asia and the world as a whole.

However, over the past three years, things have happened in a completely opposite way. A dictatorial, militarist and fascist régime, matchless in history for its ferocity, has been installed in Cambodia. The reactionary Pol Pot-Ieng Sary gang and their families have totally usurped power, sought by all means to betray the country and harm the people, causing innumerable sufferings and grief to our fellow Cambodians, and threatening our people with extermination. It is the Chinese authorities who have encouraged and backed to the hilt these traitors and tyrants. Only a few days after liberation, under the signboard "all-round, radical social revolution", and "social purification" they razed the towns and forced millions of people in cities and urban centres to leave their homes and property for the countryside to lead a precarious life and die slowly through hard labour.

They have cut all sacred sentiments of people towards their parents, between brothers, and sisters, husbands and wives, and even among neighbours. In fact, they have razed villages where out people had lived and woven sentimental ties for thousands of years. They proclaim "forcible co-operativization", "abolition of money and markets" and force people to eat and sleep in communities. In fact, they have herded our compatriots into camouflaged concentration camps, robbed our people of all means of production and consumer goods, forced them to overwork while giving them the minimum of food and clothes, forcing all strata of the population to live in misery as slaves. They classify people into different categories with a view to subduing them more easily and making them kill one another.

The crimes of the Pol Pot-Ieng Sary gang, can no longer be counted! Everywhere our people have witnessed massacres, more atrocious, more barbarous than those committed in the Middle Ages or perpetrated by the Hitlerite fascists.

They have even declared that they would not hesitate to sacrifice millions of our compatriots for the sake of building socialism the way they chose. In many places they have massacred the people of whole villages and whole hamlets. They do not even spare foetuses inside mothers' wombs! Worse still, they intend to massacre more than 1,700,000 people in the Eastern Region. In face of this situation, hundreds of thousands of people have risen up against them, tens of thousands of people whose lives are threatened have been forced to leave the motherland for abroad. Those who remain in the country live in constant fear — like fish caught in a net not knowing when their turn will come to be massacred.

The Pol Pot-Ieng Sary gang have usurped the leadership of the Party, and have forgotten all that the revolutionary people have done to feed and protect them. Immediately after seizing the top level of power, they paid back with tortures, and murders! They have betrayed their compatriots and their comrades. Many cadres, Party members authentic revolutionaries and patriots, and cadres and combatants in the armed forced who had contributed to the liberation of the country and shown absolute loyalty to the motherland have been killed *en masse* at all levels and in all places only because they did not approve the reactionary and barbarous policy of the Pol Pot-Ieng Sary gang.

They have trampled all traditions underfoot, all the fine customs and habits of our people, and committed acts of vandalism against our nation's time-honoured culture. They have banned freedom of religion, organized forced collective marriages, dislocated families, and debased our nation's habits and customs. They have destroyed pagodas and temples of Buddhism — an ancient State religion of Cambodia, and have forced monks and nuns to return to lay life. They have destroyed Hinduism, while exterminating the Champa nationality. They have razed almost all education establishments from primary schools to universities. They have forced all children of 13-14 to give up studies and enlist in the army to serve their interests: The Pol Pot-Ieng Sary régime is a régime of new-type enslavement and has nothing to do with socialism!

To camouflage their abominable crimes against our people and fool public opinion at home and abroad, to serve their dark design of building a barbarous dictatorial and militarist régime ready to kill all those who refuse to submit to them, and to serve the strategic aims of great-nation expansionism of the Chinese authorities, they have provoked a border conflict with Vietnam, thus turning friend into foe. They have transformed our revolutionary armed forces into mercenaries for the Chinese authorities, and into a tool to suppress the people's uprising movement.

Respected compatriots, Dear cadres and combatants, Dear fellow Cambodians living abroad!

The Pol Pot and Ieng Sary traitors and tyrants have drowned Cambodia in blood and tears. Boiling with anger against these barbarous acts and this policy of betrayal toward the country and people, the authentic revolutionary and patriotic forces have risen up alongside the people throughout the country to struggle resolutely against these traitors to save our country and people from slavery and extermination.

The newly founded Cambodian National United Front for National Salvation solemnly declares:

The Cambodian National United Front for National Salvation, established in the spirit of authentic independence of the Cambodian people, unites all nationalities in the country, and rallies all patriotic forces regardless of political and religious inclinations — workers, peasants, petty bourgeois, intellectual's Buddhist monks and nuns, patriots still in the ranks of the ruling clique, and compatriots now living abroad — and without distinction of age or sex, to realize with unanimity the immediate revolutionary task of the Cambodian people:

To unite the entire people and rise up to topple the reactionary and nepotic Pol Pot-Ieng Sary gang of militarist dictators, henchmen of the foreign reactionary forces; to liquidate their barbarous and blood-thirsty régime; to establish a people's democratic régime, to develop the Angkor traditions, to make Cambodia a really peaceful, independent, democratic, neutral, and non-aligned country advancing to socialism, thus contributing actively to the common struggle for peace and stability in South-East Asia.

To fulfil this historic mission, the Cambodian National United Front for National Salvation undertakes:

1. To carry out a policy of great national union, and overthrow the dictatorial militarist and nepotic régime of the reactionary Pol Pot-Ieng Sary clique. To dissolve the People's Representative Assembly created by Pol Pot.Ieng Sary. To hold general elections to a national assembly: to reorganize a people's democratic power at all levels; to work out a new constitution guaranteeing the people's rights to equality, to real freedom and democracy, and to establish the legislation of an independent, democratic State advancing to socialism.

2. To build cambodian revolutionary mass organizations affiliated to the Cambodian National United Front for National Salvation with a view to grouping various strata of the population, help them see through the anti-national and anti-popular nature of the reactionary Pol Pot-Ieng Sary gang, so that they will abandon all organizations and groups set up by this gang, and actively adhere to the youth association for national salvation, the women's association for national salvation, the trade union for national salvation, the peasants' association for national salvation, and the intellectuals' association for national salvation with a view to toppling the reactionary and nepotic Pol Pot-Ieng Sary gang and bringing to all strata of our people the right to be the real masters of the country.

3. To build and develop the Cambodian Revolutionary Army which, together with the people, has the task of crushing the reactionary Pol Pot-Ieng Sary administration, defending the revolutionary power; the people's lives and property, defending the motherland ever more effectively, firmly maintaining the independence, sovereignty and territorial integrity of Cambodia.

4. To realize the people's rights to real freedom and democracy and respect their dignity. All Cambodians have the right to return to their old native land, and to build their family life in happiness. All Cambodians have freedom of residence, movement, association, and religion, and have the right to work, recreation and education; to guaranteed freedom of person. All ethnic groups in the Cambodian social community have the right to freedom, equality, and to share the same rights and duties.

5. To carry out an independent and sovereign economic policy tending towards genuine socialism. To rebuild our war-torn country. To restore the national economy ravaged by the Pol Pot-Ieng Sary régime. The new economy shall serve the people's interests on the basis of agricultural and industrial development. It will be a planned economy with markets, meeting the needs for progress of society. To abolish the compulsory "work-and-eat-together" system, and to put an end to the Pol Pot-Ieng Sary policy of seizing the people's rice and other property. To assist and encourage mutual-aid and co-operative forms on the basis of the peasants' own volition in order to boost production and improve the people's living standards. To establish banks, issue currency, restore and develop the circulation of goods. To broaden the home trade and increase economic relations

with all foreign countries on equal footing and with mutual benefits. To abolish the Pol Pot-Ieng Sary policy of back-breaking forced labour. To carry out the policy of an eight-hour working day and pay according to labour.

6. To abolish compulsory marriage, and encourage free choice in marriage, and restore the happy life of every family. To realise sexual equality and create all favourable conditions for women to obtain education and improve their skills in order to serve society like men. To care for war invalids, families of war dead, and families which have rendered good services to the revolution. To care for the people's health, aged and infirm people and orphans. To care for and defend the legitimate interests of overseas Cambodians. To have a correct policy towards foreign residents in Cambodia.

7. To abolish the reactionary culture of the Pol Pot-Ieng Sary gang. To build a new culture of a national and popular character. To do away with illiteracy, develop the national education, build general-education schools, universities and secondary vocational schools. To give the right positions to scientific workers, technicians, artists and other educated men and women. To protect and restore historical relics, pagodas and temples, and parks destroyed by the Pol Pot-Ieng Sary gang.

8. To welcome warmly and create favourable conditions for officers and soldiers, as well as public servants in the administration of the reactionary régime to rally with the people and fight back against the Pol Pot-Ieng Sary gang to save the motherland and their own families.

Duly to punish die-hard reactionary chieftains who have committed bloody crimes against the people. To practise leniency towards those who repent sincerely. To give appropriate rewards to those with feats of arms in service of the revolution. To give humane treatment to those in the ranks of the Pol Pot-Ieng Sary administration and army who have been captured in combat and help them to become decent people, useful to society.

9. To carry out a foreign policy of peace, friendship and non-alignment towards all countries without distinction as to their political and social systems, and on the basis of peaceful coexistence, respect for each other's independence, sovereignty, territorial integrity, non-interference in each other's internal affairs, equality and mutual benefit.

10. To settle all disputes with neighbouring countries through peaceful negotiations, and on the basis of respect for each other's independence, sovereignty and territorial integrity. To put an end to the border war with Vietnam provoked by the Pol Pot-Ieng Sary gang. To restore the relations of friendship, co-operation and good neighbourhood with other South-East Asian countries, and contribute to building South-East Asia into a region of peace, independence, freedom, neutrality, stability and prosperity. Cambodia will not join any military alliance nor allow any country to build military bases on its territory or send military equipment into Cambodia.

11. To strengthen solidarity with all revolutionary and progressive forces throughout the world. To firmly support the common struggle of all nations for peace, national independence, democracy and social progress, against imperialism, colonialism and neo-colonialism.

Dear and respected compatriots, Dear cadres and combatants, Dear compatriots abroad.

Our nation is facing the danger of extermination! Our motherland is in danger!

The Cambodian National United Front for National Salvation calls on:

All fellow Cambodians of all nationalities, and all walks of life, including those living abroad, old and young, men and women, regardless of political tendencies and religious beliefs, to close our ranks under the banner of the Cambodian National United Front for National Salvation and rise up, millions as one, to overthrow the dictatorial militarist and genocidal régime headed by the nepotic and bloodthirsty Pol Pot-Ieng Sary gang.

This is the only way to save our people, our country and ourselves. In this way we can bring peace and genuine independence to our country, and freedom, real democracy and happiness to our people.

Cadres, public employees and combatants will entangled in the administration and army machinery of the reactionary Pol Pot-Ieng Sary gang! Rise up against every traitorous undertaking and policy of this gang, take an effective part in the just struggle of the people, destroy the leading torturers, and turn into genuine revolutionary armed forces of the people!

The Cambodian National United Front for National Salvation earnestly calls on the peoples and governments of all countries, international organizations, mass organizations and democratic organizations throughout the world struggling for peace, national independence, democracy and social progress to give our people's just struggle active support and assistance in all fields.

The reactionary Pol Pot-Ieng Sary régime, barbarous as it is, is shaking to its roots and is doomed to total collapse.

In the present epoch no international reactionary force, however perfidious it may be, can exterminate the heroic Cambodian people.

The genuine Cambodian revolutionary forces still have to overcome numerous difficulties and hardships. But they have a correct revolutionary line and fight for a goal, in accordance with the sacred aspiration of the nation and the trend of history. They are solidly united, millions as one, and enjoy the sympathy and support of the peoples who love peace, justice and social progress. They will win glorious victory.

The time of the revolution has come!

Cadres and combatants, unite and march forward heroically!

Struggle resolutely to overthrow the reactionary Pol Pot-Ieng Sary gang!

Our people will surely achieve a peaceful, independent, democratic, neutral, and non-aligned Cambodia which will advance to socialism! The Cambodian revolution will prevail!

Cambodian liberated zone, 3rd December, 1978.

The Central Committee of the
Cambodian National United Front
for National Salvation.[1]

[1] Members of the Central Committee of the Cambodian National United Front for National Salvation. (CNUFNS).

Heng Samrin, former member of the Executive Committee of the Party for the Eastern Region, former political commissar and Commander of the Fourth Division, President of the Central Committee of the CNUFNS;

Chea Sim, former Secretary of the Party Committee for Sector 20 of the Eastern Region, former member of the Cambodian People's Representative Assembly, Vice-President of the Front's Central Committee;

Ros Samay, Assistant Chief of Staff of unit X of the Cambodian Revolutionary Armed Forces, Secretary-General of the Front's Central Committee;

Mat Ly, former member of the Standing Committee of the Cambodian People's Representative Assembly, member of the Front's Central Committee;

Bun Mi, former Deputy Secretary of the Party Committee for Sector 3, North-Eastern Region, representative of the ethnic minorities, member of the Front's Central Committee;

Hun Sen, former Chief of Staff and former regimental Deputy Commander in Sector 21, representative of the Youth Association for National Salvation, member of the Front's Central Committee;

Mrs Mean Saman political commissar of a Cambodian revolutionary armed forces battalion, representative of the Women's Association for National Salvation, member of the Front's Central Committee;

Meas Samnang, representative of the Trade Union for National Salvation, member of the Front's Central Committee;

Neou Samon, representative of the Peasants Association for National Salvation, member of the Front's Central Committee;

Head Monk Long Sim, representative of the Buddhist clergy, member of the Front's Central Committee;

Mechanical engineer Hem Samin, representative of the Intellectuals Association for National Salvation, member of the Front's Central Committee;

Mrs Chey Kanh Nha, doctor of medicine, member of the Intellectuals Association for National Salvation, member of the Front's Central Committee;

Chan Ven, professor of physics, member of the Intellectuals Association for National Salvation, member of the Front's Central Committee;

Prach Sun, journalist, member of the Intellectuals Association for National Salvation, member of the Front's Central Committee.

Statement on Vietnam's Expulsion of Chinese Residents.*

(Complete Text). Hsinhua News Agency. 24 May, 1978.
*By Spokesman of the Overseas Chinese Affairs Office of the State Council.

On May 24 a spokesman of the Overseas Chinese Affairs Office of the State Council of the People's Republic of China gave an interview to correspondents of the Hsinhua News Agency on the question of Vietnam forcing Chinese residents there to return to China. His statement follows:

Recently, the Vietnamese side has been unwarrantedly ostracizing and persecuting Chinese residents in Vietnam, and expelling many of them back to China. The situation has been deteriorating daily.

On May 4 a responsible official of the Vietnamese side made a public statement, in which he distorted the facts in an attempt to put the blame on the Chinese side for the massive expulsion of Chinese. Under these circumstances, we cannot but set forth the facts so as to ensure a correct understanding of the matter.

Early in 1977 the Vietnamese side, in a so-called effort to "clear up the border areas," started in a planned way to expel people who had long ago moved from China to settle down in Vietnamese border areas. This subsequently developed gradually into the massive expulsion of Chinese residents in all parts of Vietnam. Out of a sincere desire to uphold Sino-Vietnamese friendship and seek a proper settlement of this question, the Chinese side repeatedly tried to persuade the Vietnamese side that it should value Sino-Vietnamese friendship and stop such extremely unfriendly practice of displacing so many overseas Chinese residents and harming the good feelings between the two peoples. But to our regret, the Vietnamese side not only failed to respond to our good wishes, but became more vicious in expelling Chinese and the number of Chinese expelled was growing. The situation became more serious. According to statistics undertaken in our border areas, more than 50,000 overseas Chinese were driven back to China in the period of one and a half months from early April to mid-May this year. Up to now, the number has exceeded 70,000, not counting those who were compelled to leave Vietnam and seek refuge in other places.

The majority of the expelled Chinese are labouring people who on their way back to China suffered various maltreatments. Some were beaten up and wounded. They lost through arbitrary confiscation most of their possessions which they had earned in long years of labour. Even the small number of personal belongings for daily use they carried with them were plundered on the way before they left Vietnamese territory. As a result, most of the Chinese had nothing left except the clothes they were wearing when they entered Chinese territory. Many old people and children suffered from hunger and disease. It was altogether a pitiful scene.

Yet, in utter disregard of the facts, the Vietnamese official made the slanderous countercharge that "some bad elements among the Chinese spread rumours to foment discord in the relations between Vietnam and China" and that the Chinese "lightly believed" the rumours and illegally crossed the border to return to their homeland.

What are the facts? Detailed investigation and checking by our border authorities have established that it is Vietnamese departments concerned and public security personnel who, acting on instructions, spread among Vietnamese people and Chinese residents the rumours that "China has committed aggression against Vietnam," that "the Chinese Government has called on overseas Chinese to return," etc., to incite hostility against the Chinese residents and threaten and intimidate them. The Vietnamese side has also used various means to restrict employment of the Chinese residents. Chinese who were on job were unjustifiably demoted or fired. Their food ration was reduced or stopped through cancellation of their residence registration. As a result, large numbers of Chinese residents have lost their means of livelihood and found it difficult to make a living and are plunged in dire distress. In Ho Chi Minh City and other places, there even occurred grave incidents of mass arrest and wounding and killing of Chinese residents. In order to cover up the truth of the expulsion of Chinese and to shirk responsibility, Vietnamese public security personnel compelled some Chinese to fill in a "Form of Voluntary Repatriation" or to copy or read out statements prepared beforehand for them which the security personnel photographed, filmed or recorded as "evidence of voluntary repatriation" of Chinese residents. Then they transported groups of Chinese to designated points on the border and drove them back to China across border rivers. A host of facts proves that the massive expulsion of Chinese back to China is a purposeful and planned line of action carried out by the Vietnamese authorities on instructions.

People will not forget that the Chinese in Vietnam have long lived in friendship with Vietnamese people and taken an active part in the Vietnamese revolution and construction. During the protracted struggle against colonial rule, and in the difficult years of wars of national salvation against French and U.S. imperialism, many Chinese residents fought shoulder to shoulder with the Vietnamese people and never flinched from bloodshed and sacrifice. They made positive contributions to the Vietnamese people's cause of liberation, to the building of the liberated areas, to postwar rehabilitation and reconstruction and to the growth of the revolutionary friendship between the two peoples, and in the process forged a profound fraternity with the Vietnamese people. After the liberation of the whole of Vietnam, however, the Vietnamese authorities have now returned evil for good by using despicable means to persecute Chinese and evict them en masse, thus greatly hurting the traditional friendship between the Chinese and Vietnamese peoples. Over this we cannot but feel strong regret and indignation.

Regarding the question of nationality of Chinese residing abroad, it has been China's consistent policy to favour and encourage their voluntary choice of the nationality of the country of residence. At the same time, we take exception to the practice of compelling them to take up against their will the nationality of their country of residence. This is the well-known and openly declared policy of the Chinese Government, which has been consistently implemented over the years. In 1955 during the discussion by the Chinese and Vietnamese Parties of the question of nationality of the Chinese residents in Vietnam, both sides agreed to abide by the principle of voluntary choice of nationality. In 1956 the reactionary Ngo Dinh Diem régime in south Vietnam compelled Chinese residents to become naturalized. The Commission of Overseas Chinese Affairs of the People's Republic of China issued a statement on May 20, 1957, strongly protesting against the Ngo Dinh Diem régime's despicable action of compelling Chinese residents to change their nationality, and solemnly stating that "the regulations of the south Vietnamese administration on changing the nationality of the Chinese residents in south Vietnam are unreasonable and unilateral," and that "the south Vietnamese administration should bear full responsibility for all the consequences arising from this unreasonable act." *Nhan Dan* of the Democratic Republic of Vietnam on May 23, 1957 carried the full text of this statement and on May 24 the same year published a signed article entitled "The Ngo Dinh Diem Clique Is the Common Enemy of the Vietnamese and the Chinese Residents," expressing its support for China's just stand. In its "Letter to Chinese Brothers and Sisters in South Vietnam" published on May 24, 1965, the South Vietnam National Front for Liberation stated that "the Chinese residents have the freedom and right to choose their nationality." But in recent years, the Vietnamese side went back on its word and abandoned the principle of voluntary choice of nationality for the Chinese residents. It resorted to a series of measures of discrimination, ostracism and persecution against the Chinese residents. It compelled them to take up Vietnamese nationality on penalty of losing their work papers, having their staple and other food rations cut, paying heavy taxes and even being deported. We feel great surprise and regret at the Vietnamese side's practice of compelling the Chinese residents to become naturalized, which violates the agreement between the two sides and runs counter to the general principles of international law.

China and Vietnam are neighbouring countries linked by common mountains and rivers, and the Chinese and Vietnamese peoples have formed a profound friendship during the protracted revolutionary struggles. We are firmly opposed to the Vietnamese authorities' arbitrary, truculent and illegal actions towards the Chinese residents. We demand that the Vietnamese side immediately stop implementing the above-mentioned erroneous policy of ostracizing, persecuting and expelling the Chinese residents and do not continue to damage the traditional friendship between our two countries and our two peoples. Otherwise, the Vietnamese Government should bear full responsibility for all the consequences arising from these unwarranted measures.

Statement by the spokesman of the Ministry of Foreign Affairs of the Socialist Republic of Vietnam.*

(Complete Text).

*Regarding the Chinese distortions of the Vietnamese Government's policy towards the Hoa people in Vietnam, 27 May, 1978.

On 24th May, 1978, the spokesman of the Overseas Chinese Affairs Office of the People's Republic of China State Council stated to the Hsinhua News Agency correspondent that Vietnam was "ostracizing, persecuting, and expelling" Hoa(1) people in Vietnam. At the same time, the Chinese press, radio, and television ceaselessly distorted the facts about the Hoa people in Vietnam. The Vietnamese people and the Government of the Socialist Republic of Vietnam are extremely surprised by these statements and energetically reject them because they are sheer fabrications utterly contrary to the policy of the Party and the Government of Vietnam.

(1) As regards Hoa people in Vietnam, as early as 1955, the Central Committee of the Vietnamese Workers' Party and the Central Committee of the Chinese Communist Party agreed that Chinese residents in Vietnam would be placed under the leadership of the Vietnamese Workers' Party and gradually turned into Vietnamese citizens. In January 1961, the Foreign Ministry of the Democratic Republic of Vietnam accepted the proposal of the Chinese Embassy in Vietnam that the Embassy would not issue passports to Hoa people.

The responsible Vietnamese services would examine the applications of those who ask to go to China to visit their relatives and would send the list of applicants to the Chinese Embassy, which would issue "tourist certificates" and visas for them to enter China.

For the past 20 years and more, the Vietnamese side has consistently respected and correctly implemented the aforesaid agreement. Hoa people in Vietnam have the same rights and obligations as Vietnamese citizens.

The great majority of the Hoa people in North Vietnam are workers employed in co-operatives, factories, state offices and mass organizations.

[1] Vietnamese generic term designating persons of Chinese descent "who can no longer be distinguished from other Vietnamese". (Ed.).

Their children study in Vietnamese schools and many of them have become teachers, engineers, doctors, high-level technicians. On the contrary, Vietnamese residents in China enjoy only very limited rights. Over the past 20 years, the Vietnamese side has repeatedly drawn the Chinese side's attention on this fact, but the situation has not been improved.

In south Vietnam, since 1956, almost all Chinese residents have adopted Vietnamese nationality. They are no longer Chinese residents but Vietnamese of Chinese origin. Since the complete liberation of south Vietnam, Vietnamese of Chinese stock have had the same rights and obligations as Vietnamese citizens. The adoption of Vietnamese nationality by Chinese residents in the south and their becoming Vietnamese of Chinese origin for the past 20 years have been a reality left by history.

At present, a campaign to transform the private capitalist commerce and industry is going on in south Vietnam.[2] Among the capitalist traders there, there are Vietnamese and Vietnamese of Chinese origin. Many of them have complied with the policies of our Party and State, but a few of them, because of their class enmity, have tried by every means to elude the

[2] On 31 March 1978 the Vietnam Government issued policy on the abolition of capitalist trade in southern Vietnam and on transferring of capitalist traders to productive activities. The policy states:

Article (1) In order to serve effectively the cause of socialist transformation and socialist construction, to restore and develop the economy and to stabilize and gradually improve the people's living conditions, the State must, through the system of socialist trade organizations, unify the administration of the circulation and supply of technical materials and other means of production for the various production and construction sectors, and provide the people with staple commodities. The State hereby decides to abolish capitalist trade carried out by the bourgeoisie, and encourages bourgeois traders to change to socialist production and to switch to production sectors and professions beneficial not only to themselves and their families, but also to national welfare and the pvople's livelihood, thereby making practical contributions to the efforts of the entire people to build a prosperous and strong country.

Article (2) Bourgeois traders may switch to production in agriculture, industry (including artisan industry and handicrafts), fishery and foresty, in conformity with the State line, policies, programmes and plans, and in accordance with the requirements of economic zoning and diversification, and of the redistribution of production forces and population throughout the country and in each locality. Households engaged in both trade and production must stop their trading operations and switch completely to production. Households which specialize in trade have priority in switching to any sector or profession they consider to be favourable and suited to their capabilities, including the production of those goods in which they are now dealing.

Article (3) The State encourages members of the bourgeoisie who switch to production to rely mainly on their own capital, manpower and means of production — which they must exploit to the fullest — and to seek State assistance only when necessary, in order to build relatively large-scale production installations in which progressive production techniques will be applied, and which will operate as joint State-private enterprises or production combinations having direct relations with the State's economic organizations through activities such as manufacturing goods on a contractual basis, organizing production in accordance with State plans and programmes, and selling all their products to the State.

Petty bourgeois who are unable to establish joint State-private enterprises may join the existing production co-operatives if their application for membership is approved by the majority of the members of these co-operatives, or they may establish new co-operatives, strictly in accordance with the regulations on co-operative organization prescribed by the State. In the initial stage of their production work, any bourgeois households unable to join State-private enterprises, co-operatives or other combinations may engage in individual production work, provided that they are duly registered, that they observe carefully all policies, procedures and regulations of the State, that they place themselves under the management of the local administration in matters concerning production guidelines and planning as well as areas and scope of operations, and that they sign contracts to sell their products to the State.

Article (4) In order to create favourable conditions for the bourgeois traders to switch to production, the State will implement the following concrete incentive policies:

(i) On the basis of its actual need for capital for the building of production installations and for the development of production, the State will help bourgeois tradesmen switch the following kinds of capital to production: all capital acquired by selling goods and materials to the State; part or all of the capital acquired by selling to the State shops, warehouses and other business facilities once used in trade operations; and capital deposited at the State banks, which will be partly or wholly shifted to production depending on production requirements and on the managerial procedures of these banks. The State encourages those members of the bourgeoisie who have other kinds of capital such as cash, jewellry, foreign currency, stocks of production materials, etc., which were not used in the past, to invest them in production operations. The State will not collect back taxes on these assets.

(ii) Bourgeois households having to move to new areas designated by the local authorities to carry out production will be given State assistance in transporting their families and property. The authorities in the new areas will provide them with land on which to build their new homes and production installations. They will be allowed to register for food rationing purposes, enjoy the same rights and have to perform the same duties as the local people. They will receive the same kind of assistance in procuring technical materials and in selling their products as that given to other production establishments having relations with the State's economic organizations.

(iii) On capital once used for trading operations but now invested in production, the State will pay interest at a rate similar to that on capital invested by the bourgeoisie in joint State-private enterprises. The State will apply different incentive rates of interest for production establishments, depending on each kind of product and on whether the product is intended for domestic consumption or for export.

(iv) Like other production establishments, while they are still in the process of building their production installation and carrying out production on an experimental basis after switching from trade, all bourgeois households will be granted tax reductions or tax exemptions by the State.

(v) Depending on investigation and decision by the tax services, in some specific cases the State may consider reducing tax arrears and excess profit tax by 30 to 50%, with a view to creating better conditions for bourgeois traders' households to pay all their back taxes and to invest more capital in production installations.

(vi) The State will provide vocational training and improve the professional skills of members of the bourgeois traders' households which have switched to production. The State will give these households the same kind of technical and professional assistance as that accorded to all newly established industrial, agricultural, forestry and fishery production installations.

(vii) Children of bourgeois tradesmen who have switched to production will be allowed to continue their schooling, will be encouraged to participate in production and all other social activities, and will be allowed to join the various mass organizations like any others of their age. (Ed.).

transformation. The socialist transformation of private capitalist commerce and industry is a correct policy in keeping with the laws of socialist revolution, which China and other socialist countries have applied. The overwhelming majority of the working people, including Vietnamese of Chinese origin in south Vietnam, have enthusiastically taken part in this campaign.

(2) Since early 1977, the Kampuchean administration has stepped up a large-scale war of aggression along the border of Vietnam, particularly since 31st December, 1977, when the Kampuchean authorities intensified their military attacks and launched a public campaign against Vietnam. Information has been spread among Hoa people in Vietnam that "China supports Kampuchea against Vietnam; war will break out between China and Vietnam; Hoa people in Vietnam will suffer losses; they must therefore find ways to leave Vietnam quickly". "The Chinese Government calls upon the overseas Chinese to come back; those wo do not do so are traitors to their country", etc. A number of bad elements among the Hoa poeple have deceived, instigated, threatened, and coerced Hoa people to leave Vietnam. This is precisely what has caused many Hoa people to be so frightened as to abandon their peaceful life in Vietnam and to return en masse to China in an illegal manner. The Vietnamese Government has advised them that they should not allow themselves to be deceived by bad elements and that they should remain in Vietnam and continue their normal life. Those who have left have taken their property with them; many have sold cumbersome articles to buy easily portable valuables. After reaching China, many have realized that they had been fooled and have escaped back to Vietnam.

Facts have shown that the deception and coercion of Hoa people in Vietnam to go to China and then the allegation that Vietnam is "ostracizing, persecuting, and expelling" Hoa people are premeditated actions aimed at creating difficulties to the construction of socialism in Vietnam, dividing Vietnamese and Hoa people, and undermining the friendship between the Vietnamese and the Chinese peoples.

(3) During the long struggle for the independence, freedom, and unification of the motherland in the past, as well as in the construction of socialism at present, the Party, Government, and people of Vietnam have always firmly stood on the position of Marxism-Leninism, and proletarian internationalism; they have strictly applied a line aimed at national and international unity, at preserving solidarity with the socialist countries, independent nationalaist countries, as well as with the working class and peace- and justice-loving people the world over. The Vietnamese people uncompromisingly struggle against the imperialists and reactionaries, but they consistently remain united with and loyal to their brothers and friends.

Formerly, in the past two patriotic wars of resistance, the Vietnamese people made a clear difference between the colonialist and imperialist aggressors — our enemy — and the French and the US people, our friends. Nowadays, although the Kampuchean authorities have kindled a frontier war against them, the Vietnamese people have all the same helped tens of thousands of Kampuchean refugees to Vietnam settle and earn their living. With regard to the nationals of a number of countries who formerly collaborated with the imperialists and indulged in hostile actions against Vietnam and who are still remaining in south Vietnam, the Vietnamese Government has applied a humane policy, and hold negotiations with the governments concerned to solve this question satisfactorily in accordance with their aspirations and in keeping with international law and practice. So have we done with the people and residents of countries formerly hostile to Vietnam. Evidently with the Hoa people who are part of the Vietnamese national community, Vietnam has no reason to "ostracize, persecute and expel" them. Even towards thousands of Chinese residents who have been persecuted and chased away by the Kampuchean authorities and who have taken refuge in south Vietnam, the Vietnamese people have given them care and assistance and share with them any means of living.

After so many years of destructive war, the Vietnamese people, more than any other people, are longing for peace and wish to have relations of friendship and co-operation will all other peoples in order to reconstruct their country. There is no reason why Vietnam should provoke a border conflict with Kampuchea. Nor is there any reason for Vietnam to create complexities in her relations with neighbouring socialist China, as the two countries have been united and supported each other in their respective revolutionary cause.

(4) The basic interests of the peoples of Vietnam and China lie in their solidarity and friendship and in their mutual support and assistance in their effort to reach the common goal of building socialism and communism. This is a decisive factor for the victory of each people's revolutionary cause. Over the past few decades the Communist Party, the Government and people of Vietnam have always made every effort to preserve and consolidate the militant friendship between the two peoples. Even when the relations between Vietnam and China were undermined by bad elements, the Vietnamese people remained unchanged in their solidarity and friendship with the Chinese people. Likewise, the Vietnamese people, imbued with genuine patriotism and proletarian internationalism, are now determined to preserve and consolidate the friendship between the two peoples, who are both "comrades and brothers" as President Ho Chi Minh has said.

Between Vietnam and China, as between a number of other socialist countries, there exist certain differences. In dealing with these differences, the Vietnamese Party and Government always stood for a negotiated settlement. Proceeding from this policy, the Vietnamese side proposes that propaganda aimed at playing upon people's feelings, harmful to the friendship between the two peoples, be stopped, and that representatives of the two governments meet soon to settle the differences over the Hoa people question in a spirit of friendship for the benefit of the two peoples.

The Vietnamese people are confident that by bringing into play their spirit of self reliance, and in addition, enjoying the support and assistance from their brothers and friends in the world, they will certainly succeed in building a peaceful, independent, unified and socialist Vietnam, thereby contributing to the cause of peace, national independence, democracy and social progress of the people of the world.

Statement of the Foreign Ministry of the People's Republic of China on Expulsion of Chinese Residents by Vietnam, 9 June, 1978.

(Complete Text). Hsinhua News Agency, 9 June, 1978.

In his statement on the question of the so-called "Hoa people in Vietnam" of May 27, 1978, the spokesman of the Ministry of Foreign Affairs of the Socialist Republic of Vietnam distorted the facts and made unfounded counter-charges in an attempt to put the blame for the expulsion of Chinese nationals on the Chinese side. With regard to this the Chinese Government cannot remain silent.

1. In his statement the spokesman of the Ministry of Foreign Affairs of Vietnam tried, in effect, to deny the objective fact that there are large numbers of Chinese nationals residing in Vietnam and wilfully distorted the agreement between the Chinese Communist Party and the Vietnamese Workers' Party on the question of Chinese residing in Vietnam, attempting thereby to deceive public opinion and justify the Vietnamese policy of discrimination against, and ostracism, persecution and expulsion of, Chinese residents. This is obviously a futile attempt.

It is well known that there are one million and several hundred thousand Chinese residents in Vietnam, the overwhelming majority of whom are working people and about 90% of whom reside in south Vietnam. In 1955 the Chinese and Vietnamese Parties exchanged views on the question of their nationality and their rights and duties. Subsequently, after repeated consultations the two sides acknowledged that the Chinese residing in north Vietnam, on condition of their enjoying equal rights as the Vietnamese and after being given sustained and patient persuasion and ideological education, may by steps adopt Vietnamese nationality on a voluntary basis. As to the question of the Chinese residing in south Vietnam, that was to be resolved through consultations between the two countries after the liberation of south Vietnam. These principles were put forward by the Chinese side out of the desire to deepen the fraternal friendship between the Chinese and Vietnamese peoples, and they are in accordance with China's consistent policy of encouraging overseas Chinese to choose, on a voluntary basis, the nationality of their country of residence, as well as with the general international rule against forcibly naturalizing foreign residents. At that time the Vietnamese Party and Government expressed approval and support for these principles and repeatedly stressed in their documents that "the adoption of Vietnamese nationality by Chinese should be a purely voluntary decision and there should be no coercion whatsoever," and that "those who are not yet willing to adopt Vietnamese nationality are still allowed all rights and may not be discriminated against. It is absolutely impermissible to use rash orders to compel them or to slight them." They also affirmed that politically the Chinese residing in Vietnam would enjoy the same rights and have the same duties as the Vietnamese, that economically they would enjoy the freedom to engage in lawful industrial and commercial undertakings, that culturally they would enjoy the freedom to run schools and papers and that their ways and customs would be respected. In recent years, however, the Vietnamese Government, running counter to the agreement between the two Parties, has compelled Chinese residents to adopt Vietnamese nationality, zealously pursued a policy of discrimination against, and ostracism and persecution of Chinese residents and seriously infringed on their legitimate rights and interests, making it difficult for the mass of Chinese residents to make a living, and has even expelled large numbers of them back to China.

In south Vietnam, the Vietnamese Government, in contravention of its publicly stated position, has continued the practice of the reactionary Ngo Dinh Diem régime and used high-handed means against the Chinese residents. On August 21, 1956 the reactionary Ngo Dinh Diem régime promulgated a decree compelling the Chinese residents to renounce their Chinese nationality and adopt Vietnamese nationality. On April 17, 1957 the reactionary régime in south Vietnam declared invalid the aliens' identity cards of all Chinese residents. On May 20, 1957 the Commission of Overseas Chinese Affairs of the People's Republic of China issued a statement strongly condemning and protesting against the unreasonable practice of the reactionary régime in south Vietnam of compelling Chinese residents to change their nationality. This just Chinese stand was at the time endorsed and supported by the Democratic Republic of Vietnam. *Nhan Dan*, organ of the Central Committee of the Workers' Party of Vietnam, published articles denouncing the Ngo Dinh Diem clique for this illegal action. In its policy statements and other relevant documents published in 1960, 1964, 1965 and 1968, the South Vietnam National Front for Liberation laid down that "all decrees and measures of the U.S.-puppet régime regarding Chinese residents shall be abrogated," and that "Chinese residents have the freedom and right to choose their nationality." However, after the liberation of south Vietnam, the Vietnamese Government abruptly changed its position and, in contravention of the spirit of the agreement between the two Parties, announced, without prior consultation with the Chinese Government, a decision before the general census in the south and the election of deputies to the National Assembly in February 1976, to the effect that Chinese residing in south Vietnam must all register under the nationality imposed upon them during the rule of Ngo Dinh Diem. Subsequently, the Vietnamese Government openly placed all kinds of harsh restrictions on those Chinese residents who retained their Chinese nationality to ostracize and persecute them. And now, the spokesman of the Vietnamese Ministry of Foreign Affairs has asserted that "back in 1956 almost all the Chinese residents in south Vietnam adopted Vietnamese nationality. They are no longer Chinese nationals but Vietnamese of Chinese origin." In this way one million and several hundred thousand Chinese nationals in south Vietnam are written off at one stroke. This is absolutely unacceptable to the Chinese Government.

Facts show that the Vietnamese side long ago thoroughly violated the agreement between the Chinese and Vietnamese Parties. Yet the spokesman of the Vietnamese Foreign Ministry now claims that the Vietnamese side "has constantly respected and strictly applied this agreement." This assertion is not convincing at all.

2. Resorting to sophistry and futile denials, the spokesman of the Vietnamese Foreign Ministry attributed the massive expulsion of Chinese residents to "information" spread by "certain bad elements among the Hoa people" and said that this was "a deliberate act." The way things developed fully shows that it is no other than Vietnam itself that, out of its needs in domestic affairs and international relations, has adopted and systematically pursued a policy of discrimination, ostracism, persecution and expulsion of Chinese residents. This is a grave anti-China step taken by the Vietnamese side in a deliberate attempt to undermine Sino-Vietnamese relations.

Indeed, there have been circulating for some time in Vietnam a number of calculated anti-China rumours to the effect that "China supports Kampuchea in opposing Vietnam, war will break out between China and Vietnam," etc. Not a few Vietnamese officials and public security personnel have used these rumours as a means to deceive and frighten Chinese residents into returning to China. In their unwarranted complaints and charges against China early this year, certain Vietnamese diplomats asserted that an "abnormal situation" had arisen along China's border, and that China was "calling for an attack on Vietnam." The similarity between these allegations and the rumours floating around in Vietnam could not possibly be a mere coincidence, but precisely shows that these rumours were deliberately fabricated and spread by the Vietnamese side.

The Vietnamese side started early in 1977 to push a policy of "purifying the border areas" in the provinces adjacent to China and expel back to China groups of border inhabitants who had moved from China to settle down in Vietnam a long time ago. In October 1977 it began to expel Chinese residents in Hoang Lien Son, Lai Chau, Son La and other provinces in north-west Vietnam. Then the measure gradually expanded into the massive expulsion of Chinese residents from various parts of north Vietnam. The Chinese Government repeatedly tried to persuade the Vietnamese Government to uphold Sino-Vietnamese friendship by taking steps to halt the expulsion of Chinese residents. The Vietnamese side, however, turned a deaf ear and created on a nationwide scale even more serious incidents of ostracizing Chinese residents. Tens of thousands of Chinese were transported overland by the Vietnamese side to such places as Lao Cai, Dong Dang and Mong Cai along the Sino-Vietnamese border and then driven back to China, while a large number of others was forced to return in small boats across the sea.' The numbers of expelled Chinese have increased daily over the past two months, from several hundred a day in early April to several thousand a day in late May, with their total exceeding 100,000 by the end of May.

It is impossible to enumerate all the persecution and maltreatment of the Chinese residents by the Vietnamese authorities. In early 1977, on the pretext of taking a general census, the Vietnamese side compelled Chinese residents to register as Vietnamese citizens. Many Chinese residents who retained Chinese nationality were then deprived of the right to employment and education. They were sacked without a just cause. Their residence registration was cancelled and their food ration stopped. The local Vietnamese authorities and public security personnel would intrude illegally at any time into their homes, ordering them to fill out the "Form of Voluntary Repatriation" and taking the opportunity to search their homes and practise extortion. Properties and possessions which many Chinese residents had accumulated through many years of hard work were illegally confiscated. Numerous families were displaced and deprived of a home. On their involuntary exodus they were subjected to all kinds of maltreatment and insult. Quite a number were beaten up for no reason at all. Some were even shot at, wounded or killed by Vietnamese troops and police. The miseries suffered by the Chinese residents in Vietnam were appalling and rarely seen in international relations.

As for the thousands of Vietnamese residents in China, the Chinese Government has never subjected them to any discrimination, but has always respected and protected their proper rights and interests. They enjoy the same rights as Chinese citizens in respect of work, education and medical care. They are given more favoured treatment than Chinese citizens in respect of the supply of necessities. This is a universally known fact which brooks no distortion.

3. The sharp increase in the number of Chinese expelled home due to aggravated discrimination against the Chinese residents by the Vietnamese side has suddenly created for China great financial and material difficulties

and burdens. In line with its consistent policy of "protecting the interests of overseas Chinese and aiding returned Chinese," the Chinese Government needs to make prompt, adequate arrangements for the resettlement of the numerous Chinese expelled by Vietnam. Therefore, it cannot but decide to cancel part of its complete-factory aid projects to Vietnam so as to divert the funds and materials to making arrangements for the life and productive work of the returned Chinese. It is clear that the cancellation of a part of China's aid projects to Vietnam is a necessary and involuntary emergency measure, it is purely a consequence of the Vietnamese policy of ostracizing the Chinese nationals.

In the past 30 years, in order to aid the Vietnamese people in their national-liberation struggle and economic construction, the Chinese people, despite their many difficulties, worked hard and practised frugality to provide Vietnam with many-sided aid without any conditions attached, and even made great sacrifices to support the Vietnamese people in their revolutionary struggle. This is a universally recognized fact. The Chinese people have always considered this their bounden proletarian internationalist duty. The Chinese Communist Party, the Chinese Government and the Chinese people feel no qualms in this respect.

A great change took place in the situation of Vietnam with the ending of the Vietnam war in 1975. On the other hand, China has encountered tremendous difficulties because of the sabotage of the "gang of four" and as a result of repeated strong earthquakes and other serious natural disasters. Even in these circumstances China has continued to give many-sided aid to Vietnam and undertake many aid projects to the best of its ability. Naturally, the annual sum of China's aid to Vietnam in peace time showed a reduction as compared with the exceptional case in the war years, but the reason is not difficult to understand. The Chinese side repeatedly explained its own difficulties to the Vietnamese side in the hope that the latter would give a respite to the Chinese people. The late Premier Chou En-lai, during his serious illness, personally said to a Vietnamese leader: "During the war, when you were in the worst need, we took many things from our own army to give to you. We made very great efforts to help you. The sum of our aid to Vietnam still ranks first among our aids to foreign countries. You should let us have a respite and regain strength." At that time Vietnamese leaders expressed understanding on many occasions. But now the Vietnamese side has seen fit to hurl vicious slanders and attacks at Chinese aid. The Chinese people are greatly pained and angered by such an action of returning evil for good.

4. In his statement, the spokesman of the Vietnamese Foreign Ministry proposed that the Vietnamese and Chinese sides "meet" to resolve their so-called "differences on the question of the Hoa people." We consider that in the present circumstances such a proposal was made purely out of propaganda needs.

The Chinese Government has always stood for the settlement of differences and disputes between states through consultation and negotiation. With respect to the Vietnamese side's ostracism, persecution and expulsion of Chinese residents, we have from the very beginning maintained that a timely solution to the problem should be sought through private consultation and we have made many efforts towards this end. The Chinese Government has made repeated representations through diplomatic channels, expressing the hope that the Vietnamese Government will take effective measures to stop the persecution and expulsion of Chinese residents. But the Vietnamese side has persisted in its course and redoubled its efforts to expel Chinese residents, and thus aggravated the situation. Now, while continuing its expulsion of Chinese nationals, the Vietnamese authorities have proposed that a meeting be held to discuss the so-called "differences on the question of the Hoa people." Since the Vietnamese side denies the existence of any Chinese nationals in Vietnam, it shows that its "Proposal" is totally false and meaningless.

5. China and Vietnam are linked by common mountains and rivers and the two peoples share weal and woe. In the long revolutionary struggles, the two peoples sympathized with and supported each other and formed a profound brotherhood and militant solidarity. It is in the fundamental interests of both the Chinese and Vietnamese peoples and it is the common desire of the two peoples to strengthen and develop steadily this revolutionary friendship and solidarity. The Chinese Communist Party and the Chinese Government and people have always valued highly this friendship and solidarity and made unremitting efforts in this connection. Though in recent years the Vietnamese side has taken a series of actions vitiating the relations between the two countries and a variety of anti-China steps, the Chinese side, mindful of the overall interest, has all along exercised self-restraint and tolerance and repeatedly expressed to Vietnamese leaders its sincere hope that the two sides would make joint efforts and take effective measures to uphold the traditional friendship between the two peoples. That the relations between the two countries should have deteriorated to such an extent is what we did not expect and what we do not want to see. The Chinese people have been and will remain devoted to consolidating and strengthening the friendship and solidarity between the Chinese and Vietnamese peoples. It is our hope that the Vietnamese side will do what it has declared, match its deeds with its words, truly value the traditional friendship and fundamental interests of the two peoples, stop forthwith its erroneous practice of ostracism, persecution and expulsion of overseas Chinese and refrain from any further acts detrimental to the friendship between the Chinese and Vietnamese peoples.

Note of the Ministry of Foreign Affairs of the People's Republic of China to the Embassy of the Socialist Republic of Vietnam in China, 12 May, 1978.*

(Complete Text).

*This document was made public by the Vietnamese Ministry of Foreign Affairs on 17 June, 1978.

The Foreign Ministry of the People's Republic of China presents it compliments to the Embassy of the Socialist Republic of Vietnam in China and has the honour to express its views regarding the serious situation caused by Vietnam's expulsion of Chinese residents as follows:

First of all, the Chinese Government would like to draw the Vietnamese Government's attention to the fact that at present the Vietnamese side is ostracizing, persecuting and expelling Chinese residents on an ever-larger scale. The situation has become more and more serious. Early in 1977, in the northern border provinces, the Vietnamese side began to expel the population of the border area who had come from China and had long settled there. In November 1977, it began expelling Chinese residents in the three provinces of Hoang Lien Son, Lai Chau, and Son La. Particularly since early April 1978, the Vietnamese side has stepped up the expulsion óf Chinese residents, extending the area of expulsion to Hanoi, Haiphong, Ha Nam Ninh, Thanh Hoa, etc. The number of expelled Chinese residents increased rapidly, within over one month, more than 35,000 have been expelled to China. Now this number has amounted to over 40,000 and seems to be continuing to increase. It should be pointed out that during the past few years, the Vietnamese side has purposefully applied a policy of discrimination, ostracism and persecution against Chinese residents. The Vietnamese Government has forced them to take up Vietnamese nationality; for a great many of them it refused to give them jobs, to admit them to colleges and universities; it even dismissed them from employment, cancelled their residence registration, cut their food ration, etc, making it impossible for them to live a normal life at their place of residence. Then, the Vietnamese side has in many ways expelled them en masse to China. In many places, Vietnamese security agents, under the pretext of controlling residence registrations, illegally searched their houses, used various means to threaten and intimidate them, and coerced them to leave Vietnam. The expelled Chinese residents are now helpless; they have not enough food and clothes, the greater part of their property, accumulated through so many years of hard work has been illegally confiscated, the little furniture they can take with them on their way back to China has also been plundered. When they enter China, most of them have nothing left, except for the clothes they are wearing.

The Vietnamese side has been transporting contingents of Chinese residents by train to places near Lao Cai, Hoang Lien Son Province, forcing them to alight and walk tens of kilometers before they can enter China. On their way to the border, they have to experience all kinds of suffering. Some are groundlessly beaten and wounded, others, old people and children included, are left hungry and sick. Their plight is miserable indeed. Moreover, in Ho Chi Minh city, of late, there has been mass arrests of Chinese residents; some have even been beaten to death or injured.

The Chinese residents have long lived in Vietnam in close friendship with the Vietnamese people; they have contributed to the Vietnamese people's revolutionary cause, to their resistance war, as well as to their national construction.

Who could expect that they should be so inhumanely persecuted? This is something really intolerable. The Vietnamese side's cruel expulsion of Chinese residents is unprecedented in the relations between socialist countries — it is also rarely seen in ordinary international relations. The Chinese people are deeply pained and greatly angered by these actions. Therefore, the Chinese Government lodges a strong protest to the Vietnamese Government.

The Chinese side has on many occasions dealt with the Vietnamese side on the massive expulsion of Chinese residents — on 27th October 1977, 6th February, 27th February, and 6th April 1976. It has repeatedly advised the Vietnamese comrades to set great store by the Sino-Vietnamese friendship and to put an end to the persecution and expulsion of Chinese residents. But to our great regret, the Vietnamese side considers China's sincere desire to preserve the Sino-Vietnamese friendship and to find a satisfactory solution to the question of Chinese residents as a weakness and thinks it can bully China. Far from reducing it in any way, it has stepped up the persecution and expulsion of Chinese residents. It is obviously a serious step taken by the Vietnamese side in undermining the relationship between China and Vietnam, seriously impairing the friendship between the two peoples. Formerly, the Vietnamese comrades had on many occasions said that they "cherished the Vietnam-China friendship", that they considered the Chinese residents "their brothers and sisters", that they "constantly united with the Chinese residents, helped them and gave them attentive care". The fact is that the Vietnamese comrades say one thing and do another.

Shirking its responsibility for the expulsion of Chinese residents, the Vietnamese side has resorted to many odious manoeuvres. In order to have proof that the Chinese residents "voluntarily" return to their country, Vietnamese security agents forced the expelled persons to write "applications saying that they return to China at their own free will" or to recopy or to re-read prepared texts so that Vietnamese security agents may tape record, photograph or film them. In order to cover up the expulsion of Chinese residents, the Vietnamese side always affirms that the Chinese residents' massive return to China is caused by the rumours spread among them. It should be pointed out that it is the Vietnamese authorities and security agents themselves who have spread rumours to deceive and intimidate the Chinese residents, saying that "the Chinese Government was calling them back to China", that "war would break out between China and Vietnam", that "those who refused to return were traitors", etc. Series of irrefutable facts have testified to this wrongdoing. The expulsion of Chinese residents has now become very serious. It is completely due to premeditated Vietnamese actions. The Vietnamese Government cannot elude its responsibility for the expulsion of Chinese residents. Now the Vietnamese side is reversing right and wrong, turning the matter upside down, in the hope of laying the blame on China. But these efforts will be in vain.

In view of the fact that Chinese residents are herded en masse by the Vietnamese side to the Chinese border, the Chinese Government, in keeping with its policy of "protecting the interests of Chinese residents and supporting them", cannot help paying attention to their lives and is compelled to make necessary arrangements for them. By the sudden massive expulsion of Chinese residents, the Vietnamese side has created a lot of difficulties to China and greatly increased the financial and material burden of the Chinese Government. Therefore the Chinese Government is obliged to cut a number of projects for which China is to supply complete equipment and to cut the money that China is to spend for these projects as aid to Vietnam, so as to finance the arrangements for the victimized Chinese residents to work and to live.

The Chinese Government would like to repeat that the Chinese side always deeply treasures the traditional friendship between the Chinese and the Vietnamese peoples; it will perseveringly endeavour to preserve this friendship. The Chinese side is reluctant to see the friendship between the people of China and Vietnam, a friendship that has been built up through the long revolutionary struggle, being continuously impaired. It hopes that the Vietnamese Government will also cherish the revolutionary friendship between the two peoples as the Chinese Government does, and that it will immediately take practical and effective measures to put an end to its absurd actions, discriminating, ostracizing, persecuting and expelling Chinese residents.

The Foreign Ministry of the People's Republic of China takes this opportunity to renew to the Embassy the assurances of its high considerations.

Note of the Government of the Socialist Republic of Vietnam to the Government of the People's Republic of China, 18 May, 1978.*

(Complete Text).

*This document was made public by the Vietnamese Ministry of Foreign Affairs on 17 June, 1978.

The Government of the Socialist Republic of Vietnam presents it compliments to the Government of the People's Republic of China and has the honour to bring the following to its knowledge:

On 12th May 1978, the Chinese Foreign Ministry sent a note to the Vietnamese Embassy in Peking informing it of the Chinese Government's decision to cut off the financial aid and complete equipment for 21 projects. The reason put forward by the Chinese side was that the amount of money would be used to arrange for the work and life of the Hoa people who had been "expelled" back to China.

The Government of the Socialist Republic of Vietnam was extremely surprised and regretful on learning of this decision, because by a mere note of its Foreign Ministry, the Chinese side has unilaterally abolished the agreements between the leaders of the two Parties and Governments. The Vietnamese Government deems it necessary to express its view as follows:

(1) Hitherto, in the struggle against imperialism and in the building of socialism, the peoples of Vietnam and China have always supported and helped one another. The great, valuable and effective assistance extended by the Party, Government and people of China to the Vietnamese people was an important contribution to the great victory of the Vietnamese people's struggle against US aggression, for national liberation. That victory is also the common victory for the two peoples, beneficial to the national defence and socialist construction of both Vietnam and China.

After the signing of the Paris Agreement on Vietnam, in the June 1973 talks between the delegation of the Party and government of Vietnam and the delegation of the Party and Government of China, Comrade Chou En-lai solemnly pledged, on behalf of the Party and Government of China, to continue their gratuitous aid to Vietnam at the 1973 level for five more years.

After the complete victory of the Vietnamese revolution, in pursuance of President Ho Chi Minh's testament, a high-ranking delegation of the Vietnamese Party and Government paid a visit to China to express their profound gratitude to the Chinese Party, Government and people for their assistance and at the same time to propose long-term co-operation in many fields with China at the new stage. The Vietnamese side has earnestly asked the Chinese side to continue its aid for a number of years more, as promised, in order to help the Vietnamese people heal the wounds of war, rehabilitate and develop the economy and rebuild the country. But it is regrettable that China has not responded to that request by Vietnam.

Since the end of 1975, China has stopped its non-refundable aid to Vietnam and since 1977 it has also cut off its loans. At the same time, the Chinese side appeared to have many difficulties in implementing the aid which had been agreed upon some years ago.

With regard to the projects now under construction, the Chinese leaders had promised to abide by the principle of activity and considered it their international obligation which they ought to fulfil. But in reality, the delivery of designs was late, the procurement of machines and equipment either delayed or non-homogeneous. Chinese experts, on many occasions, had no work; therefore the construction of many projects proceeded slowly, greatly affecting construction plans and the putting into operation of those projects. The Vietnamese side has repeatedly requested the Chinese comrades to take active measures aimed at stepping up the speed of construction of the projects, but the aforesaid situation has not been improved.

In the meantime, the Chinese side has created unnecessary difficulties to the normal activities of Chinese experts working in Vietnam. On 4th May 1978, the Chinese comrades stated that the Vietnamese had been unfriendly in taking "unilateral action" with regard to the suicide of Chinese expert Tang Hsueh-wei working in Vinh Phu textile plant. Using something which was completely untrue as a pretext, China has withdrawn all its experts working in that plant before their term expired.

Following a series of such incidents, the Chinese Government's decision to cancel a number of projects with complete equipment clearly lies in the framework of its intentions to reduce its aid to Vietnam.

(2) We have carefully studied the allegations mentioned in the Chinese note saying that Vietnam was "Ostracizing, persecuting and expelling" Hoa people. They are completely contrary to the truth and to the policy of the Party and Government of Vietnam; they are used only as a pretext for China to put into effect its intention to cut off aid to Vietnam.

As you have known, since 1955 the Central Committee of the Chinese Party and the Central Committee of the Vietnamese Party have agreed that the Chinese residents in Vietnam would be placed under the leadership of the Vietnamese Workers' Party and would gradually become Vietnamese citizens. Over the past 20 years and more, the Vietnamese Party and Government have always respected and correctly implemented that agreement. The Hoa people in Vietnam have had the same rights and obligations as Vietnamese citizens. In no other country in the world have Hoa people been as favoured and well-treated as in Vietnam. The majority of Hoa people in Vietnam are workers employed in Vietnamese collective production organizations, such as agricultural and handicraft co-operatives or state-run enterprises. Thousands of Hoa people have become cadres and members of the Communist Party of Vietnam; many of them have held leading positions at various levels of the Party, administration and Fatherland Front, and mass organizations. Their children study in Vietnamese schools and universities as do Vietnamese children, and a great number of them have become engineers, doctors, and high-level technicians working in various economic branches of Vietnam. In the emulation movement in production, hundreds of cadres and workers among Hoa people were elected "emulation fighters"; some were even awarded the title "labour hero".

Hoa people have taken part in the struggle against US aggression for national liberation and in socialist construction, making their worthy contribution to the common cause of the Vietnamese nation. The Vietnamese Party and Government have highly appreciated the contribution of Hoa people and have always cultivated among the Vietnamese people the spirit of solidarity, respect and mutual affection and assistance between the Viet and Hoa people, who have lived in harmony together in the great family of socialist Vietnam.

Deeply treasuring the friendship between Vietnam and China and imbued with their tradition of humanity, the Vietnamese people have given care and assistance to thousands of Chinese residents persecuted and expelled by the Kampuchean authorities who have taken refuge in South Vietnam, and have shared with them every means of living.

Since the Vietnam-Kampuchea incident began, rumours have been spread among Hoa people that "China supports Kampuchea against Vietnam, large-scale war will break out, Hoa people in Vietnam will suffer losses; they must therefore find ways to leave Vietnam quickly", "the Chinese Government calls on overseas Chinese to their country" etc. This is precisely what has caused many Hoa people who have been living peacefully in Vietnam to suddenly return en masse to China in an illegal manner, although the local Vietnamese administration and people have advised them to stay on without anxiety, and not listen to the bad elements' rumours.

We have enough evidence about the acts of the bad elements among Hoa people who have received, instigated, threatened and coerced Hoa people in an attempt to sabotage production, create difficulties to the economy and the Vietnamese people's life and to sow division between the Viet and Hoa people, which is detrimental to the friendship between Vietnam and China. After returning to China, many Hoa people have escaped back to Vietnam. This clearly shows that they were not expelled by Vietnam but they were deceived into going.

After being ravaged by war for many years, the Vietnamese people have now entered the stage of rebuilding their country, and have to overcome countless difficulties, so they have no reason to "expel" Hoa people in order to bring more economic and social difficulties upon themselves. There is also no reason and no interest for Vietnam to create complications in its relations with neighbouring socialist China which has stood shoulder to shoulder with Vietnam in the protracted revolutionary struggle of each country.

We deeply regret that the Chinese comrades on the basis of false reports and under the pretext that Vietnam has "ostracized Hoa people", have come to a serious unilateral decision unprecedented in the relations between the two countries. That decision has caused Vietnam many great immediate difficulties. But what is more serious is that it has damaged the age-old friendship between the two people.

(3) It is in the basic interests of our two peoples to preserve our solidarity and friendship and to strive jointly for the common goal, i.e. the building of socialism and communism. Over the past decades, the Communist Party, Government and people of Vietnam have done their utmost to preserve and consolidate the militant solidarity between the two peoples. Even when the Vietnam-China relationship was undermined by bad elements during the period of the Chinese cultural revolution or when it was hindered by the gang of four, the Vietnamese people have always been persistent and unswerving in safeguarding solidarity and friendship with China.

The Chinese Government's decision to cancel 21 projects with complete equipment in Vietnam, including essential projects for our national defence and economy, has forced us to readjust our plan in order to carry out successfully the economic construction and cultural development tasks set by our Party.

No matter what difficulties and complications there are in the relations between the two countries, the Vietnamese people will never forget the assistance extended to their revolutionary cause by the Chinese Party and Government.

Having always held firmly to their line of independence, sovereignty and unswerving solidarity, the Vietnamese Communist Party, Government and people are determined to preserve and consolidate the solidarity and friendship between our two peoples who are "both comrades and brothers", a solidarity and friendship painstakingly built up by the Vietnamese Communist Party and President Ho Chi Minh, the Chinese Communist Party and Chairman Mao Tsetung.

The Government of the Socialist Republic of Vietnam takes this opportunity to renew to the Government of the People's Republic of China the assurances of its high consideration.

Note of the Government of the People's Republic of China to the Government of the Socialist Republic of Vietnam, 30 May, 1978.*

(Complete Text).

*This document was made public by the Vietnamese Ministry of Foreign Affairs on 17 June, 1978.

Note of the Government of the People's Republic of China

to the Government of the Socialist Republic of Vietnam, Hanoi

The Government of the People's Republic of China presents its compliments to the Government of the Socialist Republic of Vietnam. The Chinese Government acknowledges receipt of the latter's reply dated 18th May 1978. We totally disagree with the unreasonable criticism of the Vietnamese side with regard to our country and wish to expound the following views on the matter.

In its note, the Vietnamese Government made every effort to elude a series of eloquent facts mentioned in the Chinese Note of 12th May 1978, fundamentally distorted the truth, even levelled slanderous charges and made criticism against China in an attempt to have a pretext for entirely shirking its responsibility. That way of confusing right and wrong has in fact surprised everyone. The Chinese Government expresses much regret at this fact.

After the sending of the 12th May Note by the Chinese Foreign Ministry to the Vietnamese side, the latter, far from stopping its ostracism against Chinese residents, has feverishly intensified it. Up to 30th May, the number of Chinese victims of Vietnamese expulsion to China has reached almost 100,000. They have not ceased to be expelled — sometimes 4,000 to 5,000 a day through Lao Cai, Dong Dang, Mong Cai and other localities of Vietnam. It is hard to imagine the plight of Chinese residents, how they are oppressed and persecuted in Vietnam and the suffering they have to endure on their way back to their country. Developments of the situation have further testified to the fact that Vietnam is deliberately carrying out a policy of discrimination, ostracism, persecution and expulsion against Chinese residents, a policy entirely stemming from its domestic and external requirements and constituting one of the serious steps of the Vietnamese side in undermining the Sino-Vietnamese relationship and in opposing China. The Vietnamese side has resorted to all tricks to compel Chinese residents to leave, then pretended that their departure was caused by so-called "false rumours" spread by bad elements, and even slanderously charged the Chinese side with instigating Chinese residents to return home. But this justification and denial can fool nobody. With extreme patience, once again the

Chinese Government advises the Vietnamese Government to take without delay effective measures to end its acts of large-scale persecution and ostracism against Chinese residents and not to run counter to the Chinese and Vietnamese people's aspirations, thereby further aggravating the situation and seriously undermining the friendship between the two peoples.

For historical reasons, China has 1,000,000 and some hundreds of thousands of Chinese residents in Vietnam. After the liberation of north Vietnam in 1955, the Chinese Party and the Vietnamese Party exchanged views on the question of Chinese residents and confirmed that as the Chinese residents enjoyed the same rights as the Vietnamese people and through a long and persevering process of ideological persuasion and education, Chinese residents in north Vietnam may, on a voluntary basis, gradually be turned into people of Vietnamese nationality. As for the question of Chinese residents in south Vietnam, it will be negotiated by China and Vietnam following the liberation of south Vietnam. This stand of the Chinese side was prompted by the desire to strengthen the fraternal friendship and the relations of friendly co-operation between the Chinese and the Vietnamese peoples. It is also in conformity with our consistent policy to approve and encourage overseas Chinese to choose the nationality of their country of residence on a voluntary basis. In the past, the Vietnamese Government agreed with these policies of the Chinese side and supported them. But over the past few years, the Vietnamese Government has on its own brazenly sabotaged the principles discussed by the two Parties in 1955 on the question of Chinese residents in Vietnam. In north Vietnam, it has feverishly pursued a policy of discrimination, ostracism and persecution against Chinese residents and compelled them to take up Vietnamese nationality, seriously trampling upon their legitimate rights, depriving many of them of their means of living, driving them into a most difficult position, and making it impossible for them to live. In south Vietnam, it has brazenly followed the proceedings of the reactionary Ngo Dinh Diem administration, and, at variance with its repeatedly and publicly stated position and regulation, it has resorted to the rudest methods to compel Chinese residents to take up Vietnamese nationality; those who refused to do so were mercilessly discriminated, persecuted and even repressed. At present, the serious and nationwide anti-China campaign generated by the Vietnamese side continues expanding. In spite of these grave facts in its Note of 18th May 1978, the Vietnamese Government categorically denied them and claimed that it had "correctly abided by this agreement". This has aroused a general indignation. It should be clearly pointed out that the Vietnamese side's proceeding is at complete variance with the spirit of the principles agreed upon by the two Parties; the Vietnamese side has long ignored and completely undermined the principles confirmed by both the Chinese and Vietnamese sides. Decidedly no rhetoric, however skilful it may be, can cover up this truth.

In its Note, the Vietnamese Government has severely criticized and attacked China regarding Chinese aid to Vietnam. This is unimaginable. In a long period of nearly 30 years, in the resistance wars against the French and the United States and in the economic construction of the Vietnamese people, the Chinese people went through hardships and difficulties, shared their means of living, and did not spare even the greatest national sacrifice to aid the Vietnamese people. Today the Vietnamese Government has resorted to an unusual way of doing and returned evil for good, making it most painful for the Chinese people. We believe that the Vietnamese people and justice-loving people the world over find it difficult to understand the attitude of the Vietnamese side.

For many years now, though faced with untold difficulties, China has given Vietnam a great amount of aid with no conditions whatsoever attached and has always considered it a proletarian international obligation to be fulfilled by China. In this connection, the Chinese Party, Government and people have nothing to be ashamed of in their conscience. In 1975, after the war in Vietnam ended, the situation in Vietnam went through very great changes. Due to the sabotage by the gang of four and successive heavy natural calamities, China had to cope with tremendous difficulties. In spite of such circumstances, China continued to extend to Vietnam a great amount of aid in many fields and within her possibilities to help Vietnam build a great number of projects with complete equipment. Of course, the yearly amount of aid to Vietnam in peace time after the war is less than that given in the critical years of war, and this is easy to understand. The Chinese side has repeatedly told the Vietnamese side about its difficulties and hoped that the Chinese people will have a respite and regain strength. Though seriously ill, Premier Chou En-lai personally told Vietnamese comrades: "In war time when you were faced with the greatest difficulties, we had supplied you with many goods taken from our troops. We had made tremendous efforts to aid you. At present, our aid to Vietnam still ranks first among our aid to foreign countries. You should let us have a respite and regain strength." At that time, the Vietnamese leaders repeatedly expressed their understanding about this fact.

It should also be pointed out that in recent years China has persistently given aid to Vietnam even though the Vietnamese side had created an unfriendly atmosphere causing the relations between the two countries to deteriorate and uncreasingly caused difficulties. In the process of building Chinese-aided projects, often there has been no appropriate co-operation of the Vietnamese side, the delivery of designing materials for which the Vietnamese side is responsible has been late, the sites for the construction of the factories changed many times; the delay caused by the Vietnamese side has constantly affected the building tempo to the extent that the equipment and material prepared by the Chinese side or handed over to the Vietnamese side have been damaged or deteriorated, no longer usable and must be disposed of or subjected to a new processing; Chinese experts came to the construction site and had nothing to do. All this has created many difficulties to the Chinese side in preparing for the construction work and resulted in enormous labour waste and financial losses.

Chinese experts in Vietnam have often been treated in a very unfriendly manner. Yet the Vietnamese Government is now making all kinds of criticisms to China. It has really confused right and wrong and called black white.

At present, the Vietnamese side has ignored the long-standing friendship between the Chinese and Vietnamese peoples, despite the repeated advice and continuous self-restraint of the Chinese side. It continues to persecute and expel Chinese residents. It has not ceased to escalate its opposition to China, and has taken a series of new grave steps in sabotaging the Sino-Vietnamese relations of friendship. Due to the Vietnamese feverish ostracism, the number of expelled Chinese has further increased by over 50,000 in only 20 days and more, thus creating more financial and material difficulties to China. The Chinese Government is therefore compelled to cancel a number of Chinese complete-factory aid projects to be built for Vietnam, together with the money to be used for these projects.

The Chinese Government wishes to reiterate that the Chinese Government and people have always treasured the long-standing friendship between the Chinese and Vietnamese peoples and have made tireless efforts to preserve the Sino-Vietnamese friendship. Today, if the Sino-Vietnamese relations have worsened to such a degree, the responsibility entirely rests with the Vietnamese side. The Vietnamese acts which have unceasingly caused serious harm to the Sino-Vietnamese friendship for the past few years have worried and upset the Chinese side. It has frankly given advice through all channels and in various forms. The Chinese leaders have repeatedly expressed their sincere attitude to the Vietnamese leaders and advised them to stop harming the friendship between the two countries. Far from properly responding to the Chinese side's goodwill, the Vietnamese side has made these relations deteriorate more quickly. Vietnamese leaders have often pledged that they would remain very faithful to President Ho Chi Minh's will to consolidate and develop the Sino-Vietnamese friendship. But it is regrettable that what the Vietnamese leaders said does not match their deeds; in fact they have engaged in deliberate acts of sabotage of the Sino-Vietnamese friendship. Once again, we would like to advise the Vietnamese leaders to respect the basic interests of the Chinese and Vietnamese peoples and the long-standing friendship between the two peoples and stop ostracizing Chinese residents and opposing China.

The Government of the People's Republic of China takes this opportunity to renew to the Government of the Socialist Republic of Vietnam the assurances of its high consideration.

Note of the Ministry of Foreign Affairs of the People's Republic of China to the Ministry of Foreign Affairs of the Socialist Republic of Vietnam, 16 June, 1978.

(Complete Text).

Ministry of Foreign Affairs of the Socialist Republic of Vietnam, Hanoi

The Ministry of Foreign Affairs of the People's Republic of China presents its compliments to the Ministry of Foreign Affairs of the Socialist Republic of Vietnam and has the honour to inform the latter of the following:

In the past 20 years or more, the Vietnamese side set up consulates-general successively in China's Kwangchow, Kunming and Nanning. The Chinese Government has always energetically given the three consulates-general all-out support and favoured treatment. In 1976 the Chinese Ministry of Foreign Affairs, with a view to promoting the friendly relations and co-operation between the Chinese and Vietnamese peoples, developing bilateral trade and handling other consular matters, proposed to the Vietnamese side to set up consulates-general in Ho Chi Minh City, Da Nang and Hai Phong; in December the same year the Vietnamese side indicated agreement to the establishment of Chinese consular missions in Ho Chi Minh City and Hai Phong, and in November 1977 it stated that the Chinese side could send an advance party to Ho Chi Minh City to prepare for the setting up of the consulate-general there. The Chinese Ministry of Foreign Affairs delivered to the Vietnamese Ministry of Foreign Affairs the letter of appointment of Wang Pu-yun as the Chinese Consul-General in Ho Chi Minh City, and the Chinese advance party for the establishment of the consulate-general in that City arrived in Hanoi long ago. Since then the Chinese side has repeatedly asked the Vietnamese Foreign Ministry to make the earliest possible arrangements for the Chinese advance party to proceed to Ho Chi Minh City to perform its duties, but the Vietnamese side has refused to do so under various pretexts, and as a result the Chinese advance party has had to stay in Hanoi for nearly three months. Such repudiation of one's own promise on the Vietnamese part is most rare in international dealings, and it has done serious damage to the friendly relations and co-operation between China and Vietnam. We express our deepest regret at it. In these circumstances, the Chinese Government could not but decide to cancel the appointment of Wang Pu-yun as consul-general and recall Consul Chou Hui-min and Deputy Consul Chung Ching-kun who were dispatched for the purpose of establishing the consular mission in Ho Chi Minh City and who remain stranded in Hanoi. On the principle of reciprocity, the Chinese Government hereby notifies the Vietnamese Government to close down forthwith its three consulates-general in China's Kwangchow, Kunming and Nanning, which are to stop all their consular activities from this date of notification and all of whose staffs are to withdraw within the shortest possible time.

The Ministry of Foreign Affairs of the People's Republic of China avails itself of this opportunity to renew to the Ministry of Foreign Affairs of the Socialist Republic of Vietnam the assurances of its highest consideration.

Note of the Government of the Socialist Republic of Vietnam to the Government of the People's Republic of China, 6 July, 1978.

(Complete Text).

The Government of the Socialist Republic of Vietnam presents its compliments to the Government of the People's Republic of China and expresses as follows its views on the note on 3rd July 1978, of the Government of the People's Republic of China.

(1) The Chinese Government, on 12th May, 1978, and 30th May, 1978, decided to cancel the major part of its complete factory aid projects to Vietnam, allegedly to divert the money and materials used on these projects to the arrangement of the life of the Hoa people "expelled" to China by Vietnam. Now the Chinese Government decides to cut all its economic and technical aid to Vietnam, and to withdraw all Chinese technicians working at the remaining Chinese aid projects in Vietnam. The reason put forward by the Chinese side to take this grave decision is Vietnam's "anti-Chinese activities and ostracism of Chinese residents in Vietnam". This, however, is sheer fabrication. Reality has rejected such a slander.

As was pointed out many times by the Vietnamese side, the friendship between the Vietnamese and Chinese people is consistently based on the stand of Marxism-Leninism and proletarian internationalism. Even when the relationship between the two countries was being undermined by bad elements, the Vietnamese people did all they could to preserve this pure and loyal revolutionary relationship. This is clear not only to the peoples of the two countries, but also to other peoples throughout the world.

Meanwhile, since the Vietnamese people won complete victory, the Chinese side has taken a series of anti-Vietnam actions: constantly giving all-out support for the Kampuchean authorities to conduct a war of aggression, committing innumerable barbarous crimes against the Vietnamese people; enticing and forcing large numbers of Hoa people to leave for China, then fabricating the story that "Vietnam expels Chinese residents"; whipping up a provocative propaganda campaign aimed to sow hatred between the two peoples; rejecting the Vietnamese side's proposals for negotiations; unilaterally scrapping all agreements on economic and technical aid to Vietnam signed by the two Governments; closing down three Vietnamese Consulates-General in China; making daily attacks and slanders — covertly and overtly — against Vietnam before world opinion, and so on. . .

These actions obviously are part of a premeditated scheme. The Chinese side has been trying to force Vietnam to give up its correct line of independence, sovereignty and international solidarity. Failing in its forcible attempt, the Chinese side step by step pushed up with its hostile policy against Vietnam. These actions of the Chinese authorities have brought anxiety to many countries and have been severely criticized by world opinion.

(2) In the relations among nations, aid is always a reciprocal affair. This view has been expressed by Chinese leaders themselves in the past. With their traditional loyalty, the Vietnamese people never forget the Chinese people's precious support and assistance to their revolutionary cause.

In their protracted struggle against imperialism, with their correct line and promoting their spirit of self-reliance and self-support, and enjoying the sympathy and strong support of brothers and friends on all continents, the Vietnamese people fought valiantly and won a glorious victory. Today, in defending and building their country, also relying on these extremely important factors, the Vietnamese people will surely overcome all difficulties and obstacles and successfully accomplish their historic tasks in the new revolutionary stage. No force, no scheme can check this iron determination of the Vietnamese people.

The friendship between the peoples of Vietnam and China is going through unprecedentedly hard trials. If the relationship between the two countries is deteriorating as seriously as it is now, this must be attributed to the wrongdoings of the Chinese authorities. The Chinese side must bear full responsibility for that situation. The people and Government of Vietnam sincerely wish that the Chinese side, out of respect for the friendship between the peoples of the two countries, give up its anti-Vietnam policy and cease actions contrary to the traditional friendship between the peoples of the two countries.

The Government of the Socialist Republic of Vietnam takes this opportunity to renew to the Government of the People's Republic of China the assurances of its high consideration.

Memorandum of the Ministry of Foreign Affairs of the Socialist Republic of Vietnam to the Embassy of the People's Republic of China in Hanoi, 3rd October 1978.

(Complete Text.).

Since the beginning of September this year, the Chinese authorities have repeatedly sent their armed forces to violate Vietnam's territory to carry out provocative activities, cause disturbances and threaten the security of Vietnam.

Following the violation of Vietnamese waters by an armed Chinese boat which shot dead a Vietnamese fisherman on 12th September, 1978, the Chinese authorities repeatedly on 13th, 14th, 15th, 21st, 22nd, 29th and 30th September, 1978, sent their armed boats across the border line into Vietnamese territory from the Tra Co rivermouth of Vietnam to the electric post No 6 in Xuan Hoa village, Mong Cai District, Quang Ninh Province, Vietnam. They detonated many mines, wrecked fishing equipment, carried out provocations and threatened the normal life of the Vietnamese fishermen.

Along the border from Mong Cai to Lao Cai the Chinese authorities many times sent their armymen police and militiamen to intrude into Vietnamese territory in many areas:

On 11th September, 20 armymen together with hooligans crossed the border and entered the area between landmarks 11 and 12 in Hanh Thanh village, Van Lang District, Cao Lang Province to carry out provocations, shout the charge and surround Vietnamese police and militia on duty on Vietnamese territory.

At 1400 14th September, 10 Chinese armymen, policemen and militiamen crossed the border between landmarks 3 and 4 in Trung Khanh village, Van Lang District, and entered 100 m deep into Vietnamese territory.

At 1600 on 20th September, 10 Chinese armymen and militiamen crossed the border at landmark 91 in Chi Phong village, Tra Linh District, Cao Lang Province, Vietnam, and penetrated 60 m into Vietnamese territory.

At 0600 20th September, 19 Chinese armymen crossed the border at landmark 53 in Dam Thu village, Trung Khanh District, Cao Lang Province, violating Lung Chang area of Vietnam.

At 2043 on 20th September eight armed Chinese armymen and policemen violated Vietnamese territory between landmarks 19 and 20 in Po Lo Po in Bao Lam village, Van Lang District, Cao Lang Province, threw stones and directed their electrical torches on a Vietnamese watch post.

On 20th September, one armyman and one militiamen of China violated Vietnam's territory between landmarks 107 and 108 in Keo Yen village, Ha

Quang District, Cao Lang Province, Vietnam. These men afterwards called in another 150 men to threaten Vietnamese police and militiamen on duty on Vietnamese soil.

On 12th, 19th and 21st September, the Chinese side sent 55 men to cross the border between landmarks 23 and 24 Lung Ly belonging to Xa Xim Cai and Son Vi villages in Meo Vac District, Ha Tuyen Province, and cleared 25,678 sq. m. of Vietnamese land.

On 21st September five Chinese crossed the border into Vietnamese territory at Lung Ly belonging to Xa Xim Cai and Son Vi villages, Meo Vac District, Ha Tuyen Province, and stole maize of the Vietnamese people.

On 25th and 26th September, 29 Chinese armymen, seven armed policemen and 64 militiamen illegally entered a lake area of Vietnam in Xim Tra hamlet, Phu Lung village, Dong Van District, Ha Tuyen Province, and penetrated about 200 m into Vietnamese territory.

Particularly serious is that at 1500 on 23rd September, 20 Chinese armymen and one militiaman crossed the border between landmarks 12 and 13 in Nam Ngat hamlet, Thanh Duc village, Vi Xuyen District, Ha Tuyen Province, and entered 70 m into Vietnamese territory, manhandled Vietnamese militia and took away a military cap, a knife and a fountain pen. At 0800 on 26th September 1978, 18 Chinese armymen, 12 armed policemen and two militiamen armed with a machine-gun and 20 CKC and AK rifles and led by Tang Kuen-chih, head of the Pac San police station, entered Keo Trinh area between landmarks 33 and 34 in Cao Lang village, Cao Loc District, Cao Lang Province, burst into the home of Mr Dau Pao and tore down a portrait of President Ho Chi Minh.

These acts of the Chinese side has caused tension at the Vietnam-China border and given the lie to the Chinese authorities' allegation that Vietnam has created a tense atmosphere at the China-Vietnam border and violated Chinese territorial sovereignty. The SRV Foreign Ministry strongly protests against and seriously condemns these wrongdoings of the Chinese authorities and demands that the Chinese side end immediately all violations of the territorial sovereignty of Vietnam and prevent the recurrence of these acts.

Note of the Ministry of Foreign Affairs of the People's Republic of China to the Vietnamese Embassy in Peking. 7th November 1978.

(Excerpts).

. . . On the morning of 1st November, over 60 armed Vietnamese personnel and militiamen intruded into the Chinese territory of the Hujun people's commune in Chinghsi County, Kwangsi Chuang Autonomous Region along the Sino-Vietnamese border, when members and militiamen of Hsinhsing and Huali production brigades of this commune were removing road blocks and sharpened bamboo stakes set up illegally by, and filling up trenches dug illegally there by Vietnamese personnel. The intruders unscrupulously made trouble and provocations against the Chinese commune members and militiamen. The Chinese inhabitants told the Vietnamese that they had intruded into Chinese territory and demanded that they return to the Vietnamese side. The armed Vietnamese personnel took no heed of the demand, attacked the Chinese border inhabitants with stones and daggers and wounded a number of them. What is more serious, a commander of the Vietnamese intruders gave a signal by firing a pistol. Then the armed Vietnamese personnel lying in ambush in advance suddenly opened fire on the Chinese border inhabitants with machine-guns, sub-machine-guns and rifles from four dug-outs nearby. More than 500 bullets were fired and 12 Chinese wounded. Eight Chinese were blatantly kidnapped.

After the incident, the Chinese border pass authorities lodged a protest with the Vietnamese border pass, demanding that the Vietnamese side return the kidnapped Chinese. This was refused by the Vietnamese side. On 3rd November, the Vietnamese foreign ministry informed the Chinese embassy in Hanoi that six of the kidnapped Chinese personnel had died.

This is a very grave incident of bloodshed deliberately created by the Vietnamese authorities at the Sino-Vietnamese border area and a new, serious step in escalating their anti-China campaign. This grave incident has aroused great indignation among the Chinese border inhabitants. The Chinese government hereupon lodges a strong protest with the Vietnamese government. The Vietnamese government must bear full responsibility for this grave incident of bloodshed, must immediately release the Chinese border inhabitants it had taken away and return the bodies of the murdered Chinese personnel. It must guarantee that such incidents would never recur. . .

Since last October armed Vietnamese personnel have on many occasions opened fire on Chinese villages and inhabitants at the Sino-Vietnamese border areas, deliberately making provocations and creating incidents. It is only because the Chinese side has exercised the greatest restraint and forbearance that these incidents have not been exacerbated.

The Chinese government warns the Vietnamese authorities in all seriousness that they should not regard Chinese restraint and forbearance as weakness and submissiveness. Should the Vietnamese authorities wilfully cling to their course and continue to intensify the anti-China provocations and armed intrusions at the Sino-Vietnamese border areas, they must bear full responsibility for all the consequences arising therefrom. . .

Treaty of Friendship and Co-operation between the Union of Soviet Socialist Republics and the Socialist Republic of Vietnam.

(Complete Text).

The Union of Soviet Socialist Republics and the Socialist Republic of Vietnam,

proceeding from the close fraternal relations of all-round co-operation existing between them, from the unbreakable friendship and solidarity which rest on the principles of Marxism-Leninism and socialist internationalis;

firmly believing that the all-out strengthening of cohesion and friendship between the Union of Soviet Socialist Republics and the Socialist Republic of Vietnam is in the vital interests of the peoples of the two countries and serves the cause of further strengthening fraternal cohesion and unity of the countries of the socialist community;

guided by the principles and purposes of a socialist foreign policy, by the striving to ensure the most favourable international conditions for building socialism and communism;

reaffirming that the two sides regard the rendering of assistance to each other in consolidating and defending socialist gains, achieved at the price of the heroic efforts and selfless labour of their peoples, as their internationalist duty;

firmly coming out for the cohesion of all forces struggling for peace, national independence, democracy and social progress;

expressing the firm resolve to promote stronger peace in Asia and throughout the world, to make their contribution to the development of good relations and reciprocally advantageous co-operation between states with different social systems;

striving to continue the development and perfection of all-round co-operation between the two countries;

attaching great importance to the further development and strengthening of the contractual-legal foundation of the relations between them;

In accordance with the purposes and principles of the Charter of the United Nations Organization;

have resolved to conclude this Treaty of Friendship and Co-operation and agreed as follows:

Article 1

In accordance with the principles of socialist internationalism the High Contracting Parties will go on strengthening relations of unbreakable friendship, solidarity and fraternal mutual aid. They will steadfastly develop political relations and deepen all-round co-operation, will give each

other all-out support based on reciprocal respect for state sovereignty and independence, equality and non-interference in each other's internal affairs.
Article 2

The High Contracting Parties will join efforts for strengthening and expanding reciprocally advantageous economic, scientific and technical co-operation with the purpose of accelerating socialist and communist construction, of steadily raising the material and cultural standards of the peoples of their countries. The Parties will continue long-term co-ordination of their national economic plans, will correlate forward-looking measures towards developing crucial branches of the economy, science and engineering, will exchange knowledge and experience accumulated in socialist and communist construction.
Article 3

The High Contracting Parties will facilitate co-operation between organs of state power and public organizations, will promote ties in the spheres of science and culture, education, literature and the arts, the press, radio and television, public health, environmental protection, tourism, physical culture and sports, and in other fields. They will stimulate the development of contacts between working people of the two countries.
Article 4

The High Contracting Parties will pursue an all-out and consistent struggle for the further strengthening of fraternal relations, of unity and solidarity among socialist countries on the basis of Marxism-Leninism and socialist internationalism.

They will bend every effort towards the consolidation of the world socialist system, will make a vigorous contribution to the development and protection of socialist gains.
Article 5

The High Contracting Parties will go on bending every effort for protecting international peace and the security of the peoples, will vigorously counteract all the designs and machinations of imperialism and reactionary forces, will support the just struggle for the final eradication of colonialism and racism in all its forms and manifestations, will support the struggle of the non-aligned countries, the struggle of the peoples of Asia, Africa and Latin America against imperialism, colonialism and neo-colonialism, for strengthening independence, in defence of sovereignty, for the right to freely dispose of their natural resources, for the estgablishment of new international economic relations free from inequality, diktat and exploitation, will support the striving of the peoples of Southeast Asia for peace, independence and co-operation among them.

They will unwaveringly come out for the development of relations between countries with different social systems on the basis of the principles of peaceful coexistence, for expanding and deepening the détente process in international relations, for the final exclusion of aggression and annexa-

tional wars from the life of the peoples, in the name of peace, national
independence, democracy and socialism.
Article 6
The High Contracting Parties will consult each other on all important
international issues affecting the interests of the two countries. In case one
of the Parties becomes the object of attack or of a threat of attack, the High
Contracting Parties will immediately begin mutual consultations for the
purpose of removing that threat and taking appropriate effective measures
to ensure the peace and security of their countries.
Article 7
The present treaty does not affect the rights and obligations of the
Parties under bilateral and multilateral agreements now in force, concluded
with their participation, nor is it directed against any third country.
Article 8
The present treaty is subject to ratification and will come into force on
the date of exchange of the instruments of ratification which shall take
place in the city of Hanoi at the earliest date.
Article 9
The present treaty is concluded for a period of 25 years and shall be
automatically prolonged every time for another 10-year period, unless
either of the High Contracting Parties gives notice of its wish to terminate if
twelve months before the expiration of the respective period.
Done in the city of Moscow this Third day of November, Nineteen
Hundred and Seventy Eight, in duplicate, each copy in the Russian and
Vietnamese languages, both texts being equally authentic.

Letter from the Presidium of the Supreme Soviet of the USSR to the Standing Committee of the Chinese National People's Congress.

(Complete Text). Peking Review, no. 13. 31 March, 1978.

The Standing Committee of the Chinese National People's Congress:
Soviet-Chinese relations assumed over the recent years a nature that
cannot but cause serious concern. The existing state of affairs leads to the
creation of the atmosphere of mutual distrust, to the heightening of
tensions in interstate relations. The vital interests of the Soviet and Chinese
peoples require adoption of definite practical measures aimed at normalizing Soviet-Chinese relations in accordance with the aspirations and hopes
of the peoples of the Soviet Union and the People's Republic of China.
The Soviet Government repeatedly advanced concrete proposals aimed
at bringing the relations between the U.S.S.R. and the P.R.C. back to the
road of good-neighbourliness, and expressed the U.S.S.R.'s readiness to

normalize relations with China on the principles of peaceful coexistence. The Government of the People's Republic of China for its part had officially stated that the P.R.C. could build relations with the U.S.S.R. on the principles of peaceful coexistence. The Soviet people sincerely wishes to see China a friendly prosperous power.

The Presidium of the U.S.S.R. Supreme Soviet, expressing the will and aspirations of the Soviet people, is once again stating its readiness to put an end to the present abnormal situation in the relations between the U.S.S.R. and the P.R.C. and to stop the dangerous process of further aggravation of relations which may lead to serious negative consequences for our countries and peoples, for the destinies of peace in the Far East, in Asia and throughout the world.

In order to materialize the desire expressed by the two sides to base their relations on the principles of peaceful coexistence and embody it in a tangible international act, the Presidium of the U.S.S.R. Supreme Soviet is suggesting that our countries come forward with a joint statement on the principles of mutual relations between the Union of Soviet Socialist Republics and the People's Republic of China. It is believed in the Soviet Union that a joint statement that the sides will build their relations on the basis of peaceful coexistence, firmly adhering to the principles of equality, mutual respect for sovereignty and territorial integrity, non-interference in the internal affairs of each other and non-use of force could advance the cause of normalization of our relations.

We suggest that if the very idea of making such a statement is acceptable for the Chinese side a meeting of representatives of both sides should be held at a sufficiently high level to agree on a mutually acceptable text of the statement in the shortest possible time.

The Soviet Union is prepared to receive representatives of the People's Republic of China. If the Chinese side deems it expedient that Soviet representatives should arrive for the afore-mentioned purpose in Peking, we agree to this. On our part, we are prepared to consider proposals of the P.R.C. aimed at normalization of Soviet-Chinese relations.

The Presidium of the U.S.S.R. Supreme Soviet

February 24, 1978.

Note of the Ministry of Foreign Affairs of the People's Republic of China to the Soviet Embassy in China.

(Complete Text). Hsinhua News Agency, 25 March, 1978.

The Soviet Embassy in the People's Republic of China:

The Ministry of Foreign Affairs of the People's Republic of China is entrusted by the Standing Committee of the National People's Congress to reply to the letter of February 24, 1978 from the Presidium of the Supreme Soviet of the U.S.S.R. as follows:

China and the Soviet Union used to be friendly neighbouring countries, and our two peoples have forged a profound friendship in their long revolutionary struggles. Responsibility for the deterioration of the relations between our two countries to what they are today does not lie with the Chinese side; China is the victim.

It is known to all that there exist differences of principle between China and the Soviet Union. The debate over these differences will go on for a long time. However, proceeding from the fundamental interests of the Chinese and Soviet peoples, the Chinese side has always held that the differences of principle should not impede the maintenance of normal state relations between the two countries on the basis of the Five Principles of Peaceful Coexistence. And to this end it has made unremitting efforts.

In September 1969 the Chinese Premier and the Soviet Chairman of the Council of Ministers held talks in Peking and reached an understanding on the normalization of relations between the two countries. The Chinese side has ever since abided by this understanding and for its full implementation has earnestly and patiently held boundary negotiations with the Soviet side for as long as eight years. However, the Soviet side not only is unwilling to implement the understanding reached by the heads of government of the two countries, it even denies the existence of the understanding itself. As a result, the boundary negotiations remain fruitless to this day. In the mean time, the Soviet Union has unceasingly increased its armed forces on the Sino-Soviet border and in the People's Republic of Mongolia, and there is not the slightest change in the Soviet policy of hostility to China. In these circumstances, the Presidium of the Supreme Soviet of the U.S.S.R. has proposed in its letter that the two countries issue a hollow statement on principles guiding mutual relations, a statement which does not solve any practical problem. Its purpose in so doing is obviously not to improve Sino-Soviet relations but lies elsewhere.

If the Soviet side really desires to improve Sino-Soviet relations, it should take concrete actions that solve practical problems. First of all, it should sign, in accordance with the 1969 understanding between the Premiers of the two countries, an agreement on the maintenance of the status quo on the border, averting armed clashes and disengaging the armed forces of the two sides in the disputed border areas, and then proceed to settle through negotiations the boundary question; and it should withdraw its armed forces from the People's Republic of Mongolia and from the Sino-Soviet border so that the situation there will revert to what it was in the early 60s. When you refuse to take such minimum actions as maintenance of the status quo on the border, averting armed clashes and disengaging the armed forces of the two sides in the disputed border areas, what practical purpose would it serve to issue a worthless "statement of principles guiding mutual relations" except to deceive the Chinese and Soviet peoples and the world public! When you have a million troops deployed on the Sino-Soviet border, how can you expect the Chinese people to believe that you have a genuine and sincere desire to improve the relations between our two countries? Isn't it fully reasonable to ask you to withdraw your armed forces from the Sino-Soviet border and restore the situation that prevailed in the early 60s?

The normalization of relations between China and the Soviet Union is the common desire of our two peoples and it accords with their fundamental interests and those of the people of the world. For its part, the Chinese side will, as always, make efforts towards this end. What the Chinese side likes to see is real deeds and not hollow statements.

The Ministry of Foreign Affairs avails itself of this opportunity to renew to the Embassy the assurances of its high considerations.

Ministry of Foreign Affairs of the People's Republic of China

Peking, March 9, 1978.

Note of the Government of the Mongolian People's Republic to the Government of the People's Republic of China.*

(Complete Text).

*The Note was delivered simultaneously in Ulan Bator and Peking on 12 April, 1978.

The Mongolian People's Republic has consistently stood for the normalization of relations with its neighbour — the People's Republic of China. Guided by sincere desire to restore the relations of good-neighbourliness and cooperation, the Mongolian side has repeatedly approached the Chinese side with specific proposals, designed to find solutions to bilateral issues.

The present state of the Mongolo-Chinese relations, however, remains to be extremely unsatisfactory. This is not because that the Mongolian side lacks good will for or interest in the improvement of normal relations with China. On the contrary, the Mongolian People's Republic has always proceeded, and continues to do so, from the premise that the restoration of good-neighbourly relations between the two countries is in complete compliance with the fundamental interests of both the Mongolian and Chinese peoples and the larger interests of peace and security in Asia and the Far East. This principled position has often been expressed in official statements by the Mongolian side.

Nevertheless, the willingness of the Mongolian side to normalize the inter-state relations has met no positive response on the part of the People's Republic of China. Moreover, the Chinese side obstinately follows a course to aggravate the Mongolo-Chinese relations and to interfere in the internal affairs of the Mongolian People's Republic.

The demand recently levelled at the Soviet Union by the Chinese authorities to withdraw the Soviet military units from the territory of the Mongolian People's Republic is considered in the Mongolian People's Republic as another fresh act of gross interference in her internal affairs. And such a demand has been made over the head of the Government of the Mongolian People's Republic. It cannot be viewed otherwise than as an attempt to disregard the Mongolian People's Republic as an independent State.

As is known, the military units of the USSR are stationed in Mongolia exclusively at the request of the Government of the Mongolian People's Republic, and in conformity with the Mongolo-Soviet Treaty on friendship, cooperation and mutual assistance.

As to the reason for the stationing of the Soviet military units at present in Mongolia, it lies in nothing else but the very policy of the Chinese authorities vis-a-vis the Mongolian People's Republic.

The ruling circles of the People's Republic of China have explicitly pronounced on various occasions their desire to integrate the Mongolian People's Republic to China. This has been accompanied by practical actions which ultimately have brought about to-day's tense state in the relationship between the two countries.

An immediate threat to the security of the Mongolian People's Republic is posed by the open war preparations by China which are being intensified with every passing year. Massive concentration of Chinese troops, construction of military and strategic installations and military exercises are being stepped up in the areas contiguous to the borders of the Mongolian People's Republic, and various subversive activities against the Mongolian People's Republic carried out too.

In the face of such a real menace, the Government of the Mongolian People's Republic was compelled to take necessary measures to strengthen the country's defence capacity and to guarantee her security. It is to this end that at the request of the Government of the Mongolian People's Republic were brought into Mongolia the Soviet military units, which now together with the Mongolian People's Army stand on guard of the national independence and territorial integrity of the Mongolian People's Republic.

Thus the presence of the Soviet military units in the Mongolian People's Republic constitutes an obliged measure necessitated exclusively by the concern to ensure her security.

No one can argue that the decision on stationing the Soviet military units in the Mongolian People's Republic is a purely internal affair of the sovereign State of Mongolia, which stems from her inalienable right to safeguard her freedom and independence.

The Government of the Mongolian People's Republic considers that the threat to Mongolia's sovereignty and independence continues to exist today, since the Chinese authorities not only haven't abandoned their expansionist design vis-a-vis Mongolia, but also keep on intensifying military preparations against the Mongolian People's Republic and her ally — the Soviet Union.

It is quite obvious that the question concerning the withdrawal of the Soviet military units from the Mongolian People's Republic may arise only then, when the reason for their presence has ceased to exist. If the Chinese leadership resigns for good from their policy of annexation with respect to the Mongolian People's Republic and embarks on the path of good-neighbourliness and cooperation with the Mongolian People's Republic and the Soviet Union, the present need for maintaining the Soviet military units in the Mongolian People's Republic would disappear on its own. It depends on the Chinese side when an how soon this will happen.

In this connection it would not be out of place to mention here that in the 1950's, when normal relations were maintained between Mongolia and China, the Mongolian People's Republic not only had no Soviet military units in its territory but it had reduced her own armed forces to the minimum and even dissolved the border troops.

The Mongolian Government reiterates that the Mongolian People's Republic will further continue to exert efforts to normalize the inter-state relations with China on the principles of peaceful co-existence and in the spirit of good-neighbourliness and mutual understanding.

The Government of the Mongolian People's Republic believes that, if sound and realistic approach would indeed be displayed by the Chinese side, the relations between the Mongolian People's Republic and the People's Republic of China could be brought back to normalcy.

Note of the Ministry of Foreign Affairs of the People's Republic of China to the Soviet Embassy in China, 11 May, 1978.

(Complete Text). Hsinhua News Agency, 11 May, 1978.

In disregard of China's sovereignty and universally-recognized principles guiding international relations, the Soviet Union side, on the morning of 9th May 1978, dispatched a helicopter to intrude into China's air space, crossing the border river Wusuli[1] and penetrating 4 km over Yueyapao district, Hulino County, Heilungkiang Province. It also dispatched 18 military boats to intrude into China's waters in the same region. About 30 Soviet troops then landed on the Chinese bank of the river. They chased and tried to round up Chinese inhabitants, shooting continually and wounding a number of them. Penetrating 4 km into Chinese territory, they seized 14 Chinese inhabitants and dragged them all the way to the riverside, giving them kicks and blows. Under the repeated protests of the Chinese inhabitants the Soviet troops finally released them. It was only due to the restraint of the Chinese side that the incident did not develop into an armed conflict.

The above-mentioned atrocities of the Soviet troops constitute an organized military provocation against China occurring at a time when the Sino-Soviet boundary negotiations had just resumed. They are a serious infringement on China's sovereignty and territorial integrity as well as a grave, calculated step to create tension on the border and vitiate the relations between the two countries. The Chinese Government hereby lodges a strong protest with the Soviet Government against this and demands that the Soviet side make an apology, punish the culprits who created this incident of bloodshed and guarantee that no similar incident would occur in future. Otherwise, the Soviet side must bear full responsibility for the consequences arising therefrom.

[1] Ussuri (Ed.).

Tass Statement

(Complete Text). 12 May, 1978.

On 11 May the New China News Agency reported a border incident on the Ussuri River, near the Krestovskiye Islands. The report alleged that the Soviet side launched an "armed provocation" on the Chinese-Soviet border "with the participation of a helicopter and gunboats." It was further alleged that Soviet servicemen opened fire and wounded a number of Chinese citizens.

This is what really happened:

On the night of May 8-9, a group of Soviet naval borderguards, who were pursuing a dangerous and armed criminal, having mistaken the Chinese bank for the Soviet Krestovskiye Islands, landed there and penetrated over a small distance into Chinese territory. The Soviet servicemen did not undertake any actions involving Chinese citizens, but, discovering that they had inadvertently landed on Chinese territory, immediately left.

Regrets have been expressed to the Chinese side over the incident.

Chinese Foreign Ministry's Oral Statement to the Soviet Ambassador.*

(Complete Text). Peking Review, no. 21. 26 May, 1978.

*The Statement was made by Vice-Foreign Minister Yu Chan during his second meeting with the Soviet Ambassador to China V.S. Tolstikov on May 17, 1978.

The Ministry of Foreign Affairs of the People's Republic of China has studied the note delivered by the Ministry of Foreign Affairs of the U.S.S.R. to the Chinese Embassy in the Soviet Union on May 12, 1978, and I am authorized to state as follows:

We have taken note of the fact that the Soviet side admitted the landing of its naval frontier guards on the Chinese bank of the river and their penetration into Chinese territory, expressed its regret over this incident and stated that it was prepared to make the culprits answer for it. However, we cannot agree to the Soviet distortion of the facts for self-justification in regard of this incident in which Soviet troops intruded into China's border and wounded Chinese inhabitants.

1. In its note the Soviet side advances the time of the Soviet military intrusion from daytime to midnight in order to justify its description of this serious intrusion of Chinese territory by Soviet troops as an inadvertent trespass. As a matter of fact, a Soviet helicopter intruded into China's airspace around 7 o'clock local time on the morning of May 9 and kept circling the area for reconnaissance till after 11 O'clock. At the same time, 18 Soviet military boats intruded into China's waters, and about 30 fully armed Soviet troops equipped with walkie-talkies landed on the Chinese bank and did not embark and leave until 10.30. One should like to ask: how could so many of your people both in the sky and on the ground fail to tell in broad daylight between the Chinese land expanse and your river island less than half a square kilometre in size?

2. Soviet military boats patrol the river all the year round, and Krestovskiy Island is very close to the base of the Soviet Dalnerechensk (Iman) frontier guards. Your frontier guards must be very clear where the Soviet island is and where the Chinese bank. While your island is less than 200 metres wide, your troops came four kilometres into Chinese territory. Did your troops really need to ask Chinese inhabitants before they knew their location and woke up to the fact that they were on Chinese territory?

3. You admit in your note that your naval frontier guards landed on the Chinese bank of the river, but then you assert that your military boats did not intrude into Chinese waters. If what you assert were true, did your guards have wings to take them to Chinese territory?

4. According to your note, the Soviet troops crossed the border in search of an armed Soviet criminal. In that case, why did your troops round up and give blows to the 14 bare-handed Chinese inhabitants, including three

women, and why did your troops drag them along as far as four kilometres?

5. The Soviet troops shot at more than 30 Chinese inhabitants, firing more than 100 rounds of ammunition, and wounded a number of them. We have in our possession the cartridge cases and even some of the bullets. In the face of witnesses and material evidence, how can you possibly deny the Soviet troops' use of force against and their firing on peaceable Chinese inhabitants?

Facts amply prove that this intrusion of Soviet troops was by no means a case of inadvertent trespass into Chinese territory, but a military provocation organized by the Soviet side, a bloody incident created by Soviet troops, and a demonstration of the Soviet policy of hostility to China and of threat or use of force against China.

The Chinese side holds to its position stated in the note of May 11, 1978 addressed by the Chinese Ministry of Foreign Affairs to the Soviet Embassy in China and demands that the Soviet side honestly admit its wrongdoing and take effective measures to guarantee against future occurrence of similar incidents.

The Chinese side awaits a formal reply from the Soviet side.

The Struggle Between the Theory of Genius and the Theory of Practice.*

(Complete Text). People's Daily. 30 October, 1978.

* Translation by the Hsinhua News Agency.

Practice is the sole criterion of truth. This elementary Marxist knowledge was for many years placed under taboo by Lin Piao and the gang of four and no one was allowed to speak of it or propagate it. This was not surprising, since Lin Piao and the gang of four were a bunch of fake Marxists and political and theoretical swindlers and could not stand the test of practice. But the problem is that now, more than a year since the smashing of the gang of four, some people who mention this elementary Marxist knowledge are still regarded by some comrades as dissidents, as if they had committed a serious crime — this fact tells us that the pernicious influence of the theory of genius has not been completely eliminated.

All of us know that Lin Piao's theoretical programme was the theory of genius. Did the gang of four have their own theoretical programme? If they did, what was it? Through the current discussion on the criterion of truth, people have obtained a better understanding of this question. The gang of four's theoretical programme was the same as Lin Piao's — the theory of genius.

In talking about the struggle between the theory of genius and the theory of practice, we cannot help recalling the 1970 Lushan conference. It is eight years since the Lushan conference was held, and, two anti-Party cliques, headed respectively by Lin Piao and the gang of four, have been smashed in turn. But to remember past errors ensures against repetition of the same errors. Recalling past history is good for us so that we can understand the facts before us. This is not aimed at settling an old account, because Lin Piao and the gang of four are on the same account. It is impossible to settle accounts with the gang of four if we do not link the criticism of them with the criticism of Lin Piao.

At the Lushan conference, Lin Piao unfurled two banners: One was "the State should have a Chairman", which was his political programme; and the other was the "theory of genius", which was his theoretical programme. He said "the State should have a Chairman" because he himself wanted to become Chairman of the State in order to usurp political power and establish the Lins' fascist dynasty. The theory of genius was precisely designed to serve this political end.

The theory of genius represents idealist apriorism, which advocates that knowledge is a priori. Whoever is wise is a genius. History is made by men of genius whose thinking is independent of time, space and concrete conditions and is the final and eternal truth. It does not come from practice, nor should it be tested by practice. On the contrary, this thinking should be regarded as the criterion of truth and the supreme judge for all the world's rights and wrongs. This theory is totally anti-Marxist and runs counter to the theory of practice.

The Marxist theory of knowledge is the theory of practice. It holds that man's knowledge can only come from social practice and that only concrete practice can tell whether it is correct or not. Of course, man cannot personally engage in practice in everything. Most of his knowledge comes from others — including books — but the knowledge of others comes also from practice. Marxism does not object to the term genius. We use this term, but explain it in a materialist way. As observed from the physiological quality of human brains and the functions of their reaction, there are differences between men. It is true that some people are wiser than others, but we must recognize the objective fact that these differences only constitute different material foundations for men's activities after birth. The direction in which a person develops and how rapidly he develops depends entirely on his social practice. No matter how wise one may be, one cannot acquire knowledge without practice. When we use the term "genius" to praise a certain great figure, we mean that he has far greater talent than others in certain fields such as politics, military affairs, engineering, techniques, science, arts or other fields. What is the source of this great talent? Practice and nothing else. The viewpoint of practice is the primary and fundamental viewpoint of the Marxist theory of knowledge.

Since Chairman Mao's "On Practice" was made public, this concept has been popularized even more comprehensively and has struck deep roots in the people's hearts. In this situation, if there are people in the Communist Party who peddle the theory of genius and oppose the theory of practice, it is because either they have never changed their world outlook and are seeking personal ends, or they have never studied Marxist works and know nothing about the concept that Chairman Mao repeatedly tried to popularize. Facts have proved that Lin Piao peddled the idealist theory of genius. His aim was to foster his individual "absolute authority" and create public opinion in order to usurp Party and State leadership. He wanted to say that he himself was a genius. However, he could not come right out and say it at that time, because the CCP and its leader Comrade Mao Tsetung enjoyed high prestige among the Chinese people. This prestige was built through the practice of protracted revolutionary struggle. The people supported the Party and cherished their own leader. They did not do this on the basis of an apriorist principle or under the signboard of "holding high" the banner. They did this on the basis of their own observations and the objective facts of their own experiences. It was for this reason that the prestige of our Party and Chairman Mao among the people was unchangeable.

In this situation, Lin Piao adopted an extremely vicious tactic by praising the proletarian leader as a "genius" and calling Mao Tsetung thought the "acme". Do you dare to oppose this theory of genius? If you do, you oppose Chairman Mao. That means you are against Mao Tsetung thought. Do you want to recognize this theory of genius? You have to admit that only Lin Piao "holds the banner highest". Then he could build his own image as a "genius" and he could thus achieve his goal. This was precisely his tactic of taking over the great banner and using it as a tiger skin to frighten people. He did this as early as the beginning of the great cultural revolution.

Chairman Mao had already discovered this incipient sign, and incessantly waged struggles against it. However, because of his own self-interest, Lin Piao blinded himself. At the second plenary session of the Ninth CCP Central Committee — the Lushan conference — he openly hoisted the banner of the theory of genius and launched an unsuccessful counter-revolutionary coup d'etat. He and his followers made boisterous noises, cried and created a foul atmosphere at Lushan as if all other people were against Chairman Mao and only they themselves held high the Red Banner. At that time, many comrades were fooled. If the struggles in the past were considered mere skirmishes, then the struggle at Lushan was an open major battle. In "My Opinion", Chairman Mao exposed with one stroke Lin Piao's anti-Party ambition, which was under the cover of his theory of genius. Because of Lin Piao's efforts over the past years in propagating the theory of genius and the confusion he caused in the minds of the people, the people were unable to distinguish between idealism and materialism. In "My Opinion", Chairman Mao put forward an extremely important theoretical question to the whole Party: who are the makers of history, the heroes or the slaves? Is a man's knowledge — one's talent also falls within the scope of knowledge — innate or acquired? Should we uphold idealist apriorism or the materialist theory of reflection? At the end of "My Opinion" Chairman Mao called on the whole Party to unite as one to win still greater victories and not to fall into the map of those who called themselves Marxists and yet knew nothing of Marxism.

It is obvious that in accordance with Chairman Mao's instruction following the Lushan meeting, a massive struggle should have been launched to criticize the theory of genius in order to eliminate the great confusion created by Lin Piao and company for many years and thus enable the whole Party and the people of the whole country to receive a profound education in Marxist materialism. But Chairman Mao's instruction was not carried out. The reason was very clear. Lin Piao was still in power; he had no intention of repenting and of course would not want to criticize himself. So the struggle to criticize the theory of genius was put off.

Reasonably, the struggle should have been launched after Lin Piao's self-destruction in 1971. Yet it wasn't. The gang of four controlled the means of propaganda and the mass media, and the struggle to criticize the theory of genius was still being suppressed.

Why didn't the gang of four criticize the theory of genius? The reason is very clear: although Lin Piao and the gang of four were the ringleaders of two counter-revolutionary revisionist lines, they were in fact jackals of the same lair, and ideologically they were of one system. If Lin Piao needed the theory of genius, then the gang of four needed the theory even more. After all, Lin Piao had fought battles and had some capital. By contrast, the gang of four hardly had any capital with which to bluff and deceive. They were the dregs of society and clowns. They didn't have any revolutionary practical experience, they were not even capable of leading a commune, and yet they attempted to rule a country with 800,000,000 people. Wasn't this pure nonsense? They wanted to assume great responsibilities but did not have practical experience; thus they could only resort to the theory of genius.

However, in appearance the gang of four's theory of genius was slightly different from that of Lin Piao. They learned a lesson from Lin Piao's failure, and they never mentioned the word "genius". On their banner was written "opposing empiricism is the key link", and that was another way of expressing the theory of genius. Lin Piao was saying that geniuses should rise to power, and the gang of four were saying that those with practical experience should step down. These were two different themes expressing the same idea; the former saying that he should rise to power, the latter saying that others should step down, both of which served their own political programmes. Lin Piao wanted the State to have a Chairman, and the theory of genius was meant to trumpet this political programme and for him to become Chairman of the State. The gang of four's political programme was that "veteran cadres are 'democrats', and 'democrats' are 'capitalist-roaders' ", and "Opposing empiricism is the key link" served this political programme — that is, to overthrow veteran cadres with practical experience. Since they described practical experience as empiricism and a bad thing and maintained that the more experienced anyone was the more necessary it was to overthrow him, it followed that the destiny of China could only be placed in the hands of "geniuses" like them.

It is apparent from both their political and theoretical programmes that the gang of four and Lin Piao were essentially the same. Therefore, asking the gang of four to criticize the theory of genius was absolutely impossible. While preventing the criticism of the theory of genius, the gang of four stepped up their opposition to the theory of practice. They not only inherited Lin Piao's principle "every sentence is truth" and quoted words and phrases out of context at will to intimidate and fool people, but in 1975 they openly suggested "opposing empiricism is the key link" and tried to carry out a massive counter-revolutionary purge.

When they put forward their theoretical programme, Chairman Mao pointed out its essence. On their theoretical programme, Chairman Mao wrote this comment: "It seems the formulation should mention opposition to revisionism, including opposition to empiricism and to dogmatism, both being revisions of Marxism-Leninism. Don't mention one and omit the other." Directing his criticism against the gang of four, that bunch of swindlers, Chairman Mao particularly pointed out: "Not many people in our Party really understand Marxism-Leninism. Some think they do, but in fact they know very little. They consider themselves always in the right and are only too ready to lecture others. This is in itself a manifestation of lack of knowledge of Marxism-Leninism." It was at that point that Chairman Mao personally initiated the struggle against the gang of four. This instruction was an extremely important document to guide the struggle. If we say that "My Opinion" was the fighting call for criticizing Lin Piao's theoretical programme, then this instruction was the fighting call for criticizing the gang of four's theoretical programme.

But neither of Chairman Mao's two fighting calls were implemented until the end of the gang of four's days, and the struggle to criticize the theory of genius never really started. Chairman Mao has now left us, and this instruction has become his behest. To carry out Chairman Mao's behests, we must fulfil this fighting call. This is exactly what the Party Central Committee headed by Chairman Hua has been doing. The third battle to expose and criticize the gang of four naturally includes criticizing the theory of genius. In depth criticism of the theory of genius is helpful in carrying the struggle to expose and criticize the gang of four through to the end and is conducive to consolidating and developing the political situation of stability and unity. To strengthen the unity of the Party and the people of the whole country, we must criticize all kinds of anti-Marxist ideas and unite the comrades of the whole Party and the people of the whole country on the basis of Marxism-Leninism-Mao Tsetung thought. Chairman Mao placed profound meaning when he linked "to unite" and "not to fall in the trap" at the end of "My Opinion". The true features of Lin Piao and the gang of four, those two bunches of swindlers, have now been exposed, but their poisonous influence has not yet been thoroughly eliminated. They have already caused extremely great chaos in the ideological field in our country. The ideological root of this chaos is the theory of genius. When we talk about unity, we must thoroughly criticize all the poison spread by Lin Piao and the gang of four, particularly their theoretical programme, the theory of genius. Only in this way can we really achieve unity on the basis of Mao Tsetung thought.

We are now at a great historical turning point. The Party Central Committee headed by Chairman Hua has led us in embarking on a new Long March to build out country into a powerful, modern socialist country in this century. In carrying out the general task for the new period, how many new things there are for us to recognize, and how many new problems there are for us to solve! One of the biggest ideological obstacles to fulfilling the general task for the new period is the theory of genius. Some comrades talk about Mao Tsetung thought every day and seem to be "holding it very high", but they often forget and even oppose the principle that practice is the only criterion of truth, which Chairman Mao especially stressed.

Do you want to solve a new problem from a practical point of view? Are you trying to take a new step forward or to articulate some new idea in light of the new historical conditions? Well, check to see whether it has been written or said by somebody! Otherwise, you will be accused of "not holding high the banner" or even "trying to pull down the banner". This is precisely what Vice-Chairman Teng said at the all-Army political work conference: "In essence, their view is that one may only copy straight from Marx, Lenin and Chairman Mao and should rest content with mechanical copying, transmitting and reproduction. They would insist that to do otherwise is to go against Marxism-Leninism-Mao Tsetung thought and the guidance coming from the Party Central Committee."

If we were to allow this kind of view and mentality to prevail, we should be doing nothing other than quoting words and phrases from books day after day, which they call "holding high the banner". But truly, this is throwing away the essence of Marxism-Leninism-Mao Tsetung thought, foregoing the revolutionary enterprising spirit of a communist and diametrically going against the line of the 11th Party Congress.

The line of the 11th Party Congress calls on us to adapt ourselves to the new historical conditions, proceed from reality in everything we do, emancipate our minds and give full play to the revolutionary creative spirit in order to realize the four modernizations as quickly as possible. This line crystallizes the objective law of socialist development and represents the strong aspiration of the 800,000,000 Chinese people. How incongruous the state of mind — the state of mind that takes Marxism not as the guidance for action but as dogma — is to the reality of our stirring society!

In short, the theory of genius spread by Lin Piao and the gang of four has for a long time been the obstacle to our country's socialist undertakings. The removal of this obstacle is urgently demanded by the vast numbers of cadres and masses. It is also dictated by the need to defend and develop Marxism-Leninism-Mao Tsetung thought and the needs of advancing history. The current discussion on the criterion of truth is in fact a campaign of criticism of the idealist theory of genius conducted under the guidance of the Marxist theory of practice. Undoubtedly, this discussion means another lively and profound education in Marxist ideology for our cadres and masses.

If there are people who hold that the recognition of practice as the sole criterion for verifying the truth obstructs their effort to hold high the banner of Marxism-Leninism-Mao Tsetung thought, it only shows that they are not really trying to hold high the banner. Marxism is truth. It fears neither criticism nor the test of practice. If Marxism were to fear criticism and the test of practice, or if it could not stand up to criticism or stand the test of practice, it would lose its usefulness. During the past century and more, the banner of Marxism has gone through numerous tests of revolutionary practice. Yet these tests have only made it more brilliant with the richness of truth. This banner has also been attacked on numerous occasions, either verbally or physically. Yet it has not been overthrown. Indeed, this banner is flying higher than ever.

If in socialist China, a banner, whatever it is, fears the test of practice and comes down whenever the phrase "Practice is the sole criterion for verifying the truth" is uttered, then that banner evidently has nothing to do with the banner of Marxism-Leninism-Mao Tsetung thought but is a sham Marxist banner. The theory of genius advocated by Lin Piao and the gang of four is precisely such a sham Marxist banner. It is only natural that sham Marxism should feel scared when it encounters geniune Marxism and that the theory of genius should collapse in the face of the theory of practice. It is an extremely good thing to overthrow this sham Marxist banner and let the Red Banner of genuine Marxism-Leninism-Mao Tsetung thought fly higher. This is our very goal in deepening the criticism of the theory of genius of Lin Piao and the gang of four.

Let us rally more closely around the Party Central Committee headed by Chairman Hua and use the theory of practice as a weapon to eliminate thoroughly the pernicious influence of the theory of genius.

The Chinese Leaders' Great Betrayal.
Editorial Granma

(Complete Text). Granma, 11 June, 1978.

The Chinese leaders' great betrayal and the sinister role of adviser Brzezinski

The visit that Zbigniew Brzezinski, national security adviser to U.S. President James Carter, has just made to Peking is the most palpable recent expression of the fact that powerful forces in the United States are joining China in an international strategy that represents a serious and real danger to world peace.

The talks which the U.S. adviser had with the top Chinese leaders — talks that were shrouded in secrecy — reflect the aim of trying to coordinate Washington's and Peking's immediate actions in the arms race; to reduce the tactical differences between the two countries to secondary importance; to establish the bases for a worldwide strategic alliance of all counter-revolutionary forces against the USSR, the rest of the socialist community and the national liberation movements; and to eliminate the anti-imperialist and socially progressive elements expressed in the Non-Aligned Countries Movement.

Shortly before his trip to China, Brzezinski declared to a U.S. *Time* magazine reporter that the United States' ties with China were constant and long-range and were based on their common interests.

Just who is this travelling adviser of Carter's?

Brzezinksi is the spawn of the monopoly interests embodied in U.S. multimillionaire David Rockefeller, president of the ultra-powerful U.S. Chase Manhattan Bank, a centre that controls enormous capitalist consortia.

Brzezinski, the son of an exiled Polish counterrevolutionary, professes a gut hatred for the socialist countries typical of renegades and expatriates. One of the men with whom Brzezinski worked as a professor at Columbia University described him privately as a gross opportunist capable of stooping to anything in order to obtain a better position.

In mid-1960, Brzezinski was a fervent champion of U.S. intervention in Vietnam. His reactionary, backward nature was brought out clearly in an article published in the June 1, 1968, issue of the weekly *New Republic*.

When U.S. authorities were confronting the growing student protests against the war in Vietnam, this troglodyte-now-turned-adviser recommended that the authorities take prompt and strong action to strip the revolutionaries of their strength and meaning, first by instituting justified reforms and then by eliminating the leaders from the scene of the revolution.

This is the philosophy of the bullies and killers in the Central Intelligence Agency, the authors of many recently revealed plots and crimes all over the world!

Can mankind live in peace and tranquility when individuals of this ilk hold such important posts in the most powerful imperialist country of our time?

To wind up this brief biographical sketch of Brzezinski, we should mention that he has also been an adviser to the Rand Corporation, one of the institutions most closely linked to the Pentagon. In 1973, when the so-called Trilateral Commission was created, these "merits" led to his being named, first director of political studies in the Commission, and then, in 1974, its president.

The Trilateral Commission is an organization that promotes a political concept aimed at coordinating and uniting the monopolies and multinational centres of the United States, capitalist Europe and Japan for a single exploiting purpose. President Carter is a distinguished member of this exclusive club.

At least one of Brzezinski's companions on his trip to China is also worth mentioning. This is Samuel Huntington, planning coordinator of the National Security Council of the United States.

This citizen was ironically described by the French *Le Monde Diplomatique* as the "brilliant inventor of the concept of forced urbanization." It was his sick, reactionary brain that dreamed up the idea of "strategic hamlets," veritable concentration camps set up in Vietnam as long as the U.S. aggression lasted.

A war criminal turned into a representative of the people of the United States, into an architect of its foreign policy! This is a great affront to the peoples.

The loathsome alliance between the most reactionary circles in the United States and the Chinese leaders that emerged more clearly with the smiles and toasts in the palace in Peking is one more proof of the Chinese leaders' great betrayal of the principles of Marxism-Leninism and of proletarian internationalism.

With ever greater assurance and in a more overt, less scrupulous way, the Chinese leaders are making common cause with the most warlike elements of the bourgeoisie of the United States, Japan and Western Europe and are clamouring against the policy of peace and détente advocated by the Soviet Union.

The representatives of the U.S. imperialist circles are rubbing their hands with glee in the delusion that China will take on the Soviet Union successfully.

Weeks before Brzezinski's visit to Peking, Richard Solomon, one of his aides, wrote in *Foreign Affairs* magazine that China had become an ally of the United States and that the Peking leadership favoured the strengthening of NATO and had offered its support to U.S. diplomacy on problems running from the Middle East to Northern Asia.

Brzezinski's visit to China took place within the context of a dirty relationship between Peking and Washington aimed not only against the Soviet Union and all the other progressive countries but also against the vital interests of the peoples of China and the United States.

AFP reported on May 22 that as a result of his anti-Soviet jokes, the U.S. presidential adviser had been dubbed the tamer of the Russian bear.

The presidential adviser visited the Great Wall of China dressed in bright sports clothes and acting like a clown, which won him pleased glances from Whang Hai-hung, Mao Tse-tung's niece and deputy minister of foreign relations.

The report says that the adventurous, irresponsible Yankeefied clown challenged his companions to a race to one of the towers of the Great Wall, telling Mao's niece that if the Chinese lost, they would have to fight the Russians in Ethiopia, but that if they won, the United States would take on the annoying job.

The insolence of the U.S. official and his scorn for the sovereignty of the peoples is summed up in this dirty and humiliating joke, which the Chinese representatives accepted with smiles of approval.

On that occasion, Brzezinski was showing off for the journalists accompanying him. All his previous actions and interviews had been secret. His private party included neither spokesmen nor journalists.

World opinion, however, takes this action seriously. The Chinese leaders have openly proclaimed that they are preparing to modernize their armed forces, and they are hurriedly building bomb shelters, saying that a Third World War is inevitable. It is suspected that one of the questions Brzezinski discussed in his meeting with the Chinese was the probability of supplying China with U.S. weapons.

There is a growing danger of world war, and this collusion between the United States and China represents a serious threat to international peace and détente.

In an article published on May 1, 1977, Hua Kuo-feng, chairman of the Council of State of China, announced the need to "speed up revolutionizing and modernizing the People's Liberation Army and strengthening war preparations."

A few years ago, Mao Tse-tung stated at a meeting of Communist and Workers' Parties: "War. So, let there be war. . . . There is no reason to fear war. If war breaks out, there will be victims. . . . In my opinion, the atom bomb is no more terrible than a sword. If half of mankind should perish in the war, that wouldn't be important. Nor would it be a terrible thing if a third of the population was left." When he made this wild and foolish statement, Mao Tse-tung was talking about a war against the imperialists.

What does the Chinese leadership seem to be after now? In its deeds, it advocates an anti-Soviet war with the same insanity. To this end, it tries to sharpen Soviet-U.S. contradictions and stir up war between the two countries. Would this be a war for China to rise up out of the ruins as the great predominating power? That would be a senseless hope, for it doesn't appreciate the extent of the devastatingly destructive power of nuclear weapons and of their current deadly stockpiling. It would certainly be a war that would entail the devastation of China itself. Moreover, it is an estimation that involves the worst political, economic and social designs for the world. But what is worse yet, the Chinese leadership seems to be thinking openly of war in alliance with the United States against the Soviet Union.

For their part, the most rabid Yankee imperialists plan to use China as a weapon to pressure the Soviet Union and the rest of the socialist community, and this prognosis does not exclude promoting conflicts and even war between China and the USSR in order to eliminate socialism and the revolutionary process.

Now, when the Special United Nations General Assembly on Disarmament is taking place in New York, it is well to recall that the Chinese leaders opposed the reduction of the military budgets of the countries that are permanent members of the Security Council.

It is also well to recall that Peking has not signed any of the international agreements aimed at limiting the arms race.

Brzezinski and the Chinese leaders understood each other very well, because they have been speaking the same language for years. Let's look at the following remarks:

In a debate held in New York in 1974, Brzezinski voiced the opinion that détente was anachronistic, dangerous and incompatible with the overall problems of the world.

This past May 20, at the welcoming banquet for Carter's adviser, Chinese Foreign Minister Huang Hua declared, "The peoples should not let themselves be lulled by illusions of peace. They should oppose the policy of détente."

During that same banquet, Brzezinski definitively stressed the interests that U.S. imperialism and the Chinese leaders had in common when they said that a secure and powerful China was in the interests of the United States and that a powerful reliable United States that had commitments around the world was in the interests of China.

The new mandarins seek to inculcate the population — and particularly the Chinese armed forces — with this philosophy.

Since the end of 1969, when the so-called Communist Party of China publicly stated that the Soviet Union was its "main enemy", there has been no end to the dirty attacks on the Soviet Union and other countries of the socialist community.

A glance at any bulletin issued by the official Chinese news agency *Hsinhua* shows that the news agency prints every bourgeois and anti-communist insult to the Soviet Union, Cuba and other socialist countries that appears anywhere in the world. In many cases, the ones who write the articles that appear in the newspapers and magazines of small groups that respond to Peking's slogans are followers in the pay of the Chinese. In other cases, the most arch-reactionary, fascist publications are echoed in the pages of the Chinese bulletins.

This cynical, opportunistic and adventuristic policy of Brzezinski's trying to wring the most our of the wild and debased Chinese leaders' betrayal of history, is completely irresponsible and insane.

What can it lead to? To the failure of the policy of détente? To unrestrained arms race? To war? To blackmailing the Soviet Union and the rest of the socialist camp? Can anyone in his right mind say that such a policy could be a benefit to a world population currently besieged by a serious economic crisis; energy shortages; and population, environmental and food problems?

Can it offer the so-called Third World countries any hope for a solution to the problem of development?

Can it be in the interests of the people of the United States, China, the Soviet Union or any other country in the world?

No one has the right to play around with the future of mankind. It is absurd to think that the progressive camp will permit itself to be intimidated by this unheard-of blackmail.

In 1969, Leonid Brezhnev, General Secretary of the Communist Party of the Soviet Union, energetically answered these provocations:

"The newspaper *Kuang Min Ribao*," Brezhnev told the International Conference of Communist and Workers' Parties held in Moscow, "has launched an appeal to 'prepare both for conventional war and for a great nuclear war against Soviet revisionism.' It is clear that between their wild cries and their real possibilities of doing what they say, there is a wide gap. The Soviet Union has enough forces to defend itself, and the Soviets have strong nerves. They are not alarmed by cries. But the orientation of official Chinese propaganda is completely clear."

The Chinese leaders' great betrayal and their anti-communist alliances

Peking's new mandarins have become the most loyal allies of the most retrogressive world bourgeoisie and the warmongering circles of the North Atlantic Treaty Organization, led by the United States.

In recent months, visits and contacts between the Chinese military and NATO dealers in war — especially those of West Germany, France, England and Japan — have been stepped up.

Naturally the United States is not lagging behind in this mad, unrestrained arms race directed toward a tempting market.

As far back as the summer of 1977, *The New York Times* leaked a secret document revealing that high levels of the Pentagon and State Department were discussing the pros and cons of supplying China with military technology, communications installations, nuclear reactors, laser equipment, planes, helicopters, antitank missiles, etc.

Chinese military delegations have become assiduous marauders of NATO arsenals.

Last fall, a Chinese military delegation headed by Yang Chen-wu, associate chief of the general staff, travelled to France. It visited land and naval bases and expressed an interest in acquiring air-to-air and surface-to-surface missiles.

China hopes to purchase vertical takeoff Harrier fighter planes in England. A British spokesman has already said in Parliament that the British were prepared to fill the Chinese request.

The NATO generals are openly delighted with these visitors who passionately defend maintaining the military bases of this aggressive pact and who unreservedly support strengthening a military alliance aimed not only against the socialist countries of Europe but also against the liberation movements and progressive governments in Africa.

It was NATO that sustained the colonialist Portuguese régime to the very end! Thousands of citizens of Angola, Mozambique, Sao Tomé and Prïncipe, Guinea-Bissau and Cape Verde were killed by the bullets and shrapnel of weapons that came from the arsenals of that military alliance!

The NATO member countries sustain, arm and incite the bloody racist and fascist régime of South Africa, which holds patents on and manufactures the most sophisticated war weapons, now being used to massacre the patriots of Zimbabwe and the fighters of Namibia and to repress the black population of Soweto and Johannesburg, bulwarks of the apartheid system.

China seeks its allies in countries such as France, whose government has been sending thousands of paratroopers to intervene in Zaire to save the corrupt and bloody régime of Mobutu Sese Seko! The French air force bombs and massacres the fighers of the POLISARIO Front who are struggling for the independence of Western Sahara!

In recent months, Peking has been a mecca for every arms salesman in the world. The list is too long to include in its entirety, but a few examples are worth giving:

— West German General Johannes Steinhoff, former chairman of the Military Committee of NATO, accompanied by Adolf Kilmanzeg and Hendrich Tretner, specialists in surprise attacks and aerial landings. Both are, of course, very closely linked to the revanchists.

— Manfred Woerner, current chairman of the Federal Republic of Germany's Bundestag Commission on Defence.

— Admiral Poser, former head of the NATO Information Service.

— James Schlesinger, former U.S. secretary of defence and current director of the U.S. Federal Energy Agency, considered to be a Pentagon Hawk and a bitter enemy of the process of international détente.

— Marshal Neil Cameron, chief of the general staff of the British army, who, while in Peking recently, stated without any beating around the bush that the British and Chinese both considered the Soviet Union to be the main enemy. This led to a diplomatic flurry and an official protest by the Soviet Government.

— Hideo Miyoshi, former chief of the general staff of the Self-Defence Forces of Japan, who stated on June 9, 1977, that visits to China by Japanese military officials would increase.

— Hisao Isashima, civilian instructor at the Japanese National Defence College, and a group of retired officers from the Self-Defence Naval Forces also paid a visit. At the same time, it became known that the Chinese authorities were in contact with high-ranking officers of the Intelligence Department of the Self-Defence Land Forces of Japan.

According to estimates made by *Far Eastern Economic Review*, a magazine that specializes in Asian affairs, China's military expenses amount to 28,000 million a year, an exorbitant investment for China's economy and one that will subject its people to ever lower standards of living.

This past April 3, the European Common Market granted China most favoured nation status, which only the United States and Japan had enjoyed up until then. This will facilitate increased trade between China and the Western European capitalist countries, for the purposes already mentioned.

In reality, however, the strategic objective goes beyond this. Through these exchanges, credits and ties with Western Europe, the new mandarins hope to find the front door open for helping themselves to the military arsenals of the capitalist countries of Western Europe.

Pravda, organ of the Communist Party of the Soviet Union, warned on February 9 that, according to a Common Market representative, this agreement set no limits on the sales of strategic material to China.

The French right-wing daily *Le Figaro* was even more explicit. It commented that the Chinese, in blackmail fashion, had let it be known that if France didn't give them what they wanted in the military field they wouldn't be in any hurry to place their orders in other branches of French industry.

The bourgeois politicians who dream of using China in their anti-Soviet manoeuvres should not forget that her hegemonic designs represent a danger for all mankind, including, of course, the capitalist states!

Have these war lords forgotten the lesson of recent history, when they protected, armed and encouraged the German imperialists and then the Nazi hordes occupied almost all of Western Europe?

Have they forgotten the lesson of recent history, when the heroic struggle of the Soviet Union, that paid a price of more than 20 million dead, was the decisive factor in freeing humanity of the fascist yoke?

The Chinese traitors have forgotten that, without the triumph of the October Revolution and the Soviet victories over Nazism and the Japanese fascist army of Manchuria, the October 1, 1949, victory of the Red Army in China — a victory that was greeted and supported by all progressive people in the world — would have been impossible!

Some petty, hackneyed theoreticians try to deny that the decay of the colonial system in the world has been possible because of the existence of the Soviet Union and the rest of the socialist community.

However, the Chinese have not limited their flirting to Europe. On February 16, China and Japan signed an important long-term private trade agreement worth more than 20,000 million dollars. Chinese heavy industry, the basis of the military modernization which they advocate, will be reinforced with Japanese technology.

At the same time, the new mandarins are using every possible stratagem to convince the Japanese Government to sign a so-called peace and friendship treaty with China.

According to an editorial in the January 6 edition of the Japanese daily *Sankei Shimbun*, the Chinese Government places special importance on this treaty because it is included in "its strategy against the Soviet Union."

The treaty contains a certain antihegemony clause which the Chinese are turning against the Soviet Union.

Under the label of "hegemonism" — which some scatterbrained politicians call by another name which, in essence, however, is used for the same purposes — the Peking leaders are keeping up an anti-Soviet barrage that the rulers of the United States, those of other capitalist countries and, of course, their puppets all find so pleasing.

This infamous, despicable policy of the Chinese leaders meshes perfectly with the strategic interests of the U.S. imperialists. This is the reason for the special attention given to these aspects by President James Carter's adviser.

For revolutionaries, this is the clearest, most categorical expression of the fact that China has taken the final step in its conscious betrayal of Marxism-Leninism, socialism, communism and proletarian internationalism and that its alliance with the imperialists is growing ever stronger!

In May last year, in an interview granted *Afrique-Asie* magazine, Fidel Castro, president of the Council of State of Cuba, said, **"We have received reliable reports stating that the Chinese secret services are working in close collaboration with the French, U.S., West German and NATO secret services. It must be said that, incredible as it seems, it is absolutely true."**

Coordination in all fields is notorious and evident. The Chinese makes no bones about their absolute coincidence of views with the imperialist countries.

Recently, the *People's Daily*, organ of the so-called Communist Party of China, dedicated an entire article to extolling the European Common Market countries' position on the political situation in Africa and the Middle East.

Referring to a meeting that the nine member countries of the Common Market held last February, the Chinese paper commented:

"The results of the deliberations on the events in Africa and the Middle East reflect **the desire of the Western European countries to increase their ties and their cooperation with the Third World so as to oppose the big power hegemonism of the Soviet Union. Their position favours the common struggle of the Third World and of the Western European Countries against the powers that seek hegemony.**"

How can anyone think that the West German Government, that has set up a missile-testing base in Zaire, favours the struggle of the "Third World?"

Is France, which has supplied South Africa with nuclear plants and weapons of all kinds, an ally of the progressive countries and the liberation movements?

Can the countries representing the system that has historically plundered Africa help in its independent development for the benefit of the African peoples?

In the case of the Middle East, the commentary is even more despicable and cunning. It says:

"The foreign minister of the nine countries of the Common Market stated that they appreciated the initiative of Egyptian President Sadat on the Middle East and asked for a general solution to the problem. **This position adopted by the countries of Western Europe constitutes support for the just struggle of the Arab peoples against Zionism.**"

So, Sadat's capitulationist attitude constitutes "support" for the struggle of the Arab peoples?

This is the height of cynicism, a slap in the face for the Palestinian people and the progressive Arab Government of Algeria, Iraq, Syria, Libya, the Democratic People's Republic of Yemen and other countries that have denounced the Egyptian president's treason!

What is the basis in doctrine for these Chinese positions?

It is the "three words" hypothesis, that was finally reformulated in 1977. According to this arch-reactionary, anti-Marxist folderol that flatly denies class struggle, the world is divided into very peculiar political areas.

The Chinese place what they call "the two superpowers" — the United States and the Soviet Union — in the "first world." Since they maintain that the USSR is the main enemy, all their attacks and all their actions are aimed against the country of the Soviets.

They place the capitalist countries of Western Europe, Japan, Canada, Australia and some other countries in the "second world." Here, too, are the European Socialist Countries, which they consider to be "exploited" by the Soviet Union.

The Chinese leaders place the underdeveloped countries of Asia, Africa and Latin America — themselves included — in the "third world."

According to the Chinese leaders, all the countries of the "third world" should unite with those of the "second" and even collaborate with the U.S. "superpower" so as to create a great alliance to destroy the Soviet Union.

These renegades consider all alliances good in the struggle against the Soviet Union, whether with the capitalist monopolies, the Bonn revanchists or the most warlike circles in the United States.

The Chinese leaders have assumed the enormous historical responsibility of having destroyed the unity of the revolutionary forces and of practicing a policy against socialism, the workers' movement and the national liberation of the peoples.

With this crafty policy, that tries to undermine the unity of the progressive forces, the Chinese leaders rendered an incalculable service to the imperialists, who, at that time, were escalating their criminal war of agression against the heroic people of Vietnam!

With this deceitful, opportunistic, unprincipled doctrine, the Chinese leaders have helped to lengthen the life of imperialism, neocolonialism, colonialism, apartheid and racism and to increase confusion and all kinds of ideological deviations.

It is a basic duty of all who struggle for peace, social progress, national liberation and socialism to expose the actions and phraseology of the Chinese leaders and their strategic alliances with the imperialists and reactionaries.

The Chinese leaders' great betrayal of the revolutionary and national liberation movement of Asia, Africa and Latin America and their alignment with Yankee imperialism

The Chinese frauds, who aspire to the leadership of the so-called Third World, provide aid and collaboration to the bloodiest and most corrupt régimes in Asia, Africa and Latin America, especially waging a hidden and traitorous struggle against the heroic people of Vietnam and the Cuban Revolution.

In their wild and frenetic campaign to insult the Soviet Union and all revolutionaries, the mandarins of Peking carefully choose their friends and allies. This is why they are frequently found in the company of corrupt rulers and in support of abominable tyrannies.

In Latin America, for example, the degree of friendship and understanding that has developed between the Chinese and the bloody Chilean dictatorship of Augusto Pinochet is scandalous.

China's ambassador to Chile, Msu Chung-fu, bade farewell to Pinochet, after receiving high honours, on October 21, 1977.

The Chilean newspaper *La Tercera* reported that, following the meeting, the Chinese ambassador declared that he was leaving with "an excellent impression of Chile and the head of its government."

This was the ambassador in charge of strengthening relations while the fascist hordes performed their macabre ballet of assessinations and disappearances that is still going on.

It is truly disgusting to note the depths of immorality to which the Chinese leaders have sunk, when even bourgeois governments keep a certain distance from the Chilean régime and some have broken relations with that sell-out government!

Very friendly links of cooperation between the Chilean military junta and the Chinese Government were established after the coup against the constitutional government of President Salvador Allende took place on September 11, 1973.

In 1974, China imported 117 million dollars' worth of Chilean products. In 1975, the Chinese purchased 8,000 tons of copper. The following year, their copper imports rose to 34,000 tons, in an effort to prop up the Chilean régime's tottering economy.

In the first half of 1977 alone, Chile sold the Chinese leaders more than 30,000 tons of saltpeter. The Chinese have also given Pinochet several generous loans.

Elsewhere in Latin America, we find the Chinese associated with the most reactionary and antinational elements or desperately trying to pick up the crumbs of the Yankee feast.

In Africa, there are several examples of the ominous Chinese alliances.

In the case of Angola, Chinese advisers and weapons were placed at the service of Holden Roberto, a long-time known agent of the CIA who was denounced as such with irrefutable proof in the U.S. Congress. There, we find aligned under the same banner the South African fascist racists; the corrupt régime of Mobutu Sese Seko, protector of Angolan counter-revolutionaries; the Chinese mandarins; and the U.S. Government and its CIA.

More recently, the Chinese régime invited the head of the so-called Liberation Front of the Enclave of Cabinda (FLEC) — an anti-Angolan counterrevolutionary organization manipulated by the French secret service — to visit its country. Thus, its actions support secessionism in Africa, in opposition to OAU Principles on the inalterability of African borders.

Another case of the Chinese leaders' open complicity with the most abject lackeys is their friendship with Mobutu Sese Seko, head of the régime in Zaire.

Mobutu granted a West German company, Orbital Transport und Raketen Adktien Gesselchaft (OTRAG), 145,522 square kilometers of national territory under a lease signed on March 26, 1976.

The company pays some 50 million dollars a year for the lease and enjoys the benefits of administering an enormous area for missile testing, while Mobutu pockets practically all the money.

According to the U.S. magazine *Penthouse*, this programme allows the West German revanchists to break the international agreements that limit rearmament, particularly the 1954 Treaty of Brussels.

The U.S. magazine added that the work being carried out in Zaire was obviously designed to equip West Germany with the most sophisticated missile systems with conventional and nuclear warheads.

Further details include the fact that this camp is located in the rich province of Shaba, the centre of huge investments by multinational companies. This new colonial enclave is supported by NATO.

It is also well to recall that China lost no time in hailing the intervention of France, Belgium and the United States in Shaba, acting in the name of NATO's "democracy" and "human rights." Hua Kuo-feng, top Chinese leader, has just sent a personal message to the servile Mobutu, congratulating him on this "victory".

Even a number of very well-known capitalist publications, including *La Monde* and *The New York Times*, have described the administration of President Mobutu, the great friend of the Chinese leaders, as "corrupt and inept."

Peking is now taking pleasure in repeating the same repugnant lies and false imputations made by Brzezinski and other Yankee spokesmen that Cuba is partly responsible for the events in Shaba. Such Chinese charges are, of course, in total agreement with the false reports the CIA has given the U.S. Government.

When, in July 1971, Gaafar el Numeiri, head of the Sudanese régime, unleashed fierce repression against the Communists and shot their main leaders, the Chinese saluted the measure jubilantly, because it was taken against a Party that "followed the Moscow line." That friendship continues.

In the case of Ethiopia, all the elements that go to make up Chinese policy are involved. They were always slyly hostile to the great antifeudal and antibourgeois Ethiopian revolutionary process, because it had enemies in Sudan, Egypt, Saudi Arabia and other reactionary governments guided by the Yankees and NATO.

While the Somalian leaders feigned acceptance of socialism and proclaimed friendship for the USSR and Cuba, they remained in the shadows, manoeuvring. Then came the treasonous invasion of Ethiopia, an imperialist plan that played on the Somalian leadership's chauvinism. China immediately expressed its support for all the enemies of Ethiopia. Somalian President Siad Barre was recently in Peking. A new alliance was forged between China and another group that has taken pro-imperialist positions. The mandarins are mortified by the crushing defeat the Somalians were dealt in the battles of Ogaden where Cuban internationalist troops played their proper role, shoulder to shoulder with the self-sacrificing, patriotic Ethiopian fighters.

The case that best illustrates the perfidious nature of the new mandarins is that of the Socialist Republic of Vietnam.

For more than a decade, the Vietnamese people, under the orientation of the Communist Party and glorious President Ho Chi Minh, waged an epic struggle against the U.S. imperialists, a struggle that won universal admiration. The sacrifices the Vietnamese made are recorded in history for all time. Mankind — particularly the revolutionaries — must thank Vietnam for having left it the example of its perseverance and unparalleled heroism and for having inflicted a tremendous defeat on the aggressors. The Vietnamese victory was an invaluable contribution to the national and social liberation of the peoples.

In the course of the war of resistance against the U.S. aggression, it was very difficult for the Chinese to criticize or blame the Vietnamese leaders, though there are indications that Peking placed every kind of obstacle in the way of transporting aid from the socialist countries — particularly from the Soviet Union during the Yankee blockade of North Vietnamese ports.

When the peace agreements on Vietnam were signed on January 27, 1973, it came out that some Chinese leaders urged that the B-52s that had spread death and destruction in Vietnam, Laos and Cambodia be kept in Thailand. They argued that this would be an important measure to prevent the increase of "Soviet influence" in that part of the world.

Some day the details of all these miserable machinations by the Chinese leaders against the Vietnamese people will become known!

Now we can refer to a recent event that proves without a doubt that the new mandarins are allied with the capitalist scum, with criminal elements, and that they are trying to slander the noble, solidary Vietnamese people.

On May 24, the official Chinese news agency *Hsinhua* released a long declaration from the Council of State office on matters concerning overseas Chinese.

This declaration accused the Vietnamese of having mistreated and expelled thousands of citizens of Chinese origin from Vietnam "for no reason."

The declaration noted that some Chinese were "victims of all types of abuses" and that "almost everything they had accumulated during the course of their long years of work was unjustifiably confiscated."

The text ended on a threatening note:

"We demand that the Vietnamese put an immediate halt to the application of this erroneous policy of ostracism, persecution and expulsion of Chinese residents and stop prejudicing the traditional friendship between our two countries and peoples. **If the Government of Vietnam does not do this, it must bear full responsibility for all the consequences of these unjustifiable measures.**"

Incredible! Do the Chinese leaders really think they can now intimidate a people that didn't yield to Yankee bombs and, long before that, had learned how to preserve its national identity over the centuries, in spite of invasions from Chinese territory?

What is the crux of the problem, and who are these "poor" Chinese residents?

Last May 5, Xuan Thuy, member of the Secretariat of the Communist Party of Vietnam, warned that some Chinese citizens had begun to leave the country illegally and asked the Chinese authorities to tell residents of Chinese origin to halt these activities.

Xuan Thuy stated in an interview with the Vietnamese news agency that those citizens who wished to leave the country should present their request to do so, which would be considered by the appropriate authorities.

What caused this situation? According to what the Vietnamese authorities could establish, certain Chinese had launched a rumour that war was going to break out between China and Vietnam and that it was advisable to leave the country as soon as possible.

Who spread the propaganda that a new war is inevitable? Who claims territory that belongs to neighbouring countries and even has maps drawn up that include Vietnam, Laos, Burma and other countries as parts of China?

While the Vietnamese liberation war was at its height, they forcibly occupied the islands Hoang Sa (Paracells) and Truong Sa (Spratly), islands that have, historically, belonged to Vietnam, taking advantage of the presence of the puppet régime in the south and foreseeing its imminent fall. The new mandarins are responsible for these deeds; they and they alone are instigating this campaign of calumnies and lies against socialist Vietnam.

Anyone who has visited northern Vietnam knows perfectly well that a large group of residents of Chinese origin have lived there for many years, that they hold all kinds of jobs and that their rights and duties are the same as those of the Vietnamese. At no time have the Vietnamese leaders sought to fan xenophobia among their people. The south also has groups of residents of Chinese origin.

The "poor" Chinese businessmen and landowners in southern Vietnam are, for the most part, people who were linked to the puppet Saigon régime and who benefitted from and collaborated with the U.S. intervention.

It is the height of shamelessness for the Chinese leaders to assume the defence of capitalists whose property has been nationalized by a sovereign state that is building socialism!

This action by Peking is a clear warning to other governments in the area, since many countries have large colonies of Chinese. Apparently Peking reserves the right to interfere in the internal affairs of other states on the pretext of "defending the interests of its nationals," just as the Governments of the United States and France do.

Another of the apparently inexplicable actions of the new mandarins is that related to the so-called border conflict between Vietnam and Kampuchea.

Various responsible publications have charged the Kampuchean authorities with acting at the instigation of China. It is evident that, without China's backing, without the aid they receive in weapons and advisers, it would be very difficult for the rulers of Kampuchea to keep up their continuous attacks on Vietnamese territory, where they have committed atrocities against the civilian population.

This is a new manoeuvre by the Chinese leaders, one explained by their expansionist policy in Asia, aimed at harassing and trying to diminish the prestige of the Vietnamese people, who accomplished one of the most admirable heroic deeds of our time and whose leaders are respected all over the world, even by the imperialist adversaries. Its objectives are to hold back Vietnam's development and force its submission and to gobble up Laos. The Chinese have a base of operations in Kampuchea and are concentrating forces along Vietnam's northern border so as to threaten that fraternal country and, eventually, intensify the armed clashes and acts of provocation of all kinds.

One of the most repugnant crimes the Chinese leadership has committed is that of whipping up the war of Kampuchea against Vietnam, one of the most heroic and long-suffering peoples of our times.

As for Cuba, Chinese propaganda rivals the imperialist press in its offences, calumny and lies.

Fine. Our people are used to measuring our abilities, successes and victories by the attacks dealt us by our enemies.

What the Chinese leaders really can't stand is that our consistent, daily practice of proletarian internationalism has become a serious obstacle to their aims of penetration in Latin America, Africa and other parts of the "Third World."

The new Chinese mandarins seek to portray our noble, courageous internationalist soldiers as mercenaries. This epithet can only arouse indignation, and not only among our people, but among other fraternal peoples, as well. In short, this serves to unmask even more, as if such were necessary, the Chinese leaders, whose betrayal has disfigured them and who cannot understand the generous sentiments of Communists and other revolutionary workers.

Moreover, as part of the services they have rendered the United States, they have even described our country as a "Soviet base" of aggression in the Caribbean. Let the peoples be the judge of this!

In May 1977, Comrade Fidel Castro told *Afrique-Asie* that, "As for Cuba, the Chinese policy is truly infamous. It uses repugnant, lying calumny to combat the solidarity our Party has given the liberation movements — calumny that meshes perfectly with the attacks U.S. imperialism has made against our homeland. China opposes the lifting of the economic blockade which the United States imposed on Cuba and the return of the territory occupied by the North Americans at the Guantánamo base."

Most recently, the Chinese have gone about openly egging the U.S. Government on to prepare a new aggression against Cuba. The *Hsinhua* news agency echoes every commentary that states that the U.S. Government should take up "the challenge of the Soviet-Cuban intervention in Africa," perversely instigating the imperialists to take measures against Cuba and promising them its plaudits.

It would seem natural for a country that calls itself socialist to support the Cuban people, but such is not the case. Cuba has set the world an example: it has not yielded. Cuba is suffering from a tight blockade, imposed by the most powerful imperialist country. Cuba neither surrenders nor sells out. Cuba is an independent, revolutionary country that is building socialism and that, for nearly 20 years, has been overcoming all attempts to subvert its revolution.

What are the Chinese doing? In effect, they are supporting the blockade, trying to destroy the Cuban Revolution. Of what are they enemies? Of socialism, of the Revolution, of a process that is loved and respected in the "Third World?" The Chinese and the Yankee imperialists hold precisely the same points of view concerning our country.

The "paper tiger" and its Chinese allies will not get their way!

It is worth stopping for a moment to analyze why these events have come about in China.

First of all, we should point out the deep antidemocratic content characteristic of Chinese institutions. The working masses, the workers, the peasants and the intellectuals have no part at all in the exercise of socialist democracy. There is no legality, and the people are subjected to the whims and caprices of those at the top levels of leadership.

The cultural revolution, begun in 1966, did away with the trade unions, youth organizations, women's federation and many other organizations.

The Communist Party of China, following its adulteration and the persecution and liquidation of many of its middle-level cadres and no small number of the members of its Central Committee, holds its congresses clandestinely. One fine day, the Chinese people learns that there is a new

Political Bureau and a new Central Committee and that figures who had been purged have been reinstated in their posts, or vice versa. These interminable palace struggles for power are well known. The last one, involving the "gang of four," was effected by imprisoning the omnipotent widow of Mao Tse-tung, almost before the "great helmsman" was buried.

Shortly before the cultural revolution, on March 13, 1966, Comrade Fidel Castro made a statement referring to China that has been fully borne out by subsequent events:

"To accept, in socialism, the method and system of absolute monarchies is the height of absurdity, because that would begin the struggle of those who aspire to be absolute monarchs."

Just a few months later, President Mao Tse-tung unleashed the "great proletarian cultural revolution," evidently aimed at purging the ranks of Party leaders. Even before succeeding to the throne, appetites for power were displayed:

As an example of the Chinese purges, we will mention the case of Teng Siao-ping, currently first deputy prime minister and chief of the general staff of the army. This is the third time he has appeared on the scene. First, he was dismissed during the cultural revolution. His second exit followed the death of Chou En-lai, in 1976. When will the next one be?

The incessant turns taken by the top Chinese hierarchs forced *Red Flag* magazine, theoretical organ of the Party, to recognize that the theory that it was impossible to understand President Mao's line clearly had been spread widely among the leaders of the revolutionary committees. (November 5, 1972). As in the Middle Ages, the "doctors" interpret selected phrases according to their own opportunistic purposes.

The present situation in China is characterized by the deification of President Mao, the constant repetition of the statement that his works contain the answer for everything and that they are the only valid interpretation of Marxism-Leninism, plus systematic, wanton propaganda cut on patterns very similar to those of fascism.

These elements explain the provocative, chauvinistic, traitorous and expansionist course aimed at obtaining true hegemony that is now being followed by the Chinese leadership.

Luckily, there are signs that, behind the apparent conformist calm that reigns in Peking and other Chinese cities, there is revolutionary restlessness.

Serious disturbances took place in Tien-an Men Square, in the centre of Peking, on April 5, 1976.

Some days later, the paper *Renmin Ribao*, organ of the Communist Party of China, accused the demonstrators of being counter-revolutionaries and, as proof of its charges, published excerpts from a wall poster that said:

"China today
is not like what it used to be,

nor are the people so bamboozled.
There is no possible return to the
feudal period
of Tsin Cheu-huang.
We need true Marxism-Leninism.
For it, we would shed blood
and risk our lives. . .''

Chauvinism is now the essential idea of the Chinese ruling clique. The most beautiful principles of proletarian internationalism have been shamelessly betrayed by an opportunistic group that has seized control of the leadership of a country whose people, not so long ago, stirred admiration and hope in the world progressive and revolutionary movement.

The Chinese are, without a doubt, a great people, and, one way or another, sooner or later, they will sweep away the scum and overcome this profouhd ideological and political crisis.

Chauvinism, a residue of narrow, reactionary, vacillating petite bourgeois nationalism, so similar to fascism in its methods and procedures, is condemned, just like bourgeois society, neo colonialism, racism and imperialism, to the garbage heap of history.

Joint Communiqué on the Establishment of Diplomatic Relations between the People's Republic of China and the United States of America.

(Complete Text). 15 December, 1978.

The People's Republic of China and the United States of America have agreed to recognize each other and to establish diplomatic relations as of 1st January 1979.

The United States of America recognizes the Government of the People's Republic of China as the sole legal government of China. Within this context, the people of the United States of America will maintain cultural, commercial, and other unofficial relations with the people of Taiwan.

The People's Republic of China and the United States of America reaffirm the principles agreed on by the two sides in the Shanghai communiqué and emphasize once again that:

— Both wish to reduce the danger of international military conflict.

— Neither should seek hegemony in the Asia-Pacific region or in any other region of the world and each is opposed to efforts by any other country or group of countries to establish such hegemony.

— Neither is prepared to negotiate on behalf of any third party or to enter into agreements or understandings with the other directed at other states.

— The Government of the United States of America acknowledges the Chinese position that there is but one China and Taiwan is part of China.

— Both believe that normalization of Sino-American relations is not only in the interest of the Chinese and American peoples but also contributes to the cause of peace in Asia and the world.

The People's Republic of China and the United States of America will exchange ambassadors and establish embassies on 1st March 1979.

President Jimmy Carter. Nationwide Address. 15 December 1978.

(Complete Text.).

"— Both believe that normalization of Sino-American relations is not only in the interest of the Chinese and American peoples but also contributes to the cause of peace in Asia and in the world.

"The United States of America and the People's Republic of China will exchange ambassadors and establish embassies on March 1, 1979."

Yesterday, our country and the People's Republic of China reached this final historical agreement.

On January 1, 1979, a little more than two weeks from now, our two governments will implement full normalization of diplomatic relations.

As a nation of gifted people who compromise one-fourth of the total population of the earth, China plays an important role in world affairs — a role that can only grow more important in the years ahead.

We do not undertake this important step for transient tactical or expedient reasons. In recognizing that the government of the People's Republic is the single government of China, we are recognizing simple reality. But far more is involved in this decision than just a recognition of fact.

Before the estrangement of recent decades, the American and Chinese people had a long history of friendship. We have already begun to rebuild some of those previous ties. Now our rapidly expanding relationship requires the kind of structures that diplomatic relations will make possible.

The change that I am announcing tonight will be of great long-term benefit to the peoples of both the United States and China — and, I believe, to all the peoples of the world.

Normalization — and the expanded commercial and cultural relations it will bring — will contribute to the well-being of our own nation, to our own national interest, and will enhance stability in Asia.

These more positive relations with China can beneficially affect the world in which we live and our children will live.

We have already begun to inform our allies and the Congress of the details of our intended action. I have already communicated with the leaders of Taiwan. But I wish also to convey a special message to the people of Taiwan, with whom the American people have had and will have extensive, close and friendly relations.

As the United States asserted in the Shanghai communiqué of 1972, we will continue to have an interest in the peaceful resolution of the Taiwan issue.

I have paid special attention to ensuring that normalization of relations between the United States and the People's Republic will not jeopardize the well-being of the people of Taiwan.

The people of the United States will maintain our current commercial, cultural, trade and other relations with Taiwan through non-governmental means. Many other countries are already successfully doing this.

These decisions and actions open a new and important chapter in our country's history and also in world affairs.

To strengthen and to expedite the benefits of this new relationship between the People's Republic of China and the United States, I am pleased to announce that Vice Premier Teng has accepted my invitation to visit Washington at the end of January. His visit will give our governments the opportunity to consult with each other on global issues and to begin working together to enhance the cause of world peace.

These events are the final result of long and serious negotiations begun by President Nixon in 1972, and continued under leadership of President Ford. The results bear witness to the steady, determined bipartisan effort of our own country to build a world in which peace will be the goal and the responsibility of all nations.

The normalization of relations between the United States and China has no other purpose than this — the advancement of peace.

It is in this spirit, at this season of peace, that I take special pride in sharing this good news with you tonight.

Statement of the Government of the People's Republic of China.

(Complete Text).

As of 1st January 1979, the People's Republic of China and the United States of America recognize each other and establish diplomatic relations, thereby ending the prolonged abnormal relationship between them. This is a historic event in Sino-US relations.

As is known to all, the Government of the People's Republic of China is the sole legal government of China and Taiwan is a part of China. The question is Taiwan was the crucial issue obstructing the normalization of relations between China and the United States of America. It has now been resolved between the two countries in the spirit of the Shanghai comm-uniqué and through their joint efforts, thus enabling the normalization of relations so ardently desired by the people of the two countries. As for the way of bringing Taiwan back to the embrace of the motherland and reuni-fying the country, it is entirely China's internal affair.

At the invitation of the United States Government, Teng Hsiao-ping, Vice-Premier of the State Council of the People's Republic of China, will pay an official visit to the United States of America in January 1979, with a view to further promoting the friendship between the two peoples and good relations between the two countries.

Hua Kuo feng. Press Conference.

(Excerpts).

Q. Chairman Hua, will you please speak about the significance of the normalization of Sino-United States relations?

A. The normalization of Sino-United States relations has long been a wish of the Chinese and American peoples. Our great leader the late Chair-man Mao Tsetung and our esteemed Premier Chou En-lai paved the way for opening Sino-United States relations. During the visit of President Nixon and Dr Kissinger to China in 1972, the Chinese and United States sides issued the Shanghai communiqué, which started the process of normalizing Sino-United States relations. Thanks to the joint efforts of the leaders, governments and peoples of the two countries in the past few years, the Sino-United States relations have now been normalized. Former United States President Ford, many of the senators and congressmen and other friends from all walks of life have all played their part toward this end. Now, President Carter, Dr Brzezinski and Secretary of State Vance have all made valuable contributions to the eventual normalization of our relations.

The establishment of diplomatic relations between China and the United States of America is a historic event. It opens up broad vistas for enhancing understanding and friendship between the two peoples and promoting bilateral exchanges in all fields. It will also contribute to peace and stability in Asia and the world as a whole. The Chinese and American peoples are happy about it and I believe the people all over the world will be happy at the news too.

Q. Chairman Hua, my question is: What policy will the Chinese Government adopt toward Taiwan in the new circumstances when relations between China and the United States of America have been normalized?

A. Taiwan is part of China's sacred territory and the people in Taiwan are our kith and kin. It is the common aspiration of all the Chinese people

including our compatriots in Taiwan to accomplish the great cause of reuni-
fying the country with Taiwan returning to the embrace of the motherland.
It has been our consistent policy that all patriots belong to one big family
whether they come forward early or late. We hope that our compatriots in
Taiwan will join all the other Chinese people including our compatriots in
Hongkong and Macao and overseas Chinese in making further
contributions to the cause of reunifying China.

*Q. Can you say that after normalization China would object to a visit to
Taiwan by an American official?*

A. The relations between China and the United States of America have
been normalized after the joint efforts of both sides which have reached an
agreement and have now issued the joint communiqué. And the answer to
your question is clearly stated in the joint communiqué which I quote: "The
United States of America recognizes the Government of the People's
Republic of China as the sole legal government of China. Within this
context, the people of the United States of America will maintain cultural,
commercial, and other unofficial relations with the people of Taiwan." So
the answer is very clear in this paragraph. There will only be unofficial
relations.

*Q. Will the United States of America be permitted to continue providing
Taiwan with access to military equipment for defensive purposes?*

A. Paragraph two of the joint communiqué which I announced just now
says:"The United States of America recognizes the Government of the
People's Republic of China as the sole legal government of China. Within
this context, the people of the United States of America will maintain
cultural, commercial and other unofficial relations with the people of
Taiwan." In our discussions on the question of the commercial relations,
the two sides had differing views. During the negotiations the United States
side mentioned that after normalization it would continue to sell limited
amount of arms to Taiwan for defensive purposes. We made it clear that we
absolutely would not agree to this. In all discussions the Chinese side
repeatedly made clear its position on this question. We held that after the
normalization continued sales of arms to Taiwan by the United States of
America would not conform to the principles of the normalization, would
be detrimental to the peaceful liberation of Taiwan and would exercise an
unfavourable influence on the peace and stability in the Asia and Pacific
region. So our two sides had differences on this point. Nevertheless, we
reached an agreement on the joint communiqué.

*Q. Mr Chairman, may I ask you please about the possibility of a wor-
sening of relations with Russia as a result of what you have announced
today, since the Russians may be very suspicious of your joining more
closely with the Americans. Do you feel that it may lead to a worsening of
relations with Moscow?*

A. We think that the normalization of relations between China and the United States of America and the signing of the treaty of peace and friendship between China and Japan are conducive to peace and stability in the Asia-Pacific region and the world as a whole. Does this mean the formation of an axis or alliance of China, Japan and the United States of America? We say that it is neither an alliance nor an axis. China and the United States of America have now normalized their relations and the relations between the United States of America and the Soviet Union have also been normalized. Therefore it is out of the question that the normalization of relations is directed at any country.

Here I would like to make an additional explanation, China has now normalized relations with the United States of America and Japan and signed a treaty of peace and friendship with Japan. This is beneficial to the development of relations between countries in the Asia-Pacific region and to the peace and stability of the Asia-Pacific region and the world as a whole. Undoubtedly, of course, it is also favourable to the struggle of all peoples against hegemonism. We have mentioned our opposition to hegemonism in our joint communiqué. We oppose both big hegemony and small hegemony, both global hegemony and regional hegemony. This will be conducive to the peace of the whole world.

Q. I would like to ask you if there were any Chinese compatriots from Taiwan involved at any stage in the discussions towards normalization.

A. No.

Historic Event. 'People's Daily' Editorial.
(Complete Text.). 16 December, 1978.

The Government of the People's Republic of China and the Government of the United States of America have announced that they will recognize and enter into diplomatic relations with each other as of 1st January 1979 and will exchange Ambassadors on 1st March. This brings to an end the prolonged abnormal state of affairs and opens a new chapter in Sino-American relations.

The establishment of Sino-American diplomatic relations is a historic event. The Chinese and the American people are both great people and have always been on friendly terms. Since the publication of the Shanghai communiqué the two countries have enhanced their understanding of each other and the friendship between the people of the two countries has been strengthened. The establishment of Sino-American diplomatic relations is the outcome of the joint efforts of the Governments and people of the two countries. The normalization of Sino-American relations is of vital significance to the maintenance of peace and stability in the Asia-Pacific region and the world at large. Consequently, the establishment of diplomatic relations between China and the United States not only conforms to the common aspirations and interests of the people of the two countries but will be welcomed by other peoples of the world and all peaceloving countries.

The joint communiqué on the establishment of Sino-American diplomatic relations reaffirms the principles to which the two sides had agreed in the Shanghai communiqué. It once again stresses that neither should seek hegemony in the Asia-Pacific region or any other region of the world, and that each is opposed to efforts by any other country or group of countries to establish such hegemony.

Hegemonism is the source of the troubles menacing world peace and the security of all nations and the cause of upheavals in the international situation. Anti-hegemonism has become the tide of history in the present era. The reaffirmation of the principle of anti-hegemony by China and the United States helps the opposition to major hegemonism as well as minor hegemonism, to global hegemonism as well as regional hegemonism. It will produce a salutary influence on the development of the world situation.

Taiwan is a part of China. Our compatriots in Taiwan are our kith and kin. The return of Taiwan to the motherland and the complete unification of the country is the common sacred cause of all Chinese people including our Taiwan compatriots; it is a behest which Chairman Mao and Premier Chou entrusted to us to accomplish without fail. We are thinking of our Taiwan compatriots all the time and the motherland is always in the minds of the Taiwan compatriots. After the establishment of diplomatic relations between China and the United States, the Taiwan compatriots will surely make greater efforts for the unification of the motherland. Patriots belong to one family, whether they come early or late. There are many patriots among the military and administrative personnel in Taiwan who will certainly make their own contributions to Taiwan's return to the motherland. It is our hope that the Taiwan authorities will make a sober assessment of the situation, adapt themselves to the demands of the times and refrain from going against the common aspirations of the entire Chinese people. We are firmly convinced that the day will definitely come when Taiwan will return to the embrace of the motherland and our fellow-countrymen there will reunite with their kith and kin on the mainland.

At present the Chinese people are continuing their great new long march towards the four modernizations. We need a peaceful international environment. Now the international situation is more favourable to us, the Chinese people will further strengthen their unity with the people of various countries and carry on an unremitting struggle in defence of world peace and security.

Over the past few years China and the United States have made increasing contacts and exchanges in the fields of science, technology, culture, sports and journalism. The establishment of diplomatic relations between the two countries opens broad vistas for the enhancement of good relations between the two countries and friendly exchanges between the two peoples. We are confident that with the joint efforts of the two Governments and peoples, the traditional friendship between the two peoples will surely develop further under the new historical conditions.

International Meetings

Communiqué on Meeting of Secretaries of Central Committees of Communist and Workers' Parties of Socialist Countries.

(Complete Text).

Regular meeting of Secretaries of Central Committees of Communist and Workers' Parties of socialist countries on international and ideological questions was held in Budapest between 27th February and 1st March.

Participating in the conference were, on behalf of the Bulgarian Communist Party, Alexander Lilov, member of the Political Bureau and Secretary of the CC, and Dimiter Stanishev, Secretary of the CC of the BCP; on behalf of the Communist Party of Czechoslovakia, Vasil Bilak, member of the Presidium and Secretary of the CC of the CPCz, Jan Fojtik, Secretary of the CC of the CPCz, and Josef Havlin, Secretary of the CC of the CPCz; on behalf of the Communist Party of Cuba, Raul Garcia Pelaez, member of the Secretariat of the CC of the CPC; on behalf of the Socialist Unity Party of Germany, Kurt Hager, member of the Political Bureau and Secretary of the CC of the SED, Herman Axen, member of the Political Bureau and Secretary of the CC of the SED, and Werner Lamberz, member of the Political Bureau and Secretary of the CC of the SED; on behalf of the Hungarian Socialist Workers' Party, Miklos Ovari, member of the Political Bureau and Secretary of the CC of the HSWP, Andras Gyenes, Secretary of the CC of the HSWP, and Imre Gyori, Secretary of the CC of the HSWP; on behalf of the Mongolian People's Revolutionary Party, Sandagiyn Sosorbaram, Secretary of the CC of the MPRP; on behalf of the Polish United Worker's Party, Jerzy Lukaszewicz, alternate member of the Political Bureau and Secretary of the CC of the PUWP, and Ryszard Frelek, Secretary of the CC of the PUWP; on behalf of the Romanian Communist Party, Dumitru Popescu, member of the Executive Political Committee of the CC of the RCP, and Secretary of the CC of the RCP, and Stefan Andrei, alternate member of the Executive Political Committee and Secretary of the CC of the CPR; on behalf of the Communist Party of the Soviet Union, Boris Ponomaryov, alternate member of the Political Bureau and Secretary of the CC of the CPSU, Mikhail Zimyanin, Secretary of the CC of the CPSU and Konstantin Rusakov, Secretary of the CC of the CPSU.

Also attending the conference as an observer was a representative of the Communist Party of Vietnam, member of the Central Committee of the CPV and head of its Department of Agitation and Propaganda Nguyen Vinh.

The heads and deputy heads of the relevant departments of the fraternal parties' Central Committees also participated in the conference.

The participants informed each other of the ideological and political work of their parties. Views were exchanged on co-operation in this sphere and on current international issues. Speakers noted with satisfaction the fruitful character of the bilateral and multilateral co-operation of fraternal countries in the field of information and propaganda, social sciences, education and culture, and expressed the resolve to develop it further. Such co-operation, which takes into account the specific conditions in which each Party is working, is helpful in dealing with problems of common interest, popularising the socialist countries' achievements, and making their domestic and foreign policy better understood.

The meeting examined the results of the events marking the 60th anniversary of the Great October Socialist Revolution. This date, which was widely observed throughout the world, and the celebration of other important anniversaries and events in the life of the fraternal parties and peoples, clearly demonstrated the importance of socialism's main achievements in all spheres of life, promoted the broader dissemination of Marxist-Leninist ideas and the great ideals of peace, freedom, national independence and socialism. Stress was laid on the need to continue marking outstanding dates of the working-class, revolutionary movement of the peoples of the socialist countries, including the 30th anniversary of the Council for Mutual Economic Assistance in 1979. The representatives of the Socialist Unity Party of Germany and the Communist Party of Cuba informed the participants of plans for next year's marking of the 30th anniversary of the German Democratic Republic and the 20th anniversary of the triumph of the Cuban revolution.

Attention was focused on the role of the mass media in present-day international policy. The view was expressed that the mass information and propaganda media should make a positive contribution to furthering detente, to curbing the arms race, to the struggle for disarmament, for strengthening trust among the peoples and promoting diverse mutually advantageous co-operation among states, irrespective of their social systems.

Special attention was drawn to the danger stemming from the continuation and intensification of the arms race, the creation of new kinds of mass destruction weapons, including the neutron bomb, which is a formidable obstacle in the path of the further normalisation of international relations. The parties taking part in the conference came out for the adoption of resolute disarmament measures, above all for nuclear disarmament. Overcoming the resistance to such measures by reactionary circles in the NATO countries and by other conservative forces is an urgent task of vital importance for all the peoples.

On behalf of their parties the participants pledged solidarity with the just struggle of the Communists, progressive, revolutionary and national-liberation forces, of all the peoples against the imperialist policy of diktat and aggression, against attempts to obstruct the free expression of their will, for national independence, sovereignty, inviolability of their borders, respect for the right of every people to decide their future themselves without outside interference, and for social progress and equitable international co-operation.

They denounced anti-Communist campaigns, attempts by imperialist and reactionary circles to distort the policy of the socialist countries and to interfere in their international affairs. They stressed their desire to promote the dissemination of objective information about the activity of all Communist and Workers' parties, on the peoples of the socialist countries and about their achievements in building a new society, in developing mutual co-operation.

Speakers stressed the significance of giving publicity to the socialist countries' constructive efforts directed at strengthening international security, and ensuring consistent and full implementation by all states participating in the European Conference of the provisions of the Final Act adopted in Helsinki. The conviction was expressed that joint efforts by all concerned, taking into account the positive experience accumulated in the sphere of co-operation between states, both big and small, irrespective of their social systems, are an important prerequisite for deepening detente and consolidating peace and security.

The participants reaffirmed the resolve of their parties to facilitate full and consistent implementation of the conclusions of the 1976 Berlin Conference of European Communist and Workers' Parties. The Communist Party of Cuba also reaffirmed that it will continue to do everything for the realisation of the conclusions of the Havana Conference of Communist Parties of Latin America and the Caribbean.

The meeting proceeded in a businesslike, friendly atmosphere, in a spirit of equality, mutual respect and internationalist solidarity.

Communiqué on the Meeting of the Committee of Ministers of Foreign Affairs of the States Parties to the Warsaw Treaty

(Complete Text).

A meeting of the Committee of the Ministers of Foreign Affairs of the states parties to the Warsaw Treaty of Friendship, Cooperation and Mutual Assistance was held in Sofia on 24 and 25 April 1978. The meeting was attended by Petyr Mladenov, Minister of Foreign Affairs of the People's

Republic of Bulgaria, Frigyes Puja, Minister of Foreign Affairs of the Hungarian People's Republic, Oskar Fischer, Minister of Foreign Affairs of the German Democratic Republic, Emil Wojtaszek, Minister of Foreign Affairs of the Polish People's Republic, Stefan Andrei, Minister of Foreign Affairs of the Socialist Republic of Romania, Andrei Gromyko, Minister of Foreign Affairs of the Union of Soviet Socialist Republics, Bohuslav Chnoupek, Minister of Foreign Affairs of the Czechoslovak Socialist Republic.

The Ministers stated that the development of the situation in Europe and the entire course of international events confirm the correctness of the assessment given in the Declaration of the states parties to the Warsaw Treaty "For New Achievements in International Détente and for the Strengthening of Security and the Development of Cooperation in Europe" which was adopted at the meeting of the Political Consultative Committee in Bucharest in November 1976.

The unshakable determination of the states represented at the meeting was reaffirmed to persist in efforts to deepen and widen international détente and to turn it into an irreversible, all-embracing process.

The Ministers of Foreign Affairs of the PRB, the HPR, the GDR, the PPR, the SRR, the USSR and the CSSR conducted an exchange of views on matters of disarmament and preparations for the special session of the UN General Assembly devoted to disarmament. It was emphasized that at present there is no more important and urgent task than to curb the arms race, to proceed to realistic and genuine disarmament moves, in particular in the field of nuclear disarmament, and to make progress on the road to general and complete disarmament.

In view of this, the special session of the UN General Assembly must become an important forum for comprehensively deliberating on matters relating to the cessation of the arms race and disarmament. It must lead to decisive progress in agreeing on respective practical measures. The special session is called upon to mobilize in significant measure the efforts of all states for implementing the objectives of disarmament and to give expression to the peoples' aspirations for greater effectiveness of the disarmament negotiations.

The Ministers manifested their states' firm resolve to contribute constructively to the work of the special session of the UN General Assembly and to strive for concrete positive results. They also declared that their states advocate the calling of a world disarmament conference with all states of the world participating.

At the meeting of the Committee of the Ministers of Foreign Affairs an exchange of views was held on matters relating to the consolidation of security and the development of cooperation in Europe. The participants of the meeting emphasized that the efforts and practical steps made by their countries with a view to implementing the provisions of the Final Act of the all-European conference, constitute an important constructive contribution towards consolidating peace and security and towards developing cooperation in Europe. Likewise, reference was made to the positive contribution made by the other peace-loving states, the communist and workers' parties, all democratic and progressive forces, the working class and the broad masses towards strengthening European security and developing cooperation. The states represented at the meeting are actuated by the necessity that all signatories to the Final Act step up their efforts for a still more effective application of the principles and arrangements adopted by the all-European conference at the highest political level.

At the same time, it was stressed at the meeting that it is at present particularly important to intensify the struggle against the imperialist policy of interference in the internal affairs of states, against the further acceleration of the arms race and the aggravation of military confrontation on the European continent.

In complete compliance with the provisions of the Final Act that the political and military aspects of security should be mutually complementary, the Ministers of Foreign Affairs, on behalf of their countries, spoke out in favour of taking as quickly as possible concrete and effective action to diminish military confrontation, promote disarmament and build up confidence in Europe.

It was stated that the well-known proposals set forth in the Declaration of the Political Consultative Committee of November 1976, serve to attain these objectives and that the states represented at the meeting submitted additional proposals to this effect. The participants of the meeting, on behalf of their states, spoke out in favour of practical deliberations on these proposals as well as those of other states in this area. The mode of reviewing them could be determined by common consent of the states which participated in the all-European conference.

The Ministers of Foreign Affairs reaffirmed their countries' endeavour to actively advance the implementation of the proposals to establish a durable and stable basis for developing mutually advantageous cooperation in the economic, scientific-technological, cultural and humanitarian fields as well as other areas within the all-European scope, in conformity with the provisions of the Final Act.

With reference to matters relating to the follow-up to the multilateral process unitiated at Helsinki, the participants in the meeting conducted an exchange of views on the outcome of the Belgrade meeting of the representatives of the states which took part in the Conference on Security and Cooperation in Europe. It was noted that the reaffirmation of the readiness of all participating countries to follow up this process, is an essential positive result of the Belgrade meeting, though it proved impossible at the meeting to reach agreement on a number of significant, constructive proposals of a practical nature, including such on military aspects of security.

The meeting of the Committee of the Ministers of Foreign Affairs of the states parties to the Warsaw Treaty proceeded in an atmosphere of mutual understanding, cooperation and fraternal friendship.

Statement of the Political Bureau of the CPSU.

(Complete Text).

The Political Bureau of the Communist Party of the Soviet Union Central Committee has examined the results of the friendly meetings held in the Crimea in July and August 1978 between Leonid Brezhnev, General Secretary of the Communist Party of the Soviet Union Central Committee and President of the Presidium of the USSR Supreme Soviet; and Gustav Husak, General Secretary of the Central Committee of the Communist Party of Czechoslovakia and President of the Czechoslovak Socialist Republic; Erich Honecker, General Secretary of the Central Committee of the Socialist Unity Party and Chairman of the State Council of the German Democratic Republic; Janos Kadar, First Secretary of the Central Committee of the Hungarian Workers Party; Edward Gierek, First Secretary of the Central Committee of the Polish United Workers Party; Nicolae Ceausescu, Secretary General of the Communist Party of Romania and President of the Romanian Socialist Republic; Todor Zhivkov, First Secretary of the Central Committee of the Bulgarian Communist Party and President of the State Council of the People's Republic of Bulgaria; and Yumjaagiin Tsedenbal, First Secretary of the Central Committee of the Mongolian People's Revolutionary Party and Chairman of the Presidium of the Great People's Hural of the People's Republic of Mongolia.

The Political Bureau of the CPSU Central Committee fully approves of the work done by Leonid Brezhnev and considers the talks that have been held to be of great significance for a further development of fraternal friendship and comprehensive co-operation of the CPSU and the Soviet State with the communist parties and peoples of the countries of the socialist community.

The Crimea meetings convincingly show that the implementation of the creative plans outlined by the congresses of the Communist and Workers' Parties of the fraternal countries is accompanied by a broadening of the ties of the socialist States in all the most important fields of public life — politics, economics and ideology. The understanding reached in the Crimea gave a fresh impetus to co-ordination of actions for both the closest and more distant prospect. They will in particular contribute to outlining and implementing the future Five-Year Plans of the countries of the socialist community under the banner of further and increasingly profound co-operation and specialization of production, in the interests of most effective development of the economy of each of the countries concerned and of a further strengthening of the world socialist system as a whole.

The Political Bureau of the CPSU Central Committee attaches high value to the fact that in the course of the Crimean meetings, a profound analysis was made of the present-day international situation, and that, in the light of this analysis, a conclusion was drawn on the need for further active efforts by the socialist States, and their co-operation, in the interests of strengthening and deepening détente as the leading trend in international life.

Recent developments — and in particular the decision of the NATO session in Washington on a further large-scale arms buildup and the subsequent approval by the US Congress of its biggest military budget of all time — have most clearly shown the real aims of those who started a noisy campaign in the West over the non-existent "military threat" from the socialist countries. Their aim is to put up a sort of propaganda smokescreen to cover up imperialist policy, which runs counter to the aspirations of the peoples demanding a lasting peace and an end to the arms race. But this camouflage will not deceive anybody.

Relations between States with different social systems are also adversely affected by the systematic attempts by the USA and some other NATO member countries to interfere in the internal affairs of the socialist States under cover of hypocritical campaigns about alleged "violations of human rights" in the socialist countries. Such attempts are a crude violation of the generally accepted standards of international law and a violation of the letter and spirit of the Final Act adopted in Helsinki.

The Political Bureau of the CPSU Central Committee stresses the serious threat which the actions of the present leaders of China constitute to the cause of peace and socialism. By pursuing its great-power, hegemonistic course, Peking is openly gambling on building up international tensions and is using all means in order to undermine the positions of the socialist community and of the revolutionary liberation forces of today.

Striving to get access to NATO's military arsenals, the Chinese rulers are advertising in every way their animosity to the Soviet Union and the other socialist countries and are advocating an unbridled arms race. This policy is all the more dangerous since it meets with support from the most reactionary forces of the imperialist States.

The Chinese leadership does not even stop short today from direct expansionist actions. Evidence of this is China's crude chauvinistic pressure on the Socialist Republic of Vietnam, its provocative role in Kampuchea's military provocations against the Socialist Republic of Vietnam and the Peking's claims on the territories of neighbouring states.

The Political Bureau of the CPSU Central Committee reaffirms the indestructible solidarity of our Party, the Soviet State and all Soviet people with the heroic Vietnamese people, who are firmly upholding the inviolability of its territory, independence and the right to carry out socialist construction in its country without hindrance, threats or pressure from the outside.

The Political Bureau of the CPSU Central Committee declares that in the present complicated international situation, the Soviet Union, guided by the decisions of the 25th CPSU Congress, intends to work persistently together with its friends and allies to deepen the process of détente, to broaden peaceful mutually beneficial co-operation among States and above all to end the arms race and to turn to disarmament.

Major issues connected with ending the arms race are already the subject of talks. It is important that the work done at these talks should not be reduced to nought, but should be crowned with substantial results. This concerns in particular, the Soviet-US SALT talks and the Vienna MBFR talks for Central Europe.

The Political Bureau of the CPSU Central Committee considers that under the present conditions it is urgently necessary to counter with firm determination any steps that could undermine the process of détente and reverse international developments back to cold war times. Now, more than ever before, it is necessary to adhere strictly to the principles of non-interference in the internal affairs of other states and respect the right of all peoples to freedom and independence and to increase efforts for the development of their peaceful co-operation, whose opportunities are clearly outlined in the Final Act of the Conference on Security and Co-operation in Europe and in the resolutions of the United Nations and other international documents.

The Political Bureau of the CPSU Central Committee expresses gratification that in the course of the meetings in the Crimea the importance was reaffirmed of the further development of the co-operation of the fraternal countries on the firm foundation of Marxism-Leninism and socialist internationalism and co-ordination of their actions in the interests of the confident progress of the cause of peace and social progress.

The meetings in the Crimea between Comrade Leonid Brezhnev and the leaders of the fraternal Parties and States marks an important step in the further strengthening of the socialist community and the deepening of the all-round co-operation between the fraternal parties, countries and peoples in the construction of socialism and communism and create favourable conditions for preparing new steps in the development of this co-operation.

The Political Bureau of the CPSU Central Committee has taken a number of decisions on concrete questions of implementing bilateral agreements reached at the friendly meetings in the Crimea.

Communique on the 32nd Meeting of the Session of the Council for Mutual Economic Assistance

(Complete Text).

The regular thirty-second Session of the Council for Mutual Economic Assistance was held in Bucharest, the capital of the Socialist Republic of Romania, from June 27 to 29, 1978.

Taking part in the Session's work were the delegations from the CMEA member countries headed by S. Todorov, Chairman of the Council of Ministers of the People's Republic of Bulgaria, G. Lazar, Chairman of the Council of Ministers of the Hungarian People's Republic, W. Stoph, Chairman of the Council of Ministers of the German Democratic Republic, C.R. Rodriguez, Deputy Chairman of the State Council and of the Council of Ministers of the Republic of Cuba, Zh. Batmunh, Chairman of the Council of Ministers of the Mongolian People's Republic, P. Jaroszewicz, Chairman of the Council of Ministers of the Polish People's Republic, M. Manescu, Prime Minister of the Government of the Socialist Republic of Romania, A.N. Kosygin, Chairman of the Council of Ministers of the Union of Soviet Socialist Republics, L. Strougal, Chairman of the Government of the Czechoslovak Socialist Republic.

Under the Agreement between the CMEA and the Government of the Socialist Federal Republic of Yugoslavia, the delegation of the SFRY headed by A. Marino, Deputy Chairman of the Federal Executive Council of the SFRY, participated in the Session's work.

Also present as observers were delegations of the Socialist Republic of Vietnam headed by Le Thanh Nghi, Deputy Prime Minister of the Government of the SRV; of the Democratic People's Republic of Korea headed by Sin In Ha, Extraordinary and Plenipotentiary Ambassador of the DPRK to the SRR; of the People's Republic of Angola headed by Jose Eduardo Dos Santos, First Deputy Prime Minister of the PRA; of the People's Democratic Republic of Laos headed by Sanan Southichak, Chairman of the Committee on Co-operation in Economy and Technology with Socialist Countries; of Socialist Ethiopia headed by Gessesse Wolde Kidane, Member of the Permanent Committee of the Provisional Military Administrative Council.

N.V. Faddeyev, CMEA Secretary, took part in the proceedings of the Session.

Present at the Session were representatives of a number of international economic organizations of CMEA member countries.

The meeting of the Session was chaired by Mr. Manescu, head of the delegation of the Socialist Republic of Romania, the Prime Minister of the Government of the SRR.

The Session considered an application from the Socialist Republic of Vietnam for admission to membership in the Council for Mutual Economic

Assistance. The participants in the Session warmly greeted the statement to this effect by Comrade Le Thanh Nghi, Member of the Politburo of the Communist Party of Vietnam, Deputy Prime Minister of the Government of the SRV. The Session unanimously resolved to admit the Socialist Republic of Vietnam to membership in the Council for Mutual Economic Assistance.

The Session of the Council considered reports on the activity of the Council for Mutual Economic Assistance between the 31st and the 32nd meetings of the Session of the Council as well as on progress and practical results in the implementation of projects contained in the Concerted plan of multilateral integrative measures of CMEA member countries for 1976-80.

It has been stated that the CMEA member countries are successfully tackling creative tasks of socialist and communist construction, are building up their economic potential. The deepening of co-operation among them plays an important role in their achievements.

On the basis of the accords reached by the leaders of the fraternal parties in 1977 in the Crimea and at other meetings, co-ordination of co-operation in the CMEA framework, carried out on a multilateral and bilateral basis, is becoming closer with the aim of implementing measures of the long-term specific programmes of co-operation.

The Session noted that as a result of the dedicated and creative labour by the working class, the peasantry, and intellectuals under the leadership of their Communist and Workers' parties, the targets of the current five-year period were being successfully fulfilled, and a foundation had been laid for the realization of the five-year national economic plans for the entire period. The national income in the CMEA member countries showed in 1977 a 12% increase over 1975, while industrial output went up 12.4%. Higher labour productivity accounted for about four fifths of the increment in industrial output. The total volume of foreign trade turnover of CMEA member countries increased by 24% in 1977 as against 1975 and exceeded 158 bln roubles.

The steady, dynamic economic growth of the CMEA member countries, in contrast to the crises and aggravation of antagonisms in the capitalist world, convincingly demonstrates the advantages of the social and political system of the socialist states and the effectiveness of their growing mutual co-operation. Industrial output in the developed capitalist countries went up 7% in 1977 as compared with the pre-crisis level of 1973, whereas in CMEA member countries it increased 32% during the same period.

Progress made in the development of economy, science and technology, the extension and deepening of the all-round mutual co-operation strengthen the might and authority of the community of the CMEA member countries, enhance its role and increase its influence on world developments. Both joint and individual initiatives of the fraternal socialist states, aimed at consolidating, deepening and materializing international detente, at halting the arms race and passing over to concrete disarmament measures, have been actively contributing to the maintenance of a lasting peace on our planet.

The Session noted that the CMEA member countries and Council's bodies had accomplished considerable work on the implementation of the Comprehensive Programme for the Further Extension and Improvement of Co-operation and the Development of Socialist Economic Integration of the CMEA Member Countries. The jointly worked out plans of concrete measures for the development of mutual trade, specialization and partnership in production, the scientific and technical co-operation, construction of projects by joint efforts, are being successfully fulfilled.

Commitments with respect to mutual deliveries of goods arising from long-term trade agreements and yearly trade protocols have been surpassed. In 1977 mutual trade amongst CMEA member countries went up 28% as against 1975 and amounted to 91 bln roubles.

During the first two years of the five-year period, capital investments totalling more than 3 bln roubles were put to use at projects envisaged in the concerted plan of multilateral integrative measures for 1976-80. The construction of a series of projects of the Soyuz gas pipeline (Orenburg — the western frontier of the USSR) will be completed by the end of the current year. It will be used for gas transport from the Soviet Union to Bulgaria, Hungary, the GDR, Poland, Romania and Czechoslovakia. The construction of this unique project exemplifies the effective work performed by the international team of many thousands of builders from the participating countries, enriches the CMEA member countries with valuable experience in joint implementation of projects of major economic significance.

The year 1978 will see the completion of work on the first intersystem 750 kV power transmission line between Vinnitsa (USSR) and Albertirsa (Hungary), thus making it possible to begin parallel operation of the interconnected power systems of the CMEA member countries and the Unified Power Grid of the USSR, to step up mutual exchange of electric power, to raise the effectiveness and reliability of power supply to countries participating in the interconnected power system.

In 1977 new capacities for the production of pellets and ferroalloys were brought into use at iron-and-steel enterprises built in the USSR, with the interested CMEA member countries participating.

Construction and assembly work is being stepped up at the Kiembai asbestos mining and dressing factory, at the Ust-Ilimsk cellulose works and at other jointly constructed projects. Under the agreements concluded, the countries participating in their construction supply, in a planned way, the necessary material resources for these projects. Their commissioning will improve the supply of the corresponding kinds of raw materials to CMEA member countries. Design and preparatory work is well under way to build, by CMEA member countries' joint efforts, a nickel factory in Cuba; a joint geological expedition is actively engaged in prospecting in the Mongolian People's Republic.

Specialization and partnership in the field of material production continues to develop and deepen among CMEA member countries together with co-operation in science and technology.

On the basis of mutual co-operation and joint efforts scientists, engineers, technicians and workers in CMEA member countries conducted research and development studies and created a number of new samples of machinery and equipment, instruments, new types of materials, advanced technologies. Their industrial application will yield a substantial national economic effect.

The participants in the Session qualified the flights of spaceships manned by international crews from among the citizens of CMEA member countries as a major event in the practical realization of the multilateral programme of co-operation in space explorations. They hailed the first flight of the Soviet-Czechoslovak crew and a new step in space explorations — the joint flight of cosmonauts from the USSR and Poland.

The Session approved the long-term specific programmes of co-operation in the field of energy, fuel, raw materials, agriculture, the food industry and machine-building for the period through 1990.

The programmes approved by the Session had been worked out in line with the decisions of the Communist and Workers' Parties of CMEA member countries and are a new important step in the implementation of the Comprehensive Programme for the Further Extension and Improvement of Co-operation and the Development of Socialist Economic Integration of CMEA Member Countries.

The Session stressed the need for taking due account, in the realization of the long-term specific programmes, of tasks regarding a gradual approximation and equalization of the development levels of the CMEA member countries, for rendering assistance and support to the Republic of Cuba and the Mongolian People's Republic in speeding up their development and raising the efficiency of their economies.

The long-term specific programme of co-operation in the field of energy, fuel and raw materials envisages as most important measures of co-operation the accelerated development of the nuclear power industry, the increased production and better use of one's own resources of solid fuels, the further development of the inter-connected electric power systems of the CMEA member countries, a more thorough processing of oil and gas, limitation on their utilization as fuel, creation by joint efforts of the interested countries of new capacities for the production of the iron and steel, chemical, paper and pulp, and microbiological products.

A major contribution to the solution of the energy problem in the European CMEA Member countries and the Republic of Cuba will be made by the construction in their territories of nuclear power stations with a total capacity of some 37,000,000 kw, as well as by the building in the USSR of another two nuclear power stations with a capacity of 4,000,000 kw each, to supply electricity to the fraternal countries. To accomplish these tasks, the CMEA member countries will organize a large-scale multilateral co-operation in the production of equipment for nuclear power stations.

To ensure a fuller satisfaction of CMEA Member countries' future requirements in diesel oil, a set of co-operation measures are being prepared to ensure a more thorough processing, and a more rational use, of oil.

The programme envisages the conduct of promising research work on the use of new sources of energy.

The problem of meeting CMEA member countries' needs for steel and ferruginous ores will be solved by way of the planned construction in the USSR of new production capacities by joint efforts of the interested countries.

Provision is made to extend co-operation of the CMEA member countries for the further development of nickel production in the Republic of Cuba.

The development of production and increased mutual deliveries of chemicals is planned between CMEA member countries.

Co-operative measures have been co-ordinated for the rational use and utmost saving of fuels and raw materials at all stages of their extraction, processing, transportation and technological utilization.

The long-term specific programme of co-operation in the sphere of agriculture and the food industry envisages the elaboration of co-operative measures conducive to the intensive development of the output of grain, livestock products and other staple agricultural produce in each CMEA member country, the improvement of the fodder supply, and an increased production of protein feeds.

It is also envisaged, on the basis of a more effective use of favourable natural conditions of the CMEA member countries, to expand the output and the mutual deliveries of a number of kinds of agricultural products and foodstuffs.

Measures have been outlined to further mechanise and chemicalize agricultural production and to strengthen the material and technical base of the food industry.

Greater use will be made of the co-operation opportunities for breeding the promising varieties of agricultural crops and highly productive breeds of animals, and developing advanced technologies in the food industry.

The long-term specific programme of co-operation in the field of machine-building is aimed at securing in CMEA member countries high rates of development of the production of modern types of equipment, machinery and instruments for better equipment of the fuel and raw-materials branches, farming, the food industry and machine-building itself with the latest machinery, and at introducing the advanced technological processes. In so doing, priority is given to measures aimed at increasing the output and mutual deliveries of equipment for nuclear power stations, for oil extraction and its thorough processing, for prospecting for, extraction and dressing of solid fuels and minerals. A set of measures will be carried out with regard to the most important kinds of equipment, including the development of specialization and partnership in production, the creation of new samples of machinery, the expansion of the existing, and the setting up of new, production capacities.

The Session stated that the approved long-term specific programme represents important documents for the further expansion of multilateral co-operation of CMEA member countries. As a main task for the successful fulfilment of these programmes, the Session recommended the countries concerned and enjoined the Counil's bodies to prepare and conclude one their basis multilateral and bilateral agreements on co-operation in the implementation of particular measures.

The heads of the delegations from the CMEA member countries, attaching great political and economic significance to the long-term specific programmes of co-operation, signed a Statement. In it they expressed the readiness of their countries to take an active part in drafting multilateral and bilateral agreements which determine the practical realization of measures included in the programmes, and to mobilize the respective national resources for the implementation of the joint projects.

The Session pronounced in favour of the need to speed up the preparation of draft long-term specific programmes of co-operation to meet the CMEA member countries' rational requirements for industrial consumer goods and to develop their transport links, as well as of the corresponding multilateral and bilateral agreements.

The Session considered it expedient that in realizing the long-term specific programmes a fuller use should be made of co-operation capabilities to raise the economic efficiency of social production in each of the fraternal countries.

The Session took note of the fact that the interested organizations of the SFRY would take part in drafting and implementing measures included ind the long-term specific programmes of co-operation on questions of mutual interest for the SFRY and CMEA member countries.

The Session stressed that the long-term specific co-operation programmes, while meeting the interests of CMEA Member countries, are at the same time fully in line with their consistent and invariable course towards the development of co-operation on the basis of equality and mutual benefit with all countries irrespective of their social system, including the realization of large-scale projects of international significance in the fields of power engineering, industry, transport, environmental protection, etc.

The Session expressed its positive attitude to the interest of the People's Democratic Republic of Laos, the People's Republic of Angola and Socialist Ethiopia in expanding their multilateral and bilateral economic, scientific, and technological co-operation with the CMEA member countries.

The CMEA member countries' determination was stressed to broaden equitable and mutually beneficial co-operation with the developing states, this helping the latter carry out measures for social, economic and cultural development in line with their national interests, strengthen their positions in the world economy, liberate themselves from the oppression by imperialist monopolies, and eliminate colonialism in all its forms.

An exchange of opinions took place at the Session concerning contacts and talks between the CMEA and the EEC.

Expressing the general opinion of the CMEA member countries' delegations, the Session underlines the expediency, on the basis of draft agreements on the basic principles of mutual relations that were forwarded by the CMEA and the EEC to each other earlier, to continue talks in order to draft an agreement between the CMEA and the CMEA member countries, on the one hand, and the EEC and the EEC member countries, on the other.

The growing scale and the deeper content of co-operation among the CMEA member countries necessitate a further improvement in the mechanism, forms and methods of the activity of the Council for Mutual Economic Assistance. Guided by the principled directives of the central committees of the Communist and Workers' Parties and the governments of CMEA member countries, the Session endorsed a set of measures for the further improvement in the organization of co-operation among the CMEA member countries and in the activity of the Council. The work of all CMEA bodies is aimed at the priority solution of co-operation tasks in the sphere of material production, primarily of those concerned with the realization of long-term specific programmes of co-operation; at the further strengthening of the planning principles in CMEA work; at raising the efficiency, effectiveness, timeliness and co-ordination in the activities of all CMEA bodies the international organizations of CMEA member countries.

The heads of government of CMEA member countries expressed their firm defermination to continue persistently to develop and deepen co-operation of the CMEA member countries in economy, science and technology, considering it an important factor actively contributing to the successful implementation of the mapped out plans for socialist and communist construction, to the strengthening of the cohesion and inviolable friendship of the peoples of socialist countries on the basis of principles of Marxism-Leninism and internationalist solidarity.

The proceedings of the 32nd meeting of the CMEA Session took place in an atmosphere of friendship, complete mutual understanding and comradely co-operation.

Declaration of the Conference of Political Consultative Committee of Warsaw Treaty Organisation Member-Countries.

(Complete Text).

The People's Republic of Bulgaria, the Czechoslovak Socialist Republic, The German Democratic Republic, the Hungarian People's Republic, the Polish People's Republic, the Socialist Republic of Romania and the Union of Soviet Socialist Republics, represented at the Conference of the Political Consultative Committee of the Warsaw Treaty Member-Countries in Moscow on November 22 and 23, 1978, considered topical questions concerning the development of the situation in Europe and had an exchange of views on some questions concerning the international situation as a whole.

The discussion centred around further steps in the struggle for the development of the process of détente and disarmament.

The participants in the Conference pointed out that in recent years the determination of the peoples and of all the forces of progress and peace to put an end to the aggressive and oppressive policy of imperialism, colonialism and neo-colonialism has become ever stronger, and the struggle for peace, for détente, for an end to the arms race, for freedom and social progress, for peaceful international co-operation on an equal footing, based on mutual respect for national independence and sovereignty and non-interference in internal affairs, has been developing ever more widely. Marked positive results have been attained in this struggle. The trend towards the relaxation of international tension, based on recognition of, and respect for, the equality of rights of all states, has emerged and has begun to have an impact on the general development of world affairs.

At the same time there has been greater activity on the part of the forces of imperialism and reaction which are seeking to subordinate independent states and peoples to their domination, to step up the arms race and to intervene flagrantly in the internal affairs of other states, which creates a threat to the process of détente and is contrary to the desire of the peoples for peace, freedom, independence and progress.

In general, developments have confirmed the assessment made by the Warsaw Treaty member-countries in their Declaration for New Frontiers in International Détente, for Strengthening Security and Developing Co-operation in Europe, adopted at the Conference of the Political Consultative Committee in Bucharest in 1976.

Those taking part in the Conference paid particular attention to questions of strengthening security and developing co-operation in Europe. They pointed out that significant changes for the better had taken place on the continent of Europe. This has been facilitated by the development of relations between the states of the continent in the spirit of the principles contained in the Final Act of the Conference on Security and Co-operation in Europe and the general recognition of the existing frontiers between the European states and their inviolability, which is of fundamental importance for international security. The overcoming of substantial obstacles on the road to an improvement in the relations between the states of Europe has helped to make these relations more even in their nature, acquiring a richer and more varied content and promoting the expansion of mutual understanding among the peoples.

In the period since the conclusion of the Conference on Security and Co-operation in Europe useful work has been done in the implementation of the principles and accords worked out at the conference and a good beginning has been made in this matter.

Developments have confirmed that the long-term programme of European security and co-operation, embodied in the Final Act of the European Conference, correctly determines the main trends of positive actions in the interests of peace and provides reliable guidance for such actions.

In the course of carrying out the Helsinki accords, meetings are being held ever more frequently between leaders of the states that participated in the European Conference, promoting the development of mutually-advantageous international co-operation on an equal footing, including co-operation on a long-term basis.

The fabric of political contacts between European states has become markedly stronger, their understanding of each other's positions, views and legitimate interests has been improved, with the expansion of bilateral relations also playing a significant and useful part in this. New possibilities have been ascertained for mutually-beneficial economic, scientific and technical co-operation among them, especially in the sphere of industrial co-operation, and definite practical steps have been outlined for the realisation of these possibilities. Preparations are under way for the convocation of a European congress on environmental protection and appropriate forums have begun considering the question of holding similar meetings on co-operation in transport, energy and a number of other fields. Cultural exchange has been extended and has become richer and more varied in content and contacts in other humanitarian spheres have been developed.

It is important that all participants in the European Conference reaffirmed at the Belgrade meeting their readiness to continue the process begun at the conference, although no concord was achieved at the meeting on a number of essential constructive practical proposals, including those related to the military aspects of security.

A useful contribution to the development of co-operation in Europe is to be made by multilateral measures on concrete questions, agreement on which was reached at the Belgrade meeting: a conference of experts for drawing up a generally acceptable method for the peaceful settlement of disputes, a European scientific forum, a conference of experts on economic, scientific technical and cultural co-operation in the area of the Mediterranean. Of positive significance is the understanding on holding in Madrid in 1980, within the framework of the multilateral process started by the European Conference, the next meeting of representatives of the states that took part in the conference. The peoples of the continent expect the Madrid meeting to help in a practical way in making progress in the cause of security and co-operation in Europe and to contribute especially towards progress in the field of military détente and disarmament. The socialist countries represented at the Conference are expressing determination to make their contribution to the success of the meeting.

However, it has been clear from the very start that a confident advance along the road paved by the European Conference, just like the strengthening of peace all over the world, can become real only in the event of all states acting consistently in this direction.

It is to be regretted that events have not been developing entirely in this way. There are clear breaches of the generally-recognised principles governing relations between states and serious threats to peace, international security, freedom and the independence of peoples. Attempts are made to halt the process of improving international relations and even to reverse it. The build-up of armed forces and arms on the continent of Europe has not been stopped and is continuing and any effective agreements in the field of military détente and disarmament have not as yet been reached, and this is endangering the process of strengthening security in Europe.

Obstacles in the way of economic, scientific and technical co-operation have not been removed, but have been even increased in some directions. Hostile political campaigns are being waged against the socialist countries the Communist and Workers' Parties and other progressive democratic forces.

Aims of aggression, revanchism and hegemonism are being pursued in the onslaught of the imperialist and reactionary forces on the positions gained by the peoples in the difficult struggle for lasting peace and international security. The states represented at the meeting of the Political Consultative Committee consider it necessary to draw the attention of all the peace forces to the fact that all this is doing serious harm to the cause of peace and security and the development of international co-operation.

The activity of the imperialist and reactionary forces aimed at complicating the international situation cannot but meet with firm opposition from all who cherish the interests of peace, a tranquil life and the labour of the peoples and from all who consider the elimination of the threat of war to be one of the most important objectives at the present time.

Convinced that the forces of peace and progress, which are constantly growing stronger, are capable of achieving new and important successes in the struggle for peace and the freedom of peoples, the states taking part in the Conference of the Political Consultative Committee declare their determination to come out jointly with other peace-loving states, with all the progressive and democratic forces and with the broad masses of the people, in order to give fresh impetus to the implementation of the Helsinki Final Act as an integral whole and reach agreement on concrete measures and steps for the development of co-operation and the attainment of genuine security on the continent of Europe and throughout the world. They are also ready to take part in a most active and energetic way in solving the most important international problems.

The main danger to peace and international security, to the relaxation of international tensions and to the independence of peoples and their economic and social development is the continuation and build-up of the arms race, the build-up of its rate and scale.

An expression of the intensification of the arms race, responsibility for which rests with the most aggressive circles of imperialism, is the adoption by the Washington session of the NATO Council of the decision to increase military appropriations by many tens of thousands of millions of dollars above the already inflated military budgets, the new programmes, designed for decades, for the development of their armed forces, the equipping of those forces with increasingly destructive types of weapons of mass destruction. These decisions, which are conducive to an increase in the arms race, as well as other actions by NATO which are in the nature of military demonstrations, are pursuing the aim of achieving military supremacy on the part of the NATO countries over the socialist and other countries of the world in order to dictate their will to the independent states, and the aim of suppressing the struggle of the peoples for national and social liberation.

These measures are entirely contrary to the provisions of the Helsinki Final Act and they create new obstacles in the way of mutual understanding and peaceful co-operation among the states and peoples of Europe. The interests of peace demand that the NATO member-countries renounce the decisions taken and set out on the road of disarmament and of creating a climate of peace, mutual understanding and confidence among all the states that took part in the European Conference.

The socialist countries that are parties to the Warsaw Treaty come out firmly against the policy of intensifying the arms race and against attempts at military blackmail. They again state that they have never sought and do not seek for military superiority: their military efforts are directed, and always will be directed exclusively towards ensuring their defence capacity. They proceed from the belief that the military balance in Europe and the world should be maintained not by increasing arms but by reducing them and by a resolute transition to concrete measures to carry out disarmament, especially nuclear disarmament. The further intensification of the arms race and the expansion of its scale and the further improvement of arms systems may have increasingly dangerous consequences for the peoples.

Accordingly, the states represented at the Conference of the Political Consultative Committee believe that the most important task in international politics in the present conditions is to bring about a rapid and resolute turn in the talks on stopping the arms race and on disarmament. This is required by the basic interests of the peoples, of all mankind, of civilisation. They note with satisfaction that this viewpoint is now widely shared everywhere in the world. The political leaders of many countries, broad public circles and ordinary people are coming out with ever greater insistence against a fresh spiraling of the arms race which jeopardises the peace and security of the states, and in favour of effective measures of disarmament.

In the conditions of the arms race, the economic and social progress of all countries is held back, co-operation between states is made more difficult, and ever greater obstacles arise in the way of efforts to close gaps in the economic development of countries and to solve other global problems on which mankind's future depends.

There can be no stable peace in conditions in which the potential of destruction is growing fast in the arsenals of states — a potential which is already sufficient, if put to use, to call in question the very survival of man on earth. The arms race is doing increasingly serious harm to the process of easing international tension.

The arms race must be stopped without delay also because the rapid development of military technology and especially the possibility of the emergence of new types and systems of weapons of mass destruction, may further complicate the search for, and the attainment of, practical solutions on matters of disarmament.

What the peoples need is not the development of new nuclear missile systems, new submarines with ballistic missiles or cruise missiles, but the complete ending of the manufacture of nuclear weapons of all types and the conversion of nuclear energy to peaceful purposes.

What meets the aspirations of mankind is not the improvement of the existing types of weapons of mass destruction and not the development of new ones, including neutron weapons, but the ending of the manufacture of all types of such weapons and their prohibition.

What the peoples need is not the further development and improvement of conventional armaments and the further enhancement of the destructive power of those weapons but the reduction of existing armed forces and armaments without diminishing the security of any state and a transition to effective measures to ease military tension and carry out disarmament.

The socialist countries represented at the Conference of the Political Consultative Committee firmly believe that it is necessary to take effective measures in all these directions, measures capable of stopping the growth of the military potential of states — in the first place, of the powers possessing big military potentials — and leading to actual disarmament.

Proposals on the entire series of problems of stopping the arms race and carrying out disarmament were submitted to the special session of the General Assembly on disarmament in the summer of this year and to the present session of the General Assembly.

The top priority task in this respect is to begin talks on stopping the manufacture of nuclear weapons of all types and on the gradual reduction of stockpiles of these weapons, up to and including their complete elimination. Parallel to this, it is necessary to press for the prohibition for all time of the use of nuclear weapons and the renunciation by all states of the use of force in relations with each other. The countries that are parties to the Warsaw Treaty are supporting proposals made on this matter by the Soviet Union and other socialist countries. They consider it necessary to reach agreement, without any further delay, on beginning talks on these questions with the participation of all the nuclear powers, and not only these powers. The sooner a definite date is fixed for such talks, the better.

The countries that are parties to the Warsaw Treaty attach great importance to the attainment of accords between the USSR and the USA on strategic arms limitation. Of tremendous importance, in their opinion, would be the early conclusion of the Soviet-American talks on the second agreement on the limitation of strategic offensive arms and a transition to the conclusion of new agreements on the reduction of these arms with the participation of other nuclear powers.

The achievement of progress in reducing strategic offensive arms would help to reduce the level of military confrontation in the world and to strengthen the trend towards détente, peace and international security. The peoples will welcome such a course of events.

The states represented at the Conference of the Political Consultative Committee express themselves in favour of the earliest possible conclusion of the present talks on other aspects concerning the limitation and ending of the arms race — on the complete and universal prohibition of nuclear weapon tests; on strengthening the nuclear non-proliferation régime on the conditions of access for all states without any discrimination to the use of nuclear energy and nuclear technology for peaceful purposes under effective international control in accordance with the IAEA standards; on banning the development of new types and systems of weapons of mass destruction; on banning and destroying chemical weapons; on the limitations and subsequent reduction of military activity in the Indian Ocean, and on the restriction of the sale and delivery of conventional arms.

Every one of the talks along these lines has a significance of its own from the point of view of the strengthening of peace and the security of the peoples. All these talks are at a more or less advanced stage in which the subject of discussion and search for agreement is not general ideas but questions of a military-material character. The socialist states which have taken part in the appropriate talks, have made and are continuing to make a great constructive contribution towards their progress and are coming up with proposals which help to overcome the obstacles which are encountered on the way. They are prepared to continue to act in this spirit in the interests of the success of the talks. But it should be absolutely clear that to achieve practical results all the participants in the talks should adopt a constructive approach.

One of the most effective and practical ways to stop the arms race is to reduce military budgets and, in the first place, the budgets of states which have great economic and military potentials.

The socialist countries are ready to reach agreement on accomplishing this big task, on cutbacks in military budgets whether by equal parts, or percentages, or in absolute terms, by magnitudes of the same order. Their proposals on this subject are being examined by the United Nations, among them being the proposal that military budgets be frozen at their present level and that their reduction be started immediately.

The implementation of this measure will not only set certain limits to the arms race, but will also release large resources for peaceful purposes — the development of industry, agriculture, science, culture and education — and for increasing aid to the developing countries in the interests of speeding up their economic and social development and also for environmental protection. This would be a tangible gain for the cause of disarmament and for the wellbeing of the peoples.

Being, as they are, European states, the socialist Warsaw Treaty member-countries naturally attach special significance to questions of military détente and disarmament in Europe.

They reaffirm their determination to work for the implementation of the well-known provision of the Final Act of the Conference on European Security and Co-operation on the necessity for carrying out effective measures directed at lessening military confrontation and at promoting disarmament, which are intended to complement political détente and strengthen security in Europe.

They are striving to contribute in every possible way towards the success of the talks on mutual reductions of armed forces and armaments in Central Europe and, with this aim, have repeatedly put forward, in the course of these talks, constructive proposals on ways of resolving the basic issues which are the subject of examination.

A new and major effort by them which is aimed at achieving decisive progress at the talks, is the proposal of June 8, 1978, embracing the whole package of the problems under discussion and ensuring the equality of the armed forces of both sides in the area of reductions with a considerable lowering of their levels as compared with the present ones. Progress will be achieved, however, only if the answer of the other side is also imbued with a constructive spirit.

Those taking part in the Conference will also make efforts to ensure that questions of military détente and of promoting disarmament in Europe are examined within the common framework of European security with the participation of all the parties who signed the Helsinki Final Act.

Whether it be on the European or on the world scale, and with reference to separate areas or the whole world, the socialist countries which are Warsaw Treaty member-states are ready to conduct talks on all aspects of the programme for ending the arms race, including aspects on which talks are not being conducted so far. This refers, for example, to the question of limiting and reducing those components of the combat potentials of both sides in Europe which are at present a source of concern for each of the sides.

There is no type of weapon that the socialist states represented at the Conference would not be ready to limit or reduce on the basis of strict observance of the principle of undiminished security of each of the sides. They are also ready to examine most attentively the proposals of other states on questions of military détente and disarmament.

Declaring their desire to make further efforts to achieve a successful solution, together with other states, to questions pertaining to ending the arms race and disarmament, the states represented at the Conference of the Political Consultative Committee consider it necessary to stress the significance of confidence in relations among states. They firmly declare themselves in favour of strict observance of the principle of refraining from the use or threat of force in relations among states and of all issues in dispute being settled solely by peaceful means, through negotiations.

In accordance with this, the socialist states represented at the Conference come out in favour of the implementation of the following measures:

The conclusion of a world treaty on refraining from the use of force in international relations which would provide for a commitment by all states on the renunciation of the use or threat of force in all of its forms and manifestations, including a ban on the use of nuclear weapons;

Strict observance by all states that took part in the European Conference of the commitment not to use force or the threat of force in their relations with one another;

The implementation of the proposal that all states that took part in the European Conference should commit themselves never to be the first to use nuclear weapons against one another, so that the NATO member-states and the Warsaw Treaty member-states should not enlarge the number of part-icipants in their alliances, so that the scale of military exercises by the sides in Europe be limited to a level of 50,000-60,000 men, and the measures for confidence on which agreement was reached at the European Conference are applied to the area of the Mediterranean;

Measures for strengthening security guarantees for non-nuclear states, including renunciation of the use of nuclear weapons against states which do not possess nuclear weapons and do not have them on their territory, as well as renunciation of the deployment of nuclear weapons on the terri-tories of states where they are not to be found at present.

The non-nuclear states which do not have nuclear weapons on their territories, have the right to receive guarantees that no nuclear weapons, and no other weapons either, will be used against them, in accordance with the principle of refraining from the use or threat of force.

The states taking part in the Conference of the Political Consultative Committee come out against force and the build-up of armaments on the territories of other states.

They have reaffirmed their consistent stand in favour of agreements being concluded on reductions of armed forces and armaments so that fresh efforts may be made on an international scale for dismantling military bases on the territories of other countries and for the withdrawal of foreign armed forces from the territories of other states and for the creation of nuclear-free zones and peace zones in various areas, including Europe.

Those taking part in the Conference also reaffirm their readiness to disband the Warsaw Treaty Organisation, simultaneously with the disband-ment of the North Atlantic Treaty Organisation, and as the first step — the elimination of their military organisations, starting with a mutual reduction of their military activity. This would be a major milestone in the construc-tion of lasting peace.

The socialist states are well aware that the solution of questions con-cerning the ending of the arms race and concerning disarmament is a diffi-cult matter calling for tremendous efforts and purposeful determination. They note the useful and important nature of the broad discussion on practical ways of ending the arms race and of disarmament at the recent special session of the U.N. General Assembly, which also adopted decisions on improving the machinery of talks with this in view. It is important now to start practical work to implement the ideas and recommendations of the final document adopted at the session and to make even more persistent efforts on an international scale in order to pass over to disarmament. A strong impetus in this whole matter could be given by the convocation, at the earliest possible date, of a world disarmament conference with all states taking part.

The states represented at the Conference of the Political Consultative Committee are also aware that there exist powerful enemies to the cause of ending the arms race, above all the imperialist circles, the monopolies that are interested in the constant expansion of the manufacture of arms and an increase of stockpiles as a means of profit and at the same time a means of subjugating independent countries and peoples, imposing their will upon them. But those taking part in the Conference are convinced that the resistance on the part of the enemies of an end to the arms race can be overcome, if all the forces of our time that are interested in preserving and strengthening peace, are mobilised and united for this purpose.

Their confidence is based on the results already achieved, which have found expression in the system of bilateral and multilateral treaties and agreements on the limitation of the arms race in some directions established in the past 15 years. The vital interests of the peoples demand that much more be done at the present time.

Decisive progress in ending the arms race is possible. All efforts must be exerted to make this a reality.

During an exchange of views on other international questions of common interest, the delegations of the People's Republic of Bulgaria, the Czechoslovak Socialist Republic, the German Democratic Republic, the Hungarian People's Republic, the Polish People's Republic, the Socialist Republic of Romania and the Union of Soviet Socialist Republics considered it necessary to emphasise that the imperialist policy directed against the peoples who are fighting for liberation from colonial-racialist oppression, against neo-colonialism, for independence and social progress, is also a source of danger to international détente.

They consider it necessary to say, above all, that the policy of imperialism pursues the same ends, although it has become more refined recently. Ever more frequently the imperialists are resorting to such methods as those of provoking enmity and conflicts between the peoples of liberated states and dispatching arms and mercenaries to help their puppets and are knocking together all kinds of military groupings of countries where pro-imperialist régimes are in power. And the significance of all this is to strengthen or, at least, to retain their domination, their positions in the economy and policy of the countries of Asia, Africa and Latin America. Nor have influential circles of the imperialist powers and international monopolies, as experience has shown, abandoned their "classical" means of keeping countries and peoples in submission — military intervention, flagrant interference in the internal affairs of independent states and infringements of their sovereign rights.

The socialist states have come out, and are continuing to come out against this policy, which is contrary to the objective requirements of mankind's historical development. They reaffirm their solidarity with the peoples' struggle against imperialism, colonialism and neo-colonialism, and against any forms of domination and oppression. They have rendered and will continue to render support to the forces that are fighting for national liberation, and to the peoples of the liberated countries who are upholding in a hard struggle their independence and freedom, including their right freely to choose their road of social development and to safeguard the territorial integrity of their countries and their independence and sovereignty.

They re-emphasise the firm intention of their countries to continue developing all-round co-operation and friendly collaboration with the young states with a socialist orientation.

The socialist states are vigorously supporting the peoples of Zimbabwe and Namibia in their dedicated struggle for the early attainment of national independence. They come out in solidarity with the just struggle of the people of South Africa for the abolition of apartheid and all forms of racialist discrimination. They condemn the attempts to impose on the peoples of Zimbabwe, Namibia and South Africa neo-colonialist solutions which are alien to them and which would create the danger of new conflicts flaring up in that region.

They reaffirm their principled position in favour of a just and lasting peace being established in the Middle East and of a comprehensive political settlement of the Middle East problems which must include: the withdrawal of Israeli armed forces from all the Arab territories they occupied in 1967; the exercise of the inalienable right of the Arab people of Palestine to self-determination, including the setting up of their own state; the safeguarding of the independent existence and security of all states of that region, including Israel. At one with the Arab states and peoples, with all the progressive forces, they will continue to strive for a settlement such as can be reached only with the participation of all the interested parties, including the Palestine Liberation Organisation.

The states represented at the Conference support the constructive proposals of the Korean Democratic People's Republic aimed at achieving the national ideal of the Korean people — the independent, peaceful and democratic reunification of the country without any foreign interference.

In their relations with the emergent countries the socialist states strictly adhere to the principles of equality, mutual respect for sovereignty and territorial integrity, non-interference in internal affairs and mutually-advantageous co-operation. In no areas of the world are socialist countries seeking any privileges for themselves, pressing for military bases or hunting for concessions. Coming out in principle against the imperialist policy of creating spheres of influence, they never take part in the struggle for such spheres.

Proceeding on the basis of their principled policy of strengthening universal peace and security, the socialist countries represented at the Conference consistently come out in favour of the settlement by Peaceful political means, by means of talks, of all disputes between young emergent states, just as among all states in general.

The participants in the Conference stress the special importance for the progress of all mankind of the struggle for the elimination of economic backwardness, for the restructuring of international economic relations on a just and democratic basis, for the establishment of a new international economic order, for the renunciation of all discrimination and for the elimination of the exploitation of the natural and human, resources of developing countries by imperialist monopolies. They regard this as a direct continuation of the struggle against imperialism and colonialism.

They also declare themselves in favour of the most active and equal participation of all states, irrespective of their social system, geographical location, size and economic and military strength, in the solution of pressing problems of world development.

The states represented at the Conference are convinced that their policy on questions related to the struggle of the peoples for their freedom, independence and social progress, is a clear and principled policy which facilitates the strengthening of peace and the success of the great cause of the freedom of the peoples.

Dangerous trends in the development of international affairs are also generated by the policy of imperialist circles which, on the one hand, encourage and support fascist and other reactionary régimes in perpetrating crude and mass violations of human rights, and on the other hand, try to utilise the problem of human rights for interference in the internal affairs of socialist and other states and for attacks on the socialist social system.

In the course of the exchange of views on this question, the delega-tions proceeded from the premise that all states participating in the European Conference recognised in the Final Act the universal importance of the main human rights and freedoms that are necessary for the development of friendly ties between them just as between all states and respect for which is a substantial factor making for peace, justice and wellbeing. In this connection they believe it to be their duty to stress that support for, and encouragement of, the fascist and racialist policy, of acts of oppression, of crude and mass violations of human rights, like the dissemination of inhuman, militaristic, neo-fascist and neo-nazi views, are in direct contradiction with the aims and principles of the United Nations Charter, the provisions of the Helsinki Final Act and other international documents.

By supporting reactionary régimes in their struggle against the democratic liberation movement of the masses of the working people, in their mockery of the rights of citizens and their barbarous crimes against their own peoples, imperialism blatantly interferes in the internal affairs of these countries. The socialist countries resolutely come out against any interference in the internal affairs of any states and for strict respect for the right of all peoples freely to shape their own destiny.

The conviction was again unanimously expressed that true democracy and true humanism are incompatible with the preservation of economic, social and political inequality and with national and racial discrimination. It is only under socialism that respect for political, civil, economic, social, cultural and other rights is ensured, as well as the free access of all members of society to work, education, culture and science, and to participation in the administration of the state. The very way in which the new social system came into being is connected with the striving to transform into reality the main right of man — the right to a worthy existence without exploitation — and to create conditions for the all-round development of the individual. The banner of human rights and freedom is a banner of socialism.

It is with all the greater sense of conviction that the socialist countries participating in the exchange of views reject the slander directed against them by the ruling classes of states whose peoples are experiencing all the calamities of mass unemployment, national and social inequality, racial discrimination, organised crime and moral degradation.

The United Nations Charter provides for the obligation of all states to facilitate respect for the implementation of human rights and basic freedoms for all, irrespective of race, sex, language and religion. In accordance with this and acting with initiative and consistency, the socialist countries have made a vigorous contribution to the drafting and adoption of the most important international treaties and agreements in this field: the covenants on human rights, the conventions on preventing the crime of genocide, the elimination of all forms of racial discrimination and many others. They are implementing in practice all the provisions of these treaties and agreements.

The states taking part in the Conference consider it necessary to build up international efforts for the resolution of vital problems concerning the interests of all mankind, and especially of the younger generation, working for the improvement of the living and working conditions of the masses of the people, the eradication of racialism and apartheid, war propaganda, violence, immorality and hatred for humanity.

International co-operation in the field of human rights has, however, nothing in common with inspiring from outside anti-socialist activity by certain persons who have set out on the path of violating their country's laws. Any attempts at such interference in the internal affairs of sovereign states constitute actions aimed at undermining international co-operation. Such interference is contrary to the U.N. Charter and the explicit commitment by the states which took part in the European Conference, in conformity with the Final Act, to respect mutually the right of all freely to choose and develop their political, social, economic and cultural systems, as well as the right to establish their own laws and administrative rules.

The socialist countries represented at the Conference have not permitted, and will not permit any interference in their internal affairs. In affirming this with the utmost determination, they stress that in this connection, too, they are guided by concern for the further positive development of international relations, so that the obstacles artificially complicating those relations are removed.

The participants in the Conference of the Political Consultative Committee have discussed issues concerning the strengthening and development of all-round co-operation among the socialist countries represented at this Conference. They noted with great satisfaction that following the Bucharest meeting of the Political Consultative Committee in 1976, this co-operation, based on the principles of Marxism-Leninism, on respect for equality, independence and national sovereignty, non-interference in internal affairs and on mutual benefit, comradely mutual assistance and international solidarity, has become even more extensive in scale and more many-sided, covering increasingly broad fields of political, economic, scientific, technical, ideological and cultural activity. These relations are not counterposed in their nature and aims to relations with other states in Europe or any other part of the world.

The states participating in the Conference declare their unswerving desire to broaden and improve multilateral ties between one another and to deepen co-operation in solving international problems of general interest. They have also expressed their wish and resolve to broaden still further the exchange of know-how as regards socialist and communist construction and increase contacts at all levels along party and state lines and also between trade union, youth, women's and other mass public organisations.

The participants in the Conference also note that great possibilities and reserves exist for the further expansion and deepening of mutually-beneficial economic relations, resting on a firm contractual basis, between the socialist countries they represent, both bilateral and multilateral relations, within the framework of the Council for Mutual Economic Assistance, in accordance with the jointly-approved principles, in the interests of accelerating the process of levelling up economic development, the progress of each socialist country and the rise in the level of their prosperity and development. They note the importance of the special programmes of multilateral co-operation in the period up to 1990, endorsed at the 32nd session of the CMEA in Bucharest and intended to facilitate the safeguarding of the requirements of the member-countries as regards fuel, energy, raw materials, food, machinery, equipment and advanced technology. These programmes are a further advance in the development and deepening of economic co-operation of the CMEA member-countries. They expand the possibilities for the ever fuller utilisation of the advantages of socialism as a social system.

Note was taken of the successful development of bilateral and multilateral co-operation among the countries represented at the Conference, in the sphere of science, culture, education, information, radio and television, contacts between people and tourism. The desire was reaffirmed to continue to expand co-operation in all these spheres, improving the popularisation of each other's achievements in building socialism and communism, in activity for the development of socialist democracy, the improvement of the guidance of social and political life and the raising of the material and spiritual standards of life of the working people.

The Conference noted with satisfaction the significance of the flights of international crews of cosmonauts of socialist countries, embodying friendship and fruitful co-operation in mankind's exploration of outer space for peaceful purposes. This co-operation will be continued.

Those taking part in the Conference of the Political Consultative Committee declare the unswerving determination of the parties and governments of their countries constantly to strengthen the friendship and the co-operation on an equal footing between them and between all the socialist states and the progressive forces of our time. They are convinced that in present-day conditions, when imperialism continues to pursue a policy of domination, oppression and inequality, the assertion of a new type of international relations and the strengthening of the unity and cohesion of the socialist countries acquires particular importance. It is precisely along this road that the interests of each people building a new society are safeguarded most successfully, that the authority of socialism in the world constantly grows and that the role of the socialist countries in stimulating the renewal of international life, the deepening of détente and the strengthening of peace is being enhanced.

Declaring once again their resolve to redouble their efforts in strengthening peace, safeguarding security, developing the process of détente and expanding international co-operation, the states represented at the Conference of the Political Consultative Committee address all European states and all the states and peoples of the world, appealing to them:

1. Resolutely to set out on the road of firm allegiance to the policy of peace, détente, renunciation of the use of force or the threat of force in international relations, peaceful settlement of all disputes, unconditional condemnation of aggressive wars, complete exclusion of wars between states from the life of mankind, an end to the arms race, and the final eradication of the vestiges of "cold war".

The dream of millions of people on all continents about a world without military conflicts is not a utopia; it can be attained and can become a reality as a result of joint efforts by all those who are prepared to fight for it.

2. To press for holding shortly negotiations of the five nuclear powers — the USSR, the USA, Britain, France and China — in order to remove

nuclear weapons of all types from the arsenals of states and to switch nuclear energy over to peaceful uses only.

Man's genius has discovered a great source of energy — the energy of the atomic nucleus — not in order to destroy civilisation with its help. Supreme wisdom today lies not in whipping up the arms race and increasing the danger of a nuclear catastrophe but in delivering mankind from the threat of a new war.

3. To insist firmly that the countries possessing considerable military and atomic potentials, and primarily the five powers that are permanent members of the Security Council and bear special responsibility for the maintenance of international peace and security, should reach agreement without delay on the reduction of their military budgets by a certain percentage or by magnitudes of the same order, as the first step, for the next three years.

The peoples cannot reconcile themselves to the ever growing burden of unproductive expenditure on the manufacture of weapons of destruction. Everywhere in the world people are waiting for greater resources to be allocated for raising their living standards and for developing the health services, improving education and meeting their cultural requirements. The developing countries demand with good reason that at least a portion of military expenditure should be converted to economic and technical assistance to them. This can and must be done.

4. To step up the efforts of states and governments with a view to concluding quickly the present talks on the limitation and ending of the arms race in its main directions and to combine the efforts of all states in drafting and implementing disarmament measures. Actively to set about implementing the ideas and recommendations which gained general approval at the special session of the General Assembly on disarmament.

Time does not wait. As regards the ending of the arms race, time can no longer be counted in years and, still less so, decades. The states participating in the talks are required to take bold steps that can ensure success for the talks. This success can be attained if the will of the peoples is duly reflected in the policy of all governments.

5. Resolutely to achieve progress in easing military tension in Europe and to take effective steps to reduce the level of the military confrontation on the continent of Europe by ensuring equal security for all European states. We call on the states that took part in the European Conference and are taking part in the Vienna talks on reductions of armed forces and armaments in Central Europe to do this.

6. To do away as soon as possible with the last remnants of colonialism and with the policy of neo-colonialist exploitation which is the main source of underdevelopment, and to pull out the roots of national and racial oppression.

It is the inalienable right of the peoples on all continents to live in conditions of peace, independence and freedom, to exercise sovereignty over their national wealth in conditions of ensured growth of their welfare, dignity and happiness for all citizens. No one has the right to interfere in the matters concerning their internal life, matters which they alone must decide. Colonial and racialist régimes in Africa and in any other area of the world should be condemned and boycotted by everyone as enemies of peace and humanity.

7. To seek persistently for a restructuring of international economic relations on a just and democratic basis, for the establishment of a new international economic order that will ensure the speedier elimination of the economic backwardness of developing countries and the dynamic progress of all peoples, of all mankind.

8. To act vigorously in the interests of securely establishing in international relations the standards of equality, non-interference in internal affairs, renunciation of the use or threat of force, respect for national independence and sovereignty and the inalienable right of every people to choose freely its own road of development in accordance with its will and aspirations; to build relations between states with strict observance of the principles adopted by the Conference on Security and Co-operation in Europe; unswervingly to pursue the policy of peaceful co-existence. In this connection, the states represented at the Conference reaffirm their determination to seek the establishment and development of extensive relations and co-operation on an equal footing among all countries of the world.

The states represented at the Conference of the Political Consultative Committee will spare no efforts in the struggle for the attainment of these aims and for the fulfilment of the just aspirations of the peoples. For the sake of all this they will co-operate still more closely and will collaborate on the international plane, while retaining fully the sovereign rights each of them.

At the same time the states represented at the Conference of the Political Consultative Committee regard as necessary for the success of this struggle the unification of the efforts sof all states irrespective of their social systems and political systems and their participation or non-participation in military alliances. They intend actively to facilitate the further development of such co-operation on the basis of peaceful co-existence and express their readiness to make a constructive contribution to that co-operation.

They are in favour of enhancing the role and effectiveness of the United Nations in accordance with the principles of its charter, in the interests of strengthening peace and international security, in the interests of deepening the relaxation of tension and of a just solution of pressing international problems and the enhancement of the cause of the freedom and progress of peoples.

In the struggle against imperialism, colonialism and neo-colonialism, for peace, security and the consolidation of the relaxation of international tension, and for ending the arms race the socialist countries represented at the Conference of the Political Consultative Committee, attach much importance to the development of co-operation and collaboration with non-aligned states. They regard the movement of non-aligned states as a positive factor in international politics and note their increased role in world affairs.

The Communist and Workers' Parties of the countries represented at the Conference will further develop fruitful comradely co-operation with fraternal parties in Europe and throughout the world. Socialist countries are prepared to conduct a constructive dialogue with socialists and social-democrats, with Christian Democrats, with religious leaders and organisations, with all public movements which stand for an end to the arms race, for removing the threat of war, for strengthening and deepening the relaxation of international tension.

The Warsaw Treaty member-countries which have assembled for the Conference of the Political Consultative Committee, are well aware of how great in scope and how difficult by its very nature is the main task — that of strengthening peace. But they are equally aware that the life, labour and better future of all peoples, regardless of their social system, the continent on which they live, or their level of economic development, depend on accomplishing this task. And they will do everything possible to ensure that this great task is accomplished and to ensure that mankind enters the 21st century in conditions of firm peace and extensive international co-operation.

Latin America

Cuba and the Movement of Non-Aligned Countries.

Statement by Carlos Rafael Rodriguez, Member of the Political Bureau of the Communist Party of Cuba and Vice-President of the Council of State and of the Council of Ministers of Cuba. Belgrade, 29 July, 1978.

(Complete Text).

Cuba, as a founder country, would never have gone to the initial conference of the Movement in Belgrade in 1961, nor would it have continued to take an active and disciplined part in the Movement if it had not agreed with the principles on which the call was based and which were explicitly set out in the first historic Belgrade Declaration.

We should first bear in mind the name of this Movement that is the heading of all summit conference declarations. It is a Movement of Non-Aligned Countries, and its basic constituent body is the Conference of the Heads of State and Government of the Non-Aligned Countries.

On more than one occasion, leaders of member countries have referred to it as the "movement of non-alignment," and even in documents of the Movement itself there have been references to the "principles of non-alignment."

But "non-alignment" is not the essence of our Movement; it is a sine qua non for being a member of the same. This is not a movement of which all countries that meet the requisite of not being party to military pacts, and therefore are not involved in those world military pacts whose dissolution is one of the objectives of the Movement, are or can be members. The Movement is a specific movement whose members are non-aligned countries that objectively subscribe to the programme and the goals for which it was set up, and that were set out in Belgrade 17 years ago and have been improved on in successive conferences of heads of state and government, but on the basis of those initial inalterable premises.

It was no accident that several countries that do not belong to military pacts and could formally also be considered non-aligned countries — for instance, Austria, Switzerland, Sweden, etc. — were not at the constituent conference in Belgrade. On analyzing the history of the non-aligned countries and the statements made by figures such as Tito, Nasser and Nehru, what becomes immediately clear is that the founding of the Movement was determined, decisively influenced, by the great historic victories of the national liberation movement of peoples fighting against colonialism, imperialism and neocolonialism between the end of World War II and the Belgrade Conference.

President Tito confirmed this in his opening speech at the current ministerial conference in Belgrade recalling that:

"The Non-Aligned Movement originated in the process of many peoples' national liberation from colonialism and the growth of a large number of newly independent countries, the greater part of them small and economically underdeveloped. This Movement has become an effective arm for their emancipation, for safeguarding their independence and for their active participation in international affairs as members of the international community with equal rights. Arising thus out of the anticolonial revolution, the Non-Aligned Movement has at the same time grown to be an active force in guaranteeing its further development and success."

Those historical origins are what have determined both the structure and composition of the Movement and its programme. This must not be forgotten.

Cuba stands firm by those principles on which the Movement of Non-Aligned Countries was founded.

We therefore agree that peace should be the first of our objectives but we also subscribe to the first postulate of the Belgrade Conference, which states that for there to be lasting peace, there has to be a world that comes of the clash between the old structure and the newly emerging national forces, a "world in which all forms of colonialist and imperialist domination have to be radically eliminated. . . ."

It was said in Belgrade, and we voice those same thoughts, that "If we are to basically eradicate the source of the conflicts, it means eradicating colonialism."

The first Belgrade Conference that, "The present-day world is characterized by the existence of different social systems." This is the starting point of all the positions Cuba takes on the international situation, and we agree with the 1961 declaration in that that difference between social systems is not in itself an obstacle to peace as long as all peoples and nations are allowed "to solve the problem of their political, economic, social and cultural system according to their own conditions, necessities and possibilities. . ." and that "Any attempt to impose one system or another on peoples by means of force is prevented. . . ."

Cuba reiterates that the countries that form part of our Movement must give our unlimited support to the full self-determination, independence and the right of peoples to choose their own road.

The first conference committed the non-aligned countries to giving their "support and encouragement to all peoples fighting for independence and equality." Cuba has made this a basic principle in its foreign policy and that is why, in all international forums and by any other means at our disposal we continue to defend the Belgrade recommendation for "the immediate, unconditional, total and definitive abolition of colonialism and the concerted effort to put an end to all kinds of neocolonialism and imperialist domination in all its forms and manifestations.''

We also continue to uphold the 1961 decision to ''demand that there be an immediate end to all armed action and all kinds of repressive measures directed against dependent peoples, that they might peacefully and freely exercise their right to complete independence.'' We also stand by ''respect for the territorial integrity of those countries.''

We have not repented having made the collective Belgrade commitment whereby the member countries of the Movement ''will scrupulously respect the territorial integrity of all states and oppose by all means any annexationist aims on the part of other nations.''

Cuba subscribed to this at the time and today ratifies its obligation as a member of the non-aligned countries to struggle in order that ''There be no intimidation, interference or intervention used against the peoples' exercising their right to self-determination, including their right to decide their own independent, constructive policies for attaining and maintaining sovereignty.''

Another basic aspect of the policy of the non-aligned countries concerns the problems of disarmament. Since 1961, our country has also contributed to outlining that policy.

At the recent United Nations Special Session on Disarmament, the Cuban delegation had the opportunity to defend all the principles on disarmament that were approved in Belgrade, at that first conference, and to maintain that ''General and complete disarmament must include the elimination of the armed forces, arms, foreign bases, arms output, plus the elimination of military training institutions and installations, except for those concerning internal unity,'' urging that the first steps be taken towards this noble objective.

At the Session, we also insisted on a principle that had come up in the early days of the Movement and is one of its main pillars: broadening the right for all countries in the international community to take part in decisions on world policy and in particular those affecting disarmament.

Those who appear surprised that Cuba should defend at that Session the idea of a world conference on disarmament, envisaged to snowball the process of general disarmament, should turn to paragraph 20 of the Belgrade Declaration, and there they will find a clear formulation of this agreement.

Lastly, as for the economic principles that are the basis for the Movement, Cuba ratifies its adherence to paragraph 21 of the Declaration which called for ''the elimination of the economic inequality inherited from colonialism and imperialism'' and all the demands that were made at the time, demands that were antecedents for the present programme of the new international economic order, which Cuba has supported and will continue to support fully.

As we have just seen, in the founding Conference of the Non-Aligned Countries held in this city, 17 years ago, there is not one postulate of our Movement that is not directed at condemning imperialism, colonialism and neocolonialism, pointing out that these reactionary forces of history are the main enemy of the peoples and inviting peoples to join with the non-aligned countries in the struggle to wipe such an infamous system of international oppression from the face of the earth.

Meeting for the second time three years later in Cairo, the Conference of Heads of State and Government had grown in number with the membership of peoples who had attained national independence in the struggle against those common enemies. It is not surprising, therefore, that the heads of state and government should first underline the fact that almost half of the independent countries of the world participated in that second Conference and go on to express their satisfaction over "the growing interest and confidence displayed by all the countries still under foreign domination and by those whose rights and sovereignty are being violated by imperialism and neocolonialism in the highly positive role of the non-aligned countries in settling international disputes. . ."

The Cairo Conference, after recognizing that some progress had been made with regard to relations between the two greatest powers, gave an alarm signal.

Why? Against which forces?

It doesn't take much to find out. The Cairo Conference on noting that "There are still forces of tension existing in many parts of the world," added, "This situation shows that the forces of imperialism" — I repeat, **the forces of imperialism** — "are still powerful and that they do not hesitate in resorting to the use of force to defend their interests and maintain their privileges."

A few paragraphs further on, the Cairo Conference expressed its satisfaction over the fact that "The national liberation movement in various regions of the world is engaged in a heroic struggle against neocolonialism, the practices of apartheid and racial discrimination."

It is not necessary to quote more from the Conferences out of which our Movement originated. On going over the documents of the Non-Aligned Movement, it will be clear that the non-aligned countries were not called together to form a new international bloc, to set themselves up as a neutral force, exclusively to defend the idea of non-alignment as a political objective, but to organize themselves into a coherent force fighting for peace, national independence, progress and democracy against a clearly defined enemy; the forces of colonialism, imperialism, neocolonialism and apartheid.

For this reason, Dr. Osvaldo Dorticós, the first representative of our country in a conference of heads of state, in Belgrade, underlined the fact that being "non-aligned," that is, not being involved in military pacts, does not mean that we should be countries with no kind of commitment. "We are committed," he said then, "to our own principles," principles that Cuba clearly identified with those set out in the first declaration.

In Cairo, Cuba's representative, on referring to the "non-aligned" nature of the member countries, said, with the approval and support of those gathered there:

"We believe this to be an opportune moment to stand scrupulously by our principles, to reiterate that, while it is true that Cuba has considered itself to have the right to participate in this Conference, in view of the fact that it is not party to any military bloc and meets all the conditions set out in the requirements to do so, we should say that for Cuba non-alignment does not mean, and nor should it for any of the countries represented here, a position of neutrality and abstention before the serious problems concerning war and peace, the aspiration common to all peoples for a more just life, the liberation movements, and the aspirations for development and progress. . . ."

The Cuban delegation clearly stressed then:

"We reject fence-sitting before the dilemma of peace and war. . . . We reject fence-sitting before the dilemma of neocolonialism on the one hand and the peoples' freedom on the other; colonialism and imperialism on one side and true social and economic independence for peoples on the other. We must speak out and take action against imperialist and neocolonialist forces. We reject fence-sitting before the dilemma of true equality for all men on the one hand and the practice of racial discrimination on the other. . . . We reject fence-sitting before the dilemma of the struggle to overcome underdevelopment and the backwardness of peoples on the one hand and the imperialist policy of exploitation that thrives on that under-development, backwardness and unequal exchange on the other. . . ."

Fourteen years later, at the celebrations for the 25th anniversary of the attack on the Moncada Garrison, Fidel Castro reiterated that it was impossible to remain neutral regarding the African peoples and their neo-colonizers, Angola and its invaders, the rights of the people of the Sahara and those occupying their territory, the Ethiopian Revolution and the Somali aggressor, the Revolution in Yemen and Arab reaction, Vietnam and those threatening and harassing that country, the people of South Africa and the South African racists, the Patriotic Front of Zimbabwe and Ian Smith, Mozambique and the Rhodesian fascists, Namibia and its colonizers, the people of Cyprus and the foreign occupiers, the progressive and right-wing forces in Lebanon, Allende and Pinochet. One cannot remain neutral before matters such as Panama's sovereignty over the Canal, the peoples of Belize and Puerto Rico's right to independence, the blockade on Cuba and the Guantánamo naval base.

Today Cuba reaffirms those principles it defended in 1961 and 1964. Cuba has not changed, nor does it want to change, the postulates of the Movement of Non-Aligned Countries. Those who changed were others, those who at one time proclaimed themselves to be socialists and yet used military force thinking that it would be easy to conquer another non-aligned country's territory; those who are again calling on neocolonial forces to defend their corrupt governments, stained with the blood of thousands of their brothers, hated tyrannies that not even the imperialists can prop up and defend; those who are out to put that neocolonizing presence and solidarity contributing to African liberation on a par with each other.

Cuba's statements to the Belgrade and Cairo Conferences were no more than a reaffirmation of the principles on which our Movement was founded. Thus, it is not surprising that at that same Cairo Conference President Tito should be heard to say categorically, "The policy of non-alignment was never and could never have been a policy of fence-sitting."

We see the Non-Aligned Movement as an association of countries with differing social and political ideas, belonging to different socioeconomic, religious or lay systems but with a bond that characterizes the participation of all in the Movement: that of not being involved in any of the global military pacts and of accepting the programme of the Movement as clearly defined at Belgrade and Cairo.

It is to that programme that Cuba is committed. If some member country wants to change the orientation of the programme of the Non-Aligned Movement, that country is not Cuba. Cuba will be opposed to it.

At the Colombo Conference, the president of the Arab Al-Yamahiria of Libya, His Excellency Muammar El Khadafi, proposed that in each summit conference there should be a review of the member countries to see which had and which hadn't carried out the previous period's programme and hadn't stood by the commitments of the Non-Aligned Movement. If this were to be done, it would have to be decided to expel from the Movement those countries that instead of giving aid to another non-aligned sister country subjected it to military invasion, for which they did not hesitate in claiming help and weapons from the imperialists and former colonizers; those that called on the military forces of the countries that had before colonized Africa, so as to crush internal rebellion against their corrupt régimes, would have to be expelled from the Movement.

When any country that proclaims itself to be non-aligned tries to refute Cuba's policy of solidarity with the peoples of Africa, it forgets above all that one of the principles reiterated at the various Conferences of the Movement has been the member countries' recommendation that they go to help other member countries of the Non-Aligned Movement whose sovereignty and territorial integrity are being threatened. That is why the best reply to those who, at the service of imperialist policy, try to contest Cuba's non-alignment because of its support for the peoples of Africa is the agreement reached by the Colombo Conference of Heads of State and Government. This agreement, after congratulating the Government and people of Angola on their heroic and victorious struggle against the racist South African invaders and their allies, "praised the Republic of Cuba and the other states that helped the people of Angola to frustrate the expansionist, colonialist strategy of the racist régime of South Africa and its allies."

Cuba believes that it is a permanent duty of a member country to work to prevent conflicts from developing among the countries making up the Movement and, in general, among the developing countries that rose to independence in the struggle against imperialism, colonialism and neo-colonialism. Cuba will spare no effort in trying to prevent such conflicts from arising. Various Cuban leaders, especially the president of Cuba, Comrade Fidel Castro, during several months gave over long work sessions to reach an understanding based on principles which would resolve the differences between Ethiopia and Somalia. These discussions were held in Havana, Colombo, Somalia and Ethiopia, and were later transferred to the People's Democratic Republic of Yemen, during the long hours in which fake intransigence on the part of the president of Somalia served as a pretext for him to block any agreement and as preamble to military aggression in Ogaden.

That is why, when the imperialists try to condemn our military presence in the Horn of Africa, we can say clearly and proudly that no country contributed more than Cuba, that no government contributed more than the Cuban Government to possible peace, based on the principles of the non-aligned countries.

Let us say a few words about the problem of so-called bloc-ism.

One of the bases of the Movement of Non-Aligned Countries in 1961 and 1964, and one that has so far not been modified, is the concept that the existence of two powerful military pacts made up of countries with enough military potential to destroy the whole of humankind has created a danger that has to be eliminated by struggling to overcome this alarming situation. This implies struggling to eliminate those and other military pacts and blocs.

But in not one of the definitions that were the basis for the Movement of Non-Aligned Countries can there be found any judgement on the political content or nature of those pacts and the membership of the pacts. In the basis of our Movement, there is no statement that identifies the two blocs equally as enemies of the non-aligned countries and of the peoples not grouped in those military pacts. Cuba would never have accepted that.

For that same reason, Cuba rejects the notion that its commitment as a member country of the Movement implies the obligation to thus identify the policies practiced by the contradictory social systems that prevail in contemporary history today.

Neither is it the case, nor has it ever been the case, that Cuba would expect the Movement of Non-aligned Countries to condemn NATO and applaud the Warsaw Pact. That is not the problem. What Comrade Fidel Castro maintained and we reiterate today here is that they are two different things and that all the documents coming out of the various conferences of the non-aligned countries, from Belgrade in 1961 to Belgrade in 1978 confirm, line by line, that the struggle that we have had to sustain and that is being sustained by the peoples of Asia, Africa and Latin America to maintain their independence, sovereignty and equality among peoples and races, to reject interference and to guarantee economic development is a struggle against the imperialists, the former colonialists, the racists and those practicing apartheid and aggressive Zionism. These, not others, are our enemies.

There has been an attempt to distort the vein and exact meaning of the courageous, historic speech made by Cuba's head of state, Comrade Fidel Castro, in Algiers, when skilful propaganda was brought into play with the powerful backing of the communications media of imperialism to spread the false idea to the effect that Comrade Fidel Castro, our Government and the Cuban delegations tried to make the Movement of Non-Aligned Countries an appendage of the socialist countries, in particular the Soviet Union.

We categorically reject this falsification. No one can distort the clear meaning and unmistakable words of President Fidel Castro in Algiers.

There he denounced the disturbing tendency of trying to pit the non-aligned countries against the socialist countries. He rejected outright the false theory of the two imperialisms. He demonstrated that nobody can reject what has been proclaimed in several ways by the founders of the Movement, by Tito, by Nehru, by Nasser, by Nkrumah: the link between the October Revolution and the end of colonialism.

But none of this implies any aim to deprive the Movement of Non-Aligned Countries of its independent role in international politics, of its identity and of the specific nature of its principles.

No one could demand that a non-aligned country, because it belonged to the Movement, should take up socialist theories or support them or even show a preference for the foreign policy of the socialist countries. But it is a fact that while the non-aligned countries may at the same time be socialist and non-aligned — as Yugoslavia and Cuba have been from the start and others later proclaimed themselves, as in the case of Vietnam, Korea and many others who have recently joined the Movement — no imperialist country, nor any country that supports or approves of imperialist policy which has been repeatedly condemned by all our Conferences, could be a member of this Movement.

This is what it's all about, nothing else. We do not expect, much less do we demand that anyone approve of our country's conviction — although

is a conviction shared by decisive forces in the Non-Aligned Movement —
that, far from being enemies of the objectives of our Movement, the
socialist countries, by the very nature of their system and their politics, are
natural allies in the struggle against colonialism, neocolonialism, imperialism, apartheid, racism and Zionism.

In 1964 on defining the policy of the non-aligned countries, President
Tito said that that policy "with its progressive action, in the common
struggle with the socialist countries and other progressive forces, has come
to be one of the most important factors in the balance of forces today, and
in changing the present state of world affairs and speeding up social
processes of a progressive nature."

Talking on the same theme at Algiers in 1965, President Tito outlined
the theoretical concept of the need for alliance, saying the following:

"If all the socialist forces, together with progressive and peace-loving
forces throughout the world, were to consistently practice a policy of co-
existence. . . the balance of forces would tip more favourably on the side of
those standing for peace and progress."

And in an interview with the editor of the Cairo newspaper *Akbar al
Yom* in 1965 President Tito stated:

"Progressive social development in the recently liberated countries. . .
means considerable backing for the socialist forces on the international
scene."

Cuba's position has been confirmed by two Conferences of Heads of
State and Government: in Algiers, clause seven of the approved declaration
stated that "The heads of state or government of the non-aligned countries
are unanimous in believing that the policy of non-alignment, together with
other peace-loving, democratic and progressive forces, constitutes an
important and irreplaceable factor in the struggle for the freedom and independence of peoples and countries, for general peace, and equal security for
all states; for the universal application of the principles of active and peaceful coexistence, for the democratization of international relations, for
overall cooperation on an equitable basis, for economic development and
social progress. . . ."

And the Declaration of the Colombo Conference, after reaffirming the
need to maintain the closest unity within the Movement of Non-Aligned
Countries, also stated that:

"They must continue to pursue their aim of cooperating with all
progressive and peace-loving forces throughout the world and thus
strengthen their ability to successfully struggle against imperialism and the
latter's desperate attempts to recover ground lost over recent years."

That is the unity we proclaim and support. That is the unity approved by
the Movement of Non-Aligned Countries. Cuba is for that alliance.

But, for the same reason, Cuba does not renounce the right — more
than a right, a duty — to reject the pretensions of some in falsifying the

principles of the Movement, principles aimed against imperialism, colonialism and neocolonialism, and trying to turn our Movement into an antisocialist one.

Cuba also rejects any country's attempt to exercise hegemony over another state by exerting its political, military or economic superiority. But we are also opposed to the use of political definitions and concepts in our non-aligned documents in a context other than that approved by the heads of state and government in our Conferences. We reject the attempt on the part of a certain known power alien to the Movement of Non-Aligned Countries — that has been accused by three small countries like Vietnam, Albania and Cuba of having hegemonic pretensions where they were concerned — to use for its own anti-Soviet propaganda purposes statements made by the non-aligned countries that are of no such nature. In Colombo, the heads of state already gave a very clear definition, which we stand by, when proclaiming in Point 32 of the Declaration issued at Sri Lanka, that:

"If colonialism, as it has been traditionally understood, is coming to its end, the problem of imperialism persists and it might well be feared to persist in the foreseeable future, under the forms of neocolonialism and hegemonic relations. . . ."

That is why the non-aligned countries were called on to be "on the alert for all forms of unequal relations and domination that go to make up imperialism."

Up to now, this is the only way we see the concept of hegemony can be dealt with in the Movement of Non-Aligned Countries.

Nevertheless, we agree that the Movement must be prepared to use the political concept of hegemony in the full sense of the word. Political and economic hegemony has been used in the history of states since the time of Greece and Rome. It came before and has come after colonialism and imperialism. It persists over time in diverse forms. As we have said, it has recently been used to define China's brutal threats against Vietnam; and many neighbouring states, some of them non-aligned, accuse each other of having hegemonic intentions. One of the tasks that we can undertake during the intervening months from Belgrade to Havana is to generalize this political concept and introduce it in the Movement's declarations, in an adequate form, acceptable to all.

From 1979 on, the role of presiding over the Non-Aligned Movement will fall on Cuba as host country. That is why we wanted to avail ourselves of this important opportunity afforded by the ministerial conference of the non-aligned countries' being held in Belgrade and to take advantage of the fruitful exchange of opinions during this meeting with many personalities representing a great number of countries and currents in the Movement, to outline, on behalf of the Cuban Government, and by way of complementing the words of our Foreign Minister Isidoro Malmierca, the principles whereby Cuba, complying with the decisions of the Conferences of Non-Aligned Countries, will set out its responsibilities in preparing for the Havana Conference and its obligations and duties from the Conference on.

Cuba shares the opinion that under contemporary conditions, the fact of being committed to participate in the Movement of Non-Aligned Countries is implicitly right away a progressive attitude. Evidently, if the principles of our programmes are acted upon, there will be a struggle for peace, for general and complete disarmament and against colonialism, neo-colonialism, imperialism, racism, apartheid, Zionism, foreign interference and all forms of domination that stem from the system of exploitation that they have engendered.

At the same time, Cuba recognizes the heterogeneous nature of the Movement, the fact that it is made up of states with different social systems, guided by different political concepts, that at times view not only the factors of the world situation but also the way in which the very programme of the non-aligned countries must be carried out in practice in very different lights.

This was the reason behind President Tito's saying in the early days of the Movement that our unity "does not force us to have unanimity."

One task we must all work at, and Cuba will certainly keep working at, is that of respecting unity and doing our utmost to reach unanimity. In this, Cuba has the right and feels under the obligation to defend its opinions sincerely and on a wide scale in all forums of the Movement.

Cuba sees the Movement as an independent force, whose purpose is not that of serving any other force active in international politics, as its tool or reserve. But, at the same time, for the reasons firmly expressed by Cuba's Head of State Fidel Castro, in Algiers, Cuba continues to believe that in the field of international action, it has become an objective need of contemporary history that there be a bond between the Movement and the forces of peace, independence and progress, in order to achieve the objectives set out in the Movement programme. The socialist countries occupy an essential place among such forces.

Lastly, we are of the opinion that the directing bodies of the Movement, its Presidency, its Coordinating Bureau, its ministerial conferences, when acting on behalf of the non-aligned countries, cannot express the opinion of any one country or group of countries, but are obliged to fully respect the Movement programme and the agreements of successive Conferences.

Soviet Union and Eastern Europe

Josip Broz Tito. The League of Communists of Yugoslavia — the Leading and Guiding Ideological-Political Force in Society.*

(Excerpts).

*Extensive excerpts from the fifth part of President Tito's Report to the Eleventh Congress of the LCY, presented on 20 June and entitled "The League of the Communists of Yugoslavia in the Struggle for Further Development of Socialist, Self-Managing and Nonaligned Yugoslavia".

. . . It is the duty of the League of Communists and other socialist forces to consolidate the self-management role of the working man in associated labour, to strengthen the position of the working class as the spearhead of the revolution. Only an organized and united working class, together with other working people, can successfully resist the various pressures from bureaucratic and technocratic monopolies, which usually demagogically represent themselves as the allged champions of the interests of associated labour or the state.

New socio-economic and political relations based on the Constitution and Law on Associated Labour cannot be instituted by spontaneous action but only by the conscious and organized ideological and political activity of the socialist forces of society, led by the League of Communists. Only in this way can our revolution go forward. It has so far won victories and achieved successes thanks primarily to the fact that it has not been a slave to any models or dogmas, nor has it fallen into the pitfall of expediency; rather, guided by the achievements of our contemporary socialist theory and practice, it has always relied on the creative and revolutionary action of the working class and the broadest strata of society.

The tasks confronting us today relate to putting our new socio-economic and political system into operation. This system, as we have conceived and constituted it, is centred on man, on his freedom and happiness, on his rights as a producer and self-manager, on his immediate and long-term interests. The revolutionary struggle of our working class and its communist vanguard is being waged for precisely these goals. Indeed, socialism is the historical process of the emancipation of labour and the working class, the emancipation of the personality, a process in which man becomes the true master of his life and work.

It is imperative for all guiding socialist forces to be active on all fronts in solving the problems of society. In the multitude of different interests pursued by self-managing entities, these forces, notably the League of Communists, stand for that which is common to our socialist society. Therefore the League of Communists must be present wherever self-managers take decisions, and it must be an inner driving force of the system and not above or beyond it. In democratic cooperation with all producers, communists must see to it that the self-managers themselves freely voice and coordinate their specific and general immediate and long-term interests, and that they adopt the most rational decisions on all matters affecting both their own life and work and the development of socio-political communities at the local and higher levels. For such democratic decision-making to succeed, the working man must be aware that his personal interests can only be satisfied if they are coordinated and brought into line with the general collective interests. It is in fostering such an awareness that the League of Communists in fact has an irreplaceable role.

The League of Communists, therefore, must be firmly established within the delegate system. It must give decisive assistance to making the delegate system a powerful instrument serving the entire self-managing society. To this end, the League of Communists should conduct a creative dialogue with the working people on a basis of equality, in close conjunction with delegations and delegates, in an organized ideological-political effort to reach the most effective solutions — in associated labour, in local communities and self-management interest unions, and in delegate assemblies, in short, in the entire political system of our socialist self-managing democracy.

The Unity of the LCY and Democratic Centralism

The ideological-political and action unity of the League of Communists, on the principles of democratic centralism, will continue in the future as heretofore to be the warranty of our successes and victories. It is the key prerequisite for the further development of socialist self-managing society and the strengthening of the equality, brotherhood and unity of the nations and nationalities of Yugoslavia.

In this connection I should like to point out that in this past period the Central Committee of the LCY has been unanimous on all the essential question of the building of socialism and our foreign policy. The leagues of communists of the socialist republics and autonomous provinces and their central and provincial committees have made a full contribution to strengthening the unity of the LCY. Their responsibility for formulating and implementing the uniform policy of the LCY was also strongly reaffirmed at the recent republican congresses and provincial conferences.

Of course, we must continue to consolidate the ideological and action unity of our ranks, primarily in day-to-day work on carrying out assignments. Only in this way will we be able to earn the confidence of the working people ever anew, just as unity itself must be reforged and reasserted at each new stage. Unity is not an abstract notion; it is achieved in the closest possible correlation with reality, with the development of socio-economic relations, through the adjustment of different interests in society, including the different interests held by various sections of the working class. Furthermore, our society has still not rid itself of various negative tendencies. The discrepancy between word and deed is particularly harmful. There is still strong resistance from various technocratic-bureaucratic monopolies. Because of differing and conflicting interests, some public organs sometimes take a biased attitude. Therefore in addition to improving the political system, we must formulate the kind of policy for the League of Communists and the entire society which will secure the greatest possible unity of action. It is in this way that we shall be able to combat all anti-self-management tendencies most effectively. The League of Communists must particularly wage a constant struggle against those who try to use the objective difficulties and contradictions in our development to prevent different interests from being reconciled in a democratic way. In doing so they are essentially refuting the equality of the nations and nationalities and denying the crucial role of the interests of the working class. . .

Democratic relations within the League of Communists itself are of special importance if it is to perform its leading role. Therefore in the future democratic centralism will remain the fundamental principle governing the internal relations, organization and overall activities of the League of Communists of Yugoslavia. It guarantees the broadest possible democracy in formulating policy and adopting decisions and the strongest unity in carrying them out. In this way each member, each organization and each leadership of the LCY can display the greatest possible initiative and creativity. Democratic centralism in the LCY is also a basic prerequisite and premise for the democratic development of our society as a whole. Therefore in the further building of internal relations and strengthening of the unity of the LCY, democratic centralism must be consistently applied and enriched.

Discussions in the League of Communists should be free and democratic. In fact, a battle of opinion aimed at seeking the best answers is a function of ideological unity. Creative, unified action is predicted on such democratic relations. The policies and decisions adopted by the majority become binding on each communist, including those who held a contrary opinion. They may maintain their view, but they must carry out the majority decision in practice. Any other behaviour would lead to clannishness and factionalism, to a disruption of the unity of the League of Communists of Yugoslavia.

The free and open expression of opinions and principled criticism are the best remedy for irresponsible criticism, demagoguery, politicking and similar ills. We are a revolutionary organization, which people join voluntarily, motivated by their ideological convictions and the desire to make a personal contribution to the revolution, to the emancipation of man and his labour. The communist must feel himself to be free, equal and needed by the working class. A creative dialogue can only be conducted in an atmosphere of democratic and comradely relations among people who freely express their opinion on every problem so that policies can be jointly formulated and concerted action taken. Therefore we must constantly foster democratic relations within the League of Communists, as the best instrument for achieving revolutionary and creative unity.

The League of Communists strives for democracy, which also entails responsibility and is a prerequisite for the effective performance of public affairs. Our unceasing efforts to achieve this kind of socialist and self-managing democracy are what distinguish us communists from the petty bourgeois, liberals and others of their ilk, who think democracy only means having rights but not also public responsibility. . .

Forms of Organization and Action of the League of Communists

The League of Communists will successfully carry out its leading ideological and political role in the new conditions as well by devising the appropriate forms and methods of action so that within the socio-economic and political system it can consistently press for socialist self-management oriented solutions to the key problems of development, about which I have already spoken. To this end we shall discuss amendments and additions to the LCY Statute at this Congress.

Special attention should be paid to the basic organization of the League of Communists, as the fundamental form of overall policy-making and ideological-political action of communists. It is in its basic organizations that the League of Communists carries out its direct communication with the working class and working people. Thanks to the formation of its basis organizations in the basic organizations of associated labour and in work and local communities, the League of Communists has become incorporated into the basic cells of society. After the Tenth Congress the proliferation of numerically small organizations continued and has had a positive effect on fostering the initiative and activity of communists and on strengthening the ideological influence of the League of Communists. Experience has shown that the Party has always been more effective when its basic organizations have been active. Today, too, communists must be exemplary revolutionaries in every way, indivisibly linked with the masses. That is why we opted for the establishment of smaller basic organizations. Since 1971, when we had 15,825 basic organizations, their number has constantly been growing from year to year. In early 1974 there were 26,575, and by the end of 1977 there were 47,212 basic organizations. The conditions have thereby been created for communists to operate even more directly and successfully.

Communists need daily dialogues and consultations with other working people directly on the job, in workers' assemblies, in labour union meetings, in the workers' council and so forth. It is here and not behind closed doors that the fundamental problems of a given environment should be discussed, that policies should be decided upon and the best answers found. In their overall activity the communists must set an example in their devotion to principles, knowledgeableness and high degree of political culture, which implies patience and respect for the opinions of others. Communists must have a keen awareness of everything that is going on around them and be attuned to the true desires of the working people. . .

The increasing success in performing the tasks set by the Tenth Congress has further strengthened the confidence of the working people in the revolutionary course and policy of the League of Communists of Yugoslavia. This fact has had a palpable effect on the growth of the League of Communists, which has swelled its ranks in the meantime from the 700,000 members registered at the end of 1977 to the present 1,629,029 members. It is noteworthy that most of the new members are young people, more than 71%, so that the League of Communists has been greatly rejuvenated, and age-wise its membership makes it one of the youngest Communist parties. This fact also shows that the policy of the League of Communists coincides with the interests and desires of the young generations as well, who see their future in socialist self-management and willingly undertake the responsibility for its further development. I have great confidence in our young generations. I am confident that our youth will courageously and with credit continue along the revolutionary path blazed by preceding generations and that they will promote the gains of our revolution with all their might.

The social composition of the League of Communists is changing for the better as well, albeit somewhat more slowly. Since the last Congress more than 166,000 workers have joined, so that today almost one third of the members of the League of Communists, or close to half a million, are direct producers. If we add to this number all the others who work in direct production in self-managing associated labour and live on their own earnings, then we can consider half the membership of the LCY to belong to the working class.

Some organizations, however, still do not take the view that efforts should be made to achieve a working class majority in the League of Communists, so that this goal remains one of our top priorities. The working class is the spearhead of the socialist revolution, and therefore it is imperative for the direct producers to form a majority in the ranks of its vanguard. In this respect, there are still certain ambiguities that must be removed in regard to the social composition of the membership. There are still incorrect views on who is today a worker. The pattern of the work force has qualitatively changed in this country, too, with the expansion of productive forces and the application of science and modern technology. There are more and more people with higher education working in the direct manufacture of material goods. In the modern technological process of production even a doctor of science is a direct producer, just like the worker behind the machine. Therefore, technicians and other educated personnel whose work is a direct function of the process of production are also a component part of the working class.

After a period of stagnation, the number of private agricultural producers in the League of Communists has slowly been climbing, and today there are close to 80,000. It must be borne in mind that in this country the migration of the rural population into towns and industry is still going on. Nevertheless, we must not be satisfied with the present number of farmers in the League of Communists. Their representation is not commensurate with their activity in the socialist transformation of the countryside and the advancement of agricultural production.

The number of women in the League of Communists has also grown, considerably, by about 160,000, so that now they account for over 23%. Special attention should be focused on admitting working women from material production and women from agricultural activities. I must say that in this respect there is still sectarianism. In some environments a conservative attitude is taken towards the role of women in socio-political life.

Working people and the youth obviously desire to be members of the vanguard, whose policies reflect their own personal aspirations and ideological-political convictions. There are, however, cases when individuals join the League of Communists to further their careers or for similar reasons, and this happens most often in places other than material production. Such people usually lapse once they have joined the Party or else leave the League of Communists. Of course, the League must not be sectarian in the future or close its doors to anyone taking part in the struggle to promote socialist self-management. Clearly there must be criteria, and admission of new members must be carried out systematically and in an organized fashion. New members should also be given greater assistance in improving their ideological and political education, so that they might successfully carry out their day-to-day tasks.

As I have always said, it is not the number of members that is crucial for a revolutionary party such as our League of Communists, but rather its ideological-political level, its ability as the leading force in society to mobilize and guide the working people in the struggle for socialism. A communist has been and remains a conscious soldier of the revolution, prepared to give his all for its ideals and goals. That is why the eyes of the nation are rightly turned towards the communists, towards what they do. It must never be forgotten that the work and behaviour of individuals affect the reputation of the League of Communists as a whole. Therefore a communist must excel in those virtues which reflect his dedication to class goals and the human values of the movement to which he belongs. He must constantly improve his ideological and moral character, must constantly study and extend his knowledge. All this is a necessary prerequisite for successful social action.

The Ideological Training of Communists

Since the Tenth Congress the organizations and leaderships of the League of Communists have been very active in the ideological-political education of communists and other working people. It is safe to say that there have been few projects carried out on such a scale in the years since the war.

As I have already said, Marxist centres have been set up in all the republics and provinces and in some large towns and work organizations. Many political schools have been established, and other forms of ideological-political education have been introduced.

The further improvement of the practices of our socialist self-management also requires ambitious undertakings as regards ideological-political education. We have opted for fostering cooperation between different spheres of work and social life, which is a new practice in many respects. Such a policy requires people to have much greater knowledge, broader horizons, and a broad culture. Our working man enjoys a status which allows him to take part at his place of work in decision-making on all matters concerning the expansion of his basic organization of associated labour, his commune and community as a whole. In order to resolve the questions, he pools part of the income which is the result of his labour, among other things. This status demands of him a profound understanding of the laws governing social development. Even more is required of the members of the League of Communists. They must have the knowledge that will enable them to analyze the relationships and situation in which they are acting, and to find answers that will strengthen socialist self-management in the multiplicity of different interests.

Ideological-political education makes communists more committed and conscious champions of further social transformations. Marxist culture changes their way of thinking and their feelings, their attitude towards other people and social problems.

Marxist education also gives communists a deeper insight into the social roots of anti-socialist and anti-self-management ideologies and the various ways in which they are manifested. In short, it equips them for the ideological struggle. . .

Personnel Policy

The League of Communists has always devoted great attention to training personnel and to personnel policy in general. This policy, which covers the entire process from ideological-political and professional training to the candidacy and election of people to specific posts, must be the concern of the working people associated in self-management and of the organized socialist forces led by the League of Communists. In pursuing this policy we take as our terms of reference the interests and goals of the working class and all working people and the practical tasks involved in building socialist self-management.

We must resolutely strengthen the class character of personnel policy and promote planning on a long-range basis. Uniform goals and criteria and democracy in implementing personnel policy make possible the all-round training and public involvement of working people as free and responsible personalities. Accordingly, the working, professional, ideological-political and moral qualities of people and their firm commitment to socialist self-management are extremely important. This particularly holds true for those who are elected to responsible positions of leadership. At the same time, we must head off tendencies of monopolization, formation of cliques and incumbency in several public offices by concluding public and democratic social compacts among the formulators of personnel policy — among whom the Socialist Alliance has a special role.

The League of Communists and all organized socialist forces must persevere in carrying out the adopted personnel policy in a consistent manner. Working people and citizens should make a greater use of their constitutional right to take direct and responsible decisions on the election and deployment of personnel to responsible jobs and positions of leadership. The League of Communists has the obligation of providing unwavering support to our millions of self-managers in their efforts to gain control over personnel policy. There should be a larger number of candidates in the process of nomination and election for each position, even the most responsible ones; of course they must meet the required criteria. Then people will truly be able, according to their own evaluation and convictions, to elect the best people who will then receive full support in their work. In this way individuals will not be able to hold the same positions for such a long time, causing them to become bureaucratized, nor will there be an unprincipled scramble for offices and positions, which is causing us serious political harm.

Individuals and groups must be prevented from deciding on personnel policy and selection without reference to elected organs and bodies, or allegedly on their behalf but in fact in contravention to the principles and criteria of our personnel policy. There have been quite a few such attempts in the recent past, and they still appear today, although less frequently.

The recent elections of delegations and delegates, and the elections in the League of Communists and socio-political organizations, clearly showed that our working people and citizens know who are the best people in their particular environments, people in whom they can have confidence and from whom they can expect the best results. There are more and more workers from direct production among the delegates and members elected to various organs and leadership bodies. There is also a larger number of young people and women. However, their representation is still not proportionate to their social role and real contribution to building socialism. The reasons for such a state of affairs are opposition from conservative individuals and groups, from bureaucratic and technocratic establishments and the insufficient involvement of various organizations and organs of the League of Communists.

The adoption of a social compact on personnel policy in the federation and its effective implementation are of great importance for the democratic and efficient solving of collective and individual problems of all our republics and provinces and for strengthening the equality and unity of our nations and nationalities. Therefore in the future we must be resolute and consistent in achieving an equal and proportional representation of personnel from the republics and provinces in the organs and organizations at the federal level.

In accordance with the character of our socialist self-managing democracy, the policy and practice should be encouraged of a non-professional performance of responsible duties in the League of Communists, socio-political organizations, delegate assemblies and other organizations and organs. It should also be arranged so that after their mandates have expired officials will return to their previous organizations, in conformity with the principle of replacement and recruitment of new people.

Personnel policy is one of the strategical considerations in our efforts to promote socialist self-management, and therefore it will continue in the future to be of special concern to the League of Communists.

* * *

Comrades,

I know that in a report it is not possible to review everything that has been achieved since the Tenth Congress. I have dwelt in more detail on those areas in which we will have the most important tasks in the coming period. These tasks will be defined in far greater detail during the discussion and in the Congress documents. However, we can already safely say that the League of Communists of Yugoslavia, as a party of revolutionary action, will achieve new victories in the struggle for socialist self-management and the all-round advancement of our country, a community of free people and equal, fraternal nations and nationalities.

Socialist, self-managing and nonaligned Yugoslavia rests on firm and enduring foundations, reliable main-stays for its future.

The strength of Yugoslavia lies in the heroism and fortitude of its nations and nationalities, who have been steeled through history and stood the test of the severest trials during the great liberation war.

Its strength lies in their unity and the consciousness that this unity in the present-day world, in which might has still not bowed to reason — is a prerequisite not only for prosperity but indeed for their very survival.

Its strength lies in the ideas which inspire us and in the goals for which we are fighting.

Its strength lies in the working class and its decisive role in society, in our working people who, although still facing many difficulties and sacrifices, have more and are better off with every passing day.

Its strength lies in our young generation, who have embraced the achievements of the revolution as their own and know that they have enjoyed a longer period of work and life in freedom and peace than any other previous generation on this soil.

Its strength lies in the system of socialist self-management, which makes it possible for the Yugoslav citizen to make free and sovereign decisions on his own work and the results of his work and which protects him from any form of enslavement or coercion, from everything that might impede the all-round development of the free human personality.

Its strength lies in the broad front of organized socialist forces, led by the League of Communists, vanguards not just in their ideological commitment and rich revolutionary experience, but also in their ability to signpost the ways and directions of further development.

Its strength lies in total national defence, with its striking force of the Yugoslav People's Army, which is characterized by ideological-moral resolve, combat readiness and up-to-date equipment.

Its strength lies in our independence and nonaligned policy, in the fact that we talk even with the greatest powers as equals and that we cooperate on a footing of equality with virtually all the countries of the world.

Its strength lies in the high prestige of socialist and nonaligned Yugoslavia, in our numerous friends throughout the world, in a position which few countries have secured for themselves in international affairs.

Therefore we look to tomorrow with confidence and optimism. I am confident that after this Congress, we shall embark upon new action to promote socialism and human happiness with a clearer view of the future and at an even quicker pace.

Resolution of the Eleventh Congress of the League of the Communists of Yugoslavia.*

(Excerpts).

* The Resolution which was adopted by the Congress on 23 June, is a lengthy document of some ten thousand words and consists of five parts. Printed below are extensive excerpts from parts III and IV dealing with the international communist and working class movement and Balkan relations respectively.

III

1. Profound changes are occurring within the workers' and other progressive movements. All organized progressive socio-political forces, parties, movements and trade unions are today in the process of continual

re-examination and adjustment of their programmes and political practice, in step with the turbulent economic-social and political change which is sweeping through the world in general and each country in particular.

In the course of this process, within workers' and other progressive movements and parties, independence and autonomy are being asserted in formulating the strategy and the tactics of their struggle. The role of communist parties is strengthening in a number of countries, and the views are prevailing on the need for cooperation among parties on new foundations. Confirmation is constantly provided that the diversity of roads and forms of the struggle for socialism the independence and autonomy of the subjects of this struggle, as well as cooperation on an equal footing and solidarity among them represent an objective law governing the development of socialism as a world-wide process. Relations among communist, socialist, socio-democratic, national, national-liberation, and other progressive and democratic movements and parties are increasingly founded on the principles of autonomy, non-interference in internal affairs, and responsibility before one's own class and people.

The League of Communists of Yugoslavia considers that only on these principles is it possible, in present conditions, to promote voluntary and equitable cooperation and internationalist solidarity of the working class of individual countries and of other progressive social and political forces, attended by mutual understanding and consideration for different interests, ideas and stances. This makes possible a more effective effort both to overcome tendencies of nationalism, or the denial of the positive experiences of others, and of declaring one's own experiences as universally valid.

These positive processes are opposed by conservative and dogmatic forces, who strive to preserve the obsolete relations, upholding, among other things, various forms of centralistic institutionalisation of the international activity of communists, or socialist and social-democratic parties. Positive processes in the workers' movement are still fraught with numerous contradictions and resistances; new forms of differentiation, division and splits occur, old mistrusts are maintained.

2. The Berlin Conference of European Communist and Workers' Parties provided a contribution to peace, security, cooperation and social progress in Europe. It was the forum where the communist and workers' parties of this Continent expressed their readiness to foster, in the struggle for peace, security and social progress, broadest cooperation with all democratically and progressively oriented social forces. This Conference has also considerably contributed to the consolidation of democratic principles in relations among communist parties, such as the right of each party to define autonomously and independently its policies, its responsibility before its working class and people, independence, equality and non-interference. Different roads in the struggle for socialism and in the development of socialism were recognized as an objective law. Another positive achieve-

ment is the fact that, for the first time in a multilateral gathering of communist parties, general consensus in decision-making and the public character
of proceedings were introduced.

The active role of the League of Communists of Yugoslavia in the preparations for the Conference, and particularly the participation of its delegation, with Comrade Tito at its head, in the Conference itself, contributed
to the assertion of new values and contents in relations among communist
and workers' parties and to the success of the Conference. The League of
Communists will continue to support the assertion of the mentioned principles in relations among communist and workers' parties, opposing the
attempts to reinstate obsolete stances and interpretations.

3. In recent years, the role and influence of some communist parties in
Western Europe, and of the Communist Party of Japan, on social developments in their respective countries have considerably increased; they have
become an important factor of national policy and international relations.
These parties have built up independent strategies and tactics of the struggle
for socialism, in conformance to the economic-social and political
conditions characteristic of the developed capitalist society, which is confronted with a crisis of the dominant social relations, the intensification of
the activity of neofascist and other reactionary social forces, as well as manifestations of anarcho-terrorism, which objectively sustain reactionary
currents and moods. They opt for the attainment of socialism through
gradual social transformation, while preserving and expanding the achievements of democratic social development.

The League of Communists of Yugoslavia supports positive trends in
the workers' movement asserting the autonomy of parties and the diversity
of roads and forms of the struggle for socialism and contributing to the consolidation of socialism as a world-wide process.

4. Communist parties in power are achieving successes in the policies of
economic, social and cultural development. They are endeavouring, with
different intensity, to perfect the existing socio-economic and political
system. They exercise influence on international relations by their policies.
The League of Communists of Yugoslavia endorses all positive tendencies
generated by these parties in their internal and international affairs.

5. The League of Communists of Yugoslavia estimates that the gradual
mutual opening up of communist and socialist, or social-democratic and
other democratic parties, is of great potential importance for socialist development as a world-wide process. This entails the search for possible points
of cooperation among the protagonists of different alternatives. This search
is naturally not devoid of certain conflicting situations. Nevertheless, the
inauguration of such a democratic dialogue contributes to the consolidation
of democracy and to the creative discovery of new, progressive solutions in
social development.

6. Intensive discussion is also conducted among communist parties on the fundamental issues of the struggle for socialism and of the construction of socialist social relations. The League of Communists of Yugoslavia considers this to be positive, necessary and indispensable; it has always upheld constructive, principled, argumented and public discussion of all open issues of the struggle for socialism, in the spirit of equality and mutual respect, and free from exclusiveness, arbitration, or labelling. Such a discussion is best suited to express most fully all the wealth of socialist ideas and practice, and to contribute to a more intensive socialist development in the world.

The League of Communists of Yugoslavia has supported such a discussion not only for the purpose of promoting democratic relations among communist parties, but above all because of the fact that contemporary socialist practice is faced with problems which did not exist either in Marx's time or in Lenin's time. Practice has confirmed — what Marx and Lenin stressed long ago — that socialism, as a transitional historical epoch and historical process which is not constrained by any dogmatic framework, is not free of conflict, a circumstance which is particularly reflected in certain relations among socialist states, and which does not preclude even wars Contemporary Marxist theory must discover the causes of such phenomena and ways to overcome such situations, but this is impossible unless responsible and democratic discussion about all these and similar problems is fostered among Marxists, among communist parties and socialist countries.

7. Numerous socialist and social-democratic parties are obliged by objective circumstances to adapt their strategies to the requirements of the contemporary West European society and to the demands of the working class, and to modify their concepts not only of economic, but also of social transformation. This is also occurring under the impact of the left in their own ranks as well as in result of the strengthening of some West European communist parties. Within the process of adaptation, socialist goals and values are mor emphasized in recent years. There are also phenomena indicating a weakening of social-democratic dogmatism and of the crudest forms of anti-communism. In recent years, however, the activity is intensified in strengthening the Socialist International as the international centre of socialist and social-democratic parties and in expanding its political and ideological influence, particularly among the parties and movements of the non-aligned and the developing countries. Such activity of the Socialist International is not conducive to the required faster liquidation of division and conflicts in the international workers' movement and may even involve attempts to introduce ideological and bloc divisions among the non-aligned countries.

8. The broadest anti-imperialist and anti-colonial struggle in the developing countries is still waged in the first place by the forces of national liberation, who have responded in the most adequate manner to the develop-

ment needs of their respective construction of their own social system, while facing great hardships in dealing with the problem of accelerated economic growth. The simultaneous occurrence of the struggle to consolidate national independence and to meet the needs of socio-economic transformation may also lead to the social-political differentiation of the leading political movements in these countries. These processes are affected by a number of factors, among them the character of the struggle and the degree of linkage of these movements with the broadest social strata. Some of them evolve into parties relying to a greater extent on socialist ideas. This process occurs at an uneven rate, and is often attended by internal upheavals, not only due to objective circumstances caused by internal differentiation but also due to the interference of various imperialist and other external interests and influences, which have been more intensive in recent years, especially on African soil.

The League of Communists of Yugoslavia opposes on principle and resolutely, forms of regional or world-wide institutionalisation of parties and movements. The revival of activities with such a character in the developing countries at the present time would tend to restore the historically transcended forms of rallying, which is contrary to the requirements of equitable cooperation among workers' and other progressive parties and movements, based on a free and autonomous choice of political solutions and roads of development, in keeping with their own conditions. Such an activity is, in substance and in form, objectively opposed to a broad political platform and action of the non-aligned countries. . .

IV

. . . In adhering steadfastly to the policy of full equality and free unfoldment of all nations and nationalities in the Socialist Federal Republic of Yugoslavia, the League of Communists of Yugoslavia upholds the respect for the national rights of those parts of the Yugoslav nations who live in other countries as national minorities. Yugoslavia regards national minorities as factors of linkage, mutual understanding and neighbourly cooperation, and looks upon the attitude towards them as a measure of the attitude also to the peoples of Yugoslavia. In striving for principled solutions to the questions of the status and all-round development of national minorities, it particularly resolutely opposes their assimilation. Such a policy practised by Yugoslavia constitutes a factor of stability, in this region and on a wider scale.

A major contribution to good-neighbour cooperation was provided by the conclusion of the Osimo agreements with Italy, whereby the state boundaries between the two countries have been definitely confirmed and some other issues settled, among which figured prominently the creation of possibilities for regulating the status and free unfoldment of national minorities.

With the Republic of Austria, our country fosters broad cooperation in the economic and scientific technological fields, in the settlement of questions concerning the conditions of life and work of our workers temporarily employed in this country, in the field of tourism, and in other areas. However, relations with this country are cumbered by the policy of assimilation, which is applied in Austria with respect to the Slovene and Croatian national minorities. The League of Communists of Yugoslavia and the Socialist Federal Republic of Yugoslavia uphold the consistent assertion of the rights of the Slovene and Croatian national minorities, as defined in the State Treaty, and support their struggle to preserve their national identity and free development.

Extremely positive results in extensive cooperation, at state and party level, have been obtained with the People's Republic of Hungary.

Extensive cooperation is evolved, and relations have been considerably promoted in all areas, between the Socialist Federal Republic of Yugoslavia and the Socialist Republic of Romania, between the League of Communists of Yugoslavia and the Romanian Communist Party.

The relations between our country and the People's Republic of Bulgaria have the same character as before the Tenth Congress of the League of Communists of Yugoslavia. Economic, cultural and other forms of cooperation are developing relatively successfully, however, the unchanged policy of Bulgaria towards the Macedonian national minority in Bulgaria and towards the Macedonian nation as a whole restricts the development of overall cooperation. The League of Communists of Yugoslavia and the Socialist Federal Republic of Yugoslavia consider that the abrogation and non-observance of the rights of the Macedonian national minority in Bulgaria is in contradiction to the United Nations Charter and the Final Act of the Helsinki Conference on Security and Cooperation in Europe. While endorsing the need for the extensive promotion of good-neighbour relations with PR Bulgaria, the Socialist Federal Republic of Yugoslavia is of the view that the restoration of the mentioned rights and the regulation of the status of the Macedonian national minority in this country would substantially contribute to the more successful and comprehensive development of cooperation between the two neighbouring countries.

Consequent on the democratic political changes in Greece, the cooperation between the two countries has revived in the political, economic and other spheres. In the endeavours to implement the Helsinki Final Act, understanding and positive contacts are being realized within the scope of the promotion of cooperation in the Balkans. The favourable development of the relations with the Republic of Greece would proceed even more favourably, freely and comprehensively if steps were undertaken in this neighbouring country to arrive at a positive solution of the status of the Macedonian national minority. This would be to the benefit of the further development of good-neighbour relations and cooperation in all spheres between our two countries.

With the People's Socialist Republic of Albania, cooperation has been developed in the economic sphere and in the sphere of education and culture. Yugoslavia is interested in the further expansion, in scope and intensity, of Yugoslav-Albanian cooperation, with full mutual respect, and on the principles of independence, territorial integrity, equality and non-interference. Yugoslavia expects the other side also to manifest the same degree of interest, since on this depends the further expansion of mutually beneficial cooperation in all spheres of relations.

Relations with the republic of Turkey have developed successfully, and new possibilities have been opened for still more intensive and comprehensive cooperation.

The Socialist Federal Republic of Yugoslavia will continue to pursue the policy of the evolvement and advancement of good-neighbour relations and cooperation, so as to make them as meaningful as possible, and the frontiers which link us with the neighbouring countries as open as possible. In addition to bilateral, Yugoslavia will also uphold the development of multilateral forms of cooperation among the Balkan countries. . .

Todor Zhivkov. Along the Road of Good-Neighbourly Relations and Cooperation.*

* Excerpts from the speech delivered by Todor Zhivkov, First Secretary of the Central Committee of the Bulgarian Communist Party and President of the State Council, at a meeting in the town of Blagoevgrad on 15 June, 1978.

When reviewing the international situation we cannot but devote particular attention to the **situation in the Balkans** — the region in which we live.

The situation in the Balkans as a whole has been developing along positive lines in recent years. Our relations with the neighbouring countries are built on lasting and stable foundations. Cooperation with them is becoming ever more varied in its forms and ever richer in content. Understanding and mutual trust is strengthening, different issues of bilateral relations are being settled faster and in a business-like manner. The dialogue on a summit level which we have established with our neighbours and are trying to maintain regularly is of great importance in this respect.

So we have sufficient reasons to be content. The time when relations between the Balkan states were unnaturally tense and strained, when prejudice and mistrust predominated in them, is increasingly becoming a thing of the past. Today our peoples are increasingly communicating, getting to know each other better and drawing ever closer. We have even begun to meet and visit each other on holidays as befits good neighbours and friends.

Your district borders on two states and you are not only witnesses to but also active participants in this good-neighbourly communication.

Naturally, if someone wishes with some impure intentions to rummage in the past of 30 or 60, 100 or more years ago, to search for black pages in Balkan interrelations, it would not be difficult to find such pages. But of what use would it be to anyone? History should be a source of lessons and not a means of poisoning present-day Balkan relations.

As for the People's Republic of Bulgaria, our deep and sincere desire is to look toward the future, to build up on new foundations the political, economic and cultural relations between the Balkan peoples and states, to move forward along the road of good-neighbourly relations and cooperation. Our policy toward all Balkan states is principled, consistent and lasting, it is not influenced by ad hoc considerations. It corresponds to the interests of the neighbouring countries and peoples and, naturally, to the vital interests of the Bulgarian people.

I would like once again most responsibly to declare: the People's Republic of Bulgaria will continue in future to stay true to its principled and constructive peace-loving policy in the Balkans which it is unswervingly pursuing as a socialist state. We have not interfered and have no intention of either interfering in the home affairs, or of taking advantage of possible internal or international difficulties of our neighbours. In our relations with them we have strictly and unswervingly adhered to the letter and the spirit of the United Nations Charter and of the Helsinki Final Act.

Comrades,

In the past there was in the Balkans only one social system — the capitalist. And it was then that the Balkans earned the sad fame of being the "Powder-keg" of Europe, as four wars broke out there in the course of 30 years. Now in the presence of two systems in our region — socialist and capitalist — the situation has radically changed. Socialism has become a strong stabilizing factor, a factor of peace in the Balkans. That is why we attach primary importance to our relations with the Balkan socialist states.

We are happy that we have close friendly relations with the **Socialist Republic of Romania**, that our cooperation is developing dynamically along an ascending line on a bilateral basis as well as on the basis of our joint participation in the Council for Mutual Economic Assistance and in the Warsaw Treaty.

We highly value the regular friendly and business contacts we maintain with the first Party and state leader of our northern neighbour — Comrade Nicolae Ceausescu. At our last meetings the beginnings were laid of a major new project — the joint building of a hydro-power complex and of two large plants on Bulgarian and Romanian soil. These projects are not only of national economic significance for both countries. For us they are something more — they can serve as an example of the extremely great potential and prospects of good-neighbourly relations between the socialist countries in the Balkans.

As regards our western neighbour — **the Socialist Federal Republic of Yugoslavia** — we are also pursuing a persistent policy of all-round development of cooperation and friendship between our countries and peoples. The last few years have seen a substantial progress in expanding economic exchange and an activization of political contacts and of ties in some spheres of science, education and culture.

We are confident that the relations between socialist Bulgaria and socialist Yugoslavia can become a model of good neighbourliness. All objective prerequisites for this are at hand. Apart from the geographic, historic and cultural proximity, these prerequisites are, most of all, the lasting and invariable common interests and aspirations of our peoples in the struggle for building socialism, in the struggle for consolidating peace in the Balkans, in Europe and the world.

It is true that there are some differences between the two countries, there are, unfortunately, complicated problems with which history has encumbered our relations. Without underestimating the importance or complexity of those issues, we, at the same time, abide by the understanding that there is only one way, only one method of overcoming difficulties arising in the relations between states — especially when they are socialist states. This way is to plant our feet firmly on the main base which unites us in a lasting and law-governed manner — the common interest of building socialism in close cooperation, in the conditions of peace and friendship. It is only by developing relations on this basis, only in the process of their constant expansion and deepening, that the so-called open questions can be successfully solved in the spirit of realism and mutual respect, through a friendly dialogue, strictly abiding by the principles of equality, non-interference in internal affairs, mutual benefit and respect for territorial integrity.

We are deeply confident that the exacerbation and pushing to the fore of the so-called open questions, the emphasis on their solution as a precondition for cooperation, the attempts to impose one's own ideas and positions on the other side — all this constitutes a wrong, futile and futureless approach.

I would like, from this high rostrum, to declare clearly and plainly: the Bulgarian Communist Party and the People's Republic of Bulgaria are filled with a sincere desire, readiness and good will to develop all-round and on a broad basis — on a large scale, in keeping with our mutual interests — the relations between our neighbouring socialist countries, between our parties and peoples. On the part of Bulgaria there are no obstacles to the promotion of such relations.

I would like furthermore to declare plainly and categorically once again that the People's Republic of Bulgaria has no territorial claims to Yugoslavia. Allegations about the existence of such claims, obviously made up according to the principle of the well-known folk proverb, are both false and speculative. We are ready to sign a joint declaration with which the People's Republic of Bulgaria and the Socialist Federal Republic of Yugoslavia shall solemnly confirm the principle of inviolability of frontiers and the mutual renunciation of territorial claims. We are ready to do this immediately, without any conditions attached, and without any delay. If only the Yugoslav side consents — I, personally, am ready to go to Belgrade tomorrow, and sign such a document together with Comrade Tito!

At the same time, I would like with the same amount of clarity and unambiguousness with which I express our readiness to develop good-neighbourly and fraternal — in the true sense of the world — socialist relations between the People's Republic of Bulgaria and the Socialist Federal Republic of Yugoslavia, to underscore our categorical "No" to the attempts to misuse our policy and constructive approach, to mislead the world public opinion, or to anyone's attempts to interfere in our internal affairs.

Our policy towards the **People's Socialist Republic of Albania** is also built on a consistent class and internationalist basis.

It is our sincere desire to have good relations and to develop a mutually advantageous cooperation. This would be in the spirit of the traditional friendship between the Bulgarian and the Albanian peoples dating back to the period of the national liberation struggles and the struggle against capitalism and fascism, in the spirit of comradely cooperation, established after the victory of the socialist revolution.

We are confident that there are no insurmountable obstacles to the complete normalization of our bilateral relations. We believe that this goal is realistic and achievable because it is in keeping with the lasting common interests of our countries and peoples in the drive for peace and socialism.

As far as we are concerned, I would like once more to point out that there is both readiness and will on our part to work towards the attainment of this goal.

Comrades,

The progressively developing process of establishing peaceful coexistence as a norm in our relations with our southern neighbours — **Turkey and Greece** — is a highly convincing expression of the positive changes which occurred in our region in the last few years.

We are happy that a positive turn has been accomplished in these relations, that the mistrust and prejudices of the past are being overcome.

Our political contacts — both on the state level and between public and political organizations, are steadily expanding and becoming regular as a result of the efforts of many years, and the political realism demonstrated, on the basis of the principle of peaceful coexistence. Economic cooperation and cultural exchange are considerably gaining in scope.

A single fact may be cited as sufficiently indicative of how much things have changed. Last month we met with Turkish Prime Minister Bülent Ecevit in Varna and had many useful, frank and friendly talks. Quite soon we will again meet with Mr Karamanlis, the Prime Minister of Greece, with whom we have been maintaining a regular friendly dialogue for several years now. Mr Korutürk, the Turkish President, also was to have come to our country, but unfortunately his visit had to be postponed because of illness. We will continue to work just as actively and in the same constructive spirit for further developing our relations with our southern neighbours, for consolidating mutual trust, for extending and deepening cooperation and contacts in all spheres.

Naturally, we are far from the intention of idealizing the situation in our region. It continues to be complex and contradictory. As in other parts of the world, some imperialist circles of NATO, and the Maoists with them, are intensifying their actions in the region, and trying to fan and use to their own ends the existing differences and problems between some of the Balkan states.

It is no secret, for instance, that the situation in the Balkans is strongly and directly influenced by the events in the Eastern Mediterranean where the fire of two of the "hotbeds" of our planet — the Middle East crisis and the Cyprus crisis, even more pertinent to our region, is still smouldering.

I would like to emphasize once again our immutable principled position on the **Cyprus question** — the position of consistent solidarity and support of the just cause of the people of Cyprus, for preserving the independence, territorial integrity and policy of non-alignment of the Republic of Cyprus, for withdrawal of foreign troops and foreign military bases from the island, for the solution to the Cyprus question by peaceful means, through negotiations, in the interest of the Greek Cypriots and the Turkish Cypriots.

As I already said, we fully take into account the whole complexity and contradictory character of the situation in our region. But we are not pessimists. We look forward to the future with optimism, we have not spared and will not spare our efforts so that here too, in the Balkans, in the former "powder-keg" of Europe, the danger of war may increasingly recede and good-neighbourly relations and understanding increasingly prevail. We are confident that this noble cause will succeed in the Balkans, as well as throughout the world, because it corresponds to the aspirations of the peoples, because th cause of peace and security has the full support of the constructive foreign policy of the great Soviet Union and the other countries of the socialist community, because this cause is supported by all peace-loving forces.

Statement by the Yugoslav Federal Secretariat for Foreign Affairs.

(in connection with Todor Zhivkov's recent speech).

(Complete Text).

We have carefully studied the speech delivered on June 15, 1978 in Blagoevgrad by Todor Zhivkov, President of the State Council of Bulgaria.

In his speech, President Zhivkov stated, among other things, that the Peoples' Republic of Bulgaria is prepared to sign a declaration with the SFR Yugoslavia on the inviolability of frontiers and on renouncing its territorial claims, and that "immediately, unconditionally and without delay". In this connection, he stated that relations between Yugoslavia and Bulgaria can become a model of good-neighbourliness.

President Zhivkov said nothing, however, about the basic problem encumbering our relations, i.e. about the fact that the People's Republic of Bulgaria is persistently negating the existence of the Macedonian national minority and is pursuing a policy of assimilation. Instead, President Zhivkov mentions "so-called open questions" and claims that insistence on their resolution is a "fruitless and pointless approach".

The general tone of President Zhivkov's speech leaves the impression that the Bulgarian side is prepared to do all it can on behalf of good-neighbourly relations, and that if it is not succeeding it is the fault of the Yugoslav and not the Bulgarian side.

Since this is a question with extremely grave implications, we feel it necessary to set forth certain relevant facts and to inform the public of the true state of affairs.

With respect to the offer of renouncing territorial claims, which President Zhivkov dramatically extends in his speech, we can say that since the end of World War II, this question has not, for us, been a disputed issue.

The Bulgarian offer would be meaningful only if it were to help create greater trust and direct recognition of the existence of the Macedonian national minority in Bulgaria and acceptance of the existence of the Macedonian nation in the SR of Macedonia, in Yugoslavia.

With regard to the offer to sign the proposed declaration "unconditionally" we should like to point out the following:

President Zhivkov's speech already clearly sets a rigid condition whereby the Yugoslav side is, in fact, asked to renounce its stand on Bulgarian recognition of the Macedonian national minority and on giving it full national rights.

There is also, the question of why President Zhivkov once again offers to carry through something "without delay" which was already on the agenda a full two years ago and has remained deadlocked precisely because the Bulgarian side set the same condition then as it is doing now. Namely, in 1976, in its proposed draft declaration on the development of relations, the Bulgarian side pursued this same line. For Yugoslavia, its acceptance would mean that Yugoslavia agrees to the policy of assimilating the Macedonian national minority which is being pursued in Bulgaria. At the time, Yugoslavia proposed to Bulgaria that the two sides sign joint documents containing the principles for removing major obstacles and laying down the groundwork for the undisturbed and all-round development of friendly good-neighbourly relations between our peoples and our two countries.

The proposed draft of the Yugoslav documents stresses the two countries' readiness to develop their relations on the basis of consistent respect for sovereignty, territorial integrity and non-interference in the affairs of other states. It also asserts the two sides' agreement that the position and protection of national minorities — the Macedonian in Bulgaria and the Bulgarian in Yugoslavia — together with consistent respect for and the realization of their rights, are an important factor in the further creation of trust, in developing and strengthening allround cooperation between the two neighbouring countries. There was also a plan for delivering special formal statements in the Yugoslav Assembly and Bulgarian Parliament on the position and rights of the Bulgarian national minority in Yugoslavia and the Macedonian national minority in Bulgaria.

In connection with the documents exchanges in Sofia in September 1976, Yugoslavia and Bulgaria held talks which came to nothing because the Bulgarian side had shown no readiness to change its attitude towards the question of the Macedonian national minority in the Peoples' Republic of Bulgaria.

As can be seen, the Yugoslav side proposed the settlement not of abstract but of quite concrete questions which are of decisive significance for the development of mutual relations, and Yugoslavia has no reason not to insist on the same now.

We should like to stress, on this occasion, that there was a time when the People's Republic of Bulgaria pursued a completely different official policy with regard to this question. Many state and official documents dating from that time show that the Bulgarian Government not only recognized the existence of a Macedonian national minority in Bulgaria, but actually used to undertake measures and obligations for improving its position. As far back as 1956, official Bulgarian statistics showed that there were 187,789 Macedonians in Bulgaria. Today, however, attempts are being made to deny that Macedonians ever lived in Bulgaria. This is an obvious departure from the political line pursued by Georgi Dimitrov in solving the question of national minorities in Bulgaria.

In view of the one-sided and false presentation of problems in Yugoslav-Bulgarian relations and in view of attempts to picture Yugoslavia as being intolerant and as interfering in the internal affairs of others, we have

decided to publish all the aforementioned documents so as to enable the
Yugoslav and world public to become fully acquainted with the objective
and hard facts.

We believe that the contents of these documents will allow everyone to
judge for himself as to which side has pursued a principled and consistent
policy and shown readiness to build relations among states in the Balkans,
in Europe and in the world at large in the spirit of the United Nations
Charter and the principles contained in the Final Act of Helsinki. As for
Yugoslavia, we can only again stress that we shall remain ready to exert, in
that spirit and on that basis, a maximum of effort for the allround development of good-neighbourly relations and cooperation with the Peoples'
Republic of Bulgaria. This means that for us the development of lasting and
stable relations is possible on the basis of complete respect for sovereignty,
independence and equality and on the basis of non-interference, which also
implies recognition and a constructive solution of the status and rights of
the Macedonian national minority in the Peoples' Republic of Bulgaria, as
is the case with the Bulgarian national minority in the Socialist Federal
Republic of Yugoslavia.

And finally, we should like to point out that respect for the right of all
nations, including national minorities, to equality and free development is
an integral part of the rights of man and of human freedom, which remains
one of the fundamental principles governing Yugoslavia's domestic and
foreign policies.

29 June, 1978.

Draft of Joint Declaration.
by the President of the Federal Socialist Republic of Yugoslavia and the Chairman of the State Council of the People's Republic of Bulgaria.*

(Complete Text).

*This document was released by the Yugoslav Federal Secretariat for Foreign Affairs on 29
June 1978. (See previous document).

The President of the Socialist Federal Republic of Yugoslavia and President of the League of Communists of Yugoslavia Josip Broz Tito and the
First Secretary of the Central Committee of the Bulgarian Communist
Party and Chairman of the State Council of the People's Republic of Bulgaria Todor Zhivkov, together with the respective associates, effected a
broad exchange of views on all question of interest to the two countries in
an atmosphere of friendship, mutual respect, understanding and frankness.

I

In doing so, the two Presidents proceeded from the long-standing experience acquired in neighbourly relations between our peoples — particularly the Serbian, Macedonian and Bulgarian nations — which demonstrates that these nations are closely linked and that their mutual friendship and cooperation have always been in their joint interest. It is upon that basis that the working class and progressive forces of the peoples of Yugoslavia and Bulgaria have cooperated, particularly in the struggle against the grand-State nationalism and hegemonism, primarily the greater-Serbia and greater-Bulgaria nationalisms of their national bourgeoisies, which have often been the cause of mutual conflicts and were particularly reflected in the fact that the just struggle of the Macedonian nation for its national freedom and equality was prevented and denied. The struggle of the progressive movements in the two countries, especially the struggle of the League of Communists of Yugoslavia and the Bulgarian Communist Party has brought about, in the new historical conditions, the creation of new socialist socio-political systems in the Socialist Federal Republic of Yugoslavia and the People's Republic of Bulgaria, systems which objectively make it possible to surmount the heavy heritage of the past and to establish closer cooperation between the workers' movements of the two countries. In this context, the cooperation during the anti-fascist liberation struggle and the socialist revolution, the exchange of messages between the Central Committee of the Communist Party of Yugoslavia and the Central Committee of the Bulgarian Communist Party at the end of 1944, agreements in Craiova in 1944 and at Bled in 1947 have a particular historical role, as well as some other subsequent encounters of the highest-ranking leaders of the two socialist countries.

Proceedings from this historical experience and the accomplishments attained, the two Presidents express their conviction that a full mutual confidence, allround fruitful cooperation and stable and developed good-neighbourly relations between the two countries and their peoples correspond to the lasting essential interests of the two countries and to the long-standing aspirations of their peoples and constitute a major contribution to cooperation in the Balkans and in Europe as well as to the cause of socialism, peace and progress in the world.

Determined to work toward realization of the objectives of the Charter of the United Nations and to contribute to the materialization of the principles and conclusions of the Final Act of the Conference on Security and Cooperation in Europe, the two Presidents consider that equality among States, the consistent respect for sovereignty, territorial integrity and inviolability of frontiers, peaceful settlement of disputes, non-interference in the internal affairs of other States, respect for the specificities of the internal system and the international position of each country, mutual understanding and confidence, constitute the fundamental principles in the development of friendly relations and cooperation between the Socialist Federal Republic of Yugoslavia and the People's Republic of Bulgaria.

With a view to strengthening their mutual confidence the two Sides decided to express in a special solemn declaration their determination to respect in their mutual relations, most consistently and reciprocally, the principle of territorial integrity and inviolability of the existing frontiers between the two States.

In view of the role and importance of the League of Communists of Yugoslavia and the Bulgarian Communist Party in the building up of the socialist society in their countries and their special responsibility concerning the state and development of relations between the two countries in general, the President of the League of Communists of Yugoslavia Josip Broz Tito and the First Secretary of the Central Committee of the Bulgarian Communist Party Todor Zhivkov pointed out that it was necessary to develop relations, and multifarious cooperation between the League of Communists of Yugoslavia and the Bulgarian Communist Party and discuss all the questions relating to their mutual relations as well as all the fundamental problems of the current struggle for peace, progress and socialism in the world. That cooperation should be developed on the basis of full mutual confidence and respect for the specificities and respect for the independent path of each country, to socialist development.

The two Presidents express their satisfaction over the firm resolve of the two Sides to develop and further promote good-neighbourly relations on lasting foundations, to exert joint efforts for surmounting the questions and problems which burden relations between the two countries.

In this context, President Josip Broz Tito and President Todor Zhivkov concur in the view that the status and protection of national minorities — the Macedonian minority in Bulgaria and the Bulgarian minority in Yugoslavia as well as the consistent respect for and realization of their national rights represent a significant factor in the further building of confidence, development and strengthening of comprehensive cooperation between the two neighbouring socialist countries. Toward that end, the Governments of the two countries, observing the international norms, including the relevant provisions of the Peace Treaty with Bulgaria signed on 10 February 1947 in Paris, and on the basis of respect for the principle of sovereign decision-making with regard to their internal affairs, shall devote their full attention to the constant promotion of the rights of national minorities, particularly in the fields of the use of their own language, education, culture, information activities and public life.

The two Presidents have decided that the Governments of the two countries, proceeding from the joint positions accepted in this Declaration, should make before their respective Parliaments a solemn declaration wherein they shall set forth the principles, measures and guarantees on the basis of which the protection of the rights of national minorities — the

Macedonian and/or the Bulgarian minorities respectively — shall be realized in their respective countries.

The two Presidents noted with satisfaction that the cooperation between the Socialist Federal Republic of Yugoslavia and the People's Republic of Bulgaria in the political, economic, cultural and other fields, as well as the cooperation between socio-political organizations registered noticeable progress. However, they are convinced that broad possibilities exist for the further expansion and promotion of that cooperation.

The two Presidents positively assessed the contacts so far between officials of State organs and representatives of socio-political organizations of the two countries at various levels and agreed that it was necessary and possible to expand and reinforce the ties between the Governments and Parliaments as well as the direct cooperation between various institutions, socio-political, work and other organizations of the two countries.

II

President Josip Broz Tito and President Todor Zhivkov noted with satisfaction that economic cooperation between the two countries was marking continuing progress as well as that mutual interest exists in and that efforts were being made for the development of advanced forms of cooperation in the fields of production, industrial production cooperation, scientific and technical cooperation, trade, communications, transport, construction of roads and railways, interconnection of energy systems, tourism as well as the promotion of cooperation in the protection of human environment. They consider that neighbourhood, mutual orientation and comparative advantages of the two economies should be utilized for the further development of economic cooperation between the two countries on lasting bases. They shall support in the future, too, initiatives of the State organs and economic organizations aiming at further promotion of economic cooperation.

The two Presidents also reviewed the state of bilateral relations in the fields of culture, science, education and mass media. They consider that determined results have been achieved in these fields, and that a number of questions regarding cooperation have already been agreed between the two Sides, and that the following should be undertaken:

— work of the commissions which should seek to ensure that questions from the histories of the two countries be correctly presented in school textbooks;

— translation of literary works, created in the two countries, into the languages of the peoples of Yugoslavia and Bulgaria;

— participation in scientific gatherings and seminars;

— access to historical archives for scientists of the two countries;

— collaboration between military historians.

In addition, other questions of cooperation, on which agreement has been reached between the two countries should likewise be implemented.

The two Presidents assessed that it was necessary to develop exchange of cultural and scientific achievements as well as exchange of experience and joint projects of scientific, cultural and educational institutions. They particularly point out the usefulness and significance of cooperation between the Serbian Academy of Sciences and Arts, the Macedonian Academy of Sciences and Arts, the Yugoslav Academy of Sciences and Arts, the Slovenian Academy of Sciences and Arts, the Academy of Sciences and Arts of Bosnia and Herzegovina, the Science Society of the SR Montenegro, the Sciences and Arts Society of Kosovo and the Bulgarian Academy of Sciences, in the study and scientific treatment of the past and, in particular, of those periods in which cooperation between the Yugoslav and Bulgarian peoples was pursued. These and other suitable forms of cooperation should ensure cultivation among younger generations of the most shining and noblest strivings of progressive and revolutionary forces, based on the traditions from the past and on the present-day aspirations of the progressive and revolutionary forces of the two countries.

President Josip Broz Tito and President Todor Zhivkov consider that direct contacts between citizens of the two countries should be developed and encouraged even more, particularly in border areas through small-border traffic, cooperation between towns, their socio-political and other organizations promotion of tourism, holding of border assemblies and in other ways, which will contribute to better mutual acquaintance and creation of confidence and strengthening of friendship between the two neighbouring socialist countries. To this end, the Governments of the two countries will examine experience gained so far in the implementation of the existing agreements and will encourage conclusion of new ones, including also those in the field of consular affairs.

The agree that a free exchange of press and information should be enabled and cooperation encouraged between information media and organizations (newspapers, periodicals, radio, television, publishing houses, etc.), as well as that cultural and information centres should be established, all with a view to better mutual acquaintance of the peoples of the two countries, of each other's successes and problems in the building of new socialist socio-economic relations.

III

The two Presidents feel that favourable conditions exist for cooperation between the two countries also on the broader international plane, considering that the views of the two Sides on numerous current international issues are concordant or similar.

They maintain that their vital interests direct them to cooperate within the United Nations with a view to strengthening peace and security eliminating hotbeds of crises and solving outstanding international issues, developing equal cooperation and establishing new, more equitable international political and economic relations in the world. Guided by the same interests, they consider it to be useful and indispensable for the two countries to cooperate and seek to have the Final Act of the Conference on Security and Cooperation in Europe in Helsinki implemented, both in the field of European security and cooperation, and on the plane of cooperation in the Balkans.

They agreed that the Governments, the ministries of foreign affairs and other ministries of two countries should expand contacts and cooperation also in this field.

President Josip Broz Tito and President Todor Zhivkov will continue to exert efforts and contribute personally to the constant promotion of stable long-term and allround friendly relations and cooperation between the Socialist Federal Republic of Yugoslavia and the People's Republic of Bulgaria as well as between their peoples.

Solemn Declaration of the Federal Executive Council in the Assembly of the Socialist Federal Republic of Yugoslavia Concerning the Bulgarian Nationality in the SFR of Yugoslavia.*

(Complete Text).

*This document was released by the Yugoslav Federal Secretariat for Foreign Affairs on 29 June 1978 — see Statement by the Yugoslav Federal Secretariat for Foreign Affairs in this volume.

The Bulgarian nationality and its members in the Yugoslav socialist community are a significant factor in the construction of the Yugoslav self-management socialist social system in which they realize their rights and socio-political, economic and cultural position.

In the spirit of the principles of the Constitution of the Socialist Federal Republic of Yugoslavia regarding the equality of nations and nationalities, the Bulgarian nationality as a whole and its members are ensured the full equality which is also guaranteed by the provisions of legislative, statutory and self-management acts.

Special attention is devoted to the realization of conditions in which the nationality continues to develop, on an equal footing, its national characteristics in all spheres of its activities.

Equality of rights and non-discrimination are manifested especially in the use of its language in the fields of upbringing, education, culture and the protection of national characteristics as well as in the sphere of socio-economic and other self-management rights, including equitable representation and access to the discharge of self-management, public and social functions within the framework of the system of socialist self-management.

In keeping with the Constitution and other laws, members of the Bulgarian nationality have the right to use their own language in exercizing their rights and duties, as well as in the procedure before the State organs and the organizations exercizing public functions, which includes the obligation to issue documents intended for the members of the nationality in two languages or to supply a translation.

Instruction in their own language is also guaranteed and ensured.

The guarantee of the possibility of expression of the Bulgarian culture, of the preservation of cultural traditions of the Bulgarian nationality, of the freedom of association and adequate participation in the mass media is one of the essential realized conditions for unimpeded development. Appropriate support to the publishing and journalistic activity in the language of the nationality is also ensured.

In addition to the clearly guaranteed position of nationalities in the constitutional and legal provisions which enable the broadest possible development of each nationality as a whole and of its members, the Government of the Socialist Federal Republic of Yugoslavia

Solemnly Declares

that it will most strictly adhere to all the principles and provisions relating to the protection and rights of the national and ethnic minorities, contained in the Charter of the United Nations, the Universal Declaration of Human Rights, the Final Act of the Conference on Security and Cooperation in Europe signed at Helsinki, the International Convention on the Elimination of All Forms of Racial Discrimination, the Convention against Discrimination in the Field of Education, the International Pact on Civil and Political Rights and other relevant international agreements;

that it will continue to undertake, in conformity with the provisions of the Constitution of the Socialist Federal Republic of Yugoslavia and constantly mindful of the development of nationalities, all the measures which are necessary for an allround development of the Bulgarian nationality in Yugoslavia in all fields.

The Yugoslavia Government is convinced that the Bulgarian nationality in Yugoslavia and the Macedonian national minority in the People's Republic of Bulgaria can and should constitute a link of friendship and understanding between the peoples of the two neighbouring and socialist States and that their free development can contribute to the strengthening and promotion of all-out good-neighbourly relations between the Socialist Federal Republic of Yugoslavia and the People's Republic of Bulgaria.

Solemn Yugoslav-Bulgarian Declaration Concerning the Respect for the Territorial Integrity and the Inviolability of Frontiers.*

(Complete Text).

*This document was released by the Yugoslav Federal Secretariat for Foreign Affairs on 29 June 1978 — see Statement by the Yugoslav Federal Secretariat for Foreign Affairs in this volume.

The President of the Socialist Federal Republic of Yugoslavia and President of the League of Communists of Yugoslavia Josip Broz Tito and the First Secretary of the Central Committee of the Bulgarian Communist Party and Chairman of the State Council of the People's Republic of Bulgaria Todor Zhivkov,

Guided by the objectives and principles of the United Nations relative to the development of friendly and good-neighbourly relations among nations as the basis of strengthening peace and security in the world,

Proceeding from the conclusions of the Final Act of the Conference on Security and Cooperation in Europe, in particular from the principle of the inviolability of frontiers stating that "The participating States regard as inviolable all one another's frontiers. . . and therefore they will refrain now and in the future from assulting these frontiers",

Expressing the lasting interest of the peoples of the Socialist Federal Republic of Yugoslavia and the People's Republic of Bulgaria in maintaining and promoting cooperation between the two socialist States,

Convinced that the strengthening of mutual confidence and cooperation will encourage a more intensive development of friendly, good-neighbourly relations in all fields between the Socialist Federal Republic of Yugoslavia and the People's Republic of Bulgaria and substantially contribute to the consolidation of peace and security in the Balkans and in Europe,

Solemnly Declare

The Socialist Federal Republic of Yugoslavia and the People's Republic of Bulgaria confirm hereby that they have no territorial claims to each other and that in their mutual relations they will most consistently adhere to the principle of full respect for the territorial integrity and inviolability of the existing frontiers between the Socialist Federal Republic of Yugoslavia and the People's Republic of Bulgaria, established in the bilateral and multilateral agreements and treaties in force.

For All-Round Development of Bulgaro-Yugoslav Relations.
Declaration of the Ministry of Foreign Affairs of the People's Republic of Bulgaria.
(Complete Text).

The policy which we are pursuing towards our western neighbour, the Socialist Federal Republic of Yugoslavia, occupies an important place in the consistent and tireless efforts of the Bulgarian Communist Party and the People's Republic of Bulgaria for the further deepening of the process of reducing international tension and turning it into an irreversible one, for the strengthening of peace and security and for the development of broad and mutually advantageous cooperation between states in an atmosphere of understanding and trust.

In the report to the 11th Congress of the Bulgarian Communist Party Comrade Todor Zhivkov indicated:

"We unswervingly follow a line of friendship and development of relations with the Socialist Federal Republic of Yugoslavia. As a result of the efforts made, progress has been scored in political contacts, in economic cooperation, in cultural ties. We attach great importance to the activation of relations between the Bulgarian Communist Party and the League of Communists of Yugoslavia and we will do everything in our power for the development of friendship between the two countries".

The policy of the Bulgarian Communist Party and the People's Republic of Bulgaria for all-round development and strengthening of ties and cooperation with the Socialist Federal Republic of Yugoslavia corresponds to the lasting common interests and aspirations of the Bulgarian and Yugoslav peoples in their struggle for national and social liberation in the past, in the struggle for peace and socialism in our days. This policy, repeatedly, clearly and authoritatively substantiated in official documents and statements of the most responsible Bulgarian leaders, is being convincingly confirmed by everyday practical actions for the all-round development of bilateral relations.

At variance with the obvious and generally known facts, this principled and consistent policy has for years now been systematically presented in an incorrect light. Unfortunately it has become practice for official institutions and responsible officials in the Socialist Federal Republic of Yugoslavia to give food to and to appear as initiators of such a distortion. All this is being done in conditions of a massed campaign in the Yugoslav mass media against the Bulgarian Communist Party and the People's Republic of Bulgaria, against the Bulgarian people and the Bulgarian Party and State leadership.

Ungrounded accusations and claims against the BCP and the PR of Bulgaria were levelled from the rostrum of the recently held 11th Congress of the League of Communists of Yugoslavia and were even included in documents of the Congress determining the policy of the LCY. Arbitrary assertions, distorting the stands and policy of the Bulgarian side on the so-called outstanding questions are contained also in the Declaration of the Federal Secretariat for Foreign Affairs of the SFRY of June 29, 1978 in connection with the speech of the President of the State Council of the PR of Bulgaria Todor Zhivkov, made in Blagoevgrad on June 15 of this year.

The Bulgarian side has not replied to this provocative approach, convinced that the difficult and complex questions must be discussed and solved only by a calm and equitable friendly dialogue. In the situation created, when the world public is being incorrectly and tendentiously informed about the positions of the Bulgarian Communist Party and the People's Republic of Bulgaria, it is necessary that the public should be acquainted with our stands on fundamental questions of Bulgaro-Yugoslav relations.

* * *

The policy which the Bulgarian Communist Party and the People's Republic of Bulgaria are unswervingly pursuing, is directed towards all-round development of cooperation with the League of Communists of Yugoslavia and the Socialist Federal Republic of Yugoslavia. Complete equality, non-interference in internal affairs, mutual advantage and observance of territorial integrity are its fundamental and inviolable principles.

The socialist system, the common communist ideals of the two parties, the identity or similarity of the views on basic problems of international life, on the one hand, and the geographic and cultural closeness between the Bulgarian and Yugoslav peoples, on the other, are a solid objective base for the existence of such relations between Bulgaria and Yugoslavia which should became a model of good-neighbourliness.

In the principled line of the Bulgarian Communist Party with respect to the League of Communists of Yugoslavia, to socialist Yugoslavia, to the Yugoslav people there have been no and there are no fluctuations. This is a line of communist solidarity, a line in support of the socialist acquisitions of the Yugoslav working people, a line of development of mutually advantageous cooperation in the realization of the common goals in the building up of socialism. This is a line of eradicating prejudices, distrust and other residues of the bourgeois past, a principled and class line.

It is a fact that besides what deeply and in a law-governed way draws the two parties and countries together, there are between them also certain differences, determined by the specific national conditions. At the same time there are difficulties and unsolved problems inherited from history.

Of extreme importance is the question how to approach these differences. **This is a major question of principle and the prospects of bilateral relations depend to a large extent on its correct formulation.**

Without underestimating the significance or complexity of the existing problems, as Comrade Todor Zhivkov said, we "adhere to the view that in relations between States — all the more so when these States are socialist — there is only one road, only one way of surmounting the difficulties that arise. This way is to stand firmly on what is essential, what lastingly and in a law-governed manner unites us — the common interest in building up socialism in close cooperation, under conditions of peace and friendship. It is only while developing relations on this basis, only in the process of their continuous expansion and deepening, that the so-called outstanding questions can be successfully solved — in a spirit of realism and mutual respect, by way of a comradely dialogue, while strictly abiding by the principles of equality, non-interference in internal affairs, reciprocal advantage and respect for territorial integrity".

Guided by precisely these positions of principle the **Bulgarian Communist Party and the People's Republic of Bulgaria are making consistent efforts to promote all-round cooperation with the LCY and the SFRY.**

It could be noted with satisfaction that in the recent years real progress has been made in the development of mutually advantageous cooperation between the two countries. Of particular significance are the renewed and activated links and exchanges between the Bulgarian Communist Party and the League of Communists of Yugoslavia. Contacts at state level, too, are expanding as are those between socio-political organizations. The headway in the promotion of trade, economic, scientific and technological cooperation is considerable. Every five years trade between the two countries doubles. A positive fact are the agreements concluded on specialization and joint industrial production. The undertakings agreed upon between the two countries on the exchanges in some spheres of culture, science and education are also being fulfilled.

At the same time the objective conditions in the two neighbouring socialist countries and their mutual interests make it possible and necessary for Bulgaro-Yugoslav cooperation to be raised to a new, higher stage.

Guided by this principle, the Bulgarian side has repeatedly proposed officially to work out jointly a comprehensive complex programme of initiatives for the development of cooperation between the People's Republic of Bulgaria and the Socialist Federal Republic of Yugoslavia in all spheres — political, economic, cultural and at all levels — party, state and public. The proposals put forward by the Bulgarian side, provide more particularly for the following trends in the development of Bulgaro-Yugoslav relations to serve as a basis for the working out of such a complex programme.

In the political sphere:

— in the first place, expansion of cooperation between the Bulgarian Communist Party and the League of Communists of Yugoslavia, exchange of views and experience between the Central Committees;

— expansion of contacts between the governments, parliaments, between socio-political and mass organizations;

— development of direct cooperation between individual departments, institutes, organizations, enterprises and twin towns;

— expansion of ties between the population in the border areas.

In the sphere of foreign policy and international relations:

— exchange of views and holding consultations between the Central Committee of the BCP and the LCY and between the Ministries of Foreign Affairs on topical issues of the international situation and of the international workers' and communist movement which are of mutual interest;

— development of cooperation between the representatives of the two countries in international organizations and forums.

In the economic sphere:

— expansion of the most modern forms of economic cooperation in implementation of the Agreement of long-term economic, scientific and technological cooperation; joint production and specialization in production and increasing trade on this basis;

— coordination of national economic plans and joint solution of major economic problems of mutual interest;

— development of cooperation in the sphere of communications, transport, road building, linking up of the power grids;

— joint appearance in third markets;

— development of cooperation in environmental protection;

— expansion of tourism;

— rise in trade between the frontier areas.

In the sphere of cultural cooperation:

— development of ties and exchange between the scientific, educational and cultural enterprises and institutes, between the academies of sciences, universities and creative unions;

— joint fundamental and applied scientific developments and research;

— exchange of artistic and performing companies, exhibitions, films, etc.;

— expansion of cooperation in the sphere of the press, radio and television, which through well-meant and objective information about the two countries to aid the strengthening of mutual respect and friendship between the Bulgarian and the Yugoslav people.

As in the past, at present too, the Bulgarian side is ready immediately to proceed to the working out and carrying through of such a complex programme. Its translation into life would undoubtedly contribute to the establishment of a most favourable atmosphere for seeking and finding mutually acceptable solutions to the existing difficulties and problems in Bulgaro-Yugoslav relations.

What are the Bulgarian side's views on the nature of these difficulties and problems?

The main difficulties on the path of developing bilateral relations, as is known, stem from the fact that the Yugoslav side lays claims on the so-called Macedonian national minority in the People's Republic of Bulgaria.

The Bulgarian side's view as regards these claims contains three principal points, which constitute its essence.

The first of these is who has the right and who is competent to determine the national composition of a given country, the national awareness of its people or of a part of its people.

In her policy on the national issue the People's Republic of Bulgaria, being a socialist state, is guided by the basic principles of the Marxist-Leninist teaching. These basic principles include on the one side the requirement of ensuring voluntary and free self-expression of the national awareness of the population and equal rights for every citizen, regardless of national origin or nationality, abolition of all national privileges. On the other hand, they include the requirement of all-round drawing together and rallying of the workers of all nationalities in the struggle for the common aims and interests — the building up of socialism and communism.

The Bulgarian Communist Party applies these Marxist-Leninist formulations of principle considering them in their dialectical unity, in their entirety and indivisibility, in compliance with the view that under the conditions of socialism it is equally wrong to underrate the role of the national-specific and the international elements. It is particularly dangerous when nationalism is harped on, when the national aspects is raised above everything else and the main, socio-class criterion is disregarded.

The national question in Bulgaria has been solved on the basis of the consistent and comprehensive application of precisely the fundamental Marxist-Leninist requirements, in accordance with the freely and democratically expressed will of the Bulgarian citizens. This has found a supreme juridical expression in the Constitution of the People's Republic of Bulgaria, adopted through a free, nation-wide referendum.

Bulgaria's national realities have been formed in the course of the historical process by the economic, social and cultural conditions of the country and have been manifested in strict observance of the inalienable right of every citizen — himself to determine his nationality under the conditions of full equality and in the absence of any discrimination. The question of the national composition of the population in Bulgaria has been solved, therefore, by those who alone are entitled to this sovereign right — the citizens of the PR of Bulgaria.

In this state of affairs to make attempts to determine from the outside the nationality of part of the Bulgarian population, and to claim the right to guardianship over it under whatever pretext this might be done, cannot be considered but as an interference in our internal affairs. This obviously is at variance not only with the principles of Marxism-Leninism but also with the generally principles of respecting the sovereignty and independence which every state, Yugoslavia included, insists, and that with complete right — on being observed in respect to it. The People's Republic of Bulgaria strictly adheres to these principles, solemnly reaffirmed also in the Final Act of the Conference on Security and Cooperation in Europe, has not interfered and does not intend to interfere in the internal affairs of anybody. She is in her own right to expect that she should be treated in the same manner.

The second question of principle refers to the population of the district of Blagoevgrad. It is no secret for anybody that when the SFRY claims on the presence of a "Macedonian national minority" in Bulgaria it is precisely the population of this district that it has in mind. These claims have no foundations whatever either in the historical facts or in the existing objective realities.

In order to give a true, objective reply to the question of the national character of the population of the Pirin area one should, on the one hand, take into consideration the present reality — the will of the population itself, and on the other — to examine the history of this population, the social, economic, political and cultural-ideological processes that have proceeded in it, to analyze the facts of the formation and development of the Bulgarian nation.

It is a generally known truth that the nation is a product of the bourgeois epoch, of the transition from the feudal to the capitalist social system. It is usually formed as a development of a nationality already existing for centuries or, as it more seldom happens, as a result of the division of a nationality, or as a result of the unification of several nationalities. The formation of new nations is, of course, possible also later, as a result of the division of a nation already created by that time, of the formation of two states, etc.

Historical science, both the Bulgarian and the world one, has established in a firm and incontrovertible fashion that the Bulgarian nation was created on the basis of the Bulgarian nationality formed in the 9th and 10th centuries in Moesia, the Dobroudja, Thrace and Macedonia. When capitalist relations emerged in the Ottoman Empire in the second half of the 18th century and the 19th century, there began also the process of the formation of the Bulgarian nation. This process was carried out in the conditions of foreign rule. It found expression also in the emergence and development of the national Bulgarian church, in the establishment of national Bulgarian schools, in the movement for an independent Bulgarian state.

There are no data to prove the existence of a Macedonian nationality and state organization in the Middle Ages and the existence of a Macedonian nation in the epoch of the National Revival Period. Historical documents incontrovertibly testify that the Bulgarians of Macedonia were among the most active in the formation of the Bulgarian nation.

They have participated most actively in the political, cultural, educational and church struggles of the Bulgarian people. From that area is for instance the father of the Bulgarian National Revival Period Paissyi of Hilendar. No one in either Bulgaria or any other country could imagine the Bulgarian National Revival Period without Paissyi of Hilendar, without his "Slav-Bulgarian History". There were born, lived and worked eminent figures of the Bulgarian National Revival, like the Miladinov brothers, Grigor Purlichev, Raiko Zhinzifov, Yordan Hadjikonstantinov — Djinot, Kiril Peychinovich and others, who felt and called themselves Bulgarians. The Bulgarian ethnic character of the Slav population in Macedonia at that time is borne out by many Turkish, Serbian, Greek, Romanian, French and other statistical data, by eminent scholars from West Europe and Serbia, the consuls of the Great Powers, etc.

To question all this would have meant to show disregard for the self-expression of the population's awareness of nation and nationality in that period, to commit violence over the historical facts and documents. No serious and conscientious scholar, from whatever country he might be, would allow any neglect of these facts and documents, their unscrupulous forgery. No one in the People's Republic of Bulgaria could agree with the distortion of the national history of the Bulgarian people, with the appropriation of their historical and cultural heritage.

The Ministry of Foreign Affairs emphasizes in a most responsible manner that these views concerning the historical past of the Bulgarian people are adduced here for the sole purpose of showing the complete groundlessness of the claims on a "Macedonian national minority" in Bulgaria. It is thoroughly illegal to ascribe topical political significance to the scientific, precisely scientific elaboration of these questions and on such a ground to make insinuations about the policy of the BCP and of socialist Bulgaria. It is also arbitrary and irresponsible to draw any parallels with the policy of the Bulgarian bourgeoisie, to blame the People's Republic of Bulgaria that she did not accept and did not recognize the existing realities in the Socialist Republic of Macedonia and in this way she was laying claims to the SFRY.

The attitude of the Bulgarian Communist Party and of socialist Bulgaria towards the anti-popular policy of the Bulgarian bourgeoisie is well-known. The Bulgarian Communist Party has always uncompromisingly condemned and still condemns this policy. No one has fought as consistently against the Great-Bulgarian chauvinistic policy of the Bulgarian bourgeoisie as the Bulgarian Communist Party. Guided by its class-selfish interests, the Bulgarian bourgeoisie conducted an anti-popular policy in the Balkans, turning itself into a tool of foreign imperialist interests. Ultimately this led it to the alliance with Nazi Germany in World War II, to violence by the Bulgarian monarcho-fascist authorities over the fighting Yugoslav peoples.

The population of Vardar Macedonia, together with the other peoples of Yugoslavia, led a heroic struggle against fascist occupation. The success of the national-liberation struggle, the victory of the socialist revolution in Yugoslavia led to the establishment of the PR of Macedonia. The People's Republic of Bulgaria greets the successes of the Socialist Republic of Macedonia scored on the road of building up socialism and expresses willingness to develop broad cooperation with it.

Strictly observing the principle of non-interference in the internal affairs of other countries, the PR of Bulgaria has repeatedly declared, she declares it again now that she recognizes the existing realities in the SFRY. These realities are regulated by the Constitution and other domestic iaws of the SFRY. What nations and what nationalities exist in the territory of Yugoslavia is a purely internal question, a question of the peoples of that country. We have never meddled so far and have no intention whatever to meddle in the future in the determination of the existing realities either in Yugoslavia or in any of the other neighbouring countries. The only thing we do not accept and to which we cannot agree is for the formation of the Macedonian State to be done on an anti-Bulgarian basis by forging generally known historical facts and by fanning up feelings of national hostility to the BCP, the PR of Bulgaria and the Bulgarian people.

Putting the principle of mutual recognition of and respect for the existing realities at the base of its approach to solving the so-called outstanding questions, the Bulgarian side in its turn, has every reason and is in its own right to expect that the SFR of Yugoslavia will also adopt this realistic approach of recognizing and respecting the realities in the district of Blagoevgrad.

For centuries — both before the emergence and development of capitalism, when the formation of nations began, and after it the population of the present-day district of Blagoevgrad has always felt to be an indivisible part of the Bulgarian people, has repeatedly and unambiguously expressed its Bulgarian national origin, has had and still has a Bulgarian awareness, a common historical destiny and common struggles with the rest of the country's population. As a result of the 1912-1913 wars this population was nationally liberated from Ottoman boundage, it was included in the boundaries of Bulgaria and continued its natural historical path as an inseparable part of the Bulgarian nation.

This area was one of the centres of the long and harsh struggle of the Bulgarian people for national and social liberation. A galaxy of Bulgarian national revolutionary figures, without whom our old and new history would have been unthinkable, have come from this district. It suffices to name only the leaders of the Bulgarian workers' and communist movement Dimiter Blagoev and Georgi Dimitrov, and the leader of the Agrarian Union, Georgi Traikov.

By the end of World War II the Yugoslav side laid a claim on annexing the Pirin area to Yugoslavia. Bulgaria in her difficult international situation then in connection with the preparations made for the realization of the well-known idea for a South-Slav Federation, held negotiations with Yugoslavia on this matter as well. At variance with Lenin's principles on the national question, as a result of a prolonged pressure, in that period an intensive campaign for forceful inculcation of a different, non-Bulgarian national consciousness in the population of the Pirin area was launched. In that campaign contrary to bilateral accords, the Yugoslav side by various ways and means interfered in the internal affairs of Bulgaria. There is abundant documentation for these actions, the witnesses of the events at that time are also living.

As a consequence of precisely that abnormal situation came the results of the censuses — the only censuses quoted in Yugoslavia.

When conditions were created for a free expression of the will of the population in the district of Blagoevgrad, it again, as always in the past, explicitly and categorically expressed and still expresses its Bulgarian national self-awareness, demonstrated that it was an organic and indivisible part of the Bulgarian nation. This is categorically confirmed by the data of the censuses of 1965 and 1975, and by the enthusiastic and mass participation of this population in the referendum for the approval of the new Constitution of the People's Republic of Bulgaria which took place in 1971.

How absurd it is to base claims on part of the population of a neighbouring state on the data of two censuses alone, carried out in the course of a decade, apart from the context of the concrete situation in which they were held, could be seen if only we try to imagine what would have meant to attach topical political significance to well-known Turkish, French, Russian, English, American, Serbian, German, Romanian, Czech and other statistical data and international inquiries of the 18th, 19th and 20th centuries, which speak of the prevailing part of the population of Macedonia as belonging to the Bulgarian nationality and nation through the centuries. . .

The documents of the 11th LCY Congress contain requests for "restoring the abolished rights" which the "Macedonian national minority" allegedly enjoyed in the PR of Bulgaria in the early post-war period. The joint documents of the bilateral inter-party and inter-governmental Bulgaro-Yugoslav talks from the respective periods are on hand. Nowhere — in either these documents or the internal legislation of the PR of Bulgaria, or any other bilateral or multilateral international treaties and agreements of our country, is there a single word about a "Macedonian minority" in Bulgaria. And the Yugoslav side is well aware of this fact.

The indisputable historical facts and documents, and the all-round free and voluntary expressions of the Bulgarian national awareness of the population of the district of Blagoevgrad in the past and today, testify in a most categorical and incontrovertible way, that there was not and there is not now any "Macedonian national minority" in Bulgaria, there is no Slav population different in its ethnic origin, in its language and culture, in its way of living and religion from the Bulgarian nation. Every one can come here and see the fact for himself.

This question for us, therefore, is not outstanding. For us it does not exist either on an internal or on an international plane. We have dealt and we are dealing with it only in so far as the Yugoslav side is raising it incessantly both in the development of bilateral relations and at international forums.

The Third question of principle refers to the approach to history. Here, as is known, difficult problems exist, inherited from the complex and contradictory past of the Balkans. Many facts and events from that past receive different contrary interpretations in the two countries.

How to proceed in such a situation?

The position of the Bulgarian Communist Party and the People's Republic of Bulgaria on this question is clear: the questions of science cannot and should not be solved in a way different from that of science and by means different from those of science. The differences in interpreting the facts and events of the historical past should be the subject of free and objective scientific research and discussion. They should be a subject of a concrete scientific debate between the expert-historians at bilateral meetings, in the respective scientific and theoretical forums and publications in the two countries. Differences of such nature could not obviously be solved politically by imposing one or another thesis, and still less — by their treatment in the mass media.

* * *

Such is the essence of the Bulgarian stands on the outstanding questions in relations between the People's Republic of Bulgaria and the Socialist Federal Republic of Yugoslavia. These stands are well known to the Yugoslav side. We have not passed over in silence, circumvented or underrated the outstanding questions. On the contrary, we have proposed and do propose realistic and mutually acceptable principles and roads for their solution.

Bilateral talks in the past few years show, however, inconsistency and lack of constructiveness in the approach of the Yugoslav side.

In 1975 in Helsinki Comrades Todor Zhivkov and J.B. Tito agreed on the setting up of a Joint Working Group to make preparations for a summit meeting with a view to raising relations between the two countries to a new, higher stage.

The sittings of the Joint Working Group, as is known, took place in Sofia in September 1976. This meeting was assessed by the two delegations as necessary and useful. It was specified on a proposal made by the Yugoslav delegation for the next meeting of the Joint Working Group to be held in Belgrade with a view to continuing the preparation of the documents for a summit meeting. The results of the talks were positively assessed by the competent Bulgarian organs. The same assessment was given to them also by the Yugoslav leadership through its official representatives.

Later, however, the Yugoslav side in point of fact revised its assessment and the mutual accords reached on continuing the preparations for the summit meeting. At the same time the leader of the Yugoslav delegation to the Joint Working Group at a press conference on Zagreb in April 1977 bound the continuation of the dialogue with the precondition of a ''definite evolution'' taking place in the position of the Bulgarian side. This in essence ultimative demand was taken up by the Yugoslav mass media.

There followed an abrupt escalation in the campaign for pressure on the People's Republic of Bulgaria and the Bulgarian Communist Party which is being conducted by Yugoslavia through the mass media, at international forums and by other means, the objective of which is to impose unacceptable and groundless stands and claims on the Bulgarian side.

This practice and this approach are at gross variance with the UN Charter and the Final Act of Helsinki.

The 11th LCY Congress confirmed and definitely deepened this line and raised it to the rank of Party and State policy.

The formations approved by the 11th LCY Congress for Bulgaro-Yugoslav relations, the Declaration of the Federal Secretariat for Foreign Affairs of the SFRY of June 29 of this year, the publication of the Yugoslav draft document of 1976 and the anti-Bulgarian propaganda campaign that followed cannot be assessed otherwise but as an attempt to obscure the fact that the Yugoslav side categorically rejects the clear and unambiguous proposal of the Bulgarian side for a mutual observance of the realities of the two sides of the frontier, for the right of the population itself to determine its nationality, for a mutual renunciation of territorial claims and the confirmation of the principle of inviolability of the frontiers.

Socialist Bulgaria sees fundamental conditions for ensuring peace and security in the recognition of the post-war territorial realities and in the inviolability of the existing frontiers. Proceeding from the first-rate significance of this question, in its desire to relax the situation and to make a step forward towards the strengthening of mutual trust, the Bulgarian side, as is known, took a new initiative. In his speech on June 15 of this year in Blagoevgrad Comrade Todor Zhivkov declared: ''We are ready to sign a joint declaration in which the People's Republic of Bulgaria and the Socialist Federal Republic of Yugoslavia solemnly confirm the principle of inviolability of the frontiers and make a mutual renunciation of territorial claims. We are ready to do this immediately, without any condition and without any postponement. If only the Yugoslav side agrees, I myself am ready to go to Belgrade first thing tomorrow to put my signature with that of Comrade Tito to such a document".

Throughout the world Comrade Todor Zhivkov's speech in Blagoevgrad and the proposals contained in it have been understood and evaluated as a considerable initiative of the People's Republic of Bulgaria for improving relations with the SFRY.

By the declaration of the Federal Secretariat for Foreign Affairs of the SFRY our proposal for immediate and unconditional confirmation of the inviolability of the frontiers and for mutual renunciation of territorial claims was rejected. At the same time in it to the Bulgarian side are ascribed — however paradoxical this may be — "territorial claims" on Yugoslavia, and the publication of the Yugoslav draft documents of 1976 obviously pursues the objective of imparting the look of authenticity to this accusation.

All the documents for the contacts and talks effected so far on the problems of bilateral relations are on hand. Neither earlier nor in the talks in 1976, nor in Comrade Todor Zhivkov's speech in Blagoevgrad, nor in the practical actions of the PR of Bulgaria even with the greatest endeavour can any ground for such accusations be found.

Things stand just the opposite way. In the declaration of the Federal Secretariat of June 29 of this year it is seen that the Yguoslav side is the one which ties up the question of the inviolability of the frontiers and the renunciation of territorial claims with the condition for the People's Republic of Bulgaria to recognize the "Macedonian minority" in Bulgaria. We reject such a binding as absolutely unacceptable. We cannot assess them otherwise than as an expression of concealed territorial aspirations to the People's Republic of Bulgaria.

When there is a question of frontiers and territories, the People's Republic of Bulgaria cannot accept any conditions. To put on such a plane the question of the frontiers after World War II and after the Helsinki is as dangerous as it is inadmissible.

Obviously the question that remains open is whether the Yugoslav side is ready or not, without any conditions and without postponement, for the PR of Bulgaria and the SFRY to confirm the inviolability of the frontiers and the mutual renunciation of territorial claims. There naturally arises the question are this practice and such an approach of the Yugoslav side to neighbouring socialist Bulgaria compatible with the role of the SFRY in the movement of the non-aligned countries and the principles continuously proclaimed by it in this movement of observing the independence, sovereignty, equality, non-interference in the internal affairs and the territorial integrity in relations between states. Or in the policy of the SFRY there exist two different mutually excluding measures for measuring: one measure is applied when it is a word of declaring principles before the representatives of distant countries, participants in the movement of the non-aligned, and quite a different measure when it is a question of applying the same principles in relations wich neighbouring countries.

As is seen there are radical differences in the positions on and the approach of the two sides to important questions of principle of their relations.

What then should be the correct, realistic road of finding mutually acceptable decisions on the questions which create difficulties in Bulgaro-Yugoslav relations?

The outstanding questions can be successfully discussed and solved only in a spirit of mutual respect and mutual consideration, by a calm and patient friendly dialogue — as befits equal, sovereign and independent states, taking into consideration that Bulgaria and Yugoslavia are socialist states which have not only national interests but also an international responsibility for the common cause of socialism and peace.

Outstanding questions are most successfully surmounted in a situation of all-round development of cooperation and contacts. Such a development is a necessary condition for getting to know each other better, for strengthening understanding and trust — the prerequisites which create a favourable atmosphere for a calm and constructive discussion of the outstanding questions.

Our country is working consistently and constructively for the overcoming of the obstacles that stand in the way of solving the outstanding questions. She has repeatedly expressed willingness for achieving an immediate, comprehensive and definitive solution to the outstanding questions on the basis of the mutual observance of the will of the population itself and the recognition of the realities on the two sides of the frontiers.

Since the Yugoslav side obviously is not ready for the immediate solution of the outstanding questions on such a basis, it remains to seek this solution persistently through systematic, though prolonged efforts of the two sides.

In this situation the Bulgarian side has proposed and proposes for the two countries to agree on the joint study, elucidation and finding generally acceptable and scientifically-grounded stands on the disputed questions, on the holding of coordinated or joint celebrations of common remarkable events and personalities in the history of the Bulgarian and the Yugoslav peoples.

It is necessary to exclude polemics and tendentious reports, to ensure objective, well-meaning and well-wishing information through the mass media about the situation in the two countries.

These are the sole realistic roads of finding mutually acceptable solutions to the so-called outstanding questions.

As is seen, the Bulgarian side does not suggest the "freezing" or "shelving" of the outstanding questions. It is in favour of joint conscientious efforts for their solution. As is a question of two sovereign and independent, and not vassal to each other states, if we want to develop good-neighbourly relations and cooperation we must talk on an equitable basis. The People's Republic of Bulgaria is always ready for such a constructive dialogue.

* * *

These are in substance the general principles of the policy of the Bulgarian Communist Party and the People's Republic of Bulgaria on Bulgaro-Yugoslav relations, including the solving of outstanding issues. They have been repeatedly expressed at various levels before the Yugoslav side. They remain in force.

In his speech in Blagoevgrad on June 15 of this year, the First Secretary of the CC of the BCP and President of the State Council of the PR of Bulgaria, Todor Zhivkov, emphasized: "The Bulgarian Communist Party and the People's Republic of Bulgaria are filled with a sincere wish, with willingness and good will to promote the relations between our neighbouring socialist countries, between our parties and peoples comprehensively, on a broad foundation and on a large scale corresponding to their mutual interests. On the part of Bulgaria there are no obstacles to the development of such relations.

The Bulgarian Communist Party and the People's Republic of Bulgaria do not reduce their policy to the LCY and the SFRY to the outstanding questions of which they quite naturally are realistically aware. In our country this policy is examined more broadly, more comprehensively, as containing all the complex of problems connected with the all-round development of the political, economic and cultural relations between our two neighbouring socialist states.

The line of our Party and State towards the LCY and the SFRY is the line which we unswervingly followed when Georgi Dimitrov stood at the head of the Party and the State and which in the same consistent way we have been pursuing for more than two decades now, since the April Plenary Session of the CC of the BCP. This is a line constant and lasting, uninfluenced by ad hoc considerations.

July 24, 1978, Sofia

Communiqué on the meeting between CMEA and EEC representatives.

(Complete Text).

Nikolai Faddeyev, Secretary of the Council of Mutual Economic Assistance, and members of his staff met on May 29 and 30 with a delegation of the European Communities led by Wilhelm Haferkamp, Vice-President of the Commission of the European Communities. The meeting, held in the CMEA offices in Moscow, was a continuation of the preliminary exchange of views which had envisaged the holding of talks with the object of concluding an agreement between the two sides.

The sides declared their common desire to reach an agreement, noting that the present relations between them are not consonant with the trend of development in Europe and that establishment of normal relations would be in keeping with the spirit of the Final Act adopted by the Conference on Security and Co-operation in Europe.

A wide-ranging exchange of opinions enabled the participants in the meeting to gain a better knowledge of the proposals advanced by the sides in the draft agreements they had submitted earlier and jointly clarify their views in regard to the agreement.

It was agreed that another meeting should be held, and to prepare this meeting a conference of experts would be held in Brussels in the near future as the next stage of the negotiations. The conference would have to define more concretely, on the basis of considerations agreed upon, the areas and terms of implementation of the proposed accord.

It was stated that the Moscow meeting marked an important stage. The participants noted the good atmosphere in which their discussions were held.

Moscow, May 30, 1978.

Businesslike contacts.
Interview with Nikolai Faddeyev, Secretary of the CMEA.

(Excerpts). Izvestia, 3 June, 1978.

Our meeting[1] — N. Faddeyev told an *Isvestiya* correspondent — was a continuation of the previous exchange of views[2] which made it possible to begin talks on establishing relations between the CMEA and the EEC by an appropriate agreement. We had a broad exchange of opinions on the range of questions envisaged by the draft agreements exchanged earlier. We expounded to each other the proposals contained in those drafts, with a view to eliciting those questions that could become the object of agreement.

[1] From 29 to 30 May, 1978 in Moscow. (Ed.).

[2] The first talks between the Community and the CMEA took place from 4 to 6 February 1975, when a delegation of Senior Commission Officials met a delegation of the CMEA Secretariat to discuss relations between the two organizations. Following this meeting, on 16 February 1976, Mr Gaston Thorn, who was President of the Community Council of

Our discussions were difficult, but frank. They proceeded from the common desire to speed the work of establishing relations between both sides. As a result of the discussion, we noted in particular, that our proposals corresponded on the need to exchange information and views by meetings of representatives and officials of the two organizations on matters of economic forecasting, statistics, the protection of the environment and standardization. In addition, it was decided that it would be useful to exchange information on the work of the organizations and to exchange documents on matters of mutual interest. Both sides were unanimous on speeding the work on the preparation of an agreement. For this purpose we agreed to hold another meeting, to be preceded by a conference of experts in Brussels in the very near future.

At the same time, a difference of approach emerged in connection with points touching on the improvement of conditions of trade and economic relations. From our point of view, together with matters of economic forecasting, statistics, protection of the environment and standardization, it would be necessary that the agreement should also reflect matters connected with improving conditions for trade and economic relations. We consider that these questions should be an integral part of our agreement, bearing in mind that they make up one of the main factors of co-operation in the spirit of the Final Act of the Conference on Security and Co-operation in Europe.

The delegation of the Commission of the European Communities, in accordance with the position it had adopted earlier, declared that questions of trade should not be included in the agreement.

At the meeting with Haferkamp,[3] we stressed our desire that the agreement should be between the CMEA and its member countries, on the one

Ministers at that time, received Mr Gerhard Weiss, the then President of the CMEA, who gave him a message from the CMEA to the EEC which proposed the conclusion of an agreement covering relations between the two organizations.

On 18 November 1976, the Council replied to the CMEA's February proposal by sending a letter containing a preliminary draft agreement setting out the forms and procedures of the relations to be established between the Community and the CMEA. These could take the form of working relations aimed at exchanges of information and contacts in the spheres of statistics, economic programming and the environment. At the same time, the Council stressed the importance which it attached to the development of Community relations, not only with the CMEA, but also with each of its member countries.

On 18 April 1977, Mr K. Olszewski, the President of the CMEA Executive Committee at that time, proposed that an exchange of ideas should take place between the President of the CMEA Executive Committee and the President of the EEC Council on the way in which subsequent negotiations should develop. The planned meeting took place on 21 September 1977 in Brussels. The CMEA representative was Mr Marinescu, the Romanian Deputy Prime Minister and President of the CMEA Executive Committee at that time. The two parties agreed to think in terms of beginning the negotiations leading to an agreement between the two organizations during the first half of 1978. (Ed.).

[3] Vice-President of the Commission of the European Communities; special responsibilities for negotiations.

hand, and the EEC and its member countries on the other. This would enable us to create favourable conditions for the development of co-operation over the whole range of relations between the organizations and their member countries. We advocated that the agreement should envisage not only an exchange of information and contacts between representatives and experts of both sides, as proposed by the Community, but also more active forms of co-operation, such as the holding of conferences, seminars and symposia, and the joint study and elaboration of problems, etc. In addition, in our opinion it would be expedient to set up a joint working body comprising representatives of the CMEA and its member countries and of the EEC and representatives of the EEC member countries to promote the implementation of the agreement.

I should like to mention our agreement that all the questions listed above, including those on which we still differ, will be discussed at future talks. In the opinion of both sides, the meeting which has taken place has been an important stage in normalizing relations and developing co-operation between our two organizations and their member countries. All the participants in the meeting noted the good atmosphere in which it took place. In conclusion, I should like to stress particularly that the signing of an agreement between both sides would be an important step in the real-ization of the agreements reached at Helsinki, and would thereby make a considerable contribution to the cause of putting detente into practice on the continent of Europe...

Note of the Ministry of Foreign Affairs of the People's Republic of China to the Embassy of the Socialist Republic of Albania in China, 7 July 1978.

(Complete Text). Hsinhua News Agency, 13 July, 1978.

The Ministry of Foreign Affairs of the People's Republic of China presents its compliments to the Embassy of the People's Socialist Republic of Albania in China and has the honour to state the following:

At the request of the Albanian Government, the Chinese Government has, since 1954, provided Albania with economic and military aid with a view to enhancing the friendship between the two peoples and the amicable relations between the two countries and in keeping with the principles of Marxism-Leninism and proletarian internationalism. Implementation of the agreements concluded between China and Albania calls for an outlay by the Chinese Government of more than ten billion yuan renminbi, most of which has already been paid out. China agreed to help Albania build 142 complete projects, 91 of which have been completed, 23 are in the main completed or under construction, and 17 others have been surveyed and are being designed. New industrial branches in Albania built with Chinese aid include iron and steel, chemical fertilizers, caustic soda, acids, glass, copper processing, paper, plastics and armaments. Projects built with Chinese aid in existing Albanian industrial branches as electricity, coal, petroleum, machine tools, light industries, textiles, building materials, communications and broadcasting helped greatly to expand their productive capacity. China provided Albania with large amounts of arms and equipment gratis. Nearly 6,000 Chinese experts were sent to Albania over the years on aid projects. China helped Albania train large numbers of economic and military technical cadres, of whom more than 2,000 were trained in China. It is evident to any unbiased person that China has conscientiously implemented and not violated its aid agreements with Albania, and that Chinese aid has served to strengthen and not impair Albania's economic development and defence building.

China has been aiding Albania while facing many difficulties itself. We delivered 1,800,000 tons of foodgrain to you when our own food supplies were inadequate. We provided you with more than 1,000,000 tons of steel products when there was not enough steel to meet our own needs. We supplied you with more than 10,000 tractors when the level of mechanization of our agriculture is still quite low, relying as we do mainly on manpower and draught animals. Though we have insufficient power generating capacity, we helped you complete or in the main complete six power stations of varying sizes with a total installed capacity of 885,000 kw, thus enabling Albania to be more than self-sufficient in electricity. We provided your armed forces with new China-made tanks and interceptors even before our own armed forces were equipped with them. We bought from abroad and re-exported to you the set of equipment, which we could not produce at the time, for the Fieri nitrogenous fertilizer plant with our much-needed foreign currency. We conducted for you special experiments and trial production over a period of more than a dozen years, spending more than a 100,000,000 yuan renminbi, for the establishment of an integrated metallurgical complex using as its raw material your paragenetic laterite ore of nickel, cobalt, iron and chromium, when we had no practical experience in this regard and when the technology and equipment required were not available on the international market. Of the 29 workshops of this complex, 20 have been completed and are in operation. The project helped Albania to produce its own iron and steel for the first time in March 1976.

China started with a weak economic and technical foundation and in recent years our national economy was affected by the sabotage of Lin Piao and the gang of four as well as serious natural disasters. It is therefore natural that we could not meet all the increasing Albanian demands for aid and could not give whatever you wanted and whenever you wanted it. But the Chinese people can say with equanimity that they scrimped on food and clothing and tried their best to aid Albania in the spirit of proletarian internationalism.

It must also be pointed out that we have continued to fulfil our aid commitments in spite of the fact that in recent years the Albanian side has repeatedly attacked China's domestic and foreign policies by insinuation. In 1975 we agreed to provide a new interest-free loan of 500,000,000 yuan renminbi and signed a new agreement on gratis military aid. Starting from the seventh congress of the Albanian Party of Labour in November 1976, the Albanian leaders began to make venomous public attacks on the Chinese people's great leader Chairman Mao and the Chinese Communist Party, seriously hurting their feelings. Even in these circumstances, China valued the friendship between the Chinese and the Albanian peoples and continued to aid Albania. The Chinese experts continued their work in pursuance of agreement. In the period from 1977 up to now, China has shipped nearly 300,000 tons of economic and military aid supplies to Albania, helped Albania to complete or in the main complete 10 construction projects, conceded the Albanian Government's request to postpone the repayment of the debt of 217,000,000 yuan renminbi due before 1980 to the period of 1991-2000, and signed an agreement on China's gratis provision of spare parts of military equipment to Albania. The sincere friendship cherished by the Chinese Government and people for the Albanian people and their good desire of maintaining the cooperation between the two countries are obvious to the broad mass of the Albanian people, cadres and soldiers.

The leaders of Albania on many occasions spoke highly of China's aid. Enver Hoxha, First Secretary of the Central Committee of the Albanian Party of Labour, said in his report at the sixth Party Congress in 1971 that China had given Albania "great and disinterested internationalist aid" and that "the Albanian people and the Party of Labour are deeply grateful to the Chinese people, the glorious Chinese Communist Party and Chairman Mao Tsetung for their fraternal aid to our socialist construction and for the prosperity and strength of our socialist motherland". Enver Hoxha and Mehmet Shehu in their message addressed on behalf of the Central Committee of the Albanian Party of Labour to Chairman Mao, Premier Chou and the Central Committee of the Chinese Communist Party in November 1975 said that "the People's Republic of China has also given the People's Republic of Albania help in the field of national defence by supplying it gratis with weapons, ammunition, means of war and equipment. The aid you have given us in the field of national defence has a major significance for our people and our Party."

But now the Albanian side, out of its own political needs in domestic and foreign policy and while intensifying its political anti-China campaign, has wantonly maligned China's aid to Albania and tried to sabotage the economic and military cooperation between the two sides. Here we just cite some of the many facts.

(1) In the first quarter of 1978 when the Albanian Vice-Minister of Industries and Mines discussed with us the question of Chinese aid for the building of an integrated metallurgical complex and other projects, he insisted that we fix a schedule for the delivery of the blueprints and equipment of the steel plate cold rolling workshop, the seamless tubing workshop and the pig iron casting workshop in the absence of results from the experiments. When we objected to this unreasonable demand, he refused any further consultations, asserted that what Albania has said was "final and categorical" and brazenly terminated the talks. This not only barred the solution of a series of questions yet to be negotiated, but also suspended work on the aid projects of the steel plate hot rolling workshop and the tube welding workshop, on which agreement had been reached.

(2) With regard to the Ballsh integrated refinery, Chinese experts long ago explained in detail to its leadership and staff the necessity of strict observance of the rules of operation, for the plant operates under high temperatures and pressures and its products are inflammable and liable to explosion. After the refinery went into operation in early 1978, however, the Albanian management ignored the technical guidance of the Chinese experts and violated operational rules, resulting in eight serious accidents within a period of three months or so. For example, there is the rule that the water content of the crude oil used in the hydrogenate refining unit must not exceed 1%. But the Albanian side in trial production used crude oil with a water content of as high as 70%, thus bringing production to a halt. What was more serious, in operating the coking unit which had been under normal operation, the Albanian side, behind the backs of the Chinese experts, closed all the valves and ran it into excessive temperature. This was obviously done to create a major accident and then put the blame on the Chinese experts and defame China.

(3) In the case of the naval base project which was being built with Chinese gratis aid, the discontinuance of the work was due to the belated discovery of seeping karst caves overlooked through poor geological survey by the Albanian side. In October 1977, the Chinese side was requested by the Albanian side to send experts to help solve the problem. It approved the request in a reply in January 1978, having had to spend some time studying the problem. But the Albanian side, on the pretext of the slowness of the reply, changed its mind by taking the work upon itself and terminated Chinese aid for this project. Moreover, it took advantage of the matter to attack China's military aid as a whole, slandering China for "damaging" Albania's national defence.

(4) In March 1978, the Chinese side informed the Albanian side that the necks of the hub shafts of the China-supplied H5 helicopters needed to be taken back to China for checking and repairs as a defect had been found in

the manufacturing process. This was done with good will and should have been positively responded to by the Albanian side. But the latter refused to send the necks back for checking and repairs and at the same time declared that the Chinese side would be held responsible for any mishaps. This is preposterous!

(5) It is provided in the agreement and it is a normal construction procedure that trial production may start only when necessary conditions have been created. But in May 1978 the Albanian side insisted that the Chinese experts act on its decision to start trial production without the necessary conditions at the newly-expanded workshop of the Enver machine tool plant and at the Valis coal mine. When the Chinese experts objected, the Albanian side went ahead on their own, while asserting that they would hold the Chinese side responsible if things went wrong. On the other hand, the Albanian side created various pretexts and, in violation of agreement, refused to sign notes on the starting of operation of projects whose trial production had been completed, such as the cinder brick factory and the blast furnace and certain workshops of the integrated metallurgical complex.

(6) It was the usual practice over 20-odd years and it was according to agreement that the Chinese side delivered invoices along with each delivery of equipment of materials for a project, and the two sides confirmed the cost of the completed project at the final settlement when balances were paid to either side as the case may be. But in May 1978 the Albanian side suddenly refused to accept the 25 invoices, totally nearly 100,000,000 yuan renminbi, which were delivered by the Chinese side for the equipment and materials and their freight for the aid projects built in the period between December 1977 and April 1978. This violation of agreement made it impossible for the continuation of normal work in the cooperation between the two countries.

(7) A scaffold was formed in the blast furnace of the metallurgical complex due to the Albanian side's disregard for the technical advice of Chinese experts. As soon as the Chinese experts discovered this on 17th March 1978, they informed the enterprise and workshop leaders. They repeatedly recommended effective measures for minimizing the harm and preventing expansion of the scaffold but were ignored. It was not until 22nd May that the Albanian machinery import corporation proposed to the Chinese side to employ a Chinese expert to blast off the scaffold. While the Chinese side was favourably studying the request and about to approve it, the Albanian Ministry of Foreign Affairs sent over a Note on 31st May 1978 stating that the Chinese side must dispatch someone to Albania within two or three days to remove the trouble and that otherwise the Albanian side would blast the scaffold on its own and would hold the Chinese side responsible for the consequences. This ultimatum-like demand was what no sovereign State could accept and was, in fact, impossible to meet. However,

in order to uphold cooperation between the two countries, the Chinese side stated that if the Albanian side truly desired to employ a Chinese expert, it should send over a Note which the Chinese side would consider. But the Albanian side refused to send over any Note. All this shows that the Albanian side is deliberately creating an issue to sabotage cooperation.

(8) In its Notes to the Chinese Embassy in Albania dated 29th April and 20th May, 1978, the Albanian Ministry of Foreign Affairs made entirely groundless charges, alleging that Chinese experts "had the deliberate intention of harming Albania's economy", and that China was "placing obstacles" in its aid to Albania "in violation of" agreements and "causing serious damage" to the Albanian economy, etc. On 7th June 1978, the Chinese Ministry of Foreign Affairs sent a reply Note to the Albanian side, expressing the hope for an exchange of views through Notes and the solution of differences in the cooperation between the two countries so that the cooperation may continue. But the Albanian Ambassador to China refused to accept the Note or solve the problems through consultation.

All the facts show that the Albanian leadership has decided to pursue the anti-China course, deliberately abandoned the agreements signed between the two sides providing Chinese aid to Albania, slandered and tried and fabricate trumped-up charges against Chinese experts, and sabotaged the economic and military cooperation between China and Albania in a planned and systematic way, making it impossible for our aid work to go on while you have blocked the way to a solution of the problems through consultation. In these circumstances, the Chinese Government has no choice but to stop its economic and military aid and its aid payments to Albania and bring back its economic and military experts now working there. The Chinese Government hopes that the Albanian Government will facilitate the return of the Chinese experts. The disruption of the economic and military cooperation between China and Albania is wholly the making of the Albanian side, which must bear the full responsibility.

The Chinese Government has always valued the friendship between the Chinese and Albanian peoples and still hopes to maintain and develop normal relations between China and Albania.

The Ministry of Foreign Affairs of the People's Republic of China avails itself of this opportunity to renew to the Embassy of the People's Socialist Republic of Albania the assurances of its highest consideration.

Peking, 7th July, 1978

Letter of the Central Committee of the Party of Labour and the Government of Albania to the Central Committee of the Communist Party and the Government of China.

(Complete Text).

On July 7, 1978 the Ministry of Foreign Affairs of the People's Republic of China handed an official note to the Embassy of the People's Socialist Republic of Albania in Peking, whereby it announces the decision of the Chinese Government "to stop its economic and military aid and its aid payments to Albania and bring back its economic and military experts" working in Albania up till that date.

With this perfidious and hostile act towards socialist Albania, you unscrupulously scrapped the agreements officially concluded between the two countries, brutally and arbitrarily violated elementary international rules and norms and extended ideological disagreements to state relations with Albania.

Taking this hostile step against socialist Albania, you seek to hit at, and damage, the economy and defence capacity of our country, to sabotage the cause of the revolution and socialism in Albania. At the same time, you gravely undermine the fraternal friendship between the Albanian and Chinese peoples. Wishing ill to a socialist country, such as the People's Socialist Republic of Albania, you give satisfaction to the enemies of socialism and the revolution. The responsibility for this reactionary and anti-Albanian act, as well as its consequences, lies completely with the Chinese side.

The Central Committee of the Party of Labout of Albania and the Albanian Government denounce the brutal cessation of aid and loans to socialist Albania before all world public opinion as a reactionary act from great power positions, an act which is a repetition, in content and form, of the savage and chauvinistic methods of Tito, Khrushchev and Brezhnev which China, also, once condemned.

The Central Committee of the Party of Labour of Albania and the Albanian Government reject the attempts made in the Chinese note to blame Albania, to groundlessly accuse the Albanian leadership of allegedly being ungrateful for China's aid and of allegedly having tried to sabotage the economic and military cooperation between the two countries. To any normal person it is unbelievable and preposterous that Albania, a small country, which is fighting against the imperialist-revisionist encirclement and blockade and which has set to large-scale and all-round work for the rapid economic and cultural development of its country, which is working tirelessly for the strengthening of the defence capacity of its socialist

Homeland, should cause and seek cessation of economic cooperation with China, refuse its civil and military loans and aid.

Inspired by the teachings of Marxism-Leninism and the principles of proletarian internationalism, the Albanian people, their Party and Government have sincerely and consistently fought for the strengthening of friendship, fraternal cooperation and mutual aid between Albania and China. The have always highly appreciated China's aid to Albania, considering it an internationalist aid of the Chinese people, an aid serving the general cause of the revolution and socialism in the world, an aid coming from a country which was called socialist. Now, as in the past, the Albanian people, their Party and Government stick to their assessments of this aid and its role, among other external factors, in the development of our country.

Socialist Albania has never considered its friendship with the peoples of other countries a means of economic profit. At the same time, it has permitted nobody to consider economic aid and cooperation an investment whereby political and ideological views, which run counter to Marxism-Leninism and socialism, are dictated to, and imposed on, our country. The People's Socialist Republic of Albania has never sold out its principles, it has never traded on them.

When the Party of Labour of Albania defended the Communist Party of China from the attack of the Khrushchevite revisionists at the Bucharest and Moscow Meetings of the Communist and Workers' Parties in 1960, it did so in full consciousness in order to defend the principles of Marxism-Leninism, and not to be given some factories and some tractors by China in return. When socialist Albania, for many years on end, defended the rights of People's China at the UNO against the US plot, it was not doing so for material interests, but for the defence of a just and principled cause. When the Party of Labour of Albania and our working class supported the strategic aims of the Cultural Revolution in China, they were not doing so for the sake of compensation, but out of their will to assist the working class, the communists and people of China to save their country from the capitalist elements who had usurped power in China.

In order to justify its cessation of aid to Albania, the Chinese Government, out of necessity, has limited itself to economic and technical "arguments" of simple common practice in interstate relations. You are doing this in order to cover up the true motives which have impelled you to take this hostile action against socialist Albania.

The cessation of aid and loans to Albania cannot be motivated with the 8 "facts" listed in the Chinese note that allegedly "the Vice-minister of Industry and Mining of Albania . . . refused further consultations . . . and brazenly terminated the talks"; that the Albanian experts "ignored the technical guidance of the Chinese experts" in the oil refinery; that the Chinese design for a military project proved successful because of "the belated discovery of seeping karst caves overlooked through poor geological survey by the Albanian side'' and that the Albanian side ''changed its mind by taking the work upon itself and terminated Chinese aid for this project''; that the Albanian side ''created various pretexts and in violation of agreements, refused to sign notes on the starting of operations of projects''; that the Albanian side ''suddenly refused to accept the 25 invoices totalling nearly 100 million yuan Renminbi''; ''that due to the Albanian side's disregard for the technical advice of Chinese experts, a scaffold was formed in the blast-furnace'', and the Albanian specialists eliminated this defect without waiting for experts to come from China; that ''the Albanian Ambassador to China refused to accept the Chinese note of June 7, 1978''.

These ''arguments'' and the ''facts'' brought forth by the Chinese Government, are not only fabricated and distorted, but even if they were not so, they could never serve as a moral and juridical basis whereupon a state could rely to justify its one-sided and brutal cessation of economic and military aid to another state, with which it has been in close alliance for a long time.

The true motives for the cessation of aid and loans to Albania have not an exclusively technical character, as the note of the Chinese Government makes out, on the contrary they have a deep political and ideological character. In their letter the Central Committee of the Party of Labour of Albania and the Albanian Government will throw full light on these political and ideological motives. But first we will stop to prove that the ''arguments'' the Chinese side resorts to in its note do not respond at all to reality.

The Government of the People's Socialist Republic of Albania will acquaint world opinion with the truth on economic relations between China and Albania and, in particular, on the questions the Chinese note takes up, by publishing the full text of the notes exchanged on these questions between the governments of the two countries. Herein we will clarify some ''facts'' mentioned in the Chinese note.

Tendentiously listing a series of figures about China's aid to Albania, the Chinese note of July 7 reflects the desire of the Chinese leadership to boast before the world. It is acting in the same way as the Soviet revisionist leadership, which with the boastfulness of the great state, constantly advertizes the ''aid'' it has once granted to Albania.

We are compelled to remind the Chinese leaders that their boasting is in utter opposition to the official declarations once made by the Chinese Government itself.

The solemn Statement on the 8 principles of the aid of the Chinese Government to other states reads: ''The Chinese Government always bases itself on the principles of equality and mutual benefit in giving aid to other countries. It never considers such an aid one-sided alms, but something reciprocal''. When visiting 14 countries in 1964 Chou En-lai stressed that

". . . in case we were to boast of our aid to others this would be great state chauvinsim".

The Albanian people, Party and Government have never denied the aid of the People's Republic of China and its role in the economic development of our country. They have acknowledged and appreciated this aid, proceeding from their sincere feelings and thinking that it came from a friendly state and was given in the spirit of the principles of socialism.

Yet, while making an exaggerated and embellished description of the Chinese economic and military aid to Albania, the Chinese note has no word about the fact that Albania, too, has aided China, as the Chinese leaders themselves have declared time and again, previously.

Appreciating the aid Albania has given China, Mao Tsetung said: "First of all, we must thank you, because you stand in the forefront, because you are in very difficult situations and persistently fight to defend Marxism-Leninism. This is a very valuable thing, this is more valuable" (From minutes of a meeting with an Albanian delegation, June 29, 1962).

On his part, Chou En-lai stated: "The Albanian comrades frequently mention China's support for, and aid to, Albania. I would like to stress here in the first place, that Albania has given us great aid and support.

". . . The Chinese people wiii never forget that at the time when the modern revisionists slandered against and attacked the Communist Party of China frenziedly, assuming a correct stand, regardless of all pressures, difficulties and dangers, the Party of Labour of Albania, courageously faced up to this opposite trend, exposed and mercilessly hit at the anti-Chinese plots of modern revisionism" ("Zëri i Popullit", January 9, 1964, speech at the Tirana rally).

On another occasion Chou En-lai said: "We are doing our internationalist duty and it will be betrayal if we do not help you . . . As the bastion of socialism in Europe, you are fighting against imperialism, revisionism and all reaction. If we do not help you, we would not be internationalist communists, but traitors. Support and assistance between us, between China and Albania, are mutual. You are a radiant beacon in Europe, and you are fighting unflinchingly and intrepidly. This is of great aid to, and support for, us and for all the peoples of the world" (From minutes of a meeting with an Albanian delegation, Peking, August 29, 1971).

A similar statement has been made also by Kang Sheng: "I have often told the comrades and I again stress that the Albanian comrades are giving us a great, colossal help. We must not consider only the nitrate amonium plant, the thermopower station, the various plants and factories we give you, they are nothing compared to the great support the Albanian comrades are giving us and the world communist movement" (From the speech at the dinner in honour of the Chinese delegation on November 13, 1966, in Tirana).

We are embarrassed when we have to mention the help Albania has given China, because what the Albanian Party and people have done for China and the Chinese people has been done with a communist sense of duty and inspired by fraternal and internationalist feelings. But you forced us to mention it, because following in the footsteps of Khrushchev and Brezhnev, you began to count the yuans and fens you have given Albania!

In its note, the Chinese Government tries to create the impression, in the public opinion, that if Albania has had any success in its economic development, this, allegedly, is due to Chinese aid. For this purpose and in order to impress the internal and international public opinion, the figures mentioned in the Chinese note are purposely inflated and fabricated. It says that the "implementation of the agreements concluded between China and Albania calls for an outlay by the Chinese Government of more than ten billion yuan Renminbi". This is an arbitrary figure which does not correspond to the truth.

First of all, it must be said that what the Chinese Government considers aid is in reality credits, obligations deriving from agreements concluded between the two governments in conformity with the desires and interests of the two sides and common international practice in the relations between sovereign states, which involve bilateral obligations. Thus, here we have nothing to do with alms or Christian charity.

On the other hand, from documents in possession of the Albanian side, it follows that from December 1954 up to July 1975, 17 government agreements on granting credits to Albania by People's China, besides agreements on military aid, have been signed between People's China and Albania. Among these 17 agreements, there are some in which the aid in credits is reckoned in old rubles, then in new rubles, later in British pounds, finally in internal yuans, or in commercial yuans or US dollars. From the convertion of the various currencies mentioned in these agreements into "commercial" yuans according to the Chinese official exchange rate fixed by the China Bank in the respective periods, it follows that the total value of Chinese economic aid in credits accorded to Albania from 1954 up to 1975, when the last agreement was signed, does not "exceed 10 billion yuans", as claimed in the Chinese note, but amounts only to 3 billion and 53 million commercial yuans. Until July 1978 Albania has utilized about 75% of this sum, reckoning the value of integral projects and general materials at the prices unilaterally set by the Chinese side. But here it must be stressed that the values included in the invoices of the China Bank for complete projects and general materials are not reckoned on the basis of the prices set "in joint consultation", but at arbitrary prices set by the Chinese side alone, without consulting the Albanian side at all, as stipulated in the agreement. Therefore, the return by the Bank of the Albanian State to the China Bank of the invoices for the projects built in Albania is no "violation of agreements", as the Chinese note makes out.

Prices for integral projects and general materials, at which the invoices sent by China are reckoned, were not set in accordance with the provisions of the official agreements between the Government of the People's Republic of Albania and the Government of the People's Republic of China of June 8, 1965, and the stipulations of the correspondence of December 22, 1971 which clearly says that: "Prices for integral projects and general materials . . . will be fixed after joint consultation according to the principles of the setting of trade prices between China and Albania".

As far as military aid is concerned, the assessments of the Chinese side are utterly arbitrary, because in agreements of this category prior to 1967, all evaluations are made in Chinese currency, without consulting the Albanian side, whereas in later agreements which comprise most of the Chinese military aid to Albania, there is no definition of concrete values, either in Chinese or any other currency.

Therefore, those billions of yuans mentioned in the Chinese note do not represent the real sum of China's economic and military aid to Albania, but represent a claim made on the basis of arbitrary, one-sided and tendentious reckonings by the Chinese side. We affirm that, in order to further its sinister aims, the Chinese side precipitated matters when it set such figures. Complete reckonings will be made according to the agreements, protocols and criteria established by both sides. Reckonings will be made taking also account of the loss and damage the Chinese side has caused our economy by failing to meet contracted obligations on time, leaving an important part of the projects incompleted, etc.

The Chinese side has not been correct in the implementation of official agreements and protocols and jointly established criteria, either. The overwhelming majority of the economic projects built in Albania on Chinese credits have always been carried out with delays, which fluctuate from 1 to 6 years. There are also projects, such as the Ferro-chrome Factory which was due to be built on Chinese credits in Albania on the basis of an agreement concluded in 1965, which for the fault of the Chinese side has not been completed to this day. Likewise, the construction of the Metallurgical Complex began with delay and to this day, also, for the fault of the Chinese side, investment in its construction has been realized only to a measure of 67 as against the volume of the total value of the Complex, and China has delivered only 74% of the equipment.

These flagrant violations of official agreements by the Chinese side have caused grave damage to the Albanian economy, and the Chinese Government bears full material and moral responsibility for this. When all this is calculated according to official documentation and concrete facts, then it will be seen who owes who and how much.

In the Chinese note China's aid to Albania is presented as the decisive factor in our country's development. But it has never been, nor could it ever be, such a factor. The decisive factor, which nobody can deny, has been the resolute, persistent and heroic work and struggle of the Albanian people, under the leadership of the Party of Labour of Albania, for the construction of socialism according to the Leninist principle of self-reliance. The brilliant successes attained by Albania in the construction of socialism and the defence of the country are the deed of the Party of Labour of Albania, of the Albanian state of the dictatorship of the proletariat, of the Albanian people, and not the result of external aid.

The aid received from China has been only an auxiliary factor. The total value of the Chinese credits utilized by Albania up to the end of 1977 amounted to a very small percentage of our national income. This is the reality, and not its false presentation by the Chinese side which tries to create the impression as if it is China that has kept the Albanian people alive.

The chauvinistic concepts of the great state have clouded the minds of the Chinese leadership and have made it speak in the language of feudal landlords. The Chinese note boasts that China has delivered 1.8 million tons of wheat, etc., to Albania. It almost stops short of saying that Albania "has kept body and soul together thanks to China's bread"! This is an offensive stand towards the Albanian people. The truth is that Albania has imported grain from China during the period of 1956-1975. Not only does this figure not correspond to reality, but it should also be said that Albania has received only 436,000 tons of bread grain on credit from China over all this period, whereas it has received the rest in the commercial way, paying for it on a clearing basis. As the Chinese note has rounded into one figure both the bread grain imported by Albania on credit and the bread grain imported by it on a clearing basis, why does the Chinese side fail to mention what it has taken from Albania, what Albania has exported to China on a clearing basis during the period 1954-1977? Albania has delivered to China over 1,7 million tons of oil, over 1,3 million tons of bitumen, about 2,7 million tons of chromium ore and chromium concentrate, etc.

By mentioning its military aid in its note and making this note public, the Chinese Government has deliberately made public the military secret of the defence of the People's Socialist Republic of Albania. By so doing, the Chinese Government has gravely impaired the defence of the People's Socialist Republic of Albania and helped its external enemies, in particular the forces of the North-Atlantic Treaty Organization and US imperialism and the forces of the Warsaw Treaty and Soviet socialimperialism. This is an act of perfidy, and the Chinese Government bears responsibility for it.

A special place in the note of the Chinese Government is occupied by attempts to accuse the Albanian working people of allegedly failing to respect and being unwilling to collaborate with the Chinese experts who had come to Albania. These are inventions through and through, and we will not take the trouble to refute them. We are convinced that, in his conscience, no Chinese expert who has lived and worked among our people will approve of these accusations. During all this time, the Albanian workers, specialists and managers have collaborated with the Chinese experts in a fraternal and friendly spirit, assessed their work correctly, respected their knowledge and experience.

Furthering definite ends, the Chinese note says that within 24 years 6,000 Chinese experts have been sent to Albania. This global figure is dished out in order to back up the claim that the credit for constructions, industry, agriculture and everything that has been made in Albania allegedly goes to these 6,000 specialists. But the construction of new Albania is the deed of the Albanian people themselves. Tens of thousands of Albanian specialists, engineers and technicians have worked everyday and continuously in the construction of various projects, without mentioning here the hundreds of thousands of technicians of medium training and the skilled workers. Without their work and knowledge no project could have been built.

As well as that, the Chinese note does not say that the experts sent by China have been paid handsomely by the Albanian people. This is not mentioned, but the note does not fail to remind us that China has allegedly spent 100 million yuans to experiment with Albanian iron! And this at the time when the Chinese experts, on orders from above, upon leaving Albania, left no blueprints to the Albanian specialists; they either burnt or took along with them all blueprints in their possession of the projects which were being built in Albania with Chinese aid.

It is natural that problems should arise between two partners, between two states about concrete economic questions for the solution of which discussions are necessary, even indispensable. The Chinese leadership, however, felt no need to conduct normal discussions, because it wanted to impose its opinions on Albania. Not only today, but for a long period of time before, the Chinese side, in various forms and manners, has brought pressure to bear on Albania over economic questions. During the talks about the signing of agreements of China's granting economic aid in credits to Albania, and then on observance of these agreements, many debates have taken place, in which the Albanian side has successfully opposed the views of the Chinese leadership which sought to impose a one-sided economic development on Albania, to inhibit its rapid and steady development.

In the lengthy debates, the pressure of the Chinese leadership reached such a degree that it threatened to have work on the designing of the hydro-power plants of Vau i Dejës and Fierza suspended, so that we should not build at all these very important industrial projects. The Chinese leadership thought that, as in their opinion, Albania had no technical cadres to design such large and complicated hydro-power plants with its own forces, it would consequently give up work on construction of these projects. But in the end, seeing that the Albanian side was undertaking to design these two hydro-power plants itself, it was compelled to accord the credit. And actually these hydro-power plants were designed and built by the Albanian specialists, whereas the Chinese experts played the role of consultants instead of designers.

Many facts and documents indicate that, at given moments, whenever the Chinese policy made great turns, to which the Albanian Party and Government did not agree, the Chinese Government resorted to pressure and various coercive economic measures. These stands are a flat denial of the clamorous and repeated statements by the Chinese Government according to which "in granting aid to other countries, the Chinese Government strictly respects the sovereignty of the recipient country and never makes it conditional on, or asks, any privilege in return".

The Chinese note says: ". . . The Albanian side out of its own needs in domestic and foreign policies . . . , has wantonly maligned China's aid to Albania. . .". This lays bare the spirit of intrigue of the Chinese leadership and its desire to see Albania politically, ideologically and economically enslaved by Soviet socialimperialism or American imperialism and the reactionary bourgeoisie. The Chinese leadership speaks so because it thinks that Albania is isolated, that it could breathe and live only through China, and that now it has remained on the streets and will fall into the trap laid by the imperialists or the socialimperialists. This is what Khrushchev and Mikoyan thought when they once said that Albania would sell itself out "for thirty pieces of silver", that "without Soviet aid it would die of starvation, within fifteen days"!

But life showed that Albania did not sell itself out, nor did it die of starvation. It forged ahead with great success in the construction of socialism. And this was done not with Chinese aid, but with the heroic work and glorious struggle of the Albanian people.

In the future, too, under the leadership of the Party of Labour of Albania, the Albanian people, relying on their own forces, will always advance triumphantly on the road of socialism, and with their own example they will demonstrate to their friends and the peoples the unconquerable strength and vitality of Marxism-Leninism, the vigour of socialism, the vigour of the people.

In our struggle for the construction of socialism and the defence of the Homeland, in our efforts to face up to and overcome with success the difficulties raised to our country by the hostile act of the Chinese Government, we have and will continue to have more internationalist aid from the genuine revolutionaries, the freedom-loving and progressive people all over the world. Albania has never been isolated, it can never be isolated.

The plans for Albania's development, as laid out by the Party, will be carried out with success in all directions, through the selfless work and resolve of our people, relying on their own forces, also on the projects which China left incomplete, as well as on more new projects which will be added to them.

The unilateral breach of the agreements on economic and military co-operation with Albania by the Chinese Government, the arbitrary violation on its part of the contracts officially concluded between the two countries, the suspension of work on many projects important to our socialist economy, the ordering back of its experts, and so on, reflect a definite political and ideological line of the Chinese leadership. They are the outcome of the departure of the Chinese leadership from Marxism-Leninism and the principles of proletarian internationalism, of its rapprochement to and collaboration with American imperialism, the international bourgeoisie and reaction, of its renunciation of aid to and support for the revolutionary and liberation forces in the international arena, of China's intentions to become an imperialist superpower.

This course of the Chinese leadership, which went through a zigzag process, has come up against the constant opposition of the Party of Labour of Albania which cherishes the cause of socialism, the revolution and the liberation of the peoples above everything else. This accounts for the emergence of serious ideological and political contradictions which have been gradually growing between the Party of Labour of Albania and the Communist Party of China. Precisely because our Party and the Albanian people did not accept and did not submit to the Chinese line and views of a great power, the leadership of the Communist Party of China and the Chinese Government went to such lengths as to cut all aid to socialist Albania, and extended ideological disagreements to interstate relations.

All along, the Central Committee of the Party of Labour of Albania has tried to settle these differences on a Marxist-Leninist road, through mutual consultations and comradely explanations, never making them public.

On this question, our Party has proceeded from the principle that differences and misunderstandings may arise among various parties and states, even when they have relations of close friendship. No matter which side is to blame, the clearing of differences and misunderstandings calls for negotiations. The more so, this principle should be implemented between two socialist countries and communist parties. Such norms, as mutual consultations and comradely explanations, are absolutely necessary, because these Marxist-Leninist norms defend pure friendship, and not hypocritical and evil-intentioned friendship, they defend the purity of our scientific theory, Marxism-Leninism, strengthen the revolution and the struggle of the peoples.

Among the Marxist-Leninist norms which regulate relations among communist parties there exists also that of the correct and reciprocal, principled and constructive, criticism of mistakes which are observed in the line and the activity of this or that party. Such a comradely criticism cannot be called polemics, as the Chinese leadership interprets this norm. Polemics, as the word itself indicates, means a state of ideological and political struggle, it is a state in which non-antagonistic contradictions are transformed into antagonistic contradictions.

In its relations with the Communist Party of China, the Party of Labour of Albania has rigorously abided by these Marxist-Leninist principles and norms which are implemented among genuine communist parties. Whenever it has seen that the Communist Party of China adopted stands and took actions in opposition to Marxism-Leninism and proletarian internationalism, in opposition to the interests of socialism and the revolution, it has pointed out the mistakes to, and criticized it in a comradely manner. This is borne out by written documents of our Party and State, which are in your possession. And what has the attitude of the Chinese leadership been? While it welcomed and highly praised the Party of Labour of Albania and the Albanian Government for their support for, and defence of, People's China, the Chinese side never welcomed the correct and principled remarks of our Party. The leadership of the Communist Party of China has never wanted the Leninist norms and methods to be implemented in relations among parties. Reasoning and acting according to the concepts and logic of a great power, of a great party and a great state, which considers itself an infallible genius, it has demonstrated that it knows no other way apart from dictate and imposition of its views on the others, especially on the smaller parties and states.

Despite the existing divergencies, the Party of Labour and the Government of Albania have publicly supported China and the cause of socialism in China, especially, at the most difficult, internal and external political junctures it has gone through, at the moments when China was isolated and made the target of attacks from all quarters, even by its present friends. Our Party and Government have done this with an open heart, convinced that by so doing they were defending the fate of the revolution in China, which was under serious threat, defending the lofty interests of proletarian internationalism, the friendship between Albania and China. In their support for China against the enemies of socialism, and their defence of its stands and actions which were taken on the right road, the Albanian communists and people fought for the strengthening of the positions of Marxism-Leninism and socialism in China.

In order to better understand the political and ideological causes which led the Chinese leadership to its arrogant act of ceasing aid to Albania, in order to understand its chauvinistic attitudes of a great power in its relations with the Party of Labour of Albania, as well as to demonstrate the sincere, fraternal and correct stand adopted by the Albanian Party, Government and people towards China and the Chinese people it is necessary to review the development of Albanian-Chinese relations.

1. Contacts between our two parties and countries were established after the triumph of the revolution in China, after the founding of the People's Republic of China. They became closer and stronger especially after 1960,

when the open struggle against Khrushchevite revisionism began. The struggle against imperialism and modern revisionism brought our parties together, but with China's departure from this struggle their roads parted.

The struggle of the Party of Labour of Albania against modern revisionism had begun even prior to the condemnation of Titoism by the Informbureau.[1] It continued more fiercely after Stalin's death, when the Khrushchevite variant of revisionism began to show up. Our Party extended and intensified this struggle more and more, rising in opposition against the anti-Marxist attitudes and actions of Khrushchev and his gang, both in their foreign policy and in their relations with the communist parties, with our Party in particular.

The Khrushchevite deviation represented the revision of the Marxist-Leninist theory in all fields and on all questions. The Khrushchevite strategy was aimed at undermining the dictatorship of the proletariat and restoring capitalism in the Soviet Union, transforming this country into an imperialist superpower, for the division and domination of the world together with American imperialism. In order to realize this strategy, Khrushchev attacked Stalin and bolshevism, he advocated extinction of class struggle both within the Soviet Union and outside it. On the pretext that the ratio of forces in the world today had changed, that US imperialism and the international reactionary bourgeoisie had become reasonable, he justified his abandonment of the key thesis of Marxism-Leninism on the violent revolution and spread illusions about the so-called peaceful road. In their relations with the communist and workers' parties, the Khrushchevites acted according to their concept of the "mother party" and "conductor's baton". They wanted the other parties to submit to their dictate and adopt their views, to transform them into tools of their foreign policy. On this road, Khrushchev, Brezhnev and others reconciled themselves to the Yugoslav revisionists and made common cause with them in the struggle against Marxism-Leninism and the revolution.

To this traitorous and counter-revolutionary line of Khrushchevism the Party of Labour of Albania responded with its determined and unyielding fight. In particular, it opposed and denounced the ideological rehabilitation of Titoism by Khrushchev, who with this act of his was clearly showing that he had completely sunk in the quagmire of opportunism and betrayal. Documents prove that, despite its waverings in its stand towards Yugoslav revisionism, at the beginning of 1960, the Communist Party of China, also, influenced by nobody, condemned the rehabilitation of Tito and his group by Khrushchev.

In June 1960, as is known, the Bucharest Meeting was held. There, the counter-revolutionary line of Khrushchev and the Khrushchevites was still

---

[1] Refers to the resolution of the Communist Information Bureau "On the situation in the Yugoslav Communist Party", issued on 28 June, 1948. (Ed.)

better confirmed. They not only attacked Marxism-Leninism in all directions, but also attacked the Communist Party of China directly. At that meeting, the Party of Labour of Albania openly went to the aid of the Communist Party of China and defended it to the end, thus drawing upon itself the fire of the anger and the weight of the pressure of all the Khrushchevite revisionists. Our Party made this principled defence in pure communist conscience, thinking and convinced that by so doing it was defending Marxism-Leninism and People's China.

The Bucharest Meeting and, later, the Conference of the 81 Communist and Workers' Parties in Moscow[2] marked the final split between the Marxist-Leninists and Khrushchevite revisionists, and the beginning of the open polemics between them. Whereas our Party initiated and carried on the fight against Khrushchevite revisionism with consistency and resolve, the Chinese leadership wavered and failed to adopt clear-cut anti-Khrushchevite stands. In the initial stage of the fierce polemics between the Party of Labour of Albania and the Khrushchevite revisionists, China was in agreement with Albania, but this only on the surface, because, in reality, as was proved later, it was seeking a reconciliation with the Soviets and the extinction of polemics with them. This was evident also in Chou En-lai's speech at the 22nd Congress of the Communist Party of the Soviet Union, where in fact, he did not defend our Party, but demanded that polemics should cease instead. The Chinese leadership called this colourless stand assistance to Albania, but the demand to cease polemics was neither to the interest of socialist Albania, nor to the interest of China itself. It benefited Khrushchev and his fight against socialism and Marxism-Leninism.

2. The wavering stand of the Communist Party of China in the struggle against revisionism became clearly manifest in June 1962. At that time the Party of Labour of Albania sent a delegation to Peking to conduct talks with the leadership of the Communist Party of China on important questions which had to do with the tactics and strategy of the common struggle of our two parties in the international arena. On this occasion, the delegation of our Party came up against the very wrong views of the Chinese leadership.

Liu Shao-chi, who next to Mao Tsetung was the principal leader of the Communist Party of China at that time, and who led the talks for the Chinese side, as well as Teng Hsiao-ping, who was then the General Secretary of the Communist Party of China, stubbornly insisted on the viewpoint of the Chinese leadership according to which the anti-imperialist front should necessarily include the Soviet Union as well, which at that time was led by Nikita Khrushchev's revisionist clique.

[2] Meeting of delegations of the Communist and Workers' Parties that had attended the Eighth Congress of the Romanian Worker's Party.(Ed.).

The delegation of our Party upheld the line of the Party of Labour of Albania, which was based on Lenin's teachings according to which no successful struggle could be waged against imperialism without simultaneously combating revisionism. Our delegation insisted on the view of the Party of Labour of Albania that not only should the anti-imperialist front not include the Soviet revisionists, but, at the same time, it should spearhead its struggle both against imperialism in general, and US imperialism in particular, as well as against Soviet revisionism.

The Chinese leadership argued its line of reconciliation with the Soviet revisionists with the need to unite "with everybody" against US imperialism, which, in its words, was the main enemy. Apart from other things, this opportunist thesis also expressed the illusions entertained by the Chinese leadership about the Soviet revisionist leaders. During the Peking talks, Teng Hsiao-ping declared to the delegation of the Central Committee of our Party: "It is impossible for Khrushchev to change and become like Tito . . . As a socialist country, the Soviet Union will never change" (From minutes of talks, June 11, 1962).

The Party of Labour of Albania accepted neither these viewpoints nor the Chinese thesis on a common anti-imperialist front, in which the Khrushchevite revisionists, also, should be included, whereas the Chinese leadership held on to its opportunist positions.

The development of later events, the stepping up of the struggle of the Marxist-Leninist forces against Khrushchevite revisionism, the deepening of Khrushchev's disruptive activity and especially the signing of the Anglo-American-Soviet Treaty of August 1963 on the banning of nuclear tests in the atmosphere, which reflected the uniting of the efforts of the two superpowers for the establishment of their domination over the world, forced the Chinese leadership to start open polemics with Khrushchev. In this manner, when the reconciliation and agreement with the Soviet revisionists, so ardently sought by the Chinese leadership, did not materialize, only then the Communist Party of China effectively entered the road of anti-Khrushchevism and agreed to the determined, consistent and principled struggle of the Party of Labour of Albania. This could not fail to rejoice the Party of Labour of Albania and the Albanian people who, single-handed, were for almost three years then facing up to the open frienzied attacks of Khrushchev and entire modern revisionism. The bonds and cooperation between our two parties in the struggle against imperialism and revisionism were strengthened even more.

Our Party made all the efforts for this struggle to be broadened and deepened, because it served the mobilization of the anti-imperialist and anti-revisionist forces for the defence of the cause of socialism and the liberation of the peoples. But the Chinese leadership, as we will see below, did not prove to be consistent and principled in this struggle.

3. In Summer 1964 Chinese propaganda took up the Sino-Soviet border problem. Referring to a talk of Mao Tsetung with a group of Japanese socialist parliamentarians, it claimed that China had been dispossessed by the Russian Czars of vast territories of hundreds of thousands of square kilometres, that in Europe, too, the Soviet Union had territorial problems which had emerged as a result of the Second World War.

The Party of Labour of Albania did not approve of Mao Tsetung's raising the problem of rectification of borders. According to the view of our Party, the Chinese leadership was making two gross mistakes. In the first place, the raising of the border problem at that moment did not assist the ideological struggle against Khrushchevism. On the contrary, it provided the Soviet leadership with a powerful weapon against China and the Marxist-Leninists in order to neutralize the effect of the ideological struggle they were waging to expose the Khrushchevite betrayal and to present our struggle as a border dispute or territorial claims. On the other hand, by calling into question the rectification of the borders of the Soviet Union with some European countries following the Second World War, J.V. Stalin was unjustly attacked, and the accusation levelled by international reaction against him for creating "spheres of influence" was backed up. The Chinese leadership agreed with Tito, who, when it came to redress the injustices Yugoslavia had suffered in the past at the hands of the victorious powers, upheld this thesis and raised his voice to the skies, while he kept completely silent about the injustices done to another people, if they were in Yugoslavia's favour.

The Chinese thesis on the rectification of borders was not as simple as that. It expressed the chauvinistic spirit of the great state and bourgeois nationalism, it was an instigation of war in Europe.

In keeping with Leninist norms, in the spirit of complete correctness and in a comradely manner, the Central Committee of the Party of Labour of Albania informed the Central Committee of the Communist Party of China and Chairman Mao Tsetung personally of its opinions on these questions in a letter addressed to them on September 10, 1964.

The letter reads in part:

"We think that raising territorial problems with the Soviet Union now would gravely harm our struggle. If we were to do this, we would be giving the enemy a powerful weapon to fight us, and this would paralyse our march forward.

"Under the pressure of Khrushchev's revisionist propaganda, under the influence of Khrushchev's slanders and calumnies, and for many other reasons, the masses of the Soviet people will not understand why People's China is now putting forth territorial claims to the Soviet Union, they will not accept this, and Soviet Propaganda is working to make them revolt against you. But we think that even true Soviet communists will not understand it, nor will they accept it. This would be a colossal loss for our struggle.

" . . . we think that we must not open old wounds, if any, we must not start a controversy and polemics over whether or not the Soviet Union has appropriated other countries' land, but our only concentrated struggle should be spearheaded against the great ulcer, against the great betrayal represented by imperialism and modern revisionism, the traitor groups of Khrushchev, Tito and all their henchmen".

The Central Committee of the Communist Party of China did not reply to the principled and correct letter of our Party. The Chinese leadership never gave our Party any explanation on this question of so great importance. Mao Tsetung limited himself to a verbal statement to the effect that "we will not reply to your letter because we do not want to stir up polemics". In our view, which is in keeping with Leninist norms, the exchange of opinions, comradely criticism and each other's enlightenment are normal things between two communist parties. They can by no means be considered polemics.

Despite this incorrect stand of the Chinese leadership, our Party did not make this disagreement public. It continued its revolutionary struggle against imperialism and revisionism together with China.

4. In October 1964 N. Khrushchev was overthrown. This event again revealed the wavering stand of the Chinese leaders towards the Soviet revisionists. The hopes for a reconciliation with, and rapprochement to, them were revived.

On October 29, 1964, on behalf of the Central Committee of the Communist Party of China and the State Council of the People's Republic of China, in the presence of the ambassadors of Vietnam, Korea, Rumania and Cuba, Chou En-lai requested the Albanian ambassador to Peking to transmit to the Central Committee of the Party of Labour of Albania the Chinese proposal that our parties send delegations to Moscow to back up the new leadership of the Soviet Union with Brezhnev at the head, and to unite with it "in the struggle against the common enemy, imperialism". He added that he had suggested to the Soviet side that an invitation should be extended to Albania, also, to attend the November 7 celebrations.

Expounding the view of the Chinese leadership at that meeting, Chou En-lai said: "Changes have taken place in the Soviet Union. Their influence and importance is not circumscribed within the Soviet Union, alone, but extends to the socialist parties and countries and the entire international communist movement, even to our common enemies and their agents. In a word, this is a good thing, a change has been made.

" . . . For these reasons we sent a message of greetings to the new leadership of the Party and Government of the Soviet Union, informing them that we support and welcome this change.

". . . Now, in Peking, from October 16 we have adopted a truce in our press.

". . . This we do in order to unite on the basis of Marxism-Leninism against our common enemy, although many major problems may not be solved for the time being".

Although Chou En-lai knew that there were no diplomatic relations between the Soviet Union and Albania, which were brutally broken off on the initiative of the Khrushchevites, he insisted that Albania should send a delegation to Moscow, and told our ambassador, "We think that the Albanian comrades must study our proposal, because this is a good opportunity to stretch a hand to, and unite with them in the struggle against the enemy".

The Central Committee of the Party of Labour of Albania could not accept this proposal, which sought the cessation of the struggle against revisionism and ideological reconciliation with it. If this line of reconciliation with the Soviet revisionists were accepted, it would spell disaster to the Marxist-Leninist movement, it would be a destructive blow at it. Therefore, our Party categorically refused the request of the Chinese leadership and turned it down flatly.

In its letter to the Central Committee of the Communist Party of China on November 5, 1964, the Central Committee of the Party of Labour of Albania explained patiently and with Marxist-Leninist correctness that the assessment made by the Chinese leadership of the changes that took place in the Soviet Union was wrong and their proposal to go to Moscow was unacceptable.

This letter reads in part:

"This event, though important and susceptible of serious consequences, has not yet led, at least until now, to the complete defeat of revisionism, has not yet marked the final victory of Marxism-Leninism over revisionism, but has only put off the decay of revisionism, has pushed revisionism close to its grave, while Khrushchev's successors are trying to prevent revisionism from falling into this grave, by implementing the policy of Khrushchevism without Khrushchev.

" . . . Although N. Khrushchev's exit from the political scene is an important victory of Marxism-Leninism, the Central Committee of the Party of Labour of Albania holds that it must not be overrated, that the vigilance of the Marxist-Leninists must not be relaxed nor should their principled struggle to smash Khrushchevite modern revisionism cease.

" . . . We are of the opinion that the open and principled polemics for the ceaseless exposure of modern revisionism must be kept up today and carried through to the end until revisionism is buried as an ideology . . . Our retreat from these positions won with struggle, would be a loss for us and a gain for the revisionists.

" . . . In these conditions, when the Soviet Government has unilaterally broken off diplomatic relations and committed dreadful anti-Marxist acts against us, we are of the opinion that it is neither permissible for us as Marxists nor is it worthy of us as a sovereign state, to ignore these things, only because of the fact that the person of N. Khrushchev has been deposed.

"For these reasons we have to express our opposition to the proposal of comrade Chou En-lai to the effect that an Albanian delegation should be invited by the Soviet Party and Government to attend the November 7 celebrations".

The Central Committee of the Communist Party of China adopted a disparaging stand towards this confidential letter of our Party. The Chinese leadership never replied to this letter and did not take into consideration its reasonable and comradely remarks.

On November 7, 1964, Chou En-lai went to Moscow at the head of a delegation of the Chinese Party and Government, to hail Brezhnev's advent to power. But, as facts were to prove, he had no success in his mission to bring about a reconciliation and agreement with the new Soviet leadership and no sooner had he returned to China than the Chinese leadership was compelled to resume polemics with the Soviet Union.

Thus, our Party's stand and its assessment of the events with regard to Khrushchev's down-fall proved correct, Marxist-Leninist. Whereas the position of the Chinese leadership was conciliatory, opportunist and utterly wrong both in its assessment of, and stand to, the new revisionist leadership of the Soviet Union. Nevertheless, although the Chinese leadership did not behave correctly and made no self-criticism, although the ideological differences deepened further, our Party went on with its struggle for the strengthening of the friendship and cooperation with the Communist Party of China, hoping that this would help the Chinese leadership to sound positions in the common struggle against revisionism and imperialism.

5. Regardless of the contradictions which had arisen between us, taking account of the difficult situations China was going through, and sincerely wishing to assist the Communist Party of China to overcome them, the Party of Labour of Albania continued to support China resolutely, especially in those political and ideological questions over which we held common views.

Our Party supported the Cultural Revolution at the personal request of Mao Tsetung, who declared to our Party that China was facing a colossal danger, and that no one knew who would win in China, the socialist forces or the revisionists (From minutes of the talk with the delegation of the Albanian Party and Government, May 1966). The Party of Labour of Albania assisted China at a very critical moment, when it was going through great upheavals and was being savagely attacked by the united imperialist-revisionist front. It supported the general line of the Cultural Revolution for the liquidation of the capitalist and revisionist elements who had usurped key positions in the Party and state power, though it did not agree over many questions of principle and methods which guided this revolution, and were used in it. By supporting the Cultural Revolution, our Party nurtured the hope that it would find the road of true revolutionary struggle, led by the working class and its vanguard, the Communist Party. The entire period of the great Cultural Revolution was a very difficult period for socialism in China, it created a complicated and chaotic situation. This situation was the logical outcome of the factional and unprincipled struggle which took place within the ranks of the Communist Party of China during the time of the struggle for the carrying out of the bourgeois-democratic revolution, and after 1949, around the road which China would follow for the further development of the revolution.

The great ideas of the Great October Socialist Revolution and the Marxist-Leninist ideology were not properly made the example for, the pillar and the compass of, the Communist Party of China in the concrete conditions of its country. This accounts for the fact that the Marxist-Leninist nucleus of the Party slipped into dangerous eclecticism, which gave rise to a chaos of unbridled struggle for power between factions, persons and groups holding various non-Marxist-Leninist views, something which seriously hampered the laying of the foundations of socialism in China. This political-ideological and organizational chaos in the Communist Party of China and the Chinese state enabled capitalist and revisionist elements to seize key positions in the Party, in the state power and in the army. In these conditions, the Cultural Revolution, inspired and led by Mao Tsetung personally, broke out.

The Party of Labour of Albania supported the general strategy of the Cultural Revolution. But we want to stress that our Party supported the strategy of this revolution and not all its tactics, it defended with determination the cause of socialism in China, defended the fraternal Chinese people, the Communist Party of China and the revolution, it did not defend at all the factionalist struggle of the anti-Marxist groups, whoever clashed and wrangled with each other, resorting even to arms, overtly or covertly, in order to retake state power.

The Cultural Revolution, more often than not, preserved the spirit and actions of an unprincipled struggle, which was not led by a genuine party of the working class which should strive for the establishment of the dictatorship of the proletariat. Thus, these clashes among factionalist groups ended in the establishment in China of a state power dominated by bourgeois and revisionist elements.

The present Chinese leadership wanted and wants the Party of Labour of Albania to denounce the Cultural Revolution according to the will and the reasons of the Chinese leadership. The Party of Labour of Albania will never accept such a dictate. Together with all the world revolutionaries it is expecting the Communist Party of China to make the true analysis of this Cultural Revolution, to have the courage to state the truth on the ideas which guided this revolution, the groups and people who carried out and led it, on those against whom this revolution was directed, and to assume clearcut stands on these questions. To this day, the leadership of the Communist Party of China has not done such a thing, because it is afraid of facts, events and their true Marxist-Leninist interpretation.

6. The Party of Labour of Albania has made all-round, powerful and open efforts to defend China in the international arena, though on many issues it held opposite views on principle. Such is the protracted and per-severing diplomatic struggle of socialist Albania for the restoration of the lawful rights of the People's Republic of China to the United Nations, denied to it by US imperialism and its allies.

China pursued a close-door policy in its relations with other countries of the world. The leadership of our Party had expressed, on special occasions and in a comradely way, its desire to the Chinese leaders that People's China should be more active in its foreign policy, extend its political, economic, cultural and other contacts and relations with various countries, particularly with its neighbouring countries. According to our view, this would be to the advantage of China itself and the cause of socialism and the revolution in the world. But your leadership found this wish of Albania's unreasonable and preferred its own isolation, excusing itself with various pretexts before all the states which expressed their wish to establish relations with it.

7. In 1968, a Party and Government delegation of Albania went to China, headed by the former member of the Political Bureau and former vice-chairman of the Council of Ministers and minister of people's defence, Beqir Balluku. This delegation was also charged with the task of presenting to the Chinese leadership our requests for aid to strengthen the defence potential of Albania.

On that occasion, Chou En-lai openly put forth to Beqir Balluku the view of your leadership according to which, Albania, as a small country, had no need of heavy armament and that it was not at all in a position to defend itself alone from foreign aggression, particularly from Soviet social-imperialism and US imperialism, no matter how much military aid it would receive from China. Therefore, according to Chou En-lai, the only road for Albania to cope with foreign aggression was that of applying the tactics of partisan warfare in the country and concluding a military alliance with Yugoslavia and with Rumania.

When our delegation came home, Beqir Balluku informed the Political Bureau of Chou En-lai's proposal. The Political Bureau of the Central Committee of our Party unanimously condemned and rejected Chou En-lai's anti-Albanian and counter-revolutionary proposal. Beqir Balluku, who formally adhered to the decision of the Political Bureau, added that he had allegedly opposed Chou En-lai's proposal. But later facts proved that Beqir Balluku had in reality been in full agreement with the proposal of the Chinese leadership and worked in secret to carry our this hostile strategic plan against the People's Socialist Republic of Albania.

Chou En-lai repeated this same thesis to the Albanian Government delegation which had gone to Peking in July 1975, to conclude an agreement on China's economic aid to Albania for the 6th Five-year Plan 1976-1980. This thesis was turned down again by our delegation in a clearcut and categorical manner.

The leadership of our Party considered Chou En-lai's proposal about the military alliance he was seeking to impose on us an attempt of a reactionary character on the part of the Chinese leadership to drive socialist Albania into the trap of warmongering plots through military alliances, with the final aim of turning the Balkan area into a powder keg, as the Soviet socialimperialists and the US imperialists are seeking to do.

We do not know if Yugoslavia and Rumania were informed of these plans of the Chinese leadership. But even at present we are witnessing that the Chinese leadership is displaying unusual zeal to interfere in the affairs of the Balkans, to mix up the cards and to kindle the fire of war in this very sensitive area of Europe. But we are confident that the Balkan peoples will never accept to be set at loggerheads with each other, they will never accept to become tools either of US imperialism, Russian social-imperialism, or Chinese hegemonism.

These acts of the Chinese leadership and the opposition of our Party to these reactionary acts had, later, very serious consequences in the relations between our two countries. Our Party has never meddled with the internal affairs of China. But the Chinese leadership, at certain moments, has criminally interfered in the internal affairs of Albania. We will make these facts public at an appropriate time. If these condemnable acts undertaken by the Chinese leadership in collusion with the Albanian traitors were realized, the People's Socialist Republic of Albania, its independence and sovereignty would have been liquidated.

8. While our Party was working to strengthen fraternal cooperation with China, while it wanted to correctly wage and intensify the struggle against imperialism, modern revisionism and reaction on a joint front also with all the Marxist-Leninist parties and forces, China saw everything only from its own angle, it wanted to dominate others, so that the latter would follow its strategy and tactics.

The events that were taking place revealed ever more clearly that the political and ideological struggle of the Communist Party of China against the Khrushchevites did not proceed from a sound basis, in reality, its aim was not to defend Marxism-Leninism, the revolution and the liberation of peoples. It was waged simply for pragmatic ends and selfish interests. This became evident in the radical change of the Chinese strategy, to which Nixon's visit to Peking officially set the seal.

In the summer of 1971, Albania, considered the closest ally of China, learned from foreign news agencies the report spread all over the world that Kissinger had paid a secret visit to Peking.[3] Negotiations, which marked a radical change in the Chinese policy, had been held with Kissinger. As in other cases, this time too, though the question was about a major political turn, a change in the strategic line, the Communist Party and the Government of the People's Republic of China did not deem it necessary to hold preliminary talks with the Party of Labour and the Government of Albania, too, to see what their opinion was. The Chinese leadership put others before an accomplished fact, thinking they had to obey it without a word.

It was clear to our Party that Nixon's visit to Peking[4] was not an up-grading of the talks that were going on till then in Warsaw between the Chinese and US ambassadors, that it was not made to promote "people's diplomacy" and to pave the road to contacts with the American people, as the Chinese leaders claimed. Nixon's visit to Peking was laying the foundations of a new policy on the part of China.

With Nixon's visit, China joined the dance of imperialist alliances and rivalries for the redivision of the world, where China, too, would have its own share. This visit paved the road to its rapprochement and collaboration with US imperialism and its allies. At the same time, the inauguration of the alliance with the United States of America also marked the abandoning on the part of the Chinese leadership of the genuine socialist countries, the Marxist-Leninist movement, the revolution and the national-liberation struggle of the peoples.

This alliance and meeting in Peking, between the Chinese leadership and the American President Nixon, were taking place at a time when the US was waging its predatory imperialist war in heroic Vietnam, when it was using all its most up-to-date means of war, except for the A-bomb, to kill the fraternal heroic Vietnamese people and to reduce Vietnam to ashes. This monstrous alliance and the Sino-US contacts were condemnable acts of disastrous consequences for the peoples.

Therefore, in view of this dangerous turn in the foreign policy of China, on August 6, 1971, the Central Committee of the Party of Labour of Albania sent a long letter to the Central Committee of the Communist Party of China, stressing in no uncertain terms that it was against this turn of China, which ran counter to the interests of People's China itself, the revolution and socialism.

[3] His secret visit took place in July. Kissinger paid an official visit to China in October of the same year. (Ed.).

[4] 21-28 February, 1972. (Ed.).

The letter reads in part:

" . . . We regard your decision to welcome Nixon in Peking as incorrect and undesirable, we do not approve of, nor do we support, it. We also hold the view that Nixon's announced visit to China will be inconceivable to, and will not be approved by, the peoples, the revolutionaries and the communists of various countries.

" . . . Welcoming Nixon to China, who is known as a frenzied anti-communist, an aggressor and assassin of the peoples, as a representative of blackest US reaction, has many drawbacks and will have negative consequences for the revolutionary movement and our cause.

Nixon's going to China and his talks there cannot fail to arouse harmful illusions among the rank-and-file, the peoples and the revolutionaries, about US imperialism, its strategy and policy.

" . . . Talks with Nixon provide the revisionists with weapons to negate the entire great struggle and polemics of the Communist Party of China to expose the Soviet renegades as allies and collaborators of US imperialism, and to put on a par China's stand towards US imperialism and the treacherous line of collusion, pursued by the Soviet revisionists towards it. This enables the Khrushchevite revisionists to flaunt their banner of false anti-imperialism even more ostentatiously and to step up their demagogical and deceitful propaganda in order to bring the anti-imperialist forces round to themselves.

" . . . The visit of the US President to China will give rise to doubts and misunderstandings among the rank-and-file who may suspect that China is changing its stand towards US imperialism and involving itself in the game of the superpowers.

" . . . Our strategy calls for close alliance with the peoples fighting all over the world, with all the revolutionaries, on a joint front against imperialism and socialimperialism, and never for an alliance with Soviet socialimperialism allegedly against US imperialism, never for an alliance with US imperialism allegedly against Soviet socialimperialism".

In conclusion, the letter points out that "the line and attitudes of the Party of Labour of Albania will always remain principled, consistent, unchanging. We will combat US imperialism and Soviet revisionism uncompromisingly and consistently". The letter expressed the hope that the remarks the Party of Labour of Albania made to a sister party "would be taken up in a comradely spirit and understood correctly".

The Chinese leadership adopted its usual stand also towards this letter. It did not deign to give any answer. By so doing, it betrayed not only big state megalomania but also its fear to face the correct and principled Marxist-Leninist arguments of our Party. It is a fact that two months after our letter, the 6th Congress of the Party of Labour of Albania was held.[5]

[5] 1-7 November, 1971. (Ed.).

That was a good occasion to exchange views with the Chinese delegation invited to the Congress and to clarify each other's positions. But in this case, too, the Chinese leadership, consistent on its road of refusing consultations and the settling of disagreements through talks, adopted a stand in contravention of all practice and internationalist relations between sister parties. It concocted some absurd excuses for its failure to send a delegation to the Congress of our Party. Practically, the Communist Party of China has ever since reduced contacts with our Party, turning relations between the two parties into a purely formal relationship.

The change of China's strategy has come about as a result of an internal struggle within its Communist Party where deep contradictions existed, "a hundred flowers blossomed and a hundred schools contended", where there were pro-Khrushchevites, pro-Americans, opportunists and revolutionaries in the leadership. This accounts for the successive changes in the political line of the Communist Party of China, its vacillating, opportunist, and contradictory attitudes towards US imperialism, modern revisionism and international reaction. The axis of the Chinese policy has changed three times over ten years, from 1962 to 1972. First, the Communist Party of China abided by the strategic formula of a "united front with the Soviet and other revisionists against US imperialism and its allies". Later on, the Communist Party of China came forward with the slogan of a "very broad united front of the proletariat and the revolutionary peoples of all countries against US imperialism, Soviet revisionism and reaction of various countries". After Nixon's visit to China, the Chinese strategy again speaks of a "broad united front", but this time includes "all those who can be united", incorporating in it even the United States of America against Soviet socialimperialism.

9. After its rapprochement with US imperialism and overtures to the United States of America and its allies, the leadership of the Communist Party of China proclaimed the anti-Marxist and counter-revolutionary theory of the "three worlds", which it presented as a strategy of the revolution, and made efforts to impose it on the Marxist-Leninist communist movement and all the peoples of the world as the general line of their struggle.

When they were fighting together against modern revisionism, and Khrushchevite revisionism, in particular, the Party of Labour of Albania as well as the Communist Party of China adhered to the principle, and stressed, that there was no "mother party" or "daughter party", that any party enjoyed the right to hold its own views on all problems, that a party was truly communist and revolutionary, when it looked at this problem from the angle of Marxism-Leninism. The Communist Party of China has violated these principles and norms in all directions. It is seeking to impose China's counter-revolutionary turn of unity with US imperialism and world reaction on all Marxist-Leninists, to have the entire revolutionary and liberation movement accept its anti-Leninist concepts and analyses of imperialism, the present-day world situation, alliances, and so on, as an absolute and incontrovertible truth.

Practice shows that in most cases, the Communist Party and Government of China have not viewed international issues from the angle of Marxism-Leninism, the interests of the revolution and the liberation struggles of the peoples. Chinese policy is a pragmatic policy, and it cannot be otherwise, in as much as its strategy and tactics are such. Therefore the world has witnessed and will witness about-faces in the Chinese strategy and politics in the future, too. These turns are passed off as Marxist-Leninist, but in reality they are anti-Marxist, they are turns catering to the interests of the big China state in its search of alliances with US imperialism, Soviet socialimperialism and world capital to create and build China into an imperialist superpower.

At present, the Chinese plan to become a superpower has found its concentrated expression in the infamous theory of "three worlds".[6] The theory of "three worlds" seeks to replace Marxism-Leninism with an eclectic amalgamation of opportunist, revisionist and anarchic-syndicalist ideas and theses, it seeks to dampen the revolutionary spirit of the proletariat and its class struggle, advocating an alliance with the bourgeoisie and imperialism. Alleging that time is not ripe for revolution, the theory of "three worlds" seeks to preserve the status quo, the present situation of capitalist, colonialist and neo-colonialist oppression and exploitation.

Under the hoax of defence of national independence from Soviet socialimperialism which it regards as the only danger and threat today, China requires the peoples to give up their struggle for national, economic, and social liberation, to submit to US imperialism and the other capitalist powers of the West, the former colonialists. It presses for the strengthening of the Common Market and the European Union, organisms set up to keep the proletariat of Europe in capitalist bondage and to oppress and exploit the peoples of other countries. By fanning up the armaments race of the superpowers and relying on such instruments of war of US imperialism as NATO and other military blocs, the theory of "three worlds" instigates imperialist world war.

The theory of "three worlds" is a smokescreen to hide China's ambition for hegemony over what it calls the "third world". It is no accident that it has included itself in the "third world" and presents itself as its leader in the international arena. It is no accident either that the Chinese leadership is flirting with the "non-aligned" and seeking to take them under its wing.

The Chinese leadership is not the first to display its "affection" and "care" for the socalled "third world". The imperialists, the social-

[6] "Chairman Mao's Theory of the Differentiation of the Three Worlds is a Major Contribution to Marxism-Leninism", in B. Szajkowski (ed.) Documents in Communist Affairs — 1977, UCCP, pp. 53-76. (Ed.).

imperialists and the other neo-colonialists have worked out various theories on the "third world" long ago before it, in order to dominate and subjugate the countries and peoples of this "world". Therefore, it is a futile effort on the part of the Chinese leadership to claim that it is the first, as early as 1974, to have produced this theory on the basis of an allegedly objective analysis of the international situations made by Mao Tsetung. It is common knowledge that the theory of "three worlds" has been concocted by world reaction.[7] The Party of Labour of Albania and the Albanian Government exposed and combated the theoretical and practical speculations in regard to the "third world" in the international arena as far back as 1960, and even before, as bourgeois-capitalist, neo-colonialist and racist manoeuvres and conspiracies to suppress the peoples who were fighting for freedom and independence.

The "contribution" of the Chinese leaders to the theory of "three worlds" consists only in its "substantiation" of the need for reconciliation of the "third world" with imperialism; they have discovered nothing; they concocted the alliance of the "third world" with US imperialism and the other imperialists to solicit their aid and to make China an imperialist super-power.

Therefore, it is not the Party of Labour of Albania which attacks the Chinese inventor or champions of this theory; it is precisely the latter who were the first to attack the Party of Labour of Albania and the struggle it has waged against this theory of world reaction, the struggle it has conducted in support of the freedom and independence of the peoples of Africa, Asia, Latin America, etc.

The implementation of the theory of "three worlds" led the Chinese leadership to unite even with the "devil", to unite with the US imperialists and the monopolists of Europe, with fascists and racists, kings and feudal lords, most rabid militarists and warmongers. Pinochet and Franco, former nazi generals of the German Wehrmacht and the Japanese imperial army, dyed-in-the-wool criminals like Mobutu and bloodthirsty kings, American bosses and presidents of multinational companies, became its allies.

This anti-Marxist line led China's leadership to unite with Tito, Carillo and other revisionists. At one time, it was against Tito, whereas now it has united with him. This testifies to its lack of Marxist-Leninist principles, to inconsistencies in its line. But our Party wants to tell the Chinese leadership: your uniting with Tito now and the suspicious alliances you are trying to piece together in the Balkans, pose a great danger to the peoples of this peninsula, to the Yugoslav, Albanian, Greek, Turkish and other peoples. Albania is well aware of the plans and ambitions of the Chinese leadership

---

[7] See: "The Theory and Practice of the Revolution", in B. Szajkowski (ed.) *op.cit.,* pp. 37-52. (Ed.).

towards the Balkans. Therefore, the peoples of the world must be vigilant towards the Chinese intrigues in this region.

10. The Party of Labour of Albania has made every effort to solve the differences arisen between the two Parties and which were becoming pronounced with the passage of time, on the Marxist-Leninist road.

Proceeding from this desire, seeing that the Chinese leadership systematically failed to answer its letters and refused to send official delegations to Albania, seeing that ideological differences with the Chinese leadership were assuming broad proportions, the Central Committee of the Party of Labour of Albania did not stay aloof, but made other efforts to engage in comradely talks with it.

Thus, in January 1974, the Central Committee of our Party proposed to the Central Committee of the Communist Party of China that a top level delegation of our Party and Government go to China for talks and that this visit be made, possibly, within the first six months of the year 1974. Though formally agreeing to the proposal of our Party, in point of fact, the Chinese leadership did not agree to our delegation going to Peking. In the beginning, the Chinese leadership told us that the delegation should arrive in the second six months of the year 1974, later it postponed its visit to the first six months of the year 1975. And, finally, it kept silent about this issue, thus barring the way to talks, at a time when kings and princes, reactionaries and fascists were welcomed with great pomp in Peking. It was clear that the Chinese leadership was persistently treading its anti-Marxist road, that in relations with our Party and country, it was guided by the concepts of great power chauvinism, that it was trying to have its line and dictate accepted unconditionally and indisputably.

In these conditions, when the Chinese leadership refused any contacts, when it avoided any discussion and consultation, when it was working arrogantly and overbearingly to impose the theory of the "three worlds" on the Marxist-Leninist movement, what had the Party of Labour of Albania to do? To connive at the anti-Marxist line of the Communist Party of China and deny itself? To give up the struggle against imperialism and modern revisionism and join the enemies of the revolution, socialism, the freedom and independence of the peoples? To break away from the Marxist-Leninist revolutionaries and unite with the opportunists and the reactionary bourgeoisie? To fail to support the national liberation struggle of the peoples against the superpowers and their agents in the ranks of these peoples?

The Party of Labour of Albania stood loyal to Marxism-Leninism and the correct and revolutionary line it has always followed resolutely, unwaveringly and consistently. It also presented this Marxist-Leninist line at its 7th Conegress,[8] where it put forward its views and stand with regard to the main international problems today, the revolution and the liberation

[8] 1-7 November, 1976. (Ed.).

struggle of the peoples. Just as at all its other congresses, at the 7th Congress, too, our Party expressed its views also on problems which have to do with the Marxist-Leninist movement in the spirit of proletarian internationalism. The line of the 7th Congress, which was unanimously approved by the entire Party, lies at the foundation of all the home and foreign policy of our country.

This Marxist-Leninist line of our Party, the independent policy of socialist Albania, the principled and resolute stand of the Albanian people, which have always run counter to the anti-Marxist big power line and policy of the Chinese leadership, are the main and real cause of the anti-Albanian attitudes and acts of the Central Committee of the Communist Party of China and the Chinese Government, which led to the arbitrary cessation of civil and military aid to Albania.

This was evident especially after the 7th Congress of the Party of Labour of Albania, when the Chinese leadership, breaking every norm of relations between sister parties, hurried to attack the 7th Congress of our Party, under the pretence that it had allegedly attacked China, the Communist Party of China and Mao Tsetung.

The accusation of the Chinese leadership is groundless. For this suffice it to read the documents of the 7th Congress, which are all made public. It is not difficult for anyone to see that it contains no attacks either against China, or against the Communist Party of China or Mao Tsetung. The Central Committee of the Party of Labour of Albania has asked the Central Committee of the Communist Party of China through a letter dated December 24, 1976, to indicate when and where our Party has attacked the Communist Party of China and Mao Tsetung. To this day the Chinese leadership, as usually, has given no reply.

But the question does not consist in "attacks" which do not exist. The anger and arrogance of the Chinese leadership towards the 7th Congress draw their source from the fact that our Party did not adopt the Chinese anti-Marxist theses and views, its counter-revolutionary theory of the "three worlds". The Party of Labour of Albania, as a genuine Marxist-Leninist Party, agrees to discuss problems, but it has never accepted orders and directives from anyone on what it must put forward and how it must put forward its view at its own congresses. Therefore, it has never allowed any Party, whether small or big, including the Communist Party of China, to interfere in its internal affairs and dictate what it should do and how it should act.

11. Continuous changes have taken place in the leadership of the Communist Party of China as to its line, strategy and composition. The Party of Labour of Albania never defended this or that group of individuals that were removed from the leadership of the Communist Party of China. We have had and still have our opinion on everything and on every person or group of the leadership acting in China. This is natural.

The present Chinese leadership wanted the Party of Labour of Albania to support its acts with regard to the changes made at the head of the Communist Party of China. As we did not do it, it comes to the conclusion that we are partisans of Lin Piao and "the gang of four". It is wrong to both aspects, and this is one of the unavowed major political, ideological reasons which have urged the Chinese leadership to cease aid to Albania. The present Chinese leadership has wanted our Party to support its illegal and non-Marxist-Leninist activity to seize state power in China. Our Party has not fulfilled and will never fulfil this desire of the Chinese leadership. The Party of Labour of Albania never tramples on the Marxist-Leninist principles, and has never been, nor will it ever be anybody's tool.

In the ideological and political differences and contradictions with the Party of Labour of Albania, in the failure of the attempts of the Chinese leadership to impose its views and line on the Party of Labour of Albania lies the real reason of the Chinese decision to cease aid to Albania. Having failed to subdue socialist Albania, the Chinese leadership is now seeking to avenge itself and harm the construction of socialism in Albania. In so doing, it is revealing its anti-Marxist and counter-revolutionary countenance even more clearly.

The cessation of credits and aid to socialist Albania on the part of the Chinese leadership is not only an episode, however grave, in the relations between China and Albania. This act assumes great international importance, it proves that China has come out against Marxism-Leninism and proletarian internationalism, that it has adopted and is applying a big power chauvinistic policy and dictate, that it is implementing hegemonic practices and it is perpetrating arbitrary and brutal acts of a superpower.

For its selfish aims, to make China a central world power, the Chinese leadership is publicizing itself as a "defender of small and middle-sized countries", that it is fighting against "the unfair division of the world economy", that it is against "economic discrimination against the developing countries by the imperialist powers", that it stands for the "development of their national economy", for "the strengthening of their independence and sovereignty", that it is fighting "against bullying of the small by the big", etc. But when the Chinese leadership behaves like an enemy towards Albania, when it ceases aid and credits because the Party of Labour of Albania does not submit to its conductor's baton, all the falsity of the Chinese line is seen through, the not in the least good-intentioned aims and lies that the Chinese leadership wants to peddle to the peoples of the "third world" in order to suppress and enslave them, to impose its will and that of the old and new colonialists on them, are also clearly understood.

By cutting short aid to socialist Albania, at a time when China receives substantial aid and credits from US imperialism and world capitalism and accords aid and credits to their agents like Mobutu and his ilk, the Chinese leadership openly shows world public opinion that it does not agree ideologically with a truly socialist country, but it agrees and is in alliance with the enemies of socialism and the reactionaries, that it is against the socialist order, against the countries and peoples who demand liberation precisely from imperialism and socialimperialism, from oppression and dictate by big state chauvinism.

We want to say to the Chinese leaders: You extended the ideological differences and disagreements also to the field of state relations with our country. With this you dealt a heavy blow at the Albanian-Chinese friendship for which the Albanian people and the Chinese people have fought so hard. You made public the disagreements and differences and began open polemics. We accept this challenge and are not afraid of polemics. But you are fully responsible for all your hostile, anti-Marxist and anti-Albanian acts before the Chinese people and the Albanian people, before all world public opinion.

In order to provide the Albanian people and the Chinese people, and all world public opinion with the possibility of becoming acquainted with, and pass judgement on, the views of your Party and Government and the Albanian Party and Government with regard to the cessation of credits and aid on the part of China to Albania, we will publish this letter as well as the note of the Chinese Government in our newspaper *Zëri i Popullit*. We hope that you will publish our letter in your newspaper *Renmin Ribao*.[9] This is a norm which China has supported in the past.

The Party of Labour of Albania, the Albanian Government and people will fight to preserve the Albanian-Chinese friendship, which is a friendship between peoples. For their part, they will make every possible effort to maintain normal state relations between Albania and China. They are sure that the Chinese people will make a correct assessment of the Albanian stand and will know how to judge the anti-Albanian acts of the Chinese leadership.

The Chinese leadership ceased economic and military aid to Albania in the belief that Albania would have either to capitulate and submit to it or to stretch its hand out to others and be discredited. But the Chinese leadership has not reckoned with the Party of Labour of Albania and the Albanian people, their determination, the strength of their unity.

The People's Socialist Republic of Albania and the Albanian people, under the consistent leadership of the Party of Labour of Albania, with Comrade Enver Hoxha at the head, will thoroughly and honourably fulfil their historic mission for the construction of socialism by relying on their own forces, further proving to the proletariat and all the peoples of the world the inexhaustible and indomitable vitality of the Marxist-Leninist

[9] The People's Daily, official organ of the Central Committee of the Communist Party of China. (Ed.).

ideology, which enables even a small country, encircled by imperialism and revisionism, as Albania is, to build socialism successfully, to defend and carry it always ahead.

Albania will never submit to anybody, it will stand to the end loyal to Marxism-Leninism and proletarian internationalism. It will march non-stop on the road of socialism and communism illuminated by the immortal teachings of Marx, Engels, Lenin and Stalin. The Albanian people, with the Party of Labour at the head, will resolutely and consistently support the revolutionary and liberation struggles of the peoples, their efforts for freedom, independence and social progress. They will fight uncompromisingly through to the very end against US imperialism, Soviet social-imperialism, modern revisionism and world reaction. Albania has never bowed its back or its head, either in the past or today, nor will it ever do so in the future.

The Chinese leadership will fail both in its sermons and in its intrigues. The reactionary act it committed against Albania is revolting to the conscience of every honest man and woman in the world. Though encircled, socialist Albania is not isolated because it enjoys the respect and love of the world proletariat, the freedom-loving peoples and the honest men and women throughout the world. This respect and love will grow even more in the future. Our cause is just! Socialist Albania will triumph!

The Central Committee of the Party of Labour of Albania

The Council of Ministers of the People's Socialist Republic of Albania

Tirana, July 29, 1978.

Michael Kaser. Note on Chinese Aid to Albania.

Sino-Albanian economic relations have been concealed from quantitative analysis by any outsider since 1964, the last year for which Albania published a country breakdown of its foreign trade. Since China has put out no partner statistics at any time, the only procedure based on an official source has been to assume that the Albanian import deficit has been wholly financed by Chinese grants. Even the country's aggregates of imports and of exports have not been explicitly published since 1964 and any series for later years has to be derived from scattered statements. The present writer's estimate (in *East European Economies Post Helsinki: A Compendium of Papers Submitted to the Joint Economic Committee, Congress of United States*, Washington, D.C., 25 August 1977, p. 1335) on those frail foundations was of Chinese supplies of goods in excess of Albanian counter-deliveries during 1961-75 of $838 mn in current prices ($744 mn at constant 1970 prices). This agreed with the upper estimate of $800 mn made from Chinese indications (A.F. Cooper, *China's Foreign Aid*, New York,

1976, Table 2.2). The statistics cited in the letters above cover a longer period, from 1954: from incomplete returns, Chinese unrequited deliveries could not have exceeded $10 mn in 1954-60, when, in any event, the USSR was the principal aid donor. A rate approaching $1 = 2yuan renminbi (RMB) is the most favourable one for application throughout the period (the cross rate through the rouble in 1961 was 1.80 RMB and the direct rate 1.78 RMB at the end of 1977), at which those estimates of the visible trade surplus of China with Albania represent 1.7 bn RMB, against the Albanian Letter's assertion of 2.3 bn (i.e. 75% utilized of 3 bn offered for 1954-75). Given the extremely rough nature of the estimates in dollars (themselves converted from leks at the official exchange rate) and the uncertainty over the RMB-lek rate (for the Albanian Letter speaks of "17 agreements. . . reckoned in old roubles, then new roubles, later in British pounds, finally in internal yuans or in commercial yuans or US dollars"), the Albanian valuation accords with what little one can verify.

The Chinese contention that "implementation of the agreements . . . calls for an outlay of more than ten billion yuan renminbi" is not however thereby rendered baseless. It must include both the 3 bn RMB which the Albanian letter accepts as the 1954-75 commitment and the 0.5 bn agreed for 1976-80 economic aid as well as an unstated provision of military equipment. Because Albania has virtually no defence industry — and its government's letter exhibits anger at being shown so dependent on Chinese supplies — it would be by no means unreasonable for the military aid (which does not figure in trade returns) to have approached economic assistance in importance. The present writer's estimate jointly with Dr. Adi Schnytzer (Deakin University, Victoria, Australia) of military hardware received in 1970 is 280 bn leks (*East European Economies Post Helsinki,* p. 643), or $56 mn or 112 mn RMB (assuming that application of the official exchange rate is valid). For the 17 years during which China was supplying defence goods that amount annually would aggregate 1.9 bn RMB. An exchange rate more favourable to the lek — the defence-good estimate is in domestic prices — would of course put the RMB value higher. It may be relevant that Soviet economic aid over 1947-61 was worth roughly $150 mn while technical and military aid was estimated at $100 mn (*ibid.*, p. 1327).

It would thus be putting a rather high figure on military aid to call it 3.5 bn RMB and, by difference from the Chinese Letter's aggregate of 10 bn, to assume that technical assistance amounted to 3 bn RMB. But even the latter can be partially supported. The Chinese Letter states for example that 100 mn RMB were spent on metallurgical research alone (a figure which the Albanian reply does not contest, though alleging that it got scant benefit due to the destruction of technical documentation). The Albanian Letter accepts that 6,000 Chinese experts worked in Albania, as claimed in the Chinese Letter, which also mentions that 2,000 Albanians were trained in China. If the annual salaries of both groups of experts was 6,000 leks (in

1970 our estimate of household consumption was 5,990 mn leks for almost exactly one million gainfully occupied, *ibid.*, pp. 580 and 583) and each expert stayed for 5 of the 24 years mentioned, some 240 mn leks, or 100 mn RMB would have been spent.

Restricting the comparisons to the safer area of civilian goods delivered without counter-delivery, viz. 2.3 bn RMB between 1954 and 1975, an estimate might be hazarded that in a year of close friendship such as 1970 represents and when aid deliveries seem to have been at a peak, Albania received just on 150 mn RMB or 370 mn leks. The 1970 net material product produced (the service-exclusive definition used for national income in Albania) was 6,839 mn leks, such that China added 5.4% by its unrequited deliveries. These latter, converted to $75 mn, were 3.7% of Chinese exports to all partners. But that sum was about the same at the United States surplus with China in the twelve months following the US lifting of export controls in mid-1972.

Any comparison of military aid must be still more hazardous, but if the very maximum of 3.5 bn RMB is effectively spread over 1961-77 (16 years) there was an annual Chinese supply of 200 mn RMB or some $100 mn to Albania. The most appropriate relationship is perhaps to Soviet arms deliveries to the Third World, which over 1972-75 averaged $2,070 mn (*Hearings before the Subcommittee on Priorities and Economy in Government of the Joint Economic Committee of the Congress of the United States*, Washington, D.C., 23 June 1977, p. 60). At a Chinese GNP of some $300 bn and a defence budget of some $27 bn (*ibid.*, pp. 45 and 112), military shipments to Albania took less than half a per cent of Chinese defence spending and an infinitesimal proportion of Chinese resources as a whole.

Political Document on the Principles of Good-Neighbourly and Friendly Cooperation between the Union of Soviet Socialist Republics and the Turkish Republic.*

(Complete Text).

*The document was signed in Moscow on 23 June, 1978, by A.N. Kosygin and Bulent Ecevit.

The Turkish Republic and the Union of Soviet Socialist Republics,

Having in mind their desire and aims further to strengthen their relations of good-neighbourly and friendly co-operation which have been developing in keeping with the principles of equality, mutual respect, non-intervention in each other's internal affairs and mutual interest;

Being convinced that the preservation — in accordance with the aims and principles of the United Nations Charter and the principles and accords of the Final Act of the Conference on Security and Co-operation in Europe — of the spirit of the mutual trust and co-operation that were established in the relations between the two states already in the period of their formation by Vladimir Ilyich Lenin and Kemal Ataturk, will be in the interests of the two countries,

Expressing confidence that the strengthening of their relations within the framework of these aims and principles will make a contribution to the process of détente in the area concerned, in Europe and throughout the world, and, consequently, to the attainment of genuine peace,

Noting that the 1972 Declaration on the Principles of Good-Neighbourly Relations between the Soviet Union and Turkey constituted an important stage along the road of improving the atmosphere of mutual good will and is helping to develop co-operation between the two countries,

Declaring that the practical implementation of the provisions of the Final Act and observance, in a balanced form, of the aims of this document, will make an important contribution to turning détente into a permanent, viable and all-embracing process,

And reaffirming their adherence to the aims and principles of the United Nations Charter!

Declare that they will be guided by the following in their actions further to strengthen the relations of good-neighbourliness and friendly co-operation between them:

The Turkish Republic and the USSR declare their determination to implement in their relations and in the consolidation of their relations the declaration of principles included in the Final Act of the Conference on Security and Co-operation in Europe;

To develop in accordance with this, in a balanced form, relations of good-neighbourliness and co-operation on the basis of respect for one another's sovereignty, equality, way of life, public order and territorial integrity, and for non-interference in internal affairs, mutual security and mutual benefit;

To preserve the borders of the two countries as borders of good-neighbourliness and friendly co-operation;

And to implement thoroughly in their mutual relations the provisions on security in Europe embodied in the Final Act, not to resort to threats of or the use of force and not to permit the use of their territory for aggression or subversive activities against other countries.

The USSR and the Turkish Republic declare their joint resolve:

To co-operate within the framwork of international organisations and conferences in those instances when this is useful and accords with their mutual interests;

To expand — taking into consideration the contribution which this will make to the strengthening of détente and to the development of bilateral relations — the mutual exchanges of views between their official representatives through contacts to be implemented through diplomatic channels;

To accord particular importance to the integrity and equivalence of the principles of the Final Act;

To press consistently for a further deepening of the process of détente in international relations and for extending it to all parts of the world by developing the political, military, economic and humanitarian aspects of this process;

To support and to strive to make a positive contribution to all efforts aimed at achieving universal and total disarmament under strict and effective international control, taking into consideration the fact that the race in the field of nuclear and conventional arms not only threatens peace and the process of détente but also leads to negative consequences both in the field of economics and from the point of view of security on the national and international level, and hampers the development of international co-operation and the effective study and solution of the problem of under-development in the world;

To display, within this framework, respect in disarmament initiatives for the complete observance of the security interests of their own countries and also of all other states as well;

And to support the efforts of developing countries in strengthening their national sovereignty and economic independence, and to oppose any forms of imperialism, colonialism and racial discrimination.

The Union of Soviet Socialist Republics and the Turkish Republic express their determination:

To exert the necessary efforts to develop economic and technical co-operation in various spheres and also trade relations in a balanced and long-term form, ensuring benefit for both countries, and to make more extensive use of the existing possibilities;

Jointly to facilitate the development of co-operation and exchanges in the fields of culture, art, science, tourism and sport with the aim of strengthening the atmosphere of mutual respect and trust between the peoples of the Soviet Union and the Turkish nation;

To develop scientific and technical co-operation between them, and for this purpose to study the possibilities for carrying out joint research in the sphere of industry, agriculture, power engineering, transport and health services, on which agreement will be reached between the two countries.

The clauses and principles of this political document, which pursues no other aims than to contribute to the cause of peace, security and mutually beneficial co-operation, and is not directed against any State, form a single whole and do not touch upon the rights or obligations of the USSR and the Turkish Republic under any agreements.

Joint Soviet—Turkish Communiqué.

(Excerpts).

The Prime Minister of the Republic of Turkey, Bulent Ecevit, paid an official visit to the Soviet Union from June 21 to 25 at the invitation of the Soviet government.

During his stay in the Soviet Union, the Prime Minister of the Republic of Turkey was received by Leonid Brezhnev, General Secretary of the CPSU Central Committee and President of the Presidium of the USSR Supreme Soviet.

Friendly and constructive talks were held between Alexei Kosygin, member of the Political Bureau of the CPSU Central Committee and Chairman of the USSR Council of Ministers, and Andrei Gromyko, member of the Political Bureau of the CPSU Central Committee and USSR Foreign Minister, and Prime Minister of the Republic of Turkey Bulent Ecevit, Foreign Minister of Turkey Gunduz Okcun and Minister of State Hikmet Cetin.

Taking part in the talks on the Soviet side were: Ivan Arkhipov, Vice-Chairman of the USSR Council of Ministers, Nikolai Baibakov, Vice-Chairman of the USSR Council of Ministers and chairman of the USSR State Planning Committee, Nikolai Patolichev, USSR Minister of Foreign Trade, Semyon Skachkov, chairman of the USSR Council of Ministers' State Committee for Economic Relations with Foreign Countries, and Alexei Rodionov, USSR Ambassador in Turkey.

Taking part in the talks on the Turkish side were: Namik Yolga, Turkey's Ambassador in the USSR, Sukru Elekdag, Director General of the Turkish Foreign Ministry, Ferit Tuzun, Counsellor of the Ministry of Industry and Technology, Atilla Candir, Deputy Counsellor of the Ministry of Power and Natural Resources, and Turgut Carikli, General Secretary for External Trade of the Turkish Ministry of Commerce. . .

During the talks, which were held in an atmosphere of mutual understanding, respect and sincereity, the sides thoroughly discussed Soviet-Turkish relations and also had an exchange of opinions on current international problems of mutual interest. The two sides pointed to the great importance of summit meetings of the leaders of the two countries, which considerably enrich relations between the Soviet Union and Turkey and make these relations more purposeful and fruitful, and confirmed their intention to continue such contacts in future. . .

During the visit, Alexei Kosygin, Chairman of the USSR Council of Ministers, and Bulent Ecevit, Prime Minister of Turkey, signed a Political Document on the Principles of Good-Neighbourly and Friendly Co-operation between the Union of Soviet Socialist Republics and the Republic of Turkey.

It was pointed t ut that the Political Document opens up new prospects for further development of good-neighbourly and friendly co-operation between the USSR and Turkey. The two sides also emphasised that the main goals of this document are fully in keeping with the Final Act of the Conference on Security and Co-operation in Europe.

Talks on the delimitation of the continental shelf in the Black Sea between the Soviet Union and Turkey were held on Turkey's suggestion. During these talks, which were held in Moscow in a constructive spirit and in an atmosphere of goodwill, the sides agreed to delimit the continental shelf in the Black Sea on the basis of the principles of justice and equality, taking into account other relevant standards of international law. As a result of this, an Agreement was signed between the Government of the Union of Soviet Socialist Republics and the Government of the Republic of Turkey on the Delimitation of the Continental Shelf in the Black Sea between the Soviet Union and Turkey.

The agreement was signed for the USSR by Andrei Gromyko, member of the Political Bureau of the CPSU Central Committee and USSR Foreign Minister, and for Turkey by Gunduz Okcun, Foreign Minister of Turkey.

The sides considered it useful and decided to exchange views on the possibility of concluding an agreement on the area of traffic supervision in the Black Sea.

The two sides exchanged views on the state and further development of economic co-operation and agreed that the Soviet side would continue to render economic and technical assistance to the Republic of Turkey in the construction of industrial and power projects. These questions will be discussed at the third meeting of the mixed inter-governmental Soviet-Turkish commission on economic co-operation, which will be held in Moscow in September.

The two sides agreed to instruct their competent bodies to prepare within a short period a long-term agreement on economic co-operation and trade relations between the Soviet Union and the Republic of Turkey.

The two sides decided to sign very soon a three-year commercial agreement aimed at increasing the volume of trade between the two countries by 100 to 150% over this period.

The two sides expressed satisfaction with the results of Soviet-Turkish co-operation in culture, science and sport and expressed their desire to intensify their contacts in these spheres. They believe that further widening of cultural, scientific and sports exchanges will promote the increase of mutual understanding between the peoples of the two countries. A programme of cultural and scientific exchanges between the two countries for 1978-80 was signed during the visit.

Assessing the development of the international situation, the two sides point out with satisfaction that many opportunities for deepening and strengthening détente now exist and stress, specifically, that the full implementation of the Final Act of the Conference on Security and Co-operation in Europe is a very important element in strengthening mutual trust and in developing co-operation. They reaffirm their strong determination to continue to promote the strengthening of détente in international relations, giving it concrete content and gradually spreading it to all areas of the world.

Special attention was paid during the talks to the state of affairs in Europe.

The Soviet Union and Turkey declare again that all states that participated in the Conference on Security and Co-operation in Europe should consistently and in full implement the principles and provisions of the Final Act so as to steadily deepen the process of the relaxation of tension and to strengthen trust and security and to develop co-operation. In this connection, the two sides noted with satisfaction that the main positive results of the Belgrade Meeting was the fact that all the countries participating in it reaffirmed their readiness to continue this process. Moreover, the importance was emphasised of the meeting to be held in Madrid in 1970.

The Soviet Union and Turkey are as convinced as ever that genuine ensurance of security in the world is inseparable from the implementation of effective measures aimed at ending the arms race and at ensuring general and complete disarmament, including nuclear disarmament, under effective international control. In this connection, the two sides attach great importance to the work of the special session of the United Nations General Assembly on Disarmament.

The two sides again emphasised the importance of strict observance of all the provisions of the nuclear non-proliferation treaty, and pointed to the need to observe international standards, taking into consideration the security of countries which renounced the production of nuclear weapons.

Pointing to the need also to strengthen détente with measures in the military sphere, the two sides reaffirmed their views about achieving agreement at the talks in Vienna on the reduction of armed forces and armaments and on associated measures in Central Europe, with due account for the agreed principle of undiminished security of each state concerned.

The Soviet Union and Turkey reaffirm, in accordance with the provisions of the Final Act of the Conference on Security and Co-operation in Europe, their support for the holding of talks on all-European co-operation in environmental protection and on the development of transport and energy.

The two sides had a useful exchange of views on the Cyprus issue. They declared themselves in favour of the speediest solution of the Cyprus issue in a peaceful way through positive and constructive talks between the two Cypriot communities on the basis of respect for the sovereignty, independence and territorial integrity of Cyprus and its policy of non-alignment, with observance of the lawful rights and interests of the Turkish and Greek communities of Cyprus and ensuring their peaceful life in an atmosphere of complete security.

The two sides expressed concern over the fact that the Middle East problem remains unsolved. They reaffirmed their identity of views with regard to the need for the withdrawal of Israeli forces from all Arab territories occupied in 1967 and recognition of the inalienable rights of the Palestinian people to decide their own future, including their right to create their own state, and with regard to the preservation of the independence and the guaranteeing of the security of all the states in the area.

Expressing concern over the latest events in Africa, both sides emphasised the need to achieve a solution of the existing problems by Africans, alone, without outside interference, in accordance with the Charters and resolutions of the United Nations and of the Organisation of African Unity. The two sides stated that they supported the efforts aimed at the undelayed and complete elimination of all kinds of racialism and colonialism and at ending apartheid.

The two sides discussed the state of affairs at the United Nations Conference on the Law of the Sea and reaffirmed their intention to continue to exert efforts to achieve a mutually-acceptable agreement on a new Convention on the Law of the Sea which would ensure the lawful rights and interests of all states, would regulate the urgent questions of the use of world's seas and its resources and would promote the strengthening of peaceful, equitable and mutually-advantageous co-operation on the high seas. . .

The two sides agreed that the talks they held were fruitful and constructive and that the results achieved were an important contribution to the further development of good-neighbourliness and friendly co-operation between the USSR and the Republic of Turkey.

Leonid Brezhnev, General Secretary of the CPSU Central Committee and President of the Presidium of the USSR Supreme Soviet, confirmed the invitation to President Fahri Koruturk of the Republic of Turkey to pay an official visit to the Soviet Union at a time convenient to both sides.

Prime Minister of the Republic of Turkey Bulent Ecevit invited Alexei Kosygin, Chairman of the USSR Council of Ministers, to pay an official visit to Turkey. The invitation was accepted with pleasure.

Nicolae Ceausescu. Speech to the Meeting of Central Party and State Active, 3 August, 1978.

(Excerpts).

Current Tendencies in World Politics and Romania's Stand

Lately, in connection with the evolution of international life, with the rapid changes worldwide, a number of Party and State activists have applied to the Party leadership to have Romania's stand on these new events and realities explained at length. . .

We — in the Executive Political Committee — have considered it useful to arrange this meeting with the Central Party and State active, in order to review the new questions of international life and to present Romania's policy with respect to them, helping the Party and State cadres, the Party members, all the citizens, better understand them. . .

As we have already pointed out on several occasions, we have been witnessing of late a sharpening of contradictions in international life, an intensification of the tendencies towards redividing the zones of influence and strengthening one's domination in various parts of the world. One can say that these contradictions and tendencies are closely connected with the economic crisis, the monetary and energy crisis, which have brought about a difficult situation in a number of states as well as with the fact that the attempts to overcome the crisis have not yielded the results expected yet. . .

We can say that, at present, we are faced with two main world tendencies in the policy of domination and redivision of the zones of influence: on the one hand, tendencies towards recourse to force, to military ways, for the promotion of domination interests, for obtaining or consolidating the zones of influence and, on the other hand, the tendency to use, in the main, the economic means, in various forms, for strengthening the domination of monopolies and multinational societies, for consolidating the influence of certain states in various regions of the world. . .

Promotion of Relations with Socialist Countries, with Developing Countries, with the Other States of the World

. . .Certain comrades have asked questions connected with the issues which have occurred in the relations among the socialist countries. Indeed, we are aware of the divergencies between China and Soviet Union which, undoubtedly, negatively influence the force and prestige of socialism in the world. That is why, the Romanian Communist Party consistently declares in favour of the normalization of the relations between these two socialist countries, of the consolidation of their friendship and collaboration. But in the meantime new issues have become apparent such as those between Kampuchea and Vietnam, China and Vietnam, China and Albania. There are also divergencies and differences of opinion among other socialist countries. Our Party cannot but deplore this negative evolution of the relations among the respective socialist countries and express its hope that those states, the communist parties, will do their best for these divergencies to be surmounted as rapidly as possible. Certainly, all these problems concern the respective countries; they have the duty to act in the spirit of mutual respect, observance of national independence and sovereignty, of fully equal rights, of the principles of socialism, to settle the issues that have arisen among them by way of direct understanding. As far as we are concerned, we will do everything possible for any problems on which opinions may differ between the Romanian Communist Party, our country, and other socialist countries or parties to be solved only by talks, negotiations to strengthen solidarity and unity.

We should never forget that the transition to the building of socialism could not remove overnight the problems accumulated during historical development, very much as it cannot prevent the appearance of divergencies of opinions on a number of problems. It is clear that the perpetuation of divergencies, their remaining unsettled, can only be detrimental to the relations among the socialist countries. This is due to the fact that the principles of socialism are not always applied in the relations among the states which build the new social system. It has always been said that among the socialist countries there cannot be misunderstandings, that all their problems are solved in the spirit of proletarian, socialist internationalism, of brotherhood and solidarity. In our opinion, the supreme interests of socialism do not require the concealment of reality but the thorough analysis in the most responsible way, of the causes that engender dissensions and litigious problems, and the taking of action for their solution on the basis of negotiations among the sides, with a view to strengthening the solidarity and collaboration in socialist construction, in the general struggle for progress and peace in the world.

Romania's policy of continual development of the friendship and collaboration relations with all the socialist countries is well known. This policy has proved correct and we must most firmly continue it. We will act in the future, too, in order to contribute to overcoming divergencies, to settling the issues existing among the socialist countries by way of direct talks among the sides concerned, in order to avoid the accentuation of differences and contradictions.

In this spirit we will militate further for the development of our relations with all the socialist countries. While openly advancing our opinion on the existing problems, we will firmly and consistently act for their solution within the relations with each socialist country separately. An important place in our foreign policy is held by the continual development of the relations of friendship, collaboration and solidarity between the Socialist Republic of Romania and the Soviet Union. In promoting this policy, we have always started both from the rich historical traditions of the relations of mutual esteem and valuation, of friendship and mutual assistance between our peoples, between the working class and the progressive forces in the two countries, between our communist parties, and from the fact that Romania and the Soviet Union are neighbouring socialist countries. The multilateral collaboration, the relations of friendship and good neighbourhood with the Soviet Union will be, in the future too, a special concern of the Romanian Communist Party of the Socialist Republic of Romania.

As is known, this spring I made official visits of friendship in five social-ist countries in Asia. These visits have been in line with our consistent policy of developing good relations of collaboration and solidarity with all the socialist countries. The visit I paid to the People's Republic of China yielded very good results and lent a fresh and strong impetus to the rela-tions of friendship between our parties and countries, to the economic, scientific and technical cooperation between the two peoples. As a matter of fact, in the latter part of this month, Chairman Hua Kuo-feng is to pay a visit to Romania at the invitation of our Party and State. Likewise, the visit to the Democratic People's Republic of Korea — to which we are linked by a Treaty of Friendship — led to the intensification of the fine Romanian-Korean relations, an example — we may call it — of collaboration between the two socialist countries. Successful were also the visits to the Socialist Republic of Vietnam, Laos and Kampuchea.

It goes without saying that in no way do we oppose our relations with China and the other socialist countries in Asia to our relations of friend-ship and collaboration with the Soviet Union or the other socialist countries in Europe and other continents, the same as we do not oppose our relations with the Soviet Union and other countries to the relations we have with the People's Republic of China and the other Asian socialist states. On the contrary, all these relations Romania has with the socialist countries, with no exception, are interrelated in a unitary whole underlain by our princi-pled, firm and consistent policy of active contribution to strengthening the unity and solidarity of all the socialist states, to enhancing the might and influence of socialism in the world. . .

Romania will not let herself be involved in any public polemics, in blaming one socialist country or another; on the contrary, she will do every-thing possible to surmount the divergencies, to strengthen solidarity.

Romania pays special attention to the development of cooperation within the CMEA. . .

We declare and work for greater collaboration and cooperation among the CMEA member countries on the basis of fully equal rights, respect of national independence and sovereignty, every side's interest and mutual advantage, to the end of bringing closer and equalizing their development levels and speeding up their advance on the path of socialism and comm-unism. Moreover, Romania takes sustained action for promoting broad economic, technical-scientific and cultural relations with all the socialist countries.

As a member of the Warsaw Treaty — which will exist as long as the North Atlantic Pact exists — Romania shall develop her military colla-boration with the other socialist countries in the membership of the Treaty. In the future too, this collaboration shall be continued, with or without the Warsaw Treaty. Likewise, we enhance our collaboration with the armies of the other socialist countries on the basis of the principles of international solidarity. We start from the necessity to strengthen and develop each national army and are concerned with increasing the combat potential of our armed forces, of the entire Romanian people so as to be able to defend the revolutionary achievements of socialism, the country's independence, sovereignty and integrity. At the same time, Romania, just like the other countries in the membership of the Warsaw Treaty, has consistently declared for the liquidation of all military blocs, for a policy of collaboration, of equality among all nations, ensuring peaceful conditions, ruling out force — war.

For Security and Peace in Europe, for Liquidation of Conflicts and for Negotiated Settlement of all Outstanding International Issues

. . .It is true that a series of divergencies have occurred between the developing countries, the non-aligned ones as well, divergencies used for dividing them, for increasing the foreign influence on them, on various regions. The most eloquent example in this respect is offered by Africa, where suchlike problems led to armed conflicts, to foreign military intervention — fact which creates great dangers for the African peoples' security and independence, for peace in general. We consider that of fundamental importance for the faster economic and social progress of the developing countries is both the enhancement of their collaboration and solidarity and the strengthening of the unity of all national forces in view of firmly defending their independence and sovereignty, carrying through new democratic reforms, chanelling the respective peoples' resources and energies to developing the productive forces and raising the standard of living. . .

Besides, although this means for us a series of efforts, we grant and shall continue to grant technical assistance to the developing countries and shall train experts from these countries in our country where currently over 12,000 foreign young people are studying. Although we have to solve problems related to ensuring tuition and accommodation, our country shall not limit but expand the activity of training students from these countries.

We consider that the further promotion of economic cooperation, technical assistance and training of experts represents a direct and important form whereby Romania can contribute to supporting the developing countries. As communists, as a socialist state it is our political and moral duty to contribute to this. In turn, Romania receives in this frame-work support from these countries. By steadily expanding our cooperation, we create a broad system of mutually advantageous help between our countries, an expression of our solidarity in the common effort for the independent socio-economic development of every people, for the promotion in the world of a new policy of equality and respect among nations, of full equity, for the abolition of the old imperialist policy of domination and oppression.

It is a fact of the present political life that the non-aligned countries — most of them developing — play an increasingly important role in the international arena. Romania participates in the non-aligned activities as invited guest. She develops broad relations with these countries, considering that they represent an outstanding force in the anti-imperialist struggle, are keenly concerned with the promotion of a new policy of full equality and equity, in defence of national independence and sovereignty. Forming an important part of the world countries, the non-aligned states work as a democratizing factor of international relations, and assert themselves ever more strongly in the solving of the major issues today. . .

We also work for the continuous development of the relations with all countries without distinction as to social system, take an active part in the international division of labour, in the world exchange of assets. As for the situation in the developed capitalist countries, we think that, in spite of all the highly negative phenomena of crisis, it would be erroneous to consider that they are no longer able to solve the problems of economic development. In spite of the difficulties they had and continue to have, the capitalist countries still have forces and continue to play an important part in the world economy. Therefore, Romania's collaboration with these states, development of multilateral relations with them — naturally in the spirit of our well-known principles — must be continued the same as so far, and in some domains even encouraged. This collaboration plays an important part in the economic and social progress of both our country and the respective countries. Likewise, we take account of the fact that the active participation in the international division of labour contributes to the promotion of the policy of détente and peace all over the world. We start from the fact that groups of countries with differing social systems — socialist, capitalist, developing countries most of which have a mixed economy and some of them firmly declare for the socialist path — will continue to exist for a long time and that all of them should develop relations of collaboration, active collaboration for the peaceful settlement of the world problems, in the service of general progress, of all the peoples' peace and security.

As for the situation in Europe, after the unsatisfactory results of the Belgrade Meeting[1] we have to think to intensify economic relations — both bilateral and multilateral — with the European countries, with a view to translating into life the Helsinki-signed documents, and to thoroughly preparing the Madrid Meeting in 1980. Besides the development of the economic, scientific, technological and cultural relations, special stress should be laid on military disengagement problems. Both the socialist and the capitalist countries participating in the Vienna[2] negotiations should

[1] The Helsinki follow-up conference in Belgrade from 4 October 1977 to 9 March 1978. (Ed.)

[2] Talks on armed forces and armaments reduction in Central Europe. The negotiations commenced on 30 October 1973. (Ed.)

work so that they may conclude with positive results before long. In my opinion, the present proposals advanced by the socialist countries, the same as those put forth by the capitalist countries, provide a good basis to come to proper understandings in a short time. The reduction of the arms and troops within the limits proposed by the socialist countries or by the capitalist countries does not affect the balance of forces at all. It is obvious that 30,000 or 50,000 people less with the corresponding equipment — as suggested in one or another proposal — from one million people existing on each side, hence from a total of two million, will make no change in the balance of forces and be no danger to either the socialist or the capitalist countries. This force reduction would have, however, a political, psychological effect on Europe and all over the world. It would demonstrate that an understanding can be reached, would build up confidence and open the path to a more serious approach to military disengagement in Europe. We must also work for the problems of military disengagement to be discussed within the general framework of European security, with the participation of all states. We should work in such a way to bring these problems in the focus of the future Madrid meeting. . .

In this connection we also have to campaign more actively for the creation of zones of understanding and peace in Europe and, in this context, in the Balkans. We should set ourselves a more comprehensive programme and carry on steadier work to take further steps towards an improved collaboration among the Balkan countries. We have, of course, good relations with all the Balkan countries. We have no problems with Bulgaria; on the contrary, our relations with that country are very good. The frequent meetings and talks with comrade Zhivkov, the understandings we reached on such occasions were a powerful impetus given to this collaboration which materialized in a series of agreements on cooperation in production, including the common use of the Danube's hydro-power potential. This collaboration makes an important contribution to the two countries' economic and social progress, to the cause of socialism, to its growing influence worldwide. There is no problem between us and Yugoslavia, with which our relations are also very good. We have systematic contacts and most fruitful talks with comrade Tito, having established numerous accords of economic cooperation, developing the joint activity for the construction of the big Iron Gates hydro-power stations which make a valuable contribution to the progress of the two national economies, while serving the cause of socialism, collaboration and peace in the Balkans. Our relations with Turkey and Greece, too, are very good. Although we have no relations on a Party line with Albania, we have good relations on a State line with it, especially in the economic field — and we should act for their further development. So, we are in a position to actually work more efficiently in order to strengthen the collaboration and peace in the Balkans. I think we should also consider a closer collaboration with the Danubian countries — I mean Hungary, Czechoslovakia and Austria — also to make better use of the Danube.

As to Romania's position to the Middle East, I would say this. We are deeply concerned about the situation in that part of the world, especially about the deterioration of the situation in the Lebanon, which creates serious dangers in that region, just as to the whole world. We therefore actively back the initiatives pursuing peace in the Middle East that would lead to the settlement of the issues through Israel's withdrawal from the Arab territories occupied in the 1967 war and the settlement of the Palestinian people's issue, through the establishment of an independent state of its own, inclusively. The deadlock in the settlement of the issue in that region is first of all generated by Israel's rigid line. It is necessary that everything possible be done to make Israel adopt a more realistic position, taking thus advantage of the favourable conditions provided for the fastest conclusion of peace in that highly troubled part of the world. We think it is necessary that the socialist countries, to which speak up for the political settlement of the Middle East conflict take a more active part in the practical efforts made for peace in that region. Conditions should be provided, in this connection, for the participation in the negotiations of all the countries concerned, including the Palestine Liberation Organization, either in the Geneva Conference or in the UN framework or with its active participation, so as to step up the efforts for the settlement of the conflict. .

Eradication of Underdevelopment and Building the New International Economic Order, Implementation of Disarmament, Democratization of Inter-State Relations

As regards the struggle for liquidating underdevelopment and for building a new international order, we must admit that the results obtained so far are not very good. . .

Some socialist countries did not seem to be preoccupied by these problems, stating that the questions of underdevelopment and of the new world economic order must concern the countries that have colonies and which therefore have the obligation to contribute to their settlement. Of late, there has been a change in their stand, but we cannot say that they have gone as far as they could. We must start from the fact that the elimination of underdevelopment and the building of a new world economic order, the promotion of economic relations based on the principles of full equality and equity are, in fact, a direct continuation of the struggle against imperialism and colonialism. That is why, the revolutionary movement and the struggle for the eradication of underdevelopment, for the building of a new world economic and political order should form a unitary whole. We believe that the socialist countries, the communist and workers' parties, the revolutionary movement, all progressive and democratic forces must actively support this struggle, and hold an important place in the efforts for the implementation of these major objectives of the world today. It is the duty of the communist parties of the developed capitalist countries as well to actively back the righteous demands of the peoples in the developing countries, to take direct and strong action in the efforts for the establishment of the new international economic order. This is in line with the principle of solidarity and internationalism.

With a view to giving an impulse to the struggle for doing away with underdevelopment — one of the most serious problems of the contemporary epoch — I think that the holding of a UN Special Session on the new world economic order is of special importance. Such a session first requires that the developing countries should agree on a clear programme and a clear orientation. A UN committee should prepare such a session, and also the documents required as was the case with the session on disarmament.

The session will have to adopt a clear and firm document establishing the principles, guidelines and ways for the elimination of underdevelopment and the establishment of international relations of a new type, based on full equality and equity. In my opinion, such a special session of the UN might conclude with still better results than the recent session on disarmament. Even the developed capitalist countries are interested in the settlement of these problems, considering that the complex economic phenomena confronting the states of the world can be solved not partially, but in the context of the general socio-economic development of all countries, of the entire mankind. The best measures should be taken for solving these questions, in order to secure the developing countries free access to modern science and technology, to the great achievements of contemporary civilization, for the speeding up of the economic and social progress of all countries laggin behind, for a faster narrowing of the gaps in the level of development of various states. . .

At the same time, taking into account the practices existing in the world, one should lay greater stress in international activity on the struggle for the independent economic development of each and every nation, for the consolidation of the national independence of all states. This is all the more necessary as the manifest tendencies for the redivision of the zones of influence directly jeopardize the independence and sovereignty of many states. Support to the national independence, to an independent economic development of all nations is at present an essential side of the entire international life. We must never think that with the winning of political independence the struggle for national liberation has ended. On the contrary, the struggle for the consolidation of political and economic independence of the new states, for a really equitable collaboration among these countries, for the ever more rapid eradication of underdevelopment is a continuation of the peoples' national liberation struggle. It is naturally for the revolutionary movement, for the socialist countries, for the communist and workers' parties, including those in the developed capitalist countries, to consider that one of their main international duties is active support to the struggle for safeguarding the peoples' national independence. They have the duty to join forces with the national liberation movement, with the peoples' struggle in defence of freedom and sovereignty, of their sacred right to be full master of their national riches, to decide their fate independently, without any interference from outside. In this way the revolutionary movement, the communist parties, the socialist countries, will really play an important part in international life, will make their contribution to the implementation of the peoples' progressive ideals, to the progressive development of human society. . .

To solve all the complex problems of our time it is necessary to provide conditions for all states, primarily the small and medium ones, to take an active part in the international life. It goes without saying that we should concern ourselves with the active participation of the small and medium-sized countries in the settlement of the international issues, starting from the fact that they are the first to fall victim to the policy of aggression, the first to be affected by the policy of domination; therefore they are keenly interested in the democratic, peaceful settlement of all international issues, in securing their independent and free development. As I have already mentioned evident in this context is the role of the developing countries, of the non-aligned countries. There is no doubt that we have never underrated and cannot underrate also the part the big countries play in international life.

New Phenomena and Realities in Communist and Working-Class Movement

. . .I should like to say that, after the Berlin Conference, there has been a more powerful development of the independent policy of the various communist and workers' parties, a broader assertion of the principles of equality, mutual esteem and respect in the relations among those parties. But, we must admit that in this period tendencies of interference in the affairs of certain communist and workers' parties have also continued to be manifest.

After the Berlin Conference,[3] both in Europe and on other continents, a number of communist and workers' parties have consolidated their positions, playing an increased part and exerting a stronger influence both in the national and in the international political life. This proves that the orientation of the parties towards an independent policy based on the national historical realities in the respective countries is entirely correct. That is why we must do our best for the powerful assertion, in the future

[3] Conference of Communist and Workers' Parties of Europe. Berlin 29-30 June 1976. (Ed.)

too, of these principles in the relations within the communist and working-class movement, for the observance of each party's right to work out its policy, its revolutionary strategy and tactics independently, in keeping with the conditions in the country where it carries on its activity, without any outside interference.

At the same time, we should choose the most appropriate ways of action for continually strengthening the international collaboration and solidarity among the communist and workers' parties. The assertion of the independent policy does not and should not run counter to the solidarity of those parties, to the development of an ever more comprehensive and close collaboration among them, for the accomplishment of the peoples' advanced ideals, for democracy, socialism and peace. Of course, we understand the concerns and the attempts made by the various parties to find solutions to the specific problems in their countries — both in Western Europe and in other parts of the world — and we consider that, on the whole, their orientations are just. I have already referred on various occasions to Euro-Communism. Certainly, this notion in itself does not convey much meaning and is not of a nature to provide a new orientation in the process of the revolutionary struggle and of the building of the socialist society, which take place in highly diverse social, economic, historical and geographical conditions. The communist and workers' parties, their revolutionary tactics and strategy cannot be considered according to the criterion of the zones or regions in which they pursue their activity, but by the way in which they solve the fundamental questions of the transformation of society, of social and national justice and equity in each country. However, we have seen in Euro-Communism an expression of the fact that the respective parties want to promote an independent policy, to act in their revolutionary struggle in concordance with the conditions in the respective country, with the interests and wishes of the large majority of the people.

Certainly, that some parties are against one model of socialist construction — and they have the right to be so — cannot entitle them to claiming to have another model worked out compulsory for the others. We must understand that socialist transformation can only be achieved by taking into account realities, not set models; there is no name that can change the revolutionary outlook on the development of human society. About this question I have had talks with the leaders of some parties in western Europe, on other continents, and in the socialist countries. We have discussed the problems directly without engaging in public polemics, even when we had certain reserves towards one stand or another. We openly expressed our own views on those questions.

As to the question about certain parties' renunciation of the notion of Marxism-Leninism, I should like to say this: of course, as you know, Marx and Engels created scientific socialism, the revolutionary theory on world and life. But Marx never claimed that this theory should be called Marxism and, no doubt, even today he would oppose scientific socialism bearing his name. In turn, Lenin made a particularly important contribution to the development of scientific socialism; but he never required that scientific socialism should be called Leninism. The notion of Marxism-Leninism was used, of course, to acknowledge the merits of these great revolutionary thinkers and militants. But one should understand that scientific socialism is not a closed doctrine, given for good and all. Our revolutionary theory is ceaselessly developing and enriching itself contingent upon the changes occurring in the social life, in the practice of the communist parties, in universal knowledge. As a matter of fact, both dialectics and materialism had existed before Marx; the founders of scientific socialism gave them a new, revolutionary interpretation, turned them into a weapon of the proletariat, of the working masses. They relied on the most advanced scientific discoveries, generalizing the knowledge of that time in keeping with the development stage of society, that of the forces of production respectively. But, using or not using the notion of Marxism-Leninism should not turn into a substantive question of the communist and working-class movement, either in one sense or in the other. Some have added the words "Marxist-Leninist" to the name of their party. Likewise, a number of political and theoretical thinking trends call themselves Marxist-Leninist, nowadays. It is the right of each and every party to choose its name, to call itself as it thinks better. After all, essential is not the fact that one party or another calls itself Marxist-Leninist or "truly Marxist-Leninist". Essential is the stress laid on the scientific content of the revolutionary theory underlying the activity of a party, the correctness of the political orientation of the parties in the revolutionary struggle, in harmony with the fundamental principles of socialism, with the demands of life. The basic problem in the conditions of our epoch characterized by the rapid growth of the productive forces, by an unprecedented revolution in science and technology, by the great upsurge of human knowledge, is the continual enrichment of scientific socialism, the growth of each party's contribution to the development of our revolutionary theory in keeping with the musts of the human society's development, of social practice. Only in that way will the communist parties, the revolutionary movement be able to develop more strongly and fulfil their historic mission of revolutionary transformation of the world, of ensuring peace.

There were also questions which referred to the criticism some Western parties make of a number of concrete problems in the life of some socialist countries, of the policy they promote in one case or another. We have discussed this problem with several parties, with parties making such criticism as well, and expressed openly our considerations and opinions. Naturally, as we have already shown, not everything is perfect in the socialist countries. Unfortunately, some problems have not been solved in these countries, Romania included. The principles of socialist ethics and equity have not always been observed and there is still much to be done for their complete assertion in life. Moreover, in a certain period abuses were made and our Party just like other parties, took a stand, at the respective time. There are, however, some problems the solution of which depends on the raising of the productive forces to a higher level, on the more intense development of science, culture, education, on the growth of the resources and means society has. In general, one cannot deny the fact that the socialist countries have made historic achievements such as the liquidation of exploitation and of the exploiting classes, the abolition of the serious economic and social inequalities of the capitalist system, the improvement of the masses' standard of living and spiritual level as well as the important successes in building socialism. It is evident that a number of reactionary, imperialist circles try to use the propaganda means they have and slander the socialist countries, to counteract the influence of the ideas of socialism on the peoples' consciousness, diminish the prestige of socialism in the world. One should not forget that renegades, déclassés still exist in the socialist countries, too, ready for a handful of coins, to betray their country, to put themselves in the service of the reactionary circles, of the enemies of their own people. Likewise, one should not forget the fact that an intense activity of espionage and diversion is being carried on under various forms, against the socialist countries. However, life shows that all this is in vain. In its victorious advance, socialism cannot be halted by any ill-meaning attacks; it is increasingly asserting itself as the only means to free mankind from exploitation and oppression, to attain all the peoples' ideals of liberty, social and national justice.

To question the entire work built in the socialist countries cannot contribute to a correct, objective understanding by the broad people's mass of the realities of socialism and, the less so, help developing the struggle of the working class, of the democratic forces in the capitalist countries. We understand that some aspects of the realities in the socialist countries may be criticized. But it is difficult to understand some communist parties' commitment in official statements against acts and events taking place in these countries. We consider that such positions serve neither the respective parties and socialist countries nor the policy of détente and international collaboration. While criticizing certain negative states of affairs, one should refer also to what is positive in the economic and social development of the socialist countries. One should make an objective presentation of the way in which socialism has solved a series of vital problems of the overwhelming majority of the people, a way quite different from and infinitely more judicious than that in which the capitalist system did and can do it. While disassociating themselves from some mistakes and abuses made in the socialist countries, the communist parties in the capitalist countries should present correctly and objectively the essential states of affairs in these countries, their huge effort for development, for raising the peoples' standard of civilization, the grand prospect socialism has opened for material and spiritual prosperity, for the liberty of mankind as a whole.

Big Ideological Confrontations in the Contemporary World

. . .Our outlook on democracy — hence on human rights — stems from the necessity of ensuring people's full equality, developing equitable economic and social relations that should allow each and every citizen to lead a dignified life, from free access to education, culture, science, to the possibility of direct participation of the people, irrespective of nationality — and first of all of the working masses — in governing the whole society. It is only such a practical approach to the question of democracy that can secure the full assertion of the human personality, serving the cause of man's liberation, for man to really be free, the master of his destiny.

We believe that, in connection with human rights, it is the duty of the revolutionary forces to work vigorously for the actual fulfilment of the fundamental demands of the working people, for the abolition of every type of exploitation of man by man, for the free expression in the sphere of material and spiritual creation of all the citizens and for their unlimited participation in the effective government of society. That is why humanitarian questions must be a central objective of the struggle waged by the revolutionary forces for progress and civilization, against the exploiting classes and reactionary circles, for the building of a better and juster world.

In the matter of human rights, certain people seek to shift the accent to marginal or formal aspects, actually trying to deflect attention from the grave social anomalies fundamentally affecting man in capitalism. In certain countries, the talk about people's rights to emigrate really pursues the aim of securing the big supernational trusts the possibility of recruiting cheap labour, particularly intellectual labour, and promoting cosmopolitan concepts that will eventually annihilate the national sense of freedom, secure the policy of domination and oppression of other nations and peoples.

Questions have also been put in connection with the emergence and development of terrorism in various countries and how our Party regards this reality. The emergence and amplification of terrorism obviously are a result and expression of the crisis and decadence of the capitalist society, of the bourgeois state's incapacity to solve the complex social and national problems confronting that system. As to our attitude to this problem, I want to emphasize that our Communist Party, the revolutionary movement in general, have always, and this includes the years of underground work, disapproved and condemned terrorist acts in all their forms. We have made and are making a clear distinction between armed struggle for national and social liberation and individual terrorist acts. We believe that terrorism cannot be a form of political struggle under any circumstances. Whatever the problems that have to be solved in a certain country, terrorism will only complicate and eventually hamper the settlement of problems. Indeed, the causes of this phenomenon must be examined and action taken for their removal; however, terrorist actions cannot and must not be justified or approved in any way. We believe that terrorist acts, whatever the pretext for them, are contrary to the cause of the peoples' national liberation, to the cause of progress and social justice. Class struggle cannot possibly be replaced by individual terrorist actions. It is only the conscious union of the working masses, of the advanced forces of society, of the peoples, a wide-ranging mass activity in various forms that can secure a just solution of social problems, the defence of democracy and citizens' rights and liberties, the triumph of the national liberation fight, of the revolutionary struggle for progress and a better life, for the revolutionary socialist transformation of the world, for peace on our Planet.

In the capitalist world, profoundly affected by phenomena of social and moral decay stemming from the fact that certain people cannot find the way to solve economic and social problems and to pass on to a new and juster social system, there appear all kinds of nihilistic and anarchical concepts — some extreme leftist — others right-oriented — which have nothing in common with the effort that is being made to settle the acute problems of the masses and transform society in a democratic, socialist manner. Unforunately, such theories may sometimes find support with certain communists, too.

We must clearly say that the revolutionary theory of democratism and human freedoms is incompatible with freedom for fascism, for terrorism, for reactionary, déclassé elements which imperil the life of people and the progressive development of society.

A number of reactionary circles are trying to resuscitate long-outdated theories about the role and place of culture and the arts in social life; what they mainly combat is their responsibility to society, saying that culture and the arts are above society. Opinions are advanced or taken up again claiming that the creators of literature and art are "chosen" people who have the monopoly of understanding what is good and what is bad in the world, the monopoly of aesthetics, of tastes. They are said to be the people who have to shape public taste and the large masses, society must passively and absolutely adopt their tastes, opinions and creations. These views strongly express a trend typical of the most reactionary ideology because they deny the role of the masses in social life, in the shaping of history, aiming at the same time to disarm and demobilize the revolutionary forces, to sever culture and the arts from these forces and place spiritual creation at the service of the exploiting classes. Moreover, attempts are being made to reduce the sphere of creation to literature and the arts alone, and to ignore scientific creation — which actually opens new roads to the civilization and progress of society — and the creation of the masses which produce the material goods, the material and spiritual wealth of the peoples. Literature and the arts certainly represent an important part of social creation and play a significant role in the life of our society. However, proper attention must be paid at the same time to the stimulation and appreciation of scientific and technical creation as well, to the material creation of the working people who hold the decisive role in securing the advance of society. Literary-artistic production should not be opposed to the broad masses of people; it must be understood that it can only develop in close connection with the growth of the forces of production, serving the people, the progressive revolutionary struggle. It is only such art that can serve the cause of progress and civilization. . .

Certain questions were also asked regarding the attitude of the Romanian Communist Party to the idea of organizing international gatherings of the communist parties and new conferences of the type held in Berlin. It is our opinion that we cannot exclude such gatherings, that we cannot renounce the organization of international meetings. We obviously believe that in the present circumstances it is not possible to have a world gathering of communist and workers' parties, but a new European gathering can be held. Naturally, this is not an immediate question, it is a question of principle, but, considering the experience gathered at Berlin, we believe that a new gathering could be held to consolidate and carry forward this experience, to help clarify certain new questions that have arisen and are continuously arising in international affairs, as well as certain ideological problems. It even appears to me that the periodical organization of international gatherings is a necessity. In the conditions of the contemporary revolutionary struggle, of the powerful development of the communist parties, of the huge diversity of conditions in which they are carrying out their activities, it is obviously impossible to try and lead the communist and working-class movement from a single centre. Life demonstrates that it is neither necessary nor possible to organize a leading centre of the communist and working-class movement. Militating for the observance of the full independence of every party, we also believe that this independence is not in contradiction with the holding of international gatherings for exchanges of opinions, for the clarification of questions, for the strengthening of solidarity among parties and achievement of a new-type unity.

It is worth noting that worldwide certain political organizations have intensified their activity, that new international centres have been set up. We are witness to a development in the activity of the Socialist International in Europe and on other continents. At the same time, there is a growing organization and coordination at the world level, of various Liberal, Christian-Democratic and other parties for the purpose of promoting their views.

It is also well known that a number of openly anti-communist extreme right-wing organizations are increasingly active and organized at international level, as well. Highly conspicuous has been the revival of organizations propagating fascist and Hitlerite theories which are a serious threat to the cause of democracy and social progress and towards which we must take a firm attitude of political and ideological exposure and opposition.

It is obvious that in the conditions existing in the world today, the communist parties, too, have to find ways of jointly discussing new theoretical, ideological and political problems and to voice unitary attitudes in connection with different aspects in the evolution of society and international affairs. The communists have to give a riposte to the various unjust trends manifest at the national and international levels. That is why we are the partisans of organizing, on a basis of full equality, European gatherings of the communist and workers' parties for exchanges of opinions and experience.

As you know, the Romanian Communist Party is developing wide relations of collaboration with Socialist and Social-Democratic parties. We believe that at the present time it is absolutely necessary to intensify collaboration between the Communist parties on the one hand and the Socialist and Social-Democratic parties on the other hand, both at the national level, in order to accelerate the progressive, democratic development of the countries concerned, and at the international level, in the struggle for security, the new economic order, disarmament and peace. We also stand for the strengthening of solidarity with the national liberation movements, with the ruling parties of the developing countries, of the non-aligned countries, with other democratic parties, including religious parties. We place this wide international collaboration in the context of the union of all the forces advocating social progress, national independence and sovereignity, friendship among peoples, peace. . .

Hua Kuo-feng. Speech at Banquet in Belgrade.

(Complete Text.). Hsinhua News Agency, 21 August, 1978.

Esteemed Comrade Josip Broz Tito, other esteemed Yugoslav leading comrades, dear comrades:

Allow me first of all to thank Comrade Tito for his invitation to visit your beautiful country. for your warm welcome and for the cordial and friendly words which Comrade Tito addressed to us a short while ago. In making use of this opportunity, I wish to convey, on behalf of the Communist Party of China, the Chinese Government and the Chinese people, to the League of the Communists of Yugoslavia, the Yugoslav Government and to the Yugoslav peoples, cordial greetings and expressions of deep respect.

This time last year; Comrade Tito paid a historical visit to our country and on that occasion we held sincere and friendly talks. After that visit, the relations between the two Parties and the two countries — China and Yugoslavia — entered a new phase of long-term, comprehensive and stable development. During the past year, our mutual understanding has further deepened, the mutual support in our joint struggle has considerably strengthened, the co-operation between our two countries in various spheres has expanded and the revolutionary friendship between our two peoples consolidated. Now we have been given the opportunity to meet again Comrade Tito and other leading comrades of Yugoslavia in Belgrade and to carry out once again a broad and fundamental exchange of views on questions of mutual interest in order to promote further our good relations, all of which represents a great satisfaction to all of us.

Both the Chinese and the Yugoslav people won victory through their difficult and persistent armed struggle; after that they have carried out independently their revolution and construction. The Chinese people are deeply impressed by the long heroic struggle of the Yugoslav people. As far back as the past years of our war against Japanese aggression we followed your struggle with great admiration. Under the leadership of the Communist Party of Yugoslavia, with Comrade Tito at its head, the nations and nationalities of Yugoslavia triumphed, with their unswerving struggle, over the German and Italian fascist aggressors, who were superior and arrogant at that time, and they liberated their homeland and thus made a great contribution to the victory of the peoples of the world in the anti-fascist war. As Comrade Mao Tsetung once said. Yugoslavia was born in the armed struggle and she came into being through great efforts. She is a heroic country. Your victories gave us inspiration.

The League of the Communists of Yugoslavia, on the basis of Marxist scientific theory and in line with the concrete conditions in its country, built up and developed the socialist self-managing system. In the past 30 years and more, your country, in which enormous changes have taken place, has been transformed from a backward country into a modern industrial-agricultural country. In Yugoslavia the system of all-people's defence and social self-protection has been built up and intensively perfected, a decisive struggle had been waged against subversive and undermining activities of internal and foreign enemies. The country is ready to rebuff at any time an enemy which would dare to carry out an invasion.

Yugoslavia is carrying out the policy of national equality and thanks to this the unity of all nations and nationalities has been strengthened and the country's unity consolidated. At the recent Eleventh Congress of the League of the Communists of Yugoslavia, the experience of the construction of socialism, acquired in the course of several decades and in particular since the Tenth Congress, had been generally approved and the general guideline of further development determined. At this Congress full confidence in Yugoslavia's future was expressed and even greater steps of the Yugoslav people along the victorious path of socialism envisaged. We are sincerely pleased about your great successes.

Yugoslavia is one of the founders of the non-aligned movement. In consistently implementing the non-aligned policy, she plays an increasingly greater role in international affairs. The non-aligned movement has today become a very important force of the peoples of the whole world in the struggle against imperialism, colonialism and hegemonism. This is precisely the reason why some see in the movement of non-alignment a serious obstacle to the implementation of their aggressive and expansionist policy. They are trying at any price to wreck the unity of the non-aligned movement, to re-orientate it and to subjugate it to their hegemonist goals. We decisely support Yugoslavia's struggle for preservation of the unity of the non-aligned movement and for the preservation of the movement's basic orientation.

The Yugoslav people love peace, the Chinese people love peace, and all the people of the world love peace. However, one cannot but see that imperialist and hegemonist forces are waging a mad race in re-arming and in preparations for war, they are carrying out everywhere aggression and expansion because of rivalry for dominance over the world and this seriously threatens the peace and security of various countries. A series of events which have taken place recently in the Near and Middle East, in Africa and in Asia clearly shows that their rivalry is becoming fiercer and that the factors of war are noticeably growing. But their actions, for their part, help the peoples to widen their horizon and to make them know gradually their true face and to rise in struggle against them. History has confirmed that it is entirely possible to defeat the initiators of war. We are convinced that the victory will go to the peoples if the peoples of the world increase their vigilance, carry out relevant preparations and wage a joint struggle.

Dear Comrades, under the leadership of the Communist Party of China, the Chinese people, have smashed the anti-Party clique "the gang of four", and in this way the socialist revolution and socialist construction in our country have entered a new period of development. We held the Eleventh Congress of our Party and the session of the Fifth National People's Congress which set the general tasks of the new period — that is that in this century our country be transformed through development into a modern and strong socialist State. By carrying high the banner of Chairman Mao Tse-tung and by consistently continuing the revolution under the conditions of the dictatorship of the proletariat, our people, firmly rallied around the Central Committee of our Party, have begun a new long march towards the implementation of the magnificent goal — modernization of industry, agriculture, people's defence, science and technology. Certainly there will also be various difficulties along this path of ours. But we also have many favourable conditions. Through persistent struggle and self-denying efforts of the people of our entire country we shall certainly achieve this goal of ours.

The relations between our two Parties and countries are based on Marxism-Leninism. We want Yugoslavia to become more prosperous and stronger and you, for your part, want China to become more prosperous and stronger. We are completely independent and equal in our mutual relations. Neither of our two countries wishes to behave badly towards the other, nor does it wish to interfere in the other's affairs or control the other. You are in the Balkans, and we are in Asia. We are linked by a similar past and a joint struggle. The relations of friendly co-operation between our two countries have a broad perspective for development. I am convinced that this visit of ours will be crowned by great successes in both political and economic co-operation between our two countries.

Now I suggest that we raise our glasses to the revolutionary friendship between our two Parties, two countries and two peoples, to the prosperity and progress of the Socialist Federal Republic of Yugoslavia and the happiness of its peoples and to the health of Comrade Josip Broz Tito, the health of the other leading Yugoslav comrades and of all the comrades present.

Chinese Warmongering Policy and Hua Kuo-feng's Visit to the Balkans.
Editorial article published by Zëri i Popullit.
(Complete Text.)

The Chairman of the Central Committee of the Communist Party and Premier of the State Council of China, Hua Kuo-feng, has just ended his long trip to Romania and Yugoslavia. Formally, this trip was advertised as one of a general character, in return for the official visits the Romanian and Yugoslav leaders paid to China last year. But from what Hua Kuo-feng stated from the public rostrums in Bucharest and Belgrade, and from the stress the Chinese press has been laying recently on some aspects of Chinese foreign policy, it follows that this clamorous tour was undertaken in pursuit of extremely diabolic aims.

Hua Kuo-feng came to Romania and Yugoslavia neither to see the high mountains and beautiful plains of the Balkans, nor because he was urged to do so by any special interest in the ancient history of the peoples of this peninsula, or to acquaint himself with their aspiration and hopes for the future. He came to the Balkans for the same aims as Khrushchev, Brezhnev, Nixon and others had had before him. They poured high-sounding words about "friendship" with and "love" for the peoples of the Balkans in torrents and gave "assurances" for freedom, independence, prosperity, in abundance. But life has shown and continues to show that US imperialism as well as Soviet imperialism have sought and are seeking by all manner of means how to subjugate and put the Balkan countries under their hegemony, how to turn them into an aggressive place d'armes against the other countries, how to enslave the peoples of this peninsula and how to hitch them to their war chariot.

The Chinese leadership is in pursuit of the same aims at present. Hua Kuo-feng, too, came to the Balkans not to bring the "spirit of sincere friendship", as he stated at the meetings, but to make use of the "friendship" offered him by someone against the other peoples of the Balkans and Europe.

Certainly, the exchange of various delegations between countries is a usual practice in their relations and we have no objection to it. But we are against the evil aims this exchange of delegations is in pursuit of, which are to the detriment of world peace and the peoples who are seeking and are fighting to live free, independent and sovereign.

The "Balkan" meetings of the Chinese leaders took place at a time when China has completely unfurled the banner of rapprochement and co-operation with US imperialism, with the big international bourgeoisie, the fascist cliques and the most reactionary groups in the world. They were held at a time when the Chinese leadership supports NATO and the Common Market in Europe, the multinational companies and a united Europe to preserve capitalist oppression and US hegemony there. They took place at a time when it stands by the military fascist juntas in Africa, Asia and Latin America, when it stands by all those that oppress and exploit the peoples.

The political and ideological affinity of the Chinese leaders, with such régimes is also shown by Hua Kuo-feng's visit to Iran. He meets and talks cordially with the Persian Shah at a time when the revolutionaries and the working people have risen against him and bloody clashes are taking place in the streets of the cities of that country. By going to Tehran in this situation, Hua Kuo-feng wants to give proof of his support for the medieval régime of the Shah. This visit is a great offence not only to the Iranian people, but also to entire democratic and progressive public opinion, which has forcefully condemned and continues to condemn the brutal acts of the régime of the Shah against the population which has risen in revolt.

The Chinese leadership dispatched a top-level delegation to Bucharest and Belgrade after it had cut off all aid and credits to Socialist Albania in a perfidious, brutal, arrogant and unilateral manner for the sole reason that she did not accept and opposed the anti-Marxist, counter-revolutionary and pro-imperialist line China has adopted. Thus, this visit to the Balkans is an act of provocation against Albania and her friendship with the peoples of Yugoslavia and Romania.

Hua Kuo-feng came to the Balkans when the Chinese leadership, proceeding from its expansionist and hegemonic aims, has instigated the bloody conflict between Cambodia and Vietnam, two neighbouring and fraternal countries.

Therefore, no matter how much the Chinese media will advertise Hua Kuo-feng's visit to the Balkans, the peoples cannot fail to see that there are not two different Chinese policies, an imperialist one towards Vietnam and a socialist one towards Romania, a hostile and chauvinist one towards Albania and a friendly and sincere one towards Yugoslavia, a policy of interference in Asia and Africa and a peaceful one in Europe. The policy of the present-day Chinese leadership is one and the same, clearly defined and consistently put into practice. It is a typically imperialist policy of a super-Power, a policy to instigate war and achieve world domination.

The first aim of the general Chinese policy and strategy is to achieve political unity with US Imperialism and the other imperialists, who are its allies for the domination of the world by the United States of Merica, China and other big capitalist countries. With the course it is pursuing, China is striving by all manner of means to create its spheres of influence, which have not existed so far. This is also the reason why it has favourably opened itself towards the capitalist countries and is in unity with the US imperialists and other imperialists.

But this claim for spheres of influence, particularly in the developing countries, such as in Africa and any other continent cannot be realized without clashing with the other continent, who have their own interests there and without leading to sharper contradictions with them. The Chinese leadership is well aware of this. Therefore at present it aims, together with the USA, to erect a fence against the expansionist ambitions of Soviet imperialism and to check the consolidation of its positions. It thinks to oppose, with the help of the United States of America, the imperialist expansion of the Soviet Union, so that China can take its place. The anti-Soviet policy of the Chinese revisionists draws its source from this aim and in no way from their "concern" and "desire" to defend the other countries from the expansion and hegemonism of the Soviet social-imperialists, or from the "struggle" for the purity of Marxism-Leninism.

This aim is also served by the treaty China signed with Japan recently, a treaty it is trying to turn into a barrier against the Soviets in the East of Asia and, at the same time, into a means for an eventual march by China on the Soviet Union. US imperialism stands behind the Sino-Japanese treaty. Decked out in an anti-social-imperialist garb by the Chinese leadership and its partners, this treaty instigates world war.

Now the expansionist policy of China's leadership is clearly evident in Africa, where it is engaging in a very feverish activity. On this continent it is acting by supporting US Imperialism and the other capitalist Powers to preserve their neo-colonialist positions. Under the guise of the protection of the peoples of Africa, it is striving to create zones of influence and markets for China, little by little and in step with the strengthening of its economy thanks to the aid accorded to it by the USA and the other capitalist countries. For its part, China has begun to "assist" some States in Africa, but this "aid", just as those of the old imperialists, is not in pursuit of such aims as the economic, political or cultural progress of these countries, it is aimed at plundering their riches and subjugating them politically to the Chinese hegemony.

These aims cannot be attained easily, of course, as the Chinese want, but through fierce political, economic and diplomatic clashes, probably with arms with the other imperialists, who have already dug in Africa, with the Soviet Union which has not been sitting by with folded arms in the efforts to create its spheres of influence on that continent. It will meet great resistance and opposition particularly by the peoples and the progressive leaderships of the African countries.

The other aim of China's foreign policy is its penetration into the Balkans. Ideologically Albania has long since engaged in struggle against the revisionist theses and political line of the Chinese leadership. Her efforts to lead the Chinese leadership on to the correct road of Marxism-Leninism clearly testify to this. When the Chinese leadership saw that it could not act with Socialist Albania according to its Great-State wishes and dictate, when their cards of hostile activity within our country had been burnt, it severed economic relations with Albania. China has fostered and continues to foster aims of transforming the Balkans into a springboard, or into a political, economic and ideological field in Europe, wherefrom it could act in the direction of the revisionist countries such as Bulgaria, Czechoslovakia, Hungary, Poland as well as the in the direction of the independent and sovereign States of Greece and Turkey. In this way it wanted to build up Chinese influence in Europe and to oppose that of the Soviet Union.

But China's opening to Europe is confined not only to the Balkans. China has declared itself an ardent defender of the European Common Market and a united Europe, that is, of European enslaving capital. It has even since entered into relations with the European Common Market and, what is more, it has its own representative to this organisation though it is not a member of it. The all-round relations between the capitalist countries of Europe and China are developing in a big way, especially with the European Common Market member countries, and particularly with the Federal Republic of Germany. Therefore, Europe is a target not only of Soviet but also of Chinese expansion.

China's opening to Europe and the creation of a favourable political and ideological field for it in the Balkans are part of the Chinese strategy of instigating war. The Chinese have been shouting themselves hoarse for many years now preaching that war is imminent in Europe, because it is precisely here and nowhere else where social imperialism will launch the war first. Therefore they are calling on NATO to increase its military budgets as much as it can, and on the USA to dispatch more soldiers and neutron bombs to Europe, to lay nuclear mines there from the North Pole to the Mediterranean, calling on the Europeans of the West to dispatch soldiers and naval fleets to the Red Sea, the Indian Ocean and around Africa in order to protect the oil and raw materials routes, in order to aboid being in dire straits as a result of the impending war.

As an aggressor it is the Soviet Union which may launch the war in Europe, but in the Far East too, also against its Number One enemy, as China declares itself. But this cannot happen, the Chinese leaders allege, because China will have to work for its "modernisation" till the year 2000. Meanwhile, let the super-Powers clash in Europe, let the European peoples be burnt and killed by the nuclear bombs, let the people be wiped out by neutron radiation. Once this apocalypse comes true, China will have been through with its "modernisation" programmes and become a super-Power, within these 20 years until the end of the century, hence it can establish its domination over the world without firing a shot.

The open statements of the Chinese leadership to the effect that the war between US imperialism and Europe, on the one hand, and the Soviet Union, on the other, will be declared by the latter in the very near future, express the Chinese strategy whose aim it is to have the Soviet Union attack Europe and shun war with China in the Far East. Within this framework it is quite clear that Hua Kuo-feng's coming to the Balkans aims at upsetting the present situation in this zone, at causing hostilities between the Balkan peoples and instigating a third world war. Regarding the Balkans as "a powder keg", just as the European and US imperialists have always done, the Chinese leadership thinks that here some "crown prince" can be easily killed and war will break out in Europe. The world must not forget Sarajevo.

But the Chinese leadership is wrong in its reckoning, not because the revisionist Soviet Union is not an aggressive imperialism and does not cherish ambition to occupy, oppress and exploit the peoples, but because the imperialist Soviet Union will surely attack first that part of the world where its interests are greatest and the link of the countries it thinks to attack is weakest. This is what the Soviet Union is doing with its various acts of interference in Africa. In the present-day situation its war is more likely to be launched against China rather than against Europe. The war of the Soviet Union against NATO would be a large-scale world war, a nuclear war. Besides, the USA wishes and strives to have the two imperialist Powers, the Soviet Union and China, clash with and destroy each other. US imperialism, just as Soviet social-imperialism and China, is well aware of its own interest and where it can draw profits.

Therefore, the calculations of Chinese imperialism to set Europe ablaze, the attempts it is making to instigate war between the Soviet Union and the United States of America and their allies for the sake of its own hegemonic interests, cannot be realized.

But the bellicose plans of the Chinese leaders cannot be realized also because of another very important reason: the fact that they run into resistance and opposition by the anti-imperialist and peace-loving forces, progressive public opinion, the revolutionaries and patriots everywhere in the world. The peoples of the Balkans and Europe have suffered a great deal from the two world wars in their countries and have learned so much as not to become a prey of the warmongering aims of the Chinese leaders. They know how to defend themselves and how to emerge victorious over the aggressors.

The peoples of the Balkans and Europe have learnt from their history that reconciliation with the policy of instigation of the imperialist war, in the name of whatever aim this has been done, has been disastrous both for freedom and national independence and for general security and peace. They can never take the torch Hua Kuo-feng brings from Peking, to set fire to the boilers of war in the Balkans and Europe, for an olive branch.

They are aware that war in Europe and the world over can be avoided not by listening to the ominous Chinese sermons which instigate imperialist war, which Lenin considered a crime, but by opposing the aggressive policy and plans for the preparation of war of US Imperialism, Soviet social-imperialism and all other imperialisms, including also that of Hua Kuo-feng's China.

Therefore, anyone who joins or plays the Chinese game today, stands in opposition not only to the lofty interests of his own people, but also creates new dangers also for the other peoples, joins those who want and instigate war.

The two sides in their press reports from Belgrade and Peking throw flowers to one another and, with general stereotyped formula, refer to various problems the two Presidents discussed at their long meetings. We do not know what they have concretely spoken about Albania, but we are convinced that they have spoken also against her. This does not intimidate the Albanian people. They have made and make it clear that nothing will catch them unawares and never will they lack vigilance. They will foil the anti-Albanian plans of whoever they may be, being convinced at the same time that they will enjoy the support of the Yugoslav people, the Chinese people and, certainly, the support of the other peoples of the Balkans.

The aim of Hua Kuo-feng's visit to Yugoslavia, as the concluded official agreements indicate, was also the public proclamation of the complete and final "reconciliation" between the Communist Party of China and the League of Communists of Yugoslavia.

In the past Hua Kuo-feng and his group, that lead China now, had allegedly adopted a pronounced "critical position towards Yugoslavia and its internal and external policies. Whereas at present it is precisely the Chinese leaders who are paying the greatest honours to the Yugoslav revisionist trend and those who lead this trend. By going to Belgrade, as a repentant son asking forgiveness from his father, Hua Kuo-feng was impatiently waiting for a redressing of the "wrongs" allegedly committed by the leadership of the Communist Party of China against this anti-Marxist trend in the past, and for calling it a "genuine Marxist-Leninist" trend, the same as the new leadership of the Communist Party of China regards itself as being "genuinely Marxist-Leninist", though in reality it is a revisionist leadership. It happened precisely the same as with Khrushchev in 1955 who, when he went to Belgrade and knelt to Tito, shifted the "fault" for the criticism of Yugoslav revisionism on to the "mistakes of Stalin". Now the Chinese leaders, too, state that "erroneous" stand towards Yugoslavia had allegedly been imposed on them by Stalin and the meetings of the communist parties. As is seen when the question is to denigrate Stalin and Marxism-Leninism, the Chinese leaders do not feel ashamed to accept and repeat by rote Khrushchev's thesis and employ his base methods.

By making self-criticism about the "Mistakes" and by bowing their back, the Chinese leaders showed themselves ready to accord economic, political, ideological and other aid to Yugoslavia, where capitalist "self-administration" has been established.

Hua Kuo-feng sought to present his visit to Yugoslavia as a testimony to the existence of a complete ideological unity between the two countries and parties "which rely on Marxism-Leninism", "on similar experience", "the common struggle", etc. In reality, he seeks unity and union with the traitors to Marxism-Leninism to fight against socialism and the revolution. Choosing Belgrade, this long-standing centre of modern revisionism, to make such statements of "loyalty" to Marxism-Leninism, Hua Kuo-feng proves himself in what quagmire of opportunism and demagogy the Chinese leadership is wriggling.

He did not fail to bring forth, as evidence of the "implementation of the scientific theory of Marxism-Leninism in the specific conditions of Yugoslavia", the policy of "national equality" which the League of Communists of Yugoslavia has been pursuing. The support for the policy of the Yugoslav revisionists as far as the alleged fair settlement of the problems of national minorities is concerned, is rendered because they are in great need of this support. Chinese logic is strange enough. Mao Tsetung considered the settlements of the post-second world war in Europe erroneous, and proposed to rectify them, while Hua Kuo-feng considers proper the unjust decisions of the Conference of the Ambassadors of the Great Powers in 1913 on the Balkans. But it should be said that Hua Kuo-feng is not able to judge whether or not the questions of national minorities in Yugoslavia have been correctly solved. The national minorities which live in Yugoslavia today are more capabm of judging this.

The Peking press with *Renmin Ribao* (*People's Daily*, Ed.) in the van has fully exploited the arsenal of Chinese compliments to describe Hua Kuo-feng's visit to Yugoslavia. The organ of the Central Committee of the

Communist Party of China writes that "Hua Kuo-feng's visit to Yugo-slavia complies with the aspirations of the peoples of the whole world". This may be the desire of the Chinese leadership, but not the viewpoint of the whole world. "The collaboration between the two Parties has deep roots", "the League of Communists of Yugoslavia is a glorious Party", writes the Chinese newspaper. No one knows where these deep roots stem from. But the Chinese propagandists are not ashamed of using hollow-sounding slogans. They do not feel ashamed either when they say that the "League of Communists of Yugoslavia applies Marxism-Leninism and builds socialism in Yugoslavia". No revolutionary and no progressive man in the world accepts the Yugoslav revisionism which Hua Kuo-feng praises and advertises as a variant of the construction of socialism. This "socialism" not only has nothing in common with the scientific theory of Marxism-Leninsim, but has also been refuted by Yugoslavia's everyday practice, which proves that socialism is not being built there.

Just as the efforts of other opportunists who have engaged in such advertising until now, the Chinese efforts, too, to deck out Yugoslav revisionism in a "socialist" and "Marxist-Leninist" garb cannot be successful either.

The policy of equilibrium of the Yugoslav leadership has never brought nor will ever bring any good to the peoples of Yugoslavia. The "great diplomacy" of President Tito, which has transformed Yugoslavia into a dependent and not independent country, now hangs it on China's hook, on another imperialist Power, as China has been transformed at present. The new friendship with China, so "deeply rooted", as *Renmin Ribao* advertises it, adds to the dangers posed to the peoples of Yugoslavia and the Balkan peoples.

The bosom friends of the Yugoslav revisionists see the dangers this acro-batic policy of Yugoslavia represents, but they instigate and allow it. In the present situation it seems to them that they are weakening Soviet social-imperialism and they think that they are omnipotent to avoid the cata-strophe when the time comes and the contradictions are aggravated. They find it natural for the Soviet naval fleet to ride at anchor at Yugoslav ports and to smile at the Chinese formula of "the struggle against hegemonism" which is known to whom it is addressed. But the peoples of the world, Europe and especially the Balkan peoples, from Greece, Turkey and Albania, do not accept this.

Uniting ideologically and politically with Yugoslavia and Romania, the Chinese leadership intends to consolidate and deepen further its political and economic positions gained in these two countries. In this case, a great role will be played by the Chinese market which is opened to Yugoslavia and Romania, which in the grave conditions of the existing crisis and the great competitive power of better quality goods of the capitalist countries, hardly find markets in the other countries of the world.

In both Romania and Yugoslavia, the Chinese delegation concluded a large number of agreements on economic, trade and technical-scientific co-operation, made various offers, etc. The Chinese promises seem very "generous" on paper, but practice will show to what extent they will be realised. But now one thing is clear: the development of this "broad co-operation", as the Chinese propaganda calls it, will be conditioned to a great extent by the influence China will succeed in imposing on these two countries, and especially by their acceptance to act according to its liking. At the same time the all-round ties of Romania and Yugoslavia with the USA and the Soviet Union do not fulfil the desires of China in this field.

In his speeches Hua Kuo-feng used some terms such as "equal friendly relations", "mutual interest free aid", "non-interference in internal affairs", "not seeking privileges", "opposition to dictate", etc. Such hypocritical and demagogic statements follow all the chauvinist, arbitrary and perfidious acts the Chinese leaders committed against our country. They who believe them will soon be disillusioned.

On his visit to Romania and Yugoslavia Hua Kuo-feng did not speak about the "third world" and the Chinese theory of the "three worlds" as he did during Tito's visit to Peking, but he made extensive and eloquent statements about the "non-aligned world". It seems that on these questions Chinese pragmatism prevails over their ideological "principled stand". But the praises lavished on Yugoslavia as "one of the founding countries" of the non-aligned movement can hardly cover up Chinese attempts to inherit the leadership of this movement.

The idea of "non-alignment" serves the counter-revolution and the pre-servation of neo-colonialism. It seeks to deceive the peoples while asking neo-colonialism to cede in regard to some worthless economic reforms, but which are important for those who give such hand-outs. Through them they want the peoples to place themselves completely under neo-colonialist hege-mony and to submit to it.

Hua Kuo-feng, who poses as the champion of the "third world", by praising "non-alignment" tries to show that his "third world" and the "non-aligned" world are one and the same thing, that the strategy of this world must suit the Chinese policy, that its centre must be in China, in Peking. When he criticizes the Soviet social-imperialists [in] that they are trying to submit the movement of the non-aligned to their expansionist aims in fact he proves that he is contending with them to achieve the same objectives and the same aims.

But the peoples of the world are in need neither of the "non-aligned" theories, nor of those of the "three worlds". These theories, advertised by the bourgeoisie and reaction with so great zeal and love, are not on the side of the revolution and the liberation struggles, but against them. They do not assist the revolutionary struggle of the working masses and the peoples to get rid of oppression and exploirtation, to do away with the national yoke and oppression, to secure freedom and national sovereignty, but assist imperialism to preserve the existing status quo, to strengthen and perpetuate the odious capitalist and colonialist system.

The truth we say openly and frankly, just as we think and judge it, will never destroy the friendship of our people with the Yugoslav peoples and the Chinese people, or with any other people. The Party of Labour of Albania and the Socialist Republic of Albania have not feared, nor do they fear, to openly air their own views without hiding them behind formulas. The friendly peoples know and appraise these views.

But when we defend our correct and principled policy, there are rumours which draw their source in Peking and Belgrade that allegedly the stand of Albania assists Soviet social-imperialism. But no one believes these insinuations. With her policy and stand, socialist Albania has proved and will prove at any time that she is an irreconcilable enemy of Soviet social-imperialism and US imperialism, or any other imperialism. The Albanian people, who know very well where dangers come from, will fight to defend their own freedom, independence and sovereignty and will make their contribution also to defend the well-wishing and peace-loving neighbours who properly understand our unflinching stand and the dangers posed by the imperialist Powers.

But the rumours which are heard from Peking and from their friends, about Socialist Albania allegedly taking the side of the Soviet Union, are spread in order to sow suspicion towards the policy of the Albanian proletarian State. The whole world should know, and must rest assured, that Albania does not stretch out a begging hand to any imperialist Power and that Albania's territorial and coastal borders and air space are inviolable.

Under the Constitution, Socialist Albania does not accept, nor will it ever accept, credits from any foreign Power. But in the capitalist and revisionist world there exists the mentality, which stems from their concrete practice, that no State, whether big or small, can survive without foreign credits. With its example, Socialist Albania will put an end to this mentality.

Just as until now, our country will continue to maintain normal trade relations with other States on the basis of mutual benefit. This does not violate in the slightest the principles sanctioned in our Constitution, but the imperialists, in pursuit of evil aims, confound trade based on mutual interest, with the granting of credits and aid, which are two entirely different things. Hence their deduction that Albania is isolated and cannot walk on its own. But the opposite happens and will happen. Being sure of their own forces and with unflinching confidence in the future, powerfully relying on the support and solidarity of international progressive opinion, the Albanian people, led by their Workers' Party, will boldly surmount the obstacles getting in their way and will carry the cause of socialism in Albania always forward.

The Party of Labour of Albania and the People's Socialist Republic of Albania have long since warned against the intrigues of the super-Powers and their attempts to introduce quarrels and conflicts into the Balkans. Comrade Enver Hoxha stated at the Sixth Congress of the PLA, in November 1971: "The Balkans did not become a powder keg of itself. It was the foreigners, the imperialists, who did this in the past, and it was they who held all the detonators in their hands. And they would like to bring about the same situation today. It is the duty of the Balkan peoples to cut all the fuses with the sword, so that peace and security may really be established in the Balkans. It is only natural that our peoples need friends. But they should never become tools of foreigners to the detriment of the interests of any one people or of all our peoples jointly."

These words of Comrade Enver Hoxha express the resolute and consistent stand of the Party. Government and people of Albania, which proceeds from the desire and determination to live always in peace and friendship with the peoples of the Balkans and of the whole world.

Statement by the Polish Social Self Defence Committee and the Charter 77 Movement in Czechoslovakia on the Tenth Anniversary of the Invasion of Czechoslovakia.

(Complete Text.).

In August, 1978 representatives of the Polish Social Self Defence Committee "KOR" met members of Charter 77 on the Polish Czechoslovak border. They exchanged information about their activities, discussed future cooperation and agreed on a common statement to mark the tenth anniversary of the Soviet led invasion of Czechoslovakia and events in Poland in 1968.

Text of Statement

Ten years have passed since the troops of five Warsaw Pact countries occupied Czechoslovakia to suppress the aspirations of its people to freedom. A brake was put on the democratisation process and on the hopes of all democratic Europe. In the name of humanistic values, the people of Czechoslovakia had developed an alternative to the totalitarian system. In the same year, the freedom aspirations of the Polish intelligentcia were suppressed by force.

The ten years that have passed have clearly proved the viability of the ideas of the Prague Spring and the democratic movement in Polish society — despite all the spokesmen for the anti-democratic order and national non-sovereignty. Many people from both countries have, because of their support for these ideas paid and still pay a very high price — being removed from public life, being deprived of work and freedom — even sometimes of life. Continuing repression is part and parcel of the life of our friends in the USSR and other countries who fight and suffer for the same aims.

In the days around this tenth anniversary we are standing together in defending truth and freedom, in defending true human rights, democracy, social justice and national independence. We declare our common intention to maintain faith in these ideals and to act in the same spirit. Human dignity as an inviolate value which gives meaning to the lives of individuals and nations is the source of all our aspirations and actions. And there springs our profound feelings of solidarity with many friends in the world who cherish the same ideas.

Statement by the Polish Social Self Defence Committee and the Charter 77 Movement in Czechoslovakia. 20th September 1978.

(Complete Text.).

A second meeting between our representatives took place on the Czechoslovak-Polish border in September 1978. The purpose of the meeting was to continue discussions concerning the cooperation between the Social Self-Defence Committee "KOR" and Charter 77, and to define more clearly the agreement reached at the first meeting. It was decided to establish permanent working groups which will supervise the swift exchange of information in order to enable us to cooperate effectively. The prospects of preparing common documents and of organising a political science seminar on the subject of independent civic initiatives in East European countries were discussed. We would wish to invite friends from other countries to participate in such a seminar.

An agreement concerning further cooperation, primarily in the field of culture and the arts, has been reached. A letter was despatched from the meeting to the defenders of human and civil rights in Armenia, Bulgaria, East Germany, Georgia, Hungary, Lithuania, Russia, Rumania and the Ukraine.

Letter to the Defenders of Human and Civil Rights in Armenia, Bulgaria, East Germany, Georgia, Hungary, Lithuania, Russia, Rumania and the Ukraine. 20th September 1978.

(Complete Text.).

Dear Friends!

We send you our warmest greetings from the second working meeting of the representatives of the Social Self-Defence Committee "KOR" and

Charter 77, taking place on the Czechoslovak-Polish border. Unfortunately a personal meeting with you does not seem possible. This is why we wish to tell you how much we value your civic stand and your willingness to fight for the right of people in our countries to live in an atmosphere of freedom and dignity. From our own experience we know the difficulties connected with this struggle. We are convinced that we are all fighting for the same ideals. We often think about all those who suffer in prison for their convictions. We think of J. Orlov, A. Scharansky, A. Ginsburg, W. Pietkus, A. Podrabinek, Bakhra, Rudenko, Tikhy, Szucewicz, Moroz, Czarnowil, Gamakhurdia, and many others. Thank you for your support of our cause. We also wish to assure you of our solidarity with you. The common fate of our nations bonds us together today more strongly than ever beofre. It is therefore important that those who attempt to improve our common destiny should join forces.

Charter 77
The Social Self-Defence Committee "KOR"

Declaration of the Founding Committee of the Polish Free Trade Unions (Baltic Seaboard Region) April 29, 1978.

(Complete Text).

The true Polish Trade Union Movement ceased to exist 30 years ago.

Forced dissolution of political parties, such as the PPS (Polish Socialist Party), the PSL (Polish Peasant Party) and other independent organisations representing various social groups in the country, preceded by imposed merger of individual Labour Unions into a single (state controlled) body — resulted in the Trade Unions becoming yet another institution representing the interests of monopolistic State employer, rather than of the employees. The Unions became an extension of the political structure of the ruling Polish United Workers Party and a lenient administrative device to operate a system of organised exploitation of all social groups in Poland.

A population deprived of its natural and necessary forms of self-defence could only react impulsively: violent eruptions of social discontent, such as in Poznan in 1956, during the "March Events" of 1968, the Baltic Coast workers revolt of 1970 and, lastly, in June 1976 — were always associated with a menacing danger of a major revolution of unpredictable national and international consequences.

The (Party) authorities, though occasionally forced to retreat — as in June '76 — or to offer a tactical and temporary appeasement — as in 1956 and in December 1970 — proved to be incapable of introducing a form of democratisation of public life. Such inaptitude resulted in a constantly aggravating social and economic crisis, leading to a crisis of State authority.

What is needed today is a process of a wide spread democratisation. The population must continue to struggle for a democratic form of government. All social strata should regain their right to self-determination and be allowed to recreate social institutions, through which their rights could be truly implemented.

Only free unions and associations can save the State; since only the process of true democratisation can lead towards integration of interests and the will of the citizen with the interests and the authority of the State. These tasks are being carried out presently by existing (dissident) social institutions, such as the "Social Self-Defence Committee-KOR", the "Movement for the Defence of Human and Civil Rights", the "Society for Academic Courses", or the "Students' Solidarity Committees".

While remembering the tragic events of December 1970 and acting in compliance with the expectations of numerous groups and millieus of the Baltic Coast region, we wish to follow the lead of our Silesian colleagues by organising independent labour unions in our area.

Today, on the eve of May Day which for over 80 years symbolised the struggle for workers rights, we hereby call into being the FOUNDING COMMITTEE OF THE FREE TRADE UNIONS OF THE BALTIC SEA-BOARD.

The aim of the Free Trade Unions is to create an organised form of defence of economic, legal and humanitarian interests of the working population. Free Trade Unions declare their willingness to assist and to protect all employees, irrespectively of their political views, or qualifications.

The Founding Committee will operate openly through their representatives, leaving our collaborators and supporters the right of decision and voicing their opinions.

Whereas we wish to identify ourselves with the guiding principles of the (unofficial) journal *Robotnik* (*The Worker*), we shall express our views on its columns, or in our own publications. We shall also inform our readers about the progress of our activities and our achievements.

We appeal to all working people — the workers, the technical, managerial and administrative staff: form your own independent Employee Representation Committees. Alternatively you may reach the same goal by introducing independent-minded activists into your Works Councils — people who would represent the electorate's interests in a true and honest manner. We would like our initiative to become a stimulus for a number of individual, varied and independent social actions.

We appeal to independent social institutions for support and widest publicity for our initiative.

We appeal to all for solidarity in the struggle for a brighter future.

Pastoral Letter of Polish Bishops for the annual Mass Media Day. Sunday, 17th September 1978.

(Complete Text.).

Beloved in Lord Jesus: In accordance with recommendation of the Holy Father Paul VI we wish to discuss today the matter of consumers of mass communication media, their expectations, duties and privileges. Since the Second Vatican Council it has been accepted that the mass communication media are understood to be the press, periodicals, radio, television, cinema and the like. As a product of human thought all of them are the property of the whole human family. Everybody has the right to use them and to receive the contents disseminated by them. The Church, through the use of the media, wishes to popularise spiritual and religious values and thereby make human unity stronger.

Alas, the Church in today's Poland, even though since the beginnings of the existence of the State it has been engaged in the co-operation of national culture, but not only been refused the right to possess the mass communication media, and in particular radio, television and the daily press, but is also not able to use them actively. All the media have been taken over by the State and given to serve the ideology which has as its aim the upbringing of human beings without God.

There is always some kind of a drama in man's creative activity. Everything created by him to serve the benefits, development and progress of people is very frequently used to harm people. This also applies to such inventions as radio, television, the cinema, press and others. Those media, in accordance with our expectations, should serve the cause of unifying the people through the exchange of cultural achievements, spiritual and religious values, and through the flow of information on problems and living conditions of people and whole human communities in various parts of the world. They should stimulate a kindly interest in others, leaving the circle of one's own interests, and should contribute towards popularising the feeling of brotherhood among people and showing all that is beautiful, noble and worth seeking and working for.

Today, however, things are not as they should be. The mass communication media are abused in order to impose one kind of view only, and one behaviour pattern only, and to spread power over people. People who have taken over today's press, radio, television and theatre consider only their own goals. Controlling the media, they feed us with their views. As citizens in our own fatherland we have rights which cannot be given up. "We have the right to expect information that is rapid, honest, objective and respectful to the hierarchy of values". Pope Paul VI reminds us in this year's message on the day of mass communication media.

We have the right and, indeed, we have the duty to pronounce criticism and to express our evaluation of the contents that are conveyed to us by radio, television and theatre. We have the right to expect that the criticism will be heard and taken into consideration when preparing programmes. To ignore our opinion, the opinion of consumers, is an expression of our treatment as objects to be freely manipulated by those who have taken over the power over citizens who have been deprived of the right to pronounce their views publicly.

Finally, we have the right of respect and of serious consideration for our convictions, our national and Christian culture, our customs and those values which for thousands of years have been the pride of our nation.

We must express regret over cases of persecution of people who have the courage to pronounce orally and in writing their judgements and opinions concerning public affairs and the content of what is published by the mass media.

All consumers of the content of mass media have important duties. Pope Paul VI says in the message: "A consumer must have an active attitude". We must, therefore, evaluate the content of what is published by press, radio, television, the cinema and theatre, remembering always their source. We must supplement the content from other, more reliable, sources. We must, if necessary, protest in the ways which are available to us. We have the moral duty to protect whenever the principles of faith and Christian morality are offended and when people who have no opportunity of defending themselves are attacked.

In order to be able to assume an active posture vis-a-vis the press, radio, television, and other mass communication media, we must take on the toil and duty of self-education, so that the pressure exerted now by these media may not blunt, or even destroy in us the ability of critical assessment. The recipient must have a triple ability in order to become a fully mature and responsible citizen, said the Pope in this year's message. He must have the ability to understand the language of the mass communication media, the ability to make a correct choice among the transmitted materials, and the ability to make an appraisal.

The first period of education in this sphere must take place within the family. The understanding, choice, and assessment of materials transmitted by these media must form part of a common plan of preparation for life. The basic duty to assist children and young people in making a choice belongs to you, parents and tutors. It is necessary, therefore, to become acquainted with publications, film and television programmes which draw the attention of young people, in order to be able subsequently to talk to them on this subject and to shape critical minds.

Parents and tutors, you cause a great moral harm to children if you permit them to watch programmes which are unsuitable for them. A constantly switched on television or radio set in your home can contribute to the breaking up of community family life, to mental impoverishment, and it can deprive you of the valuable effects of personal human ties.

We all know that the spirit of freedom is the proper climate for the full development of a person. Without freedom a person is dwarfed, and all progress dies. Not allowing people with a different social and political ideology to speak, as is the practice of the State, is unjust. State censorship has always been and remains a weapon of totalitarian systems. With the aid of censorship the desire is not only to guide the mental life of society, public opinion, but even to paralyse the cultural and religious life of the whole people. Social life requires frankness and freedom of public opinion. Censorship places blinkers on the eyes of people, said the Primate of Poland in his sermon delivered on 6th January in Warsaw Cathedral. It misinforms them and — what is even worse — releases them from responsibility for the nation.

Very often people do not know the truth, they do not know the state of affairs, and in consequence they do not feel responsible for the situation in the social, economic or moral sphere. The limitation or even abolition of the interference of censorship is the order of the moment. It is being demanded at present by all people who think in terms of the welfare of the nation, irrespective of ideological or socio-political orientation. The authorities must not ignore this generally raised demand, if they really have the welfare of the nation at heart.

The Polish people, which for a thousand years has been living and growing in the Christian culture, needs religious literature, and most of all the Holy Scripture, which is the most important book of a believing person because it contains the living word of God. We need catachisms and religious books for children and young people. For 8,000,000 children at basic and higher than basic schools, a total of only 300,000 copies of catechisms were published in Poland in 1977, which means that there was one catechism for 26 persons. We need prayer books, especially to prepare for the first Holy Communion. Older people also await them.

We are experiencing a great shortage of Catholic periodicals, and we regard as such only those publications which are guided by the truths of religion and Christian morality, and which are based on Catholic social teachings. The total edition of the three Catholic weeklies, *Gosc Niedzielny, Przewodnik Katolicki* and *Tygodnik Powszechny*, amount to only 190,000 copies, while the demand for these periodicals reaches many millions. It cannot be deemed normal when the Catholics have no possibility of purchasing a Catholic press and religious books. A Catholic society feels the need of at least one independent Catholic daily.

Just treatment of believing people demands that the Church be enabled to transmit on radio and television the Holy Mass, with a sermon on Sundays and Church holidays. This is necessary in particular for those who, for various reasons, cannot physically take part in this most important miracle of the Church.

The Episcopate has appealed many times to the authorities to make it possible to broadcast by radio religious programmes for those who are ill and suffering. We have the right to expect the voice of millions of believing citizens of our country to be heard.

Considering the need, or indeed the duty, to supplement information by using other sources, we encourage you to use the Vatican Radio, which broadcasts Church news, speeches of the Pope and religious conferences.

Putting before you our worries, we wish that they may become your concern as well. We shall all act on them and, above all, we shall pray to Him who is the Lord of Heaven and Earth, and who controls all things. We join you in this sincere prayer and we bless you in the name of the Holy Father, the Son and the Holy Ghost, Amen.

The 164th plenary conference of the Polish Episcopate.

Signed by Cardinals, Archbishops and Bishops of Poland.

Communiqué
Farmers Defence Committee — Grójec region
Provisional Farmers Defence Committee — Lublin region
Provisional Committee of Farmers Independent Trade Union

Since winter is coming and the time of coal deliveries for the villages has begun, our three committees have together appraised the situation and found the state of the deliveries reprehensibly inadequate. We have therefore resolved to initiate and organize a collective petition to the Seym in which, we believe, we will be supported by all the peasants. It is up to us and our formulation of our demands whether the villages will have decent living conditions and the necessary means of production. Even if Poland had no coal deposits, we would be justified in demanding coal deliveries from state authorities, for they exist in order to satisfy the needs of society. But as it is, Poland is first in the world in coal production per capita. This is achieved by the miners' excessive work, on Sundays and holidays, on top of the eight hour working day. And still we have no coal. Often our wives queue in the cold since midnight in order to get in the morning, after a fight with the neighbours, a tenth place in the queue, and then, maybe, get a receitp for 200 kilograms coal, or leave with nothing. We think this situation is degrading. Whole families often move into the kitchen for the winter, because it is the only heated room in our houses. Our health suffers and our property gets spoilt. We have no coal to prepare fodder for livestock, no coal to heat our greenhouses and swineries.

The whole country is waiting for our produce with impatience. Yet the authorities do not give us any possibilities to increase production, or even to maintain its present level. If the countryside is to be a fit place to live for half the population and to produce food for the whole country, we must have coal — generally available and on the free market. We demand this of the authorities.

At the same time we appeal to all farmers in Poland to sign our petition and send it to one of our committees, so that we can elect a delegation to take it to the Seym and pass it to the public opinion.

Zbrosza Duza, 8 October 1978.

Resolution of the Provisional Farmers' Self-Defence Committee of the Lublin Region. Ostrowek, 30th July 1978.

(Excerpts.). Ostrowek, 30th July 1978.

We, the farmers of the Lublin region, inhabitants of Zalesie, Kajetanowka, Kolonia Gorne, Wolka Lancuchowska, Lancuchow, Ciechanki Lancuchowskie, Antoniow, Trzeciakow, Kolonia Ostrowek, Jaszczow, Ostrowek, Maryniow, Szpica, Poplawy, Wola Korybutowa, Zawadow, Sufczyn, Klucz and other villages, assembled on 20th July 1978 at an open meeting in Ostrowek, at which some 200 people were present, demand the withdrawal of secret policement from our villages. We also demand the revocation of payment orders and the recall of bailiffs.

Last year the Parliament of the Polish Peoples' Republic passed a Bill on Old Age Penions for farmers and their families. This Bill requires farmers to pay pension contributions. In our villages these contributions have, on the whole, remained unpaid. The authorities responded by sending in the bailiffs, who, against our will, began to seize our property. At the same time the Security Service interrogated many of us, demanding to know why pension contributions were not being paid. Faced with this situation we began a farming strike. Between 28th and 30th July 1978 we refused to deliver milk. The following villages participated in the strike: Zalesie, Wolka Lancuchowska, Ciechanki Lancuchowskie, Ostrowek, Kolonia Ostrowek, Sufczyn, Klucz, Kolonia Gorne, Kajetanowska. In those villages almost all farmers joined the strike. For example: the dairy in Ciechanki, which receives approximately 3,500 litres of milk a day, managed colled just 160 litres during the strike.

We hereby give notice that, should the action directed against our villages continue, longer and more widespread strikes may follow. At the same time we are demanding that the Bill on pensions be suspended until a proper discussion on pensions for farmers can take place, as previous consultations were fictitious. We did not then know the full text of the draft and this is why we could not take a stand on it. Ever since we first refused to pay contributions we have been expecting the arrival of the authorities' representatives for a discussion on the draft and on the situation in agriculture. Bailiffs and security policemen were sent instead.

The purpose of our strike is to bring a number of problems to the attention of the authorities.

Firstly — a Bill envisaging changes in the structure of agriculture may not be passed without prior authorisation from farmers-electors.

Secondly — the contents of the Bill in its entirety, together with enabling legislation, should have been revealed in full and the wishes of the electorate taken into account.

Thirdly — given the present situation in agriculture, farmers should be able to speak out on the subject of government policy in this field and the catastophic consequences of that policy.

Fourthly — the authorities should put an end to the practice of using police methods to intimidate society.

At today's meeting we have elected the representatives of farmers from our region. They form a Provisional Farmers' Self-Defence Committee. . .

The Committee is empowered to talk to the authorities on the subject of the present strike, its consequences and the situation of farmers in our region

We empower the Committee to organise self-defence against any reprisals which may follow.

We have decided that no village will negotiate separately with the authorities.

We appeal to farmers throughout Poland to establish contact with us.

Message to the Parishes from the Conference of Lutheran Church Authorities.*

(Complete Text.).

* Concerning the planned introduction of military education in the schools of the German Democratic Republic.

Christians and Churches have increasingly recognised it as their duty to help establish peace in our world. Reconciliation, which God set against all human enmity, is the basis of our life. We owe it to all men to bear witness to it. For the sake of this mission we as the members of Christ Jesus help wherever tensions can be reduced, trust encouraged and security between the nations strengthened.

In our churches many anxious voices have been raised regarding the introduction of military education in the schools. The Committee of the Conference of Lutheran Church Authorities has taken up this anxiety and for its part requested the government not to introduce military education as a subject. It received an exhaustive statement regarding the introduction of this subject in the 9th and 10th school years. The Conference regrets that doubts on the part of the Church were not taken into account, and asked the government to reconsider its position once again. The Conference fears that through the introduction of compulsory military education, the education of young people towards peace-loving attitudes will suffer severe damage and that the credibility of the peace policies of the GDR will be called into question.

In view of this situation particular importance must be attached to peace education in our parishes and families. We must take pains to keep a space clear for attitudes of peace and reconciliation, to be seen to practice trust and openness, and not to allow pure power to have the last word in the resolution of conflicts.

Parents and parish workers bear particular responsibility for peace education. How it is to be carried out, that we must learn together and help each other.

The consciences of many are weighed down by the decisions that they have to make. We should like to assure those in moral doubt that we shall accompany them with our prayers and all possible help.

The Conference of Lutheran Church Authorities

Berlin, 14 June 1978.

Guidelines from the Conference of Lutheran Church Authorities.*

(Complete Text.).

* Concerning the planned introduction of military education in the schools of the German Democratic Republic.

In the last few months increasing anxiety had spread through our parishes concerning a measure on the part of the government, at first known only by word of mouth: the introduction of military education in the 9th classes of ordinary schools. Members of the parishes turned to ministers of the church with the urgent wish for information and advice and a decided desire that the ministers should use their influence against the realisation of any such plan. A number of petitions in this sense were sent also to the Conference of Lutheran Church Authorities in the GDR.

In this situation the Conference of Lutheran Church Authorities addressed itself to the Government of the GDR, requesting precise information on the question, putting forward doubts and objections and asking the state authorities, should such an intention actually exist, not to put it into practice.

I. Thereupon on 1 June 1978 the Secretary of State for Church Affairs informed the Chairman of the Conference and his Deputies and Secretaries about the existing plans with regard to the introduction of military education, in an exhaustive oral report.

According to this the intention is:— to introduce a subject "military education" in the 9th classes of ordinary schools as from 1 September 1978. Four double periods a year additional to the existing timetable. Attendance is obligatory for boys and girls; no marks to be given.

— Theoretical tuition to be continued on the same scale in the 10th classes.

— An intensive course of Civil Defence as from 1 September 1978, in the 9th classes, also obligatory for boys and girls, lasting two weeks of five hours per day, at the end of the school year. No weapon training.

— Parallel with these Civil Defence courses, pre-military camps lasting two weeks, on a voluntary basis. Boys only. Training includes handling of weapons (small calibre).

— In the 10th classes, from 1979, obligatory three-day final exercise in the winter holidays.

These plans were interpreted and commented on at length by the Secretary of State for Church Affairs. From the arguments resulting from further discussion with the Church representatives we select these points:

— The planned measure is not to be regarded and judged out of context, but must be seen in the connection of the whole peace policy of the government of the German Democratic Republic.

— Military education and the credibility of the peace policy are connected. The stability and state of defensive readiness of the DDR have contributed in a decisive manner to the preservation and securing of peace in central Europe.

— The introduction of military education is in complete agreement with the laws of the GDR: Constitution Article 23, Law for the Preservation of Peace, Law on the Single Socialist System of Education, Youth Law Civil Defence Law.

— Nothing new in principle is created by the introduction of Military Education (cf. existing Hans Beimler Competitions, Premilitary Training).

— Military Education as planned would fit Christians for the practical exercise of neighbourly love in the case of a catastrophe, for effective help for others in Civil Defence, Self-Defence, First Aid.

— All other socialist countries already have obligatory Military Education as part of school education and have had very good experience with it.

— The educational aims involved are discipline, sense of responsibility, activity, physical training.

— The principle of a voluntary basis is guaranteed where weapon training is involved; but a 10% participation is aimed at.

Against this presentation the Church representatives put forward anxieties and objections:

— The question whether a clear orientation towards peace education can retain its primacy when the formation of attitudes is one — sidedly influenced by the increase of Military Education.

Considerable doubts regarding the age at which Military Education is to start.* Danger of early fixation of partisan ways of thinking, habituation to force as means of solving conflicts.

— Fear that introduction of obligatory Military Education in the schools at this time (creation of measures to increase trust, relaxation of international tension, increased efforts toward disarmament) will be understood internationally as a demonstrative act and the credibility of the GDR's peace policy suffer through this.

— The effectiveness of witness for peace on the part of Protestants from the GDR in the context of the Christian churches internationally is reduced.

In case of the introduction of Military Education in the manner proposed, the representatives of the Church declared that they would support those parents and guardians who might be prevented for reasons of conscience from allowing their children to take part in this tuition. They expressed their worry that non-participation in this tuition on grounds of conscience would be taken as a sign of political unreliability.

The government side listened carefully to the considerations put forward by the representatives of the Federation of Lutheran Churches in the GDR on the basis of common responsibility for peace and for mankind. It was not apparent that the government will cancel its plans to introduce this subject. As the consequence of a special meeting on 14 June the Conference once more asked the government to reconsider the planned measures.

II. The Conference's doubts against the introduction of an obligatory school subject "Socialist Military Education" were not removed by the conversation of 1 June. In view of the impending introduction of this subject on 1 September 1978 let us once more spell them out as they appear as a result of conversations with parishes, parents and young adults communicated to us and of discussions in advisory and executive committees of the Federation:

(1) The mission of peace anchored in the Gospels demands from the churches and from each individual Christian a sober assessment of what diminishes tensions, encourages trust and serves the cause of peace in the present world situation. We do not fail to recognise the duty of the state to protect the security of its citizens; therefore we must ask ourselves what really makes us secure today. A security philosophy based on fear and threat does not, in our conviction, represent a step to greater peace, because it leads to actions which produce corresponding fear on the other side and mislead it into counter-threats. Because the intended Military Education threatens to become a part of this dangerous mechanism, it seems to us lacking in suitability as a means of securing peace.

* 9th class = approx. age 14 (transl.).

(2) Disarmament is a pressing necessity of the hour. We see an inseparable connection between global political attempts to bring about an end to the arms race, and educational efforts to bring about an informed attitude to disarmament in society. Disarmament will only be possible when it is really wanted and securely anchored in the thinking of every society. We see the danger that obligatory Military Education for minors will lead to a taking for granted of military means of solving conflicts, an attitude which in the long run could prove an obstacle to positive attitudes to disarmament. For the sake of disarmament we require an education which will enable men to settle disputes by non-violent means.

(3) Young people who have not experienced the horrors of war and who are not in a position to come to an informed judgment on the risks of the military securing of peace in the nuclear age will have their capacity to think in terms of peace seriously endangered by the planned tuition, which presupposes as natural the possibility of an armed conflict between east and west and whose content is the preparation for such a conflict. Early education into military ways of thought, attitudes and norms of behaviour in schools may lead to chances of peaceful resolutions of conflicts not even being recognised in later years.

(4) The GDR consistently supports a policy of peace and relaxation of international tensions. We fear that the credibility of this policy will be damaged abroad by the introduction of Military Education. Worldwide efforts to create non-military security systems cannot be crowned with success as long as education and training within individual states are weighted towards military security. The aim of a world without weapons, to which socialism is consciously committed, should in our view appear more clearly precisely in the area of school education and training. International Christianity expects specific help and leadership in this respect from the representatives of churches in socialist countries.

We know that the doubts and arguments once more summed up here cannot solve the conflict in which many Christian parents whose children are expected to attend Military Education find themselves, asking how in this situation they may responsibly fulfil their duty laid down in the Gospels to work for peace. But we hope that they will form the basis of a guideline for those affected and disquieted by this chain of events and that they will contribute to responsible action.

III. The introduction of Military Education as a subject makes concrete demands on the readiness and capability of us all to bring up our children in the path of peace and conciliation in personal, social and international life. Many parents and educators who are aware that our survival depends on practising and cherishing peace will have a painful sense of the disparity between such peace education and the practice of military readiness with all the emotions it arouses. They should pay attention to this in their dealings with their children and use their influence to see that the new tuition remains receptive for elements of peace education.

There will be parents who after responsible consideration will decide against their children taking part in the new tuition complex. Such a decision is to be taken as a reference to a future form of peaceful co-existence towards which we must start working today. It will only be effective in this manner if it is accompanied in a convincing manner by consistent and practical peace education in the area for which these adults are responsible. Particularly where these anxiety-arousing questions are concerned, the parish should be a centre of discussion, encouragement and support for all its members.

In the final analysis, all the things about Military Education in schools which disquiet and exercise Christian parents, educators and children can only serve to demonstrate to us how urgent it is to take steps to make peace in the co-existence of men, nations and power-blocs securer and more humane. In contemplating such steps we are aware that we tread the same path as all those men who in earlier days set up landmarks for peace and worked for trust and co-operation between nations.

We therefore see it as our particular duty to continue all efforts in the parishes towards effective peace education and to support them even more than hitherto. Peace education should impart the knowledge, values and convictions which put the individual in a position to form a balanced opinion as to what today favours peace and what increases discord. We ask parishes to consider the following points particularly:

— Force as a means of solving conflicts is self-destructive in a world full of weapons. We must start to practice non-violent means of solving disputes.

— Defensive attitudes without trust and co-operation create mistrust and fresh insecurity. We must start to explore means of defence which make not only us but also the other side more secure.

— Thinking in clichés of friend and enemy makes one incapable of perceiving the common responsibility which all men bear for the world of tomorrow. We must start to place our common points above our differences, so that we can survive in common. It is the duty of all of us to translate these realisations into action. Concrete steps towards this might be:

— Parents should bring up their children in an atmosphere of trust and renounce the use of corporal punishment. They should communicate to their children disinclination to use of physical force.

— The imagination and inventiveness of children should be directed to the peaceful solution of problems of communal existence and not to possible military conflicts. All romanticising of military life and all presentation of the inconceivable consequences of war as being of little account is to be resisted. This has consequences e.g. regarding choice of toys and reading matter bought or given by adults.

— Trips to neighbour states should be used to an even greater degree to get to know and understand the people there better; correspondingly they should be properly prepared and the correct conclusions drawn afterwards. Comprehensive information about the life, the history and the tradition of other nations is important for mutual understanding. Mutual examination of school text books might belong here: What image do our books give of the other country, what image of our country is being propagated in other countries?

— In Christian parishes it should be possible to experience how much more attractive peaceful resolutions of conflicts are than violent and loveless resolutions. The gift of the peace of Christ should be specifically celebrated in the parish occasionally.

In trust in Christ Jesus, who is our Peace (Eph. 2, 14) we pray for each other, for accompanying and intercessory prayer, and for the strength to take the necessary steps, great and small, for the realisation of peace in this world.

Appeal To the International Labour Organization and to Trade Unions in the West.

(Complete Text).

We are unemployed Soviet workers, who have come to Moscow from various cities and republics of the country. We are obliged to seek moral and material support with this APPEAL through the Western press. There are no other possibilities for us.

We have all been dismissed for exposing abuses or for speaking out against the management of enterprises where we worked. Among the issues we raised were pilfering and dilutions of materials, bribery, a high rate of industrial accidents, and flagrant violation of the Labour Code.

We are middle-aged people (35-45 years old) with more than a decade of working experience. We have been deprived of work for periods of one to five years. At first we thought that our complaints would find support, if not at local level, then at least in higher institutions and the press.

On the one hand, the Soviet Party and Government call upon citizens to correct violations wherever they occur: in industry and in the life of the state and society. On the other hand, the authorities come down with special brutality on those very people who respond to propaganda appeals by strictly observing the regulations and speaking out in the interests of the enterprise.

All our attempts to achieve justice from government authorities have been in vain.

We appealed as individuals to the central organs of Soviet power: the Central Committee of the Communist Party of the Soviet Union, the Presidium of the Supreme Soviet, the Council of Ministers of the USSR, and the All-Union Central Trade Union Council. They did not reply to us.

The legal organs decide our cases only in a one-sided manner: that is, they give meaningless bureaucratic answers and transfer us from one department to another. When we appealed to higher authorities, instead of taking positive measures, they applied unlawful methods against us for exercising our right to complain: on the pretext of registering us for an audience with the leadership, they seized us one by one and in groups, sending us to police stations and psychiatric hospitals.

This happens at the highest offices of power: in the reception-rooms of the Central Committee of the CPSU, the Presidium of the USSR Supreme Soviet and the USSR Procurator General's Office.

It is impossible to be received in a single high Soviet institution. All highly-placed personnel — our servants as they like to call themselves — are fenced off from us by the police.

We decided to unite. We began to act collectively. But just as before, they continued to expel us from Moscow with the help of the police and to put us in psychiatric hospitals.

Collectively we addressed ourselves to all social, Party, Soviet, council and trade-union organizations; to the editorial offices of major newspapers: *Pravda, Izvestia, Trud, Literaturnaya Gazeta,*; and to the magazines: *Ogonyok, Kommunist, Partiinaya zhizn,* and *Sotsialisticheskaya zakonnost.* We received no reply.

We hoped that the new Constitution of the Soviet Union would rectify the lack of rights enjoyed by the working population. But the facts concerning repression and internment in psychiatric hospitals, which we present in this Appeal, prove that the new Constitution is not taken seriously by Soviet organs, and that it merely serves as a screen with which to confuse the Soviet people and world opinion.

It was only after we made known these acts of arbitrariness and coercion that we were invited to the *Izvestia* editorial office and to the KGB committee. There, we were promised help.

But all this turned out to be a trick:

At the *Izvestia* editorial office, they had only one aim. Taking us in one at a time humouring us with promises. They brought everything round to finding out which of us was the organiser, they did everything possible to sow discord among us.

The Organs of the KGB, in seeking to find out exactly how many people supported the collective complaints as well as their addresses, had the clear aim of exiling us from Moscow or placing us in psychiatric hospitals.

And so, we decided to organize our own genuinely independent trade union. We did this in order to win the official and legal right to defend our interests. In order to enlist all those who are willing, and whose rights have been groundlessly infringed — over any matter — to enlist them in the joint struggle for their rights, that are guaranteed by the new Constitution of the USSR.

We consider that only through a union of our own, basing itself on the public opinion of workers of all countries, can we force our government to respect the ordinary workers.

In our country, there is no organ which objectively defends the workers' interests.

Soviet trade unions do not defend our rights and do not have the necessary authority, for key union posts are held by communists — that is, by people who could not succeed in their Party organizations. They are all technicians and engineers who, if not re-elected for a new term would again become subordinate to one or other higher management official. And if only for these reasons, they always need to heed the opinions of top management.

Trade-union elections take place in a purely formal manner: the chairmen of trade-union committees are elected and appointed by the management of the enterprise, the Party organizer and the regional committee of the CPSU. It happens like this. According to the rules, one delegate per ten trade-union members is elected to attend a conference, whose purpose is to hear reports and elect new officials.

It is worth noting that, in the Soviet Union, there is not one enterprise with less than 100% trade-union membership of the workers and technical-engineering employees.

All of this would be democratic, if only delegates were elected at a general meeting, in the presence of everyone. However, in practice, in order to secure support beforehand, the management and the Party committee resort to the trick of having delegates elected by shop or section. First, there is a meeting of the technical-engineering personnel at which the trade-union chairman and leaders of the Party committee lay down how the election of delegates should be "carried out".

Afterwards, the elections take place by section or shop. As a rule, the supervisor of the section or shop "recommends" (i.e., records) whichever candidates he likes. Out of gratitude to him they nominate him and the foremen. Besides all this, in each section, for the appearance of authority, one of the white collar employees is elected. These employees elect their own delegates. The workers evidently do not get a look-in. In the end, although workers outnumber employees by ten, nearly all those who attend the conference are technical-engineering personnel — that is, those for whom workers' interests are not important.

The workers' delegates receive money which they do not have to return, and the buffets abound in normally scarce products and alcoholic drinks.

To the presidium are elevated, without any invitation, the enterprise management and representatives of the district (Party) committee, the city trade unions, and the Party organisation. These then make a register of candidates, or in other words, they register on the ballot-paper anyone they like.

No other candidates are registered. That is why the election of the incoming members of the trade-union committee is ensured in advance.

The election of the chairman and the allocation of responsibilities take place at a table laden with food and spirits at public expense, and to the cheers of clanging glasses.

The "representatives" of lower trade-union organizations go on to elect territorial trade unions, and so on.

In this APPEAL, we will substantiate our arguments with newspaper items confirming that these are not individual "shortcomings", but a normal part of everyday life. In its issue of 27 January 1978, *Leninskoe Znamya*[1] carried an article "Getting Used to It" in its general column entitled "Following the anxious letters":

". . . For the second year running, the No. 3 administrative collective of the Mozhaiskovo Road building works has received a flood of anonymous letters to various local and district organizations. . . There were similar signs earlier. . . On 14 October 1977, there was a trade-union meeting to review the work and hold elections. At the end of this, the workers were given a rouble each, while the office workers went to a restaurant to drink away trade-union money. . . The enterprise manager, B.F. Stepakin [stated]: We have an old tradition; we feel that it is better to drink collectively than to hide in a corner. . . The chairman of the trade-union committee, N.I. Miroshnikov [said]: The Regional committee of the trade union puts aside special resources for such 'gatherings'."

Trud of 20 January 1978 published an article called "Strange Permits" from the town of Enakievo, Donetsk province:

". . . The statement of face-worker A.L. Todoseichuk from the platform of the election and review conference is understandable to many at the mine. A.L. Todoseichuk severely criticized the chairman of the mine committee, V.S. Sigarev, for allowing violations of the Labour Code and for the improper allocation of material assistance. The worker brought forth concrete examples. He said: Year after year, the same people use the privilege of sanitorium-resort treatment. Worse still: after absenteeism, D. Ganziuk was given a holiday; and soon after a stay in a sobering-up station, E. Litvin and A. Melikhov received permits [for accommodation at a rest-

---

[1] Leninist Banner — the organ of the Moscow provincial CPSU committee and Soviet of People's Deputies. (Ed.).

home — trans.] What is this? The managers of the mine — the general directors of the "Ordzhonikidze coal" association, N.F. Semchenko, the secretary of the association's Party committee, V.I. Gromov, and the chairman of the Enakiev territorial committee of coal industry trade unions, V.I. Kozlitin, all of whom are on the presidium, let this go by. The reaction was unexpected. A.L. Todoseichuk was a member of the mine committee. Previously he had been recommended for the new structure. But when it came to considering the candidates, the presidium did not nominate Todoseichuk. He was not included in the list for secret voting, even though this was proposed from the floor.

Sigarev was again elected chairman of the mine committee, although out of 163 delegates at the conference only 59 voted against him.[2] In broad daylight, in front of all to see, Sigarev was taken under protection, in spite of the opinions of those who openly spoke the truth about his improper conduct.

. . . A.L. Todoseichuk decided to fight for the truth. He wrote letters to the Donetsk regional and republic committees of the coal workers' trade union. He signed it with all his work-titles: face-worker, communist, honoured national miner, holder of the order of the Red Banner of Labour — but no one answered his letters.

. . . Sigarev forges signatures, sells holiday permits to a certain E.A. Sotnikova, who has nothing to do with the mine; as for the head librarian, N.I. Kuzmenko, he simply threw her out of his office (she had come to see him on official business); and the trade-union chairman paid no attention to the official requests of the city procurator. After a short period of time in office, complaints appeared in several departments from Sigarev's subordinates. Each one mentions his rude behaviour of his associates. Because of this, people are leaving "of their own volition". . . "

In our previous open letters we wrote: "there are thousands like us".

Yes, we did not exaggerate. We are convinced that every tenth worker or employee could fill our ranks.

Let us look at the press. *Pravda* of 21 January 1978 printed an article entitled "Insufficient persistence":

". . . At the Petrozavodsk enterprise no. 1126 employing a thousand workers in the town of the same name, one third of the workers left in the last year alone. . . "

The newspaper *Vechernaya Moska*[3] carried an article "A Difficult Topic". Concerning the Sokolnicheskii railwaycar repair and building works in Moscow, we read: *". . . We pay a great deal of attention to our*

---

[2] The authors of the Appeal note that according to the rules, a two-thirds majority is required. (Ed.).

[3] Evening Moscow, 21 January 1978. (Ed.).

work with cadres. . . *What is the result? The balance is not in our favour, as 24 people left while 15 were hired. . ."*

Leninist Banner of 25 January 1978 had an article entitled "Easy Parting":

"Over the past three years 262 workers have left the company. In effect, two out of three left. . ."

An article from *Pravda* of 29 March 1976, entitled "If a labout dispute occurred":

". . . Legislation of the Armenian SSR, in particular, provides for punishment of violations such as abrogation of the labour contracts with the management official or his removal from the occupied post. However, in our republic there has not yet been an occasion for the trade union to use this law. Meanwhile, all the same grounds for such sanctions are encountered. . ."

In the same article, not one tenth of the incidents of groundless dismissal of workers and employees is mentioned; and not one of these received help from the trade unions.

Here is what happened in one large metallurgical factory in the city of Enakievo, Donetsk province, where there are more than 15,000 workers. To whom is there faith entrusted? *Pravda* of 7 January 1978 headlines "The Effectiveness of Criticism":

". . . The Director of the Enakievo metallurgical works Iu. T. Cherneta became so offended at criticism in the local paper, that at the beginning of a meeting he put forward an ultimatum: 'Either me or her'. And he got what he wanted — the meeting did not begin with the 'her', the reporter from the paper, left the hall. . ."

How do the newspapers write about the cream of the cream, that is, about communists: *Pravda* of 21 January 1978:

". . . At an enterprise of 1000 workers, 75 are communists. . . The secretary of the Party committee, A. Minkowich, recently committed such a misdemeanour (?!?) that the communists had to elect a new secretary, A. Ulianov. The communists hoped that he would take matters in hand. But it did not work out: he didn't have enough character or experience. Furthermore, two other members had to be removed from the bureau: K. Asanov ended up in a sobering-up station, and V. Ushanov violated financial discipline. . ." And then 49 wrote to *Pravda*: *"The notice was not discussed in the brigades. There are no noticeable changes at the enterprise. . ."*

The whole country is gripped in a corrosive mould of bureaucratism. This has been witnessed by US and by our comrades-in-misfortune, who have grown to over 200: We worked in various enterprises in over 150 different cities and regions of the country.

We are an insignificant part of the citizens who daily occupy the reception rooms of the central apparatuses.

WE request the ILO and workers' trade unions to recognize our free trade union of working people and to give us moral and material support.

1 February 1978.

This is followed by a list of 43 signatures to the appeal as well as a list of 110 candidate members of the association.

Rules of the Free Trade Union Association of Workers in the Soviet Union.
In force from 1 January 1978 — 1 January 1979.
(Complete Text).

SECTION ONE

Members of the Free Trade Union Association in the Soviet Union

1. A member of the Free Trade Union Association of Workers, can be any manual or white collar worker, whose rights and interests have been illegally infringed by administrative, Soviet, Party and Legal Organs.

2. A member of the Free Trade Union Association has the right:—
   a) to discuss freely all the activities of the association, to make suggestions, to put forward and defend opinions, until the association has reached a decision.
   b) to participate personally in meetings, when the question of his activities or behaviour is being discussed.
   c) to engage in a tireless struggle for peace and friendship among nations.
   d) to heighten political consciousness.
   e) to observe the rules of the Free Trade Union Association.

3. A member of the association has the following advantages:—
   a) he receives proper legal Aid.
   b) he receives moral and material support so far as possible.
   c) he receives help in finding somewhere to live, if the occasion arises, he gives the same help to his comrades.

4. Acceptance into membership of the Free Trade Union Association takes place according to personal wish, after a week's preliminary consideration, stemming from the conditions and consequences of joining the association.

5. The decision about acceptance into membership made by the meeting.

SECTION TWO

Organisational Structure of the Free Trade Union Association of Workers

6. It is built on the basis of democratic centralism, which means:—

a) everyone, from the bottom to the top, is elected by the members, and is responsible to them.

b) all matters arising in the association, are decided according to the rules.

c) decisions are made by a majority vote.

7. The free and business-like discussion of aspects of the work of the association is an important principle of inner union democracy. On the basis of inner union democracy develop criticism and self-criticism, the activity and initiative of the members. On this basis a business-like and conscious discipline can grow strong.

8. The basis of the Free Trade Union Association is the association of members that grew up around the "forty three".

9. The tasks of the Free Trade Union Association are:—

a) to carry out the obligations of the collective agreement.

b) to bring manual and white collar workers into membership of the association of free trade unions.

c) to carry out the decisions of the association concerning the defence of rights and the pursuit of justice.

d) the education of members of the association in the spirit of irreconcilability to failings and bureaucratism; to "turning a blind eye"; to financial irregularities and squandering: to negligence of the popular good in general.

SECTION THREE

The Means of the Free Trade Union Association

10. The financial means of the Free Trade Union Association will consist of:—

a) the monthly membership subscriptions — depending on how much the unemployed can afford

b) not more than one percent of the pay of those in work (voluntary donations excluded).

c) revenue from non-members of the Association of the Free Trade Union for providing help of a legal nature, the printing and drawing up of complaints, the work to be charged at no more than the state rates.

d) receipts from material aid sent by foreign trade unions.

SECTION FOUR

On the Rights of the Free Trade Union Association, as a Juridical Personality

11. The Free Trade Union Association of Workers in the Soviet Union is a Juridical Personality.

As soon as the Free Trade Union Association of Workers in the Soviet Union is recognised by the ILO or the Trade Unions of Foreign Countries and we get moral and material support, we will begin a revision of the Rules, taking stock of the special position of workers in our country. But this will not be until we have been in existence for a year.

The Council of Members of the "Forty Three" Free Trade Union of Workers in the Soviet Union.

Moscow
1st February 1978

Letter to the National Union of Mineworkers from the Chairman of the Soviet Coal Mining Industry Workers' Union.

(Complete Text). Times, 8 September, 1978.

Dear Mr Gormley,

You sent us a collection of newspaper articles about a group of the so-called "unemployed Soviet workers" led by Klebanov, a former miner, who allegedly tries to organize an independent union on the grounds that the existing unions do not defend their rights and interests.

Frankly speaking, it was only after we received your newspaper clippings that we learnt about Klebanov and other persons mentioned in the articles. Klebanov has never approached with any request either the central committee of our union or the Makeevsky territorial committee of the union located in his former working area.

As we found out, it is true that Klebanov worked at Donbass mines for some years. Then, as a result of a head injury, he became a third group invalid. He was given a pension and an additional payment from the mine for partial disability. The total sum of money that he receives monthly after leaving the mine exceeds the maximum coalminers' pension.

As regards his employment, during the last years he was offered a number of various positions with consideration for his profession and state of health, including at the "Makeevougol" group of mines where he had worked before. However, he kept turning down all the jobs offered to him.

If all his behaviour is unbiasedly weighted, it will be apparent that this man is not in the least interested in getting a job, but evidently pursues some other aims.

As regards the organization of a new union, we do not understand the mere statement of this question and the ardent support given to it by the bourgeois propaganda. I should like to remind you here that the attacks on the Soviet trade unions on the part of the bourgeois press are nothing new.

There was even a period after the October socialist revolution of 1917 when the West did not recognize the Soviet trade unions. And even now attempts are made from time to time to create a wrong impression of the functions and facilities of our unions and of the nature of their activities. The Soviet miners are quite satisfied with the trade union which they set up at the dawn of the Soviet state.

Their trade union has most extensive rights that guarantee the protection of the workers' interests, effective participation in production, in labour protection, in the solution of social and other problems relating to every aspect of life of our society.

The numerous delegations of British miners that visited our country were able to see it for themselves, and there is no need to give a detailed account of it, but in relation to the questions touched upon in your letter concerning dismissals and "unemployed" miners, I want to say that in this country the administration has no right to discharge a worker or an employee without the consent of the trade union. And the trade union organizations keep a vigilant eye on that. Besides, it is well known that at present our coalmining industry and practically every coalmine experiences a shortage of labour, and any one can get a job according to his speciality.

Such are the facts of our reality, and I am sure that an unbiased person will draw only one conclusion.

Fraternally yours,

Yevgeny Efremenko.

Nicolae Ceausescu.
Speech on the occasion of the 60th Anniversary of the Foundation of the Unitary National Romanian State.*

(Excerpts.).

* Delivered on 1 December, 1978 to the Joint Session of the Central Committee of the Romanian Communist Party, National Council of the Socialist Unity Front and the Grand National Assembly.

Dear comrades,

The Meeting of the Political Consultative Committee of the Warsaw Treaty member states, which has recently taken place in Moscow, is an international event of great importance. The unanimously adopted Declaration makes a thorough review of the contemporary situation in the world and most clearly asserts the determination of the socialist countries participating in the Meeting to intensify their activity against the imperialist, colonialist policy of force and dictate, to act in close solidarity for the settlement of the complex problems of the contemporary world, through peaceful negotiations, for disarmament — primarily nuclear disarmament — for détente and peace in Europe and in the world. As you well know, the socialist countries, signatories to the Declaration are committed firmly to act for the implementation of the documents signed in Helsinki, for concrete disarmament measures in Europe, for cooperation, security and peace on our continent.

We should underline the fact that the socialist countries stand for the observance of the independence and sovereignty of all states, against interference in domestic affairs, most resolutely declaring that: *"The socialist countries do not seek privileges in any region of the world, they do not insist on obtaining military bases, they do not hunt for concessions. Standing on principle against the imperialist policy of creating spheres of influence, the socialist countries never participate in the battle for such spheres."*

In general, we can say that, by its entire content, the Declaration expresses the aspirations and the willpower of our peoples to live in friendship and peace with all the peoples of the world, whatever their social system.

That is why I wish to declare, in all responsibility, at the present joint solemn session of the Central Committee, the National Council of the Socialist Unity Front, and the Grand National Assembly, as I also did before the plenum of the Party Central Committee, and at the meetings with representatives of the working people, that the Moscow Declaration fully agrees with the will and interests of our entire people, it expresses their determination most firmly to struggle, in close unity with the socialist countries, with all peoples of the world, for détente, cooperation and peace. By signing this Declaration, on behalf of the Party and State bodies, of the Romanian people, we pledged to spare no effort for the implementation of the policy of disarmament, equal and peaceful work-together among all the nations of the world. I consider that all those present here, our entire people, will support it, that they will do their utmost for implementation of these provisions. . .

It was natural for the question to arise whether, it consideration of the present international situation, the fact that the NATO countries had decided last May, to increase military expenditures, Romania would not, take measures to increase military expenditure. As I have mentioned before, the present international situation requires that we should pay attention to strengthening the country's defence capacity and, hence, allot an important part of the national income, of our people's wealth, to adequately equip the Romanian army with fighting material. We consider, however, that the concern to strengthen the defence capacity of the country should affect in no way the country's programme of socio-economic development, of raising the material and cultural standards of our entire people. That is why, answering the questions of the working people, I declared before the -

Central Committee, before the representatives of the working people, of the other categories of working people, of the army, before our entire people, that we had not committed ourselves in any way and do not envisage to increase military expenditures above the initial provisions. I most clearly asserted that we will firmly act for steps to be taken not for an intensification of the arms race but for its reduction, that we shall do our utmost to contribute to the implementation of disarmament measures, primarily nuclear disarmament, to the reduction of armies and military expenditures.

More than once have we disapproved of the decisions taken by the NATO countries in May regarding an additional increase in military expenditure, which strongly stimulate the arms race. We consider that it is necessary to ask the NATO countries to cancel these decisions. We also consider that the socialist countries should say a firm NO to the arms race, do everything possible in order to initiate a reduction of military expenditure which is a heavy burden on all peoples, including the peoples of the socialist countries. We are firmly convinced that, if all the peoples of the world resolutely raise their voice, we will determine the governments, the states acting for arming to consider the will of the peoples and to give up the arms race. . .

It is obvious that if we allocated a larger part of the national income to military expenditure, we should no longer be able to implement the programme of economic development and the measures of raising the living standard. It is known that Romania still has much to do in order to improve its status of a developing country, to ensure its strong economic and social development, to build a solid basis for the socialist and communist society. That is why we will do everything for the implementation of the programme of the Eleventh Party Congress. It is understandable that failure to implement the economic and social development programme would also have serious repercussions on the defence and fighting potential of our people and army. It is well known that economic and social development, the successful implementation of the programme worked out by the Eleventh Congress for the building of the multilaterally developed socialist society and the improvement of the people's material and spiritual well-being help to greatly consolidate the fighting and defence capability of the country. The more significant the results in socialist construction, the more resolved our people will be to defend the revolutionary gains, the country's independence and sovereignty with all its force and at the same time to do its duty to its allies in keeping with the commitments taken. Once more we assure the Central Committee, the National Council of the Socialist Unity Front, the Grand National Assembly and the whole people that we shall not intensify military expenditure. I also want to declare in full responsibility that if the international situation deteriorates, we shall discuss the question of military expenditure in the supreme Party and State bodies and, if this seems necessary, we shall openly bring the question of allocating more funds for military needs to these bodies and to the whole people — because only the Party and State bodies, the people, are entitled to decide on such essential aspects of our general policy.

However, I once more say that the present international situation does not justifies increase in military expenditure. On the contrary, we must do everything to ensure the implementation of the programmes of economic and social development, of improvement of the people's well-being, since this guarantees the victory of socialism, collaboration and peace!

I declared before the Central Committee, before the representatives of the working people, of the whole people, and I re-state at this solemn session, that we signed no other commitment or document besides the Declaration issued, I considered and I consider it necessary to be specific, given the people's interests, of the questions I was asked in this respect.

I said before the Central Committee, the representatives of the working people, the whole people, and I once more say most clearly that we shall never sign a document committing the country, the people, the army unless it is in conformity with the Constitution and laws of the country, and the will of the entire people, unless it is approved by the whole people. At this session too, I declare that neither the president of the country, nor the Party general secretary nor anybody else can sign commitments on Romania's behalf unless he has the approval of the supreme Party and State bodies, strictly abiden by the Constitution, and has the open approval of our entire people!

I also consider necessary to declare at the joint solemn session of the Central Committee, National Council of the Socialist Unity Front and Grand National Assembly that Romania will fulfil the commitments entered through the Warsaw Treaty in case of an imperialist aggression in Europe against the socialist states which are members of this treaty. It is true we firmly advocate the concomitant dissolution of the Warsaw Pact and of NATO — and this position of the socialist countries is expressly stated in the Declaration. We believe that the policy of détente and peace demands constant work for the restriction of the activity of military pacts and the adoption of concrete measures for their concomitant dissolution. We are fully convinced that the security of our people, of all peoples, peace will be guaranteed by restricting and abolishing military blocs, not by intensifying the arms race and consolidating military blocs.

However, whether the Warsaw Treaty exists or not, in keeping with the treaties of friendship and mutual assistance we have with the friendly socialist countries, we will always fulfil our obligations to actively partici-pate in repelling every military aggression. It goes without saying that we work and shall further work for strengthening collaboration and solidarity among our armies, for cooperation in battle training. However, as I have said more than once, the relations of collaboration among the socialist countries that are members of the Warsaw Treaty must be based on the principles of socialism, equal rights, respect for the sovereignty and independence of every state and every army. It is evident that we must do everything to enhance the defence capability of every national army; we consider that our army will be able to fulfil its obligations to the homeland, to the cause of socialism in our country, and its international obligations only if it is closely linked to the entire people.

In view of the fact that the Party and State are fully responsible to the people, it is understandable that these bodies are the only ones entitled to commit the army to any kind of action. That is why, answering the numerous questions I was asked, I have considered it necessary to clearly state once again that the Romanian army will always take action only on orders from our supreme Party and State bodies, at the call of the people, and that it shall never take orders from abroad.

The Executive Political Committee of the Central Committee of the Party has thought it necessary to answer with full clarity the preoccupations and questions of the Party, of the working people in order to rule out any misunderstanding as concerns both our people and our allies.

I wish to assert once again, on this solemn occasion, the resolve of Romania, of our entire people, to spare no effort for the translation into fact of the policy of disarmament, détente and peace, to strengthen the collaboration and solidarity with the states participating in the Warsaw Treaty, with all the socialist countries, with all peoples in the world, believing there is nothing more important than the ensurance of peaceful conditions to build socialism, than the ensurance of a lasting peace throughout the world!

I should also like to refer to other aspects of Romania's international activity. This country firmly acts for the consolidation of collaboration and solidarity with the developing countries, with the non-aligned countries. At present, we have relations with more than one hundred developing countries, we collaborate ever more closely with them on an economic, technical-scientific and cultural plane, we support them in training their personnel, in turning to good account their national riches, in developing an economy of their own — the basis for the strengthening and defence of their independence. The intensification of collaboration and cooperation with the developing countries is a contribution to consolidating the anti-imperialist and anti-colonialist struggle, for defending the peoples' sovereignty, for ensuring their free, self-reliant development on the road of economic and social progress.

Particularly important is the fact that more and more peoples among them declare for the organization of society on socialist bases, which proves that in today's world only socialism offers the possibility of a rapid surmounting of the state of economic and social backwardness, of solution of the masses' fundamental, vital problems. We particularly strengthen the solidarity and collaboration with the countries which choose the socialist development path as, for instance, Guinea, the Congo, Angola, Mozambique, Somalia, Ethiopia, Algeria and others. At the same time we think it necessary to intensify our links with all developing countries, starting from the need not to oppose some of these countries to others, from the need to do our utmost for strengthening solidarity among all developing countries. This is the guarantee of solving the complex problems of under-development, of ensuring independence, of achieving the new international economic order.

In the spirit of peaceful coexistence, we expand our economic, technical-scientific and cultural relations with all developed capitalist countries, with all the countries of the world, irrespective of social system, we actively participate in the international division of labour, in the world exchange of values.

At the foundation of our relations with all countries we steadily place the principles of fully equal rights, respect for national independence and sovereignty, non-interference in internal affairs and mutual advantage, non-recourse to force or threat of force, principles ever more widely acknowledged internationally as the only ones apt to ensure the peace, progress and prosperity of all peoples and nations.

A primary concern of Romania's foreign policy is the achievement of security in Europe, the continent on which the sharpest contradictions have accumulated, where there is the highest density of arms and troops, and where the two opposed military blocs face each other. As is known, in the period following the Helsinki Conference, steps have been taken towards the normalization of relations among European states, economic, scientific and cultural collaboration has been enhanced a number of meetings have taken place among heads of states and other politicians, some under-standings have been reached on various problems. However, the results obtained are not sufficient for us to affirm with all responsibility that the aim of security is being adequately fulfilled. . .

In the opinion of our Party and State, of special importance for building security in Europe are the development of broad and unhampered relations among all European states, the removal of the barriers and discriminatory practices affecting inter-European cooperation. It is necessary also to intensify the efforts for the expansion of cultural relations, for the holding of meetings on education, science and culture, that can contribute to better mutual acquaintance, to rapprochement among all peoples.

In this context, I would like to stress especially the positive course of Romania's relations with all European states. I wish to note with satisfaction that there is a growing concern of all the states in the Balkans to intensify peaceful collaboration, détente and peace. The political relations and the general atmosphere in this zone of Europe are no special reason of concern now. Romania acted and will further act, alongside the other Balkan states, for this region to become a zone of peace, good neighbourhood, confidence and mutually advantageous collaboration, in the interest of all our peoples, of the cause of security in Europe and the world over. The problems existing between some countries in the Balkans can and must be solved only by means of negotiations, by peaceful means alone. ßin this respect, we also declare for the fastest settlement of the issues in Cyprus, for that state's independence and sovereignty to be secured, with a view to the peaceful coexistence of the two Cypriot communities in a unitary, independent state. We also attach particular importance to the intensification of the economic, political, scientific and cultural collaboration with all Danubian countries, including collaboration for the most efficient use of the big potential of the river crossing the territories of our states. Continually expanding have been our multilateral relations with the other European countries, including those in the North-Atlantic Pact, the summit meetings and contacts, the mutually advantageous exchanges and cooperation in various domains of joint interest. Romania has signed numerous joint declarations, communiqués and agreements with these countries, expressing both the will and determination for an ever more intense collaboration in achieving the major targets of our continent. We also have ever broader relations with the United States of America, just as with Canada — signatories to the Helsinki documents — we expand the political contacts and the multilateral collaboration with the states on all continents. In these broad international relations we have traced the self-same concern to seek out the ways to consolidate détente, security and peace, to avoiding a new world onclfagration. As a matter of fact, we must say it openly that with many of these states we have traditional relations of friendship, that we have always assisted each other in the struggle against foreign domination, so there is no reason for us to compete in the arms race but, on the contrary, all reasons plead for a traditional policy of friendship, collaboration, so as to secure to our peoples peace, welfare and happiness. Taking account of this, we are firmly convinced that there are real possibilities for the promotion, both in Europe and worldwide, of a new policy, of collaboration and peace among all nations. . .

In our opinion, the socialist countries ought to take new initiatives, to promote new ways and modalities of attaining these targets. Just like in the past, this would, no doubt, have a wide echo among the world public opinion, would give a powerful impetus to the fight of the people's mass in Europe and the world over to make other governments, too, take similar steps.

Setting out from the pressing need for military disengagement in Europe, we declare for a continuous narrowing of the sphere of activity of the military blocs on the Continent, with a view to providing conditions for their concomitant abolition. In this sequence of ideas, it might be useful that a zone be created between the two blocs, where neither side should locate any armies and weapons or hold any military manoeuvres and demonstrations. We are convinced that if action is taken for lessening tension, for détente, disarmament and the concomitant abolition of the NATO and the Warsaw Treaty, a new war can be prevented, the peaceful development can be ensured of the peoples in Europe and the world over. And as far as we are concerned, we have spared no effort in order to contribute to the attainment of this target. . .

Telegram to Pope John Paul II.

(Complete Text.)

On the occasion of the elevation of Your Holiness to the dignity of Pope, on behalf of the Polish nation and the highest authorities of the People's Poland, we express our wholehearted congratulations and best wishes.

This momentous decision of the conclave of the College of Cardinals is particularly pleasing to Poland. On the papal throne for the first time ever is a son of the Polish nation, which is building through the unity and co-operation of all its citizens a great and prosperous Socialist homeland; a nation known throughout the world for its particular pursuit of peace; a nation which is the champion of co-operation and friendship amongst other nations, and which has made generally acknowledged contribution to universal culture.

We express out conviction that these significant matters would serve the further development of relations between the Polish People's Republic and the Holy See.

Edward Gierek
Henryk Jablonski
Piotr Jaroszewicz

Warsaw, 17th October 1978.

Message from Pope John Paul II to the President of the Polish Council of State.

(Complete Text). 23rd November, 1978.

Having ascended St Peter's see as Bishop of Rome, I wish officially to notify the authorities of the Polish People's Republic of that fact. Let me express my gratitude for your presence, Mr President, and that of the Government delegation at the ceremony of the installation of the new

Pontificate, held on 22nd October this year. In this letter I send greetings to the entire Polish nation and express respect for its history, culture and all achievements.

The Catholic Church, basing itself on the commandment of love, strives, by its own way, to make human life on this Earth ever more worthy to man (Gaudium et Spes, No 91), according to the statement of the Second Vatican Council. The Church also wishes to serve the great cause of peace and justice in the contemporary world. With this aim in view it undertakes the work of evangelisation. I express my conviction that the work of the Church, in accordance with generally adopted principles of freedom of religion, creed and conscience, will continue to develop in our country. I extend my best wishes to all its citizens.

Statement by Polish Episcopate.

(Complete Text.).

The orphaned capital of Saint Peter has again the supreme shepherd. The words of Christ the Lord have come to pass: I shall not leave you orphaned. Cardinals of the Sacred College of the Roman Church at the conclave in the Sistine Chapel, guided by the Holy Spirit, have elected a man, who is a worthy successor of Saint Peter, Bishop of Rome. As we know, he is Karol Cardinal Wojtyla, hitherto Archbishop Metropolitan of Cracow, a son of the Polish nation. The Polish Church, as a living fragment of the Catholic Church, has given its son to the service of mankind on the supreme office of Vicar of Christ.

The new Pope has taken the name of John Paul II, indicating that he wishes to guide the Church and serve the human race in the spirit of his great predecessors, John XXIII, Paul VI and John Paul I, and first of all in the spirit of the Gospel and faith in Christ.

The Election of a Pole to the office of the Pope for the first time in the history of the Church indicates that the Holy Spirit knows no linguistic, national, racial, cultural or political barriers. Local churches make one Holy Universal Church, each one of them through their sons contributing part of its spiritual wealth to the common treasury of the entire Church. The Holy Church in Poland, for over a thousand years closely bound with the Bishop of Rome, fulfilling the redeeming mission entrusted to it by Christ, wants to serve all people, and is open for the dialogue with all people of good will in serving the entire community, nation, and all people regardless of frontiers.

The servant of the Church of Cracow and of all Poland, Deputy Chairman of the Conference of the Polish Episcopate, has been elected servant of the servants of God. We believe that it is the achievement not only of the Holy Spirit, but also of Mary, Mother of the Church, and Our Lady of

Jasna Gora, whom the newly elected Pope loves so much, and we believe that it is the result of the prayers of the entire Polish people who have received this prize for their faith and the vitality of their religion.

The entire Church rejoices at the election of the new Pope. The Church in Poland, and the entire Polish nation, are experiencing particular joy. We rejoice also because a Polish Cardinal has become the Bishop of Rome during the preparations for the celebrations of the 900th anniversary of the death of the martyr Bishop Stanislaw in Cracow, and during the preparations for the 600th anniversary of the Holy Mother of Jasna Gora in Czestochowa. We express the hope that Pope John Paul II will take part in the ceremonies. We would like to support him with our warm prayers so that he will be able to guide the helm of the Holy Church in the difficult period at the end of 20th century.

Warsaw/Rome 17th October 1978
[signed] Bishop Bronislaw Dabrowski
Secretary of the Episcopate.

Western Europe

The Belgian Communist Party in the International Communist Movement Today. Extracts from Claude Renard's Report to the Central Committee of the Belgian Communist Party.

(Complete Text). Le Drapeau Rouge, January, 1978

Our Fundamental Solidarity: A Free and National Choice.

It is vital for any Communist Party which is struggling in its own national conditions to curtail and break the grip of monopoly capitalism, to place its work in the perspective of the worldwide fight against imperialism. It is in doing so that the Party accepts both its national and international responsibilities. For 60 years the part played by the Soviet Union internationally has highlighted the relation between the extension and gathering momentum of the revolutionary process and the class character of soviet society; the contribution the Soviet Union has made to the cause of peace, national independence, democracy and socialism.

For this reason there can be no question of "distancing" ourselves from the Soviet Union: by doing so we should set *our* Party apart from the world revolutionary and democratic movement, of which the Soviet Union is still today concretely one of the main supports. This is no mere abstract theoretical question. Our Party is fully aware of the fact that imperialism is stepping up efforts to create splits within this world movement and within the Communist movement in particular. Our solidarity can never be uncritical but it is essential that the criticisms we consider necessary should never be capable of an interpretation which would put them in the same category as the biassed interpretations and slanders of the enemy.

Attempts are constantly being made to get us into this position. Of course it is easy to get unanimity on this point when it is a question of a congress report or Central Committee resolution, when the origin of these attempts (in imperialist circles) is pinpointed. Nobody in the party has a mind to give in to imperialist pressures! But life is not like that, most of the time these pressures are brought to bear indirectly, and the many forms in which they appear concretely are hardly ever plainly labelled with their real origin. They like to dress up in the guise of "objectivity". They appeal for "clear positions", following a sort of logic that must see everything as black or white.

These ideological pressures are all the more effective because they operate on the opinions of Communists and Communist sympathisers through the mediation of other currents of thought with which we cooperate in certain aspects of the political struggle but which are still, particularly in Belgium, otherwise strongly influenced by the dominant ideology.

There would be absolutely no sense in blaming other democrats because they do not share our convictions, our certainties or all the gradations of our views on internationalism; but we do not have to take our cue from them either, for the sake of getting "good conduct" certificates. Of course we have to take up clear positions, but we do not make them clearer by losing our identity.

Internationalism is as Good as its National Roots.

Relative to preceeding congresses, specially the 19th,[1] the 22nd congress[2] saw no innovation in our approach to the problem of internationalism today. On one point however, it put forward an idea of overwhelming importance: that of the necessary agreement between our action within Belgium and our international solidarity.

Our party aims to formulate its international policy in complete independence and with regard to our leading role as an integral part of the working class and democratic movement. We can however only claim an authentic leading role in as far as we are able to adapt our marxist ideas to the concrete conditions existing in our country and at the present time.

The international policy of our party is indissolubly linked to the objectives we have set ourselves and to which end we endeavour to rally all working class and progressive forces. Our party wants to find a progressive way out of the contemporary crisis of capitalism, involving a profound democratic transformation of existing social, economic and political structures, a way out which will abolish the ills from which working people are suffering at present: unemployment, insecurity, increasing material hardship, certain moral disarray particularly dangerous for younger generations, the burden of the arms race, etc. To do this the grip of the capitalist monopolies must be curbed and broken and replaced by the hegemony of the workers by hand and brain. In a country such as ours, this implies an unprecedented extension of democracy on the basis of the important gains already achieved by the democratic forces in the past.

In Belgium such an extension can only be conceived within the framework of ideological and political pluralism: we see a future which will guarantee the full expression of all human rights. Our party wishes to see the development of all the possibilities which the Helsinki agreements offer for our country and our people; the end of the arms race and the progressive dismantlement of military blocs; the resolution of international disputes by negotiation and with respect for national self-determination for all nations; the widest possible cooperation between states on a European and world scale, on a basis of equal rights for all.

[1] 15-17 November, 1968. (Ed.)

[2] 7-9 April, 1976. (Ed.).

Our Party pursues these objectives first and foremost through our work and initiatives on *our own* territory, aiming at the alliance of all working class and progressive forces. In this connection I refer back once again to our *22nd Congress*: "The Belgian Communist Party considers that at the present time the consolidation of the international solidarity of working class and democratic forces depends first and foremost on the effectiveness of the political activity of these forces in each individual country."

For this reason this session of the Central Committee will only achieve its aim if it assists the Party to work more effectively and get better results in the struggle against the domination of the monopolies in Belgium. How good our internationalism is depends on this struggle, it depends on the depths of its roots in our own country: this is a general characteristic of internationalism. At the same time we must also give our militants and party members and all those who are close to the party satisfactory explanations regarding a series of important problems, the up-to-date facts of which appear to be ignored by many comrades.

A New Era of Internationalist Relations has Opened.

One of our great problems is to update the marxist concept of internationalism, taking into account the present state of the class struggle on a world scale. A deep feeling for internationalism exists in our Party, and this is good; if it did not exist it would have to be brought into being. However it is above all a *feeling*. In its militant form it is often summed up in an attitude expressed as of principle. The Party must also be made aware of the fact that internationalism has its own history too and that its form and content have changed several times, corresponding with the advance of social forces which need to act in a concerted manner and to give mutual support in the fight against capitalist exploitation.

It is not for nothing that the weekly journal of the French Communist Party recently published the text of a talk which comrade Kanapa, a member of the Political Bureau, gave to a Party school for leading comrades. The work of comrade Kanapa is very rich theoretically, but it has obviously been elaborated in the light of French politics. We should not therefore take it over as it stands, although it would certainly be useful for a similar study to be carried out and popularised in the light of conditions in our own country. We have behind us at least four different periods in the history of internationalism and we are now on the threshold of a new period which is still in the transition stage. However it can be seen already that the essential characteristic of this new period is an unprecedented diversification of the revolutionary and anti-imperialist movement on a world scale. It is this diversification which underlies the new conception of international solidarity which was confirmed at the Berlin conference of 1976, but which nevertheless continues to evoke — wrongly — a great many reservations, particularly in some socialist countries.

However, our party is compelled to take up a position within the context of this diversification, taking care to adapt its internationalism in line with the changing complexities of the contemporary world. This necessary adaptation requires us to put an end within our ranks to old-fashioned internationalism — the 1932 solidarity model revised in 1948 — as well as to the tendency to throw out the baby with the bathwater.

I have tried in *Cahiers Marxistes* to define the type of internationalism that is going to spread and which is already spreading today. To an ever-increasing extent international solidarity will find expression through the convergence and coincidence of independent revolutionary forces around concrete objectives (I am thinking, for example, of the struggle against the neutron bomb). These forces will compare their experiences without any constraint, frequently, on the basis of similarities and analogies.

Such is the case in Western Europe, where at the same time the diversification of the revolutionary process is very real — this can be seen all the more clearly since the question of power is being posed in concrete political terms in at least two major countries: through the union of the left in France and the historic compromise in Italy (with however in both cases intermediate stages which have become much more obvious the last few months).

The idea of Eurocommunism arose out of this very diversification and there is no reason to believe that it conceals any imperialist machinations, in spite of its ambiguous nature. It must be stated that this ambiguity does not always originate in the manipulations of the class enemy. The French and Italian comrades define Eurocommunism in ways which seem valid to us, but the Spanish comrades sometimes introduce ideas which evoke the Chinese "two superpowers" thesis. These ideas hardly coincide with ours. Be this as it may, if the expression "Eurocommunism" deserves a place in our political vocabulary then hard struggles which loom in Italy and France will certainly clarify the meaning of the term — with the help of American imperialism.

The evolution of contemporary capitalism and of the crisis of capitalism have undoubtedly created a common framework within which the Communist Parties of Western Europe are carrying on the struggle in a general anti-monopolist direction, with the same perspective of a democratic road to socialism. However, one must accept that the struggle of the Portuguese comrades, for example, is not to be placed outside of this framework just because they do not claim to be "Eurocommunists". As for our French comrades, they do claim to be "Eurocommunists", but this does not prevent them from invoking the legitimate interests of French peasants when they oppose the entry of Spain into the Common Market, which the Spanish comrades, for their part, want to take place.

Thus, although there is a general relationship between the objectives of the European Communist Parties and also a *specific* solidarity arising from an obvious community of interests, the conditions in which the struggle takes place, strategy and tactics, show enormous variations from one country to another.

Let us now turn our attention to our own country: the further we progress the clearer it will become that we have to act in a *different way* from the Parties of France, Italy or Portugal if our political activity is to be effective. In solidarity, but in a different way. It is essential for our party to understand this truth. It is also necessary to bear in mind when speaking of "Eurocommunism" that in no case should this term lead us to lose sight of the fact that each Party — in Western Europe no less than elsewhere — is confronted with a unique situation, which has to be tackled with complete independence and for which the party concerned is compelled to seek a totally original solution.

The diversification of the world revolutionary process has as an inevitable consequence lack of understanding, divergencies and contradictions within the movement.

This can even go as far as armed clashes, as was recently seen on the borders of Vietnam and Cambodia. It is idle to hope to exorcize this misfortune with internationalist incantations. But it is nonetheless certain that, confronted with this sort of dramatic and often disconcerting development, parties which are fully capable of accepting the responsibilities which their independence implies have no right either to take refuge in silence or to speak carelessly. We must realize that the movement to which we belong is not necessarily and at all times capable of overcoming internal contradictions rapidly and well: impossible agreements or compromises which later remain, as it were, suspended in a void must not be sought at any price. All the same, we must look for dialogue and speak frankly and seriously, while respecting the independence of others.

Our Work on the International Plane Concerns the Whole Belgian Working-class Movement.

Within the context of present-day internationalist relations, we shall have to elaborate our ideas on the independent and original part played by our Party internationally. We shall find how to play that part here in Belgium and nowhere else. The Communist Party of Belgium has a special part to play in the international Communist movement and in inter-party relations. This role reflects our consistent practice since the beginning of the period of international conferences in 1957 up to the Berlin Conference. This practice has contributed not insignificantly to giving our Party the reputation in the movement of being a party whose views can be of use to everyone. We must safeguard and consolidate this reputation. In this way moreover we continue the best traditions of the Belgian working-class movements, which in the great days of the working-class party fought for unity in the development of the international struggle for the eight-hour day and universal suffrage, under the aegis of the Second International. Only by maintaining and consolidating this reputation can we make ourselves understood by the Belgian working-class movement itself.

Our consistent practice in international relations for many years has allowed us to encourage in a considerable measure contacts which have been established with fraternal parties in power (but not only with these) and the other working-class organisations in our own country, commencing with the Belgian Socialist Party, which in November signed a very good joint communique with the CPSU. There also we must carry on what has been started. We are in Belgium: we only represent a minority of the working-class. This minority would be nothing but a sect if it imagined it possessed a monopoly of internationalism.

What is true is that our Party in Belgium today is a rallying point for workers who have particularly well-worked out internationalist convictions, based on an ideology with universal application, but who still constitute a very small minority. Our task is to raise the whole internationalist consciousness of the whole Belgian working-class movement, and to help the movement to take up more advanced positions in the face of Schmidt, Callaghan, Soares and their ilk. That is what we have to do in Belgium today, whereas in France and Italy for example the basis for the sort of internationalism we envisage has long been strongly rooted in the majority of the working-class movement.

That is why it is so important for us to make up our minds to set out from the real situation in this respect also. That is why it is so urgent for us to overcome our own troubles by clearly defining the role our Party can have in the present stage of the world revolutionary process.

The Place of Democracy in the World Revolutionary Movement.

Another important problem to be studied which is closely linked with the preceding one: that of existing socialism and the limits of socialist democracy.

I do not need to return to the reasons for our fundamental solidarity, which I explained at the beginning of this report, I shall not refer either to my writings on the Stalin period, since my article and that of comrade Terfve[3] in *Cahiers Marxistes* have been circulated before this meeting, except for the following conclusion which my article only suggested: even under Stalin and in spite of all the aberrations of the period, the existence of the Soviet Union never ceased to be one of the great determining factors in

---

[3] Jean Terfve is Deputy Chairman of the Belgian Communist Party. (Ed.)

the liberation of the people, and it is the basically socialist nature of the Soviet Union which has made it possible to overcome Stalinism within the country.

It is true that Stalinism has only been overcome relatively lately, and indeed much too relatively for our taste.

The 20th Congress of the CPSU took place more than twenty years ago, it helped us a great deal and in general gave rise to high hopes. In retrospect we realized that we had to come to terms; one cannot blame the Soviet Union for having at a certain time overestimated possibilities of medium-term development. This happens to everybody. But that is not the question. When Krushchev was removed in 1961, our party was very perturbed and wrote to the CPSU asking them to explain to us the significance of this move for the future. The reply was that there would be no change in the course which opened with the 20th Congress. However we are obliged to state that this has not been confirmed by experience. It is true that there has been no return to the former abominations, but the least one can say is that as to the functioning of socialist democracy, socialist society today has defects which help the bourgeoisie to organize extremely effective propaganda campaigns against the whole Communist movement. The workers in our country are rightly very sensitive about everything concerning democracy and freedom. For this reason it is not surprising that in their eyes the defects of socialist democracy often obscure facts which in the economic, social and cultural fields already demonstrate the superiority of socialism over capitalism. This is obviously due to the fundamentally untrue propaganda of the bourgeoisie, but also, regrettably to facts which this propaganda is able to exploit unilaterally on a massive scale.

In spite of the extent of the crisis of the capitalist system, this hampers the struggle against domination by the monopolies.

Moreover, we have reason to believe that up to now there has been a certain tendency in the Soviet Union and other socialist countries to think that there is very little likelihood that this struggle will be able to seriously shake the domination of the monopolies and that it is better to bet on a prolonged status quo in the present European balance of forces.

In this connection I think it is useful to quote from the speech made by Comrade Brezhnev in Moscow on the occasion of the 60th anniversary of the October Revolution, in which he spoke of the struggle of the Western communists for the unity of all democratic forces against domination by the monopolies: "Their statements regarding this matter contain interesting ideas," said Comrade Brezhnev, "although one may say that not all of them are finally worked out and beyond question. This is understandable: research is research. The important thing is simply that it should be in the right direction."

This is the language of dialogue. We cannot deny the Soviet comrades the right to discuss the validity of the policies of the Western Communist parties, and it is to be noted that their doubts are expressed here with tact and moderation. In addition it is true that the work of our parties in the West is based on a series of hypotheses which, serious as they are, no less still require to be verified. However, the same can be said of all forms of revolutionary struggle, anywhere in the world.

There is every indication that our Soviet comrades are watching the struggle of the Western Communist Parties with interest, but also with a scepticism which may go as far as distrust. There is undoubtedly a connection between this scepticism, or distrust even, and the place which they assign to the development of democracy — in the Soviet Union and elsewhere — in their conception of the world revolutionary process: they do not seem to consider it to be a major political issue in the struggle. As a result, and in contradiction to what occurred immediately after the 20th Congress (but also before and during the second world war, in the face of fascism), there does not seem to be enough agreement regarding this matter between their views and those of the Western communist parties, a situation which is not without causing certain disquiet and friction.

I think that as far as we ourselves are concerned, we ought to take care not to confuse more or less debatable theories developed unilaterally with a political criticism of what seem to us to be negative features in certain socialist countries. It may be useful for some comrades to do research and to advance hypotheses, but it is not our job as Belgian communists to think up a "better" Soviet Constitution, or to wish to export our ideas on pluralism to countries where a one-party system has been created due to historical conditions. In my view in any case, the most fruitful theoretical research in this respect would be less concerned with the problems of the single party, and more with the basic conditions in which it can be transcended by setting in motion the process of the withering away of the State (and hence the disappearance of the dichotomy — party-state). This depends on internal factors, but also on external factors, which involve a new forward sweep of the world revolutionary forces. I am thinking particularly of the outcome of the struggle in Western Europe and I am also thinking of the removal of the heavy liability represented by China. Be that as it may, it is impossible for us to function as internationalists — or indeed to work politically at all — in any convincing manner, without providing our party and the working-class with detailed views on the evident limitations of democracy in the Soviet Union, and some other socialist countries.

The fact that the bourgeoisie has seen how to turn this stance to their advantage and is kicking up an enormous fuss does not make the expression of these opinions at the same time a failure of solidarity. On the contrary, we have to speak out clearly and seriously so as to be able at the same time to expose the real motives of the bourgeoisie — which have nothing to do with the defence of freedom and democracy. In this connection we must resolutely reject sweeping statements which one still hears sometimes about the different approach of the intellectuals and the working-class, even if it is true that they do not see the problem of freedom in exactly the same light and that the workers often have a better grasp of reality.

What are the sufficiently detailed opinions that can be expressed today with regard to the limitations of socialist democracy in the Soviet Union?

The Hangovers from Stalinism do not Explain Everything.

There are no grounds whatever for rebutting the Soviet assertion that the Soviet Union today has reached the stage of developed socialism. Indeed, this stage does appear to have been reached in a number of key areas. One can agree that developed socialism is the dominant characteristic of contemporary Soviet society, and that the social and economic basis already permits of an advance towards what L. Brezhnev in an article in the *World Marxist Review* termed "social and communist self-administration".[4]

But it is nevertheless true that the Soviet Union has reached the stage of developed socialism from a starting point of great historical backwardness, which has allowed deeply rooted features of under-development to persist, militating in general terms against the balanced development of a new society.

These features are particularly noticeable in the sphere of internal politics and in the way institutions function, with a recurring tendency to centralisation, giving a great deal of power and autonomy to the bureaucratic apparatuses of the State.

This does not support the image of developed socialism. It is up to those who think otherwise to try to harmonize our idea of developed democracy with the way that Comrade Podgorny was replaced by Comrade Brezhnev as head of state.

The limitations of socialist democracy and of individual rights and liberties of citizens give us some problems in expressing our solidarity, but we must think twice before ascribing these to a hangover from Stalinsim. This hangover does exist, but does not explain everything. We know for instance that in the Soviet Union in a very short space of time an enormous mixing of heterogeneous peoples took place, some of whom started out from almost medieval social and economic structures, political conditions and cultural levels. Out of this mixing, which has brought tens of millions of illiterate peasants and nomads into modern life, socialist industrialisation has in effect made a forceps delivery of a huge, educated working-class, but a working-class which has no longer anything in common with the elite proletariat which the Bolsheviks had so carefully prepared for the tasks of the revolution. As always in the history of nations, the price of this immense

[4] L. Brezhnev, 'A Historic Stage on the Road to Communism' World Marxist Review, vol. 20 no. 12. December 1977. pp. 3-14. (Ed.)

advance "on a broad front" has been the diminishing — temporary but considerable — of the style of democratic participation in relation to what it was at the beginning of Soviet power. Stalin both used and abused this situation: he certainly exacerbated everything, but he did not deliberately bring about the objective conditions which promoted, or even encouraged, the substitution of administrative decisions and orders "from above" for the democratic participation of the masses. In my view we should be making a big mistake if we thought that the Soviet Union had completely emerged from this period of upheaval: there will not be further upheavals on that scale, but the Soviet Union will have to put up with the consequences and aftermath for many years to come.

It is for this reason that the existence of firm and vigilant political power in the Soviet Union today has both internal and external justifications which it would be unrealistic not to take into account. We should avoid looking through liberal or libertarian spectacles when we criticize the limitations of socialist democracy. There is no unlimited democracy anywhere and there never will be. In here in Belgium we post the question of the extension of democracy it is not because we are especially virtuous democrats, but rather because this extension reflects an urgent need widely felt at the present stage of social development and capitalist crisis. This need is growing in the Soviet Union as well, in different economic, social, political and cultural conditions, but in general no one would deny that up to now it has only been felt acutely in certain strata of intellectual workers, a small minority of whom react to the abuses of the bureaucracy by setting themselves apart from society, giving rise to what is known as "dissidence". The most effective way of dealing with this problem is by emphasizing the fact that such limitations would be simply inconceivable here in Belgium, by reason of our specific social and political history.

With What are we in Solidarity?

But the problem of the limitations of democracy is not the principal source of our difficulties. The limitations of socialist democracy are one thing — which one can always explain, without necessarily justifying — the stifling and *distortion* of socialist democracy are quite another.

Internationalist solidarity does not in any way compel us to accept responsibility for, or to cover up, important bureaucratic deformations which do not merely limit socialist democracy, but seriously distort it.

Sending an opponent, whoever he may be, to a psychiatric asylum, is not a limitation of democracy, it is an abuse which cannot be defended.

We are in solidarity with the conquests of socialism, errors included, because they have forced capitalist exploitation and imperialism to retreat. It is for *the same reason* that it would be an absurdity, an aberration, to countenance or to cover up, in the name of internationalism, bureaucratic practices which Soviet workers were called upon by Lenin himself to oppose, including by strike action; practices which we combat ourselves when they are committed by bourgeois governments. That the socialist countries should have their police forces is normal and necessary, but we Belgian communists are under no obligation of solidarity towards that State machine; this is all the more so when we realise that, in certain countries, that machine seems to possess an autonomy of action which crosses the frontiers of the law itself.

Through the world the need for an expansion of liberties is growing in different ways and to different degrees, but with an increasing *interdependence* among all its various individual expressions. In this sense, liberty becomes truly indivisible. This need also exists, in forms appropriate to each situation, in the socialist countries, and if certain of them take too long to accord it an adequate response, that conforms with the very nature of socialism, the result will be an aggravation of political troubles which can, for the time being, still be regarded as marginal, or at least containable. We have not forgotten the cruel lessons of 1956 and 1968.

We Belgian communists also aim, by opposing the stifling and distortion of socialist democracy, to contribute as far as we are able to the prevention of such an aggravation, since it would be prejudicial to all those forces which are struggling for socialism, liberty and peace.

Comrade Terfve has written in *Cahiers Marxistes* that it was necessary to "begin to demystify the problem", and he is right.

The interest of his article lies in the fact that it not only "demystifies", but, further and more importantly, it also sets out quite clearly our marxist conception of human rights; a conception which is in absolute accordance with the principles of the international communist movement, which were explicitly defined at the Berlin conference.

Our party holds strictly to the positions of that conference, in which it participated along the lines laid down by its 22nd Congress. One still, however, comes across comrades who liken our conception of human rights to a "bourgeois democratic" conception. Of course, there does exist a bourgeois democratic conception of human rights; it favours certain individual rights at the expense of the economic and social rights which remain to be conquered in our country, and which it prefers to ignore — hence its relative narrowness. But it is not by denying or minimising the rights of the individual that one demonstrates the narrowness of the bourgeois conception of human rights. The marxist conception of human rights includes the whole contribution of the struggles of the working class for economic and social rights, and the immense contribution that the socialist countries have made to those struggles; but it also includes the whole heritage of the progressive struggles of the past against feudal reaction, and, more recently, against fascism. In the name of human rights, marxists condemn torture, and I don't suppose anyone is going to turn round and tell us that they thereby lose sight of the "class content" of the problem of torture! We condemn the occupational bans (Berufsverbote) in the Federal Republic of Germany and, by so doing, we defend the same human rights that we would defend as well and *better* in a socialist Belgium. We cannot accept that people who do no more than issue appeals in favour of the respect of individual rights should be prosecuted and persecuted, as in the case of the Charter 77 signatories in Czechoslovakia.

The situation in that country requires, moreover, some special remarks. Here we are at the tenth anniversary of the events of 1968 and we can be sure that our adversaries will make a huge anti-socialist propaganda operation out of it. That would not matter if, as is unfortunately the case, our adversaries did not in the event have too many good pretexts for so doing.

Certainly, the situation in Czechoslovakia is no longer what it was in 1968. From the economic and social point of view it has improved considerably, and the country now has a certain degree of prosperity. At this we rejoice. It is obviously not a matter of secondary importance. It does not prevent us having to recall the position which we took at the time of the military intervention of 1968; having to recall it, furthermore, as a *justified* position which still has a political bearing today. Everything that has happened confirms that that intervention (unlike that which took place in Hungary in 1956) has clumsily and for a long period of time mortgaged the functioning of democracy in Czechoslovakia. So much so that, ten years later, use is still being made of secret trials, crimes of opinion, and, no less of a serious matter, mass apoliticism.

We shall say it frankly, without any pointless idealisation of the reality of the "Prague Spring", but frankly and without expecting to be challenged for saying it.

Antisovietism and Anticommunism: A Changed Relationship.

A third problem, within the same context, which must be studied more deeply, is that posed by the current relationship between antisovietism and anticommunism.

Antisovietism and anticommunism were for a long time synonymous; they are still connected, but in a different manner.

This is due to the change in the relationship of forces which has occurred on a world scale between imperialism and the various oppositions with which it is in conflict, in particular the power of the Soviet Union itself.

Until the first half of the fifties, antisovietism was the ideological support for a strategy of driving back, whose principal variants were the military expeditions of 1919-1920, the policy of blockade and of "cordon sanitaire", the machinations of 1938-1939 (at Munich and during the drôle de guerre)[5] and finally the policy of Foster Dulles. This type of antisovietism nourished fascism, and by virtue of its own objectives it was bound to accommodate itself to fascism or to fascist methods.

In the course of time the imperialist powers came to understand the unreality of such projects and revised their propaganda accordingly. To be sure, they in no way renounced their traditional antisoviet themes, but rather added to them new, much more refined, variations. It was necessary *above all* to persuade the workers movements of the main capitalist countries, especially in Western Europe, that the achievements of Socialism, which it had become difficult to deny, could have no validity as an example to them. Even the subversive undertakings which the imperialist powers have continued to organise against the socialist countries have ended up being subordinated to this aim. The weapon of antisovietism has thus ceased to be pointed at the USSR itself, as the objective of a future crusade, to be turned towards the communist parties of the developed capitalist countries; this policy was all the more necessary for the bourgeoisie as, in the context of the ending of the cold war, it became much more difficult for it to attempt to isolate these parties by presenting them as associations of "agitators" in the service of the future enemy and of his plans for "internal aggression".

At first, above all during the period which followed the 20th Congress of the CPSU, the bourgeoisie had a fashionable theory according to which the industrial development of the capitalist countries (this was at the beginning of the monopolist expansion of the sixties) and of the socialist countries (with reference to the first sputnik) would lead them both to lose their essentially distinctive features. The Soviet Union was heading straight for "embourgeoisement" (a thesis echoed by the accusations of the Maoists) and the capitalist countries were going towards "the dissolution of classes in the consumer society".

It is perhaps necessary to recall today that that propaganda did have some effect. In any case, its aim was clear: to distort Soviet reality, as an expression of the achievement of socialism, not in order to justify any bellicose undertakings against the USSR, but to convince the workers of our countries of the uselessness of the struggle for socialism, of the uselessness of the communist parties.

This aim remains the same today. But the general conditions in which the bourgeoisie pursues it have greatly changed over the years, both nationally and internationally.

Firstly, the struggle for peaceful coexistence. The majority of communist parties, including our own, recognised twenty years ago the revolutionary significance of this struggle, which has now been crowned by

[5] Literally 'phoney war', the period from the beginning of the second World War in September 1939 to the invasion of Norway in April 1940. (Ed.)

a great victory with the signature of the Helsinki agreements, which provide
the basis for the establishment of entirely new relationships of peace and
cooperation between States.

In subscribing to these agreements, as they could not avoid doing, the
imperialist powers understood perfectly well that if they were to even half-
heartedly play the peaceful coexistence game, they would be exposing their
political power to great dangers if they allowed things to go as far as a real
improvement in understanding and cooperation between peoples.

Secondly, there is obviously no question today of trying to get the
workers to believe that we are on the way to the dissolution of classes in the
consumer society. The crisis of these last years has seen off that golden
legend, and one well understands why, at the same time as the "dissolution
of classes' fades away in the West, so does "embourgeoisement" in the
East! The seriousness of the crisis, its structural character and foreseeably
long duration evidently constitute a serious threat to monopoly capitalists'
domination, especially in conditions which, for the first time in the history
of capitalism make recourse to the traditional outlet of war extremely
difficult, if not impossible.

Thirdly, Europe has been these last few years the scene of a series of
political phenomena which have been extremely disturbing for the
bourgeoisie. These have not all been of the same order. The collapse of the
fascist dictatorships in Greece, Portugal and Spain must first of all be considered as a victory of the democratic forces and the communist parties of
those countries; however, considering the limits within which this collapse
has been contained up to now we have to say that imperialism has been able
to keep it under control and even make it fit in with the reorganisation of
the advanced defences of capitalism, in accordance with the "liberal" views
of President Carter. Nevertheless, the situation in these countries necessitates a great vigilance on the part of the ruling classes, and causes them no
little concern. This concern is turning to alarm in the cases of Italy and
France, where the communist parties are now in a position to present themselves to the masses as parties of power armed with concrete proposals for
challenging monopoly domination and for charting a way out of the crisis
from positions of power.

This combination of national and international factors has led imperialism to develop its antisoviet campaign in an unusually broad manner; this
campaign *is first and foremost for internal use* against the communist
parties, and is intended to cut them off from the popular masses, to turn
them into objects of fear by deceitfully making them appear as parties
whose first concern, once in power, would be to stifle democracy and to
suppress liberties, "as in the East". The State Department's recent declarations concerning the possible entry of communists into certain European
governments indicate, furthermore, that another aim of this campaign is to

prepare the ground for the direct, open intervention which American imperialism could be forced into by the evolution of events.

The counter-revolutionary international, whose headquarters is Washington and whose principal European subsidiary is Bonn, may have given up its former strategy of driving back, it may have dropped the Greek colonels and even withdrawn from Vietnam; it nonetheless remains faithful to itself. Clearly, Berlinguer and Marchais are not Karamanlis, and Western Europe is not Vietnam; this time the stake could be decisive, we are at the heart of one of imperialism's main redoubts.

It is in this sense that antisovietism is today at the service of anti-communism; it is aimed towards the European communist parties. It is similarly aimed at them to the extent that the high bourgeoisie is at the same time counting on this campaign to corrode the principles of internationalist solidarity which are the basis of their relationships with the socialist countries and with the Soviet Union in particular.

Thus, it is necessary to express our differing conceptions and our disagreements because we cannot allow our adversaries to make use against our cause, the cause of democracy and socialism, of situations which are foreign to us or of acts for which we cannot assume responsibility. But it goes without saying that the reason for our fundamental solidarity is as strong as ever, especially at a time when American imperialism's menacing interference in western Europe makes it quite clear that the joint struggles of the parties concerned are an integral part of a worldwide confrontation which creates, beyond the limits of "Eurocommunism", the *need* for a much greater solidarity.

An open letter to the Labour movement from the Communist Party of Great Britain, March, 1978.

(Complete Text).

Dear Comrades,

We are addressing this letter to you because we are sure that you share with us deep concern about the grave crisis facing the Labour movement.

All of us recognise that there is a serious danger of the return at the next General Election of the most reactionary Tory government for decades.

It would be led by people who have now adopted the racist policies and language of the National Front. They must be defeated in the election whenever it comes.

But this in itself is not enough. If the election results in another minority Labour government, dependent for its existence on the votes of Liberals and others, and carrying on with present policies, the country's problems will not be solved.

Mr. Callaghan recently told the cabinet and the national executive of the Labour Party that as far as unemployment was concerned, "I can see no basic solution to the problem".

The Labour movement cannot accept that attitude. The crime of mass unemployment and the other problems we face — the decline in real wages, cuts in social and public services, stagnation in industry — are the results of government policies and of an economic and political system which the Labour movement was founded to change.

They can only be tackled in the interests of the people by policies which challenge the power of the big capitalists and multi-national firms.

It is true that the rate of inflation is lower, the balance of payments more favourable, and the pound stronger. But the tragic fact is that millions of people get little or no benefit from these developments.

Hundreds of thousands of young people who have no jobs feel rejected by society. Desperate problems face the homeless, the families living in run-down city centres and concrete wildernesses, the sick and the aged. Yet thousands of millions of pounds are spent on arms and Mr. Callaghan is for adding the horrific neutron bomb to NATO's armoury.

All this provides fertile ground for the National Front and other racists to spread their poisonous doctrine. They stir up hatred between black and white people to prepare the way for attacks on all trade unionists and democrats.

People in all walks of life have reacted strongly to this danger. Many realise that it is necessary not only to oppose the National Front, but also to change the social conditions which breed racism and fascism. This encourages our belief that leadership from the Labour movement can win the majority of our people to support a policy of social advance.

We put forward for your consideration some suggestions on the main points of the overall policy which we feel is needed.

UNEMPLOYMENT, WAGES & BENEFITS

Unemployment can only be seriously combated by a policy of expanding the economy.

This means increasing home demand by raising wages, pensions and other benefits. It means expanding the social services, with a big programme of house, school and hospital building. It means increased investment in industry. The funds in the hands of big business and financial institutions, the revenues from oil, money saved by cutting arms expenditure, and the proceeds of increased taxation on the rich, should be used for these purposes. The immediate introduction of the 35-hour week and longer holidays is also vital. Free collective bargaining must be restored.

The Temporary Employment Subsidy must be continued, job creation schemes extended, and training programmes for young people developed.

RACISM
The organised Labour movement needs to take the lead in combating racist ideas and activities. It should help set up and reinforce broad campaigning committees against racism in every locality.
The provocative racist marches of the National Front should be banned. The extension of such bans to all demonstrations is a denial of democracy and must be ended.

PEACE
Britain should support the banning of the neutron bomb, close nuclear bases, phase out nuclear weapons and work for international agreement to ban them completely. Military spending should be drastically reduced.

Many of these suggestions are already the policy of Labour, Co-operative and trade union organisations. They can be won. A Labour government determined to tackle the crisis in the people's interests could carry them out and in doing so win overwhelming support.

Our appeal is that men and women in the Labour movement — trade unionists, Co-operators, Labour Party and Communist Party members and others — should at this critical moment come together to agree on and act for such a policy.

In each area, industry and workplace the issues and campaigning forms most appropriate to the local circumstances could be worked out.

In Scotland and Wales powerful wide-ranging action to win the people's votes for setting up Assemblies would establish the Labour movement as the champions of national interests as well as of their people's economic and social needs.

In all of this the Left in the Labour Movement has a great responsibility.

The general election in France shows how essential left unity is if the right is to be defeated. So do all our experiences in Britain.

Our Labour movement also needs a long-term strategy for winning socialism, as well as an immediate policy for defeating the Tories. This is why we invite you to read the new edition of our programme, "The British Road to Socialism", which has just been published.

We are confident that, despite the difficulties, the movement has the strength and resources to put our country on a new course, and realise the great aims and ideals which inspired its founders. It is in this spirit that we send you this letter.

Yours fraternally,

GORDON McLENNAN
General Secretary
On behalf of the executive committee of the
Communist Party of Great Britain.

Playing up to Imperialist Anti-Soviet Propaganda.
Concerning Some Pronouncements by Manuel Azcarate, a Leading Functionary of the Communist Party of Spain.

(Complete Text). New Times, No. 3, January, 1978.   ·

The bourgeois press, radio and television, both in America and in Western Europe, are continuing to expatiate on the subject of "Eurocommunism" interpreted, of course, from their own particular angle. A great many books and a spate of articles propounding it as an essentially anti-communist, anti-Soviet trend have been published. And congresses, seminars, symposiums and the like have been held — more are projected for the immediate future — on the problem of "Eurocommunism" and ways and means of adapting it to serve the practical needs of ruling circles in the West.

In November and December, meetings of this kind were held in Cologne and Frankfurt-on-Main in West Germany and in Lugano in Switzerland. The list of their sponsors and participants is in itself significant — we find bourgeois theorists and politicians, NATO generals and representatives of such reactionary anti-Soviet propaganda centres as *Deutsche Welle*, the CIA-financed *Radio Liberty* and *Radio Free Europe*, etc. International monopoly capital — Esso, Ford, Brown Boveri and big West German concerns — has also been prominently represented at them.

These organisations and concerns can hardly be suspected of seeking to disseminate communist ideas. On the contrary. The purpose of the assemblies they sponsor is to modernise their weapons for combating communism and to find new ways and means of dividing and weakening the international communist and working-class movement.

A recent new development is the regular invitation of representatives of West European Communist Parties to present communications and papers at such symposiums. And the representatives of some Communist Parties have accepted such invitations.

Communists, of course, are not secretarian. Already in his *"Left-Wing" communism — An Infantile Disorder*, Lenin wrote that they must make themselves heard everywhere, bourgeois parliaments and reactionary trade unions included, and must "work wherever the masses are to be found" in order to bring home to the working people the need for, and the importance of, active struggle against capitalism and for democracy and socialism.

No one is likely, however, to contend seriously that *Radio Liberty* or Ford appointees represent the masses. They speak for those who seek to suppress, intimidate and deceive the masses in order to divert them away from revolutionary struggle. It is not by chance, for instance, that the admission charge to one of the above-mentioned meetings was nearly 1,000 West German marks, or more than half the monthly wage of a West German skilled worker.

Thus invitations to monopoly seminars on "Eurocommunism" are not extended to provide a platform for the dissemination of socialist ideas among working people. And it is hard to imagine that the communists who accepted such invitations were not fully aware of this. Clearly, in agreeing to appear at gatherings of this kind they were guided by altogether different considerations. Could some of them have expected to be able to "Persuade" the monopolies to be "more obliging"? Or did they have some other ideas in mind? But let us not conjecture.

The fact remains that communists have taken part in such symposiums. The important thing, however, is how this participation tallied with communist ideology and the dignity of a communist and a champion of the workers' cause.

One of the most active participants in the meetings held so far has been Manuel Azcarate, a member of the executive committee and secretariat of the Communist Party of Spain. This is not to say, of course, that he had never before made statements hostile towards the socialist countries and, primarily, the Soviet Union. The Soviet press (for instance, the journal *Party Life* No. 4, 1974) has already replied publicly to his attacks.

It must be noted, however, that in his speeches in Cologne and Lugano and in his interview of December 12, 1977, with the West German *Der Spiegel*, Azcarate went to considerably greater lengths in directing crude attacks against the social countries and, above all, against the Soviet Union.

It is only fair to say that when one reads press comment on his perform-ance and his published statements one comes across occasional references to the desire of the Communist Party of Spain to build socialism in its country and to pursue its own specific road to that objective. All this is generally known from the party's official documents. However, it is not on this that Azcarate placed the emphasis. Nor is it this that bourgeois press writers primarily seized upon.

Their attention was attracted by two things, namely:

The fact that Azcarate disavowed the basic principles of Marxism-Leninism;
And his condemnation of existing socialism and of the experience of the Soviet Union.
Let us take a closer look at this.

First. Azcarate says: "We Spanish communists reject the concept of Marxism-Leninism. . . having long considered many aspects of Leninism as obsolete. . . we do not regard Marxism as an absolute truth."

One might ask: Did the Spanish communists authorise Azcarate to make such statements? When reading such essentially anti-communist statements, one cannot but recall that it was thanks to the epochal contribution made by Marx and Engels nearly 130 years ago by linking together the working-class movement and advanced revolutionary theory that this class movement became a powerful, militant movement. And that all the far-reaching changes that have taken place in the world in recent decades were brought about by parties and forces which based themselves on the principles of Marxism-Leninism. No other ideas have so far produced results in any way comparable with those yielded by the successful application of the ideas of Marx, Engels and Lenin.

Azcarate would have the working class return today to the remote past and reject the revolutionary ideas of Marxism-Leninism. Yet all past experience and the realities of the present day conclusively show that departure from the basic principles of Marxism-Leninism, from the historically verified laws of the class struggle and the socialist revolution, spells for the working class and all other sections of the working people only defeats and setbacks, impelling them on to the road of social reformism and submission to the policies and interests of the bougeoisie. Without the ideas of Marx, Engels and Lenin, there could be no revolutionary working-class movement, no communist movement, no genuine struggle in defence of the interests of the working class and the masses in general.

Further. There are forces which would like to see communists renounce Marxism-Leninism. They make no secret of this. These forces are the monopoly capitalists, the rightwing Social Democrats and, in Spain, the Francoists and their successors. Could following the advice of these forces bring anyone a fraction of an inch nearer to socialism?

Second. Having declared that "Eurocommunism" is a new trend in modern Marxism, Azcarate proceeded to say that "The characteristic feature of Eurocommunism is rejection of the Soviet model" and that "if the West European communists wish to work out their own concept they must openly criticise the Soviet model of society."

It is appropriate to mention — Azcarate himself, incidentally, should know this very well — that the Soviet Union has never sought to impose on anyone "its model," or the conclusions it has drawn from its own rich experience and from the international experience of contemporary socialism. It is, of course, up to every Communist Party to decide whether to study and draw on the experience of fraternal parties or whether not to do so.

Discussing the relationship between theory and practice, Leonid Brezhnev, general secretary of the CPSU central committee, said at the Berlin Conference of the Communist and Workers' Parties of Europe:

"While greatly attentive to the creative work of our comrades in the communist family, we proceed from the fact that only practical experience can be the criterion for judging whether this or that concept is right or wrong. But before practice passes its final verdict, it is possible and indeed necessary to evaluate these concepts in a comradely discussion, by comparing the points of view and experience of various parties."

As regards our party, it has for 60 years now been giving effect to the ideas of Marx, Engels and Lenin. Firmly adhering to the fundamentals of their revolutionary teaching and effectively applying it in the struggle for socialism and communism, the CPSU has led our country forward to momentous victories and achievements. This is an incontrovertible fact. At the same time our party closely studies the experience of the other socialist countries, as well as the work done in the spheres of theory and practical policy by the fraternal parties in the non-socialist countries.

Built by the efforts of the Soviet people and the peoples of the other fraternal countries, existing socialism has become a source of strength for the international working class and a powerful bulwark of peace and social progress. Its existence and growing strength open up broad opportunities for the reconstruction of society in other countries in circumstances that will be, we hope, in many cases less onerous than those with which the peoples of the USSR and other socialist countries had to cope.

Existing socialism has played a signal role in ensuring the success of the national liberation movement. Its very existence and its strength and support are now facilitating the struggle for economic independence being waged by the countries that have won independent statehood.

It is plain for all the peoples of the world to see that existing socialism has posed the task of ridding humanity of world wars on a practical plane. Moreover, it has already made a decisive contribution to the recasting of international relations along democratic lines.

The socialist countries firmly hold the initiative in the foreign policy sphere, working for such solutions of international issues as will accord with the interests of the working-class movement and of all working people and the interests of national independence, peace and security. Needless to say, in waging this struggle, the socialist countries stand solidly with the communists and all other progressive and democratic forces all over the world and highly appreciate reciprocal manifestations of solidarity on their part.

Azcarate is unable to counterpose to the living and practical experience of the USSR and other socialist countries any living, practical embodiment of his own ideas. Basing himself on an abstract and unverified scheme, he takes it upon himself categorically to reject the experience of the Communist Party of the Soviet Union, even though he does not have, and as like as not does not wish to have, any proper knowledge of that experience.

It would seem that the picture he has of the Soviet Union is derived from anti-Soviet concoctions and from the massive propaganda drive which the western mass media have mounted, making extensive use of a handful of renegades expelled from our country for hostile activity and anti-Soviet slander.

Playing up to this malicious imperialist, anti-Soviet and anti-socialist propaganda campaign, Azcarate goes so far as to say that the Soviet Union "is not really a socialist state."

Smears of this kind are not worthy of an answer. We cite them only to show how rapidly Azcarate is being sucked into the quagmire of anti-Sovietism. It is appropriate to recall that a delegation from the Communist Party of Spain, which had talks with a delegation from the CPSU in October 1974, and of which he, too, was a member, expressed in the communiqué on the visit its "deep satisfaction with the successes of the Soviet Union" and condemned anti-Sovietism as "running counter to the interests of the working class and the anti-imperialist struggle."

Considering the statements Azcarate has now been making with such self-assurance, it is legitimate to ask what positive concept he has to advance as to what a truly socialist state and socialist society should be like. But no coherent answer to this question can be found in his pronouncements. For Spain, incidentally, he puts forward the idea of socialism with all-round "pluralism" — economic, political and ideological.

In spain today there unquestionably is pluralism — in the sense of the existence of many different classes, including antagonistic ones, and parties and organisations reflecting their positions. This is perfectly natural in a capitalist country. Discerning this fact does not require too much perspicacity. The trouble is, however, that he does not go beyond this. But the working class and the masses in general want to know what is the way out of the blind alley into which their countries have been led by the domination of monopoly capitalism.

Talk about ideological pluralism as a feature of socialist society as visualised by Azcarate boils down in practical terms merely to concern for the preservation of the positions of anti-socialist ideology. And what is economic pluralism? Is it a matter of preserving capitalist property under socialism as well?

As regards pluralism as applied to our country and our state, everybody knows that we have no exploiting classes and hence no social carriers of bourgeois ideology. What, then, should we do? Cultivate class enemies so as to create pluralism to please Manuel Azcarate? Let no one expect us to do that.

Ours is an altogether different road — the road of the further strengthening and development of socialist democracy, the hallmark and consistently observed principle of which is the ever broader participation of citizens in the administration of the affairs of the state and society. Our road is the road of building communism, that is to say, of creating a society ensuring the all-round development and application of the abilities of each individual. The people of the Soviet Union take pride in their society and state and have every reason to do so; they cherish all they have achieved by their labour and struggle, and are doing everything in their power to ensure the continued advance of this society.

The true meaning of the attacks on existing socialism which are integral components of Azcarate's "Eurocommunism" can be fully assessed if they are viewed in the light of the class confrontation of the two social systems in the international arena.

Reaction and imperialism have realised that socialism has become established once and for all and cannot be overcome by frontal attack, even by using armed force. Hence their reliance, first, on slander designed to counteract the appeal socialism holds for the working people of other countries, and, second, on undermining the communist movement from within by setting the Communist Parties one against the other, and, in particular, the Communist Parties of the capitalist countries against those of the socialist countries.

The imperialists are naturally casting about for allies who may help them to achieve their ends. And, regrettably, they are not always unsuccessful. It might be mentioned in this connection that the French *Le Monde* wrote recently with obvious satisfaction about an "interesting pronouncement by Manual Azcarate" and highly praised his stand as "progressive" as compared with the stand taken by leading members of the other Communist Parties. Azcarate has thus won the plaudits of exponents of the interests of the bourgeoisie. Of this there is no doubt. What the working class thinks about it is quite another thing.

By choosing to become a detractor of existing socialism, Azcarate, in our opinion, is doing harm to his own party. History has shown time and again that anti-Sovietism is inseparable from anti-communism. Anti-Soviet campaigns or campaigns against any other socialist country can only be damaging to the entire communist movement. By virtue of its very essence anti-Sovietism inevitably tends to undermine the influence and prestige of the Communist Parties of the capitalist countries and to weaken their ties with the working class and other democratic, social and political forces.

Every anti-Soviet campaign gives encouragement to forces hostile to the communists. One cannot effectively fight for freedom and democracy in one's own country — and this applies to Spain as well — while discrediting existing socialism.

Following earlier articles published in our journal on "Eurocommunism" — from which the imperialist rulers and propagandists expect and demand, notwithstanding all the "explanations" given at various symposiums, only anti-communism, anti-Marxism and anti-Sovietism — some western press commentators felt that *New Times* had overdone it, that we had exaggerated the anti-Soviet tendency in the views and activities of the avowed ideologues of "Eurocommunism." Manuel Azcarate's latest statements testify to the contrary. The fact is that some of the most active proponents of "Eurocommunism" in fact bring grist to the mill of imperialism. It is not a matter of labels and epithets. It is a matter of stating a fact, from which we cannot but draw conclusions.

"Unity is a great thing and a great slogan," Lenin said. "But what the workers' cause needs is the unity of Marxists, not unity between Marxists and opponents and distorters of Marxism."

B. ANDREYEV

Resolutions of the 9th Congress of the Spanish Communist Party; 19-23 April, 1978.

* Printed below are four of the Resolutions adopted by the Congress.[1]

Resolution 5: A Government of Democratic Alliance

Since the Spanish Communist Party stated in July the need for a government of democratic alliance, many people have thought, and even said, that the Moncloa Agreement[2] came close to bringing about the actual formation of such a government. While it might be true that the agreement points the way to a possible government of alliance, it is nonetheless a fact that we are still a long way from having achieved this, and the country con-

[1] The following is a list of all the Resolutions adopted:
   1. Features of the present changes
   2. The policy of national reconciliation
   3. The policy of democratic alliance
   4. Significance of the Moncloa Agreement
   5. The Government of democratic alliance
   6. Social and political democracy, a step towards socialism and communism
   7. Policy on trade union affairs
   8. The liberation of women
   9. Rural areas
   10. Youth
   11. Educational and Cultural policy
   12. Cultural and civic issues
   13. Foreign and defence policy
   14. Emigration
   15. The Spanish Communist Party
   16. Small and medium-sized businesses and the self-employed
   17. Fishing and merchant shipping

[2] In early October 1977, Prime Minister Suárez invited representatives of all the parliamentary parties to talks with the Government to discuss both short-term economic measures and long-term reform of the political and economic system. The talks resulted in the Moncloa Agreement.
   The agreement was in two parts. An economic agreement (25 Oct) accepted measures to limit wage demands with a threshold clause allowing a further rise if inflation exceeded the percentage increase allowed to wages. Other measures were agreed covering monetary policy, and unemployment, together with an outline of large-scale reforms of public expenditure, taxation, social insurance etc. The parties of the left (PSOE and PCE) were

tinues to suffer the consequences of corruption, the persistence of bastions of anti-democratic authority and the failings and extravagance of an administration that has not yet been democratised.

The Communist Party has not renounced the idea of a government of alliance. Just as the Central Democratic Union Government had to turn to other parliamentary parties in order to find a possible solution to the economic and political problems it faced, the implementation of the Moncloa Agreement will prove virtually impossible in practice if the Government does not command the greater popular support that will permit the solution of the inevitable difficulties that will arise. If there is anyone who does not realise that we are facing a national emergency, it is only because he chooses to disregard a situation that is obvious to everyone else. It is not merely that we are suffering from a high rate of inflation, that unemployment continues to increase, that our overseas debt is growing and that businesses are in a financial situation for which Commercial and Company Law have a very specific term. The real problem is that much remains to be done to curb inflation, to halt the increase in unemployment, to encourage investment, to improve the conditions of those living on the land and to ensure that many thousands of small and medium-sized businesses look to the future with optimism. All these economic problems can create a rarefied atmosphere conducive to the realisation of the aims of those who have not accepted the democratic changes and could become the agents of political regression.

The national emergency, both political and economic, demands a corresponding emergency solution to the way the country is governed. Initially, it would be an important step forward to institutionalise the Moncloa Agreement at a political, economic and trade-union level, but when the difficulties become more apparent in the ensuing months and when the opposition of the old oligarchy and the tensions aroused by the right wing come to the surface, this government of alliance can be the means of preserving democracy. Otherwise, there would be no "socialist" alternative — as the Spanish Socialist Workers' Party (PSOE) said repeatedly and quite unrealistically in October — instead the only feasible alternative would be a return to the earlier form of authoritarian power, as was outlined in meetings leaked to the press. What is clear is that the forces of democracy and the mass of the people will not accept a return to the past. Such a return would cause us to lapse back into the sinister formulas that for so long oppressed the Spanish people: salary scales imposed by decree, the right to

satisfied at the Government's acceptance of some of their policies: the threshold agreement, an increase in funds for unemployment pay, that pensions were to be increased in inverse proportion, a flat-rate wage increase accounting for some 50 per cent of the total increase on the wages bill. The political agreement (27 Oct) determined measures relating to individual freedoms and the democratisation of the State that would be provisional until the adoption of the Constitution.

strike classed as sedition, the systematic censorship of everyone, imprison-ment for militant politicians and trade unionists, oppression by central government. The Spanish Communist Party could not countenance a revolt under the banner of "Save Spain" which would introduce such forms of repression. Therefore, we shall strive to show that the only solution lies in respecting, enlarging upon and strengthening the Moncloa Agreement, in advancing towards a government of democratic alliance and in emphas-ising that now is the time for solidarity.

It is the increasing possibility of governments of democratic alliance — not only in Spain, but also in other western European countries — that has prompted North American interference in the internal affairs of various nations. This is the underlying motive for the attacks on Eurocommunism, first made in an underhand way by Henry Kissinger, but now being made quite blatantly by the President of the USA, Jimmy Carter. Doubtless, they see in these governments a threat to their continued protectorate-like policy towards Western Europe.

Resolution 13: Foreign and Defence Policy
The international policy of the PCE Pays due heed to the two following basic points:

a) Spain is situated in an area of the world of great strategic importance. The international policy that we are advocating has certain basic aims: to guarantee the sovereignty and independence of Spain, the security of our frontiers and the right of our people to determine their own future free from external interference. With this aim in mind, we advocate a policy of non-alignment in which Spain's role will be to promote an international policy that will encourage the peaceful coexistence of nations, detente, disarma-ment and the breaking down of the existing military blocs; that will guarantee the right of all nations to their freedom and to self-determination; that will safeguard human rights and will foster co-operation and political, economic and cultural links between all countries in friendship and their mutual benefit. This policy will enhance the role and the prestige of Spain both in Europe and throughout the world.

b) The PCE will support the efforts being made on a world-wide scale to strengthen the working-class and anti-imperialist movement. It will continue to do all in its power to reduce and overcome the differences and divisions that at present weaken the struggle of the masses and that of individual nations against colonialism and imperialism; to develop a broad, world-wide, front against imperialism which will respect the independence and individual stance of each party and of each movement and will try to achieve unified action among all those movements and groups opposed to imperialism, whilst paying heed to their differences.

Such a policy demands that the communist movement observe the principle that there is no supreme authority, that there is no leading party or state and that all partues are independent and have equal rights. The PCE does not adhere to any International that determines our policy. There is a need to eliminate the practice of slander, condemnation and expulsion; to recognise the right to make theoretical and political criticism and to encourage an open marxist debate on the contemporary situation.

The PCE maintains fraternal relations with numerous communist parties and labour movements and it is willing to establish relations with any party on the basis of the principle of non-interference, mutual respect and equality of rights. In this connection, it will endeavour to improve relations with the Communist Party of the Soviet Union. Similarly, it wishes to normalise relations with the Communist Party of China.

On the other hand, we recognise the undeniable spread, in various quarters, of reformist tendencies and of a desire for independence.

The international policy of the PCE is set in the wider framework bounded by the correlating forces operating on the world stage. This correlation is marked by a series of setbacks inflicted upon the imperialist system. The existence of socialist countries, the decolonisation brought about by the nationalist movements, the struggle of the working class and their allies in capitalist countries, together with an unprecedented increase in production, one of whose signs is the existence of nuclear weapons, all of these factors have brought about fresh circumstances for the development of the revolutionary process.

On the other hand, there has lately been an increase in terrorist activity which is seen as the sign of a neo-fascist conspiracy which has sprung up simultaneously in several countries.

We have summarised below the PCE's position, not on the general international situation, but rather on the major issues in Spanish foreign policy today.

1. Europe: The PCE supports Spain's entry into the EEC. It is an economic and political necessity that stems from the development of the means of production, from the structure of the Spanish economy and from her trading position. Economic integration presupposes a relatively long and complex process that will not be free from strife and tension. On the other hand, it is vital that Spain should participate as soon as possible in the various bodies of the Community. Prior to the elections to the European Parliament by universal suffrage in May 1979, we demand the right of the Spanish people to take part in this election — this would include emigrant workers resident in Europe — by whatever voting system is thought most suitable. It is our opinion that the opponents of Spain's entry into the EEC are rejecting both the advantages of a progressive, democratic, process at the heart of the Community, and the opportunity to participate in the building of a balanced Europe in which the South would be able to exert its rightful influence.

Whilst advocating Spain's entry into the EEC, the PCE states its intention to work with other left-wing groups towards the modification of the present nature of the Community, dominated as it is by the big monopolies. We envisage a Europe for the workers, for the people; a Europe united on the economic and political levels; a Europe with its own independent policy that would not be subordinate to the USA or to the USSR, but which would maintain positive relations with both these powers; a Europe that would be a free agent in world politics, striving to counter the influence of the military power blocs and alter the present polarised situation, and striving to democratise international relations, enabling all nations to achieve a greater freedom and control over their own futures. The policy of detente and peaceful co-existence will thus be strengthened and given real meaning. The disarmament issue will also be approached with an increased chance of making real progress.

We support the steps taken in Helsinki and more recently in Belgrade to set up a European security system and co-operation on economic, cultural and technological matters and on human rights.

We are in favour of practical measures that will guarantee the security of all countries and nations and will slow down the arms race whose consequences seriously affect the quality of life of the mass of the population. We oppose the development of new weapons of mass destruction, like the neutron bomb.

We welcome as a step forward the normalisation of Spain's relations with the European socialist countries. Our country must develop with them economic, political and cultural relations that will be mutually beneficial.

The foreign policy of a fully democratic Spain will be conspicuous for a diversification of its international relations.

With regard to the working-class movement and the power of the multi-national companies in the European economy, we would urge the stepping up of measures — which hitherto have been quite insufficient — to develop at political and trade-union level new forms of co-operation, solidarity and co-ordinated action on an international scale.

At the present time, we are witnessing a serious crisis in the capitalist system which is having repercussions in every sphere: economic, political, social, cultural and moral. We are witnessing what is also a critical moment for the neo-capitalist aspirations of the post-war period and for the political formulae that have expressed them. In this situation, we consider it vital that the communist, socialist and social democratic parties of Western Europe initiate a bold, serious-minded and open debate aimed at seeking points of contact that would enable common action to be taken in seeking a progressive solution to the present crisis in the capitalist system. In this way, new possibilities would be opened up within democracy of making real progress towards socialism and of overcoming the barriers put up at earlier periods.

Of equal importance is a dialogue and active co-operation towards the same objectives with Christian groups amongst which certain increasingly influential elements are conspicuous for their socialist tendencies.

2. Gibraltar: Gibraltar is a part of Spain and there can be no negotiation on that point. Spain must make known to the rest of the world her demand for the return of Gibraltar by Great Britain.

At the same time, Spain must adopt a policy that offers the Gibraltarians a definite solution to the real problems that are the result of a long historical process.

We do not believe that a policy of isolation and blockade is productive. Contact between the Gibraltarians and the neighbouring population must be made easier with a view to promoting co-existence.

Meanwhile, a special statute for Gibraltar must be devised that will guarantee the population a form of self-government and respect for its way of life, bilingualism, its customs and its legal system.

3. Africa: Changes of considerable importance are taking place in Africa which are affecting the balance of world power. The continent is the setting for determined freedom movements and anti-colonial struggles.

Considerable repercussions have been caused throughout Africa by the victories of the MPLA in Angola and FRELIMO in Mozambique and the coming to power of progressive governments in Guinea Bassau and other countries that have the full support of the PCE.

The PCE will continue to develop relations with new countries born of the anti-colonial struggle, with the anti-imperialist parties or progressive movements governing those countries or which are keeping up the struggle for independence, as in Namibia, Zimbabwe and South Africa.

"Apartheid", one of the most brutal forms of racial discrimination, is a cause for shame for all mankind. It is now time for the Spanish government to put into practice the UN resolutions, i.e. to deprive South Africa's racist régime of arms supplies and to isolate it. These measures will aid the black population in their struggle to win the human rights at present denied them.

Spain requires an African policy worthy of a democratic country. We are in favour of the establishment of full diplomatic, economic and cultural relations with those African countries that have thrown off the colonial yoke.

The problem of the Sahara is especially serious. Present day Spain bears a responsibility for seeing that everything is done to correct the wrongs perpetrated in the France era, which are the result of Spanish colonialism at an earlier stage in our history.

Spain agreed to end her colonisation of the Sahara on the basis of the right of self-determination for its inhabitants. Instead of fulfilling this obligation the Arias government made way for the aggression of Morocco and Mauritania as a result of the disgraceful Madrid Agreement.[3]

The continuation of a state of war entails serious consequences and a very grave threat to Spain.

Spain needs a positive policy that will abrogate the Madrid Agreement and which will be aimed at achieving a just and peaceful settlement to the Sahara conflict.

The Spanish Communist Party recommends the following urgent measures:

a). The cessation of all arms supplies to countries engaged in the hostilities.

b). The repeal of the Madrid Agreement.

c). Action by Spain, or support for any initiative that might be made, to bring about negotiations under the auspices of the UN. These negotiations would include Morocco, Mauritania, Algeria and obviously the Polisario Front, unarguably the representative of the people of the Sahara. The aim of these negotiations would be to find a peaceful solution enabling the people of the Sahara to exercise their right of self-determination, and thereby to open the way for the restoration of peace and security in that area.

The PCE affirms its solidarity with the people of the Sahara and the Polisario Front in their struggle.

A stabilising factor and a guarantee of peace in that area would be the presence of an independent, democratic, state in the Sahara, one with which Spain could develop close relations in many spheres.

This policy is of vital importance if the security of the Canary Islands is to be strengthened. The Canary Islands are an integral part of Spain and we reject any attempt, whatever its origin, to question this self-evident fact.

The PCE is resolutely opposed to the use of Canary Islands territory for foreign military installations and bases, or to support aggression against African countries. At the same time, it will encourage every initiative among the progressive nations and movements in Africa with a view to preventing interference in the internal affairs of the Canary Islands.

4. The Middle East: We reaffirm our solidarity with the Palestinian people and with the PLO, their sole representative. We support the right of the Palestinians to create and govern their own independent state.

Any measure implying support for Israel — such as Spain's establishment of diplomatic relations — would be contrary to the interests of peace, whilst Israel keeps up her aggressive policy and continues to occupy foreign land.

---

[3] Agreement on 14 November 1975 between Morocco, Spain and Mauritania on the withdrawal of Spain from Sahara and the division of the territory between Morocco and Mauritania.

At the same time, we affirm the right of all states including Israel to exist in that area.

5. Latin America: We see a need to develop a new style of relations with the countries of Latin America, free from any outmoded paternalism.

We support the struggle being waged by the Latin American peoples for their political and economic freedom against North American imperialism and multinational companies on the one hand and national dictatorships and oligarchies on the other.

The Spanish people are deeply distressed at the plight of the oppressed peoples of Chile, Argentina, Uruguay, Paraguay and Central America who are the victims of fascist and reactionary tyrannies. Spain must assume a clear political stance in defence of human rights wherever they are violated. In the UN and similar organisations, she must join in the universal voice of protest against régimes like those of Pinochet, Videla, Ströesner etc.

Economic aid to those régimes must be halted. Spain must offer asylum to citizens of those countries who are persecuted on account of their democratic convictions, guaranteeing them full equality in society and at work with Spanish citizens.

We affirm our solidarity with the people of Puerto Rico in their effort to exercise their right to self-determination.

Close bonds of friendship link us with the socialists in Cuba. We hold in high esteem the great effort made by the Cuban Revolution to build a socialist society and to preserve the country's independence. Relations between Cuba and Spain are capable of being maintained at a higher level than at present, which would clearly be to the benefit of both nations.

On the other hand, we would emphasise the benefit to be gained from taking advantage of the considerable opportunities that have arisen to develop economic, political and cultural relations with Mexico, Venezuela, Panama and other Latin American countries. This could contribute to solving serious problems, like those of energy, fishing etc.

6. Developing countries: The underdevelopment of the so-called Third World countries is the direct result of a long period of colonial oppression and imperialism, based on unequal dealings between some countries and others. A different international economic system is needed to establish a new set of relations that would put an end to the methods and the last traces of colonialism, that would contribute in real terms to the development of both industrially advanced and underdeveloped areas to their mutual benefit. This new world order would overcome those contradictions which are intrinsic to capitalism and would be based on a meaningful respect for the political and economic independence of underdeveloped countries and on solidarity between nations.

Besides being a European country, Spain has a series of links, and not just historical ties, that should enable her to establish specific relations with the other non-aligned countries. Today, these countries make up a considerable number of the world's nations and they constitute one of the most powerful international movements working for peace and progress.

7. NATO: The PCE is quite definitely and resolutely opposed to Spain's proposed entry into NATO. This attitude is prompted by Spain's own interests and those of peaceful coexistence. Entry would lead to a strengthening of the military power blocs in Europe and a speeding up of the arms race, which would not be in the interests of peace and security. Moreover, entry would have grave consequences for the country's economy and would seriously prejudice the Spanish Armed Forces, contrary to claims made in the propaganda of interested parties. Other serious consequences would be the inclusion of all Spain, especially the Canaries and the Balearic Islands, in the strategic arrangements of the North Atlantic Alliance, under the aegis of the USA.

Furthermore, it would introduce external factors whose consequences would clearly be detrimental to the democratic process.

On the other hand, to force a decision now on the question of NATO would seriously prejudice Spanish foreign policy. There are areas concerning the EEC, Africa, Gibraltar, Latin America on which a broad consensus is possible. By developing policy along these lines, Spain will be in a position to defend her interests and to recover her prestige and independent identity in the world. To give priority to the question of NATO would be tantamount to destroying this consensus, by eliminating all possibility of it. The debate and final decision on NATO must therefore be postponed until the constitutional process has been concluded and the new Cortes, after a full-scale national debate, is in a position to take a decision whose consequences for the future require not a simple majority, but a decisive one.

We urge for Spain a non-aligned policy and we are in favour of the dissolution of the present military blocs and the simultaneous disbandment of NATO and the Warsaw Pact. The possibility of bringing about such a dissolution is not a utopian dream. The SALT talks have made important strides forward. In fact, the balance of power between the two great powers no longer rests upon the bases they have set up in various foreign countries, but on long-range nuclear weapons which both the USA and the USSR possess. Setting aside the different historical factors that brought them about, the two blocs are the apparatus of hegemony, rather than organisations responding to real military needs. Certain powerful factors are now tending to outweigh the effect of the two blocs.

On the other hand, a rejection of Spain's entry into NATO and the affirmation of a policy of non-alignment and active neutrality would go some way toward making the Mediterranean an area of peace and collaboration. It would contribute to detente, enabling a normalised situation to be created in which only the fleets of those nations bordering the Mediterranean would be permanently stationed there, thus eliminating the constant presence of fleets — equipped with nuclear weapons — belonging to the two powers without a Mediterranean seabord. They would still be granted the normal right of passage.

As far as the problem of American bases on Spanish territory is concerned, we consider it to be a situation arising solely from the existence of the two military blocs. Our aim is to remove foreign military bases from Spain and to end all agreements that diminish our national sovereignty. At the present time, the most practical step towards the removal of foreign bases and troops — of American forces from the West and of Soviet forces from the East — is the gradual disbandment of the two blocs.

Defence Policy

As a result of the francoist dictatorship's reliance on the Armed Forces for its own purposes, for forty years Spain has been without a policy or a system of national defence, modern and efficient enough to protect our borders and territory from aggression.

The PCE will aid in equipping Spain with a military strategy and strength capable of defending her independence and her frontiers.

The role of the Armed Forces is primarily to defend the sovereignty and independence of Spain and her territorial integrity and to guarantee respect for the free expression of the will of the people.

As a logical extension of these principles, the PCE advocates an active neutrality as the basis of our foreign policy and the renunciation of the use of arms as a means of political action. Nonetheless, we recognise the need to mobilise the entire nation in the event of an attack on our sovereignty or territorial integrity. In the face of aggression, the entire nation would support its Armed Forces. We therefore reject categorically the concept of a paid volunteer army and we see the need to maintain compulsory military service, although this would not be an obstacle to finding a satisfactory solution covering conscientious objection.

This policy requires operational land, naval and air forces that are properly equipped and supported by our own weapons industry whose level of technological development would allow us to be independent of foreign suppliers as far as possible.

In order to fulfil their duties more easily, members of the Armed forces must see themselves fully as part of society and as having the support of the society, thereby ensuring the total identification of the nation with its Armed Forces. The Communist Party advocates a clear division between the spheres of defence and public order, as this latter falls outside the role of the Army and involves it in duties for which it is not fit.

We realise that political choice must be exercised through civil procedures, not through the action of military units.

We advocate a more complete training system for officers that would include courses in scientific subjects, sociology and the humanities, as well as in military theory, strategy and tactics, leading to an all-round education. This education would have to be continuous in view of the rapid advances being made in science and military technology.

The high standard of training and the degree of commitment required of officers must be balanced by a satisfactory solution to their major problems, i.e. an improvement in their professional expectations and the up-dating of their duties and rights.

In the course of their military service, communists should strive to acquire every possible item of knowledge that will be useful in the defence of their country against a hostile attack.

Resolution 15: The Spanish Communist Party

The Spanish Communist Party is a revolutionary, democratic, Marxist Party which draws its inspiration from the method of analysis and theories of social development conceived by the founders of scientific socialism, Marx and Engels. In the Spanish Communist Party, the Leninist element, like that of the other great revolutionary thinkers, remains its integral part, it is still valid but only to an extent, bearing in mind that it is no longer possible today to defend the limited view that "Leninism is the Marxism of our age".

We consider ourselves the heirs of those who, under Lenin's leadership, were able to achieve in the difficult conditions of Russia in 1917 the first socialist revolution which initiated the world revolutionary process of which we are a part.

This is the basis of the historical differences that separate us from social democracy. During the First World War, the latter abandoned its international stance and placed itself at the disposition of the bourgeoisie of each country.

More recently, the policy of defending the capitalist and imperialist system has revealed the true nature of Social Democracy and demonstrated its inability to bring about true socialism. There is no evidence in the world today of a social democratic government trying to abolish capitalist exploitation. This is where we differ fundamentally from Social Democracy. We wish to change the world, to create a new society, to establish socialism. This is the *raison d'être* of all communist parties.

On the other hand, while we consider the October Revolution and all the socialist revolutions that have brought freedom to oppressed peoples to be our inheritance, we reject as alien to Marxism the phenomenon of bureaucratism, officialdom and Stalinism. Undoubtedly, a whole series of historical causes lie behind the bureaucratic and repressive elements in the democracy of the USSR. The fundamental cause was the fact that the first socialist revolution took place in an underdeveloped country — for such was Russia in 1917 — and that this revolution was not followed by revolutions in the more developed countries of Europe, as Lenin had expected.

The new-born Soviet state was attacked and placed under siege by the forces of imperialism, and was then beset by poverty, hunger and the effects of international isolation. Exposed as it was to the influence of social democracy, the proletariat of the more advanced European countries was unable to bring about revolution. This solution contributed to the creation of fresh arguments in favour of the negative approach represented by Stalinist officialdom.

These antidemocratic tendencies have entailed a significant delay in the spread of the influence of revolutionary Marxism among the workers of the advanced capitalist countries. By a process of self-examination, the Spanish Communist Party has gone beyond the premises of Stalinism and we are now re-establishing the democratic and anti-bureaucratic fundamentals of Marxism. We shall continue to advance in this direction.

The Spanish Communist Party totally rejects the dogmatic conceptions of Marxism. Marxism is scientific, not dogmatic in outlook. The Spanish Communist Party strives constantly to develop its capacity to assimilate the changes in society, new scientific discoveries and the practical experience of revolution and it strives to evaluate critically new developments in Marxist thought.

The PCE has kept up its criticism of Social Democracy and has welcomed the steps taken by certain socialist or social democratic parties, or by elements within them, towards a Marxist position. It is involved in a struggle to re-establish the unity of the world-wide working-class movement on a Marxist basis. Independently of its critique of Social Democracy, the PCE has expressed its support for the unified action of all forces of Marxist and social democratic persuasion, of all popular movements in a struggle for peace, disarmament, self-determination and the independence of all nations, co-operation between nations on a level of equality, progress, social justice and democracy and the establishment of socialism.

In the Spanish context, the PCE will persist in its determination to achieve the widest possible collaboration with the Spanish Socialist Workers' Party and other socialist organisations in order to develop and consolidate democracy and its institutions and also to further the shared libertarian ideals of socialism.

The PCE is striving to establish in Spain what our Programme-Manifesto has termed a new political movement which will embrace those parties supporting socialism, trades unions, co-operative movements and other socio-political organisations. Whilst respecting the character, independence and philosophy of each of its component elements, this movement will draw together their separate strengths and will thus constitute a viable alternative government to that of the bourgeois parties and one capable of establishing socialism within a democratic framework.

The PCE is both a militant party and a party ready to assume the responsibilities of government and to defend the interests of the working class, of all sectors of the working population and of cultural groups, both in Parliament and through mass democratic action.

With its newly won legal status, the PCE intends to act in an open, profoundly democratic manner and to strengthen its ties with the mass of the population. To this end, it will set up branches in businesses, places of work, study and cultural centres and in neighbourhoods.

The PCE, a party of the masses, but of a new order, must place great emphasis on the recruitment and encouragement of cadres. Adapted to the circumstances of our legalised position and to the present situation, the principle of a democratic central organisation according to which we operate will encourage internal democracy.

The PCE fosters among its members international solidarity with the workers and with freedom movements in every country, as well as the principles of communism and socialism.

Resolution 16

Small and medium-sized businesses and the self-employed.

Small and medium-sized businesses and the self-employed make up an important element in the context of the balanced economic, political and social life of the country. They constitute a sector whose standard of living has shown a marked deterioration during recent years particularly as a result of the policies of francoism and the concentration of capital, a tendency which has been aggravated by the economic crisis. A brief study of small and medium-sized businesses and of the self-employed will confirm the fact that their interests are at variance with those of the capitalist monopolies and with those of capitalism in general. This contradiction is all the more marked when their resources and ability to resist are limited.

The serious consequences of the economic crisis, which are a heavy burden upon the shoulders of the workers, also weigh heavily upon these groups and even threaten their very existence.

In its efforts to consolidate democracy and to advance along the road of political and social democracy and of socialism within freedom, one of the most important tasks of the Spanish Communist Party is to win the support of owners of small businesses, the self-employed and co-operative workers in the struggle of organised labour and educational and cultural groups against the monopolies and in their attempt to overcome the economic crisis.

Small and medium-sized businesses represent 99.8% of the total for Spain; they are responsible for 75% of production and services, for 70% of the Gross National Product and they account for 86% of total manpower.

They are close on 5 million self-employed workers, non-salaried workers or owners of their own means of production, in industry, business or in service industries. According to figures obtained in the 1974 industrial census, firms with less than 250 employees accounted for 6,337,113 workers, which amounts to approximately 80% of the total. Those with between 1 and 5 employees accounted for 2,094,029 workers, and those with less than 50 accounted for more than 4.7 millions which is rather more than half of those engaged in industry.

In spite of their economic importance, their political importance has been practically nil during the last forty years. In spite of the large-scale problems that they face, successive governments and the civil service have overlooked small businesses and the self-employed, whilst granting all manner of priorities and backing to the big monopolies.

Power has been denied them and they have lacked fiscal support, financial and technological aid and overseas trade, while power has remained in the hands of big business which has suffered none of these privations. The time has come to demand a greater degree of equality in the treatment of small and medium-sized businesses and the self-employed and this can be achieved only from a position of unity, based on thorough organisation, which takes account of the issues affecting them and their legitimate aspirations.

Policy of the PCE toward small and medium-sized businesses and the self-employed.

The PCE's position is based on a number of irrefutable facts:

As has just been pointed out, the first is the importance of small businesses and the self-employed in commerce and in both production and service industries. They are responsible for more than two thirds of consumer goods and investment. Given this basic role, the importance of an economic policy that accords priority to their needs is obvious.

The PCE cannot divorce itself from the interests of the mass of the population and it therefore recognises the fact that small and medium-sized businesses, skilled workers and craftsmen and the self-employed at present constitute an indispensable element in the Spanish economy, fulfilling a whole range of needs in production and service industries. If the living standards of workers are to be maintained, it will be necessary to give them support and encourage modernisation.

The second fact is the number of people that they employ. They provide the largest number of jobs for salaried staff. Given the low rate of capital investment, they account for the greatest proportion of manpower: five out of every six workers are engaged in, and receive their salary from, this kind of firm.

The third lies in the possibility of forging a broad link between organised labour, educational movements and the intermediate sectors of society with the common aim of consolidating democracy and ensuring the determined implementation of the Moncloa Agreement, especially in those matters that concern them directly.

The possibilities of forging this broad union vary according to the group or sector concerned, for the intermediate sectors do not constitute a power block. It is not possible to talk of the small and medium-sized businesses as a whole, for a distinction must be drawn between those sharing the same interests as the big monopolies on account of the extent of their capital, the number of their employees and their sphere of operation, and those able to participate in the struggle against the monopolies.

These non-aligned sectors are caught between the two directly opposing forces in society: the working class and large-scale capitalism. Within the sectors there is, moreover, a range of attitudes.

The problems involved in an alliance between self-employed workers, craftsmen and owners of small businesses who do not have salaried staff and whose income results primarily from their own efforts, are akin to those facing an alliance between the working class and agricultural workers.

Some groups do not understand that the working class can win over certain non-aligned sections of society to the antimonopolist struggle. Especially at moments of crisis, this can prompt these sections to slip back into more reactionary, or even fascist, positions.

The Employers' Association and small and medium-sized businesses.

After union elections were held in industry, the Comisiones Obreras (Workers' Commissions) and the UGT (Unión General de Trabajadores; General Workers' Union) emerged as the major representatives of organised labour, thus opening up the prospect of a unified struggle.

The financial oligarchy and its overseas allies are afraid that, now that the working class has greater confidence, it will gain greater power within society.

The CEOE (Confederación Espanola de Organizaciones Empresariales; Confederation of Spanish Employers' Organisations), i.e. the major representative of the employers that embraces both the monopolies and the banking institutions, is trying to include the owners of small businesses within its ranks. With this end in view, a subsidiary was created called CPYME (Confederación Espanola de la Pequena y Mediana Empresa; Spanish Confederation of Small and Medium-sized Businesses) and a vice-president was appointed to head it. The CEOE is seeking to become the peak of a large pyramid the base of which would be made up of small businesses which in turn would support the summit and would receive its orders from above. If the CEOE were to achieve its purpose, it would constitute a powerful pressure group capable of imposing its own objectives and ensuring that the interests of the monopoly groups prevailed.

Small businesses are more able to adapt, and sometimes to introduce innovations, than the larger companies, for the sheer size of large companies prevents them from adjustng speedily to changing demands.

Moreover, the monopolies are seeking to attract smaller businesses with a view to using them as a means of defence against the demands of the working class.

Owners of small businesses are now realising that the CEOE is endeavouring to use them to further its own designs and even to ensure that monopolist capitalism strengthens its holds over the small businesses themselves.

Owners of small businesses should surely know now who is responsible for capital evasion, for the manipulations of the official credit system, for imposing a system for financing social security and of profit margins; they know too who is reaping the benefit of special privileges, exemptions and tax dodges, manipulating public bodies as if they were private property. . . The Communist Party must make every effort to pinpoint and make known publicly the growing contradiction between the interests of the financial oligarchy and the interests and aspirations of the rest of society.

Owners of small businesses have made known a series of urgent demands that their own independent organisations must take up, develop and defend.

The process of economic and scientific development (even technical in the context of contemporary capitalism) strengthens the position and dominance of monopolist capitalism in the Spanish economy, thereby giving rise to a confrontation with the agricultural community, small and medium-sized businesses and the self-employed.

The strengthening of capitalism confronts all these sectors with the need to modernise, but also to work towards a new spirit of co-operation. Without this latter, a sizeable proportion of these sectors will be condemned to a deterioration in their standard of living or even to the loss of their position within society.

The PCE advocates that the owners of small and medium-sized businesses, farmers, and self-employed and private individuals form voluntary associations or democratic co-operatives, founded on the absolute agreement of all members and on the principle of one man, one vote.

Initially, this new co-operative organisation would not alter the legal status of its members. The aim would be to encourage consumer co-operatives and co-operation in housing, education, credit, etc. and also in buying and selling, the shared use of machinery, new activity of retailers, craftsmen, managers and industrialists and ordinary citizens, new use of products, services and overseas trade. At a later stage, we envisage a transition to workers' co-operatives, agro-industrial, commercial, industrial and service complexes whose management, administration and operation would be entirely in the power of the constituent members. This transition would depend upon the full consent of each group, but would allow for the disassociation of any one group at any time.

The state and autonomous government organisations must support the development and continued existence of this co-operative movement, which is destined to be one of the great pillars of a future free socialism.

The PCE should devote the greatest attention to the problems of these sectors of society, on the one hand urging them to set up independent organisations and, on the other, opening up a broad debate within the party so that the issues involved can be taken up by all militants.

At the same time, in defending the interests of small businesses against the state and monopolist capital, we must not forget the contradictions that exist between their interest and those of workers, especially within the firms themselves. In this context, communists support the action of the major trade unions in defence of workers' interests.

The PCE will fight for a policy supporting and encouraging small businesses, skilled workers and craftsmen and the self-employed: a policy on prices, social security, fiscal reform, credit, the encouragement of a new spirit of co-operation, organisations for the protection of small businesses, democratisation and decentralisation of government bodies that deal with these sections of society, demoralisation of planning, industrial development in rural areas, education and professional training, research and support for exporters. This is not an opportunist move. Rather it is a fundamental and constant attitude. Basically, it is a matter of demonstrating concisely and unequivocally to these sectors the need to fight for democracy. It is a question too of making them aware that at this stage in the history of capitalism their main enemies are monopolist capitalism and the power of the state and that only opposition to monopolies, combining workers' organisations and the education movement together with small and medium-sized businesses, the self-employed, under the leadership of the working class, can bring about the socio-political and economic changes that will make possible the solution of these problems.

Message from the Central Committee of the CPSU to the 9th Congress of the Communist Party of Spain.

(Complete Text). Pravda, 19 April 1978.

Dear comrades,

The Central Committee of the Communist Party of the Soviet Union sends fraternal greetings to the delegates of the Ninth Congress of the Communist Party of Spain, to all Spanish Communists and wishes them success in their work for the good of their people.

Your congress is convened at an important period when Spain is eliminating the fascist heritage, establishing democracy and forming its present-day political features. The changes taking place in Spain are the result of almost half a century of heroic struggle of the Spanish Communists, all working people and democrats against fascism. At the same time these changes became possible as a consequence of international solidarity with the Spanish democrats, as a result of deep-going favourable changes on the international arena and the changing balance of forces in favour of socialism and peace.

The Soviet people are well aware of the enormous responsibility devolving on the Spanish Communists at this stage of the country's political and socio-economic development. The historical experience of the international working-class movement clearly shows that the chief guarantee of democratic transformations and successful struggle for social progress is the existence of a strong and efficient Communist Party which is guided in its actions by the scientific theory of Marxism-Leninism and comes out as the genuine vanguard of the broad working masses.

As the Spanish Communists are well aware, for the Soviet people the problem of overcoming the régime of exploitation, class and national oppression has long since become history. Crises and inflation, high cost of living and unemployment have irreversibly receded into the past. In the Soviet Union, a developed socialist society has been built and is being continually improved, socialist democracy has been established which ensures the real rights, freedoms and interests of the working people, their effective participation in managing all the affairs of society, from top to bottom. Our achievements are the result of the heroic efforts of our working class, collective farmers and intelligentsia, the historic creativity of the masses, the vanguard role of the Soviet Communists in socialist and communist construction.

In the foreign policy sphere, the Soviet Union concentrates its attention on the struggle for peace, for the security of the peoples, against the arms race, on eliminating the hotbeds of war. At the same time the Soviet Union supports the just struggle of the peoples for national independence and social progress, rebuffing imperialist aggression.

Now that the most aggressive imperialist circles have stepped up their attempts to tilt the balance of world forces in their favour, to hamper mankind's social progress and continue to impose the arms race, it is particularly important to strengthen in every way the unity of the Communist and Workers' parties, of all democratic, anti-imperialist forces in the struggle against the main enemy of the peoples — imperialism, to firmly rebuff all attempts to undermine or weaken the positions of socialism.

The Party of Lenin, the Soviet peoples have always manifested a fighting solidarity with the courageous struggle of the Spanish Communists and democrats for a new Spain. The Spanish Communists can rest assured in the CPSU's firm fidelity to the principles of internationalism, now as well as in the future.

The Soviet Communists cherish the traditions of friendship and cooperation between our parties, sealed by the joint struggle against fascism and reaction, and consider it imperative to safeguard and multiply them in the interests of the peoples of the USSR and Spain, in the name of peace and security. The CPSU continues to come out for friendship with the CPS, for fraternal relations with it on norms and principles inscribed in the document of the 1976 Berlin Conference and in the joint communiqué of the two parties of October 16, 1974.

We wish the Communist Party of Spain success in its struggle for the vital interests of the working people, in strengthening ties with the working class, with all progressive forces, for democracy in Spain, for the triumph of the ideals of peace and socialism.

Long live friendship between the Communist Party of the Soviet Union and the Communist Party of Spain!

Long live friendship between the peoples of the Soviet Union and Spain!

Long live the invincible teaching of Marxism-Leninism!

CENTRAL COMMITTEE
COMMUNIST PARTY OF THE SOVIET UNION

Declaration of the three signatories to the Common Programme, 13 March, 1978.

(Complete Text). L'Humanité, 14 March, 1978.

For the first time for more than thirty years the majority of French men and women have just voted for the Left. That is the dominant feature of the first round of the legislative elections.[1] It expresses the country's desire for change, the hope for new policies to end the crisis, everyday problems, the injustice and neglect which characterise the policies of the Right. Despite the enormous amount of propaganda used by the parties in power and the manipulation of official statistics, this trend cannot be disguised. It opens up the prospect of a majority for the Left in the National Assembly next Sunday to ensure the advent of a government of the United Left and of a policy of progress and social justice, of decentralisation, freedom, co-operation in independence and of peace.

The parties of the Left solemnly pledge to do everything possible to bring about the formation of a common majority on a common programme for a common government of the Left.

[1] Held on 12 March, 1978. (Ed.).

With this pledge, once the country has shown its confidence in them, they will undertake negotiations aimed at lvading up to the programme, based on the Common Programme of 1972 and the provisions adopted in 1977, which will become the legislative contract to be enforced by the United Left Government.

The first task of the new government will be to meet the legitimate expectations of workers and families by adopting the important social measures which will bring them essential improvements in their living conditions and standard of life.

From its first days in office the new government will set the SMIC[2] at 2,400 F. for a 40 hour working week; raise family allowances, starting with the first child, by 50 per cent between now and 1st January 1979 and by at least half this amount from April; it will set the minimum old age pension and the allowance for handicapped adults at 1,300 F; an average revaluation of 15 per cent of retirement and other pensions; it will set the minimum unemployment benefit at two thirds of the SMIC when the person unemployed is the only wage-earner in the family, and to 50 per cent in other cases, including that of young people looking for their first job.

These measures will go hand-in-hand, as necessary, with financial relief for small businesses, for industry, for trade, and, in general, for labour-intensive industries.

At the same time, the government will make arrangements to start negotiations with trade union and professional organisations on matters concerning salaries, employment, working conditions and the structure of promotion. During these negotiations it will recommend wage increases which preserve differentials; the rapid return to a 40 hour 5 day week; an improvement in working conditions, hygiene and security; the eradication of discrimination affecting young people, women and immigrant workers; the creation of 500,000 new jobs in the first year, of which 210,000 will be in the public sector, along with any other measures needed to combat unemployment.

We will enter into negotiation with agricultural organisations with a view to confirming guarantees and raising the incomes of farming families by fixing prices to production, bearing in mind changes in farming costs, market organisation, the fight against land speculation and with a view to the discussions with our partners on a new common agricultural policy.

Right from its first session, the government will submit to Parliament bills and budgetary measures concerning: the general lowering of the retirement age on full pension to 60 and to 55 for women and for people doing unpleasant work; the fifth week of paid holiday; the repeal of the 1967 orders on social security; action in favour of health and public housing; a

[2] SMIC (salaire minimum inter-professionnel de croissance) minimum wage linked to economic growth. (Ed.).

just policy towards rents and leasing charges; the democratisation of teaching and the development of permanent education; better conditions for children and just compensation for the repatriated.

Steps will be taken and means found to establish a firm policy to fight for the protection of the quality of life against pollution and other nuisances.

In order to set in motion and carry through this essential social plan, reforms will be necessary to supply the economic, financial and political means. This will involve notably the nationalisation of banking and finance and of industrial groups which will be put before Parliament in its first session; of the indexation of savings; the reform of taxation including in particular, the creation of a wealth tax and a tax on company capital; the establishment of a democratic plan for development; the introduction of new policies relating to industry, agriculture, shipping, distribution of land and foreign policy.

Swift measures will be taken to extend the democratic rights of workers and their organisations, as well as towards equality for women in all spheres and, encouraging people's awareness, the decentralisation of power especially by the election of regional assemblies by universal suffrage based on proportional representation and the suppression of close supervision on the communes. The three parties attach particular importance to the guarantee and extension of individual and collective liberties.

The problems of the overseas territories will be settled with the populations concerned on the basis of their right to self-determination.

The government will take every appropriate measure to guarantee the independence of the country, to ensure the development of France's co-operation within the Common Market as well as with all those countries which desire it, and to progress towards general disarmament.

To put this great new policy into practice, the parties of the Left agree to govern together, each taking its place in a united government of the Left whose composition will respect the wishes of the voters and whose activities will be equally based between rights and duties, debate and solidarity.

The Socialist Party, the Communist Party and the Radicals of the Left Movement have decided on the reciprocal withdrawal of all their candidates in favour of those candidates of the Left who head the first ballot. This withdrawal of names will figure on the memorandum and will be disseminated by means of posters. The candidates who withdraw will take part in the public meetings organised to ensure the success of the candidates put forward by the union of the Left. The three parties ask their departmental organisations to meet in order to ensure that all concerned work together in a spirit of loyal co-operation.

The three parties call on their candidates and activists to mobilise and gather together in a single cause all those men and women who seek real change. Not a single vote must be lost for the Left. Everything must be done everywhere to defeat the Right.

Jean Ellenstein. From the 22nd Congress of the French Communist Party to the Defeat of the Left.

(Excerpts). Le Monde, 13, 14 and 15 April, 1978.

I. THE REVOLUTION IS NO LONGER WHAT IT USED TO BE

The defeat of the Left in the 1978 parliamentary elections is also that of all the forces which constitute it, quite apart from the responsibility of each one of them. It is therefore that of the Communist Party. It is all the more so given that its percentage of votes declined (0.8 per cent as compared with 1973), thus recording its lowest score since 1945 with the exception of the catastrophic elections of 1958 (19.2 per cent). For the first time since that same date the Socialist Party has outstripped it by about 2 per cent. These are the facts which must be looked at lucidly. Indeed there is no point in concealing the reality. A fever is not calmed by breaking the thermometer. These articles are intended to provide my contribution to the discussion to which communists have been invited by the Politburo of the PCF. . .

I would have liked to publish them in my own party's press, but it appears that this is not possible the way things stand at present. I ask those comrades who might hold this against me to consider the reasons behind such a situation and the arguments developed here, rather than curse a communist intellectual who is in the process of confiding in a non-communist newspaper. Isn't this precisely one of the problems posed by the evolution of the PCF?. : .

My disagreement with the Politburo is not founded on the spirit of the decisions taken at the 22nd Congress, but on the way in which these have been applied. Attention will be drawn to the fact that I underestimate the rôle of the bourgeoisie and that I am nourishing the anti-communist campaign of the Socialist Party. No, I do not accept this way of posing problems which leads the PCF to curl up within itself just like a besieged fortress. The Bourgeoisie has always fought the PCF and will continue to do so, but I do not see how the existence of a real public debate between communists can help it. On the contrary, it can only demonstrate the democratic vitality of a great party.

As for the Socialist Party, I have neither underestimated nor concealed its responsibilities for the crisis within the Union of the Left, which caused its defeat, but, if the Socialist Party is experiencing a social democratic drift, isn't this to a large extent because the PCF has been unable to exercise "this guiding influence", which Georges Marchais had shown to be necessary at the 22nd Congress?. . .

In short the PCF still remains incapable — unlike the Italian Communist Party — of extending its influence beyond the political and social sphere in which it moves. This is even tending to shrink a little despite the Common Programme, the right to vote at eighteen, and even the real reinforcement of the party, for the relationship between the number of members, the activity of party organizations and its electoral influence, is not a direct one.

The reasons for such a situation are numerous and cannot all be attributed to the party and its leadership. . . In my opinion the reasons for it are much older and deeper. It is the delay shown by the PCF in reforming itself and in taking new problems into account which are posed by the evolution of French society over the last twenty five years, which is the basic cause. Already in 1956, after the 20th Congress of the Soviet Communist Party, the PCF was refusing to go beyond problems posed at the time, and indeed barely confronted those. Without doubt, it condemned the military intervention in Czechoslovakia by Warsaw Pact countries in 1968, but it was satisfied with precise criticisms and took refuge in a prudent and embarrassed silence. Even today the analysis of Soviet realities remains well below the level it should attain.

L'Humanité continues to embellish this reality and conceal a certain number of features which are essential to an understanding of what is happening in the U.S.S.R. The articles devoted to Lioubimov and Rostroparitch are examples of what should be done in a penetrating fashion. Soviet foreign policy is only rarely called into question, over Africa or China for example.

The analysis of the causes of this situation remains the work of specialists to whom the columns of the communist popular press are closed. The November issue of *Nouvelle Critique* devoted to the U.S.S.R. has hardly been presented to *L'Humanité* readers. . .

Many communists, beginning with a certain number of leaders, are just not prepared to tackle these problems head on. However it seems to me that without a position of principle regarding the U.S.S.R., our interventions have little credibility and bewilder many members, without, for all that, convincing anyone outside the party.

We must have the courage to recognize that the socialism of the U.S.S.R. is imperfect and incomplete. Fragments of socialism are to be found there, an unfinished socialism, because the bureaucracy dominates and political democracy does not exist. Not only is the U.S.S.R. not a model, nor an example, but rather it serves as an anti-model. Socialism as we mean it does not exist anywhere. We don't really know what it can be, but we certainly do know what it should not be. The fact that our party bears the same name as the State — parties which rule the U.S.S.R. and other countries of this type, constitutes a heavy handicap. With regard to

French public opinion. One more reason for going all the way and setting out these problems clearly — without any anti-Soviet feeling of course: what communist can forget the sacrifice of twenty million Soviet people during the Second World War?. . .

Through this basic criticism of the U.S.S.R. we in fact came face to face with the question of the true identity of French Communism. . . The 22nd Congress was, in part, the first great attempt to clearly reject the dogmas of the past, and to sift out the foundations of a new policy. The conception of revolution itself can no longer be what it was in the France of yesteryear. The world has changed and France has been transformed. It is a question of finding a new course which is neither the traditional social democratic line nor the communist orientation associated with Tours and the Komintern.

II. THE NECESSARY TRANSFORMATION

We now know that the revolution in our country can only be the result of a long drawn out process. Great structural reforms alone will allow it, leading to economic, social and cultural transformations, from which socialism will emerge. We must not avoid the fact that this is a radically new orientation within the communist movement, and that it comes up against the tradition and what might be termed the founding myths of French communism. Too many communists are not conscious enough of these changes and the consequences they involve. Has enough been done to clarify this new orientation, and to make it understood to everyone by means of a great debate, both inside and outside the party?

To sign the Common Programme without undertaking this necessary transformation, obviously meant taking the risk of giving the Socialist Party a considerable spur. Many Frenchmen on the Left preferred to vote Socialist rather than Communist because they were not wholly convinced by the deep changes in the PCF. The Common Programme could not be electorally beneficial to the Communist Party unless the party seemed, in the eyes of the workers, the wage earners and the intellectuals, to be the best qualified to defend their interests, and the surest guarantee of a new policy which would maintain their freedom. The PCF's attitude since September 1977 has not contributed to the dispelling of their anxieties. . .

A good many qualified workers, for example in the Paris region, are in a reasonable material situation. They feel exploited but talk of absolute poverty is an old theory which must be hit on the head. Social protection is a reality in contemporary France, and it is the fruit of worker struggles. These workers often own their own flat and even a second home. They may do without some things in order to buy goods, but their situation is no longer what it used to be twenty five years ago. They did not always see themselves reflected in the "worker" language used by the party during the election campaign. Their cultural level has risen. They have often been to a technical college up to the age of seventeen or eighteen. Their children are in the grammar school or even at university. It is true that they have to work hard, that unemployment threatens, journeys to work are long, working conditions are getting more and more difficult, but you cannot speak to them as you would have done fifty years ago. They are more sensitive to qualitative problems even if quantitative claims do still exist. As for the salaried and intellectual middle classes, it may have seemed in the course of the last six months that they constituted a wasteland where the Socialist Party could recruit its voters, but which one could hardly be expected to win.

The result speeches of Georges Marchais at Lille and his last television address no longer mentioned these social classes. That shiboleth, "make the rich pay" was often used without any modifiation — where do they begin and end? One had the sensation of seeing the resurrection of those far off days when the tactic of "class against class" was used. Instead of isolating the monopolies, this kind of action turns its back on the idea of the unity of the French people ratified by the 22nd Congress. . . Let us be frank: it is towards a profound modification of party policy and its practice, with regard to the salaried middle classes, engineers, technicians, managers and intellectuals that we must advance. . . .

But all this necessitates a considerable change in our attitude towards them, a modification of our language, and above all, yes above all, the taking into account of the great problems of society, civilisation and culture which May 1968 revealed, stimulated and crystallized. One cannot set the working class and the professional and intellectual middle classes against each other. It is, on the contrary, by creating the conditions for their unity that the PCF can gain ground firstly in the big agglomerations, and it must not be forgotten that French society has now been urbanized to a great extent.

Behind the events of May 1968 we only wanted to see political leftism, and we were right to combat it. But the remainder — the fight against bureaucracy and the growing rôle of the State, self-management, feminism, hierarchical relations within companies, the problems of urban society — haven't we neglected these for too long? And even if we are beginning to take them into account, isn't it in a rather superficial fashion?. . .

That the fundamental strategic responsibility for the failure of the Left lies with the Socialist Party, few communists would question. . . but, by our way of doing things, we have — many examples show this — a certain responsibility which must not be avoided, because it is precisely the honour and greatness of a Communist Party which enable it to recognize its own faults. I simply wish that, for its part, the Socialist Party would draw the lessons of this period of time in a responsible fashion, and not take advantage of circumstances to Brush aside the spirit of the Common Programme and the Union of the Left. The defeat of the Left in March

1978, an honourable one when all is said and done, would be transformed into a real Waterloo if we continued for years on end to hurl accusations at one another and to struggle on as if the Right did not exist and was not governing France. There should be a genuine debate between communists and socialists on the great strategic options, on the very conception of socialism, on the transitional stages which a left-wing government would have to put into operation, and on the means of reaching victory. The real historic compromise in France will come via a real rapprochement between socialists and communists. The debate should be calm, fraternal and genuine, and it would be illusory to think that the Socialist Party could be the only victim of disunity. The March 1978 elections prove on the contrary that the PCF is itself likely to experience a certain weakening as soon as the division between the parties of the Left becomes established and pre-dominates.

III. GETTING DOWN TO FUNDAMENTALS.

We are not in the Russia of the Czars or in the aftermath of civil war. We are not in pre-war or occupied France, nor in the France of the cold war. It seems to me that the notion of "groupings" should be cast aside — a trend is only the first form of a grouping — just as the debate within the party should be permanent and transparent. Naturally the party leadership organisation should play its part, in its entirety, but it can only do so in direct symbiosis with communists in general. There were grounds, for example, for posing the problem of the concept of dictatorship of the pro-letariat and its renunciation. Moreover it should have been put on the agenda of the 22nd Congress, instead of contening ourselves with a too rapid debate initiated by a stand taken on television. . . Why did the defenders of this concept not take the floor at the Congress in order to uphold their ideas?. . . We have hundreds of thousands of communists who express themselves democratically in their cells, but we cannot be satisfied with a vertical circulation of ideas (from the cell to the Central Committee). A horizontal circulation is also necessary. This does not contradict democratic centralism as conceived by Lenin. It is the direct heritage of the Stalinist conception of the party which rejects this horizontal flow. . .

The party would lose its real force if it did not listen to the voices coming from the cell. On the other hand it would gain new members and would be better able to motivate the present ones, if it agreed to transform itself and, first and foremost, make the functioning of democratic centralism more democratic.

Some would like to appeal to "party spirit" in order to prevent such a public debate. That is an old trick which does not however correspond to present needs. In reality we must get down to fundamentals.* Let me

---

* Many a question asked merely stems from the evolution of contemporary France.

enumerate some of them simply to demonstrate the riches of theoretical and political debate.

What should we think of Leninism today? To what does it correspond in the current situation? Should the Communist Party defend the principles of philosophical materialism? Is it not necessary for it to be neither theist nor atheist? This would place our relations with Christians on a new footing.

Shouldn't we define more precisely our Socialist plan, its outlines and its objectives, in such a way as to show clearly what socialism "à la française" could be, as opposed to all the experiments which today claim to be of socialist origin?

Is it not necessary to study even more thoroughly our conception of democracy and freedom? Should we not make a better analysis of today's State phenomenon, and give greater consideration to the nature of the transition period in our country?. . .

Let it not be said that these are intellectual problems for intellectuals. These are real questions being asked today by communists in their hundreds of thousands. The rejection of public discussion makes the situation appear more dramatic than it really is. What would certainly be dramatic would be a persistent denial of the public discussion to which so many communists aspire. Reducing this demand to the opposition of a few intellectuals in disagreement with the 22nd Congress does not seem to me to correspond with the reality. . .

In the years to come the Left must win, and to win the French Communist Party must, to an even greater extent, be the great democratic party needed by our people to bring forth the profound changes which our society already carries within itself. An avant garde and a mass party, a party of workers, labourers, middle class wage-earners, and intellectuals, just as it really should be and should appear in the eyes of our contemporaries.

Indeed, we are not suffering from having too much of the 22nd Congress, but from not having enough of it.

Georges Marchais. Proceed Along the Line of the 22nd Congress.

Extracts from Report to the Central Committee of the French Communist Party. L'Humanité, 28 April, 1978.

. . . Our Party has once again demonstrated that it is certainly the most democratic party in this country. Since the 20th of March, in every cell, in every sectional and federal committee, Party members — all party members — members who wished to do so — have been able to express freely their point of view, criticisms and suggestions. Let those who have had a hand in trying to give us lessons, keep their own doorway clear in the first place!

Nowhere else, not even in the Socialist party where a heavy silence reigns at present, has such a free and open discussion been held.

It is obvious that this indecent campaign against our Party, constitutes the pursuit, under a new guise, of the same goal which the elections failed to attain, namely the weakening of the Communist Party in order to benefit the Socialist Party, and the creation of conditions which would enable that party to be used as a reinforcement in the implementation of capitalist policies. This time, in order to succeed, they are looking to stir up trouble within the Party and cause a split among communists. . .

All the exhortations, lamentations, and vituperations which we have seen displayed in the columns of *Le Monde* or *Le Matin*, all trying to influence the free thinking of communists, have not had the anticipated effect, despite the extraordinary publicity given to them: the broad, fraternal, democratic and responsible debate which has just been held by our Party, will, on the contrary, enable us to clarify all that has happened, reinforce the Party and to prepare the basis of its progress along the road set out by the 22nd Congress. . .

We preferred a free and democratic discussion within the Party itself, its organizations, cells, sections and federations to a public discussion. Should it not be the party members who, first of all, express their points of view and experiences in order to draw lessons from the great battle we've just fought, to state precisely our orientations and determine the tasks ahead, before going on to debate among and with the masses — this being indispensable of course, for they are affected by what we say, propose and do?

If we were to believe some people, this debate has not been a democratic one, as it was "shepherded", "confined", "enclosed", "smothered", "concealed". This inspires two reflections.

Firstly, what arrogant contempt of the 630,000 Party members, in their great diversity, leads one to think that, in the France of 1978, a point of view could be imposed upon them by leaders which they themselves have freely elected. What undervaluing and disdain regarding the intensive collective thinking which leads communist men and women, workers, employees, peasants, intellectuals, one and all, each are in the light of his own impression, to present their ideas and experiences with a view to enriching their Party's thinking and action.

Moreover, doesn't this deliberate ignorance of the general debate within the Party provide evidence of people's fear of seeing their own political viewpoint rejected by the majority following a free discussion. Most certainly it is easier to soliloquize when seated behind a desk and to write peremptory articles which will easily find a buyer, when sheltered from real life and opposition from comrades. For our part, we are committed to a free debate within our ranks which is not subject to pressure, to a constructive debate which aims to serve the workers' struggle. . .

During the battle to update the Common Programme and the parliamentary elections campaign — does it need to be said again — we only had two concerns, the one closely linked to the other: on the one hand to succeed, without bidding to highly and uncompromisingly, in updating the Common Programme, which was five years old; in other words to modify these aspects which had become outdated while scrupulously respecting the present direction and fundamental provisions. On the other hand to turn the March 1978 elections into a victory for the left and for democratic change. Must we recall the National Conference's decision to place the election campaign beneath the banner of the search for agreement? To this end we made the maximum concessions possible. Up until the last day, the last hour, we were suggesting to our partners that the discussion be resumed in order to reach the agreement which was so essential to victory. Until the last moment we made overtures which would have allowed us to reach a good compromise, without great difficulty, if our allies had shown an ounce of goodwill.

In short, our Party did not stop fighting for a political agreement, concerning, as we have said, the programme, the government and the transfer of votes. We were right to do so, and right to do so up to the end, that is March 12th, because we did not give up trying every means possible of reaching an agreement, until the last moment.

We did not manage it and it was under these circumstances that the ballot took place, and we were faced with the problem of what attitude to take towards the second round.

According to some comrades the March 13th agreement[1] is, and I quote, "a worthless and insufficient" agreement. Faced with such ignorance or misunderstanding of matters, it is necessary to recall the facts as they really are.

On the evening of the first round we reaffirmed our objective of a political agreement on the Programme, the government and the transfer of votes. The following day the Central Committee mandated our delegation to renew our proposals to the Socialist Party.

But, at the same time, after the March 12th results had become known, the Central Committee discussed the question of whether we should insist on the immediate updating of the Common Programme as a condition of the agreement, if the Socialist Party persisted in its refusal. Evidently, in that case, there would not have been an agreement.

The Central Committee therefore decided that lacking an immediate updating, we should obtain in any case a political agreement from the Socialist Party which would include a certain number of clear commitments, and which would not lead to any kind of surrender on our part.

[1] See: Declaration of the Three Signatories to the Common Programme, in this volume. (Ed.).

The main reason why the Central Committee took this position was the feeling that the results of March 12th — to the extent that they were not those anticipated by the Socialist Party, which would have given it a free hand and enabled it to impose its own law on us — would lead the Socialist Party to propose and conclude an acceptable political agreement, and also the idea that on the basis of the results of March 12th, our party would dispose of means, far beyond its September expectations, to ensure respect for the commitments which had been made.

It was in this spirit that we attended the negotiations, and what we had foreseen, did in fact take place. The agreement which we signed on March 13th did include a few steps forward on the part of the Socialist Party. This was the case with certain important social measures explicitly foreseen by the agreement, which had previously been rejected by the Socialist Party. This was true of the clear affirmation that the eventual government of the Left would include communist ministers having equal rights and duties with their partners. This agreement also called for the commitment of the Socialist Party to reopen negotiations after the 19th of March — if the Left won — starting from the present base in order to achieve a real updating of the Common Programme. For our part, while acknowledging this commitment, we did not surrender on any of our positions. . .

We must also examine objectively the behaviour of the socialist Party during the election campaign. Firstly, as I have said, having brought about the failure of the negotiations on the 22nd of September, it persisted in its refusal of all discussion until the 12th of March.

Secondly it worked hard to take away every quality of mobilization which belonged to the Common Programme by emptying it of its reformative content. In the course of the discussion which has just taken place, some comrades reproached our party's leadership for not having gone far enough in giving concessions on September 22nd.[2] To be able to say that, they must have forgotten the extent of the Socialist Party's back-sliding. Now what does giving in to the Socialist Party really mean? Quite simply it would have menat giving in on the minimum wage, giving in on the immediate rise in purchasing power, giving in on restricting the power of the hierarchy, giving in on extensive measures to be taken to curb unemployment, giving in on the obligation to employ young people when they finish their training, giving in on the reduction of working hours and on a fifth week of paid holidays as immediate measures to be passed, giving in on real estate reform, giving in on the effective nationalization of the banking and finance sectors and of the nine groups stipulated in 1972, giving in on capital and wealth tax. That would also have meant giving in on the demo-

[2] Refers to the 21-23 September 1977 meeting of the three parties of the Union of the Left during which they failed to reach agreement on their Common Programme for the March 1978 general election. (Ed.).

cratic content of the Common Programme, giving in on the paid monthly hour of union time, giving in on the free election of the presidents of nationalized firms' administrative councils, giving in on proportional representation in all elections, giving in on individual freedom, on the guarantee of being able to move freely, to choose a place to live, to cross frontiers, giving in on the rights of overseas departments and territories — freedoms and guarantees which, for a time, the Socialist Party did not want to see explicitly written into the Common Programme.

Thirdly, in order to justify the break up of the union and the renunciation of the Common Programme, the Socialist Party was led to vigorously attack the programme and our Party, while continuing to brandish the words "Common Programme" and "Union of the Left". This suicidal conduct with regard to the Left as a whole, gave the Right an unexpected chance.

In order to attack the Common Programme the Right did not invent anything new in 1978 which it had not already discovered and used in 1973 and 1974. But contrary to these two elections, it benefited this time from one considerable and invaluable advantage: the active taking over by the Socialist Party itself of all the Right's anti-communist and anti-Common Programme arguments. The Common Programme, the Right would claim was "collectivist". That's what Robert Fabre and the Socialist Party were saying about our proposals. Was it "demagogic"? That's what the Socialist Party claimed, accusing us of going too far. Did it mean "catastrophe" and "ruin" for our country? That was Michel Rocard's view about a minimum wage of 2,400 francs. . .

If the Common Programme and the alliance with the Communist Party was going to bring all the dangers vividly described for days on end by the Socialist Party, it's obvious that many voters must have thought it better to stick to Raymond Bare and the parties of the Right. . .

As for the argument that we should have given in and been content to struggle (with the Socialist Party. tr.) after the victory, it is of no value either. First of all, because it is not in the least obvious that the Left as a whole would have won under these circumstances, and then, even were this to happen, it is difficult to see, if we were unable to bring the Socialist Party to respect their commitments beforehand, how we would succeed in doing so afterwards, when, compared to us, it would have much greater strength in numbers. Moreover it is necessary to follow this reasoning to its conclusion; if we had given in, we would have compromised ourselves in the same way as the Socialist Party in abandoning the Common Programme. No, all this is obviously absurd.

In reality, the facts demonstrate this: we did everything in our power to ensure that these elections had a positive outcome, so that we could move "towards democratic change", as the Central Committee had mandated us on the 31st of March, 1977. Faced with this double problem we struggled towards one goal: to create at the same time the conditions for electoral victory and for real, effective change. It was only the obstinacy of the Socialist Party in pursuing its social democratic line of capitulation, its refusal to create the conditions for a mutually acceptable agreement, which led to defeat. It bears therefore the total responsibility for it. . .

The Left has advanced and gained new ground. This is true for our Party. Without yielding to sham optimism, which might conceal the basic reality that we did not succeed in reaching our major objective — the victory of the Left and change — nothing should drive us to despondency and pessimism.

While everyone wanted to weaken us, on the Right and Left, we emerge reinforced from these last six years of struggle. . . We may have lost 0.7 per cent in the parliamentary elections, but we gained 800,000 votes and 13 M.P.'s. Nine new departments have from now on one or several communist M.P.'s. . . At the same time we have advanced Party policy, its capacity for analysis and mobilization, and its organization which has reached 632,000 members, the highest figure since the Liberation. . .

The further reinforcement of the Party means watching over the functioning of democratic centralism and its perfecting. It is not by chance that the attacks on our Party have concentrated on democratic centralism: questioning it would be the surest way of achieving this weakening, this wiping out of the Party's fighting potential, which the bourgeoisie and the Socialist Party are seeking with such determination.

At this point I would like to make two observations. Firstly, it is necessary to state that we are sometimes asked things that are not asked of any other party. If we followed the advice of some, our cell, Central and Political committee meetings would have to be held in public — but naturally no one ever thinks of asking other political formations to do likewise. It is quite legitimate to worry about the democratic life of the Party. We do, and we have tried to improve it appreciably since the 21st Congress.

Secondly, some comrades would like to see the creation within the Party and its press of a kind of permanent discussion on anything and everything. We shall definitely not do so for two closely connected reasons. First of all, this would dispossess the leadership structures at different levels, all democratically elected by secret ballot, of their role and responsibility in putting into action the policy democratically decided by Congress. We will not allow our leadership from the cell to the Politburo, even for expediency's sake, to be denied its role and responsibilities. To be greatly concerned with the democratic life of the Party is one thing, to dismantle the Party in the name of some vague petty-bourgeois anarchism is quite another. Furthermore, it is clear to all sensible minds that permanent discussion, when all is said and done, means paralysis of decision and action. We are a democratic party not a debating society.

There is — it's a characteristic of our time — a great aspiration for democracy among the masses, a great aspiration for discussion, debate and collective reflection among communists. That's very good, very healthy — and the 23rd Congress will no doubt prolong what has already been done in this field. Having said that, we must be clear. The Communist Party is a revolutionary party, a vanguard party and there are tendencies towards the cult of spontaneity, anarchistic trends to which we would give in at the risk of foregoing the very existence of a party with an avant-garde rôle to play. .

The Communist Party does not seem to reproduce within itself, present-day society and its structures, any more than it would wish to impose its own structures on society. It is the implement of avant-garde combat for the working class and its allies, and it has chosen the structures, rules and life-style which give greatest efficiency to its combat. It is therefore futile to expect it to give these up, to water them down in a mass movement without outlines, and to abolish the vanguard characteristics which are the basis of its existence. . .

To summarize, comrades, let's go forward along the line laid down by our 22nd Congress, that is to say: to reaffirm, to specify and to enrich our perspective; to give its full dimension to a daily political practice fully expressing and serving our chosen strategy; to reinforce the influence, the organization of the Party, and to perfect unceasingly its characteristics as a revolutionary, democratic and vanguard party.

Yes, we are determined to go forward in this way. And to advance at our pace and on our terms. The complaining of one side or the other will change nothing. It is the way of common sense, of efficiency, of real boldness; it is the way of the future.

Which other party can affirm in this way, its capacity to respond to the interests and highest aspirations of the working class, the people and the nation? There aren't any. The Communist Party most certainly is, and will be, even more so, the party needed by the workers and by France.

Georges Marchais. The Reasons behind the Anticommunist Campaign.*

Excerpts from a speech delivered at the Youth Festival on 4 June, 1978. L'Humanité, 5 June, 1978.

. . . We can understand that the Giscardian right is still anxious. For they do not forget that, even if the forces of change were denied victory because of the Socialist party's mistake, it is nonetheless true that fifteen million French men and women voted in favour of real change, less than three months ago, and what has happened since has given them no reason to change their minds.

Moreover there is a second element which explains the anxiety of those in power. This is the existence in France today of a force which prevents the carrying out of a policy of "social consensus", as M. Bare would say, which has been so successful in those European countries where social democracy holds a dominant position. There is a force which is struggling obstinately against all attempts at class collaboration; a force which resolutely opposes austerity, inequalities, unemployment, all oppression — this force is the party to which the revolutionary class, the working class has given itself, the French Communist Party. This is the party, the barrier, the obstacle with which are colliding just now, all those who have an interest in causing the retreat of our democracy. And it is all the more true, now that this party, through its Central Committee, has just reaffirmed that the failure of the left would not lead to a change of strategy, that it would continue its fight for the defence by action of all who are exploited, for the unity of the working class, for the unity of manual workers and intellectuals, for the unity of the French people, for the union of the Left, in short, that it would continue the struggle for progress along the road of democracy and socialism, along the line set by the 22nd Congress.

This being so, one can understand why Giscard d'Estaing, Barre and the Socialist party are striking so many blows at our Party, why the powerful Giscardized information media are doing their utmost to wage such a campaign against it. If they could weaken it, penetrate its public, cause it to lose a part of the immense capital of trust and hope in it, borne by millions of people, what a step back that would mean for the workers' movement, what perspectives that would open up for the upper middle class and social democracy!

At the same time we can judge how serious and objectionable it is that members of our party make themselves the instruments of this campaign.

Let me explain this point further. According to these comrades, the real and great political problem, which should be given priority, is the internal life of our Party, described in the gloomiest of colours. Delighted by this unexpected boost, the great organs of the spoken and written word really let themselves go. The Communist party is like a prison, "gangland". Communists are just robots obeying orders "from above". Communist leaders are ruthless and inhuman inquisitors. I say that this campaign is unworthy and despicable, coming from those who keep quiet when the French government chooses a torturer in order to reveal its humanism in Africa. I say that the attitude of those who bring grist to this mill is unwarranted and irresponsible.

After all! In which party do personal ambitions or the flattery of leaders reign supreme? In which party do lobby scheming and party political compromises prevail, not forgetting clan disputes and the settling of scores often by the debarring of members and even whole organizations? This is the reality of the other parties, but certainly not of the Communist party, whose internal life, let us emphasize, is the most democratic of all the French political parties.

The Communist party is a voluntary gathering of men and women who have decided to become communists, precisely because they object to oppression, injustice, apathy and blind obedience. How could they endure this, therefore, in their own party? It's unthinkable.

Furthermore, struggling for the emancipation of the workers, for a society of responsible men and women, in control of their own lives, for a socialism inseparable from an ever greater freedom, the Communist party can only progress towards this end by calling upon the spirit of initiative, the intelligence and responsibility of each one of its members.

No, we have no need of Yes-men! Among us, we do not have people who think and people who act, those who decide and those who carry out. There are men and women who join together in their organizations, who discuss in complete freedom, who exchange their views, ideas, proposals and criticisms regardless of anyone else and without pressure. On this basis a decision is taken by a majority and is then applicable to everyone, because that too is democracy. But applicable without violating consciences, without reproaching anyone for maintaining his own opinion having faced up to the experience and opinion of the majority within the framework of Party life.

Finally, our leaders are democratically elected at all levels, and they have at their disposal the means to act, while being ready to submit themselves to the authority of their electors, at the proper time. For, without the existence of such a leadership, there would be no revolutionary party.

It is owing to all this, that, after the elections, a broad and free debate was initiated within the party as a whole. The Central Committee has taken this into account in making an analysis of this last battle and in defining future orientations. This analysis and these orientations have been, for more than a month, the subject of an investigation throughout the Party, and of a thorough discussion, freely held, wherever necessary and where communists wish it. And it is under these conditions that they obtain the approval of the vast majority of communists.

This then is the democratic life of the Party, a democratic life we are forever determined to perfect, in liaison with the evolution of the class struggle. Who can seriously deny that this is what we have been doing for years? And we certainly intend to continue improving this internal democracy, because life does not stop and we must always forge ahead.

It is precisely this regard for preserving the Party's democratic life, and therefore its effectiveness, which forces us to repulse the fractionary venture entered into by a small group of party members, in contempt of the basic rules of our organization. And I want to be quite clear on this point.

We have no wish, no desire to expel anyone, even if it is true that our statutes do give us this option. We don't want to, because responding to a political problem by taking administrative action is not our way. It is not the conception of the 22nd Congress. We dislike repression. We value each one of the men and women who make up this Party which bear the hopes of so many millions of people. We don't want to be less numerous but more so.

But let no one be deceived; we are determined to respond to this political problem brought about by a purposeful political struggle.

We do not want, at any price, the setting up in our Party of trends and tendencies which would ruin its democratic life, transform it into a closed shop of personal rivalries and clan disputes, which would present the class adversary with ideal means of manipulating Communists against one another, and of bringing pressure to bear on our decisions.

We do not want, at any price, a policy which would consist of committing our Party to the deceptive and eventually fatal easy way out of surrendering to social democracy. Nor do we want a doctrinal withdrawl which would transform our Party into a narrow little sect, bereft of any influence on national reality.

We do not want, at any price, one small group, suddenly overcome by dizziness and taking its support from the outside, to assume the right to change a leadership which has been democratically elected by all communists.

We do not want all that, because it would mean abandoning the line defined by our 22nd Congress. Isn't it to this that they would eventually like to constrain us? I have already said so, and I repeat: it is not in anyone's power to manage it. We will not deviate from our line; we will not give in to this destructive trend of opinion.

That is why we have called upon communists — and they have heard us — to oppose this fractionary venture with a strong political counterattack. This venture must be defeated. It will be. . .

Back to Eduard Bernstein?
Elleinstein Discards the Mask.*

(Complete Text). New Times, No. 22, May 1978.

A little over a year ago our magazine carried an article devoted to the views of Jean Elleinstein, deputy director of the Marxist Study and Research Centre of the Central Committee of the French Communist Party. We commented on a number of his writings containing sallies against the Communist Party of the Soviet Union and against our country, as well as open attacks on his own party, the PCF.

* The name Ellenstein in this text is spelt as it appeared in the New Times article.

The bourgeois press in France, Britain and the United States rallied to the defence of the "offended" author, which was only natural: attacks against the PCF and the CPSU suited them very well. Less understandable were the complaints in some fraternal newspapers that the New Times article was "Harsh" and that its tone was "excessively sharp" — as if Elleinstein himself had not trampled upon all the norms of comradely discussion among Communists by both the content and tone of his attacks on our Party and our country. Elleinstein's writings of the kind referred to in our magazine not only make a comradely exchange of opinions difficult, but give our class adversary ammunition for undermining the very foundations of the communist movement.

It should be stated outright that the evolution of Elleinstein's views in the past year not only fully confirms that the assessments of his "works" in the article in question were correct, but makes it necessary to dot the i's.

In the first place, we should say plainly, without beating around the bush, that while in his previous writings Elleinstein maligned individual pages in Soviet history, levelling outrageous, trumped-up, slanderous accusations against our people, today he has to all intents and purposes adopted a totally hostile attitude to the Soviet Union and socialism in general.

Indeed, in the past Elleinstein argued, with misplaced zeal, that the "Soviet model" of transition to socialism was inapplicable to France. Of course, on this point he was forcing an open door: no one has ever intended, or intends now, to foist any models on the French people or anyone else. Soviet Communists have maintained ever since Lenin's time that the transition to socialism in every country is bound to give rise to a diversity of forms and methods, and that each people will build socialism as they wish — of course, on the basis of the general principles and laws that distinguish socialism from non-socialism.

Today, Elleinstein regards rhetorical statements about the inapplicability of the "Soviet model" to France as a thing of the past. Deciding to go further, he declared without embarrassment in an April 13 article in *Le Monde* that the society that has been built in the U.S.S.R. is not socialism at all; moreover, that it is well-nigh an "anti-model" of socialism.

Turning immediately to problems in his own Party's policy, Elleinstein says — following his own logic — that the PCF will resolve these problems only if it "dissociates itself in principle" from the historical experience and present reality of the Soviet Union and other socialist countries. He further demands condemnation of the "consequences" of the period when his Party, proceeding from the interests of the French people, declared its solidarity with the U.S.S.R. He cracks down on *L'Humanité* for "continuing to embellish Soviet reality" and "only occasionally" calling in question "Soviet foreign policy." Echoing the opponents of peaceful coexistence, he repeats the slanderous contention that "the Soviet Union fears détente" — this at a time when the whole world acknowledges the Soviet Union's tireless and fruitful activity on behalf of détente, its efforts to consolidate détente and extend it to the military sphere.

All this is highly surprising to hear from a man who calls himself a Communist, the reader may say. It certainly is. But even this is not the limit. In an intervi :w to the magazine *Faire* Elleinstein goes so far as to draw an analogy between the roles of the state under socialism and under fascism, thereby bracketing together Hitler's state, which enslaved the whole of Western Europe, including France, and the Soviet state, which saved the world from the fascist armies.

Some of our friends may again rebuke us for "sharp language." But malicious sallies of this type against our country not only entitle us to call things by their proper names — they make it our duty to do so. It is not only the right, but the bounden duty of Soviet Communists to defend socialism, to defend the achievements of the people building a new society.

By reason of the above, we cannot but state plainly that Elleinstein's stand is anti-Soviet, anti-communist, and anti-socialist. To identify the Soviet socialist state with Hitler's nazi state is more than cynicism — it is a sacrilege.

Anti-communist and anti-Soviet attitudes play a pivotal role in bourgeois propaganda today. Worried by their weakening positions, the capitalists vilify Soviet policy and Soviet reality in order to sow distrust in socialist ideas and their bearers, the Communist parties. This accords with the logic of class struggle. But how can such vehement attacks on socialism be made by a deputy director of the Marxist Study and Research Centre of the PCF Central Committee? This is impossible to understand, let alone justify.

Elleinstein has to some extent explained the motives for his actions in his writings, and we see from these explanations that what we are up against is merely a vulgar repetition of the inglorious history of international opportunism dating from the late 19th and early 20th centuries. Judge for yourself.

Addressing the PCF national conference in January 1978, Elleinstein declared that France's road to socialism could not be found in Lenin's works or on their basis. And in his book "Lettre ouverte aux Français sur la république du programme commun" ("Open Letter to the French on the Republic of the Common Programme"), published on the eve of the parliamentary elections, he divulged, at last, the name of the prophet who can show the way. It is none other than Eduard Bernstein, the ill-famed initiator of the reformist revision of Marxism!

It will be recalled that Bernstein expressed the essence of his views in this maxim: "I say openly that I see very little sense in what is usually meant by the 'ultimate goal of socialism.' This goal, no matter what it may be, is nothing to me. . . ." Thus socialism is nothing to Bernstein. Having stated this view, he proceeded to dismiss the materialist conception of history as "untenable," reject Marx's analysis of the essence of capitalist exploitation, and embark upon a negation of the need for revolution and working-class power. There is certainly a logic in this — the logic of apostasy, the logic of betrayal of the proletarian cause. No wonder that all prominent exponents of revolutionary Marxism at the time summarily rejected Bernstein's view.

Rosa Luxemburg declared, for instance: "The person who advocates the legal road of reforms **instead of and in opposition to** the conquest of political power and a social revolution chooses, in reality, not a more tranquil, more reliable and longer road to the same **end**, but an entirely **different** end . . . he does not want to achieve a **socialist** system, but merely to reform the **capitalist** one. . . he strives to destroy only capitalism's excrescences, not capitalism itself."

Bernstein and his followers, Lenin wrote, "have not taught the proletariat any new methods of struggle; they have only retreated, borrowing fragments of outdated theories, and preaching to the proletariat not the theory of struggle, but the theory of concession — concession to the most vicious enemies of the proletariat, the governments and bourgeois parties who never tire of seeking new means of baiting the Socialists."

So much for the essence of Bernstein's theses. Clearly, these are not the theses of a revolutionary, of an adherent of scientific socialism, but of a secret ally of the bourgeoisie. But here we have Elleinstein declaring, with astonishing impudence, that Bernstein's analysis "was correct," and that it had only one "flaw" — its premature appearance. "What was utopian has now become possible," Elleinstein writes without any embarrassment.

Which of Bernstein's views are feasible today in Elleinstein's opinion? In his latest writings he advances the idea, so dear to the father of reformism, of "democratizing" the bourgeois state as the principal (sic) condition for transition from capitalism to socialism. As for the reform of capitalist society, the most important thing, Elleinstein holds, is not a reform of economic relations, i.e., capitalist property relations (the bourgeois holy of holies!) but a reform of human relations, "relations between parents and children, men and women, competent persons and incompetent persons," and so on. The class approach has totally vanished in this handling of the question.

And so, let's go back to Bernstein. Elleinstein is engagingly frank. Now everyone participating in the working-class movement can see what he is driving at, where his sympathies lie, and who his allies are.

History repeats itself. But the past is never reproduced exactly as it was. Bernstein came forward with his revision of Marxism at a time when socialism was still only an idea, a distant goal of the working-class movement. Elleinstein is prophesying at a time when socialism is already in its seventh decade, when it has proved its vitality in the severest trials, including the ordeals of World War II. Elleinstein writes his lampoons at a time when socialism is already recognized as a leading force in world development, when more and more people are turning towards its ideals and are settling about building it, when the broad masses of people pay tribute to it as the mainstay of peace and security.

In other words, Bernstein attempted to subvert the struggle for socialism before the decisive battles for its triumph, and history passed a deservedly stern judgment on him. Does not Elleinstein, who has chosen to follow in Bernstein's footsteps when one-third of mankind is already building the new society, deserve a much more severe condemnation?

But even this is not all. Today Elleinstein is coming out openly against his own Party. For instance, in a number of public utterances, including the above-mentioned *Monde* article, he blamed the electoral reverses of the Left alliance on what he calls the Party's failure to decide on "radical changes" in its essence. He demands that the Party "go all the way" in reviewing its theoretical and organizational principles.

It must be said that the "radical changes" Elleinstein urges upon the French Communists have a very definite character. In effect, he demands of the PCF what out-and-out reactionaries demand of it, namely, renunciation of the main characteristics of a revolutionary party of the working class.

For instance, he calls for founding a "new Communist Party" which would begin by disavowing the decisions of the historic Tours Congress of 1920, shedding democratic centralism, and even discarding its own name. To call a spade a spade or, as the French say, *appeler un chat un chat*, these are demands of a liquidator.

Elleinstein's writings are a hodge-podge that includes rejection of scientific socialism, praise of revisionism, impudent attacks on the Soviet Union that would do credit to its bourgeois vilifiers, and liquidationist criticism of his own Party.

However that may be, it is clear that Elleinstein has discarded the mask and appeared before the public in all his anti-socialist splendour.

No denying he has already won laurels, and quite considerable ones, but it is the class adversary that has bestowed them on him. Elleinstein's photographs, showing him sometimes in the picturesque pose of a "thinker," sometimes with a finger raised in admonition, fill the pages of the Paris pictorials. *Paris-Match*, for instance, presents him to its readers as a man who "calls everything in question" and singles out as his special virtue the fact that Elleinstein was the first among the French Communists to "criticize the U.S.S.R. openly," while *Le Nouvel Observateur*, describing Elleinstein's further "refutation" plans, bestows upon him the title of "front-page man."

It is highly indicative that the bourgeois press should praise and popularize Elleinstein. This means that what he is doing is useful to the bourgeoisie and harmful to the working-class and its parties.

Y. SEDOV

Statement of the Communist Party of France on the European Parliament.

(Complete Text). L'Humanité, 8 April, 1978.

The heads of state and government of the nine Common Market countries have reached agreement on setting the date for elections to the European Parliament for June 1979. In France these elections will be held on the basis of proportional representation.

The French Communist Party intends to take an active part in these elections.

In elaborating the programme it will put forward in this connection to the people of our country, it will be guided, fully and completely, by the interests of the French working people and the country, as well as by the demands of international cooperation that is beneficial for the peoples.

As for the French working people, whether occupied in the ferrous metal or textile industry, shipbuilding or airplane construction, and as for the French farmers and all other victims of the present European policy, the presence and activity of the PCF parliamentary representatives will serve as the best guarantee that their needs and aspirations will be taken into consideration in the European Parliament. The PCF Parliamentarians will demand broader representation of the working class and peasant trade union organisations in the institutions of the Community. They will demand that social legislation must be brought in line with the most favourable national system among the EEC member-countries. They will advance constructive proposals aimed at combating the domination of the financial oligarchy and the activity of the miltinationals.

The Communist parliamentarians will seek to defend and expand democratic freedoms in the EEC countries and will oppose all forms of political, religious, cultural or any other discrimination, any form of authoritarianism.

They will come out for genuine cooperation on the basis of equality and mutual benefit not only between the EEC members but between the EEC and other countries of Europe and throughout the world. The Europe that the Communists are working for will not aggravate the division of the world into blocs, but on the contrary, will seek rapprochement between the peoples and facilitate détente, peace, disarmament in conditions of security. The Communist parliamentarians as steadfast defenders of national independence will be everything to maintain France's freedom of action within the EEC framework. The French law forbids — thanks in particular to the efforts of the Communist deputies — any extension of the European Parliament's prerogatives or subordination to any foreign body. The PCF representatives will see that this law is scrupulously applied in the European Parliament.

The French Communists intend to promote the broadest unity of European workers and democratic forces in the name of implementing their common or coincident aims. At the same time, contrary to other parties who have already virtually become branches of foreign parties, the French Communists intend in any circumstances to proceed from the national interests, and are fully resolved to define and conduct an absolutely independent policy.

Faced with a Europe of unemployment, a Europe of the finance oligarchy which bars progressives from certain professions, the French Communist Party will advance the constructive alternative of a Europe of the people, a Europe of social progress and democracy, independence and peace.

Giorgio Amendola. The European Parties.

(Complete Text). Rinascita, 6 October, 1978.

With the elections to the European Parliament imminent, the announcement has been made, accompanied by very noisy propaganda, of the formation of European parties. Socialists, Christian Democrats and Liberals will present themselves at the next European elections with lists of candidates connected with those presented in the other EEC countries by their comrades and friends of the same political colouring. Now there has also been announced the presentation of a list of the European Right.

I do not know how much success these initiatives, presented with such loud propagandistic noises, will have at the elections. It is a known fact that the General Secretary of the PSI (Italian Socialist Party) attaches great importance to this link-up with "the great European social democracies"; perhaps he hopes to bring, by this fact alone, his own party's percentage of votes up to the far more substantial level reached by the German Social Democrats, the English Labour Party, and the French Socialists. Of course, the PSI, if it wishes to remain consistent with this stance, will have to accept in its lists also the candidates of the PSDI (Italian Social Democratic Party), a party which belongs to the Socialist International.

An attempt is being made to make people believe that the only guarantee of sincere pro-European conviction is for the Italian parties to transform themselves into sections of European ones. The fact alone that there are no plans for the formation of a European communist party is supposed, according to the zealots of the European cause, to provide proof of the scant and dubious Europeanism of the PCI (Italian Communist Party). This is a superficial and summary judgement which is not accepted for a moment.

The PCI attaches great importance to the European elections, seeing them as an important stage in the necessary process of democratisation of the Community's institutions. Of course, the possibility of creating a source of democratic legitimisation capable of giving the Parliament the real powers which are presently denied it is dependent upon the percentage of voters. It will not be easy, but the scepticism and aversion of large popular and working masses to the construction of a united Europe will have to be overcome, as too will the opposition of those middle strata of society which are still under the sway of old nationalistic ideas. Therefore, the way in which the electoral campaign is conducted will be of great importance.

So far the European Community has been an organisation without a solid democratic foundation, the result of accords between member states and of unstable and precarious compromises. None of the ambitious plans for monetary, economic and political unification has been realised because each country has sought to defend, by means of paralysing and often obstructionistic battles, not so much their own national interests, which would be their duty, but the narrow interests of sectors and corporations, often giving in to the equivocal wishes of multinational companies. The Community's activity has turned into a limited, fluctuating co-operation between barely associated states which are divided on the main issues, economic and monetary ones included. The EEC Commission, instead of being the supreme executive body, has acted as the general secretariat of the Council of Ministers, deprived of any real powers of initiative and decision-making.

Whilst the rights of the member states may thus have been formally respected, in reality the interests of the weaker countries have been ignored or infringed upon. In the absence of a democratic will representing the majority of the Community's political and social forces, the will of the stronger countries, and in particular of the Franco-German directory, has been arrogantly imposed. The most important matters are resolved at meetings of the German Chancellor with the President of the French Republic. The formal defence of the rights of the member states has not stopped the weaker ones' having to submit to the law of the stronger members. Italy in particular has had to yield, in the fields of agricultural and regional policy for example, before the coalition of the stronger states. In such a situation, one can either lock oneself up in the jealous defence of old national prerogatives — in a world which is based on interdependence, in which any kind of sovereignty is effectively a qualified one, and where a fluctuation of the dollar or in the price of oil is sufficient to bring about the closure of factories and unemployment — or one can strive to create a new multinational power. The elections to the European Parliament must mark the beginning of the reversal of the present situation; they must allow the wishes of the people, freely expressed through the ballot-box, to succeed in smashing the old yoke of individual selfishness and sectoral interests; and they must place obstacles in the way of attempts to create hegemonistic positions within the European Community.

This is why the Italian Communists, through their activity in the European Parliament, have shown their desire for the formation of a "new power" in the Community; a new, multinational power which will be able to tackle, by means of new structures and new working methods, the problems which the individual countries clearly cannot solve: money, credit, energy, health, scientific research. It is not a question of creating a new supranational state with all the powers of the old, centralised, national ones, but instead a new organisation which has a democratic foundation in a parliament elected by universal suffrage, and which has real powers of control and decision-making. It is foreseen that the new Parliament's powers will be essentially consultative. However, whether or not the new assembly will be able to win for itself the powers which it is presently denied will depend greatly on its representative strength, its political composition, the political will which animates it, and the authority and degree of commitment of the men who constitute it. The Italian Communists have always fought for an increase in the Parliament's powers. Besides, to deny the European Parliament an extension of its powers means to devalue the significance of the elections from the outset. Why should one go to the trouble of electing a body which is still denied the possibility of functioning efficiently?

If the electoral campaign wishes to strengthen the cause for a united Europe, then it ought to concern itself in effect with the concrete problems of the Community, its functioning, the stages and methods of integration, and the role which the Community must play in a world in crisis, in the relationships between East and West, and particularly with the emergent countries (if one may use such a term). This is the intention of the Italian Communists. We shall prepare our election programme in our appropriate offices, and we shall discuss it openly with our independent friends of the Left. We shall examine our activity within the European Parliament and subject it, as we do all the Party's activities, to a rigorous critical examination in the course of the preparation for our Congress. Thus we shall present ourselves at the elections with our programme and with our symbol, with an electoral list of the Italian Communist Party open also to democrats committed, in full autonomy, to join with us in the pro-European battle.

We know that there are differences of opinion, even substantial ones, between the European communist parties on the European Community's problems. We have alreasy experienced this within the European communist parliamentary group. Already, in a spirit of reciprocal respect and civilised tolerance, an Italian Communist and a French Communist have expressed opposing views on, for example, a problem which is of vital importance for the Community's future, namely its expansion to include Greece, Spain and Portugal, which we Italian Communists desire but our French comrades oppose.

Eurocommunism means a general selection of values: the inseparable bond of democracy with socialism; the rejection of all foreign models and of all foreign centres; the defence and extension of democratic liberties; and respect for the principle of political alternatives according to the wishes shown by the people. It is precisely because Eurocommunism encourages the autonomy of each communist party, and respects the individual character of each party in relation to its particular national situation, its history, its organisational structure, and also its electoral strength, that it is not translatable into the formation of a single European communist party having the same programme. All the European communist parties are committed to fight for a democratic transformation of the Community, and are concerned to see the presence in the next Parliament of a substantial communist group which will, however, respect the autonomy of the various national delegations. But each party will participate in the elections with its own autonomous programme.

We do not believe that there is anything to be gained from an electoral campaign conducted along the grand lines of Eurocommunism, Euro-socialism and Euro-Christian democracy. The formation of European parties and their participation in the elections on common platforms put at risk the necessary prominence of the Community's problems in the electoral campaign. Such formations are, in fact, made possible by the adoption of vague programmes based on considerations of principles, choices of political camp, etc. The Social Democrats and Christian Democrats will not in fact be able to come down from their generic utterances and high-sounding propagandistic proclamations to the concrete problems of the Community unless they are prepared to expose the substantial differences of opinion which separate the German Social Democrats from the English Labour Party or the French Socialists. We have had a taste of such differences in our own parliamentary experience. And the same thing happens in the camp of the Christian Democrats, where men from Zacc-agnini's Italian Christian Democracy are to be found alongside those of Strauss' German Right.

In the electoral campaign we shall conduct ourselves along the firm ground of the Community's problems and the defence of the nation's interests, and we shall not hesitate to point out the serious contradictions existing at the heart of the so-called European parties.

An electoral campaign conducted along the lines of ideological pro-clamations will end up by aggravating the divisions which already exist between the member countries, in all of which the Left borders upon but does not exceed 50% of the votes. There is not a government in Europe whose legitimacy is founded on a stable consensus of opinion of over 50% of the electorate. I do not believe that, in periods of crisis, even 51% is sufficient to give a country an effective government, comfortable in the knowledge that it has the backing of the majority of the people. But I am especially convinced that 50% is insufficient for carrying on the original task of building a united Europe. That is why it is not a matter of mechanically bringing the discussions on the alternative of the Left and the relative merits of confrontation or historic compromise on to a European level; it is a matter of laying the foundations for that greater union of democratic forces which, alone, will enable the European Community to proceed along the necessary road towards great democratic and socialist change.

PCI—CPSU Joint Communiqué, 9 October, 1978.
(Complete Text).

Enrico Berlinguer, General Secretary of the Italian Communist Party (PCI), visited the Soviet Union from October 6 to 9 at the invitation of the central committee of the Communist Party of the Soviet Union. He was accompanied by Antonio Rubbi and Antonio Tato, members of the Central Committee of the Italian Communist Party.

Leonid Brezhniv, General Secretary of the CPSU Central Committee and President of the Presidium of the USSR Supreme Soviet, received Enrico Berlinguer and had a friendly conversation with him.

Enrico Berlinguer, together with Antonio Rubbi and Antonio Tato, also had a meeting with Mikhail Suslov, member of the Political Bureau and Secretary of the CPSU Central Committee, Boris Ponomaryov, alternate member of the Political Bureau and Secretary of the CPSU Central Committee, and Vadim Zagladin, alternate member of the CPSU Central Committee.

As a result of the conversations that took place, the following joint communiqué was adopted:

The representatives of the Communist Party of the Soviet Union and the Italian Communist Party had a wide-ranging exchange of views on key problems of the present international situation.

Note was taken of the joint concern over the slowing down of détente and international co-operation, a slowing down which has been the result of the activities of certain imperialist, militarist and reactionary circles and which has brought about the growing threat of a new spiralling of the arms race.

The delegations of the CPSU and the PCI emphasised the urgent need to exert new and energetic efforts to give fresh impetus to the process of détente and international co-operation and to strengthen in Europe the constructive results achieved at the European Conference in Helsinki, through the full implementation of all the provisions of the Final Act.

In this respect, real measures aimed at preventing an intensification of the arms race would be of major importance. The two sides consider that a valuable contribution to attaining this goal would be provided by the completion, at the earliest possible date, of the strategic arms limitation talks, by concrete head-way at the Vienna talks on the reduction of armed forces and armaments in Central Europe and by the consistent implementation of the recommendations of the U.N. General Assembly's special session on disarmament.

The representatives of the CPSU and the PCI insistently emphasised the need to solve the outstanding international problems through political talks on the basis of equality and justice, with recognition of the legitimate rights of each people and without any interference whatsoever from outside. This would promote the easing of tensions and an improvement in the international situation, and would create favourable prerequisites for the solution of the most urgent problems concerning the economic, social and cultural development of the whole of mankind.

Leonid Brezhnev and Enrico Berlinguer again emphasised the full solidarity of the Soviet and Italian communists with the struggle of the peoples of Asia, Africa and Latin America for national and social emancipation from any form of oppression whatsoever and for the free and independent determination of the ways of their own development.

Of great benefit for the development of those peoples would be a policy of international economic co-operation capable of placing resources and means at the service of the cause of consistently emancipating thousands of millions of men and women from hunger, backwardness and illiteracy, a policy capable of creating the prerequisites for organising a new international economic order.

The leaders of the CPSU and the PCI pointed out that the working-class movement of the countries of Western Europe — on the basis of co-operation between the communists, the socialists and the social democrats, and other democratic forces, including Christian ones — can make its own contribution to strengthening the processes of détente and co-operation between states with different social systems and to ensuring the success of the struggle for the democratisation of international relations and the development of social progress.

The movement of non-aligned countries can make an important contribution to the attainment of these goals.

The leaders of the CPSU and the PCI reaffirmed the view in accordance with which some differences in the positions of parties are not contrary to, and must not interfere with, the strengthening and expansion of co-operation and internationalist solidarity among the Communist and Workers' Parties of all countries and continents. In the efforts aimed at achieving these goals, the two parties will be inspired by the principles formulated by the Conference of Communist and Workers' Parties of Europe held in Berlin in June 1976.

The representatives of the CPSU and the PCI exchanged detailed information about the state of affairs in their countries and the activities of the two parties. In so doing the delegation of the Italian Communist Party informed the Soviet side of the adventurist activities of criminal groupings with the help of which reactionary forces are trying, by organising terrorist acts, to impede the development of the democratic gains of the workers and the Italian people.

The representatives of the two parties condemned those terrorist activities as being absolutely contrary to the interests of the working-class and democratic movement.

During the meeting there was an exchange of views on the prospects for developing relations between the Soviet Union and Italy. Expression was given to the unanimous opinion of the two parties that the development of such relations in all fields is very important and accords with the mutual interests of the two countries and their peoples.

The representatives of the CPSU and the PCI gave a positive assessment of the relations between the two parties and expressed their desire to continue to promote the development of these relations.

While in the Soviet Union Enrico Berlinguer visited Zvezdny Gorodok (Star City), where he had a warm and comradely meeting with Soviet cosmonauts.

Index